Law and Economics of Contingent Protection in International Trade

This book discusses the regulatory framework of contingent protection in the World Trade Organization (WTO) – antidumping, countervailing duties, and safeguards – as well as an economic analysis of these instruments. The book's various chapters illuminate the basic functioning of all three protections.

Kyle W. Bagwell is the Donald L. Lucas Professor of Economics at Stanford University. Professor Bagwell is a reporter for the American Law Institute, in its study "Principles of International Trade: The WTO." He serves as well as a Research Associate at the National Bureau of Economic Research (International Trade Program). In his research, Professor Bagwell uses economic analysis to interpret and evaluate the design of the WTO. He is a Fellow of the Econometric Society.

George A. Bermann is the Jean Monnet Professor of European Union (EU) Law (a chair conferred by the Commission of the European Communities), as well as the Walter Gellhorn Professor of Law at Columbia Law School. He has been a member of the Columbia Law School faculty since 1975 teaching a range of comparative, international, and transnational law subjects, including EU law and transnational litigation and arbitration. Professor Bermann is also a member of the teaching faculty of the College of Europe in Bruges, Belgium, and also regularly teaches at the Universities of Paris I (Pantheon-Sorbonne) and Paris II (Pantheon-Assas), as well as the Institut des Sciences Politiques in Paris. More recently, Professor Bermann was Tocqueville-Fulbright Distinguished Professor at the University of Paris from June through December 2006. He is the President of the International Academy of Comparative Law, the former President of the American Society of Comparative Law, co-editor-in-chief of the *American Journal of Comparative Law,* and currently chief reporter of the American Law Institute's Restatement (Third) of the U.S. Law of International Commercial Arbitration.

Petros C. Mavroidis is the Edwin B. Parker Professor of Law at Columbia Law School, New York. He also serves as Professor of Law at the University of Neuchatel and is Research Fellow at the Centre for Economic Policy Research (CEPR), London. He specializes in the law and the WTO and serves as the Legal Advisor to the WTO in the Technical Cooperation Division, where he assists developing countries in WTO dispute settlement proceedings. He is also the chief co-reporter of the American Law Institute project "Principles of International Trade: The WTO."

Law and Economics of Contingent Protection in International Trade

Edited by

Kyle W. Bagwell

Stanford University

George A. Bermann

School of Law, Columbia University

Petros C. Mavroidis

School of Law, Columbia University

CAMBRIDGE
UNIVERSITY PRESS

CAMBRIDGE
UNIVERSITY PRESS

Shaftesbury Road, Cambridge CB2 8EA, United Kingdom

One Liberty Plaza, 20th Floor, New York, NY 10006, USA

477 Williamstown Road, Port Melbourne, VIC 3207, Australia

314–321, 3rd Floor, Plot 3, Splendor Forum, Jasola District Centre, New Delhi - 110025, India

103 Penang Road, #05–06/07, Visioncrest Commercial, Singapore 238467

Cambridge University Press is part of Cambridge University Press & Assessment, a department of the University of Cambridge.

We share the University's mission to contribute to society through the pursuit of education, learning and research at the highest international levels of excellence.

www.cambridge.org
Information on this title: www.cambridge.org/9780521769075

First published 2010
First paperback edition 2013

A catalogue record for this publication is available from the British Library

Library of Congress Cataloging-in-Publication data
Law and economics of contingent protection in international trade / edited by Kyle W. Bagwell, George A. Bermann, Petros C. Mavroidis.
p. cm.
Includes bibliographical references and index.
ISBN 978-0-521-76907-5 (hardback)
1. Foreign trade regulation – Economic aspects. 2. International trade. 3. Dumping (International trade) – Law and legislation. 4. Antidumping duties – Law and legislation. 5. Subsidies – Law and legislation. 6. World Trade Organization. 7. Competition, International. I. Bagwell, Kyle. II. Bermann, George A. III. Mavroidis, Petros C. IV. Title
K3943.L38 2009
382′.7–dc22 2008054044

ISBN 978-0-521-76907-5 Hardback
ISBN 978-1-107-68392-1 Paperback

Contents

Contributors *page* vii

Introduction 1
Kyle W. Bagwell, George A. Bermann, and Petros C. Mavroidis

1 **An Overview of the Agreement on Subsidies and Countervailing Measures – Including a Discussion of the Agreement on Agriculture** 7
Jan Wouters and Dominic Coppens

2 **Do the World Trade Organization Disciplines on Domestic Subsidies Make Sense? The Case for Legalizing Some Subsidies** 85
Robert Howse

3 **Subsidies and Countervailing Measures: Determining the Benefit of Subsidies** 103
Joseph Francois

4 **The Enduring Problem of World Trade Organization Export Subsidies Rules** 116
Andrew Green and Michael Trebilcock

4.1 ***Too Much, Too Little... Too Late?*** 168
Kyle W. Bagwell and Petros C. Mavroidis

5 **The Boeing–Airbus Dispute: A Case for the Application of the European Community State Aid Rules?** 172
Piet Jan Slot

5.1 ***Why Not Brussels? European Community State Aid Rules and the Boeing–Airbus Dispute: Comment on Piet Jan Slot*** 185
Mark Wu

6 **Antidumping: Overview of the Agreement** 197
Terence P. Stewart and Amy S. Dwyer

6.1 *A Commentary on the Stewart and Dwyer "Overview"* 241
David A. Gantz

6.2 *Comments on "Antidumping: Overview of the Agreement"* 257
Thomas J. Prusa

7 **Price Differentiation in Antitrust and Trade Instruments** 264
William E. Kovacic

8 **Nonpreferential Origin Rules in Antidumping Law and Practice** 276
Stefano Inama and Edwin Vermulst

8.1 *Nonpreferential Origin Rules in Antidumping Law and Practice: A Comment on Inama and Vermulst* 306
Piet Eeckhout

9 **The Appellate Body Interpretation of "Sunset Reviews" Provisions of Anti-Dumping and Countervailing Measures Agreements: A Critical Analysis** 309
Claudio Dordi

9.1 *Comments on "The Appellate Body Interpretation of 'Sunset Reviews' Provisions of Anti-Dumping and Countervailing Measures Agreements: A Critical Analysis"* 328
Thomas J. Prusa

10 **The Safeguards Agreement – An Overview** 334
Jasper M. Wauters

10.1 *Nondiscrimination in the World Trade Organization Safeguards Agreement: A European Perspective* 367
Marco Bronckers

10.2 *The Agreement on Safeguards: Does It Raise More Questions Than It Answers?* 374
Kamal Saggi

11 **Why Are Safeguards Needed in a Trade Agreement?** 379
Meredith A. Crowley

11.1 *How* Not *to Think about Safeguards* 401
Jeffrey L. Dunoff

Index 413

Contributors

Kyle W. Bagwell
Stanford University

George A. Bermann
School of Law, Columbia University

Marco Bronckers
Vermulst, Verhaeghe & Graafsma Advocaten, Brussels

Dominic Coppens
Junior Member, Leuven Centre for Global Governance Studies; Research Fellow, Institute for International Law, Leuven University, Brussels

Meredith A. Crowley
Senior Economist, Federal Reserve Bank of Chicago

Claudio Dordi
Associate Professor, Department of Law, Bocconi University, Milan

Jeffrey L. Dunoff
Visiting Senior Research Scholar, Program in Law and Public Affairs, and Visiting Professor of International Affairs, Woodrow Wilson School, Princeton University; Charles Klein Professor of Law and Government and Director, Institute for International Law and Public Policy, Temple University Beasley School of Law

Amy S. Dwyer
Counsel, Law Offices of Stewart and Stewart, Washington, D.C.

Piet Eeckhout
Professor of European Law and Director, Centre of European Law, King's College London; Associate Academic Member, Matrix Chambers, London

Joseph Francois
Professor, Department of Economics, Johannes Kepler University, Linz; Centre for Economic Policy Research, London

David A. Gantz
Samuel M. Fegtly Professor of Law; Director, International Trade Law Program; Associate Director, National Law Center for Inter-American Free Trade, James E. Rogers College of Law, University of Arizona

Andrew Green
Assistant Professor, Faculty of Law, University of Toronto

Robert Howse
Lloyd C. Nelson Professor of International Law, School of Law, New York University

Stefano Inama
Project Manager, Senior Customs and Trade Expert, United Nations Conference on Trade and Development, Geneva

William E. Kovacic
Commissioner, Federal Trade Commission

Petros C. Mavroidis
School of Law, Columbia University

Thomas J. Prusa
Professor of Economics, Rutgers University

Kamal Saggi
Department of Economics, Southern Methodist University

Piet Jan Slot
Professor of European and Economic Law, Law Faculty, University of Leiden; Editor, *Common Market Law Review*

Terence P. Stewart
Managing Partner, Law Offices of Stewart and Stewart, Washington, D.C.

Michael Trebilcock
University Professor, Faculty of Law, University of Toronto

Edwin Vermulst
Vermulst, Verhaeghe & Graafsma Advocaten, Brussels

Jasper M. Wauters
Associate, Law Firm of White & Case; Reporter on WTO Law, American Law Institute (ALI); Lecturer, LL.M. Programme on International and European Economic and Business Law of the University of Lausanne

Jan Wouters
Professor of International Law and International Organizations; Director, Leuven Centre for Global Governance Studies and Institute for International Law, Leuven University, Brussels

Mark Wu
Academic Fellow, School of Law, Columbia University; Former Director for Intellectual Property in the Office of the U.S. Trade Representative

KYLE W. BAGWELL, GEORGE A. BERMANN, AND PETROS C. MAVROIDIS

Introduction

This is the third volume in the series *Columbia Studies on WTO Law and Policy.* Our focus this time is on the *Law and Economics of Contingent Protection.* Our invited authors contributed chapters on antidumping, subsidies and countervailing measures, and safeguards.

Wouters and **Coppens** provide insight into the World Trade Organization (WTO) multilateral disciplines on subsidies and on measures taken to respond to subsidies (i.e., countervailing duties [CVDs]). These disciplines are articulated in the *GATT 1994*, the *Agreement on Subsidies and Countervailing Duties* (*SCM Agreement*), as well as the *Agreement on Agriculture* (*AoA*). After an overview of the historical and legal context of the *SCM Agreement*, the authors provide a systematic legal analysis of its main provisions, integrating the substantial amount of relevant case law. Finally, the specific disciplines for agricultural subsidies, as spelled out in the *AoA* in interaction with the *SCM Agreement*, are clarified.

Howse takes issue with the decision of the WTO Membership to abandon the so-called *nonactionable subsidies*, that is, subsidies against which no reaction by affected Members was permissible. These subsidies lapsed in 2001. Howse takes the view that this decision was not well thought out, and claims that developing countries might be the losers here. He offers arguments in favor of reinstating this category in the current *SCM Agreement.*

Francois provides an economist's reaction to the current regulatory framework regarding the calculation of benefit stemming from the payment of subsidy. This issue rose to prominence during the *Softwood Lumber* litigation between the United States and Canada. There, it was made clear to the WTO adjudicating bodies that the existing regulatory framework is ill-equipped to deal with "unusual" cases, such as the Canadian market for timber. Francois offers insights from economic theory on how to deal with similar concerns.

Green and **Trebilcock** examine in their chapter the WTO rules and decisions concerning export subsidies in the nonagricultural context to determine why these disputes are so prevalent and contentious, and whether the rules or their interpretation should be altered. They discuss the basic economic case against export subsidies and political economy explanations for their continued use. They then review two central concerns about the WTO rules on export subsidies. First, they examine issues surrounding identification of export subsidies, including defining what constitutes a subsidy, distinguishing export subsidies from other types of subsidies, and how closely the WTO should review domestic policies for potential (rather than actual) export subsidies. Second, they discuss the difficulty the WTO has had in finding an appropriate remedy for violations of the prohibition against export subsidies. They argue that existing WTO rules do not adequately address either set of issues. In particular, in their view, Panels and the Appellate Body should adopt a more appropriate level of penalty for the use of export subsidies, such as tying the level of penalty to the adverse trade effects from the subsidy.

In their short reaction chapter, **Bagwell** and **Mavroidis** advance some preliminary thoughts on the level of pitching in the WTO SCM Agreement. The existing regime goes, to their mind, too far toward disciplining subsidies, in particular through the absolute prohibition on use of export subsidies. In contrast, trading partners might lose the incentive to continue negotiating trade liberalization if recourse to subsidies is not regulated at all: Through subsidies, trading nations might undo the benefit granted to their trading partners in the form of tariff concessions. Something needs to be done, but what is being done is inappropriate. A legislative amendment is, to their mind, warranted, and the remaining question is whether, from a policy perspective, this is the most appropriate moment in time to start advancing thoughts in this context.

We then move to discuss a high-profile litigation in this field: The *Boeing – Airbus* dispute fits very well here. **Slot** makes the point that WTO rules do not require that local remedies be exhausted before a complaint can be brought before the *Dispute Settlement Body* (*DSB*). Nevertheless, it may be interesting to ponder whether it would be possible, or have been possible at an appropriate moment, for *Boeing*, or one of its subsidiaries, to bring a complaint before the European Community (EC) Commission alleging the granting of incompatible state aid by EC Member States. To answer this question, it is necessary to discuss the relevant EC state aid rules. In addition, it will be interesting to see whether the EC Commission has ever taken any action against individual state measures granting aid to the *Airbus* companies or one of their subsidiaries or suppliers.

Wu, commenting on Slot's chapter, notes that it highlights several advantages for companies in bringing a complaint before the European Commission under its state aid laws rather than nudging their government to pursue a subsidies violation case before the WTO. Slot's chapter raises, in his view, an interesting question: Why haven't foreign multinationals been more aggressive in bringing forward complaints before the Commission on issues of state aid? In Wu's view, Boeing's decision was nonetheless rational, and does not reflect either a systematic bias against choosing a European forum or a lack of awareness of how European state aid law operates. In discussing potential explanations for

Boeing's action, the author illuminates some of the inherent difficulties that multinationals face in adjudication before the European Commission, despite the advantages of the EC's state aid rules.

The next topic discussed in this volume is antidumping. This part kicks off with a contribution by **Stewart** and **Dwyer**. Their chapter provides an overview of the WTO Anti-Dumping Agreement. In 1994, WTO Members adopted the WTO Anti-Dumping Agreement as part of a package of multilateral trade agreements that resulted from the Uruguay Round of trade negotiations. The general overview of WTO Anti-Dumping Agreement provisions is followed by some concluding observations regarding the use of antidumping laws by WTO Members. Specifically, the authors, in the seventh section of their paper, begin by explaining that a number of the Agreement's provisions reflect the tension between the interests of exporters and importers; they then identify major users of antidumping laws over time and significant trends in WTO disputes challenging antidumping measures. To assist with further research efforts, the overview also identifies WTO Panel or Appellate Body decisions discussing particular Agreement provisions (see footnotes and Attachment 2), and contains a bibliography of books, articles, reports, and papers (Attachment 3).

In his comment to their chapter, **Gantz** asks the question, "What is the excuse for the protection thereby afforded to domestic industries, given the weak economic rationale for international antidumping rules that punish price determination?" He suggests in his commentary that the rationale is political and practical; many national governments would not agree to freer world trade without the safety valve of antidumping laws. However, despite the oversight of the WTO's DSB, the international regulatory process and implementation are deeply flawed, in large part because the WTO's Anti-Dumping Agreement fails to deal effectively with important issues such as non–market economy analysis and zeroing, or otherwise mitigate the inherent biases in the system against foreign producers. Although the number of new antidumping actions worldwide is declining, particularly among developed countries, any major future reductions in Most-Favored-Nation (MFN) tariff levels in the developing world will likely stimulate use of the antidumping remedy in the affected nations.

Prusa, who also comments on the same chapter, starts with the observation that antidumping is extremely prominent in trade law. The chapter by **Stewart** and **Dwyer** is, in his view, an excellent starting place for anyone interested in learning about the WTO Anti-Dumping Agreement. From an economic perspective, however, he considers that the chapter is severely lacking, in part because the statute itself lacks economic rationale. He also suggests that the chapter should note that pricing and sales decisions that are entirely consistent with basic economic theory are sanctionable under the Anti-Dumping Agreement.

Kovacic discusses the difference across trade and antitrust statutes in treating price differentiation. His chapter describes the original overlap of how antidumping and competition law treated price discrimination, and how the two areas diverged, with competition law encouraging price competition and antidumping (dealing only with foreign sellers) using more restrictive tests, particularly with respect to different views of what is "predatory" pricing. The first section of his chapter examines the elements that give agencies discretion to determine the impact of statutory commands. The second section describes how antitrust has adjusted controls on price differentiation. The third section considers how antitrust and antidumping treatment accords with the views of business schools and economists about how firms should make pricing decisions.

One of the thorniest issues in antidumping is that of rules of origin. This is the reason we welcomed two contributions in this area. **Vermulst** examines the role of origin rules in antidumping law and practice, with focus on the European Union (EU) system. He analyzes the use of such rules as an operative tool during the investigative process and as an enforcement mechanism once antidumping measures are imposed. He concludes that harmonization of nonpreferential origin rules remains desirable, but that such harmonization realistically should go hand in hand with the establishment of third country anticircumvention legislation.

In a separate chapter, **Inama** and **Vermulst** examine the efforts made at the multilateral level to establish disciplines on rules of origin and the various techniques that may be used in drafting rules of origin. They then discuss the role of origin rules in antidumping law and practice, with a focus on the EU system. They analyze the use of such rules as an operative tool during the investigative process and as an enforcement mechanism once antidumping measures are imposed. They conclude with an overview of the status of the Harmonization Work Programme (HWP) under the WTO Agreement on rules of origin and the recent proposals on anticircumvention made in the negotiating group on rules. Although the use of harmonized nonpreferential origin rules in the context of antidumping proceedings remains a desirable goal, it should realistically go, in the authors' view, hand in hand with the establishment of third-country anticircumvention legislation.

Eeckhout, commenting on both chapters, introduces a couple of general observations concerning the difficulties, in a globalized economy, of devising rules of origin that are appropriate for antidumping proceedings. He questions the utility and feasibility of such an exercise, in particular because the rationale for antidumping policy itself is contested.

During the Uruguay Round, the conclusion of *sunset clauses* was hailed as a major achievement in the effort to constrain abuses in antidumping practice. **Dordi** examines the Appellate Body case law in this area and notes that, in all decisions, the Appellate Body decided not to apply the same provisions regulating original investigations to the sunset review. This is a remarkable deviation, in the author's view, from the usual textual interpretation of the WTO contract that the Appellate Body follows. As a result, what was supposed to be a constraining factor ended up being a rather loose test, which essentially makes it easy for investigating authorities to keep duties in place after five years.

Prusa comments on Dordi's chapter as well, noting that it highlights a key lesson for trade negotiators. Namely, the same agreement might mean something very different to different parties. In terms of sunset rules, the agreement implied that antidumping orders would be terminated unless it could be shown that injurious dumping would be resumed. In the United States, however, a review of sunset decisions reveals that the U.S. Department of Commerce has never determined that dumping would not resume. After seeing what the United States does with sunset reviews, one wonders what trading partners will assume any new WTO agreement will mean. Clearly, the sunset provisions have shown that one must be very careful with what one negotiates with the United States.

The third and last part of this volume concerns safeguards. **Wauters** provides an overview of the disciplines imposed on WTO Members by the WTO Agreement on Safeguards. He puts safeguard measures in the broader context of the WTO system, in general, and other WTO trade remedies such as antidumping and countervailing measures in particular. The chapter examines the conditions for the imposition of safeguard measures, and addresses some specific issues relating to the application of safeguard measures such as the MFN requirements and the obligation to offer compensation. By providing an overview of the provisions of the Agreement on Safeguards and their interpretation by WTO Panels and the Appellate Body, the chapter shows that this Agreement has certain shortcomings and that, unfortunately, the Appellate Body's jurisprudence has not contributed much to rectifying these shortcomings – quite to the contrary.

Bronckers, commenting on Wauters, considers that the arguments that have traditionally been advanced in favor of a nondiscriminatory application of safeguard measures are not convincing within the regime of the WTO Safeguards Agreement. Furthermore, if selective safeguards were plainly accepted in this Agreement, it would no longer be necessary to design country-specific mechanisms, such as the China-specific safeguard clause. In the 1970s and 1980s, the EC was a major proponent of selective safeguards. However, with the advent of the WTO Safeguards Agreement, the EC seems to have lost interest in taking safeguards itself. This may change as of 2009, when the EU Reform Treaty is expected to enter into force, and the European Parliament for the first time will obtain important powers in EU trade policy.

Saggi, also commenting on Wauters, argues that whereas the economic rationale underlying the Safeguards Agreement is sound, the same cannot be said about the structure of the agreement and its subsequent interpretation by the Appellate Body. In fact, the Safeguards Agreement appears to be fraught with ambiguity, and its insistence that safeguards be used when imports are an unforeseen cause of injury to domestic industry appears to be misguided in two key respects. First, at a conceptual level, it seems difficult to see how one could ever convincingly establish that a given surge in imports was unforeseen in the past. Second, the notion of a causal link between imports and injury is devoid of economic logic: Domestic production and imports of like goods are jointly determined in the marketplace, and it makes little sense to attribute a reduction in domestic output to an increase in imports.

The thoughtful chapter by **Crowley** deals with the question of why safeguards are needed in a trade agreement. It reviews the theoretical and empirical literature on their use, and then analyzes the available data to examine two hypotheses in the economics literature, namely, that safeguards improve welfare by facilitating tariff reductions, and that safeguards improve welfare by providing insurance against adverse economic shocks. She finds that countries that undertook larger tariff reductions during the Uruguay Round conducted more safeguards investigations after the WTO was established. This finding suggests that the presence of a safeguard clause in the WTO agreement may have facilitated greater tariff reductions during the Uruguay Round. She finds no evidence that safeguards are used more intensively by countries exposed to more aggregate economic uncertainty. It thus seems unlikely that safeguards provide insurance against aggregate economic shocks.

In his comments on the Crowley paper, **Dunoff** considers whether framing an inquiry into the purpose of the safeguards mechanism in this form is likely to generate fruitful insights, or whether asking this question may instead be more likely to lead us astray. This exploration raises larger methodological questions concerning whether right now there are limits to what either legal or economic analysis can add to current understandings about the purpose and function of safeguards.

JAN WOUTERS AND DOMINIC COPPENS

1 An Overview of the Agreement on Subsidies and Countervailing Measures – Including a Discussion of the Agreement on Agriculture

Introduction

The present contribution aims to provide an insight into the World Trade Organization's (WTO's) multilateral disciplines on subsidies related to trade in goods and on unilateral measures to respond to these subsidies, in other words, countervailing duties (CVDs). In our discussion, we focus on the legal analysis and thus leave the economic analysis to other contributions in this book. As such, we offer only one part of the introduction to the Agreement on Subsidies and Countervailing Measures ("SCM Agreement"), which should be complemented with the economic analysis to evaluate the subsidy and CVD disciplines from a normative point of view.

Our legal analysis is structured around six parts. After a short overview of the legal and historical context, we clarify the object and purpose of the SCM Agreement and examine the various aspects of the definition of "a subsidy" included in the SCM Agreement. When a specific subsidy is deemed to exist under the SCM Agreement, a traffic light metaphor can be made when categorizing subsidies. Some types of subsidies are prohibited (red light), whereas all other specific subsidies are allowed as long as they do not cause adverse effects (yellow light). At present, no type of subsidy gets the green light under the SCM Agreement. Later in this chapter, we look at how WTO Members may respond to subsidies provided by other WTO Members. WTO Members can challenge red light and yellow light subsidies before the WTO adjudicating bodies (multilateral remedy), or in case subsidized imports cause injury to their domestic industry, they can opt for the imposition of CVDs (unilateral remedy). However, not all WTO Members and types of subsidies are treated equally. Therefore, in the final part of this chapter, we study the special and differential treatment provided to developing countries and the different treatment of agricultural subsidies under the Agreement on Agriculture ("AoA").

The authors would like to thank Clarisse Morgan for her helpful comments on a previous version of this paper. All views and errors are ours.

Historical and Legal Context

Originally, the General Agreement on Tariffs and Trade (GATT) 1947 was very lenient toward subsidies provided by GATT Contracting Parties. Article XVI of the GATT merely required Contracting Parties to notify subsidies that were export stimulating or import reducing and, upon request, to discuss the limitation of these subsidies if they caused or threatened to cause serious prejudice to other Contracting Parties.[1] This should be read together with Article III:8(b) of the GATT, which exempts the payment of subsidies exclusively to domestic producers from the national treatment discipline.[2] In contrast, Contracting Parties whose industry was injured by subsidized imports were allowed to impose CVDs up to the amount of the subsidy (Article VI:3 of the GATT).[3] This right was made subject to the determination by the countervailing country that the subsidy caused (or threatened to cause) material injury to its domestic industry; however, the exact procedural and substantive obligations were not spelled out.[4]

In 1955, a Review Session of the GATT included the first substantive obligations on subsidies (Section B of Article XVI of the GATT).[5] From 1958 or "the earliest practicable date thereafter," Contracting Parties had to cease to grant export subsidies on nonprimary products when they resulted in a sale at a price for export lower than that for the domestic market (bilevel pricing test) (Article XVI:4 of the GATT).[6] Only in 1960, Contracting Parties could agree on a Declaration Giving Effect to the Provisions of Article XVI:4 ("1960 Declaration")

[1] The original Article XVI was limited to paragraph 1 of the current Article XVI of the GATT. All Contracting Parties were bound by this obligation. For an elaboration of the discussions during the GATT preparatory work on subsidy disciplines, see J.H. Jackson, *World Trade and the Law of GATT – A Legal Analysis of the General Agreement on Tariffs and Trade* (Indianapolis, The Bobbs-Merrill Company, 1969), 948 pp., 368–371.

[2] For the exact scope of this exemption, see *infra.*

[3] See also Article II:2(b) of the GATT. Also pertinent in this context is Article XXIII of the GATT on the prohibition of nullification or impairment [Article XXIII(b)], given that countries can nullify or impair benefits (e.g., tariff concessions) by the use of subsidies. Moreover, the "escape clause" in Article XIX of the GATT (and the Safeguard Agreement) could also be relevant to respond to subsidies that result in increased imports that cause or threaten to cause serious injury to domestic producers.

[4] See Articles VI:3, VI:4, VI:5, and VI:6 of the GATT.

[5] The amendments were clearly inspired by the provisions of the Havana Charter but were, at the same time, not as stringent as the Havana Charter with respect to agricultural export subsidies.

[6] The second sentence of Article XVI:4 provided for a standstill obligation until the end of 1957. The expectancy was that the Contracting Parties would have agreed by that time to prohibit all nonprimary export subsidies, but an agreement was only reached in 1960 with the 1960 Declaration, which was not accepted by all Contracting Parties. Therefore, the standstill obligation was extended several times (for some Contracting Parties up to the end of 1967).

that elaborated a nonexhaustive list of export subsidies on nonprimary goods.[7] Because of the different treatment between primary and nonprimary goods, many developing countries were unwilling to adopt the 1960 Declaration, which was in the end only accepted by 17 Contracting Parties.[8] In contrast, regarding primary products,[9] the 1955 amendment only provided for an obligation to "seek to avoid" the use of export subsidies and, if Contracting Parties did grant a subsidy that had the effect of increasing exports, it was subject to a highly ambiguous standard: It could not be used in a way that resulted in a "more than an equitable share of world export trade in that product" (Article XVI:3 of the GATT).[10]

It may be noted that the 1955 GATT amendment introduced two forms of distinctive treatment that are still present in the current multilateral system. First, the multilateral system primarily targets export subsidies, which are subsidies contingent upon export, because of their direct trade-distorting effect.[11] Disciplines on other subsidies, labeled domestic subsidies, are mostly less strict. Second, disciplines on agricultural subsidies are also less severe when compared with other subsidies.[12] The latter is a result of the negotiating power of some developed countries (mainly the European Community [EC], Japan, and the United States) resistant to cutting back their agricultural subsidies.

[7] The 1960 Declaration became effective on November 14, 1962.

[8] Contracting Parties that did not accept the 1960 Declaration were thus not subject to the obligation to cease export subsidies on nonprimary products (Article XVI:4, first sentence).

[9] For the purpose of Article XVI, primary products are defined as "any product of farm, forest or fishery, or any mineral, in its natural form or which has undergone such processing as is customarily required to prepare it for marketing in substantial volume in international trade" (para. 2 of Ad Article XVI: Section B of the GATT).

[10] All Contracting Parties that accepted the 1955 amendment to Parts II and III of the GATT were subject to this obligation. See J. Jackson, *loc. cit., supra*, no. 1-376. To determine the "equitable share" of a Contracting Party, account will be taken of the shares in the product during a previous representative period and "any specific factor" affecting trade in the product (Article XVI:3 of the GATT). The fact that a Contracting Party has not exported the product in question during the previous representative period would not in itself preclude that party from establishing its right to obtain a share of the trade in the product concerned (para. 1 of Ad Article XVI:3 of the GATT). See also the exception for certain price stabilization schemes (para. 2 of Ad Article XVI:3 of the GATT).

[11] Interestingly, the "Suggested Charter for an International Trade Organization of the United Nations," proposed by the United States in 1946, already included a prohibition of export subsidies subject to the bilevel pricing test (Article 25). This prohibition of export subsidies was carried into the Havana Charter (Article 26).

[12] In fact, a differential treatment of agricultural subsidies was already inscribed in the original GATT 1947 given that Article VI:7 of the GATT excludes the possibility to countervail certain agricultural subsidies where a domestic stabilization scheme exists. The Havana Charter also provided for a more flexible treatment of agricultural export subsidies (Articles 27–28), but this differential treatment was more limited than the one inscribed by the 1955 amendment in Article XVI of the GATT.

The Tokyo Round, focusing on the use of nontariff barriers to trade, resulted in the Subsidies Code, a plurilateral agreement (accepted by 24 countries[13]) that entered into force in 1980.[14] In essence, this agreement constituted a compromise between the United States, which aimed at more stringent rules on the use of export and domestic subsidies, and the EC and other countries, which aimed at disciplining the extensive use of CVDs by the United States during the 1970s.[15] This compromise character becomes clear from the Code's provisions. On the one hand, the Subsidies Code categorically prohibited the use of export subsidies on nonprimary goods,[16] included a nonexhaustive list that built on the 1960 Declaration[17] and introduced rather flexible disciplines on the use of domestic subsidies.[18] Developing countries, however, were granted large exceptions from obligations on export subsidies.[19] On the other hand, the substantive and procedural rules on imposing CVDs were elaborated.[20] Importantly, the imposition of CVDs was made subject to an injury test, which was lacking in the CVD procedure of the United States.[21] Yet, signatories could also opt for the multilateral remedy and apply the specific procedural rules on consultation, conciliation, and dispute settlement mapped out by the Subsidies Code.[22]

[13] Some, however, with exceptions or reservations. These countries were Argentina, Australia, Austria, Brazil, Canada, Chile, Colombia, Egypt, the European Economic Community, Finland, Hong Kong, India, Indonesia, Israel, Japan, Korea, New Zealand, Norway, the Philippines, Sweden, Switzerland, Turkey, the United States, and Uruguay.

[14] In full: "Agreement on interpretation and application of Articles VI, XVI and XXIII of the General Agreement on Tariffs and Trade."

[15] T.P. Stewart (Ed.), *The GATT Uruguay Round – A Negotiating History (1986–1992)* (Deventer, Kluwer, 1993, 3 Volumes), Volume I, 1,382 pp., 817.

[16] Although it purported merely to interpret Article XVI of the GATT, the Subsidies Code was thus more stringent because it did not adopt the bilevel pricing test. See J.H. Jackson, *The World Trading System: Law and Policy of International Economic Relations* (Massachusetts, MIT Press, 2nd ed., 1997), 441 pp., 288–289. Regarding export subsidies on certain primary products (Article 10 of the Subsidies Code), signatories agreed not to grant such subsidies "in a manner which results in a more than equitable share of world export trade in such product," a benchmark elaborated on in Article 10.2 of the Subsidies Code.

[17] Articles 8 and 9 of the Subsidies Code and the Annex to the Subsidies Code.

[18] Articles 8 and 11 of the Subsidies Code. Article 11 articulated the difficult balancing act when disciplining domestic subsidies: On the one hand, signatories declared that domestic subsidies are widely used as important instruments to promote social and economic policy objectives (some of which were listed; Article 11.1), but recognized, on the other hand, that these subsidies could cause injury to the domestic industry of another signatory, nullify or impair tariff concessions, or cause serious prejudice to the industry of another signatory (Article 11.2). Disciplines on export and domestic subsidies were labeled "Track II" of the Subsidies Code.

[19] Article 14 of the Subsidies Code.

[20] Articles 2–6 of the Subsidies Code. This part was labeled "Track I" of the Subsidies Code.

[21] Article 6 of the Subsidies Code. Article VI:6(a) of the GATT already requires the determination of (threat of) material injury. However, the U.S. CVDs law (1897) dated from before GATT 1947 and was thus grandfathered from Article VI of the GATT pursuant to the Protocol of Provisional Application. See J.H. Jackson, *loc. cit., supra* no. 16, 286–287.

[22] Articles 12, 13, 17, and 18 of the Subsidies Code. Signatories could opt between a claim under Article VI and/or XVI of the GATT or under the Subsidies Code in case the other party

The economic recession in the early 1980s increased the pressure on countries to support their domestic industry and agricultural sector. The Subsidies Code proved incapable of halting the rise in subsidies. The GATT Subsidies and Countervailing Measures Committee, set up by the Subsidies Code,[23] was unable to resolve conflicts among parties because each of the parties could block the adoption of Panel Reports by the Committee and, more generally, the Committee could not agree on the interpretation or application of the Subsidies Code.[24] With the launch of the Uruguay Round, the Contracting Parties again picked up the theme of subsidies, still defending the same interests: The United States continued its "anti-subsidy crusade,"[25] whereas the EC and others, including developing countries, advocated new rules on CVDs. In parallel, the Cairns group, a coalition of developed and developing agricultural export countries,[26] aimed to liberalize trade in agricultural products, targeting the high amount of export and domestic subsidies mainly granted by the EC, the United States, and Japan. In the end, the negotiations on subsidies resulted in two multilateral agreements, which are thus applicable to all WTO Members: the SCM Agreement and the sector-specific AoA.

Before giving an overview of both agreements, it should be noted that they only deal with subsidies related to trade in goods. The SCM Agreement, elaborating the GATT rules on subsidies and CVDs, leaves subsidies for service sectors untouched.[27] Apparently, the General Agreement on Trade in Services (GATS) does not impose any substantive obligation upon WTO Members[28] to curtail subsidies, but merely obliges them to enter negotiations to develop disciplines

had also signed the Subsidies Code. See P.A. Clarke and G.N. Horlick, "The Agreement on Subsidies and Countervailing Measures," in P.F.J. Macrory, A.E. Appleton, and M.G. Plummer (Eds.), *The World Trade Organization: Legal, Economic and Political Analysis* (New York, Springer, 2005, 3 Volumes), 3120 pp., 686.

[23] See Articles 13, 16, and 18 of the Subsidies Code.

[24] The Committee was unable to adopt any Panel Report or resolve any conflict before the completion of the Uruguay Round negotiations. Only in 1994 and 1995, three of the Panel Reports that had been blocked previously were adopted by the Committee. T.P. Stewart, *loc. cit., supra* no. 15, 836; A. Clarke and G.N. Horlick, *loc. cit., supra* no. 22, 687, Footnote 35.

[25] Yet, following the election of Bill Clinton (1992), the negative stance on subsidies altered somewhat (certainly on subsidies for research and development). See G. Kleinfeld and D. Kaye, "Red Light, Green Light? The 1994 Agreement on Subsidies and Countervailing Measures, Research and Development Assistance, and U.S. Policy," 28:6 *Journal of World Trade* 1994, 43, at 43.

[26] Today, the group consists of 19 agicultural exporting countries: Argentina, Australia, Bolivia, Brazil, Canada, Chile, Colombia, Costa Rica, Guatemala, Indonesia, Malaysia, New Zealand, Pakistan, Paraguay, Peru, Philippines, South Africa, Thailand, and Uruguay.

[27] The subsidy itself can, of course, consist of the provision of a service. See Article 1.1(a)1(iii) of the SCM Agreement. See also Panel Report, *United States – Final Countervailing Duty Determination with Respect to Certain Softwood Lumber from Canada* (WT/DS257/R, adopted on February 17, 2004), para. 7.28. Abbreviation: *U.S. – Lumber CVDs Final.*

[28] Article XV.2 of the GATS only provides that, if a Member considers that it is adversely affected by a subsidy of another Member, it "may request consultations with that Member," and this request must be given "sympathetic consideration."

on subsidies (Article XV of the GATS).[29] However, the GATS does impose certain disciplines on governments when they provide subsidies.[30] First, they may not discriminate among foreign services and service suppliers pursuant to the Most-Favored-Nation (MFN) provision.[31] Second, contrary to GATT, the obligation of national treatment under the GATS does not explicitly exclude subsidies.[32] Because the GATS national treatment obligation is dependent on specific commitments, this does not curtail as such WTO Members' rights to subsidize their service sectors, but if WTO Members make commitments on specific service sectors, they seem to have to explicitly reserve their right to subsidize in a discriminatory way.[33] Otherwise, they might have to provide like treatment to foreign service suppliers with respect to subsidies.[34] Nonetheless, Matsushita et al. reject this argumentation and argue, instead, that subsidies are not covered by the national treatment provision of Article XVII of the GATS because, for the subsidies negotiations (instructed by Article XV of the GATS) to have a mandate, subsidies must by definition be discriminatory.[35] In conclusion,

[29] Article XV of the GATS. A look at the 2007 Report of the Working Party on GATS Rules to the Council for Trade in Services (S/WPGR/17, November 16, 2007, para. 4) reveals that negotiations are not yet in an advanced stage. On the little progress of these negotiations so far and GATS disciplines on subsidies, see R. Adlung, "Negotiations on Safeguard and Subsidies in Services: A Never-ending Story?" 10(2) *Journal of International Economic Law* (2007), 235–265.

[30] The scope of the GATS encompasses subsidies given that the GATS applies to "measures by Members affecting trade in services" (Article I.1 of the GATS).

[31] The MFN obligation is a general obligation (Article II.1 of the GATS), and thus is not dependent on specific commitments. At the end of the Uruguay Round, Members could schedule exceptions to this obligation (Article II.2 of the GATS). See R. Adlung, *loc. cit., supra* no. 29, 240, and 260.

[32] See Article XVII of the GATS.

[33] Some Members indeed made a (horizontal) reservation to uphold their right to subsidize in a discriminatory manner.

[34] See, for example, World Trade Report 2006, *Exploring the links between subsidies, trade and the WTO*, 223 pp., 195; G. Gauthier, with E. O'Brien and S. Spencer, "Déjà vu, or new beginning for safeguards and subsidies rules in service trade?", in P. Sauvé and R. Stern, *GATS 2000 – new directions in services trade liberalization* (Washington D.C., The Brookings Institution, 2000), pp. 165–183, 177. M. Krajewski, "Public services and Trade Liberalisation: Mapping the Legal Framework", 6(2) *Journal of International Economic Law* 2003, 341–367, 361; R. Adlung, *loc. cit., supra* no. 29, 240. The 2001 Scheduling Guidelines also adopted this approach: "Article XVII applies to subsidies in the same way as it applies to all other measures. (...) Therefore, any subsidy which is a discriminatory measure within the meaning of Article XVII would have to be either scheduled as a limitation on national treatment or brought into conformity with that article." The Scheduling Guidelines also clarify that "a binding under Article XVII with respect to the granting of a subsidy does not require a Member to offer such a subsidy to a services supplier located in the territory of another Member" because there is no obligation in the GATS that requires a Member to take measures outside its territorial jurisdiction. See Scheduling Guidelines (S/L/92, March 28, 2001), para. 16.

[35] M. Matsushita, T.J. Schoenbaum, and P. Mavroidis, *The World Trade Organization – Law, Practice and Policy* (Oxford, Oxford University Press, 2nd ed., 2006), 889 pp., 660–661. As a counterargument, one might argue that the mandate for negotiations on the basis of Article XV of the GATS remains sufficiently open given that subsidies are only disciplined by

this is indeed, as Matsushita et al. observe, an area that urgently needs clarification.[36]

Object and Purpose of the SCM Agreement

Remarkably, the SCM Agreement does not contain a preamble,[37] which might indicate the wide divergence in views on subsidies among the drafters.[38] The object and purpose of the agreement has been clarified in WTO case law. In the view of the Panel in *Brazil – Aircraft*, the SCM Agreement aims to "impose multilateral disciplines on subsidies which distort international trade."[39] In the light of the context outlined above, this description might just tell half the story. The broader description elaborated by the Appellate Body in *U.S. – Lumber CVDs Final* seems more complete: The object and purpose is "to strengthen and improve GATT disciplines relating to the use of *both* subsidies *and* countervailing measures, while, recognizing at the same time, the right of Members to impose such measures under certain conditions."[40]

Definition of Subsidy

During the Tokyo Round, participants failed to agree on a general definition of the term "subsidy," as any definition would have been considered either under- or overinclusive.[41] Instead, they focused on the effect rather than on

Article XVII insofar as Members make specific commitments in this respect. Both provisions might thus aim to tackle discriminatory subsidies, but Article XV on a multilateral basis (through negotiations) and Article XVII on a unilateral basis (when a Member makes specific commitments on reducing discriminatory subsidies).

36 M. Matsushita ea., *loc. cit., supra* no. 35, 661.

37 The Anti-Dumping Agreement also does not provide a preamble. In contrast, a preamble was included in the Subsidies Code.

38 Another explanation might be that the drafters did not consider a preamble necessary. The drafts of the SCM Agreement (Dunkel Text and Cartland Drafts) also did not contain a draft preamble.

39 Panel Report, *Brazil – Export Financing Programme for Aircraft* (WT/DS46/R, adopted on August 20, 1999), para. 7.26. Abbreviation: *Brazil – Aircraft*. See also Panel Report, *United States – Measures Treating Export Restraints as Subsidies* (WT/DS194/R, adopted on August 23, 2001), paras. 8.60–8.62. Abbreviation: *U.S. – Export Restraints*.

40 Emphasis added. Appellate Body Report, *United States – Final Countervailing Duty Determination with Respect to Certain Softwood Lumber from Canada* (WT/DS257/AB/R, adopted on January 17, 2004), para. 64. Abbreviation: *U.S. – Lumber CVDs Final*. The Appellate Body referred to its decision in *U.S. – German Steel CVDs* that described the main object and purpose as follows: "to increase and improve GATT disciplines relating to the use of both subsidies and countervailing measures." Appellate Body Report, *United States – Countervailing duties on certain corrosion-resistant carbon steel flat products from Germany* (WT/DS213/AB/R, adopted on December 19, 2002), para. 73. Abbreviation: *U.S. – German Steel CVDs*.

41 As indicated, the Subsidies Code merely provided in an annex an illustrative list of export subsidies that should not be granted.

the intrinsic nature of subsidies.[42] This implied, however, that all kinds of government interventions (and even private interventions[43]) that (potentially) distort trade could be countervailable, as was in fact the case under U.S. law.[44] As indicated, by including a definition of "subsidy," the EC and other countries aimed to curtail the coverage of these CVDs laws.[45] The inclusion of a definition in the SCM Agreement was therefore "generally considered to represent one of the most important achievements of the Uruguay Round in the area of subsidy disciplines."[46] Pursuant to the SCM Agreement, a subsidy shall be deemed to exist if two distinctive elements are present: (i) *a financial contribution by a government*[47] or *any form of income or price support in the sense of Article XVI of the GATT*[48] (ii) that confers *a benefit*.[49] To put it otherwise, it "captures situations in which something of economic value is transferred by a government to the advantage of a recipient."[50] Moreover, to be subject to the disciplines of the SCM Agreement, the subsidy must be *specific*.[51]

Financial Contribution by a Government or Income or Price Support

Financial Contribution

Article 1.1(a)(1) of the SCM Agreement points to three different kinds of financial contributions[52]:

(i) a government practice involves a direct transfer of funds (e.g., grants, loans, and equity infusion), potential direct transfers of funds or liabilities (e.g., loan guarantees);

[42] T.P. Stewart, *loc. cit., supra* no. 15, 820. As McGovern observed back in 1986: "the term 'subsidy' is one of the most frequently used and infrequently defined in the whole vocabulary of international trade regulation." E. McGovern, *International Trade Regulation – GATT, The United States and the European Community* (Exeter, Globefield Press, 1986), 629 pp. at 312.

[43] See *infra* the discussion on private subsidies.

[44] After all, countries could unilaterally define the term "subsidy" for their countervailing duty law.

[45] Panel Report, *U.S. – Export Restraints, loc. cit., supra* no. 39, paras. 8.63–8.69. They thus advocated including a (narrow) definition of "subsidy" so as to restrict the scope of subsidy disciplines as well as the potential of WTO-compatible CVDs.

[46] Panel Report, *United States – Tax Treatment for "Foreign Sales Corporations"* (WT/DS108/R, adopted on March 20, 2000), para. 7.80. Abbreviation: *U.S. – FSC*. See also T. Collins-Williams and G. Salembier, "International Disciplines on Subsidies – The GATT, the WTO and the Future Agenda," 30:1 *Journal of World Trade* 1996, 5–17, at 9–10.

[47] Article 1.1(a)(1) of the SCM Agreement.

[48] Article 1.1(a)(2) of the SCM Agreement.

[49] Article 1.1(b) of the SCM Agreement.

[50] Appellate Body Report, *U.S. – Lumber CVDs Final, loc. cit., supra* no. 40, para. 51.

[51] Article 1.2 of the SCM Agreement.

[52] We do not consider Article 1.1(a)(1)(iv) of the SCM Agreement as a type of financial contribution. It deals with the way, namely indirectly, that the government provides one of the different forms of financial contributions ([i] through [iii]) (see *infra*). This is consistent with the case law. See, for example, Panel Report, *U.S. – Export Restraints, loc. cit., supra* no. 39, para. 8.73.

(ii) government revenue that is otherwise due is foregone or not collected (e.g., fiscal incentives such as tax credits)[53];

(iii) a government provides goods or services other than general infrastructure, or purchases goods.

The Panel in *U.S. – Export Restraints* concluded that this list is exhaustive.[54] As a result, export restraints are not covered by the SCM Agreement and such measures cannot, as a consequence, be countervailed by other countries.[55] Although some authors regret such a closed list in the light of the ingenuity of governments to invent new forms of assistance, the interpretation is legally solid[56] and the three kinds of financial contributions seem to be formulated, and interpreted, broadly to cover a wide variety of financial contributions.

A look at the case law shows indeed a broad interpretation of the three different kinds of financial contributions. As to the (potential) direct transfer of funds and liabilities (Article 1.1[a][1][i]), the Appellate Body in *Japan – DRAMS Countervailing Duties* indicated that the term "funds" encompasses not only "money" but also financial resources and other financial claims more generally.[57] Consequently, similar transactions as those listed (grants, loans, and equity infusion), such as debt forgiveness, the extension of a loan maturity, and an interest rate reduction are considered direct transfers of funds within the meaning of Article 1.1(a)(1)(i) because the financial position of the borrower is improved.[58]

[53] For the exception provided by Footnote 1 to Article 1.1(a)(1)(ii) of the SCM Agreement, see *infra.*

[54] Panel Report, *U.S. – Export Restraints, loc. cit., supra* no. 39, para. 8.69.

[55] See, however, *infra* the discussion on the scope of "income or price support." Panel Report, *U.S. – Export Restraints, loc. cit., supra* no. 39, para. 8.75. In its reasoning, the Panel stressed that the requirement of "financial contribution" was precisely advocated by most countries to counter the purely effect-based definition of the United States. (paras. 8.63–8.72). The United States proposed during the Uruguay Round that the term "(actionable) subsidy" was defined as "any government action or combination of actions which confers a benefit on the recipient firm(s)." See "Elements of the Framework for Negotiations – Submission by the United States" (MTN.GNG/NG10/W/29, November 22, 1989), section II.1(a). See also Appellate Body Report, *U.S. – Lumber CVDs Final, loc. cit., supra* no. 40, para. 52, Footnote 35.

[56] In the view of Rubini, the provision presents contradictory indications on the exhaustive, or merely illustrative, nature of the list. However, the notion "i.e." in Article 1.1(a)(1) of the SCM Agreement, meaning "*id est* (Latin), that is" (*Oxford English Dictionary*) indicates that this list is closed. L. Rubini, "The International Context of EC State Aid Law and Policy: The Regulation of Subsidies in the WTO," in A. Bondi, P. Eeckhout, and J. Flynn (Eds.), *The Law of State Aid in the European Union* (Oxford, Oxford University Press, 2004), 149, at 160.

[57] Appellate Body Report, *Japan-Countervailing Duties on Dynamic Random Access Memories from Korea* (WT/DS336/AB/R, adopted on December 17, 2007), para. 250. Abbreviation: *Japan – DRAMS Countervailing Duties.*

[58] Appellate Body Report, *Japan – DRAMS Countervailing Duties, loc. cit., supra* no. 57, para. 251. The Panel in *Korea – Commercial Vessels* rejected Korea's argument that the phrase of "government practice" implies that this provision does not cover functions normally performed by banks because this phrase does not limit the scope of the provision at all. Panel Report, *Korea – Measures Affecting Trade in Commercial Vessels* (WT/DS273, adopted on April 11, 2005), para. 7.29. Abbreviation: *Korea – Commercial Vessels.*

In relation to the provision of goods or services or purchase of goods (Article 1.1[a][1][iii]), the Appellate Body in *U.S. – Lumber CVDs Final* seemed supportive of a broad definition of the term "goods," including "property and possessions," thus also immovable property.[59] Only the provision of general infrastructure is explicitly not considered a financial contribution by the government. Yet, the Appellate Body warned that only infrastructure of a general nature, and thus not all kinds of infrastructure, is excluded.[60] The case law also shows an expansive interpretation of the most contentious kind of financial contribution, namely the one whereby the government foregoes revenue that is otherwise due (Article 1.1[a][1][ii]). This category confirms that a government can subsidize not only by positive action, in other words, by providing money, goods, or services, but also by negative action, when it refrains from collecting revenue that is otherwise due. Next to social security obligations, taxes, covering direct (raised on income) as well as indirect (raised on products) taxes,[61] and import duties present the two major sources of government revenue. WTO case law has dealt with cases concerning revenue alleged to be foregone under both sources. Before discussing this case law, it should be highlighted that the SCM Agreement excludes from the definition of subsidy, and thus from the scope of the SCM Agreement, the exemption of an exported product from duties or taxes borne by the like product when destined for domestic consumption or the remission of such duties or taxes in amounts not in excess of those that have accrued.[62] The remission or exemption for exports of these indirect taxes and import duties are thus not considered as revenue foregone. The Appellate Body in *U.S. – FSC* confirmed that direct taxes, in contrast, are not covered by this exception.[63]

As to the question of when other tax measures are to be considered a financial contribution, WTO adjudicating bodies provided some insight in the

[59] The Appellate Body thereby even expanded the definition of the Panel, which understood the term "goods" in its broad ordinary meaning as "tangible or movable personal property, other than money." On this basis, the Panel concluded that standing timber was not excluded, which was upheld by the Appellate Body. See Appellate Body Report, *U.S. – Lumber CVDs Final, loc. cit., supra* no. 40, paras. 58–60; Panel Report, *U.S. – Lumber CVDs Final, loc. cit., supra* no. 27, paras. 7.23–7.30.

[60] Appellate Body Report, *U.S. – Lumber CVDs Final, loc. cit., supra* no. 40, para. 60.

[61] For a definition of "direct tax" and "indirect tax," see Footnote 58 to Annex I of the SCM Agreement.

[62] Footnote 1 to Article 1.1(a)(1)(ii) of the SCM Agreement. See also Ad Article XVI of the GATT, Article VI:4 of the GATT, and Annex I, items (g), (h), and (i) of the SCM Agreement (see *infra*).

[63] Because Footnote 1 refers to "the exemption of an exported *product* from duties or taxes *borne by the like product*" (emphasis added). See Appellate Body Report, *United States – Tax Treatment for "Foreign Sales Corporations"* (WT/DS108/AB/R, adopted on March 20, 2000), para. 93. Abbreviation: *U.S. – FSC*. The same argument holds for Ad Article XVI of the GATT (and Article VI:4 of the GATT). The exclusion of direct taxes is also confirmed by the different treatment of indirect and direct taxes under Annex I SCM Agreement (compare items [g] and [e]) (see *infra*). See on the exclusion of direct taxes in the GATT provisions, J. Jackson, *loc. cit., supra* no. 1, pp. 300–303.

U.S. – FSC case.[64] In this politically sensitive case, the EC challenged the U.S. income tax exemption for FSCs under the SCM Agreement. The U.S. tax system is a worldwide tax system because it taxes, in general, income of U.S. citizens and residents earned anywhere in the world. Nonetheless, foreign-source income of FSCs was exempted from worldwide taxation ("FSC exemption").[65] Consequently, the EC argued, and the Panel as well as the Appellate Body agreed, that the United States, by virtue of the FSC exemption, was foregoing revenue otherwise due. The Appellate Body clarified that "foregoing" suggests that the government has given up an entitlement to raise revenue that it would otherwise have raised. This cannot not refer to an "entitlement in the abstract, because governments, in theory, could tax *all* revenues," but implies "some defined, normative benchmark against which a comparison can be made."[66] As to the basis of this comparison, the Appellate Body concluded that it must be the "tax rules applied by the member in question."[67] As to the substance of this comparison, the Appellate Body (in *U.S. – FSC* and *U.S. – FSC Article 21.5*) seems to have developed a two-prong test.[68] When the measure at issue can be described as an "exception" to a "general rule," the "but for" test can be applied.[69] Here, the benchmark is the situation that would exist but for the measure at issue. Applied to the *U.S. – FSC* case, the Panel looked at whether foreign income of FSCs would be taxed higher if the FSCs scheme did not exist.[70] However, the Appellate Body realized that the "but for" test is not always workable[71] because "it is usually very difficult

[64] For comments on these cases, see: C. Carmichael, "Foreign Sales Corporation – Subsidies, Sanctions, and Trade Wars," 35 *Vanderbilt Journal of Transnational Law* (2002), 151–210; R. Howse and D. J. Neven, "United States – Tax treatment for 'Foreign Sales Corporations' Recourse to Arbitration by the United States under Article 22.6 of the Dispute Settlement Understanding and Article 4.11 of the SCM Agreement (WT/DS108/ARB)," 4:1 *World Trade Review* (2005), 101–124; R. E. Hudec, "Industrial Subsidies: Tax Treatment of 'Foreign Sales Corporations'", in E.-U. Petersmann and M. A. Pollack (Eds.), *Transatlantic Economic Disputes – the EU, the U.S., and the WTO* (Oxford, Oxford University Press, 2003), 175–205.

[65] The FSCs are foreign corporations responsible for the sale or lease of goods produced in the United States for export. If these FSCs are foreign subsidiaries of U.S. corporations, they received greater benefits under the FSC laws.

[66] Appellate Body Report, *U.S. – FSC, loc. cit., supra* no. 63, para. 90 (emphasis in the original).

[67] Otherwise, the WTO would "somehow compel Members to choose a particular kind of tax system." Appellate Body Report, *U.S. – FSC, loc. cit., supra* no. 63, para. 90.

[68] Appellate Body Report, *United States – Tax Treatment for "Foreign Sale Corporations" – Recourse to Article 21.5 of the DSU by the European Communities* (WT/DS108/AB/RW, adopted on January 29, 2002), para. 91. Abbreviation: *U.S. – FSC Article 21.5.*

[69] Appellate Body Report, *U.S. – FSC Article 21.5, loc. cit., supra* no. 68, para. 91.

[70] Panel Report, *U.S. – FSC, loc. cit., supra* no. 46, para. 7.45.

[71] Some authors read the report of the Appellate Body in *U.S. – FSC 21.5* as rejecting the "but for" test in all cases. Although some elements in paragraph 91 might underpin this reading (e.g., the last sentence), the general thrust of paragraph 91 seems to indicate that the Appellate Body is not outlawing the "but for" test in those cases where it is still possible to apply it. The wording "not (...) always *requires*" (emphasis by the Appellate Body itself) indicates that the Panels are still allowed to apply it whenever possible. The "but for" test is applicable when but for the measure at issue, the income falls under the general tax rule. The

to isolate a 'general rule' of taxation and 'exceptions' to that 'general' rule" given the variety and complexity of domestic tax systems.[72] Moreover, as the Appellate Body indicated, "it would not be difficult to circumvent such a test by designing a tax regime under which there would be *no* general rule that applied formally to the revenues in question, absent the contested measure."[73] Therefore, in most cases, Panels should use the *fiscal treatment of "legitimately comparable income"* as benchmark.[74] The Appellate Body applied this test to the ETI Act,[75] by which the United States aimed to bring its tax system in conformity with the *U.S. – FSC* ruling.[76] It compared the way the United States taxed income under the ETI Act with the way it taxed "other" foreign-source income and found a "marked contrast" between them.[77] So, without much ado, the Appellate Body considered other foreign-source income as legitimately comparable income.[78] It observed

general tax rule applies by definition to legitimately comparable income. So, the outcome of both tests would be the same. As an indication, the Panel, applying the "but for" test, and the Appellate Body, applying the "legitimately comparable income" test, came to the same conclusion in *U.S. – FSC Article 21.5*.

[72] Appellate Body Report, *U.S. – FSC Article 21.5, loc. cit., supra* no. 68, para. 91.

[73] Appellate Body Report, *U.S. – FSC, loc. cit., supra* no. 63, para. 91 (emphasis in the original).

[74] Appellate Body Report, *U.S. – FSC Article 21.5, loc. cit., supra* no. 68, para. 91. As an illustration, the Appellate Body explains that "if the measure at issue is concerned with the taxation of foreign-source income in the hands of a domestic corporation, it might not be appropriate to compare the measure with the fiscal treatment of such income in the hands of a foreign corporation." Appellate Body Report, *U.S. – FSC Article 21.5, loc. cit., supra* no. 68, para. 92.

[75] "ETI" stands for the "FSC Repeal and Extraterritorial Income Exclusion Act of 2000."

[76] This was contested again by the EC. See Panel Report, *United States – Tax Treatment for "Foreign Sale Corporations" – Recourse to Article 21.5 of the DSU by the European Communities* (WT/DS108/RW, adopted on January 29, 2002). Abbreviation: *U.S. – FSC Article 21.5*; Appellate Body Report, *U.S. – FSC Article 21.5, loc. cit., supra* no. 68. Both the Panel and Appellate Body concluded that the United States had not implemented the Dispute Settlement Body's recommendations and rulings. In response, the United States enacted the "American Jobs Creation Act of 2004." Yet, the Panel and Appellate Body determined that the United States still did not meet its obligations. Panel Report, *United States – Tax Treatment for "Foreign Sale Corporations" – Second Recourse to Article 21.5 of the DSU by the European Communities* (WT/DS108/RW2, adopted on March 14, 2006). Abbreviation: *U.S. – FSC Article 21.5 II*; Appellate Body Report, *United States – Tax treatment for "Foreign Sale Corporations" – Second recourse to Article 21.5 of the DSU by the European Communities* (WT/DS108/AB/RW2, adopted on March 14, 2006). Abbreviation: *U.S. – FSC Article 21.5 II*.

[77] Appellate Body Report, *U.S. – FSC Article 21.5, loc. cit., supra* no. 68, paras. 98–102.

[78] What if legitimately comparable income is subject to different tax rules? The Appellate Body addressed this complex question but did not solve it *in abstracto*: "We recognize that a Member may have several rules for taxing comparable income in different ways. For instance, one portion of a domestic corporation's foreign-source income may not be subject to tax in any circumstances; another portion of such income may always be subject to tax; while a third portion may be subject to tax in some circumstances. In such a situation, the outcome of the dispute would depend on which aspect of the rules of taxation was challenged and on a detailed examination of the relationship between the different rules of taxation. The examination under Article 1.1(a)(1)(ii) of the SCM Agreement must be sufficiently flexible to adjust to the complexities of a Member's domestic rules of taxation." Appellate Body Report, *U.S. – FSC Article 21.5, loc. cit., supra* no. 68, para. 91, Footnote 66.

that, "absent the ETI measure, the United States *would* tax the income under the 'otherwise' applicable rules of taxation" (emphasis added).[79] In conclusion, the "but for" test seems to examine how the income at issue *is* taxed but for the tax measure at issue from a *legal* viewpoint, whereas the "legitimately comparable income" test seems to examine how the income *would* be taxed but for the measure at issue from a *policy* viewpoint.[80] In essence, the "legitimately comparable income" test thus closes the loopholes left open by the "but for" test.[81]

The second source of government revenue consists of *import duties* (*tariffs*). It seems obvious that the imposition of tariffs as such cannot constitute a subsidy. Yet, as the Panel explained in *U.S. – Export Restraints*, a solely effect-based approach toward subsidies would encompass tariffs. Indeed, import duties are, *par excellence*, government measures that distort trade.[82] So, in the view of the Panel, the financial contribution requirement, which precisely blocks the effect-based approach, avoids that tariffs as such fall under the ambit of the SCM Agreement.[83] The imposition of tariffs is therefore not considered as a subsidy to the import competing industry. However, the government does provide a financial contribution when it foregoes revenue by providing tariff exemptions

[79] Appellate Body Report, *U.S. – FSC Article 21.5, loc. cit., supra* no. 68, para. 103.

[80] If the "but for" test is applicable, both tests would reach the same conclusion (see no. 71).

[81] If the income but for the measure at issue is not treated (legally) as the income would be treated but for the measure (policy), the government would, in absence of the measure, alter its tax system to treat the income as it treats comparable income. Theoretically, the appropriate question is thus whether the government *would* raise the revenue in the absence of the measure even if this might be harder, and more intrusive, to answer by the Panels. The question of whether the government *does* legally raise the revenue but for the measure is too limited.

[82] In the view of the Panel, "the United States seems implicitly to acknowledge that, under its approach, any government measure that *caused* an increase in the domestic supply of a good would, for that reason alone, constitute government-entrusted or government-directed provision of goods and hence a financial contribution" (emphasis in the original). Given that the imposition of tariffs would necessarily confer a benefit on some actors in the market (e.g., import competing industry), the Panel concluded that, under the effect-based approach, tariffs would constitute a subsidy within the meaning of Article 1 of the SCM Agreement. As the Panel recognized, this would raise a question of consistency with Article II of the GATT 1994, dealing with Members' schedules of concessions. If a Member applies a bound tariff rate (thus consistent with its schedule of commitment), another Member would still be allowed to argue that this constitutes an actionable subsidy if it causes adverse effects. Panel Report, *U.S. – Export Restraints, loc. cit., supra* no. 39, paras. 8.36–8.38.

[83] "It is, however, doubtful that the concept of financial contribution contained in Article 1.1(a) of the SCM Agreement seeks to bring such government action within the ambit of the SCM Agreement. To the contrary, by introducing the notion of financial contribution, the drafters foreclosed the possibility of the treatment of *any* government action that resulted in a benefit as a subsidy. (...) To hold that the concept of financial contribution is about the effects, rather than the nature, of a government action would be effectively to write it out of the Agreement, leaving the concepts of benefit and specificity as the sole determinants of the scope of the Agreement." Panel Report, *U.S. – Export Restraints, loc. cit., supra* no. 39, para. 8.38.

(similar to when it provides tax exemptions).[84] In *Indonesia – Autos*, the parties agreed that the import duty (and the sales tax) exemptions represented revenue foregone by Indonesia.[85] The Appellate Body reached the same conclusion in *Canada – Autos*, applying the "but for" test[86] as developed in the *U.S. – FSC* case: "Through the import duty exemption, Canada has ignored the 'defined, normative benchmark' that it established for itself for import duties on motor vehicles under its normal MFN rate and, in so doing, has foregone 'government revenue that is otherwise due.'"[87]

Before concluding upon these three categories of financial contributions, it seems appropriate to take one step back and reconsider the scope of Article III:8(b) of the GATT, which, as indicated above, exempts the payment of subsidies exclusively to domestic producers from the national treatment discipline.[88] Are all three types of financial contribution covered by this exemption? The answer seems to be "no" because, as the Appellate Body in *Canada – Periodicals* held, this exemption covers "only the payment of subsidies which involves the *expenditure* of revenue by a government" (emphasis added).[89] Clearly, when the government refrains from collecting revenue it would otherwise raise (type 3 of a financial contribution; Article 1.1[a]1[ii] of the SCM Agreement), the government does not spend any revenue.[90] Indeed, the GATT Panel

[84] As discussed, Footnote 1 to Article 1.1(a)(1)(ii) of the SCM Agreement provides an exception.

[85] Panel Report, *Indonesia – Certain Measures Affecting the Automobile Industry* (WT/DS54,55,59 and 64/R, adopted on July 23, 1998), para. 14.155. Abbreviation: *Indonesia – Autos.*

[86] "We note, once more, that Canada has established a normal MFN duty rate for imports of motor vehicles of 6.1 percent. Absent the import duty exemption, this duty would be paid on imports of motor vehicles." Appellate Body Report, *Canada – Certain Measures Affecting the Automotive Industry* (WT/DS139, 142/AB/R, adopted on June 19, 2000), para. 91. Abbreviation: *Canada – Autos.*

[87] Appellate Body Report, *Canada – Autos, loc. cit., supra* no. 86, para. 91. As a defense, Canada invoked the exemption provided by Footnote 1 to the SCM Agreement. Yet, the Appellate Body dismissed this argument because Footnote 1 deals with duty or tax exemptions for exported goods, whereas the measure at issue applies to imports of motor vehicles that are sold for consumption in Canada (para. 92).

[88] Article III:8(b) of the GATT elaborates that this includes "payments to domestic producers derived from the proceeds of internal taxes or charges applied consistently with the provisions of this Article and subsidies effected through governmental purchases of domestic goods."

[89] Appellate Body, *Canada – Certain Measures Concerning Periodicals* (WT/DS31/AB/R, adopted on July 30, 1997), p. 34. Abbreviation: *Canada – Periodicals.*

[90] Also, other types of financial contributions seem to fall outside the scope of Article III:8 of the GATT. In the case *Canada – Periodicals*, Canada applied reduced postal rates to Canadian publications. The provision of postal services can be considered as a financial contribution in the sense of 1.1(a)(1)(iii) SCM Agreement. The Appellate Body stated that it did "not see a reason to distinguish a reduction of tax rates on a product from a reduction in transportation or postal rates" and concluded that the reduced postal rates were not justified by Article III:8(b) of the GATT. Consequently, the Appellate Body reversed the Panel finding that considered the Canadian postal rate scheme, which provided reduced postal

in *United States – Malt Beverages*, on which the Appellate Body in *Canada – Periodicals* relied, held that the reduction of taxes on a good does not qualify as a payment of a subsidy under Article III:8(b) and is, thus, not exempted from the national treatment discipline.[91] In conclusion, this case law indicates that measures whereby the government refrains from collecting taxes that it would otherwise collect can be scrutinized under the GATT national treatment provision.[92] Such a financial contribution is, if it confers a benefit and is specific, also disciplined by the SCM Agreement. Additionally, as elaborated below, local content subsidies, which are subsidies contingent on the use of domestic over imported goods, also fall outside the scope of the exception of Article III:8(b).[93]

In conclusion, the notion of financial contribution, read together with the benefit element, shows that a subsidy does not necessarily involve a cost for the government. For example, the government can grant a loan to a private actor at an interest rate that is not available to the latter when it would borrow directly on the private market. Without any cost for the government,[94] a subsidy is provided because a financial contribution (Article 1.1[a][1][i]) is made by the government that confers a benefit upon the recipient (see *infra*).[95] Hence, the narrow focus on the "cost to government" as a necessary element of a subsidy, as proposed by the EC and some other countries when drafting the SCM Agreement, was not adopted. In contrast, the financial contribution element seems to exclude so-called "regulatory subsidies" from the scope of the SCM Agreement,

rates to Canadian publications, as compatible with Article III:8(b) of the GATT. See Appellate Body, *Canada – Periodicals, loc. cit., supra* no. 89, pp. 34–35.

91 GATT Panel Report, *United States – Measures Affecting Alcoholic and Malt Beverages* (DS23/R-39R/206, adopted on June 19, 1992), paras. 5.7–5.12. Abbreviation: *United States – Malt Beverages.* Appellate Body, *Canada – Periodicals, loc. cit., supra* no. 89, p. 34.

92 This covers at least indirect taxation, which is captured by Article III:2 of the GATT (see, e.g., GATT Panel Report, *United States – Malt Beverages, loc. cit., supra* no. 91). Direct taxes (on income), in contrast, are considered as outside the scope of Article III:2 of the GATT. See, for example, M. Matsushita ea., *loc. cit., supra* no. 35, 246 and R. Bhala, Modern GATT Law – A Treatise on the General Agreement on Tariffs and Trade (London, Sweet & Maxwell, 2005), 1269 pp., 108–110. Nonetheless, the Panel in *US – FSC Article 21.5* concluded that measures related to direct taxation can be captured by Article III:4 of the GATT on regulations: "Article III:4 applies to measures conditioning access to income tax advantages in respect of certain products" (para. 8.144). After all, as the Panel observed, "nothing in the plain language of the provision (*Article III:4*) specifically excludes requirements conditioning access to income tax measures from the scope of application of Article III (...)" (italics added). Panel Report, *U.S. – FSC Article 21.5, loc. cit., supra* no. 76, para. 8.142. See M. Daly, "WTO Rules on Direct Taxation," *World Trade Organization*, Discussion Paper number 9 (2005), 4–5; A.H. Qureshi, "Trade-Related Aspects of International Taxation: A New WTO Code of Conduct?" 30:2 *Journal of World Trade* 161 (1996), 161, at 170–171.

93 See GATT Panel Report, *Italian Discrimination against Imported Agricultural Machinery* (L/833 – 7S/60, adopted on October 23, 1958). Abbreviation: *Italy – Agricultural Machinery.*

94 After all, the borrowed sum and interest charges have to be paid back.

95 Another example is a loan guarantee provided by the government which may or may not result in an actual cost to the government (*potential* transfer of funds; Article 1.1[a][1][i] of the SCM Agreement).

which refers to the failure of a government to provide certain levels of regulation (e.g., environmental protection or labor standards).[96] Such negative action by the government cannot be labeled a subsidy because there is no (potential) direct transfer of funds (or liabilities), provision of goods or services, or revenue that is foregone.

By a Government

The financial contribution should be made by "a government or any public body within the territory of a Member." This provision covers, first of all, financial contributions by national, regional, as well as local governments.[97] But it also makes clear that the financial contribution can be made by public bodies. Although the SCM Agreement does not define the latter notion, the Panel in *Korea – Commercial Vessels* considered a public body one that is "controlled by the government," whereby government ownership of 100 percent is considered "highly relevant and often determinative of government control."[98] In addition to these direct financial contributions, Article 1.1(a)(1)(iv) of the SCM Agreement makes clear that a financial contribution can also be made indirectly by a government when it makes payments to a funding mechanism or even when the government entrusts or directs a private body to carry out such financial contribution.[99] This provision prevents governments from circumventing the SCM Agreement by channeling their contribution through an intermediary or by using a private body as a "proxy"[100] to make that contribution.[101] The Appellate Body in *U.S. – DRAMS CVD Investigation* explained that "entrustment" occurs where a government gives responsibility to a private body, and "direction" refers to situations where the government exercises its authority over

[96] See also J.H. Jackson, *loc. cit., supra* no. 16, 296.

[97] The Subsidies Code reflected, although with seemingly limited legal consequences, the concerns of federal states: "In this Agreement, the term 'subsidies' shall be deemed to include subsidies granted by any government or any public body within the territory of a signatory. However, it is recognized that for signatories with different federal systems of government, there are different divisions of powers. Such signatories accept nonetheless the international consequences that may arise under this Agreement as a result of the granting of subsidies within their territories" (Article 7, Footnote 22 of the Subsidies Code).

[98] Panel Report, *Korea – Commercial Vessels, loc. cit., supra* no. 58, paras. 7.50–7.56 and 7.352–7.356. The Panel also took other factors into account, such as the importance of the mandate of government-appointed officials.

[99] More exactly, five different requirements can be distinguished in Article 1.1(a)(1)(iv) of the SCM Agreement: (1) a government "entrusts or directs"; (2) "a private body"; (3) "to carry out one or more of the type of functions illustrated in" subparagraphs (i)–(iii) of Article 1.1(a)(1); (4) "which would normally be vested in the government"; and (5) "the practice, in no real sense, differs from practices normally followed by governments." See Panel Report, *U.S. – Export Restraints, loc. cit., supra* no. 39, para. 8.25.

[100] Appellate Body Report, *United States – Countervailing duty investigation on dynamic random access memory semiconductors (DRAMS) from Korea* (WT/DS296/AB/R, adopted on July 20, 2005), paras. 108, 115, 116. Abbreviation: *U.S. – DRAMS CVD Investigation.*

[101] See Appellate Body Report, *U.S. – Lumber CVDs Final, loc. cit., supra* no. 40, para. 52.

a private body but that the determination thereof "will hinge on the particular facts of the case."[102] An indication of entrustment or direction, although not determinative in itself, might be present if the private actor acts against its commercial interests.[103]

Apparently, as advocated by the United States and Australia during the Uruguay Round, the SCM Agreement thus also covers "private subsidies," wherein the financial contribution is made by a private body but at the direction or mandate of the government. Hence, a subsidy does not necessarily involve a financial contribution by the government itself. Nevertheless, purely "private subsidies," in other words, without any form of governmental involvement, are not targeted.[104] As indicated by the Appellate Body in *U.S. – DRAMS CVD Investigation*, "situations involving exclusively private conduct – that is, conduct that is not in some way attributable to a government or public body" – fall outside the scope of the SCM Agreement.[105]

Income or Price Support

Pursuant to Article 1.1(a) of the SCM Agreement, a "subsidy" can exist not only (1) when the government provides a financial contribution but also (2) where there is "any form of income or price support in the sense of Article XVI GATT 1994." Article XVI:1 of the GATT,[106] spelling out the notification obligation, refers to "any subsidy, including *any form of income or price support*, which operates directly or indirectly to increase exports of any product from, or to reduce imports of any product into, its territory" and thus focuses on the trade effects

[102] Appellate Body Report, *U.S. – DRAMS CVD Investigation, loc. cit., supra* no. 100, para. 116. As a result, the Appellate Body rejected the narrow definition of the Panel, which limited the terms "entrusts" and "directs" to, respectively, acts of "delegation" and "command." Such a narrow approach was also adopted by the Panels in *U.S. – Export Restraints, Korea – Commercial Vessels* and *EC – DRAMS Countervailing Measures.* Panel Report, *U.S. – Export Restraints, loc. cit., supra* no. 39, paras. 8.28–8.29; Panel Report, *Korea – Commercial Vessels, loc. cit., supra* no. 58, para. 7.368; Panel Report, *European Union – Countervailing Measures on Dynamic Random Access Memory Chips from Korea* (WT/DS299/R, August 3, 2005), para. 7.52. Abbreviation: *EC – DRAMS Countervailing Measures.*

[103] Panel Report, *Japan – Countervailing Duties on Dynamic Random Access Memories from Korea* (WT/DS336/R, adopted on December 17, 2007), para. 7.70. Abbreviation: *Japan – DRAMS Countervailing Duties.* The Appellate Body agreed with the Panel that the commercial unreasonableness is a relevant factor but stressed that "there could be entrustment or direction by the government, even where the financial contribution is made on commercially reasonable terms." Appellate Body Report, *Japan – DRAMS Countervailing Duties, loc. cit., supra* no. 57, para. 138.

[104] Such private subsidies were countervailable under U.S. law. See T.P. Stewart, *loc. cit., supra* no. 15, 898–899.

[105] Appellate Body Report, *U.S. – DRAMS CVD Investigation, loc. cit., supra* no. 100, para. 107.

[106] The Appellate Body in *U.S. – FSC* noted that Article 1.1(a)(2) of the SCM Agreement is a reference to Article XVI:1 of the GATT and not to Article XVI:4 of the GATT. See Appellate Body Report, *U.S. – FSC, loc. cit., supra* no. 63, para. 117, Footnote 135.

of the measure.[107] Consequently, trade-distortive income or price support might be targeted, but the notions of income and price support are not defined by the GATT or the SCM Agreement. Given that these provisions do not clearly demarcate the scope of this second alternative, one would hope to find some further guidance in the case law. Unfortunately, no Panel or Appellate Body Report has interpreted this second alternative so far, and what is more, some Panels and the Appellate Body sometimes seem to overlook it when they define the term "subsidy" under the SCM Agreement.[108] Most Members – and maybe also those Panels and Appellate Body Reports that neglect this second alternative[109] – might hold the view that "income or price support" is only relevant to the field of agriculture, although the reference to income and price support in Article 1.1(a)(2) of the SCM Agreement *juncto* Article XVI of the GATT is not explicitly limited to the field of agriculture.[110]

The inclusion of this second alternative in the definition of "subsidy" was, as Luengo clarifies, a way to include Article XVI of the GATT into the SCM Agreement, but no one discussed the consequences of this inclusion.[111] Whereas most authors also tend to pay little attention to this second alternative,[112] Luengo argues that it is vital for defining subsidies because it substantially broadens the

[107] See GATT Panel, *United States – Measures Affecting Imports of Softwood Lumber from Canada* (SCM/162, adopted by the Committee on Subsidies and Countervailing Measures on October 27, 1993), para. 153.

[108] See, for example, Panel Report, *U.S. – Export Restraints, loc. cit., supra* no. 39, para. 8.69; Appellate Body Report, *Canada – Measures Affecting the Export of Civilian Aircraft* (WT/DS70/AB/R, adopted on August 20, 1999), para. 156. Abbreviation: *Canada – Aircraft*; Appellate Body Report, *United States – Countervailing Measures Concerning Certain Products from the European Communities* (WT/DS212/AB/R, adopted on January 8, 2003), para. 139. Abbreviation: *U.S. – CVDs on EC Products*. In contrast, the Appellate Body in *U.S. – Lumber CVDs Final* correctly noticed that the "this range of government measures capable of providing subsidies (*Article 1.1[a][i]-[iv] SCM Agreement*) is broadened still further by the concept of 'income or price support' in paragraph 2 of Article 1.1(a)" (italics added). Appellate Body Report, *U.S. – Lumber CVDs Final, loc. cit., supra* no. 40, para. 52.

[109] It was invoked in two cases concerning agricultural subsidies. See Appellate Body Report, *European Communities – Export Subsidies on Sugar* (WT/DS265,266,283/AB/R, adopted on May 19, 2005), paras. 92 and 98. Abbreviation: *EC – Sugar Subsidies;* Panel Report, *Canada – Measures Affecting the Importation of Milk and the Exportation of Dairy Products – Second Recourse to Article 21.5 of the DSU by New Zealand and the United States* (WT/DS103/RW2 and WT/DS113/RW2, adopted on January 17, 2003), para. 5.147.

[110] As indicated, Article XVI:1 GATT refers to "subsidies, including any form of income or price support." Moreover, in the view of Jackson, the definition of "subsidy" in Article XVI:4 (on export subsidies for nonprimary products) encompasses government price-support schemes (e.g., government purchases and sales with net infusion of government funds), even though the phrase "including income or price support" is not included in Article XVI:4. See J. Jackson, *loc. cit., supra* no. 1, 397.

[111] G. Luengo, *Regulation of Subsidies and State Aids in WTO and EC Law* (the Netherlands, Kluwer Law International, 2006), 586 pp., 122.

[112] See also the World Trade Report 2006, which is rather cryptic on this issue. World Trade Report 2006, *loc. cit., supra* no. 34, 197.

scope of subsidies beyond financial contributions by a government to include any form of income or price support that causes trade distortion.[113] Consequently, the notion of "any form of income support" would capture government measures that directly or indirectly have an impact on the income of the recipient, without involving a financial contribution. For example, Luengo holds that an export restraint on a certain product can be considered a subsidy in the sense of the SCM Agreement given that it provides an indirect income support to the domestic purchasers of the product in question, who can buy the product at a reduced price.[114] So, it should have been possible for the Panel in *US – Export Restraint*, which only considered and dismissed the first alternative ("financial contribution"), to conclude that export restraints were a form of income support in the sense of Article 1.1(a)(2) of the SCM Agreement.[115]

Nonetheless, such a broad interpretation seems to render the first alternative meaningless because, at first sight, all financial contributions might have a (direct or indirect) impact on the income of the recipient. As the Panel in *US – Export Restraints* stressed, the requirement of "financial contribution" into the definition of subsidy was precisely advocated by most countries to counter the purely effect-based definition by the United States.[116] An expansive interpretation of "income or price support in the sense of Article XVI GATT" advocated by Luengo would bring the definition of "subsidy" close to such an effect-based approach, covering almost any government action that confers a benefit and causes trade distortion.

Benefit

To be labeled a subsidy under the SCM Agreement, the financial contribution, income, or price support provided by the government should confer a benefit (Article 1.1[b]). Yet, the SCM Agreement does not give any guidance on how the "benefit" element should be defined. To this end, "a highly relevant context"[117] at the disposal of the WTO's adjudicating bodies or Members aiming at imposing CVDs is Article 14 of the SCM Agreement, which sets guidelines for the calculation by the CVD investigating authority of the amount of a subsidy in terms of the benefit to the recipient. In particular, this provision prescribes[118] under

[113] See G. Luengo, *loc. cit., supra* no. 111, 120–123.

[114] G. Luengo, *loc. cit., supra* no. 111, 120.

[115] G. Luengo, *loc. cit., supra* no. 111, 120, Footnote 60.

[116] Panel Report, *U.S. – Export Restraint*, paras. 8.63–8.72.

[117] Panel Report, *EC – DRAMS Countervailing Measures, loc. cit., supra* no. 102, para. 7.173; see also Appellate Body Report, *United States – Imposition of Countervailing Duties on Certain Hot-Rolled Lead and Bismuth Carbon Steel Products Originating in the United Kingdom* (WT/DS138/AB/R, adopted on June 7, 2000), para. 57. Abbreviation: *U.S. – Lead Bars.*

[118] Indeed, calculating the benefit consistent with the guidelines is mandatory. See Appellate Body Report, *U.S. – Lumber CVDs Final, loc. cit., supra* no. 40, para. 92.

which conditions the government provision of equity capital, loans and loan guarantees, or goods and services or purchase of goods can be considered as conferring a benefit.[119]

The Appellate Body in *Canada – Aircraft* explained that "a 'benefit' does not exist in the abstract, but must be received and enjoyed by a beneficiary or a recipient."[120] This recipient can be a "person, natural or legal, or a group of persons."[121] Whereas the financial contribution element focuses on the government, in the determination of a "benefit" the focus shifts toward the recipient of the contribution.[122] As a result, the cost to the government is considered not directly relevant in this determination.[123]

The rationale behind the "benefit" concept has been adequately formulated by the Panel in *Korea – Commercial Vessels*: "[It] acts as a screen to filter out commercial conduct."[124] If the government acts as a commercial player, its action does not distort trade. After all, commercial players would as well provide the same financial contribution, implying that the government action does not give a benefit to the recipient. Hence, the case law developed the so-called *private investor test* to decide whether a "benefit" is conferred:

> "We also believe that the word 'benefit,' as used in Article 1.1(b), implies some kind of comparison. This must be so, for there can be no 'benefit' to the recipient unless the 'financial contribution' makes the recipient 'better off' than it would otherwise have been, absent that contribution. In our view, the marketplace provides an appropriate basis for comparison in determining whether a 'benefit' has been 'conferred,' because the trade-distorting potential of a 'financial contribution' can be identified by determining whether the recipient has received a 'financial contribution' on terms more favorable than those available to the recipient in the market."[125]

In the words of the Panel in *Japan – DRAMS Countervailing Duties*, "the concept of benefit is defined by reference to the market."[126] Nonetheless, the determination of the relevant marketplace may not always be clear-cut. For example, is the domestic market an appropriate benchmark when this market is distorted because of the predominant role of the government? This question was

119 The Panel in *Japan – DRAMS Countervailing Duties* indicated that "the Article 14 guidelines do not cover all eventualities." See Panel Report, *Japan – DRAMS Countervailing Duties, loc. cit., supra* no. 103, para. 7.275.

120 Appellate Body Report, *Canada – Aircraft*, *loc. cit., supra* no. 108, para. 154.

121 Appellate Body Report, *Canada – Aircraft, loc. cit., supra* no. 108, para. 154.

122 Appellate Body Report, *Canada – Aircraft, loc. cit., supra* no. 108, para. 156.

123 Appellate Body Report, *Canada – Aircraft, loc. cit., supra* no. 108, paras. 154–156; Panel Report, *Korea – Commercial Vessels, loc. cit., supra* no. 58, para. 7.84.

124 Panel Report, *Korea – Commercial Vessels, loc. cit., supra* no. 58, para. 7.28.

125 Appellate Body Report, *Canada – Aircraft, loc. cit., supra* no. 108, para. 157.

126 Panel Report, *Japan – DRAMS Countervailing Duties, loc. cit., supra* no. 105, para. 7.275.

central in *U.S. – Lumber CVDs*.[127] To impose CVDs, the U.S. Department of Commerce (DOC) relied on U.S. private stumpage fees as the benchmark for finding whether Canadian public stumpage fees conferred a benefit to Canadian lumber producers. Because the Canadian government "so dominates the Canadian market for timber that the below-market government prices suppress prices in the small private market for timber in Canada, [. . .] the use of other prices commercially available to Canadian lumber producers on the world market is the only available."[128] Canada, on the contrary, argued that whether a benefit is conferred "depends on whether the Canadian producers were better off than other purchasers who buy the same good from other sellers *in the country subject to the investigation*."[129] Although the Panel followed the view of Canada,[130] the Appellate Body concluded that other than private prices in the country of provision may be used as a benchmark "when it has been established that those private prices are distorted, because of the predominant role of the government in the market as a provider of the same or similar goods."[131]

A related issue was addressed in *Korea – Commercial Vessels*, where it was disputed whether the corporate restructuring measures (including debt forgiveness, debt and interest relief, and debt-to-equity swaps) conducted by the Korean government conferred a benefit upon the corporations involved. The Panel clarified that the complaining party, *in casu* the EC, had to demonstrate that restructurings were "commercially unreasonable."[132] To this end, the EC asserted that this "should be based on the behavior of foreign creditors/investors because these were the only creditors/investors operating outside the influence of the Korean government."[133] Referring to the Appellate Body in *U.S. – Lumber CVDs Final*, the Panel confirmed that "of course there could be circumstances

[127] This discussion concentrated on the calculation of the benefit (Article 14[d] of the SCM Agreement) but is of course highly relevant to the question of whether a benefit exists in the first place (Article 1.1[b] of the SCM Agreement). For the close link between both provisions, see Appellate Body Report, *U.S. – Lumber CVDs Final, loc. cit., supra* no. 40, paras. 84–85.

[128] Panel Report, *United States – Preliminary Determinations with Respect to Certain Softwood Lumber from Canada* (WT/DS236/R, adopted on November 1, 2002), para. 7.36. Abbreviation: *U.S. – Lumber CVDs Prelim.*

[129] Panel Report, *U.S. – Lumber CVDs Prelim, loc. cit., supra* no. 128, para. 7.31 (emphasis in the original).

[130] See Panel Report, *U.S. – Lumber CVDs Prelim, loc. cit., supra* no. 128, paras. 7.39–7.59; Panel Report, *U.S. – Lumber CVDs Final, loc. cit., supra* no. 27, paras. 7.43–7.65. For a comment, see M. Benitah, "Softwood Lumber: Exact Significance of the Recent Canadian Victory before the WTO and Prospects in the Context of the Pending Second Lumber Case," 3:2 *The Estey Centre Journal of International Law and Trade Policy* 2002, 346–356.

[131] Appellate Body Report, *U.S. – Lumber CVDs Final, loc. cit., supra* no. 40, para. 103. Yet, the Appellate Body stressed that this possibility is "very limited" and must be made on a "case-by-case basis" (para. 102). Moreover, "the benchmark chosen must, nevertheless, relate or refer to, or be connected with the prevailing market conditions in that country" (para. 103).

[132] Panel Report, *Korea – Commercial Vessels, loc. cit., supra* no. 58, paras. 7.428 and 7.494.

[133] Panel Report, *Korea – Commercial Vessels, loc. cit., supra* no. 58, para. 7.429.

in which a government influences the market to such an extent that it becomes distorted, so that private entities no longer operate pursuant to purely commercial principles.[134] However, in this case "the reasons for and the significance of the differing behavior of domestic versus foreign creditors is mixed."[135] Hence, the absence of foreign creditor participation in the restructuring was considered relevant but not decisive.[136]

Another difficult legal matter that the WTO adjudicating bodies had to resolve is whether a market price exhausts subsidization. Does the new owner who paid fair market value for a subsidized good or asset still enjoy a "benefit"? This question is addressed in two sorts of cases, namely "pass-through cases," involving countervailing of final products that have used subsidized inputs, and "nonrecurring subsidies" cases[137] involving countervailing of products produced in previously subsidized entities (e.g., privatization).[138] Previous nonrecurring subsidies case law decided that preprivatization subsidies are "extinguished" when a subsidized company is sold for fair market value.[139] However, the Appellate Body altered somewhat its position in *U.S. – CVDs on EC Products* in concluding that a market price merely creates a rebuttable presumption that a benefit ceases to exist after privatization.[140] Concerning pass-through cases, the Appellate Body held in *U.S. – Lumber CVDs Final* that the investigating authority must establish that the benefit conferred on input producers is passed through, at least in part, to producers of the processed good.[141]

Specificity

Specificity is not a constitutive element of a subsidy, but a necessary condition for subsidies to be subject to the disciplines of the SCM Agreement.[142] Accordingly, nonspecific subsidies are nonactionable under the SCM

[134] Panel Report, *Korea – Commercial Vessels, loc. cit., supra* no. 58, para. 7.434.

[135] Panel Report, *Korea – Commercial Vessels, loc. cit., supra* no. 58, para. 7.434. Additionally, the Panel stated that it had rejected the EC argument that domestic creditors had been entrusted or directed by the government (para. 7.431).

[136] Panel Report, *Korea – Commercial Vessels, loc. cit., supra* no. 58, paras. 7.487 and 7.494. Concerning another element in the case, the Panel clearly confirmed that foreign market benchmarks could be used (paras. 7.138–7.141).

[137] In general terms, nonrecurring subsidies are subsidies that are granted only once or a limited number of times. See G. M. Grossman and P. Mavroidis, "Here Today, Gone Tomorrow – Privatization and the Injury Caused by Non-Recurring Subsidies," paper prepared for the American Law Institute project on The Principles of World Trade Law.

[138] See M. Matsushita ea., *loc. cit., supra* no. 35, 350, Footnote 56.

[139] See Appellate Body Report, *U.S. – Lead Bars, loc. cit., supra* no. 117, para. 68.

[140] Appellate Body Report, *U.S. – CVDs on EC Products, loc. cit., supra* no. 108, paras. 126–127. For a critical appraisal of this case law, see G.M. Grossman and P. Mavroidis, *loc. cit., supra* no. 137.

[141] Appellate Body Report, *U.S. – Lumber CVDs Final, loc. cit., supra* no. 40, para. 146. Some authors indicate that this decision is an application of the standard set by the Appellate Body in *U.S. – CVDs on EC Products*. See M. Matsushita ea., *loc. cit., supra* no. 35, 349–350.

[142] Article 1.2 of the SCM Agreement.

Agreement.[143] The government should provide a financial contribution, income, or price support that benefits a specific recipient. As indicated, the recipient can be either a natural or a legal person.

Some authors refer to an economic rationale for the inclusion of a specificity test, given that subsidies to a specific recipient have a higher probability to be trade distorting than do general ones.[144] Others, however, doubt the accuracy of this economic justification and point to practical reasons for such a test in avoiding a review of all programs and their distorting effects.[145] Lastly, part of the rationale, in the view of Jackson, is that specificity is a useful tool to exclude from the scope of the SCM Agreement general activities by all governments (such as police or fire protection, education, roads) "which really ought not to be brought into a countervailing duty or other international process."[146] The difficult question is, of course, what is considered "general" and what degree of specificity is thus targeted.

The SCM Agreement clarifies that the subsidy should be specific to "an enterprise or industry or group of enterprises or industries."[147] Therefore, the Panel in *U.S. – Lumber CVDs Final* decided that specificity should be determined at industry level and not at product level.[148]

Prohibited subsidies, being export subsidies and local content subsidies, are presumed to be specific.[149] Consequently, only actionable subsidies should pass the specificity test in Articles 2.1 and 2.2 of the SCM Agreement, which should be based on positive evidence.[150] The SCM Agreement provides some, but arguably not sufficient,[151] guidance on the types and degree of specificity required. It targets, first of all, *de jure* specificity, whereby the subsidy is explicitly limited to

[143] This was confirmed by Article 8.1(b) of the SCM Agreement, indicating that nonspecific subsidies fell into the category of "nonactionable subsidies." Moreover, nonspecific subsidies were in any case nonactionable, in contrast to other nonactionable subsidies (see *infra*, Article 9.1 only refers to Article 8.1[a]). However, pursuant to Article 31 of the SCM Agreement, the category of nonactionable subsidy expired at the end of 1999, including thus Article 8.1(b). Nevertheless, nonspecific subsidies are still nonactionable, simply because only specific subsidies can be actionable subsidies (Article 1.2 of the SCM Agreement).

[144] See World Trade Report 2006, *loc. cit., supra* no. 34, 51, and 198; J. Jackson, *loc. cit., supra* no. 16, 296–297.

[145] L. Rubini, *loc. cit., supra* no. 56, 173.

[146] J. Jackson, *loc. cit., supra* no. 16, 297.

[147] Article 2.1 of the SCM Agreement. Pursuant to the World Trade Report, this and other provisions in the SCM Agreement referring to producers of subsidized products imply that transfers to consumers "may not be covered" by the SCM Agreement. World Trade Report 2006, *loc. cit., supra* no. 34, 54.

[148] Panel Report, *U.S. – Lumber CVDs Final, loc. cit., supra* no. 27, paras. 7.119–7.121.

[149] Article 2.3 of the SCM Agreement. To be precise, the irrefutable presumption of specificity seems not dependent on whether these subsidies are prohibited but on whether they are export/local content subsidies.

[150] Article 2.4 of the SCM Agreement.

[151] The delineation between general and specific subsidies remains vague, and it will thus have to be decided by the dispute-settlement system on a case-by-case basis. See M. Trebilcock and M. Fishbein, "International trade: Barriers to Trade," in A.T. Guzman and A.O. Sykes (Eds.), *Research Handbook in International Economic Law* (Cheltenham, Edward

certain enterprises. Hence, if objective criteria or conditions are established,[152] specificity does not exist provided that the eligibility is automatic and that such criteria and conditions are strictly adhered to.[153] However, a subsidy that is not limited in law to certain enterprises or that is based on objective criteria or objectives can still in practice benefit only certain enterprises. So, the SCM Agreement also encompasses *de facto* specificity, whereby four factors can be taken into consideration: the use of a subsidy program by a *limited number* of enterprises, *predominant use* by certain enterprises, the granting of *disproportionately large amounts* of subsidy to certain enterprises, and *the manner in which discretion has been exercised* by the granting authority in the decision to grant a subsidy.[154] If the subsidy is limited to certain enterprises within a designated geographical region, the subsidy is considered to be specific.[155] In contrast, the setting or change of generally applicable tax rates by all levels of government entitled to do so is explicitly not deemed to be specific.[156]

In Conclusion: Interplay between the Domestic and International Level

The analysis above has borne out that what constitutes a subsidy in Country A is not necessarily a subsidy in Country B. After all, the criteria and benchmarks to determine whether there exists a subsidy subject to the SCM Agreement are not all defined at the international/universal levels but depend to an important extent on circumstances at the domestic level.

Considering the specificity requirement, we indicated that the SCM Agreement puts forward general criteria encompassing *de jure* as well as *de facto* specificity. The exception for "the setting or change of generally applicable tax rates by all levels of government entitled to do" seems, nonetheless, to refer to the domestic level. First of all, the determination of "generally applicable tax rates" will be

Elgar, 2007), 640 pp., 21–22; A.O. Sykes, "International trade: Trade remedies," in A.T. Guzman and A.O. Sykes, *loc. cit., supra* no. 151, 103.

152 This means that they are neutral and do not favor certain enterprises over others, economic in nature and horizontal in application, such as number of employees or size of enterprise. Article 2.1(b), Footnote 2 of the SCM Agreement.

153 In addition to these substantive requirements, the criteria and conditions should also be "clearly spelled out in law, regulation, or other official document, so as to be capable of verification" (Article 2.1[b] of the SCM Agreement).

154 Article 2.1(c) of the SCM Agreement. Account shall be taken of the diversification of economic activities in the subsidizing country and the length of time of the subsidy program.

155 Article 2.2 of the SCM Agreement, which is much narrower than the draft text (Dunkel Text) that considered subsidies "available to *all* enterprises located within one designated geographical area" as specific (emphasis added). Clarke and Horlick reveal that this change was the result of a compromise between the United States and Canada in late 1993 in which the United States agreed upon fewer disciplines on subsidies in return for more trade-restrictive antidumping rules. See A. Clarke and G.N. Horlick, *loc. cit., supra* no. 22, 695, Footnote 82.

156 Article 2.2 of the SCM Agreement.

made by reference to the national level. Moreover, in the view of some authors, this exception implies that if a regional government aims to introduce tax incentives, it is allowed to do so because they would be treated as nonspecific, even if the central government would compensate for the shortfall in public revenue of the regional government. Conversely, according to these authors, an identical measure taken at the national level could be deemed specific.[157] Countries A and B can thus take an identical measure but, depending on the governance level, this might be specific or not.

More significantly, the benefit element is recipient specific and refers at least partly to domestic circumstances. The private investor test, as developed in the case law, uses the domestic market as the primary benchmark for deciding whether a benefit is conferred. The aim is to determine whether a benefit is conferred vis-à-vis other actors in the prevailing *domestic* market. For example, Countries A and B can provide the same goods/service against the same price, but depending on the prevailing market conditions in each country, this might confer a benefit or not.

As indicated by Matsushita ea., the financial contribution element, in particular the category of revenue "otherwise" due, is clearly determined by reference to the domestic legal regime. The "but for" test as well as the legitimately comparable income test refer to the domestic rules as the relevant benchmark. The concrete implications thereof are illustrated by the defense of the United States in the *U.S. – FSC* case. The United States argued that the European territorial tax system has the same economic effect as the FSC exemption to its worldwide tax system because both tax systems exempt foreign-source income of exporters. After all, whereas under a territorial tax system all foreign-source income is not taxed, a worldwide tax system in principle taxes all sources of income and therefore needs an exemption to exclude foreign-source income of exporters. The United States concluded that the "WTO should not penalize a country using a world-wide system for incorporating elements of a territorial system in order to obtain comparable tax treatment for its exports." Yet, the EC objected that the United States was responsible for having chosen a general tax system that puts its exporters at a disadvantage, and this view was in essence followed by the Panel:

> [T]he United States is free to maintain a world wide tax system, a territorial tax system or any other type of system it sees fit. This is not the business of the WTO. What it is not free to do is to establish a regime of direct taxation, provide an exemption from direct taxes specifically related to exports, and then claim that it is entitled to provide such an export subsidy because it is necessary to eliminate a disadvantage to exporters created by the U.S. tax system itself. In our view, this is no different from imposing a corporate income tax of, say, 75 percent, and then arguing that a special tax rate of

157 L. Rubini, *loc. cit., supra* no. 56, 173.

> 25 percent for exporters is necessary because the generally applicable corporate tax rate in other Members is only 25 percent.[158]

Hudec commented that this "your own fault" response by the Panel begs the following question: Why should one government be allowed to create subsidy-like tax effects in one case but not the other? In particular, why should the WTO reach a different result about a subsidy-like tax exemption for exporters depending on whether the country also exempts other foreign-source income? After all, the only difference between both systems is that the territorial tax systems exclude all foreign-source income, whereas the U.S. FSC exemption merely excludes foreign-source income of exporters. There seems no economic logic available to explain this different stance.[159,160]

Considered at a general theoretical level, such a different outcome is, however, inevitable given that the "but for" test, as well as the legitimately comparable income test, refers to the domestic legal order, which evidently varies among WTO Members.[161] The example of the Panel can serve as an illustration. Country A can apply a generally applicable corporate tax rate of 75 percent with an exemption of 25 percent for exporters, whereas country B might provide a generally applicable corporate tax rate of 25 percent. Moreover, the domestic level is the only appropriate benchmark in the absence of a level playing field. Indeed, the WTO adjudicating bodies cannot rely on an agreed international benchmark (e.g., a common corporate tax rate of 75 percent), and the WTO itself is not a standard-setting organization. To put it in the words of the Panel, the choice of the tax system is "not the business of the WTO" itself. So, the "but for" test, as well as the legitimately comparable income test, has to refer to the domestic legal regime of the country in question. As a consequence, Country B's tax system will probably fall outside the reach of SCM disciplines, whereas the tax exemption

158 Panel Report, *U.S. – FSC, loc. cit., supra* no. 46, para. 7.122.

159 See R.E. Hudec, *loc. cit., supra* no. 64, 190.

160 Caution should be exercised when considering the territorial tax systems as *ipso facto* SCM compatible given that the WTO did not yet have to decide on this. The United States did not file a countercomplaint. The Panel also emphasized that the "WTO-consistency of other Members' tax systems, whether territorial or otherwise, is outside our terms of reference." See Panel Report, *U.S. – FSC, loc. cit., supra* no. 46, para. 7.123. At first sight, it seems that, under both tests, the exemption of all foreign-source income under territorial tax systems would not constitute revenue otherwise due, given that the territorial tax system is the general rule and that the Appellate Body considered other foreign-source income as legitimately comparable income in *U.S. – FSC Article 21.5*. Yet, the WTO dispute settlement organs might also broaden the scope of legitimately comparable income when scrutinizing the exclusion of foreign-source income. It could be that they consider income of firms earned at home and abroad as legitimately comparable income. See commentary on the case provided by *Worldtradelaw.net*.

161 The benefit element also necessarily refers to the domestic market. The appropriate question is indeed whether a benefit is conferred to a recipient vis-à-vis other actors in the domestic market where the transaction takes place.

provided by Country A might constitute a prohibited (export) subsidy even if the economic effect upon exporters is similar.

In conclusion, whether a subsidy exists that is subject to the SCM disciplines will be determined by multilateral criteria as agreed between the WTO Members: It must be *a financial contribution (or income or price support) by a government* to *the benefit* of a *specific* recipient. Although not every governmental act that distorts trade can be considered a subsidy, the scope is nevertheless broad and wide open for interpretation by the WTO adjudicating bodies. Above all, the application of the criteria relies on a mix of uniform elements, which do not vary between countries, and domestic elements, whereby the domestic legal regime or market is considered as a benchmark. The question of whether a governmental act constitutes a subsidy thus depends partly on its domestic legal/economic environment. The broad and open scope, in combination with the domestic context, makes the determination of a subsidy a legally difficult but also a politically sensitive issue.

Categories of Subsidies

Obviously, the SCM Agreement does not ban all specific subsidies, as defined by Articles 1 and 2 of the SCM Agreement. The Appellate Body, recognizing the broad definition of the subsidy concept, explained that:

> "the granting of a subsidy is not, in and of itself, prohibited under the SCM Agreement. Nor does granting a "subsidy," without more, constitute an inconsistency with that Agreement. The universe of subsidies is vast. Not all subsidies are inconsistent with the SCM Agreement."[162]

Articles 1 and 2 merely define the concept of subsidy and specificity and do not themselves impose any obligation with respect to such "specific subsidies." These articles serve as a threshold for the application of the disciplines prescribed by Parts II, III, IV, and V of the SCM Agreement.[163] The SCM Agreement aims at targeting those subsidies that are trade distortive. To this end, the agreement as originally implemented when the WTO Agreement came into effect grouped subsidies in three categories, each imposing different disciplines (traffic light approach). On the one end, two types of subsidies are principally *prohibited* in and of themselves (red light) because of their direct trade-distortive effect, namely export subsidies and local content subsidies (Part II SCM Agreement). On the other end, three types of subsidies, in other words, for research activities, for disadvantaged regions, or for the adaptation to environmental requirements,

[162] Appellate Body Report, *Canada – Measures Affecting the Export of Civilian Aircraft – Recourse by Brazil to Article 21.5 of the DSU* (WT/DS70/AB/RW, adopted on August 4, 2000), para. 47. Abbreviation: *Canada – Aircraft Article 21.5.*

[163] See also Appellate Body Report, *U.S. – FSC Article 21.5, loc. cit., supra* no. 68, paras. 85–87.

were deemed *nonactionable* (green light) and thus in principle were allowed under the SCM Agreement (Part IV SCM Agreement). All other subsidies are *actionable subsidies* (rest category, yellow light), meaning that they can be challenged or countervailed if they cause adverse effects (Part III SCM Agreement).

However, the category of green light subsidies expired at the end of 1999.[164] Since then, just two categories exist: those subsidies that are prohibited as such (red light) and all others that can be challenged if they cause adverse effects to the interest of other WTO Members (yellow light). The category of prohibited subsidies thus circumvents the difficult proof of adverse effects[165] and provides more powerful remedies in comparison with actionable subsidies. So, subsidies that are not deemed prohibited subsidies by the WTO adjudicating bodies can still be actionable if they cause adverse affects.[166] Specific subsidies that were granted green light status are thus currently actionable if they cause adverse effects.

Prohibited Subsidies

Article 3 of the SCM Agreement targets two types of subsidies:

> (a) subsidies contingent, in law or in fact, whether solely or as one of several other conditions, upon export performance, including those illustrated in Annex I;
> (b) subsidies contingent, whether solely or as one of several other conditions, upon the use of domestic over imported goods.

These export subsidies (a) and local content subsidies (b) are prohibited and may thus not be granted or maintained[167] because they are considered trade distorting by their very nature.[168] Expansion of the red light category beyond the illustrative list of export subsidies of the Subsidies Code was one of the most contentious issues during the Uruguay Round, with the United States as its main proponent.[169] In the Doha negotiations, the United States also proposed an expansion of the red light subsidies beyond these two types of subsidies.[170]

164 Article 31 of the SCM Agreement.

165 As mentioned, prohibited subsidies are also deemed to be specific (Article 2.3 of the SCM Agreement).

166 See *infra*.

167 Article 3.2 of the SCM Agreement.

168 T.P. Stewart, *loc. cit., supra* no. 15, 886.

169 The United States aimed to expand the Illustrative List of prohibited subsidies to primary products, as well as to domestic subsidies that have a significant effect on trade or competitiveness, which should be determined on the basis of objective criteria such as the amount of the subsidy. See Negotiating Group on Subsidies and Countervailing Duties, Communication from the United States (MTN.GNG/NG10/W/20, adopted on June 15, 1988), 3–4. See T.P. Stewart, *loc. cit., supra* no. 15, 886–890.

170 See Negotiating Group on Rules, Proposal from the United States, *Expanding the prohibited "red light" subsidy category – draft text* (TN/RL/GEN/146, adopted on June 5, 2007). For example, the United States proposes to move all but one (Article 6.1[a]) of the subsidies spelled out in Article 6 of the SCM Agreement to the category of prohibited subsidies.

Before examining the substance of both types of prohibited subsidies, we look at the requirement of contingency, which is a cross-cutting issue.

The term "contingent" in these definitions should be understood as "conditional" or "depending for its existence on something else."[171] This conditionality can be *in law* but also *in fact*, which prevents governments from circumventing the provision by linking subsidies to export performance without prescribing it explicitly in their laws.[172] As to export subsidies (Article 3(1)(a)), *de jure* export conditionality should be "demonstrated on the basis of the words of the relevant legislation, regulation or other legal instrument."[173] *De facto* export conditionality is explicitly prescribed in the SCM Agreement, which even indicates how this should be determined. The complaining party should demonstrate by the facts three different substantive elements[174]: (i) the granting of a subsidy[175] is (ii) in fact *tied to*[176] (iii) actual or anticipated exportation or export earnings.[177] The mere fact that a subsidy is granted to export-oriented industries is considered insufficient in itself.[178] As far as local content subsidies (Article 3(1)(b)) are concerned, the type of conditionality is not explicitly prescribed, but case law indicates that it also covers both *de jure* and *de facto* contingency. Indeed, the Appellate Body in *Canada – Autos* disagreed with the Panel's decision that limited the scope to conditionality in law.[179] Moreover, the Appellate Body contemplated the legal standard of *de jure* contingency similar to that under Article 3(1)(a).[180]

The question arises as to what degree of conditionality is required by the term "contingent upon."[181] What is sure is that, as indicated, the mere fact that a subsidy is granted to export-oriented industries does not reach the required degree of conditionality.[182] The definitions also indicate that export performance (or local content) can be one among other conditions for receiving the subsidy

[171] Appellate Body Report, *Canada – Aircraft, loc. cit., supra* no. 108, para. 166.

[172] Appellate Body Report, *Canada – Aircraft, loc. cit., supra* no. 108, para. 167.

[173] Appellate Body Report, *Canada – Aircraft, loc. cit., supra* no. 108, para. 167. See also Appellate Body Report, *Canada – Autos, loc. cit., supra* no. 86, para. 100.

[174] See Article 3.1(a), Footnote 4 to the SCM Agreement.

[175] Appellate Body Report, *Canada – Aircraft, loc. cit., supra* no. 108, para. 170.

[176] This second element is "at the very heart of the legal standard in footnote 4." "Tied to" refers to "limit or restrict to (...) conditions." It thus requires a demonstration of a relationship of conditionality or dependence. So, "tied to" is similar to "contingent upon." See Appellate Body Report, *Canada – Aircraft, loc. cit., supra* no. 108, para. 171.

[177] Appellate Body Report, *Canada – Aircraft, loc. cit., supra* no. 108, para. 172.

[178] Article 3.1(a), Footnote 4, second sentence of the SCM Agreement.

[179] Appellate Body Report, *Canada – Autos, loc. cit., supra* no. 86, paras. 135–143. The primary reason of the Appellate Body seemed to be the circumvention argument (see para. 142).

[180] Appellate Body Report, *Canada – Autos, loc. cit., supra* no. 86, para. 123. The Appellate Body did not decide upon *de facto* contingency because of the incomplete analysis of the Panel.

[181] Article 3.1(a) and (b) of the SCM Agreement.

[182] Article 3.1(a), Footnote 4, second sentence of the SCM Agreement. Export orientation can be a relevant fact to demonstrate that the subsidy is "tied to" exportation or export earnings, provided that it is one of several other facts that are considered. See Appellate Body Report, *Canada – Aircraft, loc. cit., supra* no. 108, para. 173.

to be an export (or local content) subsidy. In other words, export performance (or local content) does not have to be a *sufficient condition* for receiving the subsidy: Other conditions might in addition be required.[183] In contrast, one could ask oneself whether export performance (or local content) must constitute a *necessary* condition for receiving the subsidy.

Whereas the text of the SCM Agreement does not provide a clear answer, the Panel in *Canada – Aircraft* considered export performance a necessary condition because it applied a "but for" test. The essential question was whether Canada would have granted the subsidy but for the export performance.[184] Although the Appellate Body agreed with the Panel's "overall approach to de facto export contingency," it dismissed the "but for" test because it did not fit into the actual language of the agreement.[185] The Appellate Body did not indicate, however, what degree of conditionality it exactly had in mind but only clarified that "it does *not* suffice to demonstrate solely that a government granting a subsidy *anticipated* that exports would result."[186]

The measure at issue in *Canada – Automotive Industry* illustrates that the question of necessary conditionality of the measure as a whole might not be decisive in all cases. First, concerning export contingency, a manufacturer could receive a certain amount of import duty exemptions (subsidies) even if he/she did not export. Yet, "the more motor vehicles a manufacturer exports (*export performance*), the more motor vehicles that manufacturer is entitled to import duty-free (*subsidy*)."[187] On this basis, the Appellate Body concluded that the

183 See Article 3.1(a) and (b), the phrase: "whether solely or as one of several other conditions." See, for example, Appellate Body Report, *U.S. – FSC Article 21.5, loc. cit., supra* no. 68, para. 111 *in fine.*

184 Panel Report, *Canada – Measures Affecting the Export of Civilian Aircraft* (WT/DS70/R, adopted on August 20, 1999), paras. 9.332 and 9.340. Abbreviation: *Canada – Aircraft.*

185 Appellate Body Report, *Canada – Aircraft, loc. cit., supra* no. 108, para. 171, Footnote 102.

186 Emphasis in the original. Appellate Body Report, *Canada – Aircraft, loc. cit., supra* no. 108, para. 171.

187 Appellate Body Report, *Canada – Autos, loc. cit., supra* no. 86, para. 106 (italics added). Two situations were distinguished by the Panel and Appellate Body. The first situation is where the production-to-sales ratio requirements are 100:100 or higher, which was a condition to be eligible for the import duty exemption. It is in essence a ratio of the net sales value of the vehicles *produced in Canada* to the net sales value of all vehicles of that class *sold* for consumption *in Canada.* So, as the Panel indicated correctly, to meet such standard, for every unit a manufacturer imports duty-free, it would have to export an equivalent unit value. Thus, exportation is, in this first situation, clearly a necessary condition for receiving the subsidy (import duty exemption). Yet, the stringent production-to-sales ratio requirements were relaxed to some extent under situation 2. For example, manufacturers with a ratio requirement of 95:100 that do not export are nevertheless entitled to import duty-free vehicles with a sales value of 5. Up to this amount, the Panel and the Appellate Body reasoned that the import duty exemption is not contingent upon export performance. For any amount above this duty-free allowance, the value of vehicles imported duty-free is strictly limited to the value of vehicles exported and, as a consequence, for that amount there is a clear relationship of contingency pursuant to the Panel and Appellate Body.

measure was contingent upon export.[188] Referring to Footnote 4 to Article 3.1(a) of the SCM Agreement, the Appellate Body thus required a "tie"[189] (i.e., a positive correlation) between the export performance and the subsidy without clarifying the required strength of the tie (the degree of correlation).[190] Second, concerning local content contingency, the import duty exemption was contingent upon certain Canadian Value Added (CVA) requirements. The definition of CVA included parts and materials of Canadian origin (thus local content) among other elements such as labor costs and manufacturing overheads. The Panel considered the subsidy as not contingent upon the use of domestic over imported goods because a manufacturer might be able to satisfy the CVA requirement without using any domestic good whatsoever. However, the Appellate Body rejected the Panel's conclusion because it had overlooked the level of CVA requirements. As an example, the Appellate Body indicated that "if the level of the CVA requirements is very high, we can see that the use of domestic goods may well be *a necessity* and thus be, in practice, required as *a condition* for eligibility for the import duty exemption."[191] The Appellate Body thus also seems to refer to "necessary conditionality," but this should be determined in relation to the level of CVA requirements.[192]

[188] Is export contingency a necessary condition to receive the subsidy? This question is indeed not fine-tuned enough to be answered for the measure as a whole. Up to a certain amount of subsidies, exportation is not a necessary condition. If a manufacturer aims to receive more duty-free (subsidized) imports, it should export the same value, and exportation becomes thus a necessary condition. The level of the amount upon which exportation becomes necessary is essential to decide whether the measure as a whole can be considered as contingent upon export. This was, however, not considered relevant by the Appellate Body.

[189] Appellate Body Report, *Canada – Autos, loc. cit., supra* no. 86, paras. 107–108. See also Panel Report, *Australia – Subsidies Provided to Producers and Exporters of Automotive Leather* (WT/DS126/R, adopted on June 16, 1999), paras. 9.55-9.71. Abbreviation *Australia – Automotive Leather.*

[190] As indicated, the level of the amount upon which exportation becomes necessary might have to be taken into consideration (see no. 188). This might be illustrated by a far-fetched example: What if the Canadian subsidy program allowed that even manufacturers with a production sales ratio of 10:100 that do not export were still entitled to import duty-free vehicles? This implies that they could import 90 percent of (the value of) their sales duty-free (subsidy) without any exportation requirement. Is this subsidy really contingent upon exportation? If the test is "whether they could import more if they exported more," the answer is nevertheless affirmative.

[191] Appellate Body Report, *Canada – Autos, loc. cit., supra* no. 86, para. 130 (first emphasis added).

[192] After all, the Appellate Body continued: "By contrast, if the level of the CVA requirements is very low, it would be much easier to satisfy those requirements *without* actually using domestic goods; for example, where the CVA requirements are set at 40 percent, it might be possible to satisfy that level simply with the aggregate of other elements of Canadian value added, in particular, labor costs. The multiplicity of *possibilities* for compliance with the CVA requirements, when these requirements are set at low levels, may, depending on the specific level applicable to a particular manufacturer, make the use of domestic goods only one *possible* means (means which might not, in fact, be utilized) of satisfying the CVA

In *U.S. – FSC Article 21.5*, the United States contended that export contingency should be understood as a necessary condition and therefore argued that the ETI measure was export neutral. After all, the ETI measure granted a tax exemption (subsidy) when goods are *sold* for use abroad and was thus available with respect to goods *not* produced in the United States.[193] Yet, the Panel and the Appellate Body came to a different conclusion by distinguishing two situations. First, when goods are *produced domestically* and sold for use abroad, exporting is obviously a necessary condition for receiving the tax exemption and the tax benefit is thus contingent upon export.[194] The Panel and Appellate Body did not decide upon the second situation, whereby goods are *produced abroad* and sold for use abroad, which does clearly not involve any exportation from the United States.[195] Importantly, the fact that the subsidies granted in the second situation might not be export contingent "does not dissolve the export contingency" arising in the first situation[196] because it concerns two different factual situations.[197] Apparently, whereas export contingency is not a necessary condition for receiving the subsidy given the ETI measure as a whole, the ETI measure with respect to the first situation is considered export contingent.[198]

This case law "clarifies" at least one element: Whether the degree of conditionality required to be contingent upon is present will be determined on a case-by-case basis. In this exercise, the text of the SCM Agreement does not provide much guidance to the dispute-settlement bodies on where it has to draw the line.[199]

requirements." Appellate Body Report, *Canada – Autos, loc. cit., supra* no. 86, para. 130 (emphasis in the original). The emphasized wording "only one *possible* means" indicates that this example is not considered a condition.

193 Appellate Body Report, *U.S. – FSC Article 21.5, loc. cit., supra* no. 86, para. 110.

194 Appellate Body Report, *U.S. – FSC Article 21.5, loc. cit., supra* no. 68, paras. 116–118.

195 Appellate Body Report, *U.S. – FSC Article 21.5, loc. cit., supra* no. 68, paras. 109 and 120.

196 "Conversely, the export contingency arising in these circumstances (*situation 1)* has no bearing on whether there is an export contingent subsidy in the second set of circumstances" (italics added). See Appellate Body Report, *U.S. – FSC Article 21.5, loc. cit., supra* no. 68, para. 119.

197 See Appellate Body Report, *U.S. – FSC Article 21.5, loc. cit., supra* no. 68, paras. 113–115. The Appellate Body indicated that the distinctiveness is confirmed by the text of the ETI measure. Moreover, the two situations "must be different since the very same property cannot be produced both within and outside the United States." So, the crux of the argument seems to be that both situations are different because they are mutually exclusive. For property produced in the United States, exportation is the only option to benefit from the tax exemption. One and the same natural or legal person may, of course, benefit under both situations at the same time (see para. 119).

198 Because exportation is a necessary condition in this situation and another sufficient condition involves a different situation. See also Appellate Body Report, *United States – Subsidies on Upland Cotton* (WT/DS267/AB/R, adopted on March 21, 2005), paras. 556–584. Abbreviation: *U.S. – Cotton Subsidies.*

199 Australia and Brazil, both raising concerns about different interpretations by the dispute-settlement bodies, introduced proposals in the Negotiation Group on Rules to amend the text of the SCM Agreement on this issue (see, e.g., WTO Negotiating Group on Rules, Communication from Australia, *Prohibited Export Subsidies* [TN/RL/GEN/34 adopted on March 23, 2005] and WTO Negotiating Group on Rules, Paper from Brazil, *De Facto Export*

Export Subsidies

Article 3.1 refers to Annex I of the SCM Agreement, which contains an "Illustrative List" of export subsidies. As the description indicates, this list, which is largely the same as the list included in the Subsidies Code,[200] is not exhaustive.[201] The Panel in *Brazil – Aircraft 21.5* clarified that measures falling within the scope of the Illustrative List are deemed to be prohibited export subsidies and that a Member should thus not first demonstrate that these are contingent upon export performance.[202] Moreover, instead of proving the 'subsidy' element under Article 1 of the SCM Agreement, complainants are allowed by panels and the Appellate Body to demonstrate subsidization on the basis of the standards set out in the Illustrative List. We discuss the different categories of examples as provided in Annex I to the SCM Agreement.[203]

Four examples of export subsidies do not need much explanation, and the WTO adjudicating bodies did not have the opportunity yet to interpret them. These are, first of all, the provision by governments of direct subsidies to a firm or an industry contingent upon export performance (item [a]). Second, currency retention schemes or any similar practice that involves a bonus on exports are also considered an export subsidy (item [b]).[204] Third, the government can

Contingency [TN/RL/GEN/88, adopted on November 18, 2005]). In response to the Panel Report in *Australia – Automotive Leather* (see *supra* no. 189), Australia raised the concern that the current rules to export subsidy would be discriminatory to the Members with small domestic markets because "WTO case law has appeared to place a greater weight on the export propensity of a product in the range of factors which are examined to determine export contingency. (...) A subsidy provided to a product by a WTO Member with a large domestic market for that product may be actionable but carry little if no risk of being found to be export contingent. The same subsidy provided to a product by a WTO Member with a relatively small domestic market may represent a very high risk of being contingent on export performance given a much higher export orientation." See WTO Negotiating Group on Rules, Communication from Australia, *Prohibited Export Subsidies* (TN/RL/GEN/22, adopted on October 19, 2004). See also T. Chen, P. Wu, and J. Juo, "Reconsidering Prohibited Export Subsidies in Doha Negotiations," in M. Matsushita, D. Ahn, and T. Chen (Eds.), *The WTO Trade Remedy System: East Asian Perspectives* (London, Cameron May, 2007), 337–355.

200 As indicated, the list of the Subsidies Code was based on the 1960 Declaration.

201 Whereas some countries had suggested during the Uruguay Round to convert it into a definitive and exhaustive list, other countries, such as the United States and the EC, had opposed this suggestion. See T.P. Stewart, *loc. cit., supra* no. 15, 888.

202 Panel Report, *Brazil – Export Financing Programme for Aircraft – Recourse by Canada to Article 21.5 of the DSU* (WT/DS46/RW/R, adopted on August 4, 2000), paras. 6.30–6.31. Abbreviation: *Brazil – Aircraft Article 21.5.* This was implicitly endorsed by the Appellate Body Report. Appellate Body Report, *Brazil – Export Financing Programme for Aircraft – Recourse by Canada to Article 21.5 of the DSU* (WT/DS46/RW/AB, adopted on August 4, 2000), para. 61. Abbreviation: *Brazil – Aircraft Article 21.5.*

203 This classification is based on A. Hoda and R. Ahuja, "Agreement on Subsidies and Countervailing Measures: Need for Clarification and Improvement," 39:6 *Journal of World Trade* 1009 (2005), 1014.

204 Siegel explains that a currency retention scheme "usually involves allowing certain exporters to retain a portion of their foreign exchange earnings notwithstanding a general rule for residents to surrender receipts of foreign exchange to local banks, or the central bank, in exchange for local currency." A surrender requirement "could give rise to a

subsidize exports by providing or mandating internal transport and freight charges on export shipments on terms more favorable than for domestic shipments (item [c]). Fourth, the last item refers to any other charge on the public account constituting an export subsidy in the sense of Article XVI of the GATT 1994 (item [d]), which seems redundant given the definition of subsidy provided by the SCM Agreement.[205] Also included in the list is the provision by governments of imported or domestic products or services for use in the production of exported good (item [d]). In particular, three elements should be present[206]: the provision of "imported or domestic products (...) for use in the production of exported goods, on terms more favorable than for provision of like or directly competitive products (...) for use in the production of goods for domestic consumption" (1). Such provision is provided by "government or their agencies either directly or indirectly through government-mandated schemes" (2).[207] Last, the terms and conditions should also be more favorable than those commercially available on world markets to their exporters (3).[208]

Furthermore, five examples of export subsidies deal with fiscal incentives (items e, f, g, h, i), which elaborate Article XVI of the GATT. It may be recalled that GATT Contracting Parties considered that indirect taxes (levied on products and services) were borne by the product, whereas direct taxes (levied on income) were not.[209] As a consequence, they are still disciplined differently under the GATT and SCM Agreement. The full or partial exemption, or deferral specially related to exports, of *direct taxes,*[210] or social welfare charges paid or payable by industrial or commercial enterprises, is a prohibited export subsidy (item e),[211]

multiple currency practice if it involved a scheme requiring a rate for the sale of the foreign exchange that is beneficial as compared to the market rate, and thus, may possibly be viewed, in WTO terms, as a bonus on exports." D.E. Siegel, "Legal Aspects of the IMF/WTO Relationship: The Fund's Articles of Agreement and the WTO Agreements," 96:3 *American Journal of International Law* 561 (2002), 596.

205 Luengo indicates that this item was included in the Subsidies Code because of the different interpretation of "subsidy" between the United States (focusing on benefit) and the EC (focusing on the cost to government or charge on the public account). G. Luengo, *loc. cit., supra* no. 111, 151.

206 See Panel Report, *Canada – Measures Affecting the Importation of Milk and the Exportation of Dairy Products* (WT/DS103,113/R, adopted on October 27, 1999), paras. 7.128–7.131. Abbreviation: *Canada – Milk/Dairy.*

207 The Panel clarified that a government-mandated scheme also includes the delegation of authority by the government to its agencies which, in turn, set up a government-mandated scheme. Panel Report, *Canada – Milk/Dairy, loc. cit., supra* no. 206, para. 7.130.

208 Annex I(d), Footnote 57 to the SCM Agreement indicates that "commercially available" means that "the choice between domestic and imported products is unrestricted and depends only on commercial considerations."

209 The 1960 Declaration considered as a prohibited subsidy the remission of a direct tax (item 3) and the exemption of exported goods from certain kinds of taxes or charges (item 4).

210 Annex I(e), Footnote 58 to the SCM Agreement defines "direct taxes" as "taxes on wages, profits, interests, rents, royalties, and all other forms of income, and taxes on the ownership of real property."

211 A tax deferral is not an export subsidy where, for example, appropriate interest charges are collected. See Footnote 59 to the SCM Agreement. In addition, also considered a

whereas the exemption or remission, with respect to the production and distribution of exported products, of *indirect taxes*[212] is considered a prohibited export subsidy only if it is in excess of those levied with respect to the production and distribution of like products when sold for domestic consumption (item g).[213,214] Yet, concerning item e on direct taxes, Footnote 59 clarifies that this is not intended to limit a Member from taking measures to avoid the double taxation[215] of foreign-source income.[216] The United States invoked this footnote as a defense with regard to the ETI measure. The Appellate Body indeed clarified that Footnote 59 constitutes an "affirmative defense" that may justify a prohibited export subsidy and that the burden of proof is on the party invoking the exception, in this case the United States.[217] At the substantive level, the Appellate Body focused on the question of whether the ETI measure targets foreign-source income[218] and concluded that it did not because it improperly combined domestic-source income and foreign-source income.[219] The Appellate Body noticed, nonetheless, that if the measure were "confined to those aspects

prohibited export subsidy is "the allowance of *special deductions* directly related to exports or export performance, over and above those granted in respect to production for domestic consumption, *in the calculation of the base on which direct taxes are charged*" (item f, emphasis added).

212 Annex I(g), Footnote 58 to the SCM Agreement defines "indirect taxes" as "sales, excise, turnover, value added, franchise, stamp, transfer, inventory and equipment taxes, border taxes and all taxes other than direct taxes and import charges." Indirect taxes are thus the residual category.

213 Also considered a prohibited export subsidy is "the exemption, remission or deferral of *prior-stage cumulative indirect taxes* on goods and services used in the production of exported goods *in excess of* the exemption, remission or deferral of like prior-stage cumulative indirect taxes on goods or services used in the production of like products when sold for domestic consumption; provided, however, that prior-stage cumulative indirect taxes may be exempted, remitted or deferred on exported products even when not exempted, remitted or deferred on like products when sold for domestic consumption, if the prior-stage cumulative indirect taxes are levied on inputs that are consumed in the production of the exported product (making normal allowance for waste)" (item h, emphasis added). Further guidelines are provided by Annex II SCM Agreement. For the definition of 'inputs consumed in the production,' see *infra* no. 222.

214 As discussed, this should be read together with Footnote 1 to Article 1.1(a)(1)(ii) of the SCM Agreement, Article XVI of the GATT, and Article VI:4 of the GATT.

215 Double taxation "occurs when the same income, in the hands of the same taxpayer, is liable to tax in different States." Appellate Body Report, *U.S. – FSC Article 21.5, loc. cit., supra* no. 68, para. 137.

216 See Annex I(e), Footnote 59 to the SCM Agreement, *in fine*.

217 The United States argued that the burden was on the complaining party, but the Appellate Body did not agree. Appellate Body Report, *U.S. – FSC Article 21.5, loc. cit., supra* no. 68, paras. 124, 126, 127, 133, 134.

218 "Foreign-source income," in Annex I(e), Footnote 59 to the SCM Agreement, "refers to income generated by activities of a non-resident taxpayer in a 'foreign' State which have such links with that State so that the income could properly be subject to tax in that State." Appellate Body Report, *U.S. – FSC Article 21.5, loc. cit., supra* no. 68, para. 145.

219 The Panel came to the same conclusion but seemed to put more emphasis on the *purpose* of the measure, namely, the avoidance of double taxation. Panel Report, *U.S. – FSC 21.5, loc. cit., supra* no. 76, paras. 8.94–8.108. See R.E. Hudec, *loc. cit., supra* no. 64, 201.

which grant a tax exemption for 'foreign-source income,' it would fall within footnote 59."[220]

Second, the remission or drawback of *import charges*[221] in excess of those levied on inputs that are consumed in the production of the exported product (making normal allowance for waste) constitute an export subsidy (item i).[222] Such remission or drawback is allowed, upon fulfilling specific conditions spelled out in item i, when a firm uses a quantity of home market inputs as a substitute for imported inputs (substitution drawback systems).[223] This item aims at detecting disguised subsidies in the form of remission or drawback of import charges in excess of the import charges actually levied on the inputs consumed.[224]

Finally, two items of the Illustrative List deal with export credit practices and spell out a cost to the government standard. In particular, *export credit guarantees*[225] *or insurance programs* are considered prohibited export subsidies if they are provided at premium rates that are inadequate to cover the long-term[226] operating costs and losses[227] of the programs (item j). The evaluation is thus made at an aggregate level and looks at the overall cost to the government.[228]

220 Appellate Body Report, *U.S. – FSC Article 21.5, loc. cit., supra* no. 68, para. 185.

221 Footnote 58 indicates that import charges "mean tariffs, duties, and other fiscal charges not elsewhere enumerated in this note that are levied on imports."

222 As discussed, this should be read together with Footnote 1 to Article 1.1(a)(1)(ii) of the SCM Agreement, and Articles XVI and VI:4 of the GATT. Inputs consumed in the production process encompass "inputs physically incorporated, energy, fuels and oil used in the production process and catalysts which are consumed in the course of their use to obtain the exported product." See Annex II, Footnote 61 to the SCM Agreement. Hence, capital goods are not covered. See also WTO, Communication from the International Monetary Fund, *Export Financing and Duty Drawbacks* (WT/TF/COH/15, adopted on February 14, 2003).

223 See item (i) and Annex II and III to the SCM Agreement.

224 See A.H. Qureshi, *supra* no. 92, at 178.

225 The Panel in *Korea – Commercial Vessels* clarified that "an instrument will guarantee an export credit if it covers default by a borrower in respect of an export credit provided to that borrower." Panel Report, *Korea – Commercial Vessels, loc. cit., supra* no. 58, para. 7.213.

226 The Panel in *U.S. – Cotton Subsidies* stated that the reference to "long term" refers to "a period of sufficient duration as to ensure an objective examination which allows a thorough appraisal of the program and which avoids attributing overdue significance to any unique or atypical experiences on a given day, month, trimester, half-year, year or other specific time period." Panel Report, *United States – Subsidies on Upland Cotton* (WT/DS267/R, adopted on March 21, 2005), para. 7.832. Abbreviation: *U.S. – Cotton Subsidies.*

227 The Panel in *U.S. – Cotton Subsidies* indicated that the term "operating costs and losses" refers "generally to an economic, financial or accounting concept," and "in that sense generally connote[s] costs and losses in administering programs," but declined to adopt an explicit definition. Panel Report, *U.S. – Cotton Subsidies, loc. cit., supra* no. 226, para. 7.838.

228 Appellate Body Report, *Canada – Measures Affecting the Importation of Milk and the Exportation of Dairy Products – Recourse to Article 21.5 of the DSU by New Zealand and the United States* (WT/DS103, 113/AB/RW, adopted on December 18, 2001), para 93. Abbreviation: *Canada – Milk/Dairy Article 21.5.* Passing this cost-to-the-government test, which is "essentially a financial one", merely requires "a finding on whether the premiums are *insufficient* (...) and not a finding of the precise difference between premiums and long-term operating costs and losses." Appellate Body Report, *U.S. – Cotton Subsidies,* supra no. 198, paras. 666 and 667 (emphasis added).

Export credits, in contrast, are considered prohibited export subsidies if they are granted at rates below those that the government in question actually has to pay for the funds so used or, alternatively, below those the government would have to pay if it borrowed similar funds on international capital markets and only insofar as they are used to secure a material advantage in the field of export credit terms (item k).[229] The term "export credit" was interpreted by the Panel in *Korea – Vessels* in a narrow sense as loans conferred upon the foreign buyer and thus not covering loans provided to exporters (supplier).[230] Additionally, prohibited also are payments by the government of all or part of the costs incurred by exporters or financial institutions in obtaining credits, insofar as they are used to secure a material advantage in the field of export credit terms (item k). Notwithstanding the benchmarks for export credit practices articulated by item j and paragraph 1 of item k, export credit practices that are in accordance with the Organisation for Economic Co-operation and Development (OECD) Arrangement on Guidelines for Officially Supported Export Credit[231] (OECD Arrangement) and are subject to its interest rate provisions are not considered to be a prohibited export subsidy pursuant to paragraph 2 of item k.

In the *Brazil – Aircraft* dispute, the WTO adjudicating bodies had the opportunity to clarify various aspects of item k. The case concerned payments made by the government of Brazil to the export of regional aircraft under the interest rate equalization component of an export-financing program (named Programa de Financiamento às Exportações). This export-financing program, set up by the government of Brazil, provided support for export credits for Brazilian export transactions, either through direct financing or interest rate equalization payments. The interest rate equalization payments by the Brazilian government to the financing institution covered, at most, the difference between the cost of the financing institution of raising the funds and the interest rate charged by the financing institution to the buyer of the exported products. So,

229 The Panel in *Korea – Commercial Vessels* held, without any explanation, that the material clause also applies to the first aspect of item k, paragraph 1. Report, *Korea – Commercial Vessels, loc. cit.*, supra no. 58, para 7.314.

230 The Panel relied on the Organisation for Economic Co-operation and Development (OECD) approach to export credits because both parties had referred to OECD sources in supporting their respective definitions. This reasoning seems not fully convincing given the tools of treaty interpretation provided by the Vienna Convention on the Law of Treaties. Panel Report, *Korea – Commercial Vessels, loc. cit., supra* no. 58, paras. 7.316–7.323.

231 With respect to export credit support, the OECD Arrangement elaborates disciplines on minimum repayment requirements, minimum interest rates (Commercial Interest Reference Rates [CIRRs]) and minimum premium rates. Given that export credit guarantees and insurance are currently not subject to the minimum interest rate requirements, such "pure cover" support cannot benefit from the safe haven. Hence, the safe haven can at the moment not be invoked to justify pure cover support violating item j and/or Article 3.1(a) *juncto* Article 1 of the SCM Agreement. The participants in this gentlemen's agreement are Australia, Canada, the EC, Japan, the Republic of Korea, New Zealand, Norway, Switzerland, and the United States. The latest revision dates from December 2008 (TAD/PG[2008]29, December 17, 2008).

in effect, the buyers could receive a reduced interest rate because the financing institution received the payments of the government. Canada argued that the payments made under the export-financing program were prohibited export subsidies (Article 3.1[a] of the SCM Agreement), which was followed by the original Panel and Appellate Body. In the Article 21.5 proceedings, Brazil conceded that the payments of the revised PROEX (PROEX II) were export subsidies under Article 3.1(a) of the SCM Agreement but advocated that the subsidies were nevertheless permitted by *the first paragraph of item k*, as these were payments by the government of all or part of the costs incurred by exporters or financial institutions in obtaining credits that are not used to secure a material advantage in the field of export credit terms item k,[232] However, the Panels held that the payments made by the Brazilian government were not payments within the meaning of the first paragraph of item k because "the costs involved are those relating to *obtaining* export credits, and not costs relating to providing them."[233] Moreover, regarding the material advantage clause, the Appellate Body indicated that it should mean something other than the benefit element in Article 1.1(b) of the SCM Agreement.[234] The determination should be based on a comparison between the actual interest rate applied to a transaction after deduction of the government payment (the net interest rate) and an appropriate market benchmark. The Commercial Interest Reference Rate (CIRR) under the OECD Arrangement is considered an appropriate market benchmark.[235] The fact that a net interest rate is less than the relevant CIRR is a "positive indication" that the government payment has been used "to secure a material advantage."[236] Yet, when the net interest rate is less than the CIRR, a WTO Member may still demonstrate that an alternative benchmark is appropriate in situations in which the CIRR does not reflect the rates available in the marketplace and the net interest rate is greater than or equal to this alternative benchmark.[237] Based on different reasonings, the WTO adjudicating bodies in the original and first Article 21.5

[232] Panel Report, *Brazil – Aircraft Article 21.5, loc. cit., supra* no. 202, paras. 6.21–6.22.

[233] See Panel Report, *Brazil – Aircraft Article 21.5, loc. cit., supra* no. 202, paras. 6.71–6.72 (emphasis in the original); Panel Report, *Brazil – Export Financing Programme for Aircraft – Second Recourse by Canada to Article 21.5 DSU* (WT/DS46/RW/2, adopted on August 23, 2001), paras. 5.223–5.224. Abbreviation: *Brazil – Aircraft Article 21.5 II.* The Appellate Body did not rule on this issue. Appellate Body Report, *Brazil – Aircraft Article 21.5, loc. cit., supra* no. 202, para. 78.

[234] Appellate Body Report, *Brazil – Export Financing Programme for Aircraft* (WT/DS46/AB/R, adopted on August 20, 1999), para. 179. Abbreviation: *Brazil – Aircraft.*

[235] Because paragraph 2 of item k refers to the OECD Arrangement, it is considered useful context for interpreting the material advantage clause. See Appellate Body Report, *Brazil – Aircraft, loc. cit., supra* no. 234, para. 181.

[236] Appellate Body Report, *Brazil – Aircraft, loc. cit., supra* no. 234, para. 182.

[237] The WTO Member must show that the benchmark on which it relies is based on evidence from relevant, comparable transactions in the marketplace. Appellate Body Report, *Brazil – Aircraft Article 21.5, loc. cit., supra* no. 202, paras. 61–76; See also Panel Report, *Brazil – Aircraft Article 21.5, loc. cit., supra* no. 202, paras. 6.82–6.92 and Panel Report, *Brazil – Aircraft Article 21.5 II, loc. cit., supra* no. 233, paras. 5.256–5.265.

proceedings concluded that Brazil was unable to meet the criteria of paragraph 1 of item k.[238] Before the Panel in *Brazil – Aircraft Article 21.5 II*, Brazil successfully argued that its amended financing program (PROEX III) was in accordance with paragraph 2 of item k, which, as mentioned, provides a safe haven for export credit practices that are in accordance with the interest rate provisions of OECD Arrangement.[239]

Three clarifications should be made regarding the safe haven provided by the OECD Arrangement, applied directly pursuant to paragraph 2 or indirectly pursuant to the material advantage concept of paragraph 1. First, as the Appellate Body remarked, a potential borrower is not faced with a single commercial interest rate to a loan in any given currency but with a range of rates depending on the length of maturity as well as the creditworthiness of the borrower. Therefore, "under the OECD Arrangement, a CIRR is the *minimum* commercial rate available in that range for a particular currency."[240] Second, the relevant version of the OECD Arrangement is the version in force at the time the financing is offered and not the version in force at the conclusion of the Uruguay Round (1995).[241] Third, conformity with the OECD Arrangement requires not merely conformity with the minimum interest rate provision, in other words, the CIRR, but also adherence to those provisions of the OECD Arrangement imposing disciplines or limits that reinforce the CIRR as a minimum interest rate.[242] This "sufficiently broad interpretation of the concept of conformity" is considered appropriate so as to guard against circumvention of the minimum interest rate provision.[243]

[238] Although based on a different reasoning, the Panel and Appellate Body in the original *Brazil – Aircraft* case, as well as the Panel and Appellate Body in the first recourse by Canada to Article 21.5, rejected the defense on the basis that Brazil did not demonstrate that the payments are not used to secure a "material advantage."

[239] The Panel previously came to the conclusion that PROEX III did not constitute an export subsidy (Article 3.1 [a]) but did not exercise judicial economy. Panel Report, *Brazil – Aircraft Article 21.5 II, loc. cit., supra* no. 233, paras. 5.17–5.55 and 5.57–5.207. Brazil did not invoke paragraph 2 directly before the original Panel because conformity with the OECD Arrangement was considered too expensive. See Appellate Body Report, *Brazil – Aircraft, loc. cit., supra* no. 234, para. 180.

[240] Appellate Body Report, *Brazil – Aircraft, loc. cit., supra* no. 234, para. 182 (emphasis in the original).

[241] Panel Report, *Brazil – Aircraft Article 21.5 II, loc. cit., supra* no. 233, paras. 5.67–5.91.

[242] According to the Panel in *Brazil – Aircraft Article 21.5 II*, this applies also in case the OECD Arrangement is invoked under the "material advantage" clause. Panel Report, *Canada – Measures Affecting the Export of Civilian Aircraft – Recourse by Brazil to Article 21.5 of the DSU* (WT/DS70/RW, adopted on August 4, 2000), paras. 5.110–5.27. Abbreviation: *Canada – Aircraft Article 21.5*. This is, however, not interpreted so broadly as to provide a safe haven for the "matching" of offers that do not comply with the OECD Arrangement (see para. 5.113 and paras. 5.124–5.140). Panel Report, *Brazil – Aircraft Article 21.5 II, loc. cit., supra* no. 233, paras. 5.102–5.118 and 5.234–5.252.

[243] Panel Report, *Brazil – Aircraft Article 21.5 II, loc. cit., supra* no. 233, para. 5.105; Panel Report, *Canada – Aircraft Article 21.5, loc. cit., supra* no. 242, para. 5.110.

In this context, the OECD Arrangement serves as a rare example of an international standard considered to be an appropriate benchmark under the SCM Agreement. Yet, as the WTO adjudicating bodies have observed, this international benchmark is not unproblematic. The Panel in *Brazil – Aircraft Article 21.5 II* recognized the "unusual" character of this provision and the possibility that "the Participants to (the most recent) OECD Arrangement could conceivably abuse their *de facto* power to modify the scope of the safe haven in a way which benefits them but does not equally benefit the rest of the WTO membership."[244] However, the Panel did not want to express a view about the relative weight to this consideration because "that is the task of the parties to a negotiation, not a dispute settlement panel."[245] Hence, Brazil proposed in the Negotiation Group on Rules altering this provision to undo this procedural unfairness and "unacceptable encroachment on the sovereignty of non-Participants."[246] Additionally, Brazil argued that items j and k raise substantive concerns, because the formulated and interpreted benchmarks would favor countries with lower perceived risks (i.e., developed countries), to the disadvantage of countries with higher risks (e.g., developing countries).[247]

In conclusion, the Illustrative List describes a number of examples (items a–l) of prohibited export subsidies. It provides a nonexhaustive list of prohibited export subsidies within the meaning of Article 3.1(a) of the SCM Agreement. However, the relationship between Article 3.1(a) and the Illustrative List is not yet fully explored. The question arises for instance whether, if the criteria set by the items of the Illustrative List are not met, this implies that the subsidy does not constitute a prohibited export subsidy pursuant to Article 3.1(a) of the SCM Agreement. Both Brazil (*Brazil-Aircraft* case) and Korea (*Korea – Commercial Vessels* case) have argued that this question should be answered in the affirmative. For this purpose they advanced an *a contrario* interpretation. In essence,

244 Panel Report, *Brazil – Aircraft Article 21.5 II, loc. cit., supra* no. 233, para. 5.87 (emphasis in the original) (see also para. 5.88). The Panel in *Canada – Aircraft Article 21.5* also mentioned that it is "quite unique in the sense that it creates an exemption from a prohibition in a WTO Agreement, the scope of which exemption is left in the hands of a certain *subgroup* of WTO Members – the Participants, all of which as of today are OECD Members – to define, and to change as and when they see fit." Panel Report, *Canada – Aircraft Article 21.5, loc. cit., supra* no. 242, para. 5.132 (emphasis in the original).

245 Panel Report, *Brazil – Aircraft Article 21.5 II, loc. cit., supra* no. 233, para. 5.89.

246 In the view of Brazil, this resulted from the evolutionary interpretation by the Panel, which refers to the version of the OECD Arrangement in force at the time the financing is offered. See Paper from Brazil, *Treatment of Government Support for Export Credits and Guarantees under the Agreement on Subsidies and Countervailing Measures* (TN/RL/GEN/66, adopted on October 11, 2005), paras. 4–10 and 18.

247 Paper from Brazil, *Treatment of Government Support for Export Credits and Guarantees under the Agreement on Subsidies and Countervailing Measures* (TN/RL/GEN/66, adopted on October 11, 2005), paras. 11–18. See also D. Palmeter, "Safeguard, Anti-Dumping, and Countervailing Duty Disputes in the Transatlantic Partnership: How to Control 'Contingency Protection' More Effectively," in E.-U. Petersmann and M.A. Pollack (Eds.), *Transatlantic Economic Disputes – the EU, the U.S., and the WTO* (Oxford, Oxford University Press, 2003), 141, at 155.

they argue that the different items of the Illustrative List cover the application of certain types of export subsidies (e.g., export credits) and that, if the criteria set by the item covering this type of measure are not met (e.g., item k), it would, *a contrario*, not be an export subsidy. Yet, the Panels do not accept such an *a contrario* defense for all items of the Illustrative List. In both cases the Panels made a distinction based on Footnote 5 (Article 3.1[a]) of the SCM Agreement, which provides that "measures *referred to* in Annex I (Illustrative List) *as not constituting export subsidies* shall not be prohibited under this or any other provision of the Agreement."[248] Footnote 5 thus governs the relationship between Article 3.1(a) and the Illustrative List. The question remains, though, what items meet the standard of "referring to measures not constituting an export subsidy." On the one hand, the Panels held that item j, dealing with export credit guarantees or insurance programs, and the first paragraph of item k, dealing with export credits, do not meet this standard because both items do not contain any affirmative statements that the measures at hand are not an export subsidy or that they are allowed.[249] An *a contrario* interpretation of these items is therefore not accepted: If a measure does not meet all the criteria set by item j or k, para. 1, it can still constitute a prohibited export subsidy if it is proven to be a subsidy (Article 1) contingent upon export performance (Article 3.1[a]). For example, an export credit guarantee under a program that runs break-even is prohibited pursuant to Article 3.1(a) of the SCM Agreement if it is a subsidy in the meaning of Article 1 of the SCM Agreement and contingent upon exportation. On the other hand, some (elements of) items are considered affirmative statements that a measure is not an export subsidy or that it is allowed, such as the safe haven for export credits in conformity with the OECD Arrangement (second paragraph of item k).[250] Thus, if an export credit is in accordance with the OECD Arrangement, it shall not be considered a prohibited export subsidy (Article 3.1[a]). Until the present, the Appellate Body has not yet revealed whether it would agree that an *a contrario* – reading of items j and k, paragraph 1 should be rejected.[251]

[248] Emphasis added.

[249] Panel Report, *Brazil – Aircraft Article 21.5, loc. cit., supra* no. 202, paras. 6.36–6.37; Panel Report, *Korea – Commercial Vessels, loc. cit., supra* no. 58, para. 7.198.

[250] The Panel in *Brazil – Aircraft Article 21.5* also referred to the first and last sentences of Footnote 59 and the clauses of items h and i. See Panel Report, *Brazil – Aircraft Article 21.5, loc. cit., supra* no. 202, para. 6.36.

[251] The Appellate Body stated that if Brazil had discharged its burden to show that its financing program did not secure a material advantage, the Appellate Body would "have been prepared to find that the payments made under the (*financing program*) are justified under item k (*paragraph 1*) of the Illustrative List" (italics added) and thus seems to accept an *a contrario* defense. Yet, the Appellate Body continued that "in making this observation, we wish to emphasize that we are not interpreting Footnote 5 to the SCM Agreement, and we do not opine on the scope of Footnote 5, or on the meaning of any other items in the Illustrative List." See Appellate Body Report, *Brazil – Aircraft Article 21.5, loc. cit., supra* no. 202, paras. 80–81. See also Panel Report, *Brazil – Aircraft Article 21.5 II, loc. cit., supra* no. 233, paras. 5.269–5.275. The Panel referred to the statement made by the Appellate Body and acknowledged that "it could be understood in the manner suggested by Brazil" but noted

Finally, it should be emphasized that, if an export subsidy in the meaning of Article 1 *juncto* Article 3.1 of the SCM Agreement is not considered prohibited on the basis of an affirmative statement in the Illustrative List, it seems still to be actionable if it is specific and causes adverse effects.[252] For example, if a subsidized export credit is in accordance with the OECD Arrangement, it shall not be considered a prohibited export subsidy, but it could still be challenged as an actionable subsidy.

Local Content Subsidies

The other category of prohibited subsidies is local content subsidies, defined as subsidies contingent upon the use of domestic over imported goods (Article 3.1[b]).[253] They are the only type of domestic subsidy that is prohibited.[254] The United States was one of the proponents during the Uruguay Round to include them in the category of prohibited subsidies, arguing that these subsidies "are as effective as any tariff in protecting domestic input supplying industries and distorting the flow of resources internationally."[255] The citation reveals that this type of subsidy is conceptually different from other kinds of subsidies, as it does not focus on the receiver of the subsidy but on the domestic input supplying industries. In other words, what is targeted is trade distortion in the input industry market and not in the market of the industry receiving the beneficial financial contribution by the government. These subsidies clearly violate the GATT's national treatment provision (Article III.4) because the regulations at hand discriminate between domestic and foreign input supplying industries. The exception provided by Article III.8(b) of the GATT is not applicable because the discrimination exists between the domestic and foreign input industries and not between the subsidized industry and the foreign industry.[256] Moreover,

that "the Appellate Body's statement does not form part of the legal basis for its disposition of the appeal, nor did the Appellate Body explain its statement" (see Footnote 214); see also Panel Report, *Korea – Commercial Vessels, loc. cit., supra* no. 58, paras. 7.193–7.207.

252 Appellate Body Report, *U.S. – FSC, loc. cit., supra* no. 63, para. 93; Panel Report, *Korea – Commercial Vessels, loc. cit., supra* no. 58, para. 7.334. See also G. Luengo, *loc. cit., supra* no. 111, 152.

253 For a discussion on the relationship between the TRIMs Agreement and the SCM Agreement, see P. Sauvé, *Trade Rules Behind Borders: Essays on Services, Investment and the New Trade Agenda* (London, Cameron May, 2003), 666 pp., 313–318.

254 Local content subsidies might in addition be contingent on export performance and thus constitute export subsidies (Article 3.1[a]). As mentioned above, "contingency" does not require that import substitution should be a sufficient condition to receive the subsidy. So, export performance can be an additional requirement. See, for example, the *Canada – Autos* case.

255 T.P. Stewart, *loc. cit., supra* no. 15, 889.

256 The GATT Panel in *Italy – Agricultural Machinery* stated that Article III:8 of the GATT was not applicable because the credit facilities were "granted to *the purchasers* of agricultural machinery and could not be considered as subsidies accorded to *the producers* of agricultural machinery" (emphasis added). GATT Panel Report, *Italy – Agricultural Machinery, loc. cit., supra* no. 93, para. 14. According to the Panel in *Indonesia – Autos*: "the purpose of Article III:8(b) is to confirm that subsidies to producers do not violate Article III, so long

local content subsidies are covered by the Illustrative List of the Agreement on Trade-Related Investment Measures (TRIMs) that are inconsistent with Article III.4 of the GATT (as local content requirements).[257] However, in contrast to the GATT and the TRIMs, the SCM Agreement does not provide any ground for justification for local content subsidies.[258]

Actionable Subsidies

Actionable subsidies, in other words, yellow light subsidies, are defined by default: If a specific subsidy (within the meaning of Article 1 of the SCM Agreement) is not prohibited, it constitutes an actionable subsidy, in other words, it can be subject to multilateral action *if* it causes "adverse effects" to the interest of other WTO Members. The main onus upon the complaining Member is to demonstrate "adverse effects," which have a threefold definition: (a) injury to the domestic industry; (b) nullification or impairment of benefits accruing to other WTO Member(s); or (c) serious prejudice to the interests of another WTO Member.[259] Members may not cause such adverse effects by subsidization. The first two types of adverse effects (a and b) codify the rules and practice of the GATT 1947, and the third type (c) significantly expands the scope of actionable subsidies.[260]

First, the term injury to the domestic industry is used in the same sense as in the context of CVD procedures where it is elaborated extensively.[261] This indicates that "injury" covers material injury as well as a threat of material injury to a domestic industry.[262] Instead of undertaking a CVD procedure (unilateral remedy), WTO Members can thus opt for the WTO dispute-settlement system (multilateral remedy) and demonstrate injury to their domestic industry (see *infra*).

Second, the concept of nullification or impairment of benefits is used and determined in the same sense as in the GATT 1994. This concept is applied in nonviolations complaints (Article XXIII:1[b] of the GATT) where three elements

as they do not have any component that introduces discrimination between imported and domestic products." See Panel Report, *Indonesia – Autos, loc. cit., supra* no. 85, para. 14.43.

257 See Article 2 *juncto* paragraph 1(a) of the Illustrative List of the TRIMs Agreement. For the relationship between the TRIMs Agreement and the SCM Agreement, see Panel Report, *Indonesia – Autos, loc. cit., supra* no. 85, paras. 14.49–14.55. The Panel concluded that measures challenged under both the TRIMs Agreement and the SCM Agreement must be reviewed under both.

258 A violation of Article III:4 of the GATT or Article 2 of the TRIMs can still be justified on the basis of the general exceptions (Article XX of the GATT and Article 3 of the TRIMs) or balance-of-payments exception (Articles XII and XVIII:B of the GATT and Article 4 of the TRIMs). It should be noted, however, that the question on the applicability of Article XX GATT to violations of the SCM Agreement is not yet settled.

259 Article 5 of the SCM Agreement.

260 A. Hoda and R. Ahuja, *loc. cit., supra* no. 203, 1060.

261 Article 5(a), Footnote 11 of the SCM Agreement. See Part V and Article 15 of the SCM Agreement.

262 Article 15, Footnote 45 of the SCM Agreement. "Injury" shall be interpreted in accordance with Article 15 of the SCM Agreement.

are established, which can also be established with regard to subsidies: (i) the use of a subsidy,[263] (ii) the existence of a benefit accruing under the applicable agreement such as tariff concessions,[264] and (iii) the nullification or impairment of a benefit (e.g., tariff concessions) as a result of the use of a subsidy.[265] Because the nonviolation remedy should remain of "an exceptional nature,"[266] the standard for determining the element of causation (iii) is set high by the adjudicating bodies: "non-violation nullification or impairment would arise when the effect of a tariff concession is *systematically* offset or counteracted by a subsidy program."[267] There is a double motivation behind nonviolation complaints. First, WTO Members have reasonable expectations that they can benefit from binding tariff concessions made by trade partners.[268] Second, these WTO Members have "paid" for the binding by making tariff concessions themselves. If trade partners offer tariff bindings for a product and would subsequently be allowed to subsidize so as to reduce market access for imports of the same product, the dynamism of reciprocal tariff concessions would be undermined.[269] This was the original rationale for disciplining subsidies under the GATT 1947.[270] In conclusion, whereas the first type of adverse effect is that caused by subsidized imports in the domestic market of other WTO Members, this second type tackles adverse effects to the export industry of other WTO Members in the market of the subsidizing country.

Third, the inclusion of serious prejudice in the definition substantially expands the scope of adverse effects. Originally, the SCM Agreement provided for a rebuttable presumption[271] that "serious prejudice" exists in the following cases: (a) the total *ad valorem* subsidization of a product exceeds 5 percent; (b) the subsidy covers operating losses sustained by an industry; (c) the subsidy covers operating losses sustained by an enterprise, other than onetime measures; or (d) direct debt forgiveness.[272] This provision facilitated the difficult demonstration by the injured Member of adverse effects, which only had to demonstrate the existence of such a specific subsidy and thus leave it upon the defending party to refute the trade effects. Yet, Article 6.1 expired at the end of 1999 because there

[263] Panel Report, *United States – Continued Dumping and Subsidy Offset Act of 2000* (WT/DS217,234/R, adopted on January 27, 2003), paras. 7.121–7.123. Abbreviation: *U.S. – Offset Act.*

[264] Panel Report, *U.S. – Offset Act, loc. cit., supra* no. 263, para. 7.124.

[265] Panel Report, *U.S. – Offset Act, loc. cit., supra* no. 263, paras. 7.125–7.131.

[266] Panel Report, *U.S. – Offset Act, loc. cit., supra* no. 263, para. 7.127.

[267] Panel Report, *U.S. – Offset Act, loc. cit., supra* no. 263, para. 7.127 (emphasis added); GATT Report, *European Economic Community – Payments and Subsidies to Processors and Producers of Oilseeds and Related Animal-Feed Proteins* (L/6627-37S/86, adopted on January 25, 1990), para. 148. Abbreviation: *EEC – Oilseeds I.*

[268] GATT Panel Report, *EEC – Oilseeds I, loc. cit., supra* no. 267, para. 148.

[269] M. Matsushita ea., *loc. cit., supra* no. 35, 279.

[270] M. Matsushita, T.J. Schoenbaum, and P. Mavroidis, *The World Trade Organization – Law, Practice and Policy* (Oxford, Oxford University Press, 1st ed., 2003), 334.

[271] Article 6.1 *juncto* 6.2 of the SCM Agreement.

[272] Article 6.1 of the SCM Agreement.

was no consensus among WTO Members to continue its existence. From the perspective of WTO law, it is rather exceptional that a stricter discipline is subject to extinction. However, the drafters of the SCM Agreement considered this stricter discipline (Article 6.1 of the SCM Agreement) as a *quid quo pro* for the inclusion of nonactionable subsidies (Article 8 of the SCM Agreement).[273] Their future was thus bound together, and both expired after a period of five years because WTO Members did not extend their application.[274,275]

Today, it is thus always the task of the complaining party to demonstrate that the subsidy causes serious prejudice[276] as stipulated in Article 6.3 of the SCM Agreement[277]:

(a) the effect of the subsidy is to *displace or impede the imports* of a like product of another Member into the market of the *subsidizing Member*;
(b) the effect of the subsidy is to *displace or impede the exports* of a like product of another Member from a *third country market*[278];
(c) the effect of the subsidy is *a significant price undercutting* by the subsidized product as compared with the price of a like product of another Member in the same market or *significant price suppression*,[279] *price depression*,[280] *or lost sales* in the same market[281];
(d) the effect of the subsidy is *an increase in the world market share* of the subsidizing Member in a particular subsidized primary product or commodity as compared to the average share it had during the previous period of three

[273] Article 31 of the SCM Agreement.

[274] See A. Hoda and R. Ahuja, *loc. cit., supra* no. 203, 1061. As indicated above, the United States proposed in the current Doha Round to bring all these types of subsidies (except for Article 6.1[a]) under the category of prohibited subsidies.

[275] See also Panel Report, *Korea – Commercial Vessels, loc. cit., supra* no. 58, para. 7.583.

[276] "Serious prejudice" includes "threat of serious prejudice." See Footnote 13 to the SCM Agreement. See also Panel Report, *U.S. – Cotton Subsidies, loc. cit., supra* no. 226, paras. 7.1494–7.1495.

[277] The rebuttable presumption shifted the burden of proof to the subsidizing party, which had to prove that the subsidization did not result in any of the effects described in Article 6.3 of the SCM Agreement (see Article 6.2 of the SCM Agreement).

[278] See also Article 6.4 of the SCM Agreement.

[279] The subsidy prevents the domestic price from increasing. In order to determine "that price suppression is the effect of the subsidy and that there is a 'genuine and substantial relationship of cause and effect'," the Appellate Body in *U.S. – Cotton Subsidies Article 21.5* agreed with the Panel's application of a "but for" test. This test had to determine whether "the world price of upland cotton would have been higher in the absence of the subsidies (that is, *but for* the subsidies)." Appellate Body Report, *United States – Subsidies on Upland Cotton – Recourse to Article 21.5 of the DSU by Brazil* (WT/DS267/AB/RW, adopted on June 20, 2008), paras. 368–375 (emphasis in the original). Abbreviation: *U.S. – Cotton Subsidies Article 21.5*.

[280] The subsidy depresses the domestic price. In its analysis, the Panel in *Korea – Commercial Vessels* applied a "but for" test: What would have been the price movements for the relevant ships in absence of the subsidies at issue? Panel Report, *Korea – Commercial Vessels, loc. cit., supra* no. 58, para. 7.537.

[281] See also Article 6.5 of the SCM Agreement.

years, and this increase follows a consistent trend over a period when subsidies have been granted.[282]

In other words, even in the absence of any prior tariff commitment, WTO Members could cause adverse effects through subsidization if this results in displacing or impeding imports of another Member into the market of the subsidizing country.[283] Moreover, adverse effects can also be caused when the subsidization results in impeding or displacing exports of another Member from a third country.[284] A threshold question under Article 6.3(a), (b), and (c) is the definition of "like product," which should, pursuant to Footnote 46 to the SCM Agreement,[285] be understood narrowly as "identical, i.e. alike in all respects" or, at least, as having "characteristics closely resembling" the product under consideration. The Panel in *Indonesia – Autos* noticed that the term "characteristics closely resembling" is "on its face (...) quite narrow" but concluded that its meaning is not confined to physical characteristics.[286]

On the other hand, circumstances are also listed in Article 6.7 in which serious prejudice in the form of displacement or impediment shall not be considered to arise, for example, in case of *force majeur* or if the policy of the complaining member itself ("unclean hands") is the cause of trade disruption. As to the question of where the serious prejudice should occur, the Panel Report in *Indonesia – Autos* clarified that a WTO Member cannot bring a claim that another WTO Member has suffered serious prejudice. The same Panel held that products not originating in a complaining Member country cannot be the object of a claim of serious prejudice. For instance, products made by a U.S. company at its European plant cannot give rise to a U.S. claim of serious prejudice. Instead, serious prejudice must occur to products made within the territory of the complaining party.[287]

[282] Emphasis added.

[283] A. Hoda and R. Ahuja, *loc. cit., supra* no. 203, 1020.

[284] See also Article 6.3(c) and (d) of the SCM Agreement.

[285] Footnote 46 to Article 15.1 of the SCM Agreement provides a definition of "like product."

[286] Moreover, the determination of "like product" must be made on a case-by-case basis. See Panel Report, *Indonesia – Autos, loc. cit., supra* no. 85, paras. 14.172–14.174.

[287] Panel Report, *Indonesia – Autos, loc. cit., supra* no. 85, paras. 14.201–14.202. The Panel in *U.S. – Cotton Subsidies* decided that allegations of other Members of serious prejudice may be taken into account "to the extent these constitute evidentiary support of the effect of the subsidy borne by Brazil as a Member whose producers are involved in the production and trade in upland cotton in the world market." However, the Panel emphasized that it did not base its decision "on any alleged serious prejudice caused to" the other WTO Members. Panel Report, *U.S. – Cotton Subsidies, loc. cit., supra* no. 226, paras. 7.1414–7.1415.

Nonactionable Subsidies

Before 2000, three categories of subsidies were nonactionable (green light subsidies). First, certain subsidies for research and development (R&D) conducted by firms or by higher education or research establishments on a contract basis with firms were nonactionable, although this was limited to a certain level and to certain types.[288] Second, assistance to disadvantaged regions was nonactionable[289] if the geographical region was clearly defined and the determination was based on neutral and objective criteria. The third category covered a type of environmental subsidy, in other words, limited assistance to promote adaptation of existing facilities to new environmental requirements.[290] Hence, three policy objectives (under specific conditions) could be pursued by means of subsidization in principle regardless of whether the subsidies caused adverse effects.[291] From an economic perspective, environmental and R&D subsidies can be legitimate to overcome market failures because without governmental intervention the market would produce a socially suboptimal level of R&D and environmental protection (positive externalities). Assistance to disadvantaged regions is an important instrument of industrial policy and legitimized on the basis of redistribution arguments.[292] Politically, this category of nonactionable subsidies was created on the demand of the EC (focusing on R&D), Canada (focusing on assistance to disadvantaged regions), and Mexico (which successfully pushed for environmental subsidies in the last days of negotiations) to place these subsidies outside the reach of U.S. CVD procedures.[293]

The SCM Agreement provided for a notification procedure for these nonactionable subsidies. Members had to notify the SCM Committee[294] of all subsidy programs they wanted to classify as nonactionable, and these notifications had to be made in advance of the implementation of the subsidy programs. When a Member disputed the nonactionable nature of a subsidy, it could start a review procedure that could end in binding arbitration.[295] If a subsidy was not notified, it could in principle not benefit from nonactionability and became thus actionable and countervailable if it caused adverse effects or injury, respectively.[296]

[288] Limited to a certain level and to certain types. See Article 8.2(a) of the SCM Agreement. Excluded from the Agreement were subsidies for "fundamental research" independently conducted by higher education or research establishments whereby the term "fundamental research" is defined as "an enlargement of general scientific and technical knowledge not linked to industrial or commercial objectives" (Footnote 26 to the SCM Agreement).

[289] Article 8.2(b) of the SCM Agreement. See Matsushita ea., *loc. cit.*, *supra* no. 270, 283.

[290] Article 8.2(c) of the SCM Agreement. See Matsushita ea., *loc. cit.*, *supra* no. 270, 284.

[291] Yet, see *infra* on multilateral remedies to nonactionable subsidies.

[292] See World Trade Report 2006, *loc. cit.*, *supra* no. 34, 61, and 200.

[293] See T. Collins-Williams and G. Salember, *loc. cit.*, *supra* no. 46, 10–11.

[294] See Article 24.1 of the SCM Agreement.

[295] See Articles 8.3–8.5 of the SCM Agreement.

[296] See Article 10, Footnote 35 of the SCM Agreement.

However – and this was the weak spot of the notification procedure – such subsidies were still nonactionable if it was found during a countervailing or multilateral proceeding that they conformed to the standards of one of the three categories.[297]

The category of green light subsidies was extinguished at the end of 1999 because there was no consensus among WTO Members to continue its application. As mentioned, the discussion was linked to the extension of Article 6.1 of the SCM Agreement. Many developing countries, such as Brazil and India, were not in favor of the extension in its existing form because in their view the categories reflected the interest of developed countries. The EC and Canada, in contrast, favored a continuation of the category of nonactionable subsidies, and the United States articulated its "mixed views on the provisions." In general, there wasn't even a consensus among either developed countries or developing countries.[298] So, it seems unlikely that WTO Members in the current Doha Round will reinstall this category in its current form.

Remedies

In addressing the remedies to subsidies, three situations, each indicating a different effect of a subsidy, should be carefully distinguished.[299] First, subsidies of country A can increase the export of product X into the *importing country*, country B, causing harm to the domestic producers of product X in country B. Second, subsidies of country A can increase the export of product X into *a third country*, country C, causing harm to the export to country C of product X from country B producers. Third, country A can subsidize domestic producers of product X to restrain the imports of product X in its *domestic market*, whereby the subsidy has thus the effect of an import barrier. Obviously, one and the same subsidy can cause these different effects cumulatively.[300]

How can country B respond to these subsidies? Only in the first situation can country B impose CVDs to offset the price effect of the subsidy. Hereby, the subsidy of country A remains, evidently, in force. In situations 2 and 3, country B cannot respond with CVDs because the harm it wishes to neutralize is not the importation of the subsidized product X.[301] Of course, in situation 2, country B may request country C to impose CVDs, but this country might in fact welcome

[297] See Article 10, Footnote 35, *in fine* of the SCM Agreement.

[298] See the minutes of the regular meeting of the Committee on Subsidies and Countervailing Measures held on November 1–2, 1999 (G/SCM/M/24) and of the special meeting held on December 20, 1999 (G/SCM/M/22).

[299] See J.H. Jackson, *loc. cit., supra* no. 16, 280; M.J. Trebilcock and R. Howse, *The Regulation of International Trade* (London, Routledge, 2005, 3rd ed.), 759 pp., 263.

[300] For example, subsidization by country A of product X can increase the imports in country B (situation 1) as well as diminish the export opportunities of country B in country C (situation 2) and country A (situation 3).

[301] See the limited exception in Article VI:6(b) and (c) of the GATT, in which a Member may impose CVDs to respond to injury that is occurring in the territory of another Member

the subsidization of product X. For example, if country C has no domestic producers of product X, the subsidized import of product X is welfare enhancing. So, how should country B respond in situations 2 and 3 if it wishes to protect the interests of its exporters of product X? From an economic viewpoint, country B can respond with an equivalent subsidy to its own producers of product X to neutralize the competitive disadvantage in countries A and C,[302] but this subsidy will also be prohibited, as an export subsidy, or actionable under the SCM Agreement. Consequently, the only option for country B is to have recourse to the WTO adjudicating bodies. If the Panel concludes that the subsidy of country A is prohibited/actionable, country A will have to withdraw the subsidy (prohibited) or at least remove the adverse effects of it (actionable).[303] Only if country A does not take these steps might country B be authorized to adopt countermeasures.

As a result, the SCM Agreement provides two remedies to take action against prohibited and actionable subsidies granted by other WTO Members, which will be discussed in depth later in this chapter. First, in all three situations, country B can follow the multilateral approach and bring the case before the WTO adjudicating bodies. Second, subject to a set of procedural and substantive requirements, country B can unilaterally impose CVDs to offset the effects of the subsidy in its domestic market (situation 1). The SCM Agreement clarifies the delineation between both options:

> "however, with regard to the effects of a particular subsidy in the domestic market of the importing Member, only one form of relief (either a countervailing duty, if the requirements of Part V are met, or a countermeasure under Articles 4 or 7) shall be available."[304]

Country B therefore can, but also should, choose between the unilateral or multilateral option to respond to the injury caused in its domestic market (situation 1). Yet, the SCM Agreement does not prohibit it pursuing the unilateral approach to offset the negative effects in its domestic market (situation 1), alongside the multilateral approach to address the negative effects of the same subsidy in its export markets (situations 2 and 3).[305]

Multilateral Remedies: WTO Adjudicating Bodies

WTO Members confronted with prohibited and actionable subsidies imposed by other WTO Members may take recourse to the WTO's dispute-settlement system. The SCM Agreement stipulates specific dispute-settlement

(which is at the same time an exporter of the product to the territory of the importing country) instead of its own.

302 M.J. Trebilcock and R. Howse, *loc. cit., supra* no. 299, 263.

303 Withdrawal is also a possible remedy for actionable subsidies.

304 Article 10, Footnote 35 of the SCM Agreement.

305 M. Matsushita ea., *loc. cit., supra* no. 35, 336.

procedure rules for prohibited subsidies[306] and for actionable subsidies,[307] which are "specific or additional" to the rules of the Dispute Settlement Understanding (DSU).[308] The deadlines and the available remedies are more stringent with regard to prohibited subsidies vis-à-vis actionable subsidies, reflecting the negative stance of WTO Members toward prohibited subsidies.

The SCM Agreement provides for an accelerated procedure available to WTO Members confronted with prohibited and actionable subsidies.[309] If consultations fail within 30 days under the prohibited subsidy procedure, the complaining Member may then refer the matter to the Dispute Settlement Body (DSB). Regarding actionable subsidies, the standard term of 60 days applies, but the term for the composition of the Panel is shorter.[310] The time limits for the Panel procedure are under both procedures substantially shorter than under the standard procedure of the DSU,[311] and those for the Appellate Body procedure are shorter with regard to prohibited subsidies.[312] Moreover, the time period for the DSB to decide upon the adoption of the Panel and Appellate Body Reports is shorter under the SCM procedures.[313] Last, if the subsidizing Member has not conformed to the DSB's ruling and recommendations within the time period indicated by the Panel (prohibited subsidies[314]) or within six months (actionable subsidies), the affected Member will have the right to request authorization to adopt counter-measures.[315]

The SCM Agreement also contains specific legal obligations and remedies. Here too, there are differences between the procedure for prohibited and actionable subsidies. If the measure is found to be a prohibited subsidy, the subsidizing Member has to "withdraw the subsidy without delay."[316] In particular, the Panel has to specify the time period within which the measure must be withdrawn. The subsidizing Member is thus not given "a reasonable period of time" to bring

306 Article 4 of the SCM Agreement.

307 Article 7 of the SCM Agreement.

308 The specific procedure is thus a *lex specialis*. In other words, the DSU is still relevant insofar as the specific procedure does not modify it: See Appendix 2 DSU.

309 See also Article 4.2 of the SCM Agreement.

310 Article 7.4 of the SCM Agreement. Compare with Articles 4.7, 6, and 8 of the DSU.

311 See Articles 4.6 and 7.5 of the SCM Agreement. Compare with Articles 12, 15, and 16 of the DSU. Under the prohibited subsidy procedure, the Panel may request assistance of the Permanent Group of Experts (PGE), composed of five experts elected by the SCM Committee, with regard to whether the measure in question is a prohibited subsidy. Although reference to the PGE is optional, the determination of the PGE is binding upon the Panel (see Articles 24.3 and 4.5 of the SCM Agreement). This might be the reason why so far no Panel has requested the determination of the PGE. See P.A. Clarke and G.N. Horlick, *loc. cit., supra* no. 22, 726.

312 See Articles 4.9, 7.7 of the SCM Agreement. Compare with Article 17.5 of the DSU.

313 Articles 4.8 and 4.9 of the SCM Agreement and Articles 7.6 and 7.7 of the SCM Agreement. Compare with Articles 16.4 and 17.14 of the DSU.

314 See *infra*: The measure will have to be withdrawn without delay.

315 Articles 4.10 and 7.9 of the SCM Agreement. Compare with the "reasonable period" stipulated by Articles 21.3 and 22.2 of the DSU.

316 Article 4.6 of the SCM Agreement.

its measure in conformity with WTO rules, as is the case under the DSU. Moreover, the subsidizing Member has no other options than to withdraw the subsidy, whereas the DSU leaves it upon the losing party to determine how to bring its measure into compliance with WTO law.[317]

A highly sensitive issue is whether the term "withdraw" may encompass repayments of previously granted prohibited subsidies. The Panel in *Australia – Leather Article 21.5*, a case involving a one-time, nonrecurring prohibited subsidy from Australia to a private company, adopted such an extensive interpretation and required that the subsidy had to be repaid in full by the private company.[318] A central motivation of the Panel was to uphold the effectiveness of the multilateral remedy if a one-time prohibited subsidy is provided:

> "If we were to accept the conclusion that 'withdraw the subsidy' does not encompass repayment, then that recommendation, far from providing a remedy for violations of Article 3.1(a) of the SCM Agreement, would grant full absolution to Members who grant export subsidies that are fully disbursed to the recipient before a recommendation to withdraw the subsidy is issued in dispute settlement, and for which the export contingency is entirely in the past."[319]

Indeed, otherwise WTO Members could easily circumvent the stringent disciplines on prohibited subsidies by providing nonrecurring subsidies. However, it is argued that this interpretation constitutes a departure from the general principle that WTO law only provides for prospective remedies, as Article 19.1 of the DSU is generally interpreted.[320] Moreover, the obligation to repay past subsidies might pose constitutional and democratic problems in some legal systems of WTO Members.[321] Lastly, Waincymer remarks that it is extremely unlikely that negotiators during the Uruguay Round would have intended to have this niche area of retroactive remedies.[322] It therefore comes as no surprise that many WTO Members criticized this interpretation of the Panel.[323] In the Doha Round,

[317] Compare Article 19.1 of the DSU and Article 4.7 of the SCM Agreement.

[318] Panel Report, *Australia – Subsidies Provided to Producers and Exporters of Automotive Leather – Recourse to Article 21.5 of the DSU by the United States* (WT/DS126/RW, adopted on February 11, 2000). Abbreviation: *Australia – Leather Article 21.5*. For a critical appraisal of this Panel Report, see G. Goh and A. Ziegler, "Retrospective Remedies in the WTO After *Automotive Leather*," 6(3) *Journal of International Economic Law* 2003, 545–564.

[319] Panel Report, *Australia – Leather Article 21.5*, *loc. cit.*, *supra* no. 318, para. 6.38.

[320] Article 19.1 of the DSU requires a Panel or the Appellate Body to "recommend that the Member concerned bring the measure *into conformity with* that agreement" (emphasis added). This provision thus does not explicitly state that only prospective remedies are covered.

[321] See G. Goh and A. Ziegler, *loc. cit.*, *supra* no. 318, 555–559.

[322] See J. Waincymer, *WTO Litigation – Procedural Aspects of Formal Dispute Settlement* (London, Cameron, May, 2002), 935 pp., 644–645.

[323] This criticism was expressed in the DSB that adopted the Panel Report. See G. Goh and A. Ziegler, *loc. cit.*, *supra* no. 318, 547–548.

Australia proposed clarifying the concept of "withdrawal" and, interestingly, its most recent contribution would allow for repayment of the ongoing benefit since the adoption of the Panel Report.[324]

If the recommendation of the DSB to withdraw the subsidy is not followed within an indicated time frame, the injured party may request to take *appropriate* countermeasures.[325] In contrast, the DSU uses the concept of equivalence (see Article 22.4 of the DSU), which is interpreted by WTO adjudicating bodies as a lower standard. The SCM Agreement clarifies, seemingly superfluously, that it is not meant to allow countermeasures that are disproportionate.[326] It does, however, not indicate whether the amount of countermeasures should be based on the amount of the subsidy or merely on the amount of the injury to the complaining party. Here again, an analysis of the case law reveals a broad interpretation, which may have opened the door for punitive damages under the WTO.[327] The Arbitrators[328] in *Brazil – Aircraft* decided that an amount of countermeasures that corresponds to the total amount of the subsidy is appropriate when dealing with a prohibited export subsidy.[329] They came to this conclusion by stressing the different purpose with respect to countermeasures under the DSU:

> "[T]he purpose of Article 4 is to achieve the *withdrawal* of the prohibited subsidy. In this respect, we consider that the requirement to withdraw a prohibited subsidy is of a different nature than removal of the specific nullification or impairment caused to a Member by the measure. The former aims at removing a measure which is presumed under the WTO Agreement to cause negative trade effects, irrespective of who suffers those trade effects and to what extent. The latter aims at eliminating the effects of a measure on the trade of a given Member."[330]

So, the different nature of prohibited subsidies, as prohibited *per se* by the SCM Agreement and not conditioned upon a "trade effects" test, legitimizes countermeasures to the full amount of the subsidy and not limited to the actual injury caused to the complaining party. Otherwise, if the injury is substantially lower than the subsidy, "a countermeasure (...) will have less or no inducement effect

[324] See WTO Negotiating Group on Rules, Communication from Australia, *Subsidies: Withdrawal of a subsidy* (TN/RL/GEN/115/Rev.1, adopted on January 24, 2007).

[325] Article 4.10 of the SCM Agreement.

[326] Article 4.10, Footnote 9 of the SCM Agreement.

[327] See, for a discussion, M. Matsushita ea., *loc. cit., supra* no. 35, 366–369.

[328] See Article 22.6 of the DSU and Article 4.11 of the SCM Agreement.

[329] Decision by the Arbitrators, *Brazil – Export Financing Programme for Aircraft – Recourse to Arbitration by Brazil under Article 22.6 of the DSU and 4.11 of the SCM Agreement* (WT/DS46/ARB, adopted on December 12, 2000), para. 3.60. Abbreviation: *Brazil – Aircraft Arbitration.*

[330] Decision by the Arbitrators, *Brazil – Aircraft Arbitration, loc. cit., supra* no. 329, para. 3.48 (footnotes deleted).

and the subsidizing country may not withdraw the measure at issue."[331] This approach was followed by the Arbitrator in *U.S. – FSC*.[332] Interestingly, the Arbitrator addressed a number of complex issues raised by his interpretation. What if there are multiple complainants, each seeking to take countermeasures in an amount equal to the value of the subsidy? Or, what if another WTO Member, subsequent to the challenge by the EC of the FSC measures, aimed to challenge the same measure? In the case of multiple complainants, the Arbitrator said that "this would certainly have been taken into account" in the determination of the appropriateness of the countermeasures, and thus implicitly indicated that an amount equal to the value of the subsidy for each WTO Member would be considered inappropriate. With regard to the second hypothetical situation, the Arbitrator realized that the "allocation issue would arise" and cited the EC's statement indicating that it would "voluntarily agree to remove some of its countermeasures so as to provide more scope for another WTO Member to be authorized to do the same."[333] In concluding, the Arbitrator emphasized that its finding did not affect the right of other complainants to subsequently request countermeasures.[334]

The legal obligations upon the subsidizing country regarding actionable subsidies are somewhat less stringent. Article 7.8 of the SCM Agreement stipulates that the subsidizing Member "shall take appropriate steps to remove the adverse effects *or* shall withdraw the subsidy."[335] The subsidizing country is therefore not required to withdraw the subsidy as long as it removes its adverse effects, which should be done within six months from the date when the DSB

331 Decision by the Arbitrators, *Brazil – Aircraft Arbitration, loc. cit., supra* no. 329, para. 3.54. The Arbitrators also rejected the claim that such an amount of countermeasures would be punitive (para. 3.55).

332 The adoption of appropriate countermeasures does not "*require* that trade effects be the effective standard by which the appropriateness of countermeasures should be ascertained, nor does it *limit* the assessment to this standard," and "there is no basis for reading Article 4.10 to be 'trade effect-oriented.'" Yet, the Arbitrator considered that an examination of trade effects would not lead to a different conclusion in this case. The injury upon the complaining party seems to serve as a minimum standard. If the adverse effects are greater than the amount of the subsidy, a Member is entitled to base its countermeasures upon the injury. See Decision of the Arbitrator, *United States – Tax Treatment for "Foreign Sales Corporations" – Recourse to Arbitration by the United States under DSU Article 22.6 / SCM Agreement Article 4.11* (WT/DS108/ARB, adopted on May 7, 2003), paras. 5.41, 5.49, and 6.33 (Footnote 84), and 6.35. Abbreviation: *U.S. – FSC Arbitration*.

333 Decision of the Arbitrator, *U.S. – FSC Arbitration, loc. cit., supra* no. 332, para. 6.29.

334 Yet, the Arbitrator indirectly included a message for a potential future Arbitrator: "(...) it need only be stated that there is, in our view, no reason to presume that an arbitrator who might be required to address such a complaint in future would not take into account all the relevant factors in determining what might, at the time it is ruling, constitute 'appropriate countermeasures' in such future case." Hereby, the Arbitrator referred to its findings in para. 6.29, including the EC's statement cited there. Decision of the Arbitrator, *U.S. – FSC Arbitration, loc. cit., supra* no. 332, para. 6.63.

335 Emphasis added.

adopts the Panel or Appellate Body Report. At the same time, the remedy available to the injured WTO Member in case of noncompliance by the subsidizing country is less powerful, which was recognized by the Arbitrator in the *U.S. – FSC* case.[336] Pursuant to Article 7.9 of the SCM Agreement, the injured WTO Member can take countermeasures "commensurate with the degree and the nature of the adverse effects." Put differently, the amount of countermeasures should be based upon the amount of injury and not on the amount of the subsidy.

Although by definition nonactionable subsidies were allowed, the SCM Agreement nevertheless provided a multilateral remedy for WTO Members to challenge nonactionable subsidies that caused "*serious* adverse effects" to their domestic industry.[337] The burden of proof for the complaining party was thus higher than in the case of actionable subsidies (referring to "adverse effects"). If consultations failed, it was up to the SCM Committee, and thus not a Panel, to decide whether this burden was met.[338] The Committee could "recommend" modifying the program in such a way as to remove these effects. Yet, if the recommendations were not followed within six months, the Committee could authorize countermeasures "commensurate with the nature and degree of the effects determined to exist."[339]

Unilateral Remedies: CVDs

Instead of following the multilateral avenue described above, a WTO Member is allowed to opt for the unilateral approach and impose CVDs to respond to the injury caused by specific subsidies in its domestic market.[340] Yet, the SCM Agreement also disciplines this unilateral avenue[341]: CVDs may only be imposed pursuant to an investigation in accordance with the procedural and substantive obligations stipulated by the SCM Agreement. This investigation should determine the existence of three substantive elements: (1) the existence of a specific subsidy, (2) injury to the domestic industry producing the like product, and (3) a causal link between the subsidized import and the injury.[342]

Procedural Requirements

An investigation can be initiated either by or on behalf of the domestic industry or by the authorities of their own accord.[343] It is made "by or on behalf of the domestic industry," if the petition is supported by domestic producers whose collective output accounts for more than 50 percent of the total production of the like product produced by that portion of the domestic industry that

[336] Decision of the Arbitrator, *U.S. – FSC Arbitration, loc. cit., supra* no. 332, para. 5.37.
[337] Article 9.1 of the SCM Agreement.
[338] Article 9.3 of the SCM Agreement.
[339] Article 9.4 of the SCM Agreement.
[340] Articles 10 and 19.1 of the SCM Agreement and Article VI of the GATT.
[341] Part V of the SCM Agreement.
[342] Article 11.2 of the SCM Agreement.
[343] Articles 11.2 and 11.6 of the SCM Agreement.

expressed its view, either for or against, in the petition. If, however, the domestic producers supporting the petition account for less than 25 percent of total domestic production of the like product, national authorities may not initiate an investigation.[344] Thus, to prevent that the CVD procedure is captured by the interests of some domestic producers, a sufficient number of domestic producers must have expressed support for the application.[345] Only "in special circumstances" can the authorities decide to initiate an investigation without an application by or on behalf the domestic industry.[346]

The written application by the domestic industry should contain *sufficient evidence* of the existence of the three substantive elements: a subsidy, injury, and a causal link injury.[347] The authorities have to review the accuracy and adequacy of this evidence to determine whether the evidence is sufficient to justify the initiation of an investigation. In parallel, the investigation can be initiated *ex officio* only if the authorities have sufficient evidence on the three substantive elements, whereby "sufficient" means there is probable cause for an investigation.[348] As a consequence, an application to investigate should be rejected and an investigation should be terminated as soon as the authorities are satisfied that there is not sufficient evidence of either subsidization or injury. It should be terminated when subsidies are *de minimis* (e.g., if the subsidy is less than 1 percent *ad valorem*)[349] or where the volume of the subsidy or the injury is negligible.[350] If an investigation is launched, it should be concluded within one year and in no case more than eighteen months after its initiation.[351] Within this period, the investigating authority that considers imposing CVDs has to demonstrate the existence of a subsidy causing injury to its domestic industry (see *infra*; substantive requirements and the imposition of CVDs).[352]

As soon as possible after an application is accepted and before the initiation of any investigation, the investigating authority has to *invite for consultations* the Members regarding the products that may be subject to such investigation.[353] Moreover, throughout the period of investigation, those Members shall be afforded a reasonable opportunity to continue consultations with

[344] Article 11.4 of the SCM Agreement (similar to Article 5.4 of the Anti-Dumping Agreement). The motive of the domestic producers that elect to support an investigation is considered irrelevant. See Appellate Body, *United States – Continued Dumping and Subsidy Offset Act of 2000* (WT/DS217/AB/R and WT/DS234/AB/R, adopted on January 27, 2003), paras. 283 and 291. Abbreviation: *U.S. – Offset Act.*

[345] The definition of "like product" is pivotal to apply the thresholds set by Article 11.4 of the SCM Agreement. Footnote 46 to Article 15.1 of the SCM Agreement defines the concept of "like product" in the context of the SCM Agreement (see also *infra*).

[346] Article 11.6 of the SCM Agreement.

[347] Article 11.2 of the SCM Agreement.

[348] M. Matsushita ea., *loc. cit., supra* no. 35, 289.

[349] The *de minimis* level is 2 percent when the subsidizer is a developing country (see *infra*) (Article 27.10[a] of the SCM Agreement).

[350] Article 11.9 of the SCM Agreement.

[351] Article 11.11 of the SCM Agreement.

[352] Article 19.1 of the SCM Agreement.

[353] Article 13.1 of the SCM Agreement.

a view to clarifying the situation and to arriving at a mutually agreed-upon solution.[354] This consultation obligation is an illustration of "due process" requirements stipulated in the SCM Agreement. With regard to the element of injury, an investigation authority is obliged, pursuant to Article 15.1 of the SCM Agreement, to make an "objective examination" of the matter. The Panel in *EC – DRAMS Countervailing Measures* clarified, thereby paraphrasing an Appellate Body Report on anti-dumping,[355] that this standard "requires that the domestic industry, and the effects of (subsidized) imports be investigated in an unbiased manner, without favoring the interests of any interested party, or group of interested parties, in the investigation."[356] Article 12 of the SCM Agreement spells out the procedural rights of interested Members and interested parties. "Interested parties" includes at least exporters of the subsidized product and the domestic producer of the like product in the importing Member.[357] The "due process" requirements therefore aim to put these interested parties, with their opposing interests, on an equal footing in the investigation.[358]

The SCM Agreement also provides for specific "due process" requirements on the gathering of *evidence*.[359] All interested Members and interested parties should have the opportunity to present all evidence that they consider relevant.[360] Moreover, the beneficiaries of the subsidy in the investigating Member (e.g., industrial users of the subsidized product and the consumers) should be given the opportunity to provide relevant information. What if an interested Member or interested party refuses access to, or does not provide, necessary information or significantly impedes the investigation? If so, the SCM Agreement allows that determinations be made on the basis of the facts available.[361] Before the final determination, the investigating authorities have to inform all interested Members and parties of the essential facts that form the basis for their decision to allow the parties to defend their interest.[362]

[354] Article 13.2 of the SCM Agreement.

[355] Appellate Body Report, *United States – Anti-Dumping on Certain Hot-Rolled Steel Products from Japan* (WT/DS184/AB/R, adopted on August 23, 2001), para. 193. Abbreviation: *U.S. – Hot-Rolled Steel from Japan.*

[356] Panel Report, *EC – DRAMS Countervailing Measures, loc. cit., supra* no. 102, para. 7.274.

[357] See Article 12.9 of the SCM Agreement. The list is not exhaustive (see para. 2), and Members may thus include other domestic or foreign parties (e.g., domestic consumer groups) as interested parties. As to the scope of the term "interested parties," see Appellate Body Report, *Japan – DRAMS Countervailing Duties, loc. cit., supra* no. 57, para. 242.

[358] Domestic consumers, which share the same interest as foreign exporters, are not explicitly mentioned as interested parties. Yet, Members may consider consumer organizations as interested parties, and at least these organizations must be heard by the investigating authority (Article 12.10 of the SCM Agreement; see *infra*). Nevertheless, the different treatment still reflects the bias toward producers' welfare in the SCM Agreement.

[359] Article 12 of the SCM Agreement. See also the disclosure of confidential information (Article 12.4 of the SCM Agreement).

[360] Article 12.1 of the SCM Agreement.

[361] Article 12.7 of the SCM Agreement. See Panel Report, *EC – DRAMS Countervailing Measures, loc. cit., supra* no. 102, paras. 7.254–7.255 and 7.259.

[362] Article 12.8 of the SCM Agreement.

Substantive Requirements

To impose CVDs, the investigating authority has to determine the existence of a specific subsidy causing injury or threat thereof to the domestic industry.[363] As to the first element, we refer to our discussion on the definition of a specific subsidy. The investigating authority should thus show a financial contribution (or income or price support) by the subsidizing government that confers a benefit to a specific recipient.[364] Although nonactionable subsidies were not fully safe for multilateral action, even though they could be investigated, they could not be countervailed even if they were not notified.[365] Because this category was extinguished, all specific subsidies can be countervailed if they cause injury to the domestic industry. Subsidies causing injury to the domestic industry of another Member are by definition actionable subsidies (Article 5.1[a]).[366] Obviously, prohibited subsidies, which are prohibited as such (without reference to any adverse effect), can also be countervailed, but injury must also be demonstrated to impose CVDs.

For the determination of the second element, the SCM Agreement elaborates upon the injury provisions of Article VI of the GATT. "Injury" refers to "material injury" or "threat of material injury" to the domestic industry or "material retardation of the establishment of a domestic injury," but these notions are not defined in more detail.[367] The determination of injury must be based on "positive evidence"[368] and involve an objective examination of (a) the volume of the subsidized imports and the effect of the subsidized imports on prices in the

363 See Articles 10, 11.2, and 19.1 of the SCM Agreement and Article VI of the GATT.

364 The specificity requirement: See Article 1.2 of the SCM Agreement, which refers to Part V on CVDs. Concerning the benefit calculation (Article 14 of the SCM Agreement), the Appellate Body clarified that the chapeau of Article 14 of the SCM Agreement sets out three requirements: (1) "any method used" for the calculation should be provided for in the national legislation or implementing regulations; (2) the application of that method in each particular case shall be transparent and adequately explained; and (3) "any such method" shall be consistent with the guidelines contained in paragraphs (a)–(d). Appellate Body Report, *Japan – DRAMS Countervailing Duties, loc. cit., supra* no. 57, para. 190.

365 Article 10, Footnote 35 of the SCM Agreement.

366 See Article 5(a) of the SCM Agreement.

367 Article 15.1, Footnote 45 of the SCM Agreement. The Appellate Body in *U.S. – Lamb Safeguards* indicated that the "material injury" standard in the SCM Agreement (and Anti-Dumping Agreement) is lower than the "serious injury" standard for safeguard measures because CVDs (and antidumping measures) counteract "unfair" trade actions. See Appellate Body Report, *United States – Safeguard Measures on Import of Fresh, Chilled or Frozen Lamb Meat from New Zealand and Australia* (WT/DS177,178/AB/R, adopted on May 16, 2001), para. 124. Abbreviation: *U.S. – Lamb Safeguards.*

368 This term "relates to the quality of the evidence that authorities may rely upon in making a determination. The word 'positive' means, to us, that the evidence must be of an *affirmative, objective* and *verifiable* character, and that it must be *credible*" (emphasis added). See Panel Report, *EC – DRAMS Countervailing Measures, loc. cit., supra* no. 102, paras. 7.226 (Footnote 191) and 7.272. The Panel relied on Appellate Body Report, *U.S. – Hot-Rolled Steel from Japan, loc. cit., supra* no. 355, para. 192.

domestic market for like products[369] as well as (b) the consequent impact of these imports on the domestic producers of such products.[370] Regarding the volume, the investigating authority has to consider whether there has been a significant increase in subsidized imports, either in absolute terms or relative to production or consumption, in the importing Member. Regarding the effect of the subsidized imports on prices, it should be determined whether there has been a significant price undercutting or a significant price depression/suppression.[371] A novelty introduced by the SCM Agreement is that it allows cumulating the effects of subsidized imports from more than one Member, all subject to CVD investigations, if specific conditions are fulfilled.[372] What can be the impact upon domestic industry of these quantitative and price effects? To this end, the investigating authority has to evaluate all relevant economic factors and indices having a bearing on the state of the industry. The SCM Agreement includes an elaborated but nonexhaustive list of factors such as (actual and potential) decline in output, sales, market share, profits, and productivity.[373] As noticed, "injury" encompasses threat of material injury, implying that CVDs can be imposed to offset subsidies that merely cause a threat to injury to a domestic industry.[374] To this end, the determination of such a threat of material injury should be based on facts and not merely on allegation, conjecture, or remote possibility. Moreover, the change in circumstances that would trigger the subsidy to cause injury must be clearly foreseen and imminent and the application of CVDs should be considered and decided with "special care."[375]

Finally, it must be demonstrated that the subsidized imports are, through the effects of the subsidy, causing injury.[376] First of all, the investigating authority should demonstrate a causal link that should be based on an examination of all relevant evidence (causal relationship requirement). In *U.S. – Lumber ITC Investigation Article 21.5*, the Appellate Body held that the investigating authority must demonstrate that further subsidized imports would cause

369 The definition of "like product" is spelled out in Footnote 46 to Article 15.1 of the SCM Agreement. See also *supra* no. 286.

370 Article 15.1 of the SCM Agreement.

371 The determination can be based on one or more of these factors (Article 15.2 of the SCM Agreement).

372 Article 15.3 of the SCM Agreement.

373 Article 15.4 of the SCM Agreement. The Panel in *EC – DRAMS Countervailing Measures* held that all factors mentioned in Article 15.4 should be evaluated. See Panel Report, *EC – DRAMS Countervailing Measures, loc. cit., supra* no. 102, para. 7.356.

374 Article 15.1, Footnote 45 of the SCM Agreement. Yet, the application of CVDs should be considered with special care (Article 15.8 of the SCM Agreement).

375 Articles 15.7 and 15.8 of the SCM Agreement. See Appellate Body Report, *United States – Investigation of the International Trade Commission in Softwood Lumber From Canada – Recourse to Article 21.5 of the DSU by Canada* (WT/DS277/AB/RW, adopted on May 9, 2006), paras. 96–99. Abbreviation: *U.S. – Lumber ITC Investigation Article 21.5.*

376 Articles 15.5 and 19.1 of the SCM Agreement.

injury.[377] Second, the investigating authority has to explicitly filter out other factors causing injury at the same time, such as contracting in demand or productivity of the domestic industry (nonattribution requirement).[378] Obviously, the injuries caused by these other factors should not be attributed to the subsidized imports.[379]

The Imposition of CVDs

Prior to the discussion on the imposition of CVDs, we have to point to an alternative.[380] This alternative refers to voluntary undertakings under which (a) the exporting Member agrees to eliminate or limit the subsidy[381] or take other measures concerning its effect or (b) the exporter agrees to revise its price so that the investigating authorities are satisfied that the injurious effect of the subsidy is eliminated.[382] Indeed, such undertakings provide an equal protection for producers in the importing country. Of course, the national welfare effects are different given that CVDs are collected by the importing Member, whereas these economic benefits in case of undertakings flow to the exporting Member (a) or the exporters (b).[383] The importing Member does not have to accept the undertaking if its acceptance is considered impractical (e.g., if the number of exporters is too great) or for other reasons such as general policy.[384] The investigating Member can accept an undertaking only after a preliminary affirmative determination of a subsidy causing injury. The investigation will nevertheless continue if either the exporting Member or the importing Member so desires. If this final determination is negative, the undertaking shall lapse except when this determination is because of the undertaking itself. If it is positive, the undertaking shall continue.[385]

Before the termination of an investigation, a WTO Member is allowed to impose provisional CVDs if (a) an investigation has been initiated at least

[377] Appellate Body Report, *U.S. – Lumber ITC Investigation Article 21.5, loc. cit., supra* no. 375, para. 132.

[378] The SCM Agreement includes a nonexhaustive list of such factors (Article 15.5 of the SCM Agreement).

[379] Article 15.5 of the SCM Agreement. See Appellate Body Report, *U.S. – Lumber ITC Investigation Article 21.5, loc. cit., supra* no. 375, paras. 133–136.

[380] The term "countervailing duty" is defined in Footnote 36 to Article 10 of the SCM Agreement and Article VI:3 of the GATT.

[381] If a subsidy is withdrawn, a Member cannot impose CVDs (see Article 19.1 of the SCM Agreement).

[382] The exporting Member should agree with undertakings from exporters (Article 18.2 of the SCM Agreement).

[383] In all situations, the negative effect on consumers in the importing country is the same (because of the higher price).

[384] Article 18.3 of the SCM Agreement.

[385] Article 18.4 of the SCM Agreement. See Article 18.2 of the SCM Agreement. See Article 21.5 of the SCM Agreement for the duration of accepted undertakings.

60 days before and interested Members and interested parties have been given adequate opportunity to submit information and make comments (procedural requirement), (b) a preliminary affirmative determination has been made on the substantive elements (subsidy, injury, and causal relation), and (c) the authorities judge provisional CVDs necessary to prevent injury being caused during the investigation (Article 17.1 of the SCM Agreement). If a final determination is made about a subsidy causing injury, a WTO Member is allowed to impose definitive CVDs unless the subsidy is withdrawn.[386] The level of (provisional or definitive) CVDs imposed by the importing Member may not exceed the amount of the subsidy.[387] It is merely "desirable" that the duty should be less than the amount of the subsidy if such lesser duty would be adequate to remove the injury (lesser duty rule).[388] So, the level of CVDs can exceed the injury caused to the domestic industry. Members are allowed to perform an investigation on an aggregate basis. As clarified by the Appellate Body in *U.S. – Lumber CVDs Final*, CVDs have to be imposed on all sources found to be subsidized, although no prior investigation of all individual exporters is required.[389] An exporter who faces CVDs but was not investigated is entitled to an expedited review so that an individual CVD rate (or no rate at all) is established.[390]

A first question with regard to the duration of CVDs is the starting point. In general, provisional and definitive CVDs can only be imposed upon products that enter into consumption after the time of the preliminary or definitive determination respectively. Only in critical circumstances may definitive CVDs be assessed retroactively; this is limited to goods imported for consumption not more than 90 days prior to the application of provisional CVDs.[391] What if there is a discrepancy between the level of provisional and definitive CVDs? If the definitive CVD is higher, the difference shall not be collected, whereas if the definitive duty is lower, the difference must be reimbursed.[392]

The application of provisional CVDs should be limited to as short a period as possible and may not exceed four months. The duration of definitive CVDs may remain in force to the extent necessary to counteract the subsidization but may in principle not exceed five years.[393] The SCM Agreement provides two review mechanisms that have an impact on the duration of definitive CVDs. First, an *administrative review* should be conducted when initiated either by the investigating authority itself where warranted or, after a reasonable period of time after

[386] Article 19.1 of the SCM Agreement.

[387] Articles 17.2 and 19.4 of the SCM Agreement.

[388] Articles 17.5 and 19.2 of the SCM Agreement.

[389] Appellate Body Report, *U.S. – Lumber CVDs Final, loc. cit., supra* no. 40, para. 152.

[390] Article 19.3 of the SCM Agreement.

[391] Article 20.6 of the SCM Agreement.

[392] Article 20.3 of the SCM Agreement. Moreover, if a final determination is negative, any cash deposit must be refunded in an expeditious manner (Article 20.5 of the SCM Agreement).

[393] Articles 21.1 and 21.3 of the SCM Agreement.

the imposition, upon request of any interested party that submits positive information substantiating the need for a review. In particular, the following elements could be requested to review or could be reviewed *ex officio*: (1) whether the continued imposition of CVDs is necessary to offset the subsidy, or (2) whether the injury would be likely to continue or recur if the duty were removed. If the investigating authorities determine that the imposition of CVDs is no longer warranted, it must be terminated immediately. In contrast, if the outcome is a positive determination and the review covered injury as well as subsidization, the five-year period restarts. Second, to extend the imposition of CVDs beyond the (original or restarted) five years, *a sunset review* must be initiated before the end of the five-year period by the investigating authority itself or on behalf of the domestic industry.[394] The CVDs can only be upheld if this sunset review determines that the expiry of the CVDs would likely lead to continuation or recurrence of subsidization and injury. The SCM Agreement thus contains an important loophole to extend the imposition of CVDs beyond five years without, however, giving much guidance on the exact standard of review.

A final question, which was also raised in the context of the multilateral remedy, is how CVDs can respond to nonrecurring subsidies. Article 19.4 of the SCM Agreement indicates, in the view of the Panel as well as the Appellate Body in *Japan – DRAMS Countervailing Duties*, that CVDs may only be imposed if there is *present subsidization* at the time of duty imposition.[395] This requirement to establish present subsidization does not mean that investigating authorities are prevented from establishing the existence of subsidization (and injury and causing) by reference to data taken from a past period of investigation.[396] Nonetheless, the Panel held that, in the case of nonrecurring subsidies, "if the review of the period of investigation indicates that the subsidy will no longer exist at the time of *imposition*, the existence of subsidization during the *period of investigation* will not suffice to demonstrate *current* subsidization at the time of imposition."[397] In other words, investigating authorities will have to establish that the CVDs are imposed on products that are still benefiting from the nonrecurring subsidy. One such method, adopted by Japan in this case, is to allocate (spread out) the amount of the benefit conferred by the nonrecurring subsidy

394 Yet, CVDs can remain in force during the sunset review, even if this extends beyond the five-year period.

395 Panel Report, *Japan – DRAMS Countervailing Duties, loc. cit., supra* no. 105, para. 7.355; Appellate Body Report, *Japan – DRAMS Countervailing Duties, loc. cit., supra* no. 57, para. 210.

396 Indeed, the Panel recognized that investigating authorities have no choice because of the procedural requirements to establish the existence of subsidization (and injury) on the basis of past periods of investigation. Panel Report, *Japan – DRAMS Countervailing Duties, loc. cit., supra* no. 105, para. 7.356; Appellate Body Report, *Japan – DRAMS Countervailing Duties, loc. cit., supra* no. 57, para. 209.

397 Emphasis added. See Panel Report, *Japan – DRAMS Countervailing Duties, loc. cit., supra* no. 105, para. 7.357.

over the useful life of the product. The useful life of the subsidized production facilities in this case was determined by Japan as five years (2001–2005). The Panel did not question this "useful life" approach in general or the determination by Japan but concluded that this five-year allocation period is a finding that the benefit will expire after a period of five years and that Japan thus failed to demonstrate subsidization at the time of the imposition of CVDs (year 2006).[398] In the Negotiating Group on Rules, proposals are made to introduce rules on how subsidy benefits should be allocated.[399]

Differential Treatment

We have discussed the general disciplines on subsidies in the SCM Agreement. However, these disciplines are not horizontally applicable to all countries or all goods. In this last part, we focus on differential treatment for developing countries and agricultural goods. In fact, both special regimes might be contrasted with each other, as the first was established on the demand of developing countries whereas the second was created on the demand of developed countries with a vulnerable agricultural industry. Of course, the division of interests toward agriculture does not fully correspond to the division between developed and developing countries: Whereas developed agriculture exporters such as Canada and Australia are firm proponents of liberalizing agriculture, net food-importing developing countries will be hurt by reduced subsidization in agriculture.[400]

Ratione personae: Special and Differential Treatment for Developing Countries

Article 27 of the SCM Agreement elaborates special and differential (S&D) treatment provisions for developing countries. As if it were a preamble, it declares that "Members recognize that subsidies may play an important role in economic development programs of developing countries."[401]

Regarding prohibited subsidies, the disciplines on *export subsidies* contained in Article 3.1(a) do not apply to (i) least-developed countries (LDCs)[402] and (ii) some other low-income countries listed in Annex VII until their gross

398 The Panel also remarked that Japan's determination does not suggest that there might continue to be a subsidy after the period during which the benefit conferred by that (nonrecurring) subsidy has expired. See Panel Report, *Japan – DRAMS Countervailing Duties, loc. cit., supra* no. 105, para. 7.360.

399 See, for example, Negotiating Group on Rules, Communication from the United States, *Allocation and Expensing of Subsidy Benefits* (TN/RL/GEN/130, adopted on April 24, 2006); Negotiating Group on Rules, Paper from Brazil, *Allocation of Subsidy Benefits* (TN/RL/W/192, adopted on November 23, 2005).

400 The United States also aims at eliminating agricultural export subsidies, which are mainly provided by the EC.

401 Article 27.1 of the SCM Agreement.

402 Annex VII to the SCM Agreement. LDCs are designated by the United Nations.

national product (GNP) per capita income has reached $1,000 per annum. The Doha Ministerial Conference decided to raise this threshold to $1,000 in constant 1990 dollars for three consecutive years.[403] The Ministers in Doha emphasized that these countries "have flexibility to finance their exporters, consistent with their development needs."[404] Yet, this right extinguishes for products that have reached export competitiveness. In that case, these subsidies have to be phased out within eight years.[405]

Other developing countries were given eight years to phase out export subsidies but they could request the SCM Committee, considering all their relevant economic, financial, and development needs, to extend this period. The SCM Committee has to review the necessity of maintaining the subsidies for which extension is granted. If the SCM Committee makes a negative determination, the export subsidy should be phased out within two years from the end of the last authorization period.[406] Here again, the Doha Ministerial Conference provided some more flexibility without, however, extending the eight-year period in general. First, the Ministers instructed the SCM Committee to avoid different treatment for countries in similar circumstances.[407] Second, certain small trading developing countries[408] were granted, without a substantive review,[409] annual extensions to 2007 for export subsidy programs in force in 2001 that provided full or partial exemptions from import duties and internal taxes.[410] Nevertheless, the level of subsidies still benefiting from this transitional period may not be raised (standstill obligation).[411] Moreover, products that have reached export competitiveness must be phased out over a period of two years. This procedure was extended by the General Council in July 2007.[412] Until December 31, 2013, the SCM Committee shall continue these authorizations, subject only to an

403 Moreover, Ministers agreed that the country in question will be re-included in it when its GNP per capita falls to less than $1000. See Ministerial Conference, *Implementation Related Issues and Concerns* (WT/MIN(01)/17, adopted on November 14, 2001), paras. 10.1 and 10.4.

404 Ministerial Conference, *Implementation Related Issues and Concerns* (WT/MIN(01)/17, November 14, 2001), para 10.5.

405 Article 27.5 of the SCM Agreement. Article 27.6 of the SCM Agreement defines "export competitiveness."

406 Article 27.4 of the SCM Agreement.

407 The SCM Committee must thus take into account relative competitiveness in relation to other developing countries that requested extension.

408 Developing countries whose share of world merchandise export trade was not greater than 0.10 percent and whose gross national income (GNI) for the year 2000 was less than or equal to $20 billion.

409 The annual review merely verifies transparency and standstill requirements.

410 SCM Committee, *Procedures for Extensions under Article 27.4 for Certain Developing Country Members* (G/SCM/39, adopted on November 20, 2001).

411 Article 27.4 of the SCM Agreement. See Panel Report, *Brazil – Aircraft, loc. cit., supra* no. 39, paras. 7.58–7.67.

412 General Council, *Article 27.4 of the Agreement on Subsidies and Countervailing Measures* (WT/L/691, adopted on July 31, 2007).

annual review of the transparency and standstill requirements.[413] Consequently, the remaining export subsidies should be phased out no later than December 31, 2015. In conclusion, the gradual prohibition of export subsidies by these developing countries can be seen as the main novelty of the SCM Agreement on this issue, given that export subsidies by developed countries were already disciplined by the Subsidies Code.[414]

Today, developing countries are not benefiting from S&D treatment with regard to *local content subsidies* because the transitional period provided by Article 27.3 expired. All local content subsidies, even those of LDCs, are therefore prohibited. Arguably, flexibility for local content subsidies would be anyway less meaningful, because Article III.4 of the GATT and TRIMS also outlaws these subsidies.

Export subsidies that are not prohibited because of S&D treatment may nonetheless be actionable if they cause "adverse effects."[415] Indeed, all subsidies by developing countries that cause adverse effects are actionable subsidies. Yet, not all three forms of adverse effects caused by developing countries can be challenged as such. "In the usual case,"[416] a Member can only proceed against injury to their domestic industry as well as against nullification or impairment of tariff concessions undertaken by the subsidizing developing country. Complaints on the basis of "serious prejudice," which is the broadest form of adverse effects, are less evident and might even be impossible today. Article 27.8 explicitly states that the presumption of serious prejudice described in Article 6(1) of the SCM Agreement could not be invoked against developing countries, but WTO Members can nevertheless demonstrate by positive evidence that serious prejudice is caused in those four cases.[417] Other cases of serious prejudice caused by subsidizing developing countries can surely not be challenged.[418] As the presumption in Article 6(1) expired at the end of 1999, Article 27.8 no longer has legal value today. More importantly, some authors argue that, with the expiration of the presumption, the four cases of subsidies of which serious prejudice could be demonstrated have also disappeared. As a consequence, developing countries may not be subject to a claim that their subsidies have caused serious prejudice.[419] In contrast, one might also argue that the expiration of the presumption did not alter the four cases upon which serious prejudice can be based.[420]

413 The list of programs in countries eligible for continuation of extensions under the procedures is annexed to the General Council decision (see *supra* no. 412).
414 For a list of beneficiary countries and their export subsidies that are still exempted, see Report (2007) of the SCM Committee (G/L/840, adopted on November 12, 2007), paras. 17–18.
415 Article 27.7 of the SCM Agreement.
416 Panel Report, *Indonesia – Autos, loc. cit., supra* no. 85, para. 14.156.
417 Article 27.8 of the SCM Agreement.
418 Articles 27.8 and 27.9 of the SCM Agreement.
419 A. Hoda and R. Ahuja, *loc. cit., supra* no. 203, 1029.
420 Indeed, Article 27.9 seems to refer to the types of subsidies spelled out in Article 6(1) and not to the presumption. See also A. Clarke and G.N. Horlick, *loc. cit., supra* no. 22, 728–729.

So as to stimulate privatization programs, direct forgiveness of debts and subsidies to cover social costs when directly linked to privatization can never be challenged as actionable subsidies. To benefit from this exception, these subsidies should be granted for a limited time period and notified to the SCM Committee, and the program should result in eventual privatization of the enterprise concerned.[421]

The S&D treatment provisions described so far do not restrict the use of CVDs against developing countries but merely have an impact on the use of multilateral remedies. Indeed, the limited exemptions for disciplines on prohibited and actionable subsidies do not exclude that Members impose CVDs to offset subsidies from developing countries causing injury to their industry. Nevertheless, Article 27.10 of the SCM Agreement raises the *de minimis* standard for imposing CVDs upon products originating from developing countries. These CVD investigations should be terminated if the overall level of subsidies is less than 2 percent *ad valorem* (in contrast to 1 percent otherwise[422]) or if the volume of subsidized imports is less than 4 percent of the total imports.[423]

In contrast, the substantive and detailed procedural requirements to impose CVDs are not relaxed with regard to developing countries. Given the limited resources of LDCs and small low-income developing countries, the attractiveness of this trade remedy is clearly lower than in large emerging developing countries or developed countries.

Ratione Materiae: AoA

Trade liberalization of agricultural products always deserved a separate discussion when discussing international trade liberalization disciplines. Differential treatment is not based on an economic rationale here but should be understood, as noted by the 2006 World Trade Report, "in terms of asymmetries in negotiating power."[424] During the GATT area, the differential treatment was partly apparent in the text of the GATT 1947 and in the Subsidies Code. For example, the fundamental rule on the prohibition of quantitative restrictions (Article XI of the GATT) was not fully applicable to agricultural products.[425] In addition, when disciplining export subsidies, the GATT reserved a separate position for subsidies on the export of primary goods: They were permitted as long as they did not lead to "more than an equitable share of world export trade" for

421 Article 27.13 of the SCM Agreement. To date, there have been no such notifications.

422 Article 11.9 of the SCM Agreement.

423 Yet, this second exception does not apply if imports from developing countries the individual shares of which are less than 4 percent collectively account for more than 9 percent of total imports. Article 27.10 of the SCM Agreement.

424 World Trade Report 2006, *loc. cit., supra* no. 34, 194.

425 Article XI:2 of the GATT.

the subsidizing country.[426] Furthermore, more leniency was provided by waivers (e.g., the United States to subsidize), protocols of accession (e.g., Switzerland), and low tariff bindings (e.g., the EC using variable levies in its Common Agricultural Policy [CAP]). As mentioned, during the Uruguay Round, the Cairns group pushed for trade liberalization in this area. Their interest, in combination with the rise of agricultural disputes and the heavy financial burden of subsidization in the EC and United States, was the incentive for concluding an AoA aiming to achieve greater liberalization of trade in agriculture.[427] But the preamble of the AoA also expresses the arguments of opposing forces when noting nontrade concerns, such as food security, environmental protection, and the negative effects on LDCs and net food-importing developing countries. The AoA reflects recognition "that the long-term objective of substantial progressive reductions in support and protection resulting in fundamental reform is an ongoing process."[428]

The conclusion of the AoA was thus a starting point for liberalizing trade in agriculture and – like the GATS in the area of services – the agreement offers a framework for further liberalization. The framework consists of three main pillars. The first pillar on market access requires WTO Members to convert nontariff barriers[429] into ordinary customs duties (tariffication) and to subsequently bind and reduce the latter (progressive liberalization).[430] The other two pillars deal with subsidies and will be discussed below. The second pillar consists of commitments and general disciplines on domestic support,[431] and the third pillar covers the same with regard to export subsidies.[432] Contrary to the SCM Agreement,[433] the AoA makes a clear difference between domestic and export subsidies. In this discussion, the interplay with the SCM Agreement also deserves

426 This exception was considered the "Achilles heel" of the GATT to constrain subsidy programs. A difficult legal question was the correct interpretation of "equitable share." Another difficulty was the proof of the causal relationship between the grant of a subsidy and the acquisition of more than an equitable share of world trade. The Subsidies Code did not overcome these legal problems (see Article 10.2 of the Subsidies Code). See J. Josling and S. Tangermann, "Production and Export Subsidies in Agriculture: Lessons from GATT and WTO Disputes Involving the U.S. and the EC," in E.-U. Petersmann and M.A. Pollack (Eds.), *Transatlantic Economic Disputes – the EU, the U.S., and the WTO* (Oxford, Oxford University Press, 2003), 606 pp., 215; See J. McMahon, *The WTO Agreement on Agriculture – a Commentary* (Oxford, Oxford University Press, 2006), 333, pp. 90.

427 For the coverage of the AoA, see the definition of agricultural products in Annex 1 AoA.

428 Article 20 of the AoA.

429 See Footnote 1 to the AoA for a nonexhaustive list of such measures.

430 See Part III of the AoA (see Articles II and XI of the GATT). See exceptions provided by Article 5 of the AoA and Annex V. Developed countries committed themselves in the Uruguay Round to an average reduction of 36 percent over 6 years, whereas developing countries had to reduce their tariffs by 24 percent over 10 years. Least-developed WTO Members were only required to tariffy and bind their tariffs but did not have to make any reduction commitment. See J. McMahon, *loc. cit., supra* no. 426, p. 30.

431 Articles 3.1 and 3.2 of the AoA and Part IV of the AoA.

432 Articles 3.1 and 3.3 of the AoA and Part V of the AoA.

433 As mentioned, the SCM Agreement also prohibits local content subsidies, whereas other domestic subsidies are merely actionable if they cause adverse effects.

special attention. The expiration of the peace clause partly removed the distinction between disciplines on agricultural and other subsidies.

Export Competition

Parallel to the SCM Agreement, the AoA defines export subsidies as "subsidies contingent upon export, including the export subsidies listed in Article 9 of (*the AoA*)."[434] Yet, contrary to the SCM Agreement, the term "subsidy" is not further defined. The Panel in *U.S. – FSC* held that Article 1 of the SCM Agreement is "highly relevant context for the interpretation of the word 'subsidy' within the meaning the Agreement on Agriculture" but did "not say that the definition in the SCM Agreement (...) is directly applicable to the Agreement on Agriculture."[435] Indirectly, the WTO adjudicating bodies seem to rely on the definition provided by the SCM Agreement in Article 1 or the Illustrative List unless the contrary is to be inferred from the AoA.[436] Furthermore, pursuant to the Appellate Body Report in the same case, the interpretation of "contingent upon export subsidy" in case law on the SCM Agreement can also be applied in the context of AoA.[437]

The AoA also includes a nonexhaustive list of export subsidies. Article 9.1 lists six types of export subsidies: (a) direct subsidies contingent upon export performance,[438] (b) the sale or disposal for export of noncommercial stocks of agricultural products at a lower price than for buyers in the domestic market, (c) payments on the export of an agricultural product financed by virtue of governmental action,[439] (d) subsidies to reduce the costs of marketing exports of agricultural products, (e) more favorable provision of internal transport and freight charges, and (f) subsidies on agricultural products contingent on their incorporation in exported products (upstream subsidies).

However, in contrast to the SCM Agreement, the list included in the AoA not only facilitates the determination of an export subsidy but also has an impact on the applicable disciplines under the AoA, although the case law has largely

[434] Article 1(e) of the AoA.

[435] Because Article 1 of the SCM Agreement refers to "for the purpose of this Agreement." The Panel considered that a subsidy within the meaning of the SCM Agreement is also a subsidy within the meaning of the AoA unless the contrary is to be inferred from the AoA. As an example of the latter, the Panel mentioned that "[f]or instance, a measure which is listed as an export subsidy in Article 9.1 of the Agreement on Agriculture is an export subsidy for the purposes of the Agreement on Agriculture independently of the definition of subsidy in the SCM Agreement." See Panel Report, *U.S. – FSC, loc. cit., supra* no. 46, para. 7.150 (see also Footnote 702).

[436] See, for example, Appellate Body Report, *U.S. – FSC, loc. cit., supra* no. 63, paras. 136–142.

[437] Appellate Body Report, *U.S. – FSC, loc. cit., supra* no. 63, para. 141.

[438] This includes payments-in-kind. The Appellate Body clarified that this refers to a transfer of economic resources in a form other than money but rejected that a payment-in-kind is necessarily a direct subsidy. See Appellate Body Report, *Canada – Measures Affecting the Importation of Milk and the Exportation of Dairy Products* (WT/DS103 and 113/R, adopted on October 27, 1999), paras. 84–92. Abbreviation: *Canada – Milk/Dairy*.

[439] See Appellate Body Report, *EC – Sugar Subsidies, loc. cit., supra* no. 109, paras. 227–278.

neutralized the difference between both sets of disciplines for listed and nonlisted export subsidies. First, considering the types of export subsidies provided in the list, a distinction should be made between unscheduled and scheduled agricultural products in the Schedule of Commitments of the Member in question. With regard to unscheduled agricultural products, listed types of export subsidies are prohibited as such. In contrast, considering scheduled agricultural products, the listed types of export subsidies are prohibited only to the extent that they are in excess of the budgetary outlay and quantity commitment levels of the Member in question.[440] Developed WTO Members committed themselves in the Uruguay Round[441] to reducing their level of export subsidies by the year 2000 by 36 percent in value terms and by 21 percent in volume terms from a 1986–1990 base period, and this on a commodity-by-commodity basis.[442] Developing countries had to reduce their level of support by 24 percent in value terms and 14 percent in volume terms over ten years, and LDCs did not have to make any commitment.[443] In conclusion, contrary to the SCM Agreement, Members can uphold the listed types of export subsidies upon agricultural products if these products are included in their schedule and up to the financial and quantitative level committed.[444] Hence, only those Members having scheduled agricultural products have a limited right to offer listed types of export subsidies (except for S&D treatment for developing countries in Article 9.4).

Second, with regard to nonlisted types of export subsidies, they are subject to the anticircumvention discipline described in Article 10.1 of the AoA, regardless of whether the subsidized agricultural product at issue is scheduled or not.[445] The *U.S. – Cotton* case made it clear that these nonlisted types of export subsidies include subsidized export credits, export credit guarantees, or

440 Article 9.2(a) of the AoA. Regarding the burden of proof, see the special rule provided by Article 10.3 of the AoA, which only applies to scheduled goods. Appellate Body Report, *U.S. – Cotton Subsidies, loc. cit., supra* no. 198, paras. 644–645. On the interpretation of the schedule of commitments, see Appellate Body Report, *EC – Sugar Subsidies, loc. cit., supra* no. 109, paras. 159–226.

441 See Negotiating Group on Market Access, *Modalities for the Establishment of Specific Binding Commitments under the Reform Programme* (MTN.GNG/MA/W/24, adopted on December 20, 1993), para. XI. Abbreviation: *Modalities Agreement.*

442 This was a compromise between the United States, demanding full elimination of export subsidies over ten years, and the EC, refusing to make any commitment. Some more flexibility is provided by Article 9.2(b)(i)–(iii) of the AoA.

443 Moreover, developing countries did not have to undertake commitments on two listed types of export subsidies during the implementation period (Article 9.4 of the AoA) and this period was extended by the Hong Kong Ministerial Declaration until five years after the end-date for elimination of all forms of export subsdies. See Modalities Agreement, *loc. cit., supra* no. 441, paras. XV and XVI; Hong Kong Ministerial Declaration (WT/MIN(05)/DEC, adopted on December 22, 2005), para. 6.

444 See also WTO, Committee on Agriculture – Special Session, Note by the Secretariat – Revision, *Export Subsidy Commitments* (TN/AG/S/8/Rev.1, adopted on February 2, 2005).

445 See Appellate Body Report, *U.S. – FSC, loc. cit., supra* no. 63, paras. 143–147; Panel Report, *U.S. – Cotton Subsidies, loc. cit., supra* no. 226, para. 7.665.

insurance programs.[446] Although Article 10.2 of the AoA stipulates that Members undertake to work toward disciplines on these types of export subsidies, they are already subject to the anticircumvention discipline (Article 10.1 of the AoA).[447] Pursuant to this discipline, nonlisted types of export subsidies may not be applied in a manner which results in, or threatens to lead to, circumvention of export subsidy commitments.[448] Circumvention is present if nonlisted export subsidies (e.g. subsidized export credit guarantees) are offered to unscheduled agricultural products or to scheduled agricultural products above their level of commitment.[449]

In conclusion, contrary to the SCM Agreement, export subsidies are not *per se* prohibited under the AoA.[450]At the Hong Kong Ministerial Conference in December 2005, Members agreed to the elimination of all agricultural export subsidies by the end of 2013. However, the implementation of this decision is uncertain because the conclusion of the Doha Development Round is still undecided.

Domestic Support

The AoA also aims to reduce domestic support for agricultural products. To this end, the AoA categorizes domestic support measures in terms of the degree to which they are deemed to distort markets. On the one hand, some domestic subsidies are considered trade distorting. These are labeled amber box subsidies and are in principle subject to reduction commitments.[451] Yet, if these trade-distorting subsidies are contingent upon production reductions, they are not subject to reduction commitments, and this subcategory of amber box subsidies is labeled blue box subsidies. On the other hand, other domestic subsidies,

[446] Appellate Body Report, *U.S. – Cotton Subsidies, loc. cit., supra* no. 198, paras. 608–628. According to the Appellate Body, international food aid is also covered by Article 10.1, and "Article 10.4 provides specific disciplines that may be relied on to determine whether international food aid is being 'used to circumvent'" (para. 619).

[447] One Member of the Appellate Body disagreed with this conclusion: "'work toward the development of disciplines' strongly suggests to me that disciplines do not yet exist." Appellate Body Report, *U.S. – Cotton Subsidies, loc. cit., supra* no. 198, paras. 632–639.

[448] The Appellate Body in *U.S. – Cotton Subsidies* clarified that "the ordinary meaning of the term 'threaten' refers to a *likelihood* of something happening; the ordinary meaning of 'threaten' does not connote to a sense of certainty" (emphasis in the original). Appellate Body Report, *U.S. – Cotton Subsidies, loc. cit., supra* no. 198, para. 704.

[449] Panel Report, *U.S. – Cotton Subsidies, loc. cit., supra* no. 226, paras. 7.875 and 7.881.

[450] However, recall that some items of the Illustrative List (e.g. item k, para. 2) can be used as an affirmative defense (see *supra* no. 250).

[451] In the literature, some authors define amber box subsidies as those subsidies that are subject to reduction commitments in the AoA (narrow definition), whereas others adopt a broader definition and include all trade-distorting subsidies (so all subsidies that are not green box subsidies). We adopt the broader definition and thus consider blue box subsidies to be a subcategory of amber box subsidies, which highlights the exceptional nature of blue box subsidies (as trade distorting but nevertheless not subject to reduction commitments).

called green box subsidies, are considered at most minimal trade distorting and should therefore not be reduced.

Domestic subsidies are thus placed in the green box if they are not, or are minimally, trade distorting.[452] To meet this requirement, the AoA stipulates general and policy-specific criteria. First, the two general criteria are that the support must be provided through a publicly funded government program (including government revenue foregone) not involving transfers from consumers and that it must not have the effect of providing price support to producers. In addition, the support program must fit into the list of programs provided by the AoA and meet the policy-specific criteria in question.[453] In broad terms, the list covers government service programs and decoupled direct payments (including revenue foregone) to producers. Government service programs include general services (e.g., research and training services), public stockholding for food security purposes, as well as domestic food aid.[454] Decoupled direct payments are payments that are decoupled, i.e., delinked, from various aspects of production decisions and thus considered to be not trade distorting because they do not stimulate production.[455] Decoupled income support and all non-listed types of direct payments must be decoupled from type or volume of production, domestic or international prices, and factors of production employed, and, additionally, must not require any production to receive the payment.[456] Specific criteria are stipulated for listed types of direct payments, which include income insurance and income safety-net programs, payments for relief of natural disasters, structural adjustment assistance provided through retirement programs or investment aid, and payments under environmental and regional assistance programs. If the general as well as policy-specific criteria are fulfilled, these domestic support measures are put in the green box, implying that they are not subject to reduction commitments and may thus even be increased.

All other subsidies are put in the amber box and are thus in principle subject to reduction commitments. Yet, two categories of subsidies as well as a limited amount of subsidies should not be reduced. First, as indicated, domestic subsidies should not be reduced if they are direct payments made under production-limiting programs (blue box subsidies). To this end, these payments must be made based on a fixed acreage and yields or on 85 percent or less of the base level production, or, in case of livestock payments, on a fixed number of head.[457] There are no limits on providing such blue box subsidies. So, in contrast to direct payments put in the green box, these payments are not decoupled from production.[458] These subsidies are considered trade distorting, but output

[452] See Annex 2, para. 1 of the AoA.

[453] See Annex 2, paras. 2–13 of the AoA.

[454] Annex 2, paras. 2–4. See also the specific criteria that should be fulfilled.

[455] Annex 2, paras. 5–13. See also the specific criteria that should be fulfilled. See Appellate Body Report, *U.S. – Cotton Subsidies, loc. cit., supra* no. 198, para. 321.

[456] Annex 2, paras. 5 and 6 of the AoA.

[457] Article 6.5(a) of the AoA.

[458] The EC and the United States insisted during the Uruguay Round on including blue box subsidies because they were unwilling to decouple their domestic support.

will nevertheless fall over time and so will the demand for trade protection.[459] Therefore, some countries consider blue box subsidies as a necessary first step to converting distorting subsidies into green box subsidies, whereas others, however, aim to limit or to abandon the blue box category. Second, measures of assistance, whether direct or indirect, to encourage agricultural and rural development provided by developing countries should not be reduced (sometimes labeled as "S&D box subsidies"). In particular, three forms of assistance are included: investment assistance generally available to agriculture, input subsidies generally available to low income or resource-poor producers, and support to producers to encourage diversification from growing illicit narcotic crops.[460] Third, a limited amount of amber box subsidies can also be provided (*de minimis* level). In case of product-specific subsidies, support up to 5 percent of the value of production of the product in question can be given and, in case of nonspecific subsidies, support up to 5 percent of the value of total agricultural production can be provided. These *de minimis* thresholds are raised to 10 percent with regard to developing countries.[461]

In conclusion, exempted domestic support includes green box subsidies, blue box subsidies and *de minimis* subsidies, as well as S&D box subsidies in the case of developing countries.[462] All domestic support that is not exempted is considered subject to reduction commitments.[463] This leftover category captures product-specific subsidies as well as non–product-specific subsidies. Included product-specific subsidies are market price support, non-exempt direct payments, and other non-exempt policies such as input subsidies or marketing cost reduction measures.[464] For example, market price support covers the gap between the price that should be received by producers and the lower world market price and thus obviously has an impact on production decisions.

To apply reduction commitments, the exact amount of non-exempted subsidies should first be quantified. To this end, the concept of Aggregate Measure of Support (AMS) refers to the annual support, in monetary terms, provided for non-exempted product-specific and non–product-specific subsidies.[465] For each basic agricultural product, a specific AMS is established and all non–product-specific support is totaled into one non–product-specific AMS. Subsequently the sum of all these AMS[466] delivers the Total AMS, in other words, one single figure representing the full amount of domestic subsidies subject to reduction (with

[459] See M. Matsushita ea., *loc. cit., supra* no. 35, 306.

[460] Article 6.2 of the AoA.

[461] Article 6.4 of the AoA.

[462] The EC and United States are the two main providers of domestic support, with the EC clearly taking the lead. See WTO Secretariat, *Members' Usage of Domestic Support Categories, Export Subsidies and Export Credits* (G/AG/NG/S/12/Rev.1, adopted on March 12, 2001).

[463] Article 6.1 of the AoA.

[464] Annex 3 of the AoA.

[465] Article 1(a) and Annex 3 of the AoA. If the calculation of the AMS is impracticable, an "Equivalent Measurement of Support" is used (Article 1[d] and Annex 4 of the AoA).

[466] And all the "Equivalent Measurements of Support" if this is used.

the Current Total AMS of year X indicating the Total AMS for year X). Importantly, reduction commitments are made at this aggregate level. So, in contrast to export subsidies, commitments are not made at a product level, which implies that Members can maintain (and even increase) high levels of support to sensitive agricultural products. The reduction commitments were calculated on the basis of the Base Total AMS, which represented the average amount of non-exempted subsidies[467] from 1986 through 1988.[468] All Members with nonexempted subsidies during this period had to undertake reduction commitments.[469] The developed countries had to reduce their Base Total AMS by 20 percent over six years, whereas developing countries committed to a reduction of 13.3 percent over ten years and LDCs were exempted from commitments.[470] Yet, because of the high level of the Base Total AMS,[471] the level of support for 1995 (Current Total AMS of 1995) of some developed countries was already close to, or even less than, their final commitment level for 2000 (Final Bound Level of Commitment).[472] Needless to say, the reduction commitments on domestic support resulting from the Uruguay Round were not far-reaching for the major subsidizing countries. This Final Bound Level of Commitments, which had to be implemented by 2000 for developed countries and by 2004 for developing countries, still serves as the ceiling for nonexempted domestic support, because no new reduction commitments are agreed upon.[473] Disagreement on further reduction commitments for

[467] However, some exempted subsidies, such as blue box subsidies, were taken into account in the calculation of the Base Total AMS, whereas they were excluded from the Current Total AMS. The AoA was not clear on this point: Article 1(a), on the calculation of the AMS, only excludes green box measures, whereas Article 6, on the subsidies subject to reductions, also excludes the other types of exempted subsidies ("set out in this article"). Including blue box subsidies clearly increased the Base Total AMS, implying that Members started from a higher benchmark.

[468] Yet, upon insistence of the EC, "credit *(was)* allowed in respect of actions undertaken since the year 1986" (italics added). If the amount of subsidies diminished over the period from 1986 through 1988, Members could thus use the higher 1986 amount of subsidies to calculate the Base Total AMS. The aim, again, was to set the amount of the Base Total AMS as high as possible. See Modalities Agreement, *loc. cit., supra* no. 441, para. VIII.

[469] Thirty Members (counting the EC as one) were in this situation. If no Total AMS Commitments existed, the Member was not allowed to provide support to agricultural producers in excess of the *de minimis* level (Article 7.2[b] of the AoA).

[470] Modalities Agreement, *loc. cit., supra* no. 441, paras. VII, XV, and XVI. The reductions had to be implemented progressively, implying that a developed country had to reduce its level of AMS each year of the implementation period with roughly 3.3 percent ("Annual Bound Level of Commitments"). The Current Total AMS in a certain year could not exceed the corresponding Annual Bound Level of Commitments. At the end of the six-year period, the Base Total AMS was thus reduced by 20 percent, resulting in the Final Bound Level of Commitments.

[471] See *supra* no. 467 and 468.

[472] For example, in 1995, the EC and the United States were already below their final bound level.

[473] Yet, this might have to be nuanced somewhat because the levels are set in nominal terms and inflation may thus make these ceilings more constraining over time.

domestic support measures is one of the main reasons for the retardation in the conclusion of the Doha Development Round.

Relationship between the SCM Agreement and AoA

In comparison with the SCM Agreement, the AoA is more lenient vis-à-vis export subsidies and domestic subsidies. However, the crucial question is to what extent agricultural subsidies are shielded from the stricter disciplines imposed by the SCM Agreement. In general, the AoA articulates in Article 21 that "the provision of GATT 1994 and of other Multilateral Trade Agreements in Annex 1A to the WTO Agreement (e.g., the SCM Agreement) shall apply subject to the provisions of this Agreement."[474] This provision should be read together with the peace clause (Article 13 of the AoA), which limited the applicability of the SCM Agreement for AoA-conform subsidies during an implementation period. Export subsidies in conformity with the AoA disciplines could not be considered prohibited or actionable subsidies but could be countervailed, although "due restraint" had to be shown in initiating CVDs investigations. Regarding domestic subsidies, green box subsidies could not be considered actionable subsidies and could not be countervailed, whereas all amber box subsidies (including blue box subsidies, S&D subsidies, and *de minimis* subsidies) were countervailable, subject to the exercise of due restraint, and could not be considered actionable subsidies if the support granted to a specific commodity was not in excess of the support provided during 1992. However, this peace clause expired at the end of 2003, which enlarged the applicability of the SCM Agreement disciplines.

With regard to agricultural export subsidies, scheduled agricultural products are only prohibited in excess of their commitment level under the AoA. Hence, if an agricultural export subsidy is in conformity with the AoA, could it nevertheless be prohibited or actionable pursuant to the SCM Agreement, given that the peace clause has lapsed? Three positions can be distinguished.[475] In this discussion, apart from Article 21 of the AoA and the aforementioned peace clause, an important role is played by Article 3 of the SCM Agreement, according to which "except as provided in the Agreement on Agriculture," export and local content subsidies are prohibited.

First of all, some authors argue that, with the expiration of the peace clause, agricultural export subsidies are subject to Article 3 of the SCM Agreement and are therefore prohibited as such.[476] Remarkably, next to the Cairns Group, some U.S. trade negotiators have also taken this position, probably because of the much higher level of agricultural export subsidies provided by the EC. In this

474 Article 21 of the AoA.

475 See R.H. Steinberg and Timothy E. Josling, "When the Peace ends: the Vulnerability of EC and U.S. Agricultural Subsidies to WTO Legal Challenge," 6 *Journal of International Economic Law* June 2003, 369, at 377–378.

476 See D.E. McNiel, "Furthering the Reforms of Agricultural Policies in the Millennium Round," 6 *Minnesota Journal of Global Trade* 2001, 41, at 72.

view, regardless of the commitment level or type of export subsidies, no agricultural export subsidy can be provided pursuant to the SCM Agreement. Implicit in this reasoning is that the clause "except as provided in the AoA" merely refers to the peace clause. The peace clause explicitly exempts export subsidies in conformity with the AoA from action on the basis of Article 3 of the SCM Agreement on prohibited subsidies. This provision would have had no legal meaning if this were already the case in the absence of the peace clause.[477]

Second, some EC negotiators have taken the opposite view and have based their argument on Article 3 of the SCM Agreement *juncto* Article 8 of the AoA, which provides that Members undertake "not to provide export subsidies otherwise than in conformity with this Agreement and with (their) commitments (...)." In their view, these provisions imply that export subsidies in conformity with the AoA are not prohibited and are not even actionable pursuant to the SCM Agreement.

Third, Steinberg and Josling – correctly in our view – adopt a middle position and reject both extreme approaches because both fail to distinguish between legality and actionability.[478] The peace clause only constrained the actionability and did not alter the question of legality. After the end of the peace clause, agricultural export subsidies that are in conformity with the AoA are still legal (and thus not prohibited) but may be actionable.[479] Although dating from before the end of the peace clause, the Appellate Body Report in *Canada – Dairy Article 21.5* seems to agree that AoA-conform export subsidies are not prohibited by the SCM Agreement even after expiration of the peace clause. After all, the Appellate Body concluded that the WTO consistency of an export subsidy should be examined, in the first place, under the AoA and, importantly, it based this conclusion on Article 3.1 of the SCM Agreement. This conclusion is merely borne out, in other words, confirmed/supported by the peace clause.[480]

477 Implicitly, the Panel in *Canada – Dairy* also seemed to adopt this approach: "(...) *by virtue of Article 13(c)(i)* of the Agreement on Agriculture, export subsidies that conform fully to Part V of the Agreement on Agriculture are exempt from actions based on Article 3 of the SCM Agreement *for the duration of the 'implementation period'* (*in casu*, up to 31 December 2003)" (emphasis added). So, the peace clause exempts export subsidies from the scope of Article 3 of the SCM Agreement but merely for a limited period of time. However, the Appellate Body seemed to disagree (see *infra* no. 480). See Panel Report, *Canada – Milk/Dairy, loc. cit., supra* no. 206, para. 7.21.

478 The same position is adopted by H.N. Siuves, in "The Expiry of the Peace Clause on Agricultural Export Subsidies – the Outlook Post-Cancun," 31(1) *Legal Issues of Economic Integration* 2004, 25, at 32–34.

479 So, they stress that prohibited subsidies are illegal *per se* whereas all other subsidies are legal but could be actionable if they cause adverse effects.

480 "The relationship between the Agreement on Agriculture and the SCM Agreement is defined, in part, by Article 3.1 of the SCM Agreement, which states that certain subsidies are 'prohibited' except as provided in the Agreement on Agriculture. This clause, therefore, indicates that the WTO consistency of an export subsidy for agricultural products has to be examined, in the first place, under the Agreement on Agriculture. This is *borne out* by Article 13(c)(ii) of the Agreement on Agriculture (...)" (emphasis added). Appellate Body

It therefore seems that AoA-conform agricultural export subsidies are not prohibited by the SCM Agreement. In contrast, the argument in favor of the actionability pursuant to the SCM Agreement of agricultural export subsidies as well as domestic agricultural subsidies seems solid. About this second category, the question is whether agricultural subsidies, regardless of their status under the AoA (e.g., in which box they are placed), are actionable under the SCM Agreement. Part III of the SCM Agreement on actionable subsidies explicitly exempts from its scope "agricultural products as provided in Article 13 (peace clause) of the Agreement on Agriculture."[481] The exemption is therefore clearly dependent on the existence of the peace clause, which also seems to be indirectly confirmed by the Panel and Appellate Body in *U.S. – Cotton Subsidies.*[482] Moreover, as Steinberg and Josling indicate, nothing in the AoA saves AoA-conform subsidies from actionability under the SCM Agreement.[483] Consequently, domestic agricultural support is actionable under the SCM Agreement. As in all actionable subsidy cases, it requires that the complaining party show the existence of a specific subsidy as well as "adverse effects" to its interests.

Finally, it should be noted that agricultural subsidies, regardless of whether they are AoA-conform or not, can be countervailed under the SCM Agreement. As indicated, the peace clause only partially narrowed this unilateral venue. With the end of the peace clause, these limitations also expired.[484] Of course, the procedural and substantive requirements set out in the SCM Agreement must be met.

Report, *Canada – Milk/Dairy Article 21.5, loc. cit., supra* no. 228, paras. 123–124. Because Brazil made no claim that there may be a violation of Article 3 of the SCM Agreement in respect of *all* exports, including those in conformity with the Agreement on Agriculture, the Panel in *U.S. – Cotton Subsidies Article 21.5* did not solve this question. Panel Report, *United States – Subsidies on Upland Cotton – Recourse to Article 21.5 of the DSU by Brazil* (WT/DS267/RW, adopted on June 20, 2008), Footnote 785. Abbreviation: *U.S. – Cotton Subsidies Article 21.5.* The *U.S. – Cotton Subsidies* case has confirmed that agricultural export subsidies *not* in conformity with the AoA can subsequently be scrutinized under Article 3 of the SCM Agreement.

481 Articles 5 and 6.9 of the SCM Agreement.

482 In contrast, as indicated, Article 5.1 of the SCM Agreement (on prohibited subsidies) refers to "except as provided in the Agreement on Agriculture." Because the domestic support challenged by Brazil did not meet the conditions of the peace clause (which was still applicable at that time), it was actionable under Articles 5 and 6 of the SCM Agreement. See Panel Report, *U.S. – Cotton Subsidies, loc. cit., supra* no. 226, para. 7.608; Appellate Body Report, *U.S. – Cotton Subsidies, loc. cit., supra* no. 198, paras. 319 and 394.

483 R.H. Steinberg and Timothy E. Josling, *loc. cit., supra* no. 475, 388. If AoA-conform domestic subsidies could be challenged under Article 5 of the SCM Agreement (actionable subsidy), there is no reason why AoA-conform export subsidies could not be challenged similarly given that export subsidies are typically disciplined more severely. Moreover, export subsidies for nonagricultural products that are not prohibited on the basis of the Illustrative List (e.g., OECD Arrangement) also still seem to be actionable (see above).

484 See Article 10 of the SCM Agreement. No provision in the SCM Agreement or AoA points in the opposite direction.

Conclusion

At one time, one could claim in the U.S. Congress that "the definition of a subsidy, like that of beauty, varies with the beholder whose eye is focused on the object under scrutiny."[485] Looking at the full spectrum of government (and even private) actions, an "open-minded" beholder could detect subsidies everywhere. An effective fire or police service or educational system could be regarded as a subsidy because they clearly benefit the domestic industry. A creative beholder could even label negative action by the government as a "regulatory subsidy" when this government refrains from providing a certain level of regulation (e.g., environmental or labor standards). Indeed, the range of subsidies will vary depending on the views of the beholder on the proper role of the government and the market. However, since 1995, the SCM Agreement has narrowed the field of vision of the beholder. A specific subsidy exists when a government makes a financial contribution or provides income or price support that confers a benefit to a specific recipient. Whereas general governmental services and regulatory subsidies fall outside its scope, the reach of the SCM Agreement is, nonetheless, broad and wide open for interpretation by the WTO's adjudicating bodies. The determination of the different elements relies on a combination of uniform and domestic elements. In the absence of international benchmarks, the existence of a subsidy depends partly on the regulatory framework of the country in question. The definition of "subsidy" serves a double purpose: It opens the door to the substantive disciplines on subsidies but it also limits, at the same time, the measures against which a WTO Member is allowed to impose CVDs.

The variety of specific subsidies within the meaning of the SCM Agreement is subject to the substantive obligations of the SCM Agreement. Two types of subsidies, namely export subsidies and local content subsidies, are flatly prohibited in principle (red light). All other subsidies are not prohibited but may not cause adverse effects to the interests of other WTO Members (actionable subsidies). Since the expiration of the green light subsidies, the SCM Agreement is merely concerned with the effect of the subsidy on other WTO countries. The economic (e.g., overcome market failure) or social (e.g., redistribution) objectives of the subsidy in question are irrelevant. Of course, subsidies pursuing such objectives (like all other subsidies) can still fall outside the scope of the SCM Agreement if they are based on objective criteria.[486] Moreover, regarding the interests of the other WTO Members, only the effect on the industry and not on the consumers,

[485] U.S. Congress, House Committee on Agriculture (1972), cited by G. Schwartz and B. Clements, "Government Subsidies," 13(2) *Journal of Economic Surveys* 1999, 119, at 120.

[486] Yet, the strict conditions set out in Article 2.1(b) and Footnote 2 of the SCM Agreement should be fulfilled, and the subsidy may not be *de facto*-specific either. See World Trade Report 2006, *loc. cit., supra* no. 34, 201.

benefiting from the subsidized imports, is taken into account. Their industry can be affected in a threefold way: Their domestic industry can be hurt by increased imports (1), and the export opportunities of their industry to third countries (2) as well as to the subsidizing country (3) can be affected.

WTO Members can challenge these prohibited and actionable subsidies before the WTO's dispute-settlement system. Moreover, accelerated procedures as well as more stringent enforcement measures are at their disposal. On the other hand, WTO Members may also opt for the unilateral approach to react against injury caused to their domestic industry by specific subsidies: Provided detailed procedural and substantive obligations are met, they are allowed to impose CVDs to offset the effect of the subsidy.

Nonetheless, WTO Members have recognized that subsidies play an important role in economic development programs of developing countries and, therefore, have offered some more flexibility towards these countries. However, it is debated among academics whether the provided S&D treatment is wide enough to recognize the role that subsidies play for economic development. Whereas some academics consider the S&D treatment flexible enough, others argue that the SCM Agreement does not offer enough "policy space" for developing countries to spur their economy.[487] The thrust of their argument is that developed countries in their early stage of development also relied on subsidies that are disciplined today by the SCM Agreement. Moreover, they advance evidence from the developmental experience of various countries that there exists no single road to development, and that the WTO, including the SCM Agreement, should provide more flexibility to experiment with different industrial policy strategies. In the Doha Round, developing countries also plead for more policy space in the area of subsidies, rejecting the mere re-inclusion of the three types of green light subsidies that reflect too much the interest of developed countries.

No economic underpinning (but only an imbalance in negotiating power) explains the enhanced flexibility to provide agricultural subsidies as elaborated in the AoA. The Doha negotiations show that this imbalance is still very much alive today. Legally, however, the favorable treatment has seemed to be substantially reduced since the expiration of the peace clause. Agricultural

[487] See, in general, K. Gallagher (Ed.), *Putting Development First – The Importance of Policy Space in the WTO and International Financial Institutions* (New York, Zed Books, 2005), 301 pp; see also F.A. Ayala and K.P. Gallagher, "Preserving Policy Space for Sustainable Development: The Subsidies Agreement at the WTO," *International Institute for Sustainable Development* (December 2005), 28 pp.; Y.-S. Lee, "Facilitating Development in the World Trading System – A Proposal for Development Facilitation Tariff and Development Facilitating Subsidy," 38(6) *Journal of World Trade* 2004, 935–954; J.S. Mah, "Export Promotion and Economic Development," 40(1) *Journal of World Trade* 2006, 153–166; J.E. Stiglitz and A. Charlton, "A Development Round of Trade Negotiations?" Proceedings from the Annual Bank Conference on Development Economics, Washington, 2004, 28 pp.

subsidies causing adverse effects to other WTO Members might be challenged before the WTO adjudicating bodies (multilateral remedy). In addition, WTO Members can impose CVDs to offset the injury caused by subsidized agricultural products (unilateral remedy). Given the delay in the conclusion of the Doha Development Round, affected WTO Members might shift their focus to these remedies.

ROBERT HOWSE

2 Do the World Trade Organization Disciplines on Domestic Subsidies Make Sense? The Case for Legalizing Some Subsidies

Introduction

Prior to the Uruguay Round, the multilateral trading system did not contain any enforceable legal disciplines on domestic subsidies. The treatment of such subsidies in the General Agreement on Tariffs and Trade (GATT) was ambiguous: On the one hand, their legitimacy as tools of public policy was affirmed while their capacity to distort trade was also acknowledged. On the other hand, self-help against such subsidies was permitted in the form of countervailing duties (CVDs), provided that the subsidies caused "material injury" to domestic industry in the importing country. The Uruguay Round Agreement on Subsidies and Countervailing Measures (SCM Agreement) introduced a category of domestic subsidies[1] called "actionable," which can be challenged in World Trade Organization (WTO) dispute settlements, thus for the first time providing a multilateral legal remedy against subsidization. For a subsidy to be challenged in a WTO dispute settlement as actionable, it has to fall within the definition of subsidy in Article 1 of the SCM Agreement, which means it must entail a "financial contribution" governmental financial assistance to firms (from cash payments to equity infusions to provision of goods and services below market prices), and also

[1] It should be noted that export subsidies are placed in the category of "prohibited" in the SCM Agreement. These subsidies, aimed at enhancing the export performance of the subsidizing Member in competition with other WTO Members, raise somewhat different economic and political economic issues, including the issue of subsidies wars for market share in third countries. There may be good reasons to reconsider the prohibition on such subsidies in the SCM Agreement, but a different analysis is required. I have left that analysis for another time. I would only note that the analysis in this chapter cannot simply be applied to the case of export subsidies. See, for example, Bagwell and Staiger, "Strategic Export Subsidies and Reciprocal Trade Agreements: The Natural Monopoly Case," *Japan and the World Economy*, Vol. 9, 1997, 491–510.

I am grateful to Kyle Bagwell, George Bermann, Bob Staiger, Petros Mavroidis, and Andre Sapir for comments on an earlier version of this chapter, which was first presented in the Columbia WTO Seminar, and to Bagwell, Staiger, Al Sykes, and Joe Stiglitz for conversations on some of the economic issues discussed in the chapter.

confer a "benefit" on an enterprise; the subsidy must also be "specific," either *de jure* (legally targeted at a particular industry or enterprise or group of industries or enterprises) or *de facto* (in fact used only or disproportionately by a particular industry or enterprise or group of industries or enterprises).

If these criteria are met, then the subsidy in question will be actionable, which means that if the importing country can further show the existence of certain "adverse effects" on the interests of other WTO Members, then it can either request in WTO dispute settlement the legal remedy of removal of the offending measure or it may countervail the subsidy (provided the CVD action complies with the various procedural and substantive requirements in the SCM Agreement that apply to countervail). If any of these criteria are not met, not only will a dispute settlement action fail, but the imposition of CVDs will be illegal.

The SCM Agreement (Article 8) originally entailed a defined list of subsidies to be *deemed* "nonactionable"; in other words, subsidies immunized from challenge in WTO dispute settlement as well as CVD action, even if they were to be found to meet the criteria discussed above. This list included certain subsidies for research and development, for environmental protection, and to disadvantaged regions. However, this provision for deemed non-actionability applied provisionally, for only the first five years that the SCM Agreement was in force. Since its effective expiration, WTO Members have been unable to agree either to continue with the list as it now stands or to create a different list. Therefore, today there are no subsidy programs that are explicitly protected as nonactionable.

During the current Doha Round negotiations, proposals from developing countries (most notably Venezuela and Cuba) emerged for the reinstatement of a category of non-actionable subsidies. These proposals need to be seen in a context of renewed and more sympathetic attention by economists to the question of industrial policy and the role of various instruments of government policy, including subsidies, in achieving economic development goals through industrial policy.[2] At the same time, an important and provocative article by Bagwell and Staiger has raised fundamental issues about the economic rationality of the SCM Agreement disciplines on domestic subsidies, suggesting that these rules may do more harm than good to the world trading system.[3] The 2006 World Trade Report of the WTO Secretariat focuses extensively on the issue of subsidies and entertains the possibility that the SCM rules may, in some respects, end up disciplining efficient domestic policy interventions.

In light of recent debates about subsidies and trade in the economics and trade policy literature, this chapter aims to revive the case for creating a "safe haven" of nonactionable subsidies in the SCM Agreement. It begins by looking at different rationales for, or ways of, conceptualizing the discipline of subsidies

[2] For an overview of the recent literature, see D. Rodrik, "Industrial Policy for the Twenty-First Century," September 2004, available at www.ksg.harvard.edu.

[3] K. Bagwell and R.W. Staiger, "Will International Rules on Subsidies Disrupt the World Trading System?" 96(3) *The American Economic Review* June 2006, 877–895.

in WTO law. It then examines against this framework some important recent work in economics and trade policy on the question of subsidies and WTO law. In light of this analysis, this chapter continues by examining the extent to which the existing rules on domestic subsidies in the SCM Agreement are desirable and optimal in light of the justificatory framework developed in the first part of the chapter. Finally, the chapter considers proposals for reintroducing non-actionability and asks whether and how creating a safe haven for defined subsidies would improve outcomes under the SCM Agreement.

Justifying Domestic Subsidies Disciplines in the WTO

The debate about subsidies must be seen in light of a fundamental dissensus among both scholars and practitioners about why the WTO exists.[4] For economists like Bagwell and Staiger, the purpose of WTO rules is to facilitate internationally efficient outcomes through negotiated improvements in market access, consistent with states' domestically efficient outcomes (taking their policy objectives as given). Much different is the notion of the WTO as a global economic constitution, a charter of rights for free and fair competition in world markets (Ernst-Ulrich Petersmann). A further, alternative conception of the WTO rules is that they serve to entrench a view of what are good domestic public policies and tie the hands of governments in their choice of policies, helping them to pursue rational rather than irrational domestic policies, despite demands of concentrated domestic interest groups for the latter (what I shall call the "good governance approach"). Then there is the view that I have propounded with Kalypso Nicolaidis[5]: a renewed "embedded liberalism." This view begins with the notion that the trading system is about assisting domestic political communities to achieve their chosen collective objectives in a manner that reinforces and does not undermine global community goals: peace and security as the Bretton Woods planners had in mind in thinking of the social and political effects in the interwar period of spiraling protectionism, but now also sustainable development as reflected in the preamble to the WTO Agreement and human rights, many of which have achieved the status of customary law, binding on all states to the extent that they have not contracted out (in the case of nonpreemptory norms).

The Howse and Nicolaidis approach, in its emphasis on empowerment of domestic polities as *the starting point* for the determination of optimal trade rules, is quite compatible with the framework of analysis of economists like Bagwell and Staiger in most respects; it simply adds a further evaluative criterion, asking whether or how the rules advance or undermine the goals of the

[4] See D. Regan, "What Are Trade Agreements For?" 4(4) *Journal of International Economic Law* 2006, 951–988.

[5] R. Howse and K. Nicolaidis, "Enhancing WTO Legitimacy: Constitutionalization or Global Subsidiarity?" 16(1) *Governance* 2003, 73–94.

emerging global juridical community as a whole. In this specific sense, our approach could be called "constitutionalist," but, unlike Petersmann's, it is outward looking toward global order as a whole,[6] not inward looking to the WTO system as itself constitutional. At the same time, the goals of the emerging global juridical community (as, e.g., Habermas and Teitel have emphasized), although global, are hardly autonomous from the basic values internal to liberal democracies, and these values are dependent for their globalization not simply or perhaps even primarily on classic international law but also on political transition within domestic political communities and the emergence of formerly "domestic" actors – individuals, peoples, nongovernmental organizations (NGOs) – as global actors.[7]

Finally, there is a political bargain view of the WTO that understands the rules as a set of political compromises with which the parties are able to live; governments may well have accepted rules in some areas that reduced domestic welfare (say, the Agreement on Trade-Related Aspects of Intellectual Property Rights [TRIPs] or subsidies or antidumping) in return for benefits flowing from other agreements (such as agriculture). From this approach, it makes little sense to ask whether particular rules are efficient or welfare-improving for all WTO Members, at least without bearing in mind the underlying political tradeoffs, including across issue areas. From the political bargain perspective, the legal constraints on subsidies could, even if not otherwise efficient, be a desirable cost of a bargain that curbs the unilateral use of CVDs against subsidies, if this is the necessary price for getting users of CVDs (historically the predominant user is the United States) to accept such curbs.

How Well Do the Existing Rules Perform (i.e., Absent Nonactionability)?

From the first perspective, which I will call "domestic efficiency," Bagwell and Staiger make a powerful case that the existing rules are suboptimal and perhaps even worse than the *status quo ante* (the GATT with the Tokyo Round Code). Bagwell and Staiger ask us to assume (from a domestic efficiency perspective) that subsidies may in certain cases be desirable policy instruments; as they point out, this assumption is actually reflected in the language on subsidies

[6] See the conception of constitutionalization in Habermas, *The Divided West*, "Does the Constitutionalization of International Law Still Have a Chance?" Polity Press, 2006. For a conception of cosmopolitanism in ethics consistent with and supportive of national and other forms of difference while able to underpin the goals of global juridical community, see A. Appiah, *Cosmopolitan Ethics*. See also Ruti Teitel's elaboration of the evolving global juridical order and its normative foundations in terms of "humanity": Teitel, "Humanity's Law," Cornell Law Review, 2002. Nicolaidis and I are currently at work on a reformulation of our vision that draws considerably on the work of these authors to understand global economic governance in terms of the political ethics of rights-based democracy.

[7] Ibid.

in the GATT and the statements of WTO Members. At the same time, Bagwell and Staiger acknowledge that a subsidy may undermine a tariff binding; a government, by subsidizing a domestic producer and thus lowering the cost of production of a domestic good relative to the imported like product, may produce the kind of price differential in favor of the domestic good. This differential undermines all or some of the value of the tariff concession in terms of market access for the imported like product. Thus, if there were no discipline whatever on a government's ability to erode the value of tariff concessions in this way, one would expect few such concessions to be made.

The question, therefore, is "What kind of legal rule can maximize domestic efficiency by providing enough legal security against erosion of tariff concessions to facilitate efficiency-enhancing tariff reductions while, however, not unduly constraining the achievement of domestically efficient policy outcomes through subsidization, such that the cost of such constraint to domestic efficiency is less than the gains from tariff reductions facilitated by the constraints?" Bagwell and Staiger consider the disciplines available pre-Uruguay Round (the possibility of a Non-Violation Nullification and Impairment)[8] [NVNI] complaint and of countervailing consistent with GATT rules including those in the Tokyo Round code) and compare them with the disciplines now added in the SCM Agreement.

What is distinctive and innovative in their formal analysis is that they entirely logically assume that, whereas too few constraints on subsidization will deter tariff concessions (because the value of the concessions will be too insecure, arguably), too many constraints will also deter tariff concessions, because uncertainty as to whether they can use subsidization to achieve policy goals may lead states to want to retain greater capacity to use tariffs.

On the basis of their formal modeling, Bagwell and Staiger conclude that, assuming governments have a variety of policy instruments available to them (what they call "policy redundancy"), the GATT rules produce an efficient outcome: Negotiated market access through tariff concessions is protected by the NVNI possibility. Although states' parties will have to pay a price in terms of other adjustments (compensation) if the NVNI complaint is successful, they will not have to remove the subsidy. (Similarly, the imposition of a CVD imposes a price on the choice of subsidization as the policy instrument but does not require the abandonment of that instrument, obviously). When Bagwell and Staiger add the additional SCM disciplines to the mix, which actually provide removal of

[8] A Non-Violation Nullification and Impairment complaint entails the complaining WTO Member establishing that a policy change by another Member has nullified or impaired the benefits that the complaining Member could reasonably expect to flow from specific binding market access commitments (such as tariff bindings) made by the defending Member. As a matter of the actual jurisprudence, few such complaints have succeeded in the history of the GATT and the WTO; this does not detract from the value of the Bagwell and Staiger analysis, which is aimed at theorizing an ideal multilateral regime for disciplining subsidies. The existing legal test for NVNI is expounded by the Panel in the *Kodak/Fuji* ruling (United States-Film).

the subsidy as a remedy, they conclude that, in a variety of scenarios, the result will be that some efficient outcomes in tariff negotiations may well be prevented because of these additional disciplines. Only under the assumption of limited domestic policy instruments (little policy redundancy) and where use of subsidies is of minor importance in domestic policy do the WTO rules produce a more efficient outcome than the GATT.

In their model, Bagwell and Staiger introduce only three features of the "new" WTO disciplines:

> First, a subsidy that is successfully challenged under the SCM Agreement must be removed to achieve compliance (i.e., subsidy complaints under the SCM Agreement are "violation" complaints), whereas under an NVNI claim the subsidizing government would simply be expected to make a policy adjustment that returned market access to its original level – it would be under no obligation to remove the subsidy [footnote omitted]. Second, there is no distinction in the SCM Agreement between 'new' subsidies and subsidies that were known to exist at the time of market access negotiations. And, third, there is no requirement that a government challenging a subsidy under the SCM Agreement had previously negotiated a tariff commitment with the defendant government. (p. 32)

Have Bagwell and Staiger correctly identified and understood the relevant features of the new WTO rules? One feature that they clearly do not take into account in their model is that the new constraints on subsidies come along with new constraints on CVDs. Thus, CVDs can be challenged not only on the grounds that existed in the Tokyo Round subsidies code but also on grounds that the subsidy in question is not "actionable" within the meaning of the SCM Agreement. The SCM Agreement thus provides a new legal remedy against improper use of CVDs as well as a new legal remedy against subsidies. To the extent that the Bagwell and Staiger model does not take into account the effects of this new remedy against improper countervailing, it may not present a comprehensive picture of the difference in outcomes from the present situation of the law as opposed to the GATT *status quo ante*. Indeed, from the political bargain perspective, this may explain the status quo: The Uruguay Round rules may be efficient in the sense that, in terms of the costs of engaging in domestically efficient subsidies policies, subsidizing WTO Members are better off by accepting this particular set of disciplines as a *quid pro quo* for some constraint of the unilateral threat of CVDs against subsidization.

Second, Bagwell and Staiger do not take into account other differences in the legal criteria for entitlement to a remedy between NVNI in the GATT era and what is the case now under the SCM Agreement. The SCM Agreement does more than extend disciplines to subsidies that existed at the time of tariff concessions and on goods for which no tariff concessions have been negotiated. In the case of subsidies that are new and on which tariff concessions have been negotiated, and thus where under the GATT *status quo ante* an NVNI complaint might have been brought, the WTO Agreement allows a complaint to be brought even *if* nullification and impairment of benefits cannot be established on GATT principles for NVNI complaints, provided that the subsidy causes injury to domestic industry or "serious prejudice" as defined in 6.3 of the SCM Agreement. In contrast, it is arguable that, given the nature of the WTO system of treaties as an "integrated system,"[9] the NVNI remedy itself has been transformed by virtue of the concept of nullification and impairment of benefits being incorporated as one basis for an entitlement to a legal remedy in the case of an "actionable subsidy." This possibility is reinforced by the language of the provision of the SCM Agreement in question, which mentions "in particular, benefits of concessions bound under Article II of GATT 1994" and in a footnote refers to GATT practice on nullification and impairment. Thus, to successfully pursue an NVNI complaint against a subsidy, the complainant would arguably have to comply both with Article 23 of the Dispute Settlement Understanding (DSU), incorporating the NVNI remedy from the GATT, as well as the relevant provisions of the SCM Agreement defining an "actionable" subsidy. In such a case, the shift from GATT to WTO would make an NVNI unavailable against any subsidy that was not specific. (In contrast, the WTO rules, as Bagwell and Staiger of course do take into account, shift the remedy from compensation to removal of the subsidy, where the nullification and impairment of benefits arise from an actionable subsidy.)

In the *European Community (EC)-Commercial Vessels* case, the panel noted (Footnote 369) that Part III of the SCM Agreement defined causes of action that differed somewhat from those in Article 23 of the DSU but then drew a distinction between an action based on NVNI and one based on the obligation not to cause adverse effects from actionable subsidies in Part III. Although this is not entirely clear, the panel does seem to have assumed that that an action based on NVNI and one based on the adverse effect being nullification and impairment of benefits from tariff concessions bound in the WTO would both be possible in the WTO system. There is an open interpretative issue about whether the meaning of "actionable" under the SCM Agreement encompasses "actions" for NVNI.

It would be useful to refine the formal analysis by Bagwell and Staiger to take into account the other features of the WTO rules discussed above, including the legal uncertainty concerning whether an NVNI complaint still exists autonomously of the remedy for adverse effects from an actionable subsidy in the SCM Agreement Part III. However, one implication of their approach is that the possibility of states agreeing on certain subsidies as exempt from the WTO disciplines (nonactionable) is that one could capture the benefits of the WTO disciplines where there is limited policy redundancy and subsidies are not important to government's attainment of their efficient outcomes while

[9] See Appellate Body ruling in *Dessicated Coconut.*

avoiding the drawbacks where subsidization is significant, in other words, by in these latter cases designating the subsidies in question as non-actionable. "Non-actionability," depending on what provides more efficient outcomes, could be defined clearly as either including or excluding the traditional GATT NVNI remedy.

Finally, consistent with the Bagwell and Staiger logic is the possibility that gains can be had if states are enabled to remove or reform nontariff market-access-limiting measures through using non-actionable subsidies. This kind of role for non-actionable subsidies already has a precedent in the "green box" of the Agreement on Agriculture, where some subsidies that play a positive role in adjustment to liberalization are given a carve-out. States may be more prepared to liberalize in sectors such as water and electricity, for example, if they have clear rights to provide subsidies that ensure that the universal access/universal service goal is achieved under a deregulated and/or privatized market structure.

The second, "competition charter" perspective on the SCM Agreement implies a focus not only on the possibility for subsidies to undermine the market access benefits from tariff concessions but more generally to undermine the competitive relationship between domestic and imported products. The competition charter perspective is perhaps most visible in the evolution of European Union (EU) law on state aids, as part and parcel of EU competition law. Article 87 of the EC Treaty prohibits only those state aids that distort or threaten to distort competition in particular markets as well as affect trade between the Member States.

There are a number of features of WTO subsidies rules that appear to support the competition charter perspective. First of all, there is the requirement that a subsidy confer a benefit for it to be actionable. As interpreted by the Appellate Body,[10] "benefit" means a competitive advantage as measured against the benchmark of an undistorted market. Having focused, however, on this concept of competitive advantage in interpreting the word "benefit," the Appellate Body has arguably not applied it in a rigorous manner, and has failed to use appropriate economic analysis to determine whether in fact competition-distorting effects can be attributed to particular subsidies.[11]

Second, the SCM Agreement excludes nonspecific subsidies from actionability. This is consistent with a "competition charter" – based approach in that subsidies that are generally available, and widely used, by many actors throughout the economy are less likely to distort competition in a particular product

[10] See particularly *Canada – Aircraft I, US – Lead Bars* and *US – Softwood Lumber CVDs.*

[11] See the critique of the analysis of benefit in the first Appellate Body ruling in Lead Bars by G. Grossman and P.C. Mavroidis, "*United States – Imposition of Countervailing Duties on Certain Hot-Rolled Lead and Bismuth Carbon Steel Products Originating in the United Kingdom:* Here Today, Gone Tomorrow? Privatization and the Injury Caused by Non-Recurring Subsidies." Gene M. Grossman and Petros C. Mavroidis, in Case Law of the WTO 2001, Cambridge University Press, 2003.

market or between particular firms. It should be noted that EC provisions on state aids only discipline those subsidies granted to a particular enterprise or enterprises.

Third, the way in which adverse effects is defined in Articles 5 and 6.3 of the SCM Agreement arguably also focuses on certain kinds of effects that indicate a distortion of competition, such as price effects (see Article 6.3).

The difficulty with applying a distortion of competition approach in the interpretation and application of the SCM provisions discussed above is that many markets are imperfect (i.e., absent subsidization by the importing country) and subsidies may be used to correct market imperfections in some cases (e.g., where there are public goods or externalities that markets do not adequately internalize).

The challenge of determining whether a subsidy confers a benefit in an environment where government action pervasively influences the shape of the market was recognized in the context of privatization by the WTO Appellate Body in its second decision in the *Lead Bars* dispute:

> The Panel's absolute rule of 'no benefit' [in the case where a subsidy was granted to a state enterprise that has subsequently been privatized in a 'market' transaction] may be defensible in the context of transactions between two private parties taking place in reasonably competitive markets; however, it overlooks the ability of governments to obtain certain results from markets by shaping the circumstances and conditions in which markets operate. Privatizations involve complex and long-term investments in which the seller – namely the government – is not necessarily always a passive price taker and, consequently, the 'fair market price' of a state-owned enterprise is not necessarily always unrelated to government action. In privatizations, governments have the ability, by designing economic and other policies, to influence the circumstances and the conditions of the sale so as to obtain a certain market valuation of the enterprise. (Para. 124)

This statement by the Appellate Body has huge implications, far beyond the context of privatizations. In effect, the Appellate Body is suggesting that the concept of "benefit" as competitive advantage cannot be applied without considering how other government actions (and perhaps more generally by implication) and private anticompetitive activity have already distorted competition. The Appellate Body implies that the concept of "benefit" may have a different application in a "reasonably competitive market" than in a market that is not "reasonably competitive." In the *Softwood Lumber* case, the Appellate Body was faced by the argument of the United States that the benchmark for determining "benefit" in the SCM Agreement, a comparison between the price of timber based upon the government measure that the United States viewed as a subsidy and the price of timber on private markets in the country of exportation (in this case Canada), was nonfunctional because government sales of timber pervasively influenced prices in private markets. The United States claimed that in these circumstances it was justified in using U.S. private market prices as the appropriate benchmark against which to compare governmentally determined prices in Canada. The Appellate Body, in a not entirely coherent finding, said, on the one hand, that in these circumstances, the United States might be justified in using a benchmark other than Canadian private market prices, but on the other hand, it could not simply revert to U.S. private market prices, either. What alternative benchmark did the Appellate Body have in mind? The problem is that none is present in the SCM Agreement. These two examples illustrate the challenge, working with the SCM legal text, of adopting an approach focused on distortion of competition, in other words, without the practical institutional possibilities that exist in the EC for specialized rule making under the treaty as well as in an EC context of broader competition rules including those that reach private behavior, which can be drawn on in the interpretation of rules on state aids.

First, carve-outs for "nonactionable subsidies" could well enhance the possibility of applying in a principled way a "competition charter" approach to WTO subsidies disciplines. For example, WTO Members might be able to explicitly exempt from discipline subsidies that correct market failures and distortions. Thus, the inclusion of R&D subsidies in the list of nonactionable subsidies in the SCM Agreement may reflect the well-accepted market failure rationale for some R&D subsidies: the benefits of R&D have public goods features: R&D may end up benefiting market actors other than the private firm that pays for the R&D; thus, the latter will underinvest, because its level of expenditure will reflect only the benefits it is able to internalize. Second, a list of nonactionable subsidies might include subsidies in certain particular sectors where markets are pervasively influenced by government policies (regulated industries). In such cases, a competition approach may only be coherent through specialized sectoral norms that take account of the full range of government instruments shaping the marketplace (e.g., energy). Finally, a competition approach may not necessarily imply (and normatively overreaches, I would argue, if it is taken to that extreme) that other social goals may not in appropriate cases trump the goal of fair and free competition in markets. Thus, a competition approach is consistent with governments deciding to exclude from discipline subsidies that are directed toward such social goals.

The list of exclusions in the EC Treaty reflects, I would argue, this latter recognition. The list is as follows:

The following shall be compatible with the common market:

(a) aid having a social character, granted to individual consumers, provided that such aid is granted without discrimination related to the origin of the products concerned;
(b) aid to make good the damage caused by natural disasters or exceptional occurrences;

(c) aid granted to the economy of certain areas of the Federal Republic of Germany affected by the division of Germany, insofar as such aid is required in order to compensate for the economic disadvantages caused by that division.

The following may be considered to be compatible with the common market:

(a) aid to promote the economic development of areas where the standard of living is abnormally low or where there is serious underemployment;
(b) aid to promote the execution of an important project of common European interest or to remedy a serious disturbance in the economy of a Member State;
(c) aid to facilitate the development of certain economic activities or of certain economic areas where such aid does not adversely affect trading conditions to an extent contrary to the common interest;
(d) aid to promote culture and heritage conservation where such aid does not affect trading conditions and competition in the Community to an extent that is contrary to the common interest;
(e) such other categories of aid as may be specified by decision of the Council acting by a qualified majority on a proposal from the Commission.

It should be noted that this list also discloses that the EU approach to state aids includes an element of "community interest," which is analogous to the Howse and Nicolaidis perspective, to be discussed later in this chapter, which would take into account global community goals in considering appropriate multilateral disciplines on subsidies.

On the third, "good governance" perspective, subsidies disciplines should entrench good governance. WTO disciplines will improve domestic welfare if they prevent governments from granting subsidies that are domestically inefficient. Governments might be forced to do this if they cannot otherwise resist the pressures from special interests. This perspective has a range of problems with it that are worth mentioning from the outset. The first is that it *presumes* that inefficient outcomes are resulting from distortions in the democratic process and not from legitimate noneconomic considerations and constraints in the choice of policy instrument, which may lead to a choice of instrument other than the theoretically most efficient one to attain a given goal (this might include communitarian and cultural values that militate against solving the economic problem at issue using the more efficient instrument). Intellectually consistent economists such as Bagwell and Staiger simply fully account for such considerations in their understanding of what is a domestically efficient outcome: Cultural and communitarian, and indeed other noneconomic considerations, are merely aspects of the revealed preferences of a society that determines the meaning of an efficient outcome in that society. Trade policy experts have often not been so careful in their approach to efficiency in instrument choice.

The second difficulty with using the "force us to do what is good for us" approach to subsidies disciplines is that there is considerable disagreement and debate about the role of subsidies in producing efficient versus inefficient domestic outcomes.[12] In the 1980s and 1990s, the economic orthodoxy was in general against the use of targeted industrial policies, including many kinds of subsidies. In contrast, as Rodrik suggests more recently, theoretical and empirical work, taking account of information economics and the dynamics of innovation and technological development, presents a much more complex and messy picture, suggesting that in a variety of situations, targeted industrial policy may be indispensable to economic development in a society.[13] Moreover, the new work tends to stress the importance of experimentation in determining which strategies may work in a given country and which may not work. Overall, this newer economic analysis of industrial policy raises the question of whether one can generate at all a set of rules applicable across countries and sectors and different phases of economic development of any particular country, which could properly differentiate between the properties of "good" subsidies (from a dynamic [i.e., development-friendly] domestic efficiency standpoint) and "bad" ones.

One plausible consequence may be that there should be no disciplines on subsidies beyond the remedy of compensation in the case of nonviolation nullification and impairment (arguably necessary to protect the value of tariff concessions and viability of tariff negotiations). However, an alternative to such a radical reversal in WTO law might well be to identify subsidies that have had a positive effects on economic development and make those subsidies nonactionable. Although such a list would be underinclusive (in the sense that there might be other subsidies in some contexts and countries that could also have positive effects, but we simply can't identify all these *ex ante* and on the basis of existing empirical research and theory) and overinclusive (in that some of the subsidies on the list might not work or have positive effects in all contexts and countries even though they have proven to be successful in *some*), nevertheless such a list would align WTO disciplines closer with the best available information on the domestic welfare effects of subsidies, including dynamic effects.

Rodrik himself has produced some tentative conclusions from an overview of the empirical literature concerning what seems to work and what doesn't from a dynamic domestic efficiency perspective. These conclusions could be of use in evaluating the adequacy of existing rules as well as proposals for a list of nonactionable subsidies. For example, Rodrik suggests:

> It is common for investment promotion agencies to specify their priorities in terms of sectors or industries – e.g., tourism, call centers, or biotech. This leads to the misdirection of industrial promotion efforts. The targets of

[12] On how, in the domestic constitutional context, disagreement complicates the case for precommitment, see Jeremy Waldron, "Precommitment and Disagreement."

[13] And see, for example, S. Teitel, Exports and Poverty, ICER, 2007.

> public support should be viewed not as sectors but as activities. This facilitates structuring the support as a corrective to specific market failures instead of generic support for this or that sector. Rather than providing investment incentives, say, for tourism or call centers, government programs should subsidize bilingual training, feasibility reports for nontraditional agriculture, infrastructure investment, adaptation of foreign technology to local conditions, risk and venture capital, and so on. Cross-cutting programs such as these have the advantage that they span several sectors at once and are targeted at market failures directly. (p. 23)

The specificity test in Article 2 of the SCM Agreement would appear to track fairly closely Rodrik's recommendation here; although some of the instruments he mentioned might still be found "specific" on grounds that *de facto* they are *used* exclusively or disproportionately by particular firms or sectors, nevertheless, 2.1(b) appears to be aimed at guaranteeing some policy space for such cross-sectoral instruments:

> "Where the granting authority, or the legislation pursuant to which the granting authority operates, establishes objective criteria or conditions governing the eligibility for, and the amount of, a subsidy, specificity shall not exist, provided that the eligibility is automatic and that such criteria and conditions are strictly adhered to. The criteria or conditions must be clearly spelled out in law, regulation, or other official document, so as to be capable of verification."

Beyond this, the principles that nonactionable subsidies should be subsidies to activities and targeted to an identifiable and specific market failure could be used as a basis for formulating a list of carved-out "nonactionable" subsidies.

Another of Rodrik's guiding principles, based on the evidence about where industrial policy has worked and where it has failed, is that there should be a built-in "sunset" clause: "One way to ensure that resources (both financial and human) do not remain tied up for a long time in activities that are not paying off is to phase out support by default. Hence, every publicly supported project needs to have not only a clear statement *ex ante* of what constitutes success and failure, but also an automatic sunset clause for withdrawing support after an appropriate amount of time has elapsed" (pp. 22–23). Here, in terms of a possible list of nonactionable subsidies, the implication would be that a time limit should be put on nonactionability status. As a matter of legal drafting, this might be a tricky business: How can a WTO Member be prevented from avoiding the time limit by simply replacing the old subsidy program with a "new" subsidy of equivalent affect?

The Howse/Nicolaidis "global subsidiarity" perspective views the multilateral trading system as primarily about obtaining gains from liberalization in a manner consistent with the political and regulatory choices of societies and citizens and not about shaping, changing, or overriding those choices. At the same time, this perspective acknowledges that sustaining bargained trade liberalization is not possible without *some* constraint on those choices, if only to preserve a sense of security in the value of the bargained liberalization (i.e., that it not be undermined by domestic policies). This dilemma is addressed through the idea of global subsidiarity. As already noted, the Howse/Nicolaidis perspective would also take into account certain global community goods that are widely recognized and reflected in general public international law and certain of its specialized regimes (biodiversity and human rights being two examples).

In terms of global subsidiarity, the heightened disciplines in the SCM Agreement would appear undesirable, generally speaking, for much the same reasons as those advanced by Bagwell and Staiger. An NVNI approach addresses the problem of cheating on the "bargain" while interfering as little as possible with the Member's instrument choice (albeit, the requirement of compensation makes the choice more costly than it otherwise would be, but global subsidiarity recognizes the need for *some* trade-off if one is to have a meaningful liberalization bargain at all).

From a global subsidiarity perspective, the asymmetry between the policy space possible when using nonsubsidy instruments and that possible with subsidy instruments is troubling. Thus, Article XX of the GATT applies to allow a WTO Member to maintain otherwise GATT-illegal measures for purposes of *inter alia* protecting public morals and human and animal life and health, where the measures are necessary for the achievement of these purposes. The SCM Agreement contains no analogous exceptions. The 2006 World Trade Report of the WTO Secretariat, in its legal analysis, suggests: "While Article XX in principle would apply to subsidies, the more specific rules of the SCM Agreement in any case are explicitly geared to remedying trade distortions from subsidization." (p. 201)

It is not easy to determine what exactly this statement means. It could appear to suggest that, because the SCM Agreement is simply a *lex specialis* to the GATT provisions on subsidies, Article XX can be used as a defense against any claim of violation of the more specialized rules in the SCM Agreement. At some level, this would be consistent with the "integrated system" approach to the relationship between the SCM Agreement and the GATT in the Appellate Body *Desiccated Coconut* ruling. Such an interpretation would also take account of the absurd result of not applying Article XX: WTO Members would have more policy space to enact much more obviously and severely trade-distorting measures such as import bans and quotas than what are generally understood to be less distortive measures, namely domestic subsidies. The lack of textual support for such a reading, however, makes it unlikely that the Appellate Body would accept an Article XX defense to a claim under the SCM Agreement.

The concern of the global subsidiarity approach with the general interests of the global juridical community goals would, at a minimum, suggest that the SCM Agreement not be applied so as to prevent a WTO Member from fulfilling its obligations under customary international law. The adopted *Korea – Government Procurement* Panel confirmed that customary international law obligations should be respected in the application of the WTO Agreements by the dispute settlement organs, unless there is an explicit contracting out of customary obligations, something not to be lightly inferred. Some human rights obligations have arguably achieved the status of custom (indeed, a few are *ius cogens*). If, arguably, nondiscrimination rights and certain minority rights have the status of custom, then, for instance, subsidies for affirmative action purposes or to protect the linguistic and cultural rights of minority groups might be, in a given context, indispensable to the discharge of customary obligations. The case of obligations that are not custom but are binding on a WTO Member as a party to another treaty is more complex. How a possible conflict of obligations is resolved might depend on factors such as the temporal relationship between the other treaty and the WTO SCM Agreement (the Vienna Convention on the Law of Treaties "later in time rule"), whether the other treaty is *erga omnes partes* and whether the SCM obligations are regarded as bilateral or *erga omnes partes*, and whether the other treaty is regarded as a modification of WTO obligations as between the parties to the other treaty, as provided for in the Vienna Convention on the Law of Treaties, Article 41.[14]

Furthermore, it would be appropriate to interpret "objective criteria and conditions" in 2.1(b) of the SCM Agreement (discussed earlier in this chapter) based upon relevant general international law, which (for interpretative purposes could include "soft law," such as declarations of multilateral organizations). The footnote to 2.1(b) stipulates that such criteria must be "economic in nature." The meaning of "economic" here should be interpreted in light of international human rights instruments that affirm the interconnection of economic and other human rights (civil, political, social, and cultural).[15] In light of the objective of sustainable development and its connection to economic development as articulated in the Preamble of the WTO Agreement, "economic" would also surely include criteria and conditions that go to sustainable development including biodiversity and protection of the environment more generally (and indeed such instruments would meet a narrower definition of "economic" as well, inasmuch as they address externalities, i.e., market failures).[16]

[14] Cite Joost Pauwelyn; also see The Report of the Study Group of the International Law Commission on Fragmentation.

[15] See R. Howse and R. Teitel, *Beyond the Divide: The Covenant on Economic, Social and Cultural Rights and The World Trade Organization*, Ruti Teitel, co-author. Occasional Paper #30, Friedrich Ebert Stiftung, Geneva, April 2007.

[16] See the 2004 Dakar Declaration of Trade Ministers from Least-Developed Countries: "27. Recognising that subsidies applied by LDCs may play an important role in economic development and poverty alleviation programs in these countries, we further call upon Members:

a. to treat as nonactionable, subsidies required by LDCs for development, diversification, and upgrading of infant industries;

All this said, from a "global subsidiarity" view, greater certainty and legal security for domestic subsidy policies to fulfill international obligations might be obtained if these were to be explicitly defined as "nonactionable."[17]

Nonactionable Subsidies in the Doha Round

The notion of reviving the category of nonactionable subsidies has, in the Doha Round, been put forward primarily from the perspective of the needs of developing countries. In 2002, Venezuela tabled a proposal based on the notion that "Non-actionable subsidies might be one of the tools needed to implement certain development policies in the framework of the multilateral trading system, under which a country can promote the transformation of its economic fabric, including production diversification and increased value-added output, in a sustainable manner consistent with its national economic and social policy objectives."[18] Venezuela suggested that the reintroduction of nonactionable subsidies could be guided by paragraph 10.2 of the document on Implementation-related Issues and Concerns accompanying the Doha declaration. On this basis, Venezuela proposed that subsidies should be considered for nonactionable status if they are "aimed at achieving legitimate development goals such as regional growth, technology research and development funding, production diversification and development and implementation of environmentally sound methods of production." However, Venezuela did not suggest beginning afresh but rather starting from the categories of nonactionable subsidy that were provisionally included in the Uruguay Round SCM Agreement. Moreover, Venezuela endorsed the principle that that such subsidies should be "least trade-distorting." On the basis of comments and questions from, among others, Australia[19] and Egypt on its original document, Venezuela (and later Cuba, which joined Venezuela in support for the initiative) clarified its proposal. Reactions to the proposal suggested some interest but considerable skepticism.

b. to treat as nonactionable, subsidies provided by LDCs for research activities, adaptation of new environmental requirements, and development of industries;
c. to grant exemption from export competitiveness thresholds, export subsidies applied by LDCs.

[17] Conversely, subsidies that undermine or violate such obligations would certainly be excluded for the "nonactionability" category; for example, subsidies to fossil fuels that undermine Kyoto objectives, or other subsidies that encourage nonsustainable exploitation of natural resources.

[18] "Improved Rules under the Agreement on Subsidies and Countervailing Measures – Non-Actionable Subsidies: Paragraph 10.2 of the Document on Implementation-related Issues and Concerns: Proposal by Venezuela," TN/RL/W/41.

[19] "Egyptian Paper Containing Questions and Comments on the Contributions Submitted in the Framework of the Doha Negotiations on the Subsidies and Countervailing Measures Agreement," TN/RL/W/57, adopted on February 10, 2003; "Comments From Australia on Venezuela's Submission on Non-Actionable Subsidies Under the Agreement on Subsidies and Countervailing Measures" (Document TN/RL/W/41, adopted on February 11, 2003.

Part of the skepticism was based on the fact that little use was made of the "nonactionable" subsidy provisions in the SCM Agreement while they were in force; it was also suggested (by Australia) that, generally speaking, least-trade-distortive subsidies continue to be nonactionable in the sense that these would be found "nonspecific" in dispute settlement. In replying to such comments, Venezuela and Cuba rightly noted that the provisional list of nonactionable subsidies in the Uruguay Round Agreement was accompanied by stringent conditions and ceilings, including notification requirements, which made this list of little practical use, generally speaking, in carrying out effective development policies. These problems would point to formulating a better list and more appropriate conditions, rather than abandoning the "nonactionable" category altogether.

With respect to trade distortion, the assumption that the concept of "specificity" is sufficient to remove non- or minimally trade-distorting subsidies from WTO discipline needs to be questioned. Although (as argued above) the specificity rules in the SCM Agreement have *some* correspondence to economic thinking concerning distortive versus market-failure-correcting subsidies, clearly the work of Bagwell and Staiger raises the possibility that one could enhance internationally efficient trade liberalization by some relaxation of the existing disciplines. In the revised proposal, Cuba and Venezuela suggest that, starting from the categories in the Uruguay Round SCM Agreement, it might be possible to develop an indicative list of nonactionable subsidies that could be included in an Annex to the SCM Agreement.[20]

Conclusion

Many reasons have been advanced for the failure of the Doha negotiations, but in my mind a crucial reason is that those involved have not really come to grips with the implications of dissensus about the very purpose or nature of the WTO as a rules-based system. This chapter has proceeded on the basis of a stylized account of the different views; of course, actors within the system often do not have a consistent view; there may be elements of more than one of the stylized accounts included in their vision. What is interesting is that, from all of these perspectives, one can find reasons to revisit the existing SCM disciplines and a highly plausible role for a nonactionable carve-out in improving them. Of course, it is another issue whether the possible gains from any of these perspectives would be worth the transaction costs of negotiation of such changes. Finally, it is possible, from a political bargain perspective, that even if one can improve the WTO rules on subsidies, suboptimal features of the existing rules may constitute a necessary price to pay in return for the constraints the SCM

[20] "Second Contribution by Cuba and Venezuela to the Negotiating Group on Rules Expanding on the Proposal Concerning Non-Actionable Subsidies," TN/RL/W/131, adopted on July 11, 2003.

Agreement imposes on unilateral action against subsidies in the form of CVDs. The United States, the predominant user of CVDs, plausibly would not have agreed to curb CVDs unless the WTO disciplines closely tracked U.S. law on subsidies and CVDs as it existed at the time. It is an open question whether the gains from the constraint on unilateral action outweigh the costs of suboptimality in the legal disciplines themselves. How valuable has the SCM Agreement actually been as a constraint on the use of CVDs against subsidies defensible under the normative perspectives discussed above? As the political economy of protection shifts within domestic polities and as the dynamics of multilateral bargaining evolves, new political bargains may be possible. Thus, even from a political bargain perspective, if the SCM disciplines on domestic subsidies could be viewed as welfare improving, taking account of the realities that existed at the time it was negotiated, it is still important to reopen the underlying normative question of what an optimal set of multilateral disciplines would look like. Furthermore, we should recall that even the original bargain did contain (an albeit quite limited) list of nonactionable subsidies.

JOSEPH FRANCOIS

3 Subsidies and Countervailing Measures: Determining the Benefit of Subsidies

Introduction

The writers of the unfair trade laws captured the moral high ground early in the twentieth century and have held it ever since. It is one thing to argue for trade in general. It is another to argue for trade that is perceived as "unfair." Indeed, Bhagwati (1988) has even gone as far as comparing the purchase of unfair goods to accepting stolen goods. In theory, the General Agreement on Tariffs and Trade (GATT) 1994 Agreement on Subsidies and Countervailing Measures (SCM Agreement) regime and its implementation in national law are supposed to be there to protect us all from unfair competition linked to subsidized trade. Whether they do or not is a matter open for debate (and academic research). The evidence is rather strong that in reality political forces manipulate these processes.[1]

Although little noticed, the accountants captured the analytical high ground as countervailing duty (CVD) practice has evolved, seemingly at the expense of economic analysis. Indeed their approach was carried over, more or less intact, from U.S. law into the SCM Agreement. Since then, however (and as discussed later in this chapter), the World Trade Organization's (WTO's) Dispute Settlement Body (DSB) has placed emphasis on market-based interpretations of benefit.

What exactly is the benefit conferred by a subsidy? Somewhat tautologically, under Paragraph 1 of Article 1 of the SCM Agreement, a subsidy is defined as a "financial contribution by government" that confers a benefit. A "benefit" is understood to consist of something better than the market would provide.[2] The governmental practices that would constitute a "financial contribution" are set out in some detail in the first three of four subparagraphs of Paragraph 1(a) of Article 1. These practices include grants, loans, equity infusions, and tax incentives. Subparagraph (iv) is an anticircumvention provision encompassing the financial contributions detailed in the first three subparagraphs when those

[1] See Boltuck and Litan (1991), Tharakan (1996), and Blonigen and Prusa (2003).

[2] Appellate Body Report, *Canada – Measures Affecting the Export of Civilian Aircraft*, WT/DS70/AB/R, adopted on August 20, 1999, DSR 1999:III, 1377, para. 157.

contributions are made by a private body that a government "entrusts or directs" to make them.

Paragraph 2 of Article 1 further provides that CVDs may be imposed only on subsidies that are "specific" to an enterprise or industry, or group of enterprises or industries. Thus a subsidy is the provision of a financial contribution that confers a benefit to a specific enterprise or industry or group of enterprises or industries.

This chapter focuses on the calculation of benefit, given that estimated benefits are used both to determine injury and to set CVDs. My approach in this paper is a deliberately naïve one. Notwithstanding the political, psychological, and systemic logic behind why we might actually need and use fair trade laws, I will assume here that CVDs actually are simply meant to do what they claim – protect us from unfair trade by exactly (to the extent possible) offsetting the benefits of subsidies in trade. Based on this premise, I will ask what the appropriate measure of benefit actually is. Emphasis is placed on the concept of "competitive benefit." Notwithstanding the doubtlessly important legal aspects of CVD case law, we will deliberately ignore and/or pass quickly through much of this, focusing instead on economic factors, combined with a bit of speculation and discussion on what the concept of "benefit" actually means when the goal is to counter such benefit through selective, punitive tariffs. I will not focus on strategic trade issues, although they are discussed in the third section.

This chapter is organized as follows. The next section discusses the justification for focusing on economic benefit rather than on accounting definitions of benefit. The third section focuses on the measurement of economic or competitive benefit, and how this may differ from an accounting definition of a subsidy in practice. The last section is devoted to general discussion.

Accountants versus Economists

When does a government action confer an unfair benefit, how big is this benefit, and what should be done about it? The set of GATT/WTO Panel and Appellate Body Reports on subsidies makes it clear that there is a presumption that actionable subsidies confer an (unfair) benefit when they lead to an outcome in which a firm has an advantage in the marketplace as a direct result of government action. For example, in the Appellate Body Report on the Canada Aircraft dispute, we are told:

> We also believe that the word "benefit," as used in Article 1.1(b), implies some kind of comparison. This must be so, for there can be no 'benefit' to the recipient unless the 'financial contribution' makes the recipient 'better off' than it would otherwise have been, absent that contribution. In our view, the marketplace provides an appropriate basis for comparison

> in determining whether a 'benefit' has been 'conferred,' because the trade-distorting potential of a 'financial contribution' can be identified by determining whether the recipient has received a 'financial contribution' on terms more favourable than those available to the recipient in the market.[3]

The text of the Agreement and the case law build on this concept and includes requiring that actionable government credits and loans be those at nonmarket rates. Government supply of inputs is actionable when they are supplied at below prevailing market rates.

The SCM Agreement, therefore, seems to be about preventing subsidies from conferring unfair advantage in the marketplace. To quote another DSB report:

> We turn to the object and purpose of the SCM Agreement. We note, first, that the Agreement contains no preamble to guide us in the task of ascertaining its object and purpose. In Brazil – Desiccated Coconut, we observed that the 'SCM Agreement contains a set of rights and obligations that go well beyond merely applying and interpreting Articles VI, XVI and XXIII of the GATT 1947.
>
> The SCM Agreement defines the concept of "subsidy," as well as the conditions under which Members may not employ subsidies. It establishes remedies when Members employ prohibited subsidies, and sets out additional remedies available to Members whose trading interests are harmed by another Member's subsidization practices. Part V of the SCM Agreement deals with one such remedy, permitting Members to levy countervailing duties on imported products *to offset the benefits of specific subsidies bestowed on the manufacture, production or export of those goods* (emphasis added). However, Part V also conditions the right to apply such duties on the demonstrated existence of three substantive conditions (subsidization, injury, and a causal link between the two) and on compliance with its procedural and substantive rules, notably the requirement that the countervailing duty cannot exceed the amount of the subsidy. Taken as a whole, the main object and purpose of the SCM Agreement is to increase and improve GATT disciplines relating to the use of both subsidies and countervailing measures.[4]

Benefit would therefore appear to mean a measure of the change in competitive position in the marketplace, yet this is not quite the way the system operates in practice. There are important departures from this approach. First is the arbitrary nature of benefit calculations. Their valuation is supposed to reflect departures from market prices for inputs, credits, and the like. The body

[3] Appellate Body Report, *Canada – Aircraft*, para. 157.

[4] Appellate Body Report, *US – Carbon Steel*, paras. 73–74.

of SCM Panel and Appellate Body reports makes this point repeatedly. However, although this is inherently an economic approach to pricing benefits, the corresponding benefit calculations do not then take the next step forward and focus on the economic effect of subsidies. Rather, they take an oblique turn and focus on an accounting sense of the benefit and subsidy rate when duties are set. The result is an eclectic mix of government interventions that have been countervailed over the years. These have included:

- state loans and credits at below-market rates
- export restrictions on upstream inputs
- production subsidies
- export subsidies
- targeted tax credits
- state supply of inputs at below-market prices
- subsidies paid for domestic sales but not for export

Like the Sesame Street children's matching game, one can make a list of accounting-based subsidies that have been countervailed and try to spot the ones that do not belong based on economic effects. The classic example is Norwegian cheese (the last item in the list). Applying a strict accounting approach, the United States applied duties because Norway paid a subsidy to cheese producers when they sold cheese domestically. The subsidy was not paid if cheese was exported. (These rules reflected a food-independence policy grown out of food shortages during World War II.) An economist would call this an export tax. The accountants called it a subsidy. In the end, although benefits are, in some ways, subject to market-based benchmarking requirements, this is a long way from really focusing on the competitive benefit following from a subsidy. There is a disconnect between the payment of subsidies and their implications in terms of economic behavior.

Another departure involves the programs that are exempted from the disciplines that the SCM imposes on CVDs. These are important exceptions, and quite surprising from an economic point of view. We know from the economic literature on trade and interaction between firms that government subsidies for research and development (R&D) can confer critical competitive advantage (Leahy and Neary, 1999). Yet R&D support is exempted – it is "nonactionable." We also know that many of the more harmful impacts of subsidies on developing countries involve agricultural subsidies, yet although there is hope that the subsidy regime may limit such subsidies,there are also important carve-outs for agriculture. In addition, although the negative impact of subsidies may be on competing exports to third markets, the legal standing for seeking redress is heavily biased toward domestic industry. CVDs are about domestic competition with imports. Third-country exporters do not have the same channels for legal redress.

In addition to the exceptions, there are also oddities in the way subsidies and CVDs are determined that point to a political rather than technical role for CVD in supplying import protection. If one works through the issues covered by the body of GATT/WTO reports on subsidies, it is notable that many of the disputes appear, at least to this nonlegal reader, to be about governments going too far in their pursuit of supplying protection for political reasons. This is an obvious signal that the teams of bureaucrats calculating rates are not insulated from politics.

Competitive Benefit

The political origin of CVD practices are mixed with those of antidumping laws, and indeed modern U.S. practice in both CVD and antidumping law originates with the Tariff Act of 1930. CVDs through legislation date back earlier. The American Tariff Act of 1890 imposed a duty on refined sugar that received subsidies above that paid for unrefined sugar. This regime was expanded to all subsidized imports by 1897 (See Viner, 1923), approaching its current form with the Tariff Act of 1930.

The justification for these laws is the protection of domestic producers from subsidized imports. Basically, the premise is that fair competition is one thing, but whatever the logic for import protection in general, domestic firms merit protection from unfair competition. Under this narrow interpretation, duties are meant to reset competitive positions, leveling the playing field and undoing any unfair competitive advantage. In this section, this will be our assumption. As such, we focus on the concept of competitive benefit.

Ignoring politics and taking the naïve approach, we will focus on the impact on an import-competing industry in a country contemplating a CVD. We will refer to this market as the countervailing market. We proceed under the working assumption that we are resetting the domestic playing field in the countervailing market, neutralizing the impact of production or export subsidies on competing domestic producers.

A Basic Analytical Framework

Conceptually, we should draw a distinction between the amount of a subsidy and the competitive benefit of the subsidy. The point is illustrated in Figure 1. In the figure, we assume we have an industry in the exporting country. This industry sells either at home or in the countervailing market. The left panel represents the domestic market in the export market. The line S indicates the schedule of supply by the subsidized industry, mapping different combinations of producer price and shipments. The demand schedule D then indicates domestic demand, mapping domestic sales to price. The excess supply in this market (the difference between supply and demand in the export market) then defines

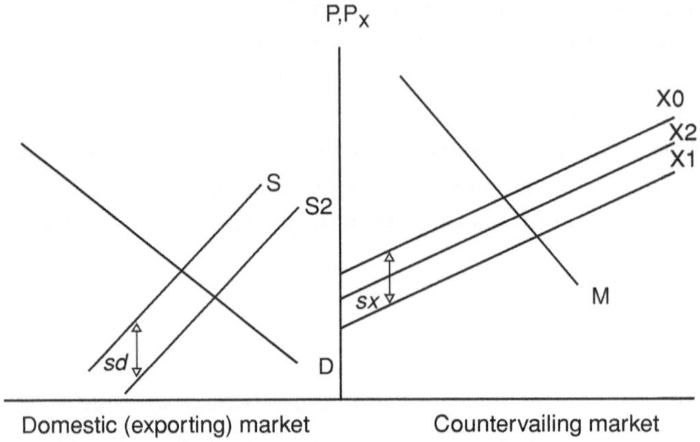

Figure 1. The competitive benefit of subsidies.

the supply for the countervailing market. Demand in the countervailing market is a function of available domestic supply, as well as available third-country imported substitutes for the subsidized import. Import demand for the subsidized import is indicated by schedule M : $X: QX_s = Q_s - Q_d$

Formally, we can represent domestic supply Q^s and demand Q^d as functions of price (inclusive of domestic subsidy sd). To keep things simple we use constant elasticity functional forms.

$$S: Q_s = k_s(P(1 + sd))^{\varepsilon s} \tag{1}$$

$$D: Q_d = k_d(P)^{\varepsilon d} \tag{2}$$

In equations (1) and (2), the terms εs and εd are supply and demand elasticities, and the k terms are constants. The term sd is a production or output subsidy. The difference between supply and demand is export supply QX_s.

$$X: QX_s = Q_s - Q_d \tag{3}$$

Import demand QX_d is defined as also being a function of domestic price P and the export subsidy sx.

$$M: QX_d = k_m P \varepsilon m \tag{4}$$

Market clearing conditions in the export market, which implies the market clearing in the domestic market as well, can be specified as follows:

$$QX_s = QX_d \tag{5}$$

$$\Rightarrow k_m P \varepsilon m(1 + sx)^{-\varepsilon m} = k_s(P(1 + sd))^{\varepsilon s} - k_d(p)^{\varepsilon d} \tag{6}$$

We will focus on the price impact of a subsidy. To do this, we need to define the wedge between domestic price P and export price P_x, which follows from the export subsidy *sx*.

$$P = P_x(1 + sx) \tag{7}$$

Defining the Benefit in the Countervailing Market

Given our basic analytical framework, we now turn to defining the concept of competitive benefit. Consider first a per-unit export subsidy of *sx*. As we have only one export market, we therefore can also consider this an export subsidy that targets the countervailing market. This concept of a targeted export subsidy will serve as our benchmark. The question we will ask is, "How does this subsidy compare to a targeted export subsidy in terms of the impact on the countervailing market?" Such a targeted export subsidy shifts the export supply curve down by the full amount of the subsidy. We have shown this in Figure 1 with a shift in the export supply curve from X0 to X1. The competitive benefit of the export subsidy, with respect to the countervailing market, is then reflected by the unit subsidy rate *sx*. Indeed, to restore the subsidy-free equilibrium, we need a CVD equal to the subsidy rate *sx*. In this sense, the accounting definition of subsidy rate reflects the competitive benefit.

Now suppose instead that we introduce an identical subsidy, but on total production rather than just on production destined for the countervailing market. We will set this subsidy rate as $sd = sx$. This is represented in the left panel of Figure 1 by a downward shift in the entire industry supply curve from S0 to S2. What happens to export supply? Recall that the export supply curve is the excess supply to the countervailing market. In the case of our "identical" output subsidy, we have some of the benefit of the subsidy being absorbed by the domestic market. A consequence of this is that the export supply schedule shifts by less than the amount of the output subsidy itself, from X0 to X2.

Formally, if we differentiate around the subsidy-free equilibrium, we can show that, from equations (1)–(7), the shift in export supply to X2 will be as if we had an export subsidy sx^*:[5]

$$sx^* = \frac{1}{1+\theta} sd \tag{8}$$

$$where\ \theta = \frac{|\varepsilon d\, Q_d|}{\varepsilon s\, Q_s}$$

From equation (8), if domestic sales are zero, then (logically) an export subsidy is identical to a production subsidy. Otherwise, the greater the domestic share of total output, the less the impact of an output or production subsidy relative to a comparable export subsidy. From Figure 1 and equation (8), we make the following observation.

[5] See Francois (1991).

Observation 1: An output subsidy has less effect on export markets than does a targeted export subsidy set at an identical rate.

Corollary 1: The duty needed to offset the competitive benefit conferred by an output subsidy is less than the subsidy rate itself.

Our corollary follows directly from the partial pass-through of output subsidies to the countervailing market. Because the pass-through will be only partial, we need a duty set at less than the subsidy rate itself to offset the benefit of the subsidy. In other words, for export markets, the competitive benefit from a subsidy in the export market is less than the overall benefit.

We can actually go a step further. We should be drawing a distinction as well between general export subsidies and export subsidies that target a particular market. The discussion so far implicitly assumes that our export subsidy targets a particular market whereas the output or production subsidy is general. Consider instead an export subsidy for exports to the world. Obviously, the countervailing market is only a subset of the world market. As such, we can also expect that, for general export subsidies, the competitive benefit they confer will again be less than the rate of the subsidy itself. Formally, we can summarize this as follows:

Observation 2: A general export subsidy has less effect on a given export market than does an identical (in a per-unit subsidy sense) targeted export subsidy.

Corollary 2: The duty needed by one country to offset the competitive benefit conferred by a general export subsidy is less than the subsidy rate itself.

Observation 2 can be proven formally simply by relabeling the markets in Figure 1 as the total export market (the left panel) and the countervailing export market (the right panel). Although some of the increase in exports will go to the countervailing market, some of it will also be absorbed by the other export markets. Hence the impact is again less than that of a targeted export subsidy. By implication, because the competitive benefit is less than the full subsidy, the duty needed for an individual country to offset an export subsidy will again be less than the subsidy rate itself.

What Happens When Many Countries Countervail?

We have so far been discussing a world where one country countervails, such that we can calculate the competitive benefit of a subsidy taking the rest of world as given. However, what happens when a group of countries sets out to countervail at the same time? To phrase it another way, if we look at the full set of export markets, what is the competitive benefit that is conferred on exports?[6]

[6] A similar issue came up with the U.S. imposition of safeguard duties on steel. The European Union became quite alarmed that this would divert steel to the European market.

For the markets viewed collectively, it will be the full amount of the export subsidy. Indeed, if all countries collectively calculate the competitive benefit for the purpose of imposing a duty, it will then be the full rate of the general export subsidy. We can summarize this point as follows:

> *Observation 3:* The competitive benefit of an export subsidy, defined over a set of export markets, is greater than the benefit defined with respect to an individual market.
>
> *Corollary 3:* The duty needed to offset the competitive benefit of a general export subsidy for a set of countries imposing duties will be greater than the duty needed for an individual country. The limit is the actual export subsidy rate itself.
>
> *Corollary 4:* The duty needed to offset the competitive benefit of a production subsidy for a set of countries will be greater than the duty needed for an individual country to offset the same subsidy. The limit is the actual general export subsidy equivalent of the production subsidy.

In general, we should draw a distinction between the amount of a subsidy and the competitive benefit conferred by the subsidy. The competitive benefit is what translates a subsidy at the input, output, or export level into a shift in the condition of a competing domestic industry. What Corollaries 3 and 4 highlight is the beggar-thy-neighbor aspect of CVDs. When an individual country imposes duties appropriate when acting in isolation, the result is that the subsidized imports are redirected to third markets. If these other markets also take action, then imports are rerouted back to the original countervailing market. For this reason, although the impact in individual markets of a general export subsidy is less than the subsidy itself, collectively the general export subsidy rate may be the appropriate estimate of competitive benefit if all relevant markets are expected to impose duties.

Fungibility and Capital Subsidies

Three of four substantive paragraphs in Article XIV of Part V of the SCM, which defines the scope for using CVDs, are devoted to subsidized access to capital. This includes below-market loans, equity infusions, and loan guarantees. This seems relatively straightforward, yet for firms engaged in multiple activities, the specificity of capital can be relatively weak. Consider, for example, a firm engaged in two activities – bottling cola and making steel pipe. The firm faces limits on access to capital, such that the supply curve for capital services to the firm is upward sloping. Given the total supply of capital, the firm then allocates capital services to cola bottling and pipe manufacturing based on the marginal benefit of each activity, in terms of its total profit. This is represented in Figure 2. In the left panel, we have total supply of capital services to the firm K and the marginal benefit of adding capital to steel pipe production, MB1. The

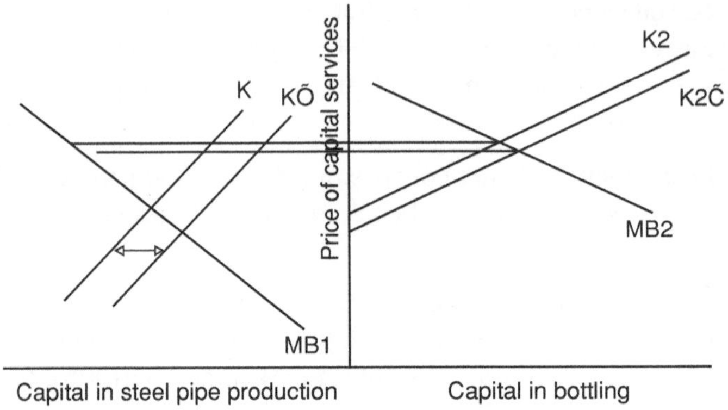

Figure 2. Capital allocation in a multiproduct firm.

right side represents allocation of capital services to the bottling activity. The marginal benefit in bottling is MB2. The firm's willingness to allocate capital to the second activity is reflected by the curve K2. The K2 curve reflects, for higher returns in bottling, the amount of capital that will be allocated to bottling instead of steel pipe. This is the difference between the K curve and the MB1 curve in the left panel. Given the intersection of the MB2 and K2 curves, we can find total capital costs and quantity.

In this setting, suppose the government injects capital into the steel pipe activity. This action has the effect of shifting the K curve to the right to K′. The result is that the K2 curve will also shift to the right to K2′. Indeed, the firm will change the way it allocates nongovernment capital, with a shift toward other firm activities. In essence, public capital injections to a multiproduct firm can be expected to leak to other activities. The net impact is that, for the targeted activity, capital injections, even when "specific," may be diluted depending on the structure of the firm.

> *Observation 4:* For capital constrained, multiproduct firms, capital injections and public credit, loan subsidies, and loan guarantees will be diluted across other (technically nonsubsidized) firm activities.

The point to be taken away here is that, even for capital subsidies, actual government assistance, even when properly measured in an accounting sense, may not have full effect in an economic sense.

Lobbying and Government

From the literature, there are (at least) two reasons why we may observe subsidies. One is that they reflect lobbying, and the other is that government is itself acting strategically. The discussion earlier in this chapter has abstracted from strategic aspects of subsidies. There is indeed a large literature – falling under the rubric of "old new" trade theory – that explores strategic application of production and export subsidies by governments. Under this theory, firms have market power, so that they are interacting strategically and so that government subsidies are themselves entered strategically to influence the outcome of the interaction between firms. CVDs can serve to neutralize strategic incentives for subsidies. This is not necessarily the case, however. Policy equilibria can include a mix of tariffs and subsidies, and every case is potentially unique, without clear scope for generic guidelines. A good review of this literature is provided by Brander (1995). It is clear that governments do engage in such games. Even so, for the vast majority of cases involving steel, leather, fish, and other products in competitive markets, the approach discussed earlier in this chapter is appropriate for addressing the economic benefit of a subsidy. Where strategic decisions come into play (like aircraft introduction in the ongoing Boeing-Airbus), extension will need to be case specific. Even so, a focus on economic benefit, as a concept, may serve to keep the SCM focused on actionable outcomes.

Discussion

The SCM-based strictures on CVDs involve an eclectic mix of economics and accounting. Although the text of the Agreement stresses market-based measures of benefit in a monetary sense, we do not have the same emphasis on benefit in terms of effect. In a sense, this is the role of the injury stage of CVD investigations. (However, the U.S. CVD code was grandfathered into the WTO, so for the United States the connection to draw is not between subsidy and injury but between imports and injury, unlike Article VI.) One can hope that, if not reflected in the set of accounting-based measures of benefit, the economic aspects of subsidy schemes are reflected in the establishment of causation. Regardless of what happens at the injury stage, identifying benefits correctly is also important if we want to rebalance the market by setting duties correctly. This calls for a nuanced approach that combines the information from accounting definitions of subsidy with an economic sense of competitive benefit. In this chapter we have examined the extent to which accounting benefits and competitive benefits may (or may not) coincide. It is not meant to provide a comprehensive method for determining economic benefit, but rather to illustrate that economic benefit, contrasted with the accounting approach, can itself serve as a useful conceptual benchmark.

There may be important systemic reasons to get the economics right in calculating the benefits of subsidies. It is well established that, for domestic policy objectives, direct domestic subsidies are the preferred direct tool (Bhagwati & Ramaswami, 1963). If they have unintended effects on the trade front, the WTO subsidy rules allow Members to countervail and even pursue the removal of the subsidies. As Bagwell & Staiger (2004) have stressed, such limits on legitimate domestic policy tools may limit the willingness of WTO Members to make trade policy commitments. This problem is handled, in part, by language in the WTO

SCM that states that subsidies can be legitimate policy tools. Hence we have carve-outs; for example, for R&D, regional subsidies, and adjustment assistance. It seems logical to also focus on the trade-related economic impact of subsidies when calculating benefits for CVD purposes. To do otherwise (in particular, to focus on an accounting approach to large domestic programs) may lead to inflated trade remedies, greater strictures on legitimate policy tools, and further reluctance from WTO Members to make commitments.

REFERENCES

Bagwell, K., and R. W. Staiger. 2004. Subsidy Agreements. National Bureau of Economic Research Working Paper Series, paper no. 10292, February.

Bhagwati, J. 1988. *Protectionism.* Cambridge, MA: MIT Press.

Bhagwati, J., and V. K. Ramaswami. 1963. "Domestic Distortions, Tariffs and the Theory of Optimum Subsidy." *Journal of Political Economy* 71(1):44–50.

Bloningen, B., and T. J. Prusa. 2003. Antidumping. In *Handbook of International Trade,* eds. E. K. Choi and J. Harrigan. Oxford: Blackwell Publishing.

Boltuck, R., and R. E. Litan. 1991. *Down in the Dumps: Administration of the Unfair Trade Laws.* Washington, DC: The Brookings Institution.

Brander, J. 1995. Strategic trade policy. In *The Handbook of International Economics,* Volume III, eds. Gene M. Grossman and Kenneth Rogoff. North Holland-Amsterdam: Elsevier Science.

Diamond, R. 1991. Comment on conceptual and procedural biases in the administration of countervailing duty law. In *Down in the Dumps: Administration of the Unfair Trade Laws,* ed. R. Boltuck and R. E. Litan. Washington, DC: The Brookings Institution.

Dixit, A. K. 1988. "Antidumping and Countervailing Duties under Oligopoly." *European Economic Review* 32:55–68.

Eaton, J., and G. Grossman. 1986. "Optimal Trade and Industrial Policy under Oligopoly." *Quarterly Journal of Economics* 101:383–406.

Francois, J. F. 1991. "Countervailing the Effects of Subsidies." *Journal of World Trade Law.*

Leahy, D., and J. P. Neary. 1999. "Learning by Doing, Precommitment and Infant-Industry Protection." *Review of Economic Studies* 66:447–474.

Tharakan, P. K. M. 1996. "Political Economy and Contingent Protection." *Economic Journal* 1550–1664.

Viner, J. 1923. *Dumping: A Problem in International Trade.* Chicago: University of Chicago Press.

Appendix

Article 14

Article 14: Calculation of the Amount of a Subsidy in Terms of the Benefit to the Recipient

For the purpose of Part V, any method used by the investigating authority to calculate the benefit to the recipient conferred pursuant to Paragraph 1 of Article 1 shall be provided for in the national legislation or implementing regulations of the Member concerned, and its application to each particular case shall be transparent and adequately explained. Furthermore, any such method shall be consistent with the following guidelines:

(a) government provision of equity capital shall not be considered as conferring a benefit, unless the investment decision can be regarded as inconsistent with the usual investment practice (including for the provision of risk capital) of private investors in the territory of that Member;
(b) a loan by a government shall not be considered as conferring a benefit, unless there is a difference between the amount that the firm receiving the loan pays on the government loan and the amount the firm would pay on a comparable commercial loan which the firm could actually obtain on the market. In this case the benefit shall be the difference between these two amounts;
(c) a loan guarantee by a government shall not be considered as conferring a benefit, unless there is a difference between the amount that the firm receiving the guarantee pays on a loan guaranteed by the government and the amount that the firm would pay on a comparable commercial loan absent the government guarantee. In this case the benefit shall be the difference between these two amounts adjusted for any differences in fees;
(d) the provision of goods or services or purchase of goods by a government shall not be considered as conferring a benefit unless the provision is made for less than adequate remuneration, or the purchase is made for more than adequate remuneration. The adequacy of remuneration shall be determined in relation to prevailing market conditions for the good or service in question in the country of provision or purchase (including price, quality, availability, marketability, transportation, and other conditions of purchase or sale).

ANDREW GREEN AND MICHAEL TREBILCOCK

4 The Enduring Problem of World Trade Organization Export Subsidies Rules

This chapter examines the World Trade Organization (WTO) rules and decisions concerning export subsidies in the nonagricultural context to determine why these disputes are so prevalent and contentious and whether the rules or their interpretation should be altered. It discusses the basic economic case against export subsidies and political economy explanations for their continued use. It then reviews two central concerns about the WTO rules on export subsidies. First, it examines issues surrounding identification of export subsidies, including defining what constitutes a subsidy, distinguishing export subsidies from other types of subsidies, and how closely the WTO should review domestic policies for potential (rather than actual) export subsidies. Second, it discusses the difficulty the WTO has had in finding an appropriate remedy for violations of the prohibition against export subsidies. It argues that existing WTO rules do not adequately address either set of issues. In particular, Panels and the Appellate Body should adopt a more appropriate level of penalty for the use of export subsidies, such as tying the level of penalty to the adverse trade effects from the subsidy.

Introduction

Export subsidies have been at the center of a long series of high-profile disputes at the WTO. For example, in the 1990s, Canada and Brazil initiated reciprocal complaints that each gave subsidies for the export of domestically made regional aircraft.[1] A number of countries challenged the United States over its

[1] This dispute has been the subject of a number of Panel and Appellate Body decisions including *Brazil – Export Financing Programme for Aircraft (Complaint by Canada)* (1999), WTO Doc. WT/DS46/AB/R (Appellate Body Report); *Canada – Measures Affecting the Export of Civilian Aircraft (Complaint by Brazil)* (1999), WTO Doc. WT/DS70/AB/R (Appellate Body

The authors wish to thank Vivien Milat for excellent research assistance and aid in earlier drafts of this chapter as well as Kyle Bagwell, the participants in the Columbia Seminar on WTO Law and Policy, the University of Pennsylvania Law and Economics Workshop, and the American Law and Economics Association meetings for their helpful comments on earlier drafts.

rules for "foreign sales corporations." The dispute centerd on billions of dollars of tax exemptions for these corporations that the WTO eventually found to be, in some cases, prohibited export subsidies.[2] On the agricultural side, export subsidies have also been central to the negotiations in the Doha Round and have been subject to a range of disputes such as recent challenges to the U.S. policies on cotton.[3] The recent dispute between the United States and the European Community (EC) regarding alleged export (and other) subsidies to their respective manufacturers of large civil aircraft is another in this line of highly contentious disputes.

Export subsidies are, in a general sense, subsidies "granted only to products when they are exported."[4] Economists view export subsidies as beneficial to the subsidized producers in the exporting country and to consumers in the importing countries. However, they also tend to see them as harmful in many cases to the welfare of the subsidizing country as a whole, with a possible exception of situations in which export subsidies provide a country's producers with a first mover advantage in imperfectly competitive markets.[5] Furthermore, export subsidies are harmful to more efficient producers of the good in other countries, whether in the importing country or in third-country exporters. In some cases, there may, on net, be global benefits from subsidized exports because, for example, the harm to the more efficient producers in the importing country is more than offset by the gain to consumers.[6] Even though there are possible global gains from export subsidies in certain cases, the Agreement on Subsidies and Countervailing Measures (SCM Agreement) adopted by the WTO during the Uruguay Round contains a broad prohibition on export subsidies for nonagricultural products.[7] The Uruguay Round's Agreement on Agriculture permits some

Report); (*Brazil – Export Financing Programme for Aircraft – Recourse by Canada to Article 21.5 of the DSU* (2000), WTO Doc. WT/DS46/AB/RW (Panel Report); *Brazil – Export Financing Programme for Aircraft – Second Recourse by Canada to Article 21.5 of the DSU* (2001), WTO Doc. WT/DS46/RW/2 (Panel Report) and *Canada – Export Credits and Loan Guarantees for Regional Aircraft (Complaint by Brazil)* (2002), WTO Doc. WT/DS222/R (Panel Report).

[2] *United States – Tax Treatment for "Foreign Sales Corporations" (Complaint by the European Communities)* (2000), WTO Doc. WT/DS108/AB/R (Appellate Body Report) and *United States – Tax Treatment for "Foreign Sales Corporations" – Recourse to Article 21.5 of the DSU by the European Communities* (2001), WTO Doc. WT/DS108/AB/RW (Appellate Body Report).

[3] *United States – Subsidies on Upland Cotton (Complaint by Brazil)* (2005), WTO Doc. WT/DS267/AB/R at paras. 578–583 (Appellate Body Report).

[4] John H. Jackson, *The World Trading System* (Cambridge, The MIT Press, 1997) at 279.

[5] Paul Krugman and Maurice Obstfeld, *International Economics: Theory and Policy* (7th ed.) (Boston, Addison Wesley, 2005), pp. 101–102. See Part II for a more detailed discussion of the economic and political economy rationales behind export subsidies.

[6] Michael J. Trebilcock and Robert Howse, *The Regulation of International Trade*, 3rd ed. (London/New York, Routledge, 2005) at 283.

[7] Article 3.1(a) of the SCM Agreement.

export subsidies subject to reduction commitments and a prohibition on export subsidies used to circumvent these commitments.[8]

Despite what appear to be rather clear rules, disputes over export subsidies (high profile and otherwise) constitute a significant share of all cases that have gone to Panels since the WTO was formed (roughly 10.5 percent).[9] Panels have been established in ten cases (including both agricultural and nonagricultural disputes). Seven of these Panel findings were appealed to the Appellate Body. In five cases, there were further compliance proceedings under Article 21.5 of the Dispute and Settlement Understanding (DSU), with a further three cases going before an Article 21.5 Panel a second time. In three cases, the respondent country refused to withdraw its subsidies, leading to arbitration proceedings to determine the appropriate imposition of countermeasures.[10] These numbers do not include export subsidy disputes that are settled before a Panel is appointed. They also only include disputes about measures that the complaining party alleged were export subsidies; as we will discuss, in some cases, complaining parties prefer to allege other forms of subsidies instead.

This chapter examines the WTO rules and decisions concerning export subsidies in the nonagricultural context to determine why these disputes are so prevalent and contentious and whether the rules or their interpretation should be altered. The next section discusses the basic economic case against export subsidies and political economy explanations for their continued use. Then the chapter briefly sets out the history and structure of WTO rules concerning nonagricultural export subsidies. The chapter then reviews two central concerns about the WTO rules on export subsidies. We examine issues surrounding identification of export subsidies, including defining what constitutes a subsidy, distinguishing export subsidies from other types of subsidies, and how closely the WTO should review domestic policies for potential (rather than actual) export subsidies. We discuss the difficulty the WTO has had in finding an appropriate remedy for violations of the prohibition against export subsidies. This chapter concludes by discussing the difficulties posed by high-profile, high-stakes disputes such as the dispute between the United States and the EC over subsidies for large commercial aircraft.

[8] Articles 3.3, 9.2(a), and 10 of the Agreement on Agriculture.

[9] As of the end of 2005, 105 Panel Reports had been circulated. See Kara Leitner and Simon Lester, "WTO Dispute Settlement from 1995 to 2005 – A Statistical Analysis" 9 *Journal of International Economic Law* 2006, 219 at 226.

[10] *Brazil – Export Financing Programme for Aircraft – Recourse to Arbitration by Brazil under Article 22.6 of the DSU and Article 4.11 of the SCM Agreement* (2000), WTO Doc. WT/DS46/ARB (Arbitration Report); *United States – Tax Treatment for "Foreign Sales Corporations" – Recourse to Arbitration by the United States under Article 22.6 of the DSU and Article 4.11 of the SCM Agreement* (2002), WTO Doc. WT/DS108/ARB (Arbitration Report); and *Canada – Export Credits and Loan Guarantees for Regional Aircraft – Recourse to Arbitration by Canada under Article 22.6 of the DSU and Article 4.11 of the SCM Agreement* (2003), WTO Doc. WT/DS222/ARB (Arbitration Report).

Why Prohibit Export Subsidies?

The SCM Agreement's prohibition of nonagricultural export subsidies reflects what appears to be a long-standing near-consensus that export subsidies are undesirable and that their primary purpose is to distort trade. The main reason for this proposition's appeal is undoubtedly its intuitiveness: If the intent was not to distort trade, why would the subsidy not apply to both domestic and foreign sales? Such a subsidy would allow domestic consumers to receive at least some of the benefits, whereas in the case of an export subsidy, foreign consumers derive most of the benefits.

However, export subsides are, in general, welfare reducing for the subsidizing country (with the possible exception of the strategic trade theory explanation discussed later in this chapter). Although they provide a benefit to the producers of the exported good, they worsen the country's terms of trade – the rate at which a country can trade its exports for imports from other countries. The terms of trade worsen because, for example, the subsidy increases the domestic (and, if not a small economy, the world) supply of the good, thereby causing the relative price of the good to fall.[11] Moreover, export subsidies distort resource allocation toward the higher-cost subsidized good and, because the subsidizing government needs to increase revenues to finance the subsidies, generally impose a deadweight loss on the economy.[12] Furthermore, Sykes (2003) argues that, even when there is some domestic reason that may point to the need for subsidies (such as a market failure of some form), export subsidies never appear to be the best response and other policy responses would usually be more efficient and effective. He argues that the prohibition of nonagricultural export subsidies is "useful and sensible from an economic perspective."[13]

Export subsidies cannot therefore be explained in terms of a benefit to the subsidizing country. Instead, the most prominent explanation is the political economy story of the political officials of a particular country providing benefits to concentrated interests – the subsidized exporting industry.[14] These exporting producers benefit, as do foreign consumers, from the lower cost of the good. However, domestic consumers lose because of the higher relative cost of the good (and worsened terms of trade), taxpayers lose because they

[11] Krugman and Obstfeld (2005), pp. 99–102 and 186–187, Donald Regan, "What are Trade Agreements For? Two Conflicting Stories Told by Economists, with a Lesson for Lawyers," 9(4) *Journal of International Economic Law* 2006, 951–988, and Kyle Bagwell, "Remedies in the WTO: An Economic Perspective" (Draft manuscript, January 9, 2007).

[12] Alan O. Sykes, "The Economics of WTO Rules on Subsidies and Countervailing Measures," 2003, University of Chicago Law & Economics, Olin Working Paper No. 186 at 9.

[13] Sykes (2003) at 2.

[14] Regan (2006) notes that "an export subsidy (by which I mean any subsidy to an exporting industry, not just a subsidy conditioned on export performance) must be primarily motivated by protectionism (in the broad sense of being a law designed to enhance the competitiveness of domestic producers), because it has a perverse terms-of-trade effect" (p. 29).

have to pay for the increased subsidies, and/or the government loses revenue.[15] The political officials may provide these subsidies to gain an advantage from these concentrated interests (such as revenue for reelection campaigns or future employment). The officials may face losses (such as a loss of votes or revenue for reelection) because they have imposed costs on consumers and taxpayers (and an overall loss to the country as a whole). However, these losses are likely to be lower than the benefits to concentrated interests because the more diffuse consumer and taxpayer interests face information and collective action asymmetries.[16]

A possible exception to this view of export subsidies as beneficial to the subsidizing industry (and to political officials of the subsidizing government), but harmful to the country as a whole, derives from strategic trade theory. As was first shown by Brander and Spencer (1985), in certain circumstances it can actually be welfare increasing for a government to provide export subsidies.[17] They demonstrate that, in a simple Cournot oligopoly model with two firms (one in each exporting country) selling to third-country markets, where governments set subsidy levels before these firms make their decisions, subsidies allow the domestic firm to capture a larger share of the international market and increase its profits. Such a subsidy may increase domestic welfare (by increasing the profits of the subsidized firm) despite worsening the terms of trade.

Strategic trade theory typically views benefits to export subsidies as arising in imperfectly competitive markets, with the commercial aircraft industry being a paradigmatic example.[18] However, to gain the benefits, governments need a significant amount of information, including the costs of both the domestic and foreign industries and the demand for the good.[19] The need for this information raises concerns about government failure – either subsidizing an industry when it is not necessary or providing too high or too low a subsidy.

There may be some other benefits from export subsidies. For example, Bagwell and Staiger find a potential use for export subsidies where foreign buyers are unaware of the quality of an exporting firm's product.[20] They argue that higher-quality exporting firms may not be able to credibly inform foreign consumers

15 Krugman and Obstfeld (2005), pp. 101–102.

16 Krugman and Obstfeld (2005), pp. 219–220; Sykes (2005).

17 James A. Brander and Barbara J. Spencer, "Export Subsidies and International Market Share Rivalry," 18 *Journal of International Economics* 1985, p. 83. See also Elhanan Helpman and Paul R. Krugman, *Trade Policy and Market Structure* (Cambridge, The MIT Press, 1989) at 83–115.

18 See, for example, Krugman and Obstfeld (2005), pp. 262–263 (using a hypothetical dispute between Airbus and Boeing to explain strategic trade theory). But see Kyle Bagwell and Robert W. Staiger, *The Economics of the World Trading System* (Cambridge, The MIT Press, 2002) at pp. 168–179 (adding a political economy component to the basic Brander–Spender framework to apply it to agricultural export subsidy disputes [a perfectly competitive market]).

19 Krugman and Obstfeld (2005), pp. 264–265.

20 Kyle Bagwell and Robert W. Staiger, "The Role of Export Subsidies When Product Quality Is Unknown," 27 *Journal of International Economics* 1989, p. 69.

of their high quality especially with respect to 'experience goods' (goods whose qualities are difficult to observe prior to competition). As such, they must initially sell at the low-quality price until they have established a reputation for high quality. If, given the higher costs of producing a high-quality product, they cannot do so profitably, then they would be unable to enter this foreign market. An export subsidy can allow the firm to export profitably in this initial period until it can develop a reputation for quality. This need for aid in building a market may explain why developing countries, whose products would be more likely to be perceived as low quality in developed country markets, would have bargained for a temporary exemption from the export subsidy prohibition. It also explains why this exemption is temporary: Developed countries would have an incentive to restrict the use of export subsidies for their producers to benefit from informational asymmetries.

Political interests of the subsidizing country therefore often appear to favor export subsidies (and such subsidies may in some cases be good for the country). Furthermore, importing countries tend to gain when other countries use export subsidies because the gain to domestic consumers in general more than offsets any losses to domestic producers of the good (leading to the claim that importing countries should not complain about export subsidies but instead send thank-you notes).[21] Why then did the General Agreement on Tariffs and Trade (GATT) Contracting Parties and later the WTO members agree to prohibit export subsidies?[22] Any attempt to tie the prohibition merely to the desire to reduce harm in the exporting country appears to be mere paternalism. There have been a number of other explanations proposed. First, governments may be attempting to "tie themselves to the mast" – that is, they may wish to adopt an international prohibition to be able to resist the pressure from exporting industries for (domestic welfare-reducing) subsidies.[23] The difficulty with this explanation is that it is not clear why, if governments could overcome domestic exporting interests to agree on the prohibition, they could not simply say no to the demands for export subsidies. Regan suggests one possible answer – the framing of the issue makes one result possible and the other not.[24] It may be, for example, that framing a broad prohibition against export subsides as a "fairness" issue enables mobilization of more general public support for a prohibition than would be possible for resisting a particular claim by a domestic industry

21 Trebilcock and Howse (2005), p. 283.

22 See, for example, Regan (2006), p. 17 (noting that the prohibition on export subsidies is puzzling because of the benefits to importing countries).

23 Merit E. Janow and Robert W. Staiger, "Canada – Measures Affecting the Importation of Dairy Products and the Exportation of Milk" in Henrik Horn and Petros C. Mavroidis (Eds.), *The WTO Case Law of 2001* (Cambridge, Cambridge University Press, 2003) 236 at 247. See also Giovanni Maggi and Andres Rodriguez-Clare, "A Political-Economy Theory of Trade Agreements" (March 2007), online: http://pantheon.yale.edu/~gm329/index_files/downloadable%20papers_files/mrworkingpapermarch14.pdf.

24 Regan (2006).

for export subsidies.[25] The "fairness" claims would be that foreign governments are unfairly subsidizing their exports and harming either the domestic industry in the importing country or exporters to third-country markets. These claims of "unfair" trade may be sufficient to overcome potentially subsidized exporting interests where countries (such as the United States) are both importers and exporters.[26]

Second, although (in general) importing countries appear to benefit from export subsidies, there may be reasons why importing countries are harmed and therefore may agree to a prohibition on export subsidies. For example, Sykes (2003) argues that there may be special cases in which export subsidies harm the importing country by providing the exporting country's industry with monopoly profits (including strategic trade policies).[27] However, these are special cases, and in general, importing countries would be expected to benefit on net and therefore not agree to a prohibition. Janow and Staiger offer a more general argument for why importing countries may agree to a prohibition. They argue that export subsidies are welfare enhancing for importing states unless those states are concerned about injuries to domestic producers *and* lack the ability to respond.[28] Countries cannot respond by raising tariffs directly under the GATT if they are bound. However, they may be able to respond in other ways such as renegotiation of tariff bindings or countervailing duties (CVDs). They may wish to prohibit export subsidies if the transaction costs of using these other measures are too high.

Finally, exporting countries may wish to prohibit export subsidies because they feel that a prohibition will on balance aid their exporting industries. For example, export subsidy prohibitions may be the result of negotiations among exporters to restrict trade. Such restrictions, by decreasing trade volumes and increasing prices, come at the expense of importers.[29] Furthermore, exporting governments may wish to avoid a subsidies war. Under strategic trade theory, for example, the subsidizing country has the advantage of providing a subsidy to its industry so that it can gain an advantage over the competing industry in another country. Of course, the government in the other country also has the same opportunity to benefit from an export subsidy, but if both countries subsidize exports,

[25] For a general discussion of fairness debates in trade, see, for example, Ronald A. Cass and Richard D. Boltuck, "Antidumping and Countervailing-Duty Law: The Mirage of Equitable International Competition" in Jagdish N. Bhagwati and Robert E. Hudec (Eds.), *Fair Trade and Harmonization. Vol. 2, Legal Analysis: Prerequisites for Free Trade?* (Cambridge, The MIT Press, 1996), 351.

[26] Krugman and Obstfeld (2005), pp. 101–102.

[27] Sykes (2003), p. 11.

[28] Merit E. Janow and Robert W. Staiger, "Canada – Measures Affecting the Importation of Dairy Products and the Exportation of Milk," in Henrik Horn and Petros C. Mavroidis (Eds.), *The WTO Case Law of 2001* (Cambridge, Cambridge University Press, 2003), 236 at 242.

[29] Janow and Staiger (2003) at 250, and Bagwell (2007) (discussing the terms of trade effect of restricting export subsidies).

no advantage is gained. At that point, the exporting countries' welfare could be increased through a mutual reduction in subsidies. These countries face a form of prisoners' dilemma: If the countries could cooperate and reduce their subsidies, they would both benefit. The result may be a commitment by these countries not to subsidize exports.[30]

As the economic literature provides a breadth of diverging arguments both for and against the prohibition of export subsidies, it is unclear which argument might have provided Uruguay Round negotiators with the primary motivation for adopting a broad prohibition. Looking at the case law, however, we observe several trends. First, several cases (the Canada–Brazil and now United States–EC disputes over civil aircraft are the best examples) have involved two-firm industries similar to those in the Brander–Spencer strategic trade model. Second, the cases tend to involve disputes over sales to third-country markets, not exports to the complaining party's domestic markets. Third, the complaints have been filed by rival countries, not importers, which suggests that subsidy competition is not considered to be harmful by importers who lack a competing industry. Fourth, we observe, especially in the context of Article 21.5 compliance proceedings, a clear desire by subsidizers to "cheat," as predicted again by the Brander–Spencer model. Overall, these trends suggest that some version of the strategic trade policy argument may best describe real-world subsidy policy and disputes.

Export subsidies then seem to be welfare reducing in most cases for the exporting country but may be politically advantageous for the government of the exporting country. Given that they should in general spark gratitude in the importing country (as the gain to consumers tends to outweigh any loss to domestic producers), we need to consider whether export subsides are on balance beneficial globally. If so, the prohibition on export subsidies may either be paternalism (to stop harm in the subsidizing country) or be reducing (global) efficiency to provide a benefit to certain parties. The answer appears to be that export subsidies "are (normally) globally inefficient," although there may be limited cases in which they are efficient.[31] Consider first a single country without any exports or imports. Economists in general do not favor subsidies (with the potential exception of certain instances of market failure) because they induce consumers to demand too much of the (lower-priced) good and producers to produce too much.[32] For example, subsidies to electricity producers induce consumers to increase their use of electricity and electricity producers to increase

[30] Spencer and Brander (1985); Krugman and Obstfeld (2005), p. 265; Sykes (2003), p. 9; and Bagwell and Staiger (2001).

[31] Regan (2006), p. 17. But see Bagwell (2007), at 29 ("While it is certainly true that important circumstances exist in which the use of export subsidies can decrease welfare, the competing-exporter models support the following basic conclusion: the economic case for rules that facilitate a reduction in export subsidies is much weaker than the economic case for rules that facilitate a reduction in import tariffs").

[32] See Sykes (2003) and Green (2006) discussing some of the potential rationales for subsidies in some circumstances.

their supply. There is a distortion of resource allocation away from other, more efficient uses of resources (or lower-cost suppliers in the case of subsidies to specific firms) because of the subsidy.

The same holds true when we consider a three-country world in which two countries are exporting a good to a third country. The export subsidy squeezes out producers in the other exporting country and in the importing country in favor of less efficient producers in the subsidizing country.[33] The consumers in the importing country consume too much, the producers in the subsidized country produce too much, and there is a misallocation of resources across producers. The same amount of the good could be produced with fewer resources. Even in the cases where strategic trade theory appears to provide a domestic benefit greater than the cost of the subsidy, from a global perspective the result is merely a transfer from one (potentially lower-cost) exporting country to another, and may allow monopoly profits (harming importing countries).[34] Furthermore, Sykes (2003) argues that, as export subsidies undermine market access expectations under existing trade agreements, they reduce the value of such agreements and thereby the likelihood of such agreements.[35] To the extent that such agreements increase global welfare, the reduced probability is a concern. Finally, as noted above, export subsidies may lead to a waste of resources such as in the case of rent seeking or subsidies wars.

As a result, although export subsidies may benefit the economy of the importing country, they appear likely to be globally inefficient. However, there may be some situations in which export subsides are efficient. First, if there is an oligopoly (as in the classic Brander–Spencer model), there may be too little of the particular good produced. To the extent that the export subsidy not only transfers production from one company (country) to another but increases overall production, there may be a global benefit. In addition, if there are import tariffs for a particular good, an export subsidy could be seen as merely overcoming an existing distortion by reducing the net tariff for the particular good. Furthermore, Bagwell (2007) argues that "the economic case for rules that facilitate a reduction in export subsidies is much weaker than the economic case for rules that facilitate a reduction in import tariffs."[36] The ban on export subsidies may be the result of countries creating a cartel to increase profits by restricting trade.[37] Such an increase in profits would then come at the expense of importing countries. He agrees that production may be diverted to less efficient firms by an export subsidy but notes that these welfare costs can arise with tariffs as well.[38] He concludes that a complete ban on export subsidies is therefore "not well supported by the terms-of-trade approach to trade agreements."[39]

[33] Sykes (2003).

[34] Sykes (2003), p. 11 (arguing that strategic trade policy may result in monopoly pricing).

[35] Sykes (2003), p. 9.

[36] Bagwell, above n 11 at 29.

[37] Bagwell, above n 1, at 28–29.

[38] Bagwell, above n 1, at fn 40.

[39] Bagwell, above n 1, at 30.

Lawrence raises a different argument in favor of export subsidies. He argues that export subsidies are beneficial to developing countries.[40] He notes that the special rules in developing countries' "export zones" may allow greater growth where it is difficult to introduce more wholesale institutional and policy changes in the rest of the country. He argues that export subsidies may promote knowledge spillovers by increasing exporting.[41] These arguments fit within the broader infant industry literature, where Chang has argued that export subsidies are an important part of a targeted protectionist agenda designed to generate sufficient economies of scale and overcome the initial learning period in the production of experience goods.[42] Even if these arguments have some validity, however, given the potential for injury to other countries, Lawrence and Stankard acknowledge that not all export subsidies should be permitted. Rather, there may be certain cases in which developing countries should face more lenient penalties than other countries.[43]

Export subsidies therefore appear in general to be inefficient from a welfare perspective, although they may sometimes have positive welfare effects such as in the case of experience goods or oligopolies. Lawrence and Stankard have taken the potential for such positive welfare effects as evidence that theory does not justify the ban on export subsidies.[44] However, even if it is true that export subsidies are efficient in some circumstances (i.e., that we may want some flexibility concerning their use), the optimal export subsidy provisions will depend not only on the efficiency of export subsidies in certain cases but on a number of other factors. As Kaplow notes in his discussion of rules versus standards, the optimal form and content of legal commands will depend on relative costs and benefits.[45] First, there are *ex ante* costs of promulgating a law and, in particular, the information costs related to identifying and specifying the various aspects of a rule in advance of its being applied.[46] Second, the parties subject to the legal command face costs in obtaining information about what the command requires. Third, there are enforcement costs, including the costs of monitoring

[40] Lawrence and Stankard, above n 6, at 30–31.

[41] Lawrence and Stankard, above n 6, at 30–31. See also Devesh Roy and Arvind Subramanian, "Who Can Explain the Mauritian Miracle: Meade, Romer, Sachs, or Rodrik?" (IMF Working Papers Series, No. 01/116, 2001).

[42] Ha-Joon Chang, "Industrial Policy and East Asia – The Miracle, the Crisis, and the Future" (World Bank workshop on "Rethinking the East Asian Miracle," February 16–17, 1999, San Francisco), http://www.econ.cam.ac.uk/faculty/chang/wbip-pdf.pdf, at 10.

[43] Lawrence and Stankard, above n 6, at 31 (arguing for relaxed rules, especially where the developing country has a small share of world trade). See below n 126 for a discussion of the transitional provisions for developing countries in the SCM Agreement.

[44] Lawrence and Stankard, above n 6, at 30.

[45] Louis Kaplow, "Rules Versus Standards: An Economic Analysis," 42(3) *Duke Law Journal* 1992, 557.

[46] See, for example, in the trade context Horn, Maggi, and Staiger, above n 43, at 2–3 (formalizing the costs of contracting and discussing WTO agreements as incomplete contracts) and Schwarz and Sykes, above n 1.

compliance and litigating any enforcement action. Finally, Kaplow discusses the benefits that arise from the complexity of the legal command. These benefits can be thought of as a benefit to complexity or as a cost where there are errors as to the appropriate rule. A related issue, which arises from the law and economics literature concerning remedies generally and trade remedies in particular, is the cost of bargaining between the affected parties after a violation has occurred.[47] To design the optimal provisions (including remedies) concerning export subsidies, each of these sets of costs must be examined. The identity of the institution or party involved in decision making will affect the various costs, including the likelihood of error in reaching decisions.[48]

WTO provisions concerning export subsidies could provide flexibility to allow efficient export subsidies in two ways. First, the requirements relating to export subsidies could be flexible. These requirements could take the form of a rule (in which the requirements are specified *ex ante*) or a standard (which is broadly expressed with the details of the requirement to be determined through adjudication).[49] Both rules and standards can be more or less complex. Second, the flexibility could arise through the remedies used to enforce the requirement. After describing the relevant provisions under the SCM Agreement in the next sections, the rest of this chapter will draw on this discussion of the economics of export subsidies to examine the optimality of the actual wording and interpretation of the prohibition. It will first discuss the flexibility of the ban itself and then analyze the remedies for noncompliance with the ban.

The WTO Framework for Export Subsidies

Pre-Uruguay Round Export Subsidy Rules

The search for a mechanism to discipline export subsidies dates back to the early 1950s.[50] The 1947 GATT created few substantive rules governing subsidies, although Article VI did permit CVDs as a response. However, CVDs were authorized only when subsidized imports caused material injury to the importer's competing domestic industry. Amendments to GATT in 1955 introduced the first rules on export subsidies. For nonprimary goods, Article XVI provided that parties should cease to grant subsidies on exports if the subsidy would result in the export price being lower than the domestic price. For primary goods, Article XVI

[47] See, for example, Schwartz and Sykes, above n 1 and Trachtman, above n 1.

[48] Kaplow, above n 67, at 608–611. For a discussion of rules versus standards in the context of export subsidies remedies, see Andrew Green and Michael Trebilcock, "Enforcing WTO Obligations: What Can We Learn from Export Subsidies?" 10(3) *Journal of International Economic Law* 2007, 653.

[49] On the difference between rules and standards, and the overlap between them, see Kaplow, above n 67, at 559–566.

[50] See Jackson (1997) at 285–293.

specified that parties avoid the use of export subsidies and no subsidy was to result in a more than "equitable share" of the world market. For various reasons, few countries were prepared to accept the declaration implementing these provisions, so these commitments were binding on only a few GATT-Contracting Parties.[51] GATT contained no specific enforcement mechanism relating to export subsidies.

Negotiations in the Tokyo Round resulted in a 1979 Subsidies Code, the "first general comprehensive multilateral discipline of the use of subsidies."[52] This agreement established two tracks. Track I governed unilateral responses to subsidies (CVDs), but did not clearly define a countervailable subsidy. Track II prohibited the granting of export subsidies on nonprimary products and requested that signatories not use export subsidies on primary products to increase their share of world trade beyond what was equitable. The Code did not contain a precise definition of what constituted an export subsidy. Instead, an annex to the Code contained an Illustrative List of Export Subsidies describing practices that were deemed to be export subsidies.[53] Track II sets out a procedure for consultations, adjudication by a Panel, and the possible authorization of countermeasures by a Committee on Subsidies and Countervailing Measures.

This framework proved only modestly effective,[54] and by the end of Uruguay Round negotiations in 1994, only twenty-four countries had ratified the Tokyo Round Code.[55] Because of the weaknesses in this system, the Uruguay Round included negotiations over new subsidies rules. These negotiations resulted in the SCM Agreement to which all WTO members are parties.

The WTO Framework on Export Subsidies

The SCM Agreement divides subsidies into three categories: prohibited, actionable, and nonactionable. Subsidies contingent on export performance, along with import-substitution subsidies, are expressly prohibited.[56] Other subsidies are subject to less stringent disciplines. Actionable subsidies are nonagricultural subsidies that are "specific" and cause "adverse effects" to the interests of another member.[57] In the case of actionable subsidies, the subsidizing

[51] See Jackson (1997) at 286.

[52] Jackson (1997) at 288.

[53] Michael J. Trebilcock and Robert Howse, *The Regulation of International Trade*, 3rd ed. (London/New York, Routledge, 2005) at 265.

[54] Trebilcock and Howse (2005) at 266.

[55] Jackson (1997) at 290.

[56] Article 3 of the SCM Agreement states: "Except as provided in the Agreement on Agriculture, the following subsidies, within the meaning of Article 1, shall be prohibited: (a) subsidies contingent, in law or fact, whether solely or as one of several conditions, upon export performance, including those illustrated in Annex I; (b) subsidies contingent, whether solely or as one of several other conditions, upon the use of domestic over imported goods." [footnotes omitted]

[57] As discussed below, the term "specific" is poorly defined in the SCM Agreement but is intended to capture subsidies targeted at a relatively narrow range of firms or industries

member can be required to remove the adverse effects or withdraw the subsidy, or, alternatively, the member claiming injury can impose CVDs against the subsidizing member.[58] Finally, the SCM Agreement initially recognized a category of nonactionable subsidies that included certain subsidies for research and development, regional development, and environmental upgrades to existing facilities. However, this nonactionable category expired in 2000.[59]

There are a few provisions in the SCM Agreement central to the analysis of export subsidies. Article 1 defines the term "subsidy." Article 3.1(a) explicitly prohibits subsidies contingent, in law or in fact, on export performance. Annex I complements this prohibition with an Illustrative List of governmental actions that are deemed to be export subsidies.[60] Finally, Article 4 creates an expedited process for dispute resolution, which, under Article 4.7, leads to a mandatory requirement of withdrawal of subsidies found to be prohibited. These provisions and the jurisprudence surrounding them will be examined in detail later in this chapter.

This framework applies "except as provided in the Agreement on Agriculture."[61] Unlike the SCM Agreement, the Agreement on Agriculture authorizes some export subsidies, subject to reduction commitments.[62] These subsidies must be disclosed in the subsidizing member's schedule to the Agreement.[63] The Agreement prohibits export subsidies used to circumvent these commitments.[64] Although this chapter focuses on nonagricultural subsidies, the Appellate Body has found at times that certain substantive requirements (such as export contingency) are the same under both Agreements.[65] The jurisprudence under the Agreement on Agriculture can therefore sometimes be

(Articles 1 and 2). "Adverse effects" include injury to another member's domestic industry, nullification or impairment of benefits under the GATT 1994, and serious prejudice to the interests of another member, as defined in Article 6 of the SCM Agreement. See Article 5 of the SCM Agreement.

58 Article 7.8 of the SCM Agreement.

59 Article 31. See A. Green, "Trade Rules and Climate Change Subsidies," 5(3) *World Trade Review* 2006, 377 (discussing environmental subsidies and the nonactionable category). See also Trebilcock and Howse (2005) at 269.

60 The Uruguay Round Illustrative List is substantially identical to the Illustrative List in the Tokyo Round Subsidies Code.

61 Article 3.1 of the SCM Agreement.

62 Article 9.2(a) of the Agreement on Agriculture. For a brief summary of the Agreement on Agriculture's export subsidies provisions, see, for example, Karen Halverson Cross, "King Cotton, Developing Countries and the 'Peace Clause': The WTO's *US Cotton Subsidies* Decision," 9 *Journal of International Economic Law* 2006, 149 at 164–165, or Michael J. Trebilcock and Robert Howse, *The Regulation of International Trade*, 3rd ed. (London/New York, Routledge, 2005) at 337–339.

63 Articles. 3.3 and 10 of the Agreement on Agriculture.

64 Article 10.1 of the Agreement on Agriculture.

65 *United States – Tax Treatment for "Foreign Sales Corporations" (Complaint by the European Communities)* (2000), WTO Doc. WT/DS108/AB/R at para. 141 (Appellate Body Report).

relevant to the analysis of the SCM Agreement and will be discussed later in this chapter, where relevant.[66]

One final provision is important to mention at the outset. Article 27 of the SCM Agreement exempts developing country members from the prohibition on export subsidies. The developing countries listed in Annex VII are exempt until they achieve export competitiveness in a product, at which point they are required to phase out export subsidies for that product over a period of eight years. Other developing countries were given eight years from the date of entry into force of the WTO Agreement (1995) to phase out their export subsidies. For those countries, the exemption has now expired. In the one case involving export subsidies where the respondent country sought to rely on this exemption, the Appellate Body upheld the Panel's ruling that the exemption did not apply.[67] Brazil had increased the level of its export subsidies in violation of Article 27.4, so the general Article 3.1(a) prohibition on export subsidies was held to apply to Brazil.[68]

What Is an Export Subsidy?

A key issue that arises from the SCM Agreement is how to identify an export subsidy. As noted above, separating export subsidies from other types of subsidies is important because export subsidies are prohibited *per se*, whereas other types are merely actionable (requiring evidence of specificity and some form of harm to be successfully challenged). How export subsidies are identified determines whether the requirement is a rule or a standard and its flexibility. There are three questions central to identifying export subsidies. First, does the government action fall within the general definition of a "subsidy" under the SCM Agreement? Second, if so, is the subsidy "contingent on export performance"? Finally, is the enabling domestic legislation mandatory or discretionary – that is, does it require that the government provide a prohibited export subsidy or is such a subsidy merely a possibility within the discretion of the government? Each of these questions will be discussed in turn.

[66] Conversely, the SCM Agreement is relevant in the agricultural context: The Appellate Body has stated that it is erroneous judicial economy for a Panel not to consider parties' SCM Article 3 claims even if the Panel has already made a determination under the Agreement on Agriculture. *European Communities – Export Subsidies on Sugar* (*Complaints by Thailand, Brazil and Australia)* (2004), WTO Doc. WT/DS283/AB/R (Thailand)/WT/DS266/AB/R (Brazil)/WT/DS265/AB/R (Australia) at para. 335 (Appellate Body Report).

[67] *Brazil – Export Financing Programme for Aircraft (Complaint by Canada)* (1999), WTO Doc. WT/DS46/R at para. 7.86 (Panel Report) and *Brazil – Export Financing Programme for Aircraft (Complaint by Canada)* (1999), WTO Doc. WT/DS46/AB/R at para. 164 (Appellate Body Report).

[68] Article 27.4, which provides for the gradual phasing out of developing country export subsidies, prohibits developing country members from increasing the level of their export subsidies.

What Is a "Subsidy"?

Article 1.1 of the SCM Agreement sets out the operative definition of a subsidy:

> 1.1 For the purpose of this Agreement, a subsidy shall be deemed to exist if:
> (a)(1) there is a financial contribution by a government or any public body within the territory of a Member (referred to in this Agreement as "government"), i.e., where:
>
> (i) a government practice involves a direct transfer of funds or liabilities (e.g., loan guarantees);
> (ii) government revenue that is otherwise due is foregone or not collected (e.g., fiscal incentives such as tax credits);
> (iii) a government provides goods or services other than general infrastructure, or purchases goods;
> (iv) a government makes payments to a funding mechanism, or entrusts or directs a private body to carry out one or more of the type of functions illustrated in (i) to (iii) above, which would normally be vested in the government, and the practice, in no real sense, differs from practices normally followed by governments;
>
> or
> (a)(2) there is any form of income or price support in the sense of Article XVI of the GATT 1994;
> and
> (b) a benefit is thereby conferred.

For a measure to be classified as a subsidy under the SCM Agreement, it needs to satisfy two main requirements: First, there must be a financial contribution by a government or public body; second, a benefit must be conferred.

The various elements of the financial contribution requirement are relatively straightforward and have not been the source of extensive controversy, particularly in export subsidy cases.[69] The definition is broad and encompasses most government action that would be considered a subsidy. One contentious issue has been the term "otherwise due" discussed in the various *United States – Foreign Sales Corporations* (*U.S. – FSC*) cases. The difficulty is finding an appropriate baseline – should "otherwise due" be seen in reference to what other countries generally do or solely in reference to other actions of the member whose actions have been challenged? The Appellate Body stated that "otherwise due" meant revenue that would otherwise be taxed by the member state but for

[69] For a broader analysis of the definition of "subsidy" in the SCM Agreement generally, see, for example, Mark Clough, "Subsidies and the WTO Jurisprudence" 8 *International Trade Law and Regulation*. 2002, 109, and Marc Bénitah, *The Law of Subsidies under the GATT/WTO System* (The Hague, Kluwer Law International, 2001).

the contested measure – that is, the baseline is the actions of the particular member, not other states.[70]

The definition of "benefit" is more problematic. Sykes (2003) argues that it is difficult to define a subsidy other than in theory. Although in theory a subsidy is a government measure that changes the market equilibrium, there is no pure market equilibrium that exists without government intervention.[71] Any pure definition of subsidy therefore should take account of all government action (including all other subsidies and taxes) to determine whether the measure is distortionary (which is an unrealistic standard), and a subsidy should be found only where the action has an impact on the subsidized industry's production levels.[72]

The Appellate Body in Canada – *Measures Affecting the Export of Civilian Aircraft* (Canada – Aircraft), an early case on export subsidies, held that a financial contribution will confer a benefit only if it was provided on terms more advantageous than those the recipient could have obtained on the market.[73] This approach is administratively simple, as the existing market provides a straightforward comparator. However, it catches actions that may merely offset other government measures (such as taxes or regulations) rather than provide any advantage. This definition of benefit therefore appears overly broad. For domestic (nonexport) subsidies, such an offsetting effect may be seen to be part of an effort to adjust for a market failure (by, e.g., providing subsidies to environmentally friendly industries that offset subsidies to more harmful industries).[74] However, there is, in principle, no reason to provide such subsidies contingent on export, rather than have these subsidies available for all products that are potentially disadvantaged through other government measures.[75] An overly broad in the definition of "benefit" therefore seems acceptable if the export contingency requirement (discussed in the next section) appropriately separates export from domestic subsidies.[76]

Furthermore, the use of the market as a comparator for whether a benefit has been conferred captures actions that may have no actual impact on exports of the subsidized firm. The "subsidy" under this definition may have no actual impact on export levels or costs of production and yet be potentially prohibited (e.g., a subsidy for decommissioning a hazardous plant).[77] In one sense, the government measure should decrease the marginal costs (and increase the

[70] *United States – Tax Treatment for "Foreign Sales Corporations" (Complaint by the European Communities)* (2000), WTO Doc. WT/DS108/AB/R at para. 90 (Appellate Body Report).

[71] Sykes (2003).

[72] Sykes (2003).

[73] *Canada – Measures Affecting the Export of Civilian Aircraft (Complaint by Brazil)* (1999), WTO Doc. WT/DS70/AB/R at paras. 149–161 (Appellate Body Report).

[74] For a discussion of this over-breadth in the context of domestic environmental subsidies, see Green (2006).

[75] Sykes (2003).

[76] The export contingency requirement is discussed in Part IV(b) below.

[77] Sykes (2003), pp. 20–21.

production) of the subsidized good to have the negative efficiency impacts discussed earlier in this chapter. However, this is not necessarily the case. A threat of a production benefit may be sufficient to deter investment by foreign competitors under strategic trade theory. The actual impact on production and costs is therefore less of a concern for export subsidies than potentially is the case for domestic subsidies.

There is one further issue that arises under Article 1. Article 1.2 of the SCM Agreement requires that a measure be "specific" to fall within the terms of the SCM Agreement. Although the SCM Agreement does not clearly define the term "specific," it states that a subsidy must be specific to "certain enterprises," which include "an enterprise or industry or group of enterprises or industries."[78] This specificity requirement is intended to capture subsidies that are targeted to a few industries and to exclude generally available government-provided benefits such as transportation infrastructure or public education. In part, this requirement is intended to identify distortionary or protectionist measures. Broad-based measures are argued not to cause distortion as any effects are spread across the whole economy and, given their nontargeted nature, to be less likely to be protectionist (i.e., less likely to be the result of interest group pressure).[79]

However, the SCM Agreement deems all prohibited subsidies (including export subsidies) to be specific.[80] The result is that all export subsidies fall within the terms of the SCM Agreement even if they would not otherwise be "specific." This deemed specificity reflects a consistent concern about distortion and protectionist action. As discussed earlier in this chapter, export subsidies in general create distortions (on both a global and domestic level). Moreover, the most plausible general explanation for export subsidies is protectionism – the desire to promote domestic industry at the expense of foreign competitors. There is therefore no general reason to separate out more specific from more broadly based export subsidies. Specificity is thus not an issue in Article 3.1(a) export subsidy cases.

The definition of "subsidy" under the SCM Agreement therefore is broad, capturing a wide range of government measures (whether specific or not) that provide any advantage relative to the market. For domestic (non-export) subsidies, this definition seems overly broad. However, for export subsidies, this wide scope is less of a concern as it responds to the concerns about the distortionary

[78] Article 2 of the SCM Agreement.

[79] Sykes (2003), pp. 19–20, John H. Jackson, *The World Trading System* (Cambridge, The MIT Press, 1997) at pp. 296–299 and Trebilcock and Howse (2005). But see Sykes (2003) [arguing that "where a principled justification for a subsidy exists, it will likely arise narrowly and case-by-case, so that the policy response will often appear specific" (p. 20) and that relatively broadly applicable measures may be protectionist such as subsidies to the entire agricultural sector]. Sykes (2003) and W. Wilcox, "GATT-Based Protectionism and the Definition of a Subsidy" 16 *Boston University International Law Journal* 1998, 129.

[80] Article 2.3.

or protectionist nature of export subsidies. A key issue then is whether the SCM Agreement adequately separates domestic subsidies from export subsidies.

Is the Subsidy "Contingent . . . Upon Export Performance"?

For a subsidy to be prohibited as an export subsidy, it must fall within the scope of Article 3.1(a), which prohibits "subsidies contingent, in law or in fact, whether solely or as one of several other conditions, upon export performance, including those illustrated in Annex I." Contingency on export performance can be demonstrated in two ways: either *de jure* or *de facto*. In *Canada – Aircraft*, its first decision involving this issue, the Appellate Body explained that the word "contingent" expresses a single legal standard.[81] Contingent means conditional or "dependent for its existence on something else."[82] The difference between *de jure* and *de facto* contingency lies in the evidence that is used to demonstrate this relationship. In a *de jure* case, contingency is "demonstrated on the basis of the words of the relevant legislation, regulation or other legal instruments." In *Canada – Autos*, the Appellate Body added that *de jure* contingency does not have to be set out expressly, but can also be derived by necessary implication from the terms of a legal instrument.[83] Accordingly, it upheld a finding that ratio requirements for duty-free imports of motor vehicles constituted a *de jure* export subsidy.[84]

As the Appellate Body acknowledged in *Canada – Aircraft*, *de facto* contingency, which seeks to prevent circumvention of the prohibition against *de jure*–contingent export subsidies, is more difficult to establish.[85] The Appellate Body attempted to articulate a standard beginning with footnote 4 of the SCM Agreement, which specifies some requirements for contingency "in fact." Footnote 4 states "This standard is met when the facts demonstrate that the granting of a subsidy, without having been made legally contingent upon export performance,

[81] *Canada – Measures Affecting the Export of Civilian Aircraft (Complaint by Brazil)* (1999), WTO Doc. WT/DS70/AB/R at para. 167 (Appellate Body Report).

[82] *Canada – Measures Affecting the Export of Civilian Aircraft (Complaint by Brazil)* (1999), WTO Doc. WT/DS70/AB/R at para. 166 (Appellate Body Report).

[83] *Canada – Certain Measures Affecting the Automotive Industry (Complaint by Japan and the European Communities)* (2000), WTO Doc. WT/DS139/AB/R / WT/DS142/AB/R at para. 100 (Appellate Body Report).

[84] *Canada – Certain Measures Affecting the Automotive Industry (Complaint by Japan and the European Communities)* (2000), WTO Doc. WT/DS139/AB/R/WT/DS142/AB/R at paras. 106–109 (Appellate Body Report). The Canadian measure at issue allowed manufacturers who produced motor vehicles in Canada to import motor vehicles duty-free if the ratio of their sales in Canada to the ratio of their production in Canada met or exceeded a required ratio. In the Panel and Appellate Body's view, this implied that the only way for a manufacturer to increase the amount of duty-free imports it was entitled to was to export more cars produced in Canada. That made the subsidy contingent on exports (see paras. 103–104).

[85] *Canada – Measures Affecting the Export of Civilian Aircraft (Complaint by Brazil)* (1999), WTO Doc. WT/DS70/AB/R at paras. 167–168 (Appellate Body Report).

is in fact tied to actual or anticipated exportation or export earnings. The mere fact that a subsidy is granted to enterprises which export shall not for that reason alone be considered to be an export subsidy within the meaning of this provision." The Appellate Body held that *de facto* contingency requires that three different elements from footnote 4 be demonstrated: "the *granting* of a subsidy," "*tied... to...*," and "actual or anticipated exportation or export earnings."[86]

"The *granting* of a subsidy" implies a focus on the granting authority.[87] The granting authority must have imposed a condition based on export performance. Because the prohibition is against *granting* subsidies, not against *receiving* them, the Appellate Body explicitly rejected arguments that the contingency analysis should focus on the reasonable knowledge of the recipient.

"Tied to" refers to the relationship between the granting of the subsidy and actual or anticipated exports.[88] This relationship must be one of conditionality or dependence. The Appellate Body stated that it is not enough that a subsidy was granted in anticipation of exports, although the export-orientedness of the recipient's business may be one of the factors to be taken into consideration. The granting of the subsidy must have been tied to (or contingent upon) actual or anticipated exports. The Appellate Body did not elaborate on this distinction, except for linking it to the second sentence of footnote 4, which it viewed as a specific expression of the "tied to" requirement.[89]

"Anticipated" implies that exports were expected.[90] The Appellate Body stated that there must be an examination based on objective evidence to determine whether exports were anticipated or expected. This inquiry is separate from the inquiry conducted to determine whether a subsidy is *tied to* actual or anticipated exports. The Appellate Body seemed concerned about relying on the granting authority's claims about its expectations of exports; this seems like a natural extension of its concerns about circumvention.[91]

The earlier Panel decision in *Australia – Automotive Leather* had reached a result that is consistent with this standard.[92] In that case, the Panel found that

[86] *Canada – Measures Affecting the Export of Civilian Aircraft (Complaint by Brazil)* (1999), WTO Doc. WT/DS70/AB/R at para. 169 (Appellate Body Report).

[87] *Canada – Measures Affecting the Export of Civilian Aircraft (Complaint by Brazil)* (1999), WTO Doc. WT/DS70/AB/R at para. 170 (Appellate Body Report).

[88] *Canada – Measures Affecting the Export of Civilian Aircraft (Complaint by Brazil)* (1999), WTO Doc. WT/DS70/AB/R at para. 171 (Appellate Body Report).

[89] The second sentence in footnote 4 reads "The mere fact that a subsidy is granted to enterprises which export shall not for that reason alone be considered to be an export subsidy within the meaning of this provision."

[90] *Canada – Measures Affecting the Export of Civilian Aircraft (Complaint by Brazil)* (1999), WTO Doc. WT/DS70/AB/R at para. 172 (Appellate Body Report).

[91] It is important to remember that the Appellate Body considered that the purpose behind the *de facto* contingency language was to prevent circumvention of the *de jure* prohibition; just as it is worried that legal instruments could mask the export contingency of a subsidy, it could have been concerned that granting authorities might mask anticipation of exports.

[92] *Australia – Subsidies Provided to Producers and Exporters of Automotive Leather (Complaint by the United States)* (1999), WTO Doc. WT/DS126/R at paras. 9.71 and 9.74 (Panel Report).

grants conditional on the subsidized company achieving a level of production that was only possible through increased exports were contingent on exports. Conversely, it held that a loan to the parent company that could be repaid using revenue from any of its subsidiaries was not contingent on exports.

This methodology generally reflects an attempt to balance the purpose of the *de facto* standard with the provision in Footnote 4 that a subsidy to an exporter is not, by that fact alone, an export subsidy. However, although the Appellate Body has been fairly clear on what facts do not alone establish *de facto* contingency, it has been far less precise about what *does* establish *de facto* contingency. Indeed, in *Canada – Aircraft*, it cautioned that "there can be no general rule as to what facts or what kinds of facts *must* be taken into account."[93] Whereas with *de jure* contingency a single document will usually be determinative of contingency, in the *de facto* situation the Appellate Body favors a more holistic approach. The use of this approach may reflect a concern that a precise standard of *de facto* contingency would defeat the anticircumvention purpose.

An interesting question has arisen in cases where the challenged measure is part of a larger framework of subsidies. In the Article 21.5 compliance proceedings in *U.S. – FSC*, the Appellate Body considered a tax exemption that was available both for property produced within the United States and held for use outside the United States and for property both produced and held for use outside the United States. The Appellate Body separated the two circumstances, finding that the export contingency in the first circumstance had no bearing on whether the second circumstance created an export contingency.[94]

A similar situation arose in *U.S. – Cotton*.[95] The United States' Step 2 program provided subsidies both for export and for the domestic use of United States–grown cotton.[96] The United States argued that, because payments were also available to domestic users, the whole Step 2 program was not contingent on exports. The Panel observed that the subsidy for domestic use was an import substitution subsidy prohibited by the SCM Agreement (under Article 3.1[b]).[97] It stated that joining two prohibited subsidies within a single measure could not somehow "unprohibit" these subsidies – "two wrongs cannot make a

[93] *Canada – Measures Affecting the Export of Civilian Aircraft (Complaint by Brazil)* (1999), WTO Doc. WT/DS70/AB/R at para. 169 (Appellate Body Report).

[94] *United States – Tax Treatment for "Foreign Sales Corporations" – Recourse to Article 21.5 of the DSU by the European Communities* (2001), WTO Doc. WT/DS108/AB/RW at para. 119 (Appellate Body Report).

[95] See Karen Halverson Cross, "King Cotton, Developing Countries and the 'Peace Clause': The WTO's *US Cotton Subsidies* Decision" 9 *Journal of International Economic Law* 2006, 149 at 170–171.

[96] The Step 2 program, officially called the Upland Cotton User Marketing Certificate Program, "provides subsidy payments for documented sales by exporters or purchases by users of US-grown cotton when the lowest price for US cotton exceeds a benchmark price for Northern European cotton over a consecutive four-week period." See Cross (2006) at 157.

[97] *United States – Subsidies on Upland Cotton (Complaint by Brazil)* (2004), WTO Doc. WT/DS267/R at para. 7.738 (Panel Report).

right."[98] The Appellate Body upheld the Panel's findings,[99] citing its previous holding from *U.S. – FSCs (Article 21.5)* that "the fact that the subsidies granted in the second set of circumstances *might* not be export contingent does not dissolve the export contingency arising in the first set of circumstances."[100]

The Illustrative List (Annex I to the SCM Agreement) provides examples of practices that are deemed to be export subsidies. As Article 3.1 refers to subsidies contingent on export performance as "including those illustrated in Annex I," the Illustrative List is not to be read as an exhaustive list of prohibited subsidies. Measures explicitly prohibited by the Illustrative List include direct export-contingent subsidies,[101] discounted domestic shipping on export shipments,[102] various forms of preferential tax treatment for exports,[103] and the provision of export credit at below-market rates.[104]

As well as using the Illustrative List to identify prohibited export subsidies, members have invoked it in two different ways to defend measures that would *prima facie* be prohibited. First, they have argued that a particular item in the Illustrative List, by setting out certain requirements for a particular type of prohibited subsidy, implicitly permits subsidies of that nature that do not meet that requirement. Second, members have argued that a particular measure fits within the subsidies explicitly allowed in the Illustrative List.

Several respondent countries have attempted the first (*a contrario*) interpretation of the Illustrative List, arguing that, because a particular measure does not meet one of the requirements stated in the relevant item of the Illustrative List, it is not prohibited. This use of the Illustrative List as an affirmative defense has been unsuccessful. Brazil, in its defense of its PROEX export subsidy program, contended that the program was not prohibited, as it did not provide a "material advantage" as required by item k of the Illustrative List.[105] The Appellate Body rejected this argument because Brazil had not provided sufficient evidence to make a *prima facie* case supporting its contention in light of the Appellate Body's

[98] *United States – Subsidies on Upland Cotton (Complaint by Brazil)* (2004), WTO Doc. WT/DS267/R at para. 7.742 (Panel Report).

[99] *United States – Subsidies on Upland Cotton (Complaint by Brazil)* (2005), WTO Doc. WT/DS267/AB/R at paras. 578–583 (Appellate Body Report).

[100] *United States – Tax Treatment for "Foreign Sales Corporations" – Recourse to Article 21.5 of the DSU by the European Communities* (2001), WTO Doc. WT/DS108/AB/RW at para. 119 (Appellate Body Report).

[101] Annex I, item a.

[102] Annex I, item c.

[103] Annex I, items e, f, g, and h.

[104] Annex I, items j and k.

[105] The first paragraph of item k prohibits "the grant by governments (or special institutions controlled by and/or acting under the authority of governments) of export credits at rates below those which they actually have to pay for the funds so employed (or would have to pay if they borrowed on international capital markets in order to obtain funds of the same maturity and other credit terms and denominated in the same currency as the export credit), or the payment by them of all or part of the costs incurred by exporters or financial institutions in obtaining credits, *in so far as they are used to secure a material advantage in the fields of export credit terms.*" (emphasis added)

standard for material advantage.[106] The Appellate Body thereby avoided addressing the broader question of the availability of *a contrario* interpretations.[107]

In the subsequent Article 21.5 proceeding, Brazil argued that its revised program did not provide a material advantage. The Panel explicitly rejected the use of item k as an affirmative defense.[108] In its subsequent analysis, however, the Appellate Body was again able to reach a decision without considering the availability of item k as an affirmative defense. It thus deemed the Panel's finding on this question to be "moot, and thus, . . . of no legal effect."[109] When this issue arose again in the second Article 21.5 proceeding in this dispute, the Panel referred to its earlier decision on the question and adopted its previous reasoning.[110] More recently, the Panel in *Korea – Vessels* again rejected an *a contrario* interpretation of item k as well as of item j.[111]

Panels have therefore tended to treat *a contrario* interpretations of items in the Illustrative List as unavailable, although the Appellate Body has not examined this issue. This position is consistent with a broad interpretation of export contingency. It also comports with the language of Article 3.2 of the SCM Agreement, which implies that the Illustrative List is not exhaustive.[112]

As noted above, in addition to asking for *a contrario* interpretations, respondent countries have also sought to rely on the specific exceptions in the Illustrative List. As provided for by Footnote 5 of the SCM Agreement, the Illustrative List expressly permits some measures that might otherwise be deemed to be export subsidies.[113] Panels and the Appellate Body have generally interpreted these

[106] *Brazil – Export Financing Programme for Aircraft* (1999), WTO Doc. WT/DS46/AB/R at para. 184 (Appellate Body Report). It was agreed that, as the party raising the affirmative defense, it was up to Brazil to make a *prima facie* case supporting its alleged defense. Brazil would have had to show that the net interest rates resulting from PROEX subsidies were not below the OECD's Commercial Interest Reference Rates (CIRRs) to establish that PROEX did not provide a material advantage (para. 183).

[107] *Brazil – Export Financing Programme for Aircraft (Complaint by Canada)* (1999), WTO Doc. WT/DS46/AB/R at para. 187 (Appellate Body Report).

[108] *Brazil – Export Financing Programme for Aircraft – Recourse by Canada to Article 21.5 of the DSU* (2000), WTO Doc. WT/DS46/AB/RW at para. 6.66 (Panel Report).

[109] *Brazil – Export Financing Programme for Aircraft – Recourse by Canada to Article 21.5 of the DSU* (2000), WTO Doc. WT/DS46/AB/RW at para. 81 (Appellate Body Report).

[110] *Brazil – Export Financing Programme for Aircraft – Second Recourse by Canada to Article 21.5 of the DSU* (2001), WTO Doc. WT/DS46/RW/2 at para. 5.275 (Panel Report).

[111] *Korea – Measures Affecting Trade in Commercial Vessels (Complaint by the European Communities)* (2005), WTO Doc. WT/DS273/R at paras. 7.310 and 7.207 (Panel Report). Item j prohibits "the provision by governments (or special institutions controlled by governments) of export credits guarantee or insurance programmes, of insurance or guarantee programmes against increases in the cost of exported products or of exchange risk programmes, at premium rates which are inadequate to cover the long-term operating costs and losses of the programmes." Korea argued its program was charging premium rates that were adequate to cover its long-term operating costs and losses.

[112] See also Marc Bénitah, *The Law of Subsidies under the GATT/WTO System* (The Hague, Kluwer Law International, 2001) at pp. 145–146.

[113] Footnote 5 specifies that "Measures referred to in Annex I as not constituting export subsidies shall not be prohibited under this or any other provision of this Agreement."

exemptions narrowly. For example, item e of the Illustrative List prohibits "the full or partial exemption, remission, or deferral specifically related to exports, of direct taxes or social welfare charges paid or payable by industrial or commercial enterprises." However, Footnote 59 states that item e of the Illustrative List is "not intended to limit a Member from taking measures to avoid the double taxation of foreign-source income earned by its enterprises or the enterprises of another Member." The United States sought to rely on Footnote 59 to defend tax exemptions for exporters that it argued were necessary because the use by the United States of a worldwide income-based tax system created a competitive disadvantage for its exporters. The Appellate Body rejected this argument in the Article 21.5 proceeding in *U.S. – FSC.*[114] For the Appellate Body, this provision is restricted to measures that exempt from taxation income actually earned through foreign activities that might form a basis for taxation by a foreign state, which was not the case with the challenged American FSC Repeal and Extraterritorial Income Exclusion Act of 2000 (ETI Act).[115]

Similarly, Panels have read relatively narrowly the second paragraph of item k of the Illustrative List, which is an important exemption relied on in several disputes involving export subsidies. It states that export credit practices in conformity with the interest rate provisions of an international undertaking on official export credits (or its successor) to which at least twelve original Members of the SCM Agreement are parties as of January 1, 1979, are not to be considered a prohibited export subsidy.[116] After several other item k arguments had been rejected, Brazil successfully convinced a Panel that its revised PROEX III export subsidy program could be administered in compliance with the interest rate provisions of the *Organisation for Economic Co-operation and Development (OECD) Arrangement* and thus managed to take advantage of this safe haven.[117]

However, in *Canada – Export Credits and Loan Guarantees for Regional Aircraft* (*Canada – Export Credits for Aircraft*), the Panel examined whether the

[114] The item e argument had been made to the Appellate Body in the first *United States – Foreign Sales Corporations* proceeding, but as it had not been submitted to the Panel, the Appellate Body refused to consider it. See *United States – Tax Treatment for "Foreign Sales Corporations" (Complaint by the European Communities)* (2000), WTO Doc. WT/DS108/AB/R at para. 103 (Appellate Body Report).

[115] For a summary of the Appellate Body's analysis, see Robert E. Hudec, "Industrial Subsidies: Tax Treatment of 'Foreign Sales' Corporations" in Ernst-Ulrich Petersmann and Mark A. Pollack (Eds.), *Transatlantic Economic Disputes: The EU, the US, and the WTO* (Oxford, Oxford University Press, 2003), 175 at 201–202.

[116] This is an oblique reference to the *OECD Arrangement on Officially Supported Export Credits.* For a description of the *Arrangement* or of export credits generally, see OECD, *The Export Credit Arrangement: Achievements and Challenges 1978–1998* (Paris, Organization for Economic Cooperation and Development, 1998) at 16–21.

[117] *Brazil – Export Financing Programme for Aircraft – Second Recourse by Canada to Article 21.5 of the DSU* (2001), WTO Doc. WT/DS46/RW/2 at para. 5.207 (Panel Report). The PROEX III program could also be administered in ways that were not compliant with the *OECD Arrangement,* but under the mandatory/discretionary distinction, which is discussed subsequently, that is not relevant.

second paragraph of item k allowed Canada to match export credits offered by Brazil that derogated from the *OECD Arrangement*. It concluded that the matching of a derogation, although permitted under the *OECD Arrangement*, was not in conformity with the *Arrangement*'s "interest rates provisions."[118] Therefore, this matching fell outside of the second paragraph of item k and constituted a prohibited subsidy under the SCM Agreement. The Panel justified its conclusion by relying on a general prohibition against self-help in the WTO system.[119] Its reasoning has been called "clearly erroneous" by commentators who point out that the WTO system, instead of prohibiting self-help, implicitly permits it by allowing states to take unilateral countervailing measures against prohibited subsidies.[120]

Panels and the Appellate Body have therefore fairly broadly interpreted the export contingency requirement under the SCM Agreement. Article 3.1(a) already has a wide ambit on its face, as it captures both *de jure* and *de facto* contingency. This wording has been made more inclusive with the contextual reading of the *de facto* contingency requirement and the use of the Illustrative List in a manner that allows a wider reach for the prohibition. This broad interpretation is consistent with the view of the prohibition as an attempt to resist political pressure because it aims at prevention of even hidden forms of protectionism. It also is consistent with the view that export subsidies are globally inefficient, as it requires a close tie between the subsidy and exports in an attempt not to capture domestic subsidies that may be legitimate. At the same time, it allows Panels to examine the actual measures closely to determine if the respondent country is cheating on its commitment. The desire to identify cheating comports with the view that exporting countries may be trying to use the prohibition to further their own welfare either by restricting the supply of the good or by overcoming the prisoners' dilemma arising under strategic trade theory. Under such a view, each country has an incentive to attempt to cheat on its commitment and obtain added benefits of the arrangement at the expense of other exporters. The wording of the SCM Agreement and its interpretation lacks clarity in many respects (and could potentially be improved with a bright line [although somewhat arbitrary] rule such as, for example, where some high percentage [e.g., 80 percent] of the output of an industry is exported and subsidized, the measure is deemed to be an export subsidy regardless of any *de jure* or *de facto* export contingency analysis). However, the export contingency requirement seems generally to be consistent with both the positive and normative reasoning behind the prohibition.

[118] *Canada – Export Credits and Loan Guarantees for Regional Aircraft (Complaint by Brazil)* (2002), WTO Doc. WT/DS222/R at para. 7.180 (Panel Report).

[119] *Canada – Export Credits and Loan Guarantees for Regional Aircraft (Complaint by Brazil)* (2002), WTO Doc. WT/DS222/R at para. 7.170 (Panel Report).

[120] Robert Howse and Damien J. Neven, "Canada – Export Credits and Loan Guarantees for Regional Aircraft (WT/DS222/R: A Comment) in Henrik Horn and Petros C. Mavroidis (Eds.), *The WTO Case Law of 2002* (Cambridge, Cambridge University Press, 2005) 88 at 96–97.

Is the Enabling Legislation Mandatory or Discretionary?

Although Panels and the Appellate Body have adopted a rather broad definition of export contingency and a very narrow interpretation of subsidies explicitly permitted under the Illustrative List, they have been willing to rely on another principle to avoid finding measures to be in violation of the SCM Agreement's prohibition on export subsidies: a long-standing[121] distinction in public international law and GATT/WTO law between mandatory and discretionary measures.[122]

Mandatory legislation requires the government of the member state to violate its WTO obligations. Mandatory measures can be challenged *as such:* If a Panel finds a measure to be mandatory, then it can require that that measure be withdrawn. Legislation that grants a member government discretion as to whether to apply it consistently with its WTO commitments is described as discretionary. Discretionary measures can only be challenged *as applied:* The complaining member must prove that these measures have been applied in a way that contravenes the WTO Agreements.

The use of this distinction in WTO export subsidy jurisprudence dates back to one of the first cases, *Canada – Aircraft.* In that case, the Panel used the distinction to reject Brazil's assertion that the Export Development Canada (EDC) program was a *per se* prohibited export subsidy.[123] The Panel was unable to find evidence that EDC's mandate required the grant of export subsidies, and therefore classified the EDC program as discretionary legislation. The Panel then examined and rejected the claim that the EDC program, *as applied,* provided prohibited export subsidies.

In the *Canada – Aircraft* case, the Panel could successfully undertake this two-step analysis because EDC had operated for years, and there was therefore available evidence as to its operation. However, the mandatory/discretionary argument in the second Article 21.5 compliance proceeding in *Brazil – Export Financing for Aircraft* arose in a different context. The Brazilian government's PROEX export-financing program had been deemed to be a prohibited export subsidy in two previous proceedings. Following these decisions, Brazil modified the program (now called PROEX III) such that it was discretionary whether or

121 For the history of this rule, see Kwan Kiat Sim, "Rethinking the mandatory/discretionary legislation distinction in WTO jurisprudence," 2 *World Trade Review* 2003, 33 at 8–21.

122 For a review of the use of this distinction in GATT/WTO law, see Sharif Bhuiyan, "Mandatory and Discretionary Legislation: The Continued Relevance of the Distinction under the WTO," 5 *Journal of International Economic Law* 2002, 571.

123 *Canada – Measures Affecting the Export of Civilian Aircraft (Complaint by Brazil)* (1999), WTO Doc. WT/DS70/R at paras. 9.124–9.129 (Panel Report). Brazil alleged that Canada's Export Development Corporation (EDC) was providing a variety of financial and risk absorption services, the combination of which made EDC itself an export subsidy program. See *Canada – Measures Affecting the Export of Civilian Aircraft (Complaint by Brazil)* (1999), WTO Doc. WT/DS70/R at paras. 6.1–6.2 (Panel Report).

not the financing would exceed what the previous Panels and the Appellate Body had said was acceptable under item k of the Illustrative List. The second Article 21.5 Compliance Panel applied the mandatory/discretionary principle and found that PROEX III, as such, could be applied in conformity with the requirements of item k, and therefore that it was not a prohibited export subsidy *per se.*[124] Because there was no evidence relating to the actual application of PROEX III, the Panel ended its inquiry there. Canada would have to return to the WTO should the Brazilian authorities actually provide prohibited subsidies by exercising their discretion in the administration of PROEX III in a manner that exceeded what is permitted by item k.

This dichotomy has been weakened in several cases not involving export subsidies. In *US – Section 301*, the Panel examined U.S. legislation that gave officials discretion to impose measures without following the procedures in the DSU Agreement.[125] Given that the U.S. Trade Representative could nonetheless act in compliance with the DSU procedures, the United States sought to defend its measure by classifying it as discretionary legislation. The Panel disagreed. It found that some WTO obligations were such that they were violated by inconsistent discretionary legislation that, by its mere existence, had the potential to create a "chilling effect."[126] As the Panel decision was not appealed, this move away from a rigid application of the mandatory/discretionary distinction was not reviewed by the Appellate Body.

The Appellate Body, in *U.S. – Corrosion-Resistant Steel Sunset Review*, which also did not involve export subsidies, stated that it saw "no reason for concluding that, in principle, non-mandatory measures cannot be challenged 'as such.'"[127] It added that it has not "been required to pronounce generally upon the continuing relevance or significance of the mandatory/discretionary distinction" but "caution[ed] against the application of this distinction in a mechanistic fashion."[128] Furthermore, the Appellate Body appeared to adopt the more contextual approach of the Panel in *US – Section 301*, as it noted that "the import of the 'mandatory/discretionary distinction' may vary from case to case."[129]

124 *Brazil – Export Financing Programme for Aircraft – Second Recourse by Canada to Article 21.5 of the DSU* (2001), WTO Doc. WT/DS46/RW/2 at paras. 5.206–5.207 (Panel Report).

125 See, for example, Kwan Kiat Sim, "Rethinking the Mandatory/Discretionary Legislation Distinction in WTO Jurisprudence," 2 *World Trade Review* 2003, 33 at 48–50.

126 *United States – Sections 301-310 of the Trade Act of 1974 (Complaint by the European Communities)* (1999) WTO Doc. WT/DS152/R at para. 7.88 (Panel Report).

127 *United States – Sunset Review of Anti-Dumping Duties on Corrosion-Resistant Carbon Steel Flat Products from Japan (Complaint by Japan)* (2003) WTO Doc. WT/DS/244/AB/R at para. 88 (Appellate Body Report).

128 *United States – Sunset Review of Anti-Dumping Duties on Corrosion-Resistant Carbon Steel Flat Products from Japan (Complaint by Japan)* (2003) WTO Doc. WT/DS/244/AB/R at para. 93 (Appellate Body Report).

129 *United States – Sunset Review of Anti-Dumping Duties on Corrosion-Resistant Carbon Steel Flat Products from Japan (Complaint by Japan)* (2003) WTO Doc. WT/DS/244/AB/R at para. 93 (Appellate Body Report). See Yuka Fukunaga, "Securing Compliance Through the WTO

Although the Panel in the latest export subsidy case, *Korea – Vessels*,[130] reiterated a commitment to the traditional approach, the Appellate Body subsequently in *U.S – Zeroing of Dumping Margins* referred to its statement in *U.S – Corrosion-Resistant Steel Sunset Review* that "the import of the 'mandatory/discretionary distinction' may vary from case to case."[131]

It remains to be seen whether future Panels will continue to apply the mandatory/discretionary distinction rigidly, or whether they will follow the Appellate Body's apparent move toward a more contextual approach. The purpose of the distinction is to respect states' sovereignty by affording them a presumption of good faith in the application of legislation. Furthermore, without such a distinction, states are exposed to spurious complaints.[132] However, the contextual approach signaled by the Appellate Body is more consistent with the economic theory behind the export subsidy prohibition than is the former rigid classification. The contextual application of the distinction would require examination of the content and purpose of the obligation in question as well as the purpose and effect of the challenged measure.[133]

In the context of export subsidies, the obligation is a prohibition on export subsidies that has as its apparent purpose the avoidance of trade distortions and protectionist measures (thereby potentially enhancing global welfare). The purpose could also be seen as overcoming a prisoners' dilemma that fosters competing export subsidies. Either of these purposes would lead to a desire for a broad restriction on export subsidies, including on discretionary legislation that may impact the actions of foreign producers. Strategic trade theory, in particular, is based not only on actual subsidies but also on the threat of subsidies that deter entry into a market. Discretionary legislation can impact behavior through threats as well as actions.[134] Given this purpose, it seems reasonable for a complaining party to be able to raise the possibility that a discretionary measure, even though not yet applied, has a "chilling effect" that benefits the producers in the respondent member.

The contextual approach signaled by the Appellate Body accords with the purposes underlying the prohibition on export subsidies. The distinction between mandatory and discretionary legislation could be interpreted as a presumption in favor of the legitimacy of discretionary legislation subject to rebuttal by the complaining party based on a consideration of the purpose and effect of

Dispute Settlement System: Implementation of DSB Recommendations," 9(2) *Journal of International Economic Law* 2006, 383 at 393.

130 *Korea – Measures Affecting Trade in Commercial Vessels (Complaint by the European Communities)* (2005), WTO Doc. WT/DS273/R at paras. 7.60–7.67 (Panel Report).

131 *United States – Laws, Regulations and Methodology for Calculating Dumping Margins (Zeroing) (Complaint by the European Communities)* (2006), WTO Doc. WT/DS294/AB/R at para. 214 (Appellate Body Report).

132 Sim (2003), pp. 59 and 63.

133 Sim (2003), p. 62, and Fukunaga (2006), p. 393.

134 Sim (2003), pp. 63–64 (citing a claim about section 301 of the US Trade Act of 1974 that it has an impact on foreign governments largely through the threat of its possible application).

the measure.[135] Such a presumption would aid in reducing colorable challenges and yet still allow challenges where the threat of subsidies has an impact on trade. As will be discussed in the following section, however, one of the major difficulties for both actual and potential measures that have been found to violate the prohibition is the appropriate remedy.

Remedies

In the previous section, we examined how the SCM Agreement and its interpretation by Panels and the Appellate Body have sought to identify prohibited export subsidies. In large measure, it found that, in form, the SCM Agreement establishes a simple rule banning export subsidies. Such a simple ban may have benefits including the facts that it is not costly to design and it is easily understood by the members. However, there is a potential loss of efficiency if there are instances where export subsidies are in fact efficient. The current rule as interpreted has some flexibility built into it. One option to obtain greater flexibility, and therefore hopefully greater efficiency, would be to build more complexity into the rule by specifying which export subsidies are efficient and therefore permitted. However, a more complex rule would require much more information *ex ante* and greater between-member agreement, which would likely be difficult to obtain. A second option would be to shift to more of a standard, such that there would be a ban on "inefficient" export subsidies. However, any such standard would require Panels and the Appellate Body to have significantly more information and the ability to determine which types of subsidies are efficient and inefficient.[136]

A third option, discussed more fully in this section, is that the flexibility is achieved not in the requirement but in the remedy. Although, as we have seen, the identification of export subsidies has been contentious, the remedies for violations of the prohibition have proven even more vexing, leading at times to a lack of compliance and multiple recourse to the Dispute Settlement Body (DSB). This section of the chapter will examine the three main types of remedies for violations of export subsidies: withdrawal of the subsidy, countermeasures, and unilateral domestic measures. As noted earlier in this chapter, WTO agreements may be viewed as agreements that either foster the joint economic welfare of the member countries or maximize the welfare of the governments (and, in particular, the political officials) of those countries.[137] Each view may lead to a

[135] Sim (2003), p. 59.

[136] This discussion of the costs and benefits of different options for increasing the flexibility of export subsidies requirements is based on Green and Trebilcock (2007).

[137] See, for example, Bagwell (2007); Joel Trachtman, "The WTO Cathedral," 43(1) *Stanford Journal of International Law* 2007, 127; and Warren Schwartz and Alan O. Sykes, "The Economic Structure of Renegotiation and Dispute Resolution in the World Trade Organization," 31 *Journal of Legal Studies* 2002, S179.

different view of the purpose and therefore form of remedy.[138] Relatedly, there is a debate about the proper function of remedies for noncompliance with trade agreements. They may be aimed at fostering compliance with the agreements in all cases, which would imply a form of property rule requiring compliance in all cases subject to a severe penalty. Alternatively, they may allow noncompliance with the agreements where it is efficient so that the (necessarily incomplete) agreements allow adjustment as conditions change.[139] Such a view would point to a liability rule – that is, a penalty that requires payment by the breaching party at a level that deters inefficient breach but is not so large as to deter efficient breach (i.e., where the benefit of the breach exceeds the costs arising from nonperformance).[140]

Flexibility in remedies can arise in two ways. First, the remedy may be a property rule but there may be bargaining by the parties around the remedy.[141] Such bargaining will occur only if the transaction costs of bargaining are low. If the transaction costs are high, the parties will not be able to bargain around the requirement, and whatever it requires will likely be achieved.[142] The latter situation is advantageous if the requirement is always efficient, but problematic if there are instances where compliance with the requirement is inefficient. As Schwartz and Sykes note, a property rule is in general preferable if breach is inefficient in all cases.[143] The question then becomes how to choose the level

[138] Bagwell (2007) (arguing that there is a need to understand the purpose of trade agreements before designing remedies) and Trachtman (2007).

[139] There is a continuing debate about the nature of the WTO regime and the appropriate positive and normative approach to remedies. For recent discussions of the different approaches and of concerns with WTO remedies, see Schwartz and Sykes (2002); Joost Pauwelyn, "Optimal Protection of International Law: Navigating Between 'European Absolutism' and 'American Voluntarism'" (Draft, November 15, 2006) (applying Calabresi and Melamed's framework for approaching remedies to international law generally with examples from the WTO); Marco Bronckers and Naboth van den Broek, "Financial Compensation in the WTO: Improving the Remedies of WTO Dispute Settlement," 8(1) *Journal of International Economic Law* 2005, 101; Jide Nzelibe, "The Case Against Reforming the WTO's Enforcement Mechanism" (Northwestern University School of Law Public Law and Legal Theory Series No. 07-12, April 2, 2007); Bagwell (2007); and Trachtman (2007).

[140] The "efficient breach" approach to WTO remedies has generated controversy. See, for example, Trachtman (2007); Schwartz and Sykes (2002); Joseph Pelzman and Amir Shoham, "WTO Enforcement Issues," 7(1) *Global Economy Journal* 2007, 1; Pauwelyn (2006); Nzelibe (2007); and Bagwell (2007).

[141] This chapter will discuss the alternatives of a property rule and a liability rule, although there is also the potential to view WTO remedies (and export subsidies rules in particular) as inalienable (see Pauwelyn (2006) for a discussion of inalienable rules, property rules, and liability rules).

[142] See Green and Trebilcock (2007) (arguing that the transaction costs of *ex poste* bargaining in the case of export subsidies appear high).

[143] This general description of the law and economics of contract remedies is based on Schwartz and Sykes (2002), pp. S181–S183. See also Pauwelyn (2006) (arguing that international rules in general and most WTO rules in particular can and should be seen as default property rules) and Trachtman (2007).

of penalty for breach. In theory, an optimal level of deterrence should take into account both the level of benefit from providing the export subsidy as well as the probability that the prohibited activity will be detected and punished. The member state would then compare the expected penalty (taking account of the probability of detection and punishment) and the expected benefit.[144]

Second, the remedy for noncompliance could be a liability rule. Such a remedy permits the parties to "buy" their way out of noncompliance with the agreement and therefore avoids the need for bargaining and any error costs associated with an inefficient rule or standard.[145] In standard law economics, the remedy should be set at expectation damages, which are sufficient to place the harmed party in the position in which it would have been had the contract not been breached. A party will therefore only breach if it is efficient (the benefits of breach exceed the value of the prior agreement) – either in terms of global welfare or the political welfare of the governments involved.[146] The difficulty with liability rules is determining the appropriate level of expectation damages and therefore creating the proper incentive for breach.[147] If the level of payment is too low or too high, then members will have an incentive to engage in too much or too little noncompliance. If it is difficult to estimate the appropriate level of the remedy, a property rule may be more beneficial.[148]

The following discussion will examine the three existing remedies in light of these basic ideas of the purpose and form of remedies.

Withdrawal Without Delay

Article 4.7 of the SCM Agreement states that "If the measure in question is found to be a prohibited subsidy, the panel shall recommend that the subsidizing Member withdraw the subsidy without delay." The Panel is required to specify the time period within which the measure is to be withdrawn. Unfortunately, although it seems clear the agreement seeks rapid compliance with the prohibition, it has often not been clear what exactly withdrawing the subsidy actually entails. As a result, this question has motivated several Article 21.5 compliance proceedings.[149]

The Article 21.5 disputes concerning exports have proven controversial, particularly the first of these proceedings, *Australia – Automotive Leather*. In that

[144] See, for example, Pauwelyn (2006), p. 57 (discussing property rules and "back up enforcement" in the international law context) and Trachtman (2007).

[145] Trachtman (2007), Schwartz and Sykes (2002), and Pauwelyn (2007).

[146] Schwartz and Sykes (2002) and Trachtman (2007). See Green and Trebilcock (2007) for a more complete discussion of the advantages and disadvantages of property and liability rules in the context of export subsidies.

[147] See, for example, Pauwelyn (2006), Trachtman (2007), and Bagwell (2007).

[148] Trachtman (2007)

[149] Article 21.5 of the DSU provides for disagreements about compliance with recommendations and rules to be decided by a Panel, preferably the original Panel.

case, the Panel required Australia to obtain repayment of the prohibited subsidy that the Australian government had provided to Howe, a manufacturer of automotive leather. A number of critical issues relating to the withdrawal remedy that arise out of the *Automotive Leather* Article 21.5 decision have also arisen in subsequent cases. First, is withdrawal to be interpreted as a retrospective or a prospective remedy? Second, how should preexisting subsidy commitments be treated? Third, are any obligations under domestic law to be taken into consideration?

Retrospective or Prospective Withdrawal?

At first glance, the withdrawal of the subsidy should at least partially remove the benefit from the granting of the export subsidy. The company will be returned to its prior cost structure, and any increase in production resulting from the subsidy should end. Both the protective and terms of trade impact of the export subsidy should cease. However, the effect of the remedy is closely related to the issue of whether the withdrawal should be interpreted as retrospective or prospective. This issue arose in *Australia – Automotive Leather*, the third Panel decision involving export subsidies that, unlike the previous two (the disputes between Canada and Brazil over regional aircraft), was not appealed to the Appellate Body. Whereas the dispute between Canada and Brazil went through the appeal process, the *Australia – Automotive Leather* dispute continued on to an Article 21.5 compliance proceeding. As a result, the Panel's decision in that proceeding was the first Article 21.5 decision involving export subsidies.

Faced with the initial Panel order to withdraw the subsidy that had been found to be prohibited, Australia entered into an agreement with Howe.[150] Howe repaid the part of the subsidy that the Australian government considered to be the "prospective element."[151] The government also terminated all existing obligations under the grant contract. In exchange, the government gave Howe's parent company a new loan.[152] The United States argued under Article 21.5 that this was insufficient and proposed an alternate formula for calculating how much

150 *Australia – Subsidies Provided to Producers and Exporters of Automotive Leather – Recourse to Article 21.5 of the DSU by the United States* (2000), WTO Doc. WT/DS126/RW at paras. 1.3–1.4 (Panel Report). The subsidy consisted of a grant contract that provided for three payments by the Australian government to Howe. The first payment was made upon signing the contract, whereas the two later payments were conditioned on Howe meeting targets. *Australia – Subsidies Provided to Producers and Exporters of Automotive Leather* (1999), WTO Doc. WT/DS126/R at para. 9.62 (Panel Report). All three payments, including the first one, were found to be contingent on exports: *Australia – Subsidies Provided to Producers and Exporters of Automotive Leather* (1999), WTO Doc. WT/DS126/R at paras. 9.71–9.72 (Panel Report).

151 *Australia – Subsidies Provided to Producers and Exporters of Automotive Leather – Recourse to Article 21.5 of the DSU by the United States* (2000), WTO Doc. WT/DS126/RW at para. 6.3 (Panel Report).

152 A similar loan had been found not to be contingent on exports in the original Panel decision.

Howe should repay based on the "prospective portion" of the subsidy.[153] In addition, it alleged that the new loan was structured in a way that negated any financial impact on Howe from the repayment.[154]

Both of these approaches to remedies were entirely prospective; indeed, the Panel noted that "Australia, like the United States, contends that only a 'prospective' remedy is envisioned under Article 4.7 of the SCM Agreement."[155] The Panel refused to limit itself to the arguments that the two countries had made.[156] Instead, it examined what exactly withdrawal of the subsidy entails. In the Panel's view, withdrawal is not limited to purely prospective actions, but may encompass repayment of prohibited subsidies.[157] The Panel concluded that repayment of the entire subsidy at issue, although without interest, was required.[158] Accordingly, it found that Australia had not withdrawn the subsidy.

The decision in *Australia – Automotive Leather* was unexpected, and several members reacted against it. When the Canada–Brazil regional aircraft dispute subsequently entered the Article 21.5 process, both countries were adamant that they were not seeking a retrospective remedy against the other.[159] In addition, the EC made a third-party submission on this point. Using strong language, they criticized the *Australia – Automotive Leather* Panel on two grounds. The first was procedural: They argued that the Panel should not consider alternatives beyond what the complaining party had raised. The second was substantive: They argued against the availability of retroactive remedies. In the *Canada–Brazil*

153 The "prospective portion" was calculated by estimating the value of the benefits that Howe would continue to receive after the Panel decision from the assets it invested in. See *Australia – Subsidies Provided to Producers and Exporters of Automotive Leather – Recourse to Article 21.5 of the DSU by the United States* (2000), WTO Doc. WT/DS126/RW at para. 6.10 (Panel Report).

154 *Australia – Subsidies Provided to Producers and Exporters of Automotive Leather – Recourse to Article 21.5 of the DSU by the United States* (2000), WTO Doc. WT/DS126/RW at para. 6.13 (Panel Report). The American argument was that the loan was such that, after using part of the loan to repay the required portion of the prohibited subsidies, Howe could conservatively invest the remainder of the loan at a rate of return that would enable it to repay the whole loan at maturity.

155 *Australia – Subsidies Provided to Producers and Exporters of Automotive Leather – Recourse to Article 21.5 of the DSU by the United States* (2000), WTO Doc. WT/DS126/RW at para. 6.14 (Panel Report).

156 *Australia – Subsidies Provided to Producers and Exporters of Automotive Leather – Recourse to Article 21.5 of the DSU by the United States* (2000), WTO Doc. WT/DS126/RW at para. 6.18–6.19 (Panel Report).

157 *Australia – Subsidies Provided to Producers and Exporters of Automotive Leather – Recourse to Article 21.5 of the DSU by the United States* (2000), WTO Doc. WT/DS126/RW at para. 6.42 (Panel Report).

158 *Australia – Subsidies Provided to Producers and Exporters of Automotive Leather – Recourse to Article 21.5 of the DSU by the United States* (2000), WTO Doc. WT/DS126/RW at para. 6.48 (Panel Report).

159 Gavin Goh and Andreas R. Ziegler, "Retrospective Remedies in the WTO after *Automotive Leather*," 6 *Journal of International Economic Law* 2003, 545 at 548.

aircraft case, the Article 21.5 Panels restricted their discussion to the prospective remedies discussed by the parties. These remedies were essentially limited to ensuring that reforms made by both countries to their respective measures made those measures compliant with the SCM Agreement.[160]

Subsequent Article 21.5 Panel and Appellate Body rulings have also limited themselves to prospective remedies, leading two commentators to conclude that "Canada's comments [...] – that the findings [in *Australia – Automotive Leather*] will be treated by WTO Members 'as a one-time aberration of no precedential value' – have therefore proved prophetic."[161] The requirement for remedies to be prospective currently appears to be solidly anchored in WTO law, notwithstanding the *Australia – Automotive Leather* anomaly.

The retrospective approach provides strong incentives to member states not to provide subsidies because they know that the recipient firm will not be able to keep the subsidy if it is successfully challenged through the WTO. It would have a dramatic impact in a case such as *U.S. – FSC* in which billions of dollars of subsidies were granted to many recipients over an extended period of time. It also would discourage reliance on governmental measures with the potential of being deemed contingent on exports due to a well-founded fear that, years later, governments would be forced by the WTO to recover subsidies from firms or, even worse, export buyers. The use of a retrospective remedy would therefore be consistent with a view of the prohibition on export subsidies as responding to negative global and domestic welfare effects. The penalty would be severe and therefore discourage their use.[162]

The prospective remedy avoids these issues, but at a serious potential incentive cost. The reasoning of the Article 21.5 Panel in *Australia – Automotive Leather* is convincing in this regard – without retrospective remedies, nothing could be done in the case of a one-time subsidy contingent on export performance.[163] The prospective nature of the remedy therefore accords with a view of the prohibition and its remedy as providing scope for "efficient" breach where efficiency corresponds to the political interests of political officials rather than global or domestic economic welfare.[164] The remedy allows for short-term, one-time breaches but not for ongoing violations. It provides a form of political safeguard allowing

[160] In the Brazil case, there were also issues relating to subsidies that Brazil had committed to provide before being ordered to withdraw the subsidies, but that had not been paid. These issues, which arose solely because a prospective approach was used, will be discussed below in Part (a)(ii).

[161] Gavin Goh and Andreas R. Ziegler, "Retrospective Remedies in the WTO after *Automotive Leather*," 6 *Journal of International Economic Law* 2003, 545 at 545.

[162] There would, however, be other impacts, such as potentially greater unwillingness of counties to enter into trade agreements (see, e.g., Pauwelyn [2006]).

[163] *Australia – Subsidies Provided to Producers and Exporters of Automotive Leather – Recourse to Article 21.5 of the DSU by the United States* (2000), WTO Doc. WT/DS126/RW at paras. 6.33–6.45 (Panel Report).

[164] See Trachtman (2006) (arguing that prospective remedies are too low to be a welfare-based remedy).

governments to respond if necessary to significant interest group pressure but not over the long term. Each country appears to be willing to allow others to use this safeguard while reserving its own ability to do so, which may explain the "marked reluctance... of complainants to claim retrospective withdrawal."[165]

However, there is another concern about this remedy. In many cases, the "prospective" interpretation of withdrawal of the subsidy may eliminate the impact going forward, although not the impact in the past. However, if (according to strategic trade theory) the impact were to deter entry of foreign competitors and provide a first-mover advantage to the subsidized industry, removal of the subsidy would not have an impact. The damage would already have been done, and the subsidized industry would have control of the market. The prospective remedy therefore would not respond to the prisoners' dilemma arising from strategic trade theory, as the subsidy that gives rise to the harm (the diversion of trade from the initial subsidy) is not eliminated.

As a result, the prospective interpretation of the requirement to remove the subsidy without delay points toward the remedy for export subsidies being a liability rule tied to the political interests of governments.[166] It ensures that the remedy for the violation is not too severe – including potential bankruptcy of the industries involved. It creates an incentive for short-term efficient breach (a form of political safeguard subject only to informal sanctions such as the international reputation of the subsidizing government) but not for ongoing violations.[167] It may also allow room for good faith differences in opinion about interpretations of the SCM Agreement.[168] Unfortunately, such an interpretation does not eliminate the use of export subsidies for strategic trade purposes. If the concern were with the negative effects of the export subsidies on global and domestic welfare (including the elimination of strategic trade measures), the remedy would be retrospective. Such a rule would make the remedy more akin to a property rule, as the penalty could conceivably be high. However, such a remedy is likely politically infeasible, particularly in the case of large subsidies to important domestic industries such as commercial aircraft.

Preexisting Commitments

Often there is a delay between the time when a legal entitlement to a subsidy is created and the time that the subsidy is actually paid out. In the meantime,

[165] Gavin Goh and Andreas R. Ziegler, "Retrospective Remedies in the WTO after *Automotive Leather*," 6 *Journal of International Economic Law* 2003, 545 at 549.

[166] See, for example, Schwartz and Sykes (2002) (arguing that WTO rules should be seen as liability rules) and Trachtman (2006). But see Pauwelyn (2006) (arguing that the WTO rules should not necessarily be seen as liability rules) and Nzelibe (2007).

[167] There is the potential for other sanctions from noncompliance with WTO rules including reputation. See Pauwelyn (2006) (discussing the "community costs" of noncompliance with international law, which include reputation) and Trachtman (2006) (discussing the effect of reputation).

[168] Schwartz and Sykes (2002), p. S201.

a Panel's recommendation to withdraw the subsidy could be adopted. In *Australia – Automotive Leather*, this was not an issue because the last payment was made in July 1998 and the Panel Report was issued in May of the following year.[169] Even if payments had been scheduled for later, the broad retrospective remedial approach adopted by the Panel would have led to the result that, if past payments had to be returned, no future payments could be made. With the more common prospective interpretation of withdrawal, however, this timing issue can become significant.

The prohibition on export subsidies (Article 3.2) states that a "Member shall neither grant nor maintain [prohibited] subsidies." Article 4.7, when read within the context of the entire Article 4, requires that Members that are found to have granted or maintained prohibited subsidies withdraw these measures without delay. A prospective remedy implies that subsidies granted (or maintained) prior to the deadline set by the Panel under Article 4.7 are unaffected, but that the Member State must not grant further subsidies after that date. A question that arises therefore is, "When is a subsidy actually 'granted'"? Is it granted when the legal entitlement to it is created, or is it when the subsidizing state actually pays the subsidy?

This question was tangentially examined in *Australia – Automotive Leather* in the context of a procedural argument. As the final payment had been made after the Panel had been established, Australia sought to have it excluded from the Panel's terms of reference.[170] The Panel rejected this argument and stated that the government's commitment to make payments constituted part of the grant of the subsidies.[171] In this factual context, that reasoning was sensible and allowed for the inclusion in the Panel's terms of reference of something that common sense would dictate should be included.

In the *Brazil – Export Financing for Aircraft* case, the factual situation was substantially different. Under Brazil's PROEX program, prior to concluding a formal agreement with a buyer, Embraer would submit details of the proposed transaction to the committee administering PROEX.[172] The committee would issue a letter of commitment to Embraer in which the government of Brazil pledged to provide support provided that the sales contract was entered into in the subsequent ninety days. After an aircraft is delivered (exported) and paid for, bonds are issued by the Brazilian National Treasury through the Banco de Brasil (the Brazilian central bank) to the bank that is financing the transaction.

169 *Australia – Subsidies Provided to Producers and Exporters of Automotive Leather* (1999), WTO Doc. WT/DS126/R at para. 2.3 (Panel Report).

170 *Australia – Subsidies Provided to Producers and Exporters of Automotive Leather* (1999), WTO Doc. WT/DS126/R at para. 9.37 (Panel Report).

171 *Australia – Subsidies Provided to Producers and Exporters of Automotive Leather* (1999), WTO Doc. WT/DS126/R at para. 9.39 (Panel Report).

172 *Brazil – Export Financing Programme for Aircraft – Recourse by Canada to Article 21.5 of the DSU* (2000), WTO Doc. WT/DS46/RW at paras. 2.5–2.6 (Panel Report).

Under this structure, a number of years could elapse between the time the Brazilian government makes the commitment and the issuance of the bonds that make up the actual subsidy. An additional complication is that the bonds are issued directly to the buyer's bank or its Brazilian agent, not to Embraer. A prospective remedy would not affect the bonds that have already been issued, and withdrawing the subsidy implies not issuing further letters of commitment. It is not, however, as obvious what happens in the case in which the Brazilian government has committed to providing these bonds, but has not actually done so and may not do so for years.

This situation was examined by the Panel and the Appellate Body in the first Article 21.5 compliance proceeding. The Panel observed that, in the previous proceedings, the Appellate Body had said that, for the purposes of Article 27.4 (the developing country exemption), PROEX subsidies were granted when the bonds were issued. Despite Brazil's objections that applying this interpretation would constitute a retrospective remedy and that it would raise issues within domestic law, the Panel concluded that, for Article 3.2 purposes, the subsidies were granted when the bonds were issued.[173] Accordingly, the Panel found that, by continuing to issue bonds under letters of commitment issued prior to the Panel decision, Brazil had not withdrawn the subsidy.

The Appellate Body upheld this conclusion, although it did not discuss the Panel's reasoning.[174] The Appellate Body's approach was simpler: PROEX had been found to be a prohibited export-contingent subsidy. The Appellate Body determined that withdrawing such a subsidy entailed not making any additional payments under the prohibited program. Issuance of the bonds constituted payments under the program after the date by which Brazil was required to withdraw its subsidy, and thus Brazil was not in compliance.

Brazil did not comply with this recommendation, and countermeasures were authorized. Brazil's reluctance to comply is understandable: Not only are there potential domestic civil liability issues, which will be discussed in the subsequent section, but the structure of the program makes it difficult for Brazil to comply. Given that the Brazilian government paid the bonds directly to the purchaser's bank and not to Embraer, either the purchaser or its bank (depending on the legal arrangements between them) would have to absorb the loss of the subsidy should the Brazilian government not issue the bonds.[175] Brazil's defense in the initial proceeding was that its subsidies were needed to offset a negative perception of Brazil and "Brazil risk" in world capital markets. Causing international

[173] *Brazil – Export Financing Programme for Aircraft – Recourse by Canada to Article 21.5 of the DSU* (2000), WTO Doc. WT/DS46/RW at para. 6.17 (Panel Report).

[174] *Brazil – Export Financing Programme for Aircraft – Recourse by Canada to Article 21.5 of the DSU* (2000), WTO Doc. WT/DS46/AB/RW at para. 47 (Appellate Body Report).

[175] They could also not take delivery of the Embraer planes, but that might raise its own set of contractual legal issues; it would also frustrate whatever business activities the customers had planned in reliance on the Embraer order.

financial institutions to lose substantial amounts of money on their customers' purchases of Embraer planes would no doubt aggravate this negative perception. Canada, of course, would potentially benefit from the resulting impairment of Brazil/Embraer's credibility in world capital and regional aircraft markets, which may explain why this was an important element of the Article 21.5 proceedings. Ironically, in the subsequent *Canada – Export Credits for Aircraft* case, Canada faced exactly the same dilemma and it, too, openly refused to withdraw the subsidies.[176]

A similar situation arose in the *U.S. – FSC* case. The United States' FSCs tax mechanism was found to be a prohibited subsidy. The United States subsequently repealed it but transitionally allowed all transactions made by existing FSCs to receive the subsidy for an additional year, whereas transactions made under contracts prior to the withdrawal deadline could receive FSC tax treatment indefinitely. The Panel in the Article 21.5 proceeding, citing the Appellate Body's reasoning in *Brazil – Export Financing for Aircraft* (Article 21.5), found that the United States had not fully withdrawn the prohibited subsidy.[177] The Appellate Body upheld this decision, adding that "a Member's obligation to withdraw prohibited export subsidies, under Article 4.7 of the SCM Agreement, cannot be affected by contractual obligations that private parties may have assumed *inter se* in reliance on laws conferring prohibited export subsidies."[178]

Subsequently, the United States introduced legislation that not only maintained these grandfathered FSC subsidies, but also grandfathered some subsidies under the replacement measure, the Extraterritorial Income Exclusion Act of 2000 (ETI Act). The ETI Act had been deemed a prohibited subsidy in the first Article 21.5 proceeding. The Panel and the Appellate Body had no difficulty finding that the United States had not fully withdrawn the subsidy.[179]

The rule, then, seems to be clear: The conferral of benefits through prohibited subsidies must stop at the date set by the Panel, no matter when or how the state had made the commitment. This interpretation seems to be an attempt by Panels and the Appellate Body to compensate for some of the weaknesses inherent in the prospective approach. Their deciding that a subsidy was granted when

[176] *Canada – Export Credits and Loan Guarantees for Regional Aircraft – Recourse to Arbitration by Canada under Article 22.6 of the DSU and Article 4.11 of the SCM Agreement* (2003), WTO Doc. WT/DS222/ARB at para. 3.106 (Arbitration Report).

[177] *United States – Tax Treatment for "Foreign Sales Corporations" – Recourse to Article 21.5 of the DSU by the European Communities* (2001), WTO Doc. WT/DS108/RW at paras. 8.168–8.170 (Panel Report).

[178] *United States – Tax Treatment for "Foreign Sales Corporations" – Recourse to Article 21.5 of the DSU by the European Communities* (2001), WTO Doc. WT/DS108/AB/RW at para. 230. (Appellate Body Report).

[179] *United States – Tax Treatment for "Foreign Sales Corporations" – Second Recourse to Article 21.5 of the DSU by the European Communities* (2005), WTO Doc. WT/DS108/RW2 at para. 7.65 (Panel Report) and *United States – Tax Treatment for "Foreign Sales Corporations" – Second Recourse to Article 21.5 of the DSU by the European Communities* (2005), WTO Doc. WT/DS108/AB/RW2 at para. 100(b) (Appellate Body Report).

the legal entitlement to it was created would have enabled subsidizing governments to create long-term subsidy arrangements that could effectively never be withdrawn. This approach ensures that only payments that were already made are "immune" from withdrawal, at the cost of creating potential problems under domestic law (which will be discussed in the next section).

Obligations Under Domestic Law

Export subsidies are often provided through contracts between subsidizing governments (or their agencies) and either the exporting firm or foreign buyers. Such legal arrangements can lead to two potential conflicts if the subsidy is ordered to be withdrawn. First, a Panel could order the subsidizing government to make the subsidized firm retrospectively repay the subsidy after the subsidy had been entirely, or partly, paid out, as happened in *Australia – Automotive Leather*. As was observed by commentators and the Australian government, the Australian government had no basis in domestic law for demanding repayment of its money.[180] Furthermore, such repayment could constitute a form of expropriation or breach of contract, for which the firm might be entitled to compensation under domestic law.[181] Payment of this compensation might itself amount to a failure to withdraw the subsidy.

Second, the subsidizing government might have entered into an agreement committing it to pay subsidies at a later date and, consistent with the definition of "grant" outlined in the previous section, a Panel may order it to withdraw the subsidy before the date at which the subsidy is to be paid. The government would be breaching its agreement to provide the subsidy by not making the payment when it is due, and it would potentially be exposed to liability under domestic law for breach of contract. This issue was central in the first Article 21.5 proceeding in *Brazil – Export Financing for Aircraft*, which was discussed previously. In that case, Brazil was required not to issue bonds that it had committed to issuing under domestic law. The Panel and the Appellate Body dismissed Brazil's argument that it could not do so because not issuing the bonds might give rise to liability under domestic law.[182]

The WTO has not concerned itself with the domestic legal issues that might arise from its recommendations, reflecting a principle in international law that

[180] Daniel Moulis and Benjamin O'Donnell, "Does Withdraw the Subsidy Mean "Repay the Subsidy"? The Implications of the Howe Leather Case for Firms in Receipt of Government Subsidies," 6 *International Trade Law and Regulation* 2000, 168 at 170.

[181] Goh and Ziegler (2003) at 556.

[182] *Brazil – Export Financing Programme for Aircraft – Recourse by Canada to Article 21.5 of the DSU* (2000), WTO Doc. WT/DS46/RW at para. 6.16 (Panel Report) and *Brazil – Export Financing Programme for Aircraft – Recourse by Canada to Article 21.5 of the DSU* (2000), WTO Doc. WT/DS46/AB/RW at para. 46 (Appellate Body Report). Brazil did not comply and continued to issue the bonds, so any analysis of what might have happened had a case been brought in Brazilian courts is entirely hypothetical.

domestic law cannot be an excuse for not performing treaty obligations.[183] Although this stance may initially appear problematic, the rationale behind it is that, if domestic legal issues were taken into consideration, a subsidizing government would be able to structure its domestic law and domestic legal arrangements to frustrate the withdrawal of prohibited subsidies. This concern was explicitly recognized by the *Brazil – Export Financing for Aircraft* Article 21.5 Panel.[184]

However, in either of the two situations outlined above, there is a potentially serious problem should the subsidy's recipient decide to enforce its rights under domestic law. If the recipient is successful, the member state could face the following paradox: Domestic law requires the government to either pay damages for breach of contract or provide compensation for the seizure of property, but any such payment might, under the *Australia – Automotive Leather* reasoning at least, constitute a failure to withdraw the subsidy.[185] In such a case, the government would be unable to comply with its WTO obligations without violating domestic law. This problem may prove to be largely theoretical in cases involving a subsidy paid directly to a domestic firm. In practice, the relationship between the government and the subsidized firm may be so close that the firm would not have to sue the government to enforce its domestic law right to the subsidy because the government would try to find solutions that comply with the WTO (including negotiations with the importing country). As seen in the case of *Australia – Automotive Leather*, governments will go to great lengths to avoid actually taking back the subsidy.[186]

The greater danger may be in cases such as the Brazilian PROEX program, where the government provides the subsidy to a foreign buyer or its agent. A foreign buyer that bought a particular product in reliance on a substantial subsidy might be inclined to pursue all available remedies under the subsidizing state's domestic law (or under another country's laws pursuant to choice of law and choice of forum clauses) if that state repudiated the subsidy contract. If what happened in the Brazil case or the subsequent *Canada – Export Credits*

[183] This principle is laid out explicitly in Article 27 of the Vienna Convention on the Law of Treaties and states that "A party may not invoke the provisions of its internal law as justification for the failure to perform a treaty." See Goh and Ziegler (2003) at 555–556.

[184] *Brazil – Export Financing Programme for Aircraft – Recourse by Canada to Article 21.5 of the DSU* (2000), WTO Doc. WT/DS46/RW at para. 6.16 (Panel Report).

[185] The damages or compensation would presumably be in the same amount as the subsidy that was to have been provided. See Goh and Ziegler (2003) at 556.

[186] In that case, the Australian government reached a settlement with the United States that required Howe to repay a portion of the subsidy over twelve years, but agreed to make substantial concessions on other products. This settlement shows the extent to which the Australian government was willing to compromise in other areas to spare Howe. See Daniel Moulis and Benjamin O'Donnell, "Does 'Withdraw the Subsidy' Mean "Repay the Subsidy"? The Implications of the Howe Leather Case for Firms in Receipt of Government Subsidies," 6 *International Trade Law and Regulation* 2000, 168 at 171.

for Aircraft case is any indication, however, the subsidizing state may rather not comply and face countermeasures than breach such a contract.

These situations could be avoided if domestic law incorporated WTO norms in a way that made a contract in violation of the WTO Agreements unenforceable and explicitly permitted governments to require repayment.[187] However, not only would most countries object to giving direct domestic legal effect to WTO norms, but such domestic law might have a chilling effect on trade and investment. Would an aircraft buyer, for instance, have purchased Embraer planes for delivery years later if it knew Brazilian law left it with no remedy if the government was forced to retract its commitment to provide the subsidy? Would an export-oriented industry invest in new facilities if it knew it risked being ordered to repay the subsidy? Member states may rather promote reliance on their subsidy programs, including making those subsidies enforceable under domestic law, even if this enforceability entails being unable to comply with a WTO recommendation and facing countermeasures. Such a view is consistent with the view of export subsidy remedies as responding to domestic political interests. It would promote efficient subsidies to the extent that the subsidizing country negotiates a settlement with the harmed country or, as discussed in the next section, submits to an appropriate level of countermeasures.

Countermeasures

The current interpretation of the requirement to withdraw export subsidies without delay therefore appears to correspond to a liability rule. The prospective interpretation of the requirement (including the approach to preexisting commitments) permits breaches of the agreement in the form of one-time payments but not long-term, ongoing subsidies. It ensures that the penalty for export subsidies is not so high as to completely deter breaches and therefore allows governments short-term responses to political pressures. However, the effect of this interpretation and the prohibition in general depends on the penalty for non-compliance with the requirement to withdraw the subsidy.[188]

The apparent aim of the dispute settlement process is that the subsidy be withdrawn or that some other "mutually acceptable" settlement be reached between the parties.[189] If the parties fail to reach a settlement and the prohibited subsidy is not withdrawn, Article 4.10 of the SCM Agreement requires the DSB to authorize the complaining member to take "appropriate countermeasures"

[187] Of course, such legislation might raise constitutional issues in some countries that constitutionally mandate due process or compensation for expropriation. See Goh and Ziegler (2003) at 556 (suggesting that constitutional amendments might be necessary to permit requiring repayment).

[188] Pauwelyn (2006) terms such penalties "back-up enforcement."

[189] Article 3.7 of the DSU.

unless the DSB decides by consensus to reject the request.[190] The complaining state decides what countermeasures are appropriate. If the member that provided the subsidy considers that the complaining state's countermeasures are not appropriate, it can submit the countermeasures to arbitration under Article 22.6 of the DSU.[191] The SCM Agreement does not define what "appropriate" countermeasures are except to note, somewhat cryptically, that "this expression ["appropriate countermeasures"] is not meant to allow countermeasures that are disproportionate in light of the fact that the subsidies dealt with under these provisions are prohibited."[192]

There have been three Article 22.6 arbitrations in the Article 4.11 export subsidy context. They involve, unsurprisingly, the three disputes discussed previously in which the subsidizing country refused to withdraw a portion of the subsidies and failed to reach an agreement with the complaining state: *Brazil – Export Financing for Aircraft, U.S. – FSC,* and *Canada – Export Credits for Aircraft.* In *Brazil – Export Financing for Aircraft,* the parties agreed that what Canada was proposing (the suspension of concessions or other obligations on various Brazilian products) qualified as countermeasures.[193] However, the arbitrator had to determine what constituted the subsidy about which Canada could take action: Was it all PROEX payments in the relevant time period, or only the portion of PROEX payments that exceeded what was permissible under item k of the Illustrative List? The Arbitrators concluded that, as it was the whole PROEX program that had been deemed a prohibited subsidy in the prior proceedings, calculation of the countermeasure should be based on the full amount.[194]

The Arbitrators then went on to consider precisely what "appropriate" countermeasures entail. They found that "when dealing with a prohibited export subsidy, an amount of countermeasures which corresponds to the total amount of the subsidy is 'appropriate.'"[195] Brazil attempted to exclude from the calculation the subsidies it had committed to providing under domestic law. The Arbitrators,

[190] The obligation under Article 4.10 of the SCM Agreement that countermeasures be "appropriate" is somewhat different from the general requirement under Article 22.4 of the DSU that countermeasures be "equivalent" to the nullification and impairment. See Holger Spamann, "The Myth of 'Rebalancing' Retaliation in WTO Dispute Settlement Practice," 9(1) *Journal of International Economic Law* 2006, 31 (discussing the issue of whether retaliation leads to rebalancing of concessions).

[191] Article 4.11 of the SCM Agreement.

[192] Footnotes 9 and 10 to the SCM Agreement.

[193] *Brazil – Export Financing Programme for Aircraft – Recourse to Arbitration by Brazil under Article 22.6 of the DSU and Article 4.11 of the SCM Agreement* (2000), WTO Doc. WT/DS46/ARB at para. 3.29 (Arbitration Report).

[194] *Brazil – Export Financing Programme for Aircraft – Recourse to Arbitration by Brazil under Article 22.6 of the DSU and Article 4.11 of the SCM Agreement* (2000), WTO Doc. WT/DS46/ARB at para. 3.40 (Arbitration Report).

[195] *Brazil – Export Financing Programme for Aircraft – Recourse to Arbitration by Brazil under Article 22.6 of the DSU and Article 4.11 of the SCM Agreement* (2000), WTO Doc. WT/DS46/ARB at para. 3.60 (Arbitration Report).

explicitly citing the reasoning used to dismiss that argument in the Article 21.5 proceeding, held that those subsidies should be included.[196] They undertook their own calculations about what an appropriate amount of countermeasures would be and, citing Article 22.8 of the DSU, emphasized the temporary nature of the countermeasures.

Different issues arose in *U.S. – FSC*. The United States sought to argue that countermeasures should be calculated based on the impact the infringing measures had on the EC. The Arbitrators disagreed, finding that "the entitlement to countermeasures is to be assessed taking into account the legal status of the wrongful act and the manner in which the breach of that obligation has upset the balance of rights and obligations as between Members."[197] They also stated that "members may take countermeasures that are not disproportionate in light of the gravity of the initial wrongful act and the objective of securing the withdrawal of a prohibited export subsidy, so as to restore the balance of rights and obligations upset by that wrongful act."[198]

This approach led the Arbitrators to conclude that the EC was entitled to countermeasures based on the total amount that the United States continued to spend on its FSC/ETI subsidies after the deadline for withdrawal (approximately $4 billion/year). In their view, countermeasures are a response to an initial wrongful violation (the granting of subsidies) of obligations owed by the United States. Accordingly, the EC was entitled to respond by suspending a numerically equivalent obligation that they owed the United States.[199] Thus, the Arbitrators found that suspending around $4 billion in tariff concessions owed by the EC to the United States was appropriate. They noted that there was only one complaining state in this case; if there had been more, there could have been issues regarding allocation of the countermeasures among the multiple complainants.[200]

The third case is *Canada – Export Credits for Aircraft*, where Canada was ordered to withdraw subsidies that, *as applied*, constituted prohibited subsidies. Unlike the previous two cases, in which the amount of the subsidy was used to calculate countermeasures, Brazil sought to base its countermeasures

[196] *Brazil – Export Financing Programme for Aircraft – Recourse to Arbitration by Brazil under Article 22.6 of the DSU and Article 4.11 of the SCM Agreement* (2000), WTO Doc. WT/DS46/ARB at para. 3.65 (Arbitration Report).

[197] *United States – Tax Treatment for "Foreign Sales Corporations" – Recourse to Arbitration by the United States under Article 22.6 of the DSU and Article 4.11 of the SCM Agreement* (2002), WTO Doc. WT/DS108/ARB at para. 5.24 (Arbitration Report).

[198] *United States – Tax Treatment for "Foreign Sales Corporations" – Recourse to Arbitration by the United States under Article 22.6 of the DSU and Article 4.11 of the SCM Agreement* (2002), WTO Doc. WT/DS108/ARB at para. 5.41 (Arbitration Report).

[199] *United States – Tax Treatment for "Foreign Sales Corporations" – Recourse to Arbitration by the United States under Article 22.6 of the DSU and Article 4.11 of the SCM Agreement* (2002), WTO Doc. WT/DS108/ARB at para. 6.19 (Arbitration Report).

[200] *United States – Tax Treatment for "Foreign Sales Corporations" – Recourse to Arbitration by the United States under Article 22.6 of the DSU and Article 4.11 of the SCM Agreement* (2002), WTO Doc. WT/DS108/ARB at para. 6.28 (Arbitration Report).

on what it claimed were the adverse effects of the Canadian subsidies. The Arbitrators rejected this basis for countermeasures, along with the calculations used by Brazil. Canada argued that, as the subsidies were granted in response to the imminent granting of prohibited subsidies by Brazil, countermeasures should have been lowered. However, the Arbitrators found that Canada was not entitled to take the law into its own hands.[201]

In the Article 22.6 proceeding, Canada openly admitted that it had no intention of withdrawing any portion of the subsidy, including portions that had not yet been granted.[202] Given that, in their view, countermeasures are intended to end breaches, the Arbitrators found that Canada's intention not to comply mandated higher countermeasures than what Canada deemed appropriate.[203] Brazil also raised concerns about the need to deter so-called "hit and run" actions – the granting of one-time subsidies that cannot be ordered withdrawn. Here, the mandatory/discretionary distinction intervened again on Canada's side: The Panel found that the countermeasures cannot extend to subsidy programs that, as such, are not prohibited.[204] The Panel noted that doing otherwise would negate the difference between mandatory and discretionary legislation. They did, however, increase the countermeasures by 20% more than what they had calculated to account for Canada's stated unwillingness to comply.[205] Finally, the Arbitrators expressed their opinion that a mutually satisfactory agreement dealing with the broader context of this dispute would be the most appropriate solution.

These Article 22.6 Arbitration decisions have been therefore, at least in the rhetoric of Panels, based on a property rule approach to the export subsidy prohibition.[206] The Arbitrators have stated that the principle behind countermeasures is to bring about compliance, and the penalty must be sufficiently large

[201] *Canada – Export Credits and Loan Guarantees for Regional Aircraft – Recourse to Arbitration by Canada under Article 22.6 of the DSU and Article 4.11 of the SCM Agreement* (2003), WTO Doc. WT/DS222/ARB at para. 3.98 (Arbitration Report).

[202] *Canada – Export Credits and Loan Guarantees for Regional Aircraft – Recourse to Arbitration by Canada under Article 22.6 of the DSU and Article 4.11 of the SCM Agreement* (2003), WTO Doc. WT/DS222/ARB at para. 3.06 (Arbitration Report).

[203] *Canada – Export Credits and Loan Guarantees for Regional Aircraft – Recourse to Arbitration by Canada under Article 22.6 of the DSU and Article 4.11 of the SCM Agreement* (2003), WTO Doc. WT/DS222/ARB at para. 3.107 (Arbitration Report).

[204] *Canada – Export Credits and Loan Guarantees for Regional Aircraft – Recourse to Arbitration by Canada under Article 22.6 of the DSU and Article 4.11 of the SCM Agreement* (2003), WTO Doc. WT/DS222/ARB at para. 3.110 (Arbitration Report).

[205] *Canada – Export Credits and Loan Guarantees for Regional Aircraft – Recourse to Arbitration by Canada under Article 22.6 of the DSU and Article 4.11 of the SCM Agreement* (2003), WTO Doc. WT/DS222/ARB at para. 3.121 (Arbitration Report).

[206] Robert Howse and Damien J. Neven, "United States – Tax Treatment for 'Foreign Sales Corporations' Recourse to Arbitration by the United States under Article 22.6 of the DSU and Article 4.11 of the SCM Agreement (WT/DS108/ARB) A Comment," in Henrik Horn and Petros C. Mavroidis (Eds.), *The WTO Case Law of 2002* (Cambridge, Cambridge University Press, 2005) 36. See also Pauwelyn (2006) (arguing that most WTO rules are property rules) and Trachtman (2006).

to do so. Furthermore, the arbitrator in *Canada – Export Credits for Aircraft* even added an extra penalty for deliberate noncompliance. A property rule approach to countermeasures is consistent with the view of the prohibition on export subsidies as a resolution of a prisoners' dilemma (a high penalty is required to stop cheating) as well as with the view that export subsidies are in most cases globally (and domestically) inefficient. It therefore is consistent with both a political economy explanation of the prohibition and an economic welfare approach.

However, Arbitrators have used a poor measure on which to base the level of the "appropriate" countermeasure if they wished to create a property rule. The Arbitrators have chosen the level of the subsidy provided as the basis for the countermeasure (with, in some cases, an additional penalty). However, there is no clear or necessary connection between the level of the subsidy and incentives to comply (and, in *U.S. – FSC*, the Arbitrators never really considered the incentive effects of this level of countermeasure).[207] In some cases it could be higher than the level of benefit (judged either in terms of economic welfare or the political interests of officials) obtained by the subsidizing government. A high penalty would be desirable under a property rule, as the intention is to stop noncompliance.[208]

However, a level of penalty calibrated by reference to the size of the subsidy will often be too low – much lower than the level of benefits provided to the subsidizing country by the subsidy. In such a case, the countermeasure does not provide an incentive to comply and it becomes in effect a liability rule.[209] For example, in strategic trade theory, the subsidy may provide profit to the subsidized firm (and economic benefit to the subsidizing country) in excess of the subsidy.[210] In other cases, the subsidy may inflict economic harm on the subsidizing country as a whole but provide significant gain to the political interests of the government officials because of the benefit to a specific concentrated interest. The issue then becomes whether a series of retaliatory measures set at the level of the subsidy will sufficiently harm the political interests of the subsidizing government so as to end the subsidy. They may have such a result, particularly if the subsidizing country and the complaining country have a sufficiently large trade in the particular good such that the subsidized industry feels the full extent of the countermeasures. However, in cases where the countermeasures are levied

[207] Howse and Neven (2005), Trachtman (2006), and Spamann (2006).

[208] Spamann (2006), at 74 (stating that "[w]ith the current regime, it is hard to see what exactly it achieves, except generating huge suspension awards.") There may also be a concern that a high penalty violates the principle of proportionality in international law (Howse and Neven, 2005). See Bagwell (2007) (arguing that neither the broad prohibition on export subsidies nor the use of disproportionate remedies to back this prohibition is firmly supported by a terms of trade approach).

[209] See Trachtman (2006) and Schwartz and Sykes (2002) arguing that WTO rules are in effect liability rules, but see Pauwelyn (2006) arguing that WTO rules are property rules despite what appear, at first glance, to be low penalties.

[210] Spamann (2006).

because of subsidies to exports to third countries and/or the complaining member needs to impose countermeasures on other goods, the impact of the countermeasure will depend on the political interests that these countermeasures harm. There is no necessary reason to believe that in such a case the level of countermeasure will be sufficiently large so as to induce compliance.[211] As Howse and Neven point out, the more appropriate remedy in terms of a property rule would be the benefit to the subsidizing country, however measured.[212] Such a measure (assuming it is possible to quantify) would negate the incentive for noncompliance.

The insufficiency of the penalty would be exacerbated if the complaining party could only bring countermeasures to the extent that it was harmed (in some proportion to its trade with the subsidizing country, as the United States argued in *U.S. – FSC*).[213] In such a case, the strength of the complaining member's countermeasures will depend on the volume of trade between the complainant and the respondent. The Arbitrator's approach in *U.S. – FSC*, in contrast, entitles the complaining party to take countermeasures equal to the full subsidy even if it is not the only member that is harmed. Although there may be concerns about the basis of such an approach in international law,[214] it at least has the virtue of making it more likely that the penalty will be sufficiently large to induce compliance. There is, of course, the concern with WTO remedies that the complaining party may often not practically be able to impose sufficient harm where trade between the noncomplying country and the complaining country is not extensive and that the actual countermeasures themselves may harm the complaining country.[215]

However, there is a potential further concern with the current approach to "appropriate" countermeasures. Even if the penalty is sufficiently high to induce compliance with the prohibition, it may leave no scope for efficient breaches. Recall that a property rule leads to efficiency where the transaction costs are not too high to prevent bargaining.[216] If the transaction costs of bargaining around the prohibition are too high, then countries will never breach the prohibition. Transaction costs are not a concern to the extent that export subsidies are viewed as always inefficient from a global welfare perspective. However, as noted earlier

[211] See Nzelibe (2007) (examining remedies from a public choice perspective).

[212] Howse and Neven (2005), p. 115.

[213] See Trachtman (2006) (arguing for taking into account harm to all members).

[214] Howse and Neven (2005).

[215] Pauwelyn (2006), Spamann (2006) at 74 (stating "it is almost inconceivable that the retaliating Member will ever have all at once the ability, the economic incentive, and the need to use 'appropriate countermeasures' to 'skim off' the subsidy"), Nzelibe (2007), and Bronckers and Broek (2005). In terms of the harm to the complaining country, see Trachtman (2006) and Pauwelyn (2006), but see Bagwell (2007).

[216] Schwartz and Sykes (2002), but see Pauwelyn (2006) (citing arguments that an efficient breach approach is inappropriate for WTO rules) and Nzelibe (2007) (arguing that this measure of "harm" may be all that the WTO can obtain in an international setting without centralized enforcement).

in this chapter, Janow and Staiger argue that export subsidies may sometimes be efficient provided that the transaction costs are not too high for a country to respond to the export subsidies.[217] There may also be instances where, from the perspective of political officials, there may be a desire to allow noncompliance where there are large political gains that exceed the (political) harms caused in other countries.

The issue then becomes whether the transaction costs are too high in the context of export subsidies to allow efficient breach either from an economic welfare or political perspective. Howse and Neven argue that, in some cases, a property rule may bring about efficient breaches even in the absence of explicit bargaining, as the complaining party (or parties) may have an incentive to set the countermeasure high enough to provide it with the benefits of the countermeasures (such as political benefits from protecting certain industries) but not so high as to induce compliance (such that the complaining party continues to receive the benefits of the countermeasure).[218] Transaction costs do not appear to be low in the case of export subsidies for a number of reasons, including the potentially large number of parties sometimes involved and the ability of any of these countries to obtain a remedy for the full amount of the subsidy regardless of the extent to which they are harmed.[219] However, if, as Janow and Staiger argue, one of the reasons for the prohibition may be that the transaction costs of bargaining are too high to allow efficient adjustments for importing countries, these transaction costs may be reduced by the use of the WTO mechanism for countermeasures. Requiring the approval of the Arbitrator before any level of countermeasures can be imposed limits the ability of countries to be holdouts.[220] It sets an upper limit on the complaining countries' claims and defines the parties who are to be included in the negotiations.

If the desire is to permit globally efficient breach, the main alternative to a property rule would be to interpret "appropriate" countermeasures as a form of liability rule with the level of the remedy set at harm to other countries.[221] However, the arbitrators in the *U.S. – FSC* decision rejected the use of harm or injury as a basis for countermeasures.[222] Such a rule would allow for efficient buyout of compliance by the subsidizing country – that is, the government would subsidize when the benefits of the subsidy (in terms of either welfare or political interest) exceed the harm that the subsidy causes to others.[223] Using the level

[217] Janow and Staiger (2003) and Bagwell (2007).

[218] Howse and Neven (2005).

[219] See Green and Trebilcock (2007) for a discussion of the transaction costs of bargaining in the case of export subsidies.

[220] See Pauwelyn (2006) and Schwartz and Sykes (2002) discussing holdouts and liability rules in the international context.

[221] Trachtman (2006) and Pauwelyn (2007).

[222] Howse and Neven (2005).

[223] Note, however, that there are political economy concerns with this depiction, given that governments' decisions may reflect public choice concerns in terms of both who is paying for the penalty and who receives any compensation. See, for example, Nzelibe (2007) and Pauwelyn (2006).

of subsidy as the basis for countermeasures does not necessarily correspond to such expectation damages – that is, the harm from the breach of the agreement in terms of either economic welfare loss in other countries or harm to political interests of other governments. It may be larger than the harm in some cases (in which case it would overdeter efficient activities [whether efficiency is judged in terms of economic welfare or political interests]) and smaller than the harm in others (resulting in underdeterrence and fostering inefficient breach).[224]

The level of subsidy, however, is relatively easy to calculate. The harm caused by the subsidy would in contrast be very difficult for arbitrators to estimate.[225] From a global welfare perspective, the arbitrator would be required to estimate the impact of the subsidy on the markets in the complaining country as well as the harm in other, noncomplaining countries.[226] Moreover, to be complete, it would also require estimating the harm caused to the welfare of the subsidizing country (such as from the terms of trade effect). From a political economy perspective, the remedy should equate in at least a rough sense the harm the subsidy has imposed on other countries' governments in political terms. The subsidizing country would then assess its political benefits against the political costs it is imposing on other countries. The notion of "equivalent" concessions used as the basis of remedies for other violations of WTO agreements may correspond to this political harm.[227] In either case (welfarist or political), however, the arbitrators in all likelihood would have difficulty making such estimations yielding either excessive breach (if the estimate is too low) or deterrence of efficient breach (if the estimate is too high).[228] Furthermore, as noted above, there are concerns when the complaining country does not have sufficient trade with the subsidizing country to impose this level of damages and that, even if it did, the "compensatory" measures (countermeasures) would actually cause it harm rather than place it in the position it would have been in but for the subsidy (as is generally the case for a liability rule).[229]

As a result, the potential use by arbitrators of a property rule as a basis for "appropriate" countermeasures means that they do not face the potential costs

224 Trachtman (2006). Schwartz and Sykes (2002) p. S192, argue that, in the case of a complaint about a tariff, when the complaining party is able to withdraw substantially equivalent concessions, there is at least some connection between the costs and benefits of breach. However, the use of the level of subsidy does not appear to create any such connection.

225 See Spamann (2006) (discussing the difficulty in determining appropriate measures).

226 The harm can be seen in not just trade volumes but also importantly in the terms of trade effect. See Bagwell (2007) and Trachtman (2006).

227 Sykes and Schwartz (2002), pp. S187–S188.

228 Pauwelyn (2006), Spamann (2006), Bagwell (2007), and Pelzman and Shoham (2007).

229 Such concerns about the effectiveness of remedies for noncompliance with WTO obligations have led to a range of reform suggestions such as monetary compensation, auctioning of retaliation, and collective remedies. See, for example, Trachtman (2006), Pauwelyn (2006), Pelzman and Shoham (2007), Bronckers and Broek (2005), Bagwell (2007), and Nzelibe (2007). In the context of export subsidies, see Green and Trebilcock (2007).

of mistakes in estimating harm (as is the case for a liability rule) but are confronted with a potential lack of bargaining in the case of subsidies that are efficient (in terms of either economic welfare or political interests) and transaction costs of bargaining that are high.[230] In terms of a prisoners' dilemma explanation of the prohibition or the view that export subsidies are always inefficient, such a trade-off makes sense. Furthermore, bargaining (or at least efficient subsidies) may be possible under a property rule interpretation, allowing efficient breach in some cases. However, arbitrators have used total subsidy as the basis for the remedy that is inappropriate for a property rule, as in many cases it provides insufficient incentive to deter subsidies and potentially leads to excessive breach.

Unilateral Domestic Remedies

Countries harmed by export subsidies have an alternative remedial option under the SCM Agreement – the unilateral imposition of CVDs.[231] In fact, as Schwartz and Sykes note, unilateral domestic remedies have provided an important source for ensuring compliance with trade agreements.[232] If a country uses unilateral remedies, exporting countries may challenge their use before the WTO. Although Panels and the Appellate Body have reviewed many countervailing decisions, in none of these cases were CVDs imposed in response to an alleged export subsidy.

Challenges to countervailing measures may not involve export subsidies because there may be significant strategic advantages to treating a subsidy as an actionable subsidy instead of an export subsidy in such challenges. The SCM Agreement requires evidence of injury to the domestic industry (which is one form of adverse effects) for the imposition of CVDs, no matter what kind of subsidy is being countervailed.[233] Assuming that the country is in a position to countervail the subsidy, classifying it as export-contingent would carry the additional burden of having to prove export contingency. Classifying it as actionable, in contrast, leads to an additional requirement that the subsidy be "specific." Whether the complaining party will wish to proceed by classifying the subsidy as prohibited or actionable will depend in part on whether it is easier for the complaining country to obtain information about specificity than about export contingency in some cases. Furthermore, classifying a subsidy as actionable and imposing CVDs is not a workable solution in certain circumstances.

[230] Pauwelyn (2006) discusses some of the trade-offs in the choice of property rule versus liability rule, such as the difficulty in setting the proper remedy, flexibility, credible commitment, and stability.

[231] Michael J. Trebilcock and Robert Howse, *The Regulation of International Trade*, 3rd ed. (London/New York, Routledge, 2005) at 272. ("Countervailing duties may only be imposed in respect of actionable or prohibited subsidies as defined in the Agreement.")

[232] Schwartz and Sykes (2002), pp. S198–S200.

[233] Article 11.2(iv) of the SCM Agreement.

The additional requirement of specificity for actionable subsidies would prohibit countervailing broadly available export-contingent subsidies such as the American measures in the various *U.S. – FSC* cases.[234]

In addition, although there are drawbacks to the arbitration process, countries may not want to use unilateral domestic remedies in the case of export subsidies because of benefits provided by the arbitration process for countermeasures under the SCM Agreement. The drawbacks to the arbitration process include, for example, that it may take longer to impose a penalty by pursuing the WTO process than if the country imposes the penalty unilaterally. During the arbitration process, the complaining country will need to challenge the measure successfully and then seek arbitration of the appropriateness of the level of the countermeasure. In contrast, it has more control over how quickly it can invoke countervailing measures, although the time difference between domestic and multilateral remedies for export subsidies is reduced by an expedited procedure in the SCM Agreement for claims concerning prohibited subsidies. However, the benefit of the arbitration process may be that any remedy through this process is evaluated by a neutral third party before it is imposed.[235] This resort to a neutral third party before any imposition of a remedy may reduce the potential for retaliation by the subsidizing country. The subsidizing country can always challenge the countervailing measure before the WTO, but it may not wish to wait for a response before taking such retaliation.[236]

There is, however, another important difference between the unilateral and multilateral tracks – the size of the potential remedy is greater under the multilateral track. The amount of CVD allowed under WTO rules would be the same whether the subsidy is classified as actionable or prohibited.[237] Furthermore, the SCM Agreement sets an upper limit on CVDs at the amount of the subsidy found to exist and notes that it is "desirable" that the duty be lower if it would be sufficient to remove the injury.[238] Given that, as discussed above, "appropriate" countermeasure has been interpreted as the amount of the subsidy and may include an additional penalty for deliberate noncompliance, the upper limit on countermeasures is potentially higher than for CVDs.

Furthermore, and more importantly in many cases, CVDs may not even be a potential remedy. CVDs, unlike countermeasures authorized by the DSB, must

[234] In such a case, the subsidy could presumably be countervailed as a prohibited subsidy instead of an actionable one, although it seems difficult to imagine a country applying the single-product-centric countervailing procedures of the *SCM Agreement* on essentially every product it imports from the subsidizing country. In such a case, attacking the subsidy measure itself through the multilateral track would be more practical.

[235] Schwartz and Sykes (2002) and Pauwelyn (2006).

[236] The use of unilateral sanctions may not be constrained by reputational impact from other countries (i.e., other countries may not be able to sanction excessive countervailing measures) given that these other countries would have poor information about the harms of the subsidy or the legitimacy of the challenge. See Schwartz and Sykes (2002).

[237] Article 19.4 of the SCM Agreement.

[238] Article 19.2 of the SCM Agreement.

be imposed on the subsidized product.[239] For these CVDs to have an impact, the complaining country must be an importer of the subsidized good. In many cases, there is little trade in the subsidized products between the two parties. Instead, as in the case of the Canada–Brazil disputes involving regional aircraft, both parties' producers are rivals competing in larger third-country markets. Those third countries would be the ones able to impose effective CVDs. However, given that their consumers benefit from the export subsidies and that they typically lack a significant domestic industry in that sector, these countries would have nothing to gain from doing so. In addition, under the multilateral track, if the subsidy is not withdrawn, the complaining country is able to impose countermeasures on *any* goods it imports from the subsidizing country. However, CVDs may be imposed only on the subsidized product and, even then, only to the extent that those imported products are causing injury.[240]

This increased retaliatory ability through the use of countermeasures presumably increases the likelihood of withdrawal of the export subsidy. Furthermore, unlike actionable subsidies, where removing the adverse effects of the subsidies is enough, the SCM Agreement requires the withdrawal of the export subsidies. Although countries do not necessarily always do so, they may suffer a reputational impact from not withdrawing the subsidy, which may add to the incentive to eliminate the subsidy.[241] These differences in the size of the remedy (as well as potentially the decreased risk for retaliation) may have led members to rely more on the multilateral response than unilateral responses to export subsidies.

Conclusion

The rules relating to export subsidies have been, and continue to be, the subject of numerous disputes. The design of the requirement and the remedy involves trade-offs involving such factors as the costs of promulgation, information, enforcement, error, and bargaining. To allow optimal flexibility (including in some cases no flexibility), the trade-offs across these costs must be considered as well as the nature of the institutions that make decisions under each alternative.[242] A simple ban on export subsidies as currently exists may give rise to inefficiencies. Flexibility to reach efficient solutions could come from a more complex rule or standard. However, it will be costly (particularly considering

[239] Articles 19.3 and 19.4 of the SCM Agreement.

[240] Article 19.3 of the SCM Agreement.

[241] For a discussion of reputation, see, for example, Sykes and Schwartz (2002) and Trachtman (2007).

[242] These costs are relevant across all measures. For example, tariffs may also raise trade-offs favoring a ban, although other costs (such as adjustment and political economy costs) may be sufficiently large to support a more flexible rule. Reciprocity in negotiating tariff reductions and gradualism in phasing in the reductions may be a means of moderating these adjustment and political economy costs.

information costs and competency) for either the WTO members as a whole to set a sufficiently complex rule or the Panels or Appellate Body to set an appropriate standard. Flexibility could also come through the form of the remedy. The current prospective remedy is not optimal, as it permits short-term breach at no cost, thereby increasing the use of inefficient subsidies. As the *ex post* costs of bargaining in the case of export subsidies are likely high (particularly under the current rules), a liability rule may be preferable to a property rule. To achieve a reasonable valuation cost, the liability rule should be based on trade effects, as is the case for other violations. Such a rule would at least be an improvement over the current rule setting the remedy at the level of subsidies, which is both over- and underinclusive.[243]

What does this lack of clarity and interpretation of countermeasures mean for the continued use of subsidies by members? The current dispute between the United States and the EC about subsidies to commercial aircraft illustrates the ongoing problem. The U.S. government, for example, claims that the EC provided (and is providing) subsidies or "launch aid" to support in the design and development of Airbus aircraft that would not be commercially viable without the aid.[244] The definition of "subsidy" in the SCM Agreement is broad enough to capture the provision of most types of financial aid that the United States claims that the EC has provided to Airbus, including provision of interest at below-market rates (with no requirement to repay the financing if the aircraft is not successful) and financing through the European Investment Bank to Airbus for "large aircraft design, development and other purposes" (including for the A380).[245]

The issue of *de facto* contingency may be more contentious. The current contextual approach makes it easier to prove that there has been *de facto* contingency, but there remains a lack of clarity in what actually is required for a showing of *de facto* contingency. In particular, the export-orientedness of the industry is one factor (but not the sole factor) to take into account in determining whether the subsidy is "tied to" exports. It is unclear, however, what other factors are to be taken into account or how "export oriented" an industry must be for this factor to be a dominant consideration.

The remedy for the United States will prove even more difficult assuming it can prove that there have been prohibited subsidies. First, given the prospective nature of the remedy, any subsidies that have already been granted by the time of the decision will not be required to be withdrawn. The aid that the EC has

243 Green and Trebilcock (2007).

244 *European Communities and Certain Member States – Measures Affecting Trade in Large Civil Aircraft* (Request for Panel) (2005) WT/DS316/2, p. 1 and *European Communities and Certain Member States – Measures Affecting Trade in Large Civil Aircraft* (Request for Panel) (2006) WT/DS316/6.

245 *European Communities and Certain Member States – Measures Affecting Trade in Large Civil Aircraft* (Request for Panel) (2005) WT/DS316/2, pp. 2 and 4.

given in terms of development of new models may therefore already have been provided and not subject to any countermeasures. The main exception would be any preexisting commitments made by the EC which, as noted above, the EC would not be permitted to fulfill. In any event, the return of already-provided subsidies is not likely politically realistic given the competitiveness of the civil aircraft industry and the significant negative political effects that the repayment of subsidies would likely entail.[246]

Second, for the ongoing subsidies, if the EC refuses to withdraw the subsidies, the United States can apply to impose "appropriate countermeasures." As noted earlier in the text, these countermeasures would likely be set at the level of the total subsidy. This level of penalty may not be sufficient to induce the EC to eliminate its subsidies given the potential benefits from financing the civil aircraft industry. The benefits of the subsidy can be large, as "the civil aircraft industry remains a catalyst of economic growth and competitiveness, both because it provides a lot of high paying jobs, and because it exhibits leading-edge technological spillovers that benefit other sectors."[247] The United States may therefore impose countermeasures on the EC but not bring about its hoped-for elimination of the subsidies. Although in some cases the total level of subsidy will be very large and therefore provide an inducement to eliminate the export subsidies, it may be the case that that remedy would be insufficient in the case of subsidies to an industry such as civil aircraft with large spillovers. A penalty geared to the benefit to the subsidizing country from the subsidy would be more likely to induce compliance.

The existing rules on remedies may therefore not address the prisoners' dilemma problem that appears to lie at the heart of the prohibition of export subsidies, nor do they prevent export subsidies to the extent that they are globally inefficient. They may encourage large, up-front subsidies such as launch aid that can be provided (and can provide strategic benefits) before the WTO can hear a complaint. The existing remedies cannot affect these subsidies. The countermeasures may be sufficiently punitive to encourage the parties to negotiate a new agreement on the financing of civil aircraft.[248] In such a case, the parties may bargain to an efficient solution on export subsidies. However, given the low level of the penalty, the bargaining may result in the subsidizing countries having more bargaining power (the complaining party having a lower threat point) than would be the case with a more appropriate level of penalty (i.e., a penalty tied at least to the adverse trade effects from the subsidy). Panels and the Appellate Body will need to rethink the remedies issue to find a better solution to the ongoing problems and disputes surrounding export subsidies.

[246] On the competitiveness of the civil aircraft industry, see Marc L. Busch, "Testimony to the House Aviation Subcommittee" (May 25, 2005) (http://www.aei.org/events/eventID.1356/event_detail.asp, last accessed August 2006).

[247] Busch (2005), p. 1.

[248] Busch (2005).

KYLE W. BAGWELL AND PETROS C. MAVROIDIS

4.1 *Too Much, Too Little... Too Late?*

In this short chapter, we advance some preliminary thoughts on the level of pitching (neither over- nor underregulate) in the World Trade Organization (WTO) Agreement on Subsidies and Countervailing Measures (SCM Agreement). The existing regime goes, to our mind, too far toward disciplining subsidies, in particular through the absolute prohibition on the use of export subsidies. In contrast, trading partners might lose the incentive to continue negotiating trade liberalization if recourse to subsidies is not regulated at all: Through subsidies, trading nations might undo the benefit granted to their trading partners in the form of tariff concessions. Something needs to be done, but what is being done is inappropriate. A legislative amendment is, to our mind, warranted, and the remaining question is whether, from a policy perspective, this is the most appropriate moment in time to start advancing thoughts in this context.

Too Much

The WTO SCM, as it now stands,[249] distinguishes between prohibited and actionable subsidies. The distinction is, *inter alia*, functional because different remedies are associated with each form: Whereas prohibited subsidies must be withdrawn (Article 4 of the SCM), it might suffice that actionable subsidies be adjusted (Article 5 of the SCM). The severity of the remedy becomes more obvious in case of nonimplementation (e.g., in case a prohibited subsidy is not withdrawn, or an actionable subsidy has not been adjusted). A WTO Member that has not adjusted an actionable subsidy might face countermeasures up to the level of the injury it has caused to its trading partners. The injury would, typically, cover the trade lost by the nonsubsidizing WTO Members to the subsidizing

[249] The provision for nonactionable subsidies (Article 8 of the SCM Agreement) was of transitional value. Because WTO Members did not renew it, it has expired (Article 31 of the SCM Agreement).

partner. In the case where a prohibited subsidy has been granted, though, the subsidizing Member could face countermeasures up to the level of the subsidy paid. On occasion, such countermeasures could be substantially higher than the injury suffered by the complainant. This has been arguably the case in the *United States – Foreign Sales Corporations (U.S. – FSC)* litigation, where the European Union was awarded the right to impose countermeasures exceeding four billion dollars against the United States.[250]

Does it make sense to provide such rigid remedies? Some research in economics suggests that there are good reasons why this should not be the case. Consider first subsidies to domestic production. As Bagwell and Staiger (2006) discuss, a domestic production subsidy can be a "first-best" instrument with which to address market failures that result in underproduction; furthermore, severe restrictions on domestic production subsidies may have a "chilling" effect on the willingness of governments to make tariff concessions. Intuitively, if governments are unable to stimulate domestic production with a subsidy, then they may attempt to achieve this goal by setting a high import tariff. Such a policy substitution would be unfortunate, because a domestic production subsidy is a more efficient instrument with which to stimulate domestic production.

Consider second export subsidies. When a country offers an export subsidy, the world price of its export good is lowered. It is thus sometimes argued that the importing country should send a "note of thanks" for the opportunity to consume the export good on more favorable terms. Of course, a complete assessment of an export subsidy must also recognize the harm that the consequent lower world price imposes on firms from other exporting countries. The famous Brander–Spencer model of strategic trade policy is useful here.[251] In this model, there are two exporting countries, and each exporting country has one firm. All consumers reside in a third country. If a country offers an export subsidy to its firm, the world price of the export good falls; consequently, the consumers in the third country benefit and the rival exporting firm loses. In this model, however, the chosen export subsidy results in an overall gain to economic efficiency. The reason is that the market was initially distorted, because of the market power and consequent low output that is associated with a duopolistic market structure. An export subsidy results in an increase in overall production, pushing the market output level closer to the competitive ideal.[252] Our intention here is not to claim that all export subsidies should be encouraged; rather, we simply observe that the net effect of an export subsidy on global economic efficiency may be positive

[250] U.S. exports to the European Union – 27 EU Members amounted to 214 billion dollars, and imports 333 billion dollars in 2005.

[251] See Brander and Spencer (1985).

[252] A similar point can be made when the market is initially distorted because of the presence of an import tariff. In this case, an appropriate export subsidy could offset the import tariff and result in a more efficient trade volume.

when a preexisting distortion is present. This observation calls into question the wisdom of a blanket prohibition on the use of export subsidies.

It is also relevant to compare the treatment of subsidies and tariffs. In particular, one might legitimately ask the following question: Why should the framers punish subsidies so severely while allowing tariffs? An export subsidy expands trade and benefits foreign consumers, whereas an import tariff restricts trade and harms foreign exporters. It is not clear why an export subsidy should be prohibited while an import tariff is negotiable. Similarly, when a country raises its import tariff, it may face countermeasures in the event that its applied tariff exceeds the bound tariff rate to which it agreed in a previous negotiation; by contrast, a domestic subsidy may be actionable, even if the subsidizing country did not previously negotiate a bound tariff rate on the product in question. In this respect, it is not clear why domestic subsidies should be treated more severely than import tariffs. This puzzle gets more complicated when it is recalled that a domestic production subsidy can be a first-best instrument with which to address market failures that lead to insufficient production.

Too Little

The analysis in the previous section suggests that the framers of the SCM may have overshot by placing such severe disciplines on subsidies. Should they have stayed idle and done nothing? Indeed, some authors have hinted that such should be the regulatory output, in light of the difficulty in defining what a subsidy is, not to mention the problems posed by the specificity requirement.[253] First do no harm is, in essence, what this trend in literature suggests.

The problem with this approach is that subsidies can act as a concession-erosion instrument. Suppose that country A promises a maximum tariff of 10 percent on imports of wheat into its market. Subsequently, country A pays a hefty subsidy to its own producers of wheat, and as a result, firms in country B cannot export wheat to country A anymore. Country B, however, has "paid" for county A's concession on wheat by promising to lower its own tariff on products of export interest to county A. Besides fairness-type arguments, country B might have little incentive to continue negotiating with country A if it anticipates that country A might behave similarly in the future with respect to other product markets. Some discipline on the use of domestic production subsidies is thus needed to insure that the value of (negotiated) concessions will not be eroded over time. Insurance against concession erosion, in turn, provides trading partners with the continued incentive to negotiate and lower tariffs. We thus conclude that some disciplines on subsidies are needed to protect the value of negotiated tariff concessions.[254]

[253] See, on this score, the analysis in Sykes (2003).
[254] See Bagwell et al. (2002).

Too Late (?)

What we have suggested so far is that something needs to be done to discipline subsidies, but probably too much has already been done. What we would suggest is a twofold strategy.

(i) On the one hand, WTO Members should get rid of the absolute prohibition for some types of subsidies. This would require a legislative amendment;
(ii) On the other hand, they could stick to what we already know as a remedy: nonviolation complaints (NVC). An alternative approach that might warrant further consideration would be for WTO Members to adopt the farm products liberalization model for all subsidies, and start negotiating volumes of subsidies for particular product markets.

Is a legislative amendment feasible? Probably this is not the best time to add to the negotiating agenda. In light of the difficulties that the Doha Round is currently experiencing, the world trading system will be better served if items were removed rather than added to the existing agenda. At this stage of the game, a legislative amendment concerning subsidies deserves attention but is not the highest priority issue. By the same token, exporting the farm products liberalization model is too ambitious a proposal at this point in time.

It seems to us that keeping NVC as the sole response to subsidies (beyond imposition of countervailing duties [CVDs]) is an adequate response. WTO Members that might lose market access[255] as a result of payment of subsidies will be in a position to request compensation for such losses. At the same time, WTO Members that do not wish to counteract subsidies will be in a position to benefit from lower prices.

REFERENCES

Bagwell, K., P. C. Mavroidis, and R. W. Staiger. 2002. "It Is All About Market Access." *American Journal of International Law* 96:56–76.
Bagwell, K., and R. W. Staiger. 2006. "Will International Rules on Subsidies Disrupt the World Trading System?" *American Economic Review* 96:877–895.
Brander, J., and B. Spencer. 1985. "Export Subsidies and International Market Share Rivalry." *Journal of International Economics* 18:83–100.
Sykes, A. O. 2003. "The Economics of the WTO Rules on Subsidies and Countervailing Measures." John M. Olin program in Law & Economics Working Papers, No. 186, University of Chicago.

[255] As we argue in another article, market-access concerns are the dominant motivation for WTO members to adhere to the multilateral trading system. See Bagwell, Mavroidis, and Staiger (2002).

PIET JAN SLOT

5 The Boeing–Airbus Dispute: A Case for the Application of the European Community State Aid Rules?

Introduction

World Trade Organization (WTO) rules do not require that local remedies be exhausted before a complaint can be brought before the Dispute Settlement Body (DSB). Nevertheless it may be interesting to ponder whether it would be possible, or have been possible at an appropriate moment, for Boeing, or one of its subsidiaries, to bring a complaint with the European Community (EC) Commission alleging the granting of incompatible state aid by EC member states. To answer this question, it is necessary to discuss the relevant EC state aid rules. In addition, it will also be interesting to see whether the EC Commission has ever taken any action against individual state measures granting aid to the Airbus companies or one of its subsidiaries or suppliers. These rules will be described in the second section of this chapter.

The analysis of the compatibility of state aid measures normally can be properly undertaken only if we have a thorough knowledge of the company structure of Boeing; in particular, we want to know whether Boeing has subsidiaries or important suppliers in the EC (this seems likely). The following quote from the front page of Boeing's Web site illustrates this point:

> Headquartered in Chicago, Illinois, U.S.A., Boeing employs more than 155,000 people in some 67 countries. This represents one of the most diverse, talented and innovative workforces anywhere. More than 83,800 of our people hold college degrees – including nearly 29,000 advanced degrees – in virtually every business and technical field from approximately 2,800 colleges and universities worldwide. Our enterprise also leverages the talents of hundreds of thousands more skilled people working for Boeing suppliers worldwide.[1]

[1] http://www.boeing.com/companyoffices/aboutus/.

Thus we may assume that Boeing has subsidiaries in the EC that could be considered competitors of Airbus or its subsidiaries or suppliers.[2]

Another point concerns the alleged subsidies. As can be seen from the Request for Consultation by the United States,[3] the list forwarded by the U.S. government includes a large number of aid measures granted by governments of European Union (EU) Member states and local authorities as well as the European Investment Bank.[4] I will limit my contribution to a discussion of the *state aid measures* (which means that I will only discuss financial contributions by governments, whether central or local).

EC State Aids Law

Introduction

Article 87 of the EC, which lays down the substantive rules on state aid, and Article 88 of the EC, which provides for the procedural rules, form part of the chapter on competition in the EC Treaty. These rules have been supplemented by secondary legislation.

There are several important pieces of such legislation. The first is Regulation 994/98/EC applying Articles 87 and 88 of the EC.[5] The gist of the Regulation is that the Commission is authorized to adopt block exemptions for certain categories of aid. On this basis the Commission has adopted a number of regulations, which will be discussed later in this chapter.

The most important regulation on procedure is Regulation 659/99/EC, which lays down detailed rules for the application of Article 88 of the EC.[6] The regulation is largely a codification of the case law of the Court of Justice and the Court of First Instance (CFI). In recent years, the substantive rules have been developed in the case law of the Court of Justice and the CFI as well as in a number of Commission documents called guidelines, frameworks, notifications, or communications.[7] These rules have been further developed in the many decisions given by the Commission in individual cases.

[2] Even if Boeing had not had subsidiaries in the EC, it would have been easy for it to "set up shop"; in other words, establish a subsidiary in the EC that would allow Boeing to be treated as an EC company, according to Article 48 of the EC Treaty.

[3] See the complaint in the electronic document.

[4] Footnote 3 of the document notes that the complaint does not include EIB financing to airline customers for the purchase of new aircraft.

[5] [1998] OJ L141/1.

[6] [1999] OJ L83/1.

[7] *Cf.* Commission, *Competition Law in the European Communities, Vol. II: Rules applicable to State Aids, Situation at 31 December 1994*, Brussels, 1995. The terminology is not very consistent: The central feature of all of these rules is that they are not adopted on the basis of an article in the Treaty or secondary legislation.

Material Principles

The structure of Article 87 of the EC requires a systematic analysis of the different elements contained in this chapter. The following four criteria must be satisfied to establish a contravention of Article 87: The existence of "state aid" must be shown, it must operate in a "selective" manner, and there must be an effect on competition as well as on trade between the Member States. We will now examine each of these criteria in turn.

The Concept of "State Aid"

The Treaty is silent on the matter of definition, but the case law of the Court of Justice has made it clear that the concept of "aid" is wider than that of a subsidy.[8] The definition is in fact very wide. The outer limit was defined in *Sloman Neptune*[9]: Only benefits granted directly or indirectly from state resources are to be regarded as a state aid. In its *PreussenElektra* judgment, the Court held that the charges levied by the state on particular companies to finance environmental objectives were not to be treated as state aid measures.[10] Nevertheless, this still leaves a broad range of benefits covered by the scope of Article 87 of the EC: direct subsidies, interest subsidies, low interest loans, interest-free loans, capital injections, grants, asset revaluation, compensation for government-imposed financial burdens, the foregoing of recovery of sums due, preferential terms, price reductions, public supply contracts, reduction in social security charges, state guarantees, state participation in capital tax concessions, and the foregoing of state revenue.

The aid must be effected by a Member State or through state resources. An example of the latter is the preferential tariff accorded to the fertilizer industry by the Dutch gas company, Gasunie.[11]

Selectivity

The prohibition of Article 87 of the EC does not apply if all undertakings within a Member State benefit from assistance, without any distinction being made between them. General measures of economic policy, such as the lowering of the tax rate applicable to corporate profits, are outside the scope of Article 87 of the EC.

[8] Case 30/59 *De Gezamenlijke Steenkolenmijnen in Limburg v. High Authority of the ECSC* [1961] ECR 1, at 19, recently confirmed in Case C-387/92 *Banco de Crédito Industrial SA, now Banco Exterior de España SA v. Ayuntamiento de Valencia* [1994] ECR I-877.

[9] Cases C-72/91 and C-73/91 *Sloman Neptune* [1993] ECR I-887.

[10] Case C-379/98 *PreussenElektra AG v. Schleswag AG* [2001] ECR I-2099. The important point to note about this judgment is that it is generally assumed that the Court's decision would have been different had the undertakings concerned been owned or controlled by the state, whether by the central government or the local government.

[11] Case 67/85 *Kwekerij Gebroeders van der Kooy BV and others* v *Commission* [1988] ECR 219.

The distinction between general and specific measures is not always easy to apply. Thus, the Italian reduction in the rate of social security contributions was deemed to constitute a state aid because it specifically benefited the Italian textile industry.[12] The Italian government claimed that the reduction was only restoring the competitive position of the textile industry because the textile industry employed a very high percentage of female workers, which created a situation whereby the contributions for the social security system exceeded the benefits.[13]

Effect upon Competition and Trade between Member States

The granting of benefits must result in a distortion of competition to be caught by Article 87(1) of the EC. For this purpose, it is necessary to consider whether the aid strengthens the position of the beneficiary enterprise compared with other enterprises operating in the same line of trade.[14] It is, however, not necessary for the Commission to produce a fully fledged analysis of the relevant product and geographical market along the lines of the analysis required by Article 81 and especially Article 82 of the EC.[15] Nevertheless, the Commission must produce something more than a statement that competition has been or may be distorted.[16] The Court of Justice has so far not endorsed a *de minimis* rule, which would require a minimum effect of the measure. Nevertheless, the Commission will have to show that the aid will have an impact on trade between the Member States.[17]

The *de minimis* rule has now found a legal basis in Article 2 of Regulation 994/98/EC and in the block exemption Regulation on *de minimis* aid.[18]

It should further be noted that in practice, the effects on competition and those on trade between the Member States will almost always coincide. It is therefore common practice to use these two concepts interchangeably even though there is a theoretical difference.

[12] Case 173/73 *Italy* v *Commission* [1974] ECR 709.

[13] The benefits of Italian social security were based on the needs of the family of the worker, and the contributions were levied on the basis of the wage costs of each company. The Italian textile sector had a disproportionately low percentage of male workers who could claim such benefits as head of a family. As a result, the textile industry was paying substantially more to the system than the benefits its male workers received.

[14] Case 730/79 *Philip Morris Holland BV v. Commission* [1980] ECR 2671.

[15] See Cases C-72/91 and C-73/91 *Sloman Neptune* [1993] ECR I-887.

[16] Cases 296 and 318/82 *The Netherlands and Leeuwarder Papierwarenfabriek BV v. Commission* [1985] ECR 824. For the United Kingdom's Office of Fair Trading (OFT)'s suggestions on how to use an economic approach to address the question of the distortion of competition caused by state aid, see its recent proposals in *European state aid control* (OFT 821) (November 23, 2005) (available on the internet at: http://www.oft.govuk/NR/rdonlyres/F346B4FF-4C97–4970-BD95–70E9EB56ADBE/0/OFT821.pdf) (last visited December 31, 2005).

[17] Case 248/84 *Germany v. Commission* [1987] ECR 4013.

[18] Regulation 69/2001/EC [2001] OJ L10/30.

NB. It is important for the purposes of this chapter to note that neither the criterion "effect on trade between the Member States nor the effect on competition" would seem to constitute a bar to challenging state aids by Boeing or its subsidiaries or suppliers.

The "Market Economy Investor Principle"[19]

Many state aid cases involve aid to public companies. In such cases it is sometimes difficult to distinguish between "normal financial contributions" by the owner (i.e., the state) and aid. An important concept to enable the Commission to distinguish between benefits granted by governments that are prohibited by Article 87(1) of the EC and those that are not is the market economy investor principle. The concept was especially developed in the context of government participation in the capital of enterprises.[20] According to this principle, government actions that take place under market conditions and terms do not give rise to the application of Article 87(1). If the provision of funds by the state has been made subject to certain conditions that would also have been required by a private investor, such action will not be considered to amount to a grant of aid.

The market economy investor principle has become an important instrument to discriminate between lawful and unlawful government assistance. In its communication of October 1991 on the application of what are now Articles 87 and 88 of the EC and Article 5 of Commission Directive 80/723/EEC to public enterprises in the manufacturing sector, the Commission has clarified matters further.[21] It is not the intention of the Commission to replace the investor's judgment. It recognizes that the investor has a wide margin of judgment. Only when there are no objective justifications for the investment will the Commission consider Article 87(1) of the EC to be applicable. In the recent *Chronopost* judgment, the Court held that, where the principle is applied to a company that performs services of public importance, the relevant comparison that must be made is with the cost price of the performance of those services by *that* company and not with that of a company in the market sector.[22]

NB. The market economy investor principle may also be relevant in the context of subsidies to the Airbus industry or its affiliates because many companies are wholly or partially owned by governments. This was precisely the argument forwarded by the Spanish government in the decision of 97/807.[23]

19 For recent trenchant criticism of this principle and its application, see Parish, "On the Private Investor Principle" 28 *European Law Review* 2003, 70.

20 Cases 296 and 318/82 *Leeuwarder Papierwarenfabriek*: note 16, above.

21 [1991] OJ C273/2. The Commission's notice was annulled by the European Court of Justice in Case C-325/91 *France v. Commission* [1993] ECR I-3283. The Commission has incorporated the rules in a further Directive, amending Directive 80/723: [1993] OJ L254/16.

22 Cases C-83, 93 and 94/01 P *Chronopost SA v. Ufex* [2003] ECR I-6993.

23 See the electronic document.

Exceptions

When a government measure granting certain benefits meets the conditions of Article 87(1) of the EC, it is incompatible with the common market. It can then only be exempted by the provisions of Article 87(2) or 87(3) of the EC or the provisions of Articles 73 or 86(2) of the EC. Assuming that the financial benefit in question *does* qualify as a state aid, there are still means to exempt such aid from the prohibition of the EC Treaty, which we discuss in the following text.

(i) Aid that is compatible with the Common Market, Article 87(2) of the EC:

This provision provides for three categories of aid which *shall* be compatible with the Common Market. The word "shall" is taken to imply that the Commission does not enjoy a discretion to decide whether the exemption applies. Similar wording is used in Article 73 of the EC. I will omit a discussion of these provisions because they are not relevant to our topic.

(ii) Aid that may be compatible with the Common Market, Article 87(3) of the EC:

This provision lists four categories of aid that, in the discretion of the Commission, may be exempted. It is important to note that this provision, as an exemption from the general principles of the Treaty, has been interpreted in a restrictive manner. Thus in its judgment in *Philip Morris*,[24] the Court of Justice supported the Commission interpretation according to which state aids can be allowed only to the extent that they are necessary for the achievement of objectives accepted under Article 87(3) of the EC.

In summary, the requirements are as follows:

(i) The aid must promote or further a project that is in the Community interest as a whole.
(ii) The aid must be necessary for the achievement of this result, and the objective could not have been obtained in the absence of this measure.
(iii) The duration, intensity, and scope of the aid must be proportionate to the importance of the intended result.[25]

The second element has been specified by the Commission as follows:

> State aids are in principle incompatible with the common market. The discretionary power of the Commission should only be exercised when the aids proposed by Member States contribute to the achievement of the Community objectives and interest set out in Article 87(3). The national interest of a Member State or the benefits obtained by the recipient of the aid in contributing to the national interest do not by themselves justify the positive exercise of the Commission's discretionary powers.

[24] Case 730/79 *Philip Morris Holland BV v. Commission* [1980] ECR 2671.

[25] See the Commission's 12th Report on Competition Policy (1983), para. 160.

The Court of Justice accepted the validity of the compensatory justification principle in its *Philip Morris* judgment. These principles of interpretation have strengthened the Commission's hand considerably.

It is only relatively recently that block exemptions have been enacted to clarify the above outlined exemptions. Regulation 994/98/EC, applying Articles 87 and 88 of the EC, authorizes the Commission to adopt block exemptions for certain categories of aid.

To provide guidance as to how it will apply the exemptions of Article 87(3) of the EC, the Commission has traditionally published guidelines, codes, frameworks, communications, and notifications. Although the designations are not consistent, these instruments all serve the same purpose. They can be classified as rules for sectoral,[26] general or specific, regional, and other horizontal aid.[27] For the purpose of this chapter, the Community framework for State aid for research and development (R&D) is important.[28]

NB. The Commission applied this framework in decision 97/807, the case of aid of the Spanish government.[29]

Procedural Rules, Article 88 of the EC and Regulation 659/99/EC

Introduction

The procedural rules are embodied in Regulation 659/99/EC, which has been developed by Regulation 794/2004/EC. The latter Regulation includes a notification form for new aid.

Chapter VI defines the rights of interested parties: These include (among others) the intended beneficiaries and complainants, which will usually be competitors.

Article 88 of the EC reads as follows:

> 1. The Commission shall, in cooperation with Member States, keep under constant review all systems of aid existing in those States. It shall propose to the latter any appropriate measures required by the progressive development or by the functioning of the common market.
>
> 2. If, after giving notice to the parties concerned to submit their comments, the Commission finds that aid granted by a State or through State resources is not compatible with the common market having regard to Article 87, or that such aid is being misused, it shall decide that the State concerned shall abolish or alter such aid within a period of time to be determined by the Commission. If the State concerned does not comply with this decision

26 In 1998, the Commission published a single text of its guidelines on regional aid [1998] OJ C74/9. It also published a multisectoral framework on regional aid for large investment projects, [1998] OJ C107/7.

27 Examples of the latter are rules for R&D and environmental protection aid.

28 OJ 1996 C 45, pp. 5–6; OJ 1998, C 48, p. 2; OJ 2001, C 78, p. 24; OJ 2002, C 111, p. 3; OJ 2005, C 310, p. 10.

29 See electronic document.

> within the prescribed time, the Commission or any other interested State may, in derogation from the provisions of Articles 226 and 227, refer the matter to the Court of Justice direct.
>
> On application by a Member State, the Council may, acting unanimously, decide that aid which that State is granting or intends to grant shall be considered to be compatible with the common market, in derogation from the provisions of Article 87 or from the regulations provided for in Article 89, if such a decision is justified by exceptional circumstances. If, as regards the aid in question, the Commission has already initiated the procedure provided for in the first subparagraph of this paragraph, the fact that the State concerned has made its application to the Council shall have the effect of suspending that procedure until the Council has made its attitude known.
>
> If, however, the Council has not made its attitude known within three months of the said application being made, the Commission shall give its decision on the case.
>
> 3. The Commission shall be informed, in sufficient time to enable it to submit its comments, of any plans to grant or alter aid. If it considers that any such plan is not compatible with the common market having regard to Article 87, it shall without delay initiate the procedure provided for in Paragraph 2.
>
> The Member State concerned shall not put its proposed measures into effect until this procedure has resulted in a final decision.

It is of the greatest importance for an understanding of this area of law to draw a distinction between *existing aid* (para. 7.4.3.2) and *new aid* (para. 7.4.3.3). Control of existing aid takes place *ex post*, whereas new aid is controlled *ex ante*.

Existing Aid

According to Article 88(1) of the EC, aid existing in Member States must be kept under constant review by the Commission. According to Article 18 of the Regulation, the Commission proposes measures to the Member States if the aid is not or is no longer compatible with the Common Market. Member States shall be bound by the Commission's proposals if they accept them. If the Member State does not accept the proposals, the Commission is entitled to proceed with the formal examination procedure of Article 88(2) of the EC. This procedure is examined later in this chapter. Existing aid is defined in Article 1 of the Regulation. The most important categories are aid that has been authorized by the Commission, aid applied in a Member State before the entry into force of the EC Treaty,[30] or before accession of a new Member State.

[30] An example can be found in Case C-44/93 *Namur-Les Assurances du Crédit SA v. Office National du Ducroire and Belgium* [1994] ECR I-3829. This case also demonstrates how difficult it can be to draw the distinction between the two categories.

Existing aid cannot be challenged in national courts. However, such aid can be challenged by bringing a complaint to the Commission.

New Aid

New aid, in other words, any plans to grant or alter aid, must, under Article 88(3) of the EC, be notified to the Commission in sufficient time to enable the Commission to communicate its comments. Regulation 794/2004/EC (referred to as "the Regulation" in what follows) includes in its Annex I the necessary notification form. Its Article 4 also provides that

> [a]n alteration to existing aid shall mean any change, other than modifications of a purely formal or administrative nature which cannot affect the evaluation of the compatibility of the aid measure with the common market. However an increase in the original budget of an existing aid scheme by up to 20% shall not be considered an alteration to existing aid.

As a result, such small changes need no longer be notified as "new" aid; Article 4 goes on to subject alterations to existing aid outside this definition to a simplified notification procedure (using the form included in Annex II of the Regulation). These aids concern budget increases greater than 20%, the prolongation of an existing aid scheme by up to six years, and any tightening of the criteria for application of an authorized aid scheme.

On the basis of Article 88(3) of the EC, the Commission may, after summary examination, either conclude that the aid is compatible with the Common Market or open the procedure provided for in Article 88(2) of the EC. This is called the preliminary examination procedure specified in Article 4 of the Regulation. New aid that has not been notified may, according to the last sentence of Article 88(3), not be put into effect until this procedure; in other words, the procedure of Article 88(3) and/or Article 88(2) of the EC, has resulted in a final decision. This is called the "standstill clause."

The last sentence of Article 88(3) of the EC has direct effect. New aid within the scope of the block exemptions referred to earlier in text does not have to be notified.[31]

Under the preliminary procedure, the Commission has a period of two months to make up its mind. If it finds that the aid is compatible with the Common Market, it will inform the Member States concerned accordingly. Such a decision may be reviewed by the CFI.[32] Judgments of the CFI may be appealed to the Court of Justice on points of law only.

[31] The block exemption regulations oblige the Member States to forward a summary of the aid they provided under these regulations.

[32] This may be intended beneficiary of the aid or a competitor that manifested itself clearly, Case C-198/91 *William Cook plc v. Commission* [1993] ECR I-2487. Until April 2004, appeals by Member States were reviewed by the ECJ.

If the Commission is of the opinion that it needs more time to complete the review of the state aid, it must open the procedure of Article 88(2) of the EC. The decision to open the Article 88(2) of the EC procedure is a contestable act within the meaning of Article 230 of the EC.[33]

If the Commission fails to act, the Member State concerned may, according to Article 4(6) of the Regulation, implement the aid after giving notice to the Commission. The aid then becomes an existing aid.[34]

The Article 88(2) of the EC procedure is laid down in Articles 6 and 7 of the Regulation. It is called the "formal investigation procedure." It is a contentious procedure, which means that the parties concerned may submit comments. The Commission will publish a notice in the *C Series of the Official Journal of the EC*, describing the aid plans and inviting comments. In practice, it is quite common for Member States, beneficiaries and interested parties, competitors, as well as trade associations to provide comments. Such comments strengthen the hand of the Commission considerably. The comments will be submitted to the Member State concerned.

It is important to note that Boeing, its subsidiaries, or its suppliers can bring and/or could have submitted comments in EC state aid procedures.

According to Article 7(6) of the Regulation, the Commission has eighteen months for adopting a decision. If that period has lapsed, the Member State concerned can request the Commission to make a decision within two months. This brings the total time for the Commission under this procedure to twenty months. The combination of the two procedures, Article 88(3) and 88(2) of the EC, leads to a maximum of twenty-two months.

After completing the EC Article 88(2) procedure, the Commission may either:

(i) declare the aid compatible with the Common Market, with or without conditions, or
(ii) declare it incompatible with the Common Market.

Either decision may be subject to review by the CFI with a possibility of appeal to the European Court of Justice (ECJ) on points of law.

A final positive decision ends the operation of the standstill clause of Article 88(3) of the EC. A positive decision may be accompanied by conditions that should alleviate the effect on competition.[35] The Commission's decision in the *Air France* case provides a good example of this practice.[36] In this case, the Commission imposed a series of conditions that included the requirement that

[33] Cases C-312/90 *Spain* v *Commission* and C-47/91 *Italy v. Commission* [1992] ECR 1–4117 and 4145.

[34] Case 120/73 *Gebrüder Lorenz GmbH* v *Germany* [1973] ECR 1471.

[35] According to Article 87(3)(c) and (d) of the EC, "such aid should not affect trading conditions and competition in the Community to an extent that it is contrary to the common interest."

[36] [1994] OJ L254/73.

Air France was not to use any of the aid received for the purpose of increasing its aircraft fleet. A positive decision may also approve the aid in successive tranches whereby the approval of the next tranche is subject to the satisfactory implementation of a restructuring programme.[37]

In the case of a negative final decision, the standstill clause [contained in the last paragraph of Article 88(3) of the EC] does *not* lapse after the Commission concludes the EC Article 88(2) procedure: Instead, the standstill obligation is henceforth based on the negative decision.

Complainants have, according to Article 20 of the Regulation, a right to inform the Commission of any alleged unlawful aid or the misuse of aid. The Commission has published a form for the submission of complaints.[38] Complainants can bring an action under Article 232 of the EC if the Commission fails to act.[39] Furthermore, as the Court of Justice observed in the *Sytraval* judgment, complainants (as third parties that are "directly and individually concerned") will have a right to challenge state aid decisions addressed to governments of Member States.[40] The Court also pointed out that, although the Commission is not obliged to hear complainants, it must nevertheless respond to facts and points of law raised by the complainant.

NB. It is important for the purposes of this chapter to note that there are no inherent limitations to the bringing of complaints, and any company claiming that its interests are affected is entitled to bring a complaint. This would, of course, include Boeing or any of its subsidiaries or suppliers. Boeing, its subsidiaries, or its suppliers can also challenge subsequent Commission decisions before the CFI.

Unlawful state aid is not automatically incompatible with the Common Market. The Commission also has a duty to review such aids.[41] According to Article 13(2) of the Regulation, the Commission shall not be bound by the normal time limits in case of nonnotified aid. It also has powers to issue injunctions to suspend or provisionally recover the unlawful aid (Article 11 of the Regulation).

Because of the direct affect of the last sentence of Article 88(3) of the EC, national courts have an important role in enforcing the procedural requirements of the EC state aid regime. They can enforce the standstill clause. National courts may also award damages in cases of unlawful aid.[42] They may also grant injunctions. Such remedies may be of vital importance in aid cases in which the timing is often a crucial element in rescue operations. The role of national courts

[37] This was the case in *Air France* as well as in *Aer Lingus*: Decision 94/118, [1994] OJ L54/30. This decision was challenged in Case T-140/95 *Ryanair Ltd v. Commission*, [1998] ECR II-3327.

[38] OJ 2003, C 116, p. 3.

[39] Case T-95/96 *Gestevision Telecinco SA v. Commission* [1998] ECR II-3407.

[40] Case C-367/95 P *Commission v. Chambre Syndicale (Sytraval)* [1998] ECR I-1719.

[41] Case C-301/87 *France v. Commission (Boussac)* [1990] ECR I-307.

[42] Case C-354/90 *Fédération Nationale du Commerce Extérieur des Produits Alimentaires and Syndicat National des Négociants et Transformateurs de Saumon v. France* [1991] ECR I-5523.

has recently been stressed in a Commission Communication on the cooperation between national courts and the Commission in the field of state aids.[43] It has been further highlighted in the judgment of the ECJ in the *SFEI* case.[44] The ECJ held in this judgment that national courts seized of a request relating to an infringement of Article 88(3) of the EC, which is also under review by the Commission, are not required to declare that they lack jurisdiction or stay the proceedings until such time as the Commission has adopted a position.

In case of doubts about the question of whether a measure constitutes an aid in the sense of Article 87(1) of the EC, national courts may refer a question to the ECJ or consult the Commission. The Commission may also be consulted about matters of procedure.[45] When national courts consult the Commission or refer questions to the ECJ, they must decide whether it is necessary to order interim measures to safeguard the interests of the parties pending final judgment. A national court requested to order repayment must grant that application if it finds that the aid was not notified to the Commission.

NB. Boeing, its subsidiaries, or its suppliers could also have brought suit in national courts of the EC Member State granting the aid.

According to Article 14 of the Regulation, the Commission has the power to order recovery of illegally implemented aid.[46] The Commission may order recovery-of-interest advantages, where unlawful aid has been implemented prior to Commission approval.[47] See decision 97/807 Article 2.[48]

When ordered to recover aid, a Member State cannot invoke a rule of domestic law to oppose recovery orders.[49] In this context, it is important to note that the Commission has, for many years, when publishing notices under the EC Article 88(2) procedure, warned the enterprises concerned that illegally implemented aid can be recovered.

Commission decisions ordering recovery of illegally implemented aids normally require the Member States concerned to report to the Commission which measures have been taken to implement the decision. See Article 3 of Decision 97/807.[50]

The second paragraph of Article 88(2) of the EC states that the Commission or an interested Member State may bring an action before the ECJ in derogation

[43] [1995] OJ C 312/8.

[44] Case C-39/94 *Syndicat Français de L'Express International (SFEI) and others v. La Poste and others* [1996] ECR I-3547.

[45] The judgment of the ECJ follows a structure similar to its judgment in case C-234/89 *Delimitis* [1991] ECR I-935, concerning the application of Articles 81 and 82 of the EC by national courts.

[46] Case 70/72 *Commission v. Germany* [1973] ECR 175.

[47] Case 310/85 *Deufil GmbH & Co KG v. Commission* [1987] ECR 901.

[48] OJ 1997, L 331, 10. See the electronic document.

[49] Case 94/87 *Commission v. Germany* [1989] ECR 175; and, in particular, Case C-24/95 *Land Rheinland-Pfalz v. Alcan Deutschland GmbH* [1997] ECR I-1591.

[50] OJ 1997, L 331, 10. See the electronic document.

of the provisions of Articles 226 and 227 of the EC[51] if the State concerned does not comply with the Commission's decision.[52]

Conclusion

The EC state aid rules provide ample opportunities for competitors of (intended) beneficiaries of subsidies to challenge such measures by Member States. The opportunities apply both to the substantive as well as the procedural state aid rules.

The EC Commission has taken a number of decisions on state aid to the aircraft manufacturing industry and its suppliers. Many have been wholly or partially approved, often under the R&D framework.

Interesting decisions in this respect are:

(i) 97/807 in the electronic document,
(ii) decision C 27/06, OJ 2006, C 196, p. 7,
(iii) a decision to recover 103 million Euros from Fokker,[53]
(iv) a decision approving 70 million aid for projects concerning the main parts of the engines for the Airbus 380,[54] and
(v) a decision authorizing a reimbursable advance to Rolls Royce to develop engines for large civil aircraft.[55]

This conclusion raises, of course, the question of why Boeing has never bothered to lodge complaints and provide comments in EC state aid procedures. Is it possible that Boeing prefers to have the U.S. government represent its interests?

[51] This means that the Commission does not have to give a reasoned opinion, as is required by Articles 226 and 227 of the EC. Therefore, the procedure of Article 88(2) of the EC is much more expedient.

[52] The Commission followed this procedure in Case 70/72 *Commission v. Germany (Kohlegesetz)* [1970] ECR 487; Cases 31/77R and 53/77R *Commission v. United Kingdom* [1977] ECR 921; Case 203/82 *Commission v. Italy* [1983] ECR 2525; Case 52/83 *Commission v. France* [1983] ECR 3707; Case 93/84 *Commission v. France* [1985] ECR 829; Case 52/84 *Commission v. Belgium* [1986] ECR 89; Case 213/85 *Commission v. Netherlands* [1988] ECR 281; Case C-5/89 *Commission v. Germany* [1990] ECR I-3437.

[53] Competition report 1998, p. 260.

[54] OJ 2002, C 309, 16.

[55] Competition Policy Newsletter 1998 No. 2, June p. 85.

MARK WU

5.1 *Why Not Brussels? European Community State Aid Rules and the Boeing–Airbus Dispute: Comment on Piet Jan Slot*

Piet Jan Slot's chapter (Chapter 5) highlights several advantages for companies to bring a complaint before the European Commission (EC) under its state aid laws rather than nudging their government to pursue a subsidies violation case before the World Trade Organization (WTO). First, a successful complainant can obtain more extensive remedies through the Commission. European state aid laws allow for recovery of any illegally implemented aid,[1] whereas the WTO limits remedies to prospective measures. Second, Regulation 659/99/EC includes a standstill clause, mandating that certain forms of aid shall not be put into effect while the Commission undertakes a preliminary examination.[2] In contrast, a government is free to continue implementing the disputed subsidy while a WTO case is being litigated. Third, if the complainant should win its case, it is much more certain of obtaining enforcement of a Commission judgment in an EC Member State's national court. A WTO judgment, in contrast, could very well go ignored.[3]

Given these advantages, Slot raises an interesting question: Why haven't foreign multinationals been more aggressive in bringing forward complaints before the Commission on issues of state aid? Indeed, as Slot rightly notes, multinational companies are increasingly taking advantage of other realms of European law to serve their commercial interests.[4] Why not state aid? In particular, Slot asks

[1] Council Regulation 659/1999, Article 14, 1999 O.J. (L 83) 1, 6 (EC).

[2] Ibid., Article 3, at 4.

[3] For a specific discussion of this risk in the Boeing–Airbus dispute, see N. Meier-Kaienburg, "The WTO's 'Toughest' Case: An Examination of the Effectiveness of the WTO Dispute Resolution Procedure in the Airbus-Boeing Dispute Over Aircraft Subsidies," 71 *J Air Law Commerce* 2006, 191, 226–231.

[4] For example, opponents of the General Electric–Honeywell merger successfully persuaded European regulators to block the merger when their American counterparts had already approved it. Similarly, Sun and other software companies successfully obtained a Commission decision against Microsoft for its anticompetitive practices, which was upheld by the Court of First Instance. Opponents of the Google–DoubleClick merger have also managed to stall it by pressing the Commission to examine the deal's market impact more thoroughly.

this question of Boeing. In its ongoing WTO dispute with Airbus, Boeing, through the Office of the U.S. Trade Representative (USTR), raises concerns about several aid measures granted by EC member governments that are arguably subject to Article 87 rules. Why then did Boeing choose to adjudicate before the WTO, especially in light of the important advantages noted above in seeking recourse through the EC?

I argue that Boeing's decision is rational, and does not reflect a systematic bias against choosing a European forum or a lack of awareness of how European state aid law operates. In discussing potential explanations for Boeing's action, I hope to illuminate some of the inherent difficulties that multinationals face in litigating before the EC, despite the advantages of the EC's state aid rules.

The Subsidies at Issue in the Boeing–Airbus Dispute

Before discussing the rationale for Boeing's decision, one needs to understand generally the types of subsidies at issue in the Boeing–Airbus dispute. Boeing is alleging that Airbus benefits from five major types of subsidies: (1) launch aid from EC member governments, (2) loans from the European Investment Bank (EIB), (3) subsidized infrastructure aid from EC member governments, (4) capital contributions from EC member governments, and (5) research and development (R&D) funding.[5] Each type is introduced briefly.

By far, the largest, and therefore most important, subsidy being attacked by Boeing and the United States is financing provided by European governments to their aircraft manufacturers, which the United States has labeled "launch aid."[6] Launch aid is described by the United States as "a form of highly-preferential financing that the Airbus governments designed and use to offset the enormous costs and extremely high risks" of developing large civil aircraft.[7] Essentially, the governments provide long-term, unsecured loans to Airbus at zero or

[5] Chapter 5.1 does not take a position on whether any of these categories actually constitute subsidies. Instead, it considers all five of these categories because they form the underlying basis of the allegations of the United States and Boeing.

[6] The EC has objected to the terminology of "launch aid" on the grounds that it is suggestive and oversimplistic, and instead describes the collective program as "member state financing." See First Written Submission of the European Communities, *European Communities – Measures Affecting Trade in Large Civil Aircraft*, para. 290, WT/DS316, available at: http://trade.ec.europa.eu/doclib/docs/2007/april/tradoc_134551.pdf (hereinafter EC First Submission). While recognizing this objection, I will use the term "launch aid" in this chapter because it focuses on the forum for the arguments of Boeing and the United States.

[7] See Executive Summary of the First Submission of the United States, *European Communities – Measures Affecting Trade in Large Civil Aircraft*, para. 5, WT/DS316 (adopted on November 25, 2006), available at: http://www.ustr.gov/trade-topics/enforcement/dispute-settlement-proceedings/wto-dispute-settlement/measures-affecting-t-0. There is a link at the bottom of the Web page for the document referenced in this footnote.

below-market interest rates with repayment contingent on the aircraft's commercial success. The loan is repaid through a per-aircraft levy, which typically increases over the course of the repayment period.[8] If sales are insufficient to repay the loan, then the outstanding balance is indefinitely extended or forgiven. As a result, the government assumes much of the risk for the development and marketing of each aircraft line, but does not charge Airbus a premium for assuming the risk. The United States asserts that, during the past thirty years, the French, British, German, and Spanish governments have provided an estimated $15 billion in launch aid to Airbus and its predecessors.[9] This includes $4 billion for the A380 and $1.7 billion for the A350, Airbus's two most recent aircraft lines.[10]

Second, Boeing and the United States are also challenging loans from the EIB. The EIB is a legal and financially autonomous institution within the European Union (EU) that acts as its long-term lending bank. It raises money on capital markets that it then lends on favorable terms to projects that further EU policy objectives. The EIB provided €1.6 billion in loans to European aircraft manufacturers associated with Airbus, including €700 million for the A380 project.[11] Boeing and the United States contend that these loans constitute subsidies because they were provided at terms more favorable than those available in the market.

Third, Boeing and the United States are challenging infrastructure and infrastructure-related grants that they allege unfairly subsidize Airbus. The initial U.S. submission identifies fifteen such grants.[12] Ten of these concern grants given by the Spanish government or regional governments to various projects in Andalusia and Castilla-La Mancha.[13] Another focuses on aid for a runway extension at Bremen Airport, allegedly to accommodate transport flights for Airbus wings manufactured there.[14] The remainder center on land and/or facility developments. For example, the United States contends that German authorities subsidized Airbus by converting a wetland area in Hamburg into a production

[8] EC First Submission, *supra* note 6, paras. 320–321. If the debt and interest are repaid in full, the manufacturers may also be required to make royalty payments for subsequent aircraft deliveries.

[9] First Submission of the United States, *European Communities – Measures Affecting Trade in Large Civil Aircraft*, para. 81, WT/DS316, available at: http://www.ustr.gov/assets/Trade_Agreements/Monitoring_Enforcement/Dispute_Settlement/WTO/Dispute_Settlement_Listings/asset_upload_file292_10235.pdf (hereinafter U.S. First Submission).

[10] Ibid. para. 89. Note that the EC takes issue with these figures and notes that no commitments have been made for the A350. EC First Submission, *supra* note 6, paras. 345–359.

[11] U.S. First Submission, *supra* note 9, para. 387. The EC contends that the United States fails to demonstrate that any of the EIB loans from 1988 through 1993 were provided to the company that produces large civilian aircraft today (i.e., Airbus SAS). See EC First Submission, *supra* note 6, para. 1057.

[12] See U.S. Executive Summary of the First Submission of the United States, *supra* note 7, paras. 44–59.

[13] U.S. First Submission, *supra* note 9, paras. 494–513.

[14] Ibid., paras. 450–454.

facility for Airbus's A380 project and providing the site to Airbus for less than adequate remuneration. The United States alleges that the site is one that the commercial market would not have independently converted.[15] Another example is a French government grant of €200 million to transform agricultural land surrounding Airbus's headquarters in Toulouse to an aeronautics industrial park known as "AeroConstellation."[16]

Fourth, Boeing and the United States also are raising questions about the legality of a series of capital contributions made by the French and German governments to their respective aerospace manufacturers. Boeing alleges that the French government subsidized Aerospatiale through a series of equity infusions and share transfers.[17] It also alleges that the German government subsidized Deutsche Aerospace by transferring its ownership share in Deutsche Aerospace without compensation, and by forgiving DM 7.7 billion of Deutsche Aerospace's debt in the course of its takeover by Daimler-Benz.[18]

Finally, Boeing and the United States are challenging measures undertaken by the Commission and four European governments to help fund Airbus's R&D efforts. These have largely taken the form of pure cash grants, often provided through the vehicle of the EC Framework Programmes, although in a few instances, they have also taken the form of noncommercial loans.[19] The United States estimates the total grants from the Commission to exceed €1 billion[20] and those from the four member governments to be several hundred million euros.[21]

For each of these five categories of alleged subsidies, I argue that Boeing would face difficulties persuading the Commission to decide that the measures in question are illegal under EC state aid law. The reasons for Boeing's difficulties differ depending on the category at issue.

[15] Ibid., paras. 423–433, 437–442.

[16] Ibid., para. 456.

[17] Boeing and the United States claim that four equity infusions totaling FF 7.15 billion by the French government made during an eight-year period, as well as the French government's share transfer of its 45.76% share of Dassault's capital to Aerospatiale (translating into a FF 5.28 billion equity infusion) are specific subsidies to Airbus because they are inconsistent with the usual investment practices of private investors. U.S. Executive Summary, *supra* note 7, paras. 63–64.

[18] Ibid., paras. 60–62.

[19] U.S. First Submission, *supra* note 9, para. 621.

[20] The United States claims that it is unable to estimate the full value of the grants under some of the EC Framework Programs because the publicly available information does not break down the value of the grants for the aeronautics research projects in which Airbus participates. Nonetheless, the United States claims that it is able to identify that the EC provided at least €19 million under the Second Framework Program, €509 million under the Fifth Framework Program, and at least €450 million under the Sixth Framework Program. See ibid., paras. 628, 631, 636, 641, and 646.

[21] The United States is claiming that the German federal government subsidized €695 million of grants for Airbus's research and development. See Ibid., para. 654. It has not publicly released a figure for the precise subsidies from the German subfederal government, or the French or British governments, or for the submarket loans from the Spanish government. When these are factored in, the precise sum is likely to exceed €1 billion as well.

The Difficulties Posed By the Commission's Past History on Launch Aid

Because elimination of launch aid is Boeing's top priority, I focus first on this form of alleged subsidy. It is highly unlikely that the Commission would have found launch aid to be illegal under the EC's state aid rules for two reasons.

First, the Commission has clearly endorsed the notion of launch aid in the recent past. In 2003, when responding to the Strategic Aerospace Report, the Commission itself decreed that the provision of launch aid is a "crucial responsibility" of member governments and is necessary for retaining and improving the global competitiveness of European aerospace.[22] This view was again reinforced by a Commission official in 2006.[23] Having itself mandated that governments provide launch aid, it is hard to fathom that the Commission would now backtrack and declare such actions to be illegal.

Second, an examination of recent Commission rulings also suggests that the Commission would authorize launch aid as compliant with European state aid law, given the existing market conditions in the large civil aircraft sector. The Commission has ruled on launch aid twice in the last decade. Slot mentions one case that has been touted as possible evidence that the Commission would decide that launch aid is incompatible with EC state aid rules. In 1997, the Commission decided that 1.9 million pesetas worth of aid granted by the Spanish government to the aerospace company Construcciones Aeronauticas, SA (CASA), was illegal under the laws governing state aid.[24] What is unmentioned, however, is the existence of a second case decided the following year. In late 1998, the Commission did the opposite; it approved launch aid provided by the French government to Aerospatiale for the Airbus A340–500/600 project.[25]

Why did the Commission find launch aid to be illegal under state aid laws in the *CASA* case, but not so in the *Aerospatiale* case? Note that the cases differ in two important ways. First, the aerospace products at issue are different. The *CASA* case concerned small regional aircraft, whereas the *Aerospatiale* case concerned large civil aircraft. Quite likely, the Commission found the Community to have greater strategic interests in the latter than the former. In its 2003 report on the aerospace sector, the Commission stated, "The overall development of the market for large civil aircraft and the competitiveness of Airbus are the key elements for the future development of the European [aerospace]

[22] Commission of the European Communities, *A Coherent Framework for Aerospace – a Response to the STAR 21 Report*, at 12, COM (2003) 600 final (October 13, 2003) (hereinafter Coherent Framework for Aerospace).

[23] Caterine Ebah-Moussa, European Commission DG-Enterprise, Commission Communication COM (2003) 600: A Coherent Framework for Aerospace – a Response to the STAR 21 Report 14 (March 28, 2006), available at: http://www.abgs.gov.tr/tarama/tarama_files/20/SC20EXP_Aerospace.pdf.

[24] Commission Decision 97/807, 1997 O.J. (L 331) 10.

[25] Commission Decision N 369/98, 1998 O.J. (C 52) 10.

industry."[26] No mention is made by the Commission of regional aircraft, although numerous other aerospace-related products (e.g., helicopters, unmanned aircraft, satellites) are also discussed.

Second, the market conditions are different. In the *CASA* case, the market for European regional aircraft faced overcapacity and was dominated by intra-EC competition. This was not the case in the market for large civil aircraft in the *Aerospatiale* case. As a result, the Commission's rulings suggest that it is likely to be more tolerant of intense, longer-term state aid when the European market is not facing overcapacity or fierce internal competition.

Obviously, a Boeing challenge to launch aid for ongoing Airbus projects would much more closely parallel the *Aerospatiale* case than the *CASA* case. Thus, despite the favorable *CASA* ruling mentioned by Slot, it is unlikely that Boeing would be able to prevail before the Commission. To do so, it would need to differentiate the launch aid at issue from that considered in the *Aerospatiale* case. It is difficult to fathom upon what facts Boeing would have drawn to do so successfully.

The *Aerospatiale* case, combined with the Commission's recent declarations about the central importance of launch aid to European aerospace, no doubt reflect a clear Commission position that launch aid constitutes permissible state aid. Indeed, Airbus is so confident of this fact that it has publicly gone on record to declare launch aid commitments to be "legally binding."[27] In light of this past history, for Boeing to challenge launch aid under EC state aid rules would clearly have been a futile exercise.

Potential Difficulties in Challenging Other Categories of Alleged Subsidies

For Boeing, without a doubt, the most important issue in its ongoing legal dispute is launch aid.[28] The unlikelihood of obtaining a favorable Commission ruling on launch aid alone should suffice to deter Boeing from challenging Airbus under EC state aid rules. However, Boeing's difficulties are not confined to launch aid. Boeing would face potential problems before the Commission on each of the four other forms of alleged subsidies as well.

First, consider the EIB loans to which Boeing objects. The problem here is jurisdictional. Article 87 governs "any aid granted by a Member State or through State resources in any form whatsoever." It is unlikely that the Commission would have found that Article 87 provides it with authority to review EIB loans. Although the EU member states are the EIB's shareholders and are responsible for capital contributions, the EIB functions as an independent institution and

[26] Coherent Framework for Aerospace, *supra* note 22, at 4.

[27] Airbus Says It Has "Binding" Aid Pledges, *Chicago Tribune*, October 8, 2005, at C8.

[28] See *John Newhouse, Boeing Versus Airbus*, 58–63 (2007) (emphasizing how the launch aid issue was Boeing's primary concern); see also Meier-Kaienburg, *supra* note 3, at 205 (describing launch aid as "the center of this dispute").

cannot be considered to be an extension of any state. The European Court of Justice has confirmed this point, noting that "the bank has a legal personality distinct from that of the Community and that it is administered and managed by organs of its own accordance."[29] To fund its loans, the EIB borrows on the international capital markets and does not draw on the budgets of any Member State.[30] As a result, although Boeing and the United States can credibly argue that the EIB loans constitute a subsidy under the WTO Agreement on Subsidies and Countervailing Measures (SCM Agreement),[31] they would have faced severe difficulties in establishing that EIB loans constitute state aid under Article 87.

Second, consider the various infrastructure-related aid to which Boeing also objects. The bulk of Boeing's infrastructure-related objections relate to aid grants given by Spanish authorities to the Andalusia and Castilla-La Mancha regions. Article 87(3), however, provides an exception for state aid "to promote the economic development of areas where the standard of living is abnormally low or where there is serious unemployment." Because both Andalusia and Castilla-La Mancha are economically weaker areas of Spain, the Commission has recognized, on multiple occasions, the legality of the underlying aid scheme for several such grants.[32]

Slot does not mention these rulings, but they are major impediment to Boeing's ability to rely on EC state aid rules to challenge these Spanish grants. Instead, he only notes, rightly, that Boeing has a general right to submit comments during the Commission's review and, more importantly, a right to challenge the Commission's decision before the Court of First Instance, but it is difficult to fathom how Boeing could have made a persuasive legal argument. The aid scheme was clearly earmarked for regional development; therefore, the Commission appears fully entitled to consider it to qualify for the exception under Article 87(3)(a). Recourse to the WTO, therefore, is Boeing's best option for several of these infrastructure-related grants.

Moreover, even for those infrastructure projects for which the Commission did not review and endorse the state aid, Boeing likely would face challenges. For example, consider Boeing's objection to aid given by German authorities to support the extension of Bremen Airport's runway.[33] Several past cases hint at the

[29] Case C-85/86, *Comm'n v. Board of Governors of the European Investment Bank*, para. 28, 1988 E.C.R. 1281, 1320.

[30] Protocol on the Statute of the European Investment Bank, Article 22.

[31] U.S. First Submission, *supra* note 9, para. 387.

[32] Commission Decision N 507–00, 2001 O.J. (C 263) 8; Commission Decision N 773–99, 2000 O.J. (C 184) 22; Commission Decision N 442–99, 2000 O.J. (C 121) 17.

[33] Boeing and the United States are asserting that the project was done solely for Airbus's benefit and that use of the runway extension is restricted to Airbus by regulation. U.S. First Submission, *supra* note 9, at paras. 451–454. However, the EC contends that the claim by the United States is factually incorrect. It notes that "the extension of the runway can be used by any airline," and that no specific benefit is conferred because "Airbus pays fees for

difficulty of successfully challenging state aid for aerospace-related infrastructure projects. The traditional view of the Commission is that an infrastructure investment project, such as the enlargement of an airport, "represents a general measure of economic policy which cannot be controlled by the Commission on the Treaty rules on state aid."[34] Even in recent years, when the Commission has been more open to reviewing such aid, it has approved public financing specifically for runway extensions, similar to Bremen's, at both Derry Airport in Northern Ireland[35] and Kiel-Holtenau Airport in Germany.[36] The Commission has also approved government financing for general airport infrastructure improvements in Ireland,[37] Poland,[38] and Germany.[39] Indeed, since the Commission issued its 2005 guidelines clarifying the five criteria for consideration in any state aid case concerning public financing for airports, it has yet to reject an infrastructure expansion case on the basis of any of the listed criteria.[40] Again, Boeing's decision not to pursue the matter before the Commission is not altogether irrational.

In addition, Boeing would also face an uphill battle with respect to its objections to grants for land and facilities development projects that it alleges benefit Airbus. EC state aid rules are fairly accepting of measures to fund infrastructural works and industrial sites, so long as it is not for the exclusive benefit of a single

the use of Bremen airport that are in accordance with the general fee schedule applicable at Bremen airport." EC First Submission, *supra* note 6, paras. 868–873.

[34] U. Soltesz, "The New Commission Guidelines on State Aid for Airports – A Step Too Far . . . ," *European State Aid Law Quarterly 2006,* 719, 721; *accord* C.H. Bovis, "The Application of State Aid Rules to the European Union Transport Sectors," 11 *Columbia Journal of European Law* 2005, 557, 583; M.N. Muller, "State Aid to the Aviation Sector," in M.S. Rydelski (Ed.), *The EC State Aid Regime: Distortive Effects of State Aid on Competition and Trade* (2006), 423, 437. Cameron-May, London.

[35] Commission Decision NN 21/2006, 2006 O.J. (C 272) 13.

[36] Press Release, European Commission, State Aid: The Commission Considers that the German State Aid Scheme for Kiel-Holtenau Airport Conforms to the Joint Task Scheme Already Approved in 2005, IP/07/1686 (November 13, 2007).

[37] Commission Decision N 353/06, 2006 O.J. (C 280) 4.

[38] Press Release, European Commission, State Aid: Commission Approves Aid to the Rzeszow Jasionka Airport in Poland, IP/07/1582 (October 23, 2007).

[39] Commission Decision N 644i/2002, 2005 O.J. (C126) 12.

[40] In examining public financing of airport infrastructure, the Commission has stated that it will examine whether: (a) construction and operation of the infrastructure meets a clearly defined objective of general interest, (b) the infrastructure is necessary and proportional to the objective which has been set, (c) the infrastructure has satisfactory medium-term prospects for use, (d) all potential users have access to it in an equal and nondiscriminatory manner, and (e) the development of trade is not affected to an extent contrary to the Community's interest. European Commission Communication, Community Guidelines on Financing of Airports and Start-up Aid to Airlines Departing from Regional Airports, 2005 O.J. (C 312) 1, December 9, 2005 (EC). If Boeing were to challenge the Bremen Airport runway extension before the Commission, it likely would have argued that the airport's use restrictions are unequal and discriminatory. Whether this is factually accurate, however, is open to debate. See *supra* note 33.

user.[41] European governments, in defending their grants, would certainly resort to such an argument. For example, German authorities, in defending funds spent to reclaim wetlands for an Airbus production site, would contend that the project constitutes general public infrastructure that can be reused for other purposes.[42] French authorities too would use a similar argument in addressing Boeing's complaints about aid to develop the AeroConstellation site in Toulouse, highlighting that the site is an industrial park servicing multiple companies rather than Airbus alone.[43] Were it to press its case before the Commission, Boeing would face the tough task of persuasively refuting these governments' claims.

Third, consider the capital contributions made by the French and German governments to which Boeing is also raising objections. Again, it is not likely that the Commission would have found these to be in violation of state aid rules. Like some of the infrastructure-related aid, the Commission has also previously reviewed the French government's equity infusion. Although no documents on the Commission's state aid review are publicly available, the EC notes that "no negative decision prohibiting the 1994 capital contribution has been issued."[44]

In addition, it is unlikely that the Commission would have found the German government's restructuring package for Deutsche Airbus to be illegal, despite Boeing's contention that the restructuring resulted in the forgiveness of DM 750 million of debt, tantamount to illegal state aid.[45] The Commission has laid out specific guidelines for reviewing state aid in the context of restructuring.[46] Because Deutsche Airbus teetered on the edge of bankruptcy as a result of under-capitalization and external shocks,[47] it would have qualified as a "firm in difficulty" under the guidelines.[48] Its restructuring plan would likely have met the guideline's requirements for permissible state aid, as the Daimler-Benz takeover allows for the restoration of the firm's long-term viability.[49] Moreover, the Commission has looked more favorably upon restructuring aid given in parallel with

[41] See C. Quigley, and A.M. Collins, EC State Aid Law and Policy (2003) 58–59. Hart Publishing, Oxford; Leigh Hancher et al., E.C. State Aids, (2nd ed., 1999) para. 2–010. Sweet and Maxwell, London.

[42] See EC First Submission, *supra* note 6, para. 791 ("Hamburg has not sold the land in the reclaimed Area to Airbus Germany. To the contrary, Hamburg retains ownership of the property and the possibility to use the newly created land for other purposes after a possible termination of the lease arrangement.")

[43] See ibid., paras. 913–916 (highlighting the general interest works undertaken and the fact that every company paid the same price).

[44] Ibid., at Footnote 938.

[45] The EC disputes this allegation and argues that there was no debt forgiveness because the amount repaid represented the fair market value of the repayment claims. See Ibid., paras. 1175–1176.

[46] Community Guidelines on State Aid for Rescuing and Restructuring Firms in Difficulty, 2004 O.J. (C 244) 2 (hereinafter EC Restructuring Guidelines).

[47] EC First Submission, *supra* note 6, para. 1177.

[48] EC Restructuring Guidelines, *supra* note 46, paras. 10–11, at 3.

[49] See Ibid., paras. 32–51, at 6–8, for a discussion of the specific conditions for the authorization of restructuring aid.

private industrial investors, such as Daimler-Benz.[50] Therefore, again, Boeing would have faced serious difficulties in challenging the German and French capital contributions before the Commission.

Finally, Boeing also acted rationally in not challenging the R&D grants received by Airbus and other European manufacturers before the Commission. Had it done so, it would have had little chance of success. As was the case with launch aid, the Commission itself played an active role in authorizing these grants. Therefore, it is unlikely that the Commission would subsequently decree them illegal. A significant portion was directly approved by the Commission and the European Parliament under the Framework Programmes.[51] The Sixth Framework Programme specifically called for the funding of "community aeronautical research activities... in order to increase the competitiveness of the European industry with regard to civil aircraft, engines, and equipment."[52] Similarly, the current Seventh Framework Programme emphasizes the importance of "improving industrial competitiveness" in aeronautics.[53]

Moreover, the Commission has generally adopted a favorable attitude toward R&D aid for aerospace projects.[54] Its framework for assessing R&D state aid specifically provides an exemption for aid for "important projects of common European interest," pursuant to Article 87(3)(b).[55] Most R&D projects related to Airbus could fall under this exemption. In addition, in its assessments, the Commission has tended to look favorably on R&D aid for activities connected with the development of new technologies[56] and which serve overall European

[50] See M. Lienemeyer, "State Aid to Companies in Difficulty – The Rescue and Restructuring Guidelines," in *The EC State Aid Regime, supra* note 33, at 183, 194–195; see also Quigley and Collins, *supra* note 41, at 161 (describing financial restructuring, in the form of capital injections and debt reduction, as usually linked to a viable restructuring plan).

[51] See, for example, European Parliament and Council Decision 1982/2006/EC, 2006 O.J. (L 412) 1; European Parliament and Council Decision 1513/2002/EC, 2002 O.J. (L 232) 1; European Parliament and Council Decision 182/1999/EC, 1999 O.J. (L 26) 1.

[52] European Parliament and Council Decision 1513/2002/EC, Annex 1, § 1.1.4, 2002 O.J. (L 232) 1, 12.

[53] European Parliament and Council Decision 1982/2006/EC, Annex 1, 2006 O.J. (L 412) 1, 7.

[54] See, for example, Commission Decision N 453/02, 2003 O.J. (C 195) 16.

[55] Community Framework for State Aid for Research and Development and Innovation § 4, 2006 O.J. (C 323) 1, 12–13. The current version of the framework requires the Commission to apply a three-part balancing test that considers whether the aid measure: (1) is aimed at a well-defined objective of common interest, (2) is well designed to deliver the objective of common interest, and (3) limits the distortions of competition and effect on trade such that the overall balance is positive. Ibid., § 1.3.1, at 5. Although the Framework is not a binding legal act, "the Commission regularly and openly applies such 'soft law' measures when investigating and deciding on R&D aid." M.N. Muller, "The Community Framework for State Aid for Research and Development," in S. Bilal and P. Nicolaides (Eds.), *Understanding State Aid Policy in the European Community* (1999), 101, 106. Kluwer Law International, The Hague.

[56] C. Quigley, "Framework for State Aid for Research and Development," in *The EC State Aid Regime, supra* note 34, at 271, 273.

policy considerations to boost industrial competitiveness.[57] As a result, the EC has confidently proclaimed that the R&D aid for certain programs being challenged by Boeing and the United States operate in line with its state aid rules.[58] Furthermore, like launch aid, the Commission has also decreed that it is a "crucial responsibility" of Member States to provide R&D funding for aerospace programs.[59] Given this history, it would be futile for Boeing to challenge Airbus's R&D grants through the Commission.

Therefore, for all five categories of alleged subsidies, Boeing would have faced difficulties obtaining a favorable judgment through the EC state aid regime. Past Commission reviews of the forms of aid received by Airbus and its related manufacturers have almost invariably found such aid to be compatible with the common market. Without a doubt, an important factor driving acceptance of such state aid is Europe's desire to preserve its competitiveness in aerospace through Airbus. Quite understandably, Boeing chose to press its case through Geneva rather than Brussels.

Conclusion

All this is not to detract from Slot's main point – that companies should seriously consider litigation in local venues as an alternative to the WTO. This is particularly true when the substantive rules of the local venue offers advantages over those of the WTO, as is the case with the EC's state aid regime. When confronted with competitors subsidized by European governments, multinationals should weigh the possibility of seeking recourse through Brussels.

Multinationals also need to be aware of the limits of such an approach. What Slot does not discuss is that, although the EC state aid rules may appear advantageous, European industrial policy and political economy considerations can seriously hamper the efforts of multinationals to obtain favorable outcomes before the Commission. In sectors such as aerospace, the competitiveness of which the Commission has decreed to be a top priority, EC state aid rules may offer minimal hope for multinationals. As I have tried to illustrate with Boeing, companies in such sectors do not seek recourse in Brussels, not because their lawyers are unaware of the EC's state aid rules or are systematically biased

[57] Quigley and Collins, *supra* note 41, at 181.

[58] See EC First Submission, *supra* note 6, para. 1265. ("This programme operates on the same procedural lines ... as provided for in EC State aid rules.") See also, for example, Commission Decision N 741/02, 2002 O.J. (C 154) 9 (authorizing Germany's funding for aviation research programs during 2003–2007 under the Commission's state aid review); Commission Decision NN 15/00, 2001 O.J. (C 19) 5 (authorizing the U.K.'s funding for civil aviation research and technology program under the Commission's state aid review).

[59] Coherent Framework for Aerospace, *supra* note 22, at 12; Ebah-Moussa, *supra* note 23, at 14.

against choosing the EC as a venue. Rather, past Commission policies and past Commission decisions on state aid in the sector often make it an unattractive option. Despite the EC's well-established state aid rules, appealing to one's government to seek recourse through the WTO may indeed sometimes prove to be the most rational and smartest move.

TERENCE P. STEWART AND AMY S. DWYER*

6 Antidumping: Overview of the Agreement

Background

Dumping is generally defined as the act of an exporter selling a product in an export market at a price below that which is charged for the same or comparable merchandise in the home market.[1] Where dumping has the effect of causing injury to the domestic industry in the importing country, the General Agreement on Tariffs and Trade (GATT) and World Trade Organization (WTO) Antidumping Agreement permit antidumping measures, in the form of increased duties, to counteract or offset the dumping.

In fact, the Contracting Parties to the GATT, as well as the Members of the WTO, have recognized that injurious dumping is "to be condemned."[2] The reason for such strong language is that, although consumers of dumped products may benefit in the short term from lower prices, dumping sends false market signals about the underlying competitive positions of market participants.[3] As U.S. Assistant Attorney General Samuel Graham put it in 1916:

> [G]enerally accepted principles of political economy hold that it is not sound policy for any Government to permit the sale in its country by foreign citizens of material at a price below the cost of production at the place

[1] See General Agreement on Tariffs and Trade 1994, April 15, 1994, Article VI, in *World Trade Organization, The Results of the Uruguay Round of Multilateral Trade Negotiations* 17, 424, 430 (2001) ("GATT") (GATT 1994 includes the provisions of the GATT 1947 as rectified, amended, or modified by the terms of legal instruments that entered into force before the date of entry into force of the WTO Agreement); see also Agreement on Implementation of Article VI of the GATT 1994, April 15, 1994, Article 2.1, in *World Trade Organization, The Results of the Uruguay Round of Multilateral Trade Negotiations* 147 (2001) ("Antidumping Agreement").

[2] GATT, Art. VI:1.

[3] See T.P. Stewart, Administration of the Antidumping Law: A Different Perspective, in R. Boltuck and R.E. Litan (Eds.), *Down in the Dumps: Administration of the Unfair Trade Laws* (1991), 288. The Brookings Institution, Washington, DC.

* J. Daniel Stirk was an associate with Stewart and Stewart, Washington, D.C., from 2003 to 2007 and contributed to the 2006–2007 version of this chapter.

> produced, for the reason that such a system, in its final analysis and on a sufficient scale, spells bankruptcy.[4]

Hence, governments use antidumping measures to protect their domestic industries from injury caused by unfair international price discrimination.

Though antidumping measures are provided for in the GATT and the WTO Antidumping Agreement, the antidumping remedy came into existence well before these multilateral accords. The antidumping remedy was originally enacted in national legislation by various countries beginning in the early twentieth century. Canada passed the first antidumping law as part of its Customs Act of 1904.[5] This law was soon followed by the enactment of antidumping laws by, *inter alia*, New Zealand in 1905, Australia in 1906, and South Africa in 1914.[6] The United States enacted its first antidumping law as part of the Revenue Act of 1916,[7] although the modern U.S. law has its origins in the Antidumping Act of 1921.[8]

When the original Contracting Parties to the GATT agreed to a comprehensive multilateral trade agreement in 1947, provision was made at the outset for antidumping measures in Article VI of the GATT. As noted above, injurious dumping was a concern of many governments, and the ability to counteract unfair trade, including dumping as well as subsidization, and also to mitigate the injury from unexpected increases in fair trade through safeguard measures,[9] was politically necessary to enable the Contracting Parties to open their markets as contemplated by the GATT. Though the overall economic benefit of trade liberalization is undisputed, rapid expansion of international trade can nevertheless be disruptive. Domestic industries and workers, and their representatives in legislatures, want assurances of a level playing field, no unfair trade, and a smooth transition to a more open trading regime. Thus, the availability of an antidumping remedy has been an integral part of the multilateral trading system from the beginning and plays a significant role in facilitating further trade liberalization.

The language in Article VI of the original GATT 1947 was relatively simple and short. It provided a broad outline of the circumstances under which action

[4] S.J. Graham, letter to the editor, *New York Times*, July 4, 1916.

[5] An Act to Amend the Customs Tariff, 1897, 4 Edw. VII, I Canada Statutes 111 (1904).

[6] See *Antidumping and Countervailing Duties: Secretariat Analysis of Legislation*, GATT Doc. No. L/712 (October 23, 1957), at 4.

[7] The 1916 Act established civil and criminal penalties for dumping, including treble damages. The law was rooted more in antitrust policy than in international trade and tariff policy. It was rarely used because of the level of proof required and the need to show intent to injure a domestic industry. Japan and the EC successfully challenged the 1916 Act in WTO dispute settlement proceedings as violating provisions of the Antidumping Agreement. See *United States – Antidumping Act of 1916*, WT/DS136 and WT/DS162. The law was repealed in 2004. Miscellaneous Trade and Technical Corrections Act of 2004, § 2006, Pub. Law 108–429, 118 Stat. 2434, 2597 (December 3, 2004).

[8] Antidumping Act of 1921, ch. 14 §§ 201–212, Pub. Law 67–10, 42 Stat. 9, 11–15 (19 U.S.C. §§ 160–171).

[9] See Article XIX of the GATT.

could be taken and the type of action the Contracting Parties agreed was permitted, but Article VI did not provide a precise set of rules or guidelines for implementation. The article consists, *in toto*, of just eight paragraphs, only the first two of which discuss dumping and antidumping exclusively.[10] However, these paragraphs, although brief, nevertheless contain almost all of the elements of the antidumping remedy that would be elaborated on in later plurilateral and multilateral agreements, and which are still the subject of ongoing multilateral negotiation today. Concepts such as dumping, margin of dumping, normal value, ordinary course of trade, export price, constructed normal value, due allowances or adjustments, like product, material injury, and threat of material injury are all noted under Article VI of the GATT. The brevity of the provision, however, left nearly all the detail of implementing the rights and obligations under Article VI to the discretion of the Contracting Parties.

Such discretion led to, or rather perpetuated, significant differences in the national antidumping systems adopted by the Contracting Parties. Over time, with more experience and increased international trade, a host of issues arose in the area of antidumping, and there was an increased desire among the Contracting Parties to clarify certain concepts, promote consistency, and prevent abuse of the antidumping remedy. A series of plurilateral antidumping "codes," and eventually the multilateral WTO Antidumping Agreement, were thus negotiated to elaborate the rights and obligations of Article VI of the GATT.

The first Antidumping Code resulted from the Kennedy Round of Multilateral Trade Negotiations concluded in 1967.[11] Article 1 of the Kennedy Round Code provided that "[t]he imposition of an anti-dumping duty is a measure to be taken only under the circumstances provided for in Article VI of the General Agreement" and that the provisions of the Code "govern the application of this Article, in so far as action is taken under anti-dumping legislation or regulations."

[10] Article VI of the GATT, paras. 1–2, provide in pertinent part:

> 1. The Contracting Parties recognize that dumping, by which products of one country are introduced into the commerce of another country at less than the normal value of the products, is to be condemned if it causes or threatens material injury to an established industry in the territory of a Contracting Party or materially retards the establishment of a domestic industry. For the purposes of this Article, a product is to be considered as being introduced into the commerce of an importing country at less than its normal value, if the price of the product exported from one country to another
> (a) is less than the comparable price, in the ordinary course of trade, for the like product when destined for consumption in the exporting country, or
> (b) in the absence of such domestic price, is less than either
> (i) the highest comparable price for the like product for export to any third country in the ordinary course of trade, or
> (ii) the cost of production of the product in the country of origin plus a reasonable addition for selling cost and profit.
> Due allowance shall be made in each case for differences in conditions and terms of sale, for differences in taxation, and for other differences affecting price comparability.
> 2. To offset or prevent dumping, a Contracting Party may levy on any dumped product an antidumping duty not greater in amount than the margin of dumping in respect to such product. For the purposes of this Article, the margin of dumping is the price difference determined in accordance with the provisions of paragraph. 1.

[11] Agreement on Implementation of Article VI of the GATT, July 1, 1967, Basic Instruments and Selected Documents (BISD) 15S/24 (1968).

Thus, the Code was an elaboration of the antidumping rules already established in Article VI of the GATT. The Kennedy Round Code expanded the rules from a handful of paragraphs to ten pages of fairly detailed provisions covering five main substantive areas, including determination of dumping, determination of material injury, investigation and administrative procedures, antidumping duties and provisional measures, and antidumping actions on behalf of third countries. As detailed in Appendix 1 to this chapter, the Kennedy Round Code established a structure that was, for the most part, maintained as the rules were further expanded in subsequent negotiated texts. The Code, however, was a plurilateral, rather than a multilateral agreement, and not all GATT Contracting Parties were bound by it. Indeed, the United States, because of internal political pressures, implemented the Kennedy Round Code only to the extent that it did not conflict with its existing antidumping laws.

The next iteration of the Antidumping Code resulted from the Tokyo Round of Multilateral Trade Negotiations, concluded in 1979.[12] As reflected in the table in Appendix 1, the Tokyo Round Code maintained the structure of the Kennedy Round Code but expanded or revised several articles, adding further specificity and detail to a number of provisions across a variety of substantive issues. Like the Kennedy Round Code, the Tokyo Round Antidumping Code was a plurilateral agreement, so not all GATT Contracting Parties were bound by it. However, the major users of the antidumping remedy agreed to be bound by, and implemented, the Code.

The WTO Antidumping Agreement, part of the package of Multilateral Trade Agreements adopted at the conclusion of the Uruguay Round in 1994, represents the first truly multilateral agreement on antidumping rules, as all WTO Members must agree to be bound by its provisions. The text of the Antidumping Agreement is nearly double the length of the prior codes, and includes significantly greater detail in the provisions governing the main areas of determination of dumping and injury, imposition of antidumping measures, procedures and evidence, and review of existing measures. These areas are discussed in greater detail later in this chapter to provide a general overview of the current rules under the Antidumping Agreement. Following this overview discussion are some concluding observations regarding the use of antidumping laws by WTO Members.

The Determination of Dumping

The Price Comparison

The obligations within Article VI of the GATT 1994 regarding dumping must be read together with those in the WTO Antidumping Agreement.[13] "Dumping"

[12] Agreement on Implementation of Article VI of the GATT, January 1, 1980, BISD 26S/171 (1980).

[13] Indeed, the official title of the WTO Antidumping Agreement is the "Agreement on Implementation of Article VI of the General Agreement on Tariffs and Trade 1994."

is defined in both Article VI:1 of the GATT 1994 and Article 2.1 of the Antidumping Agreement as a form of price discrimination between markets. When a foreign exporter's products are imported at an "export price" (EP) that is less than the products' "normal value" (NV), the products have been "dumped" into that market. The determination of dumping, therefore, is based on the answer to a simple, objective mathematical question: Is EP < NV? The answer to that question does not depend on the exporter's intent or the price charged by domestic producers for the same product.

The Antidumping Agreement envisions that "authorities" in the WTO Members will investigate allegations of dumping and make dumping determinations. Footnote 3 of the Agreement defines the term "authorities" to mean "authorities at an appropriate senior level." In the United States, the U.S. Department of Commerce's International Trade Administration is charged with determining whether a foreign producer or exporter is dumping products into the U.S. market.[14]

The General Rule

Article 2.1 states that the normal value of a product is based on the product's price in the exporter's home market. Specifically, the normal value is the "comparable price, in the ordinary course of trade, for the like product when destined for consumption in the exporting country." According to Article 2.6, the term "like product" means "a product which is identical; that is, alike in all respects to the product under consideration, or in the absence of such a product, another product which, although not alike in all respects, has characteristics closely resembling those of the product under consideration." Other provisions of the Antidumping Agreement permit the use of alternative bases for normal value and export prices.

Normal Value Options

Third Country Prices and Constructed Normal Value

There will be times when a product is either not sold in the exporter's home market "in the ordinary course of trade" or when a particular market situation or a low volume of home market sales makes it necessary to compare export prices to another benchmark. In such a case, Article 2.2 permits alternative normal values based on (1) third country prices or (2) a constructed normal value based on the product's cost of production in the country of origin plus a reasonable amount for administrative, selling, and general costs (SG&A) and for profits.

Uruguay Round negotiators focused on creating specific rules to address the proper calculation of costs when home market prices were unreliable. Article 2.2.1 explains that home market or third country sales may be treated as not

[14] 19 U.S.C. §§ 1673b(b), 1673d(a), 1677(1); see *Import Administration Antidumping Manual* (1998), available at http://ia.ita.doc.gov/admanual/index.html.

being "in the ordinary course of trade" if they are below per unit (fixed and variable) costs of production plus SG&A. Sales below cost may be disregarded in determining normal value only if they (1) are made within an extended period of time in substantial quantities, and (2) are at prices that do not provide for the recovery of all costs within a reasonable period of time. Articles 2.2.1.1 and 2.2.2 further explain how costs should be calculated for purposes of constructing normal value and determining if sales are below cost.

Intermediate Country Prices

If the product is not exported directly to the country of importation but is instead exported through an intermediate country, Article 2.5 provides that the normal value will usually be based on intermediate country prices unless (1) the products are merely transshipped through the intermediate country, (2) the products are not produced in the intermediate country, or (3) there is no comparable price for such products in the intermediate country.

Non–Market Economy Prices

If the product is exported from a non–market economy country in which the government has a monopoly on trade and fixes domestic prices, Article 2.7 read in conjunction with the Ad Note 1 to Article VI:1 of the GATT recognizes that special difficulties may exist in determining price comparability. Accordingly, WTO Members may find that a strict comparison with domestic prices in a non–market economy country is not appropriate. Because the Antidumping Agreement does not indicate what WTO Members should do when such a comparison is not appropriate, WTO Members have adopted their own methodologies to calculate dumping margins. For example, the United States constructs the normal value by using values from a surrogate market–economy country(ies) for each factor of production used in producing the merchandise (including labor, raw materials, energy/utilities, and capital costs) to arrive at a total cost of manufacture for the product to which amounts for general, administrative, and selling expenses; profits; and packing are added.[15]

Export Price Options

Article 2.3 of the Antidumping Agreement and Ad Note 1 to Article VI:1 of the GATT also account for instances in which there is no export price or where the export price is considered to be "unreliable." An export price could be unreliable because the exporter (1) is associated with (or related to) the importer or (2) has a compensatory arrangement with the importer for consignment sales.[16] If the export price cannot be used, Article 2.3 permits alternative export prices to be constructed based on (1) the importer's or consignee's resale price to an

[15] 19 U.S.C. § 1677b(c)(1) and (3).

[16] Article 2.3 implements Ad Note 1 to Article VI:1 of the GATT about "hidden" dumping.

independent buyer or, if unavailable, (2) such reasonable basis as the authorities may determine.[17]

Selecting and Adjusting the Prices to Be Compared

Since the Kennedy Code, Article 2 has required dumping determinations to be based on a "fair comparison" between the export price and the normal value by requiring that the two ex-factory prices (the price at the factory door before delivery costs) be compared at the same level of trade with respect to sales made as nearly as possible at the same time. Rarely can the prices of products sold in two markets be compared without making some sort of mathematical adjustment to account for differences in the products or their circumstances of sale. Therefore, Uruguay Round negotiators focused on adding specific rules to address how export prices should be compared to normal values.

Article 2.4 requires authorities to make "due allowance" for (1) differences in the conditions and terms of sale, (2) differences in taxation, (3) differences in levels of trade, (4) differences in quantities, (5) differences in physical characteristics, and (6) other differences affecting price comparability. Additional adjustments are made to constructed export prices for costs, including duties and taxes, those incurred between importation and resale, and for profits accruing. If price comparability has been affected by the use of constructed export prices, Article 2.4 further requires authorities to establish the normal value at a level of trade equivalent to the level of trade of the constructed export price or to make other "due allowance" as warranted.

In addition to selecting and adjusting prices to make a "fair comparison," Article 2.4.1 addresses the issue of the conversion of currencies and fluctuations in exchanges rates. Article 2.4.2 further addresses the determination of dumping margins in investigations. According to Article VI:2 of the GATT 1994, the "margin of dumping" is the price difference determined when a product is imported at less than its normal value. The margin of dumping can be expressed as a monetary figure or as an *ad valorem* percentage of the total export price:

Normal Value	–	Export Price	=	Margin of Dumping
$10.90		$10.00		$0.90 = 9%

Specifically, Article 2.4.2 identifies three different price comparison methodologies to be used to determine dumping margins in investigations. Article 2.4.2 requires authorities to establish the existence of margins of dumping on the basis of a comparison of (1) weighted-average normal values and weighted-average export prices or (2) transactions. If the authorities find a pattern of export prices that differ significantly among different purchasers, regions, or time periods,

[17] See Antidumping Agreement, Article 9.3.3 (regarding calculation of constructed export price according to Article 2.3).

however, the price comparison may be based on a comparison of (3) a weighted-average normal value to prices of individual export transactions, if an explanation is provided as to why such differences cannot be taken into account by using the first two price-comparison methodologies.

The Limitations of Article 2

An important part of understanding what Article 2 of the Antidumping Agreement requires WTO Members to do is to understand the scope and limits of the Agreement itself. The Antidumping Agreement was not drafted to cover each and every possible question or concern that might arise regarding the dumping margin calculation. At the most rudimentary level, the Antidumping Agreement reflects the level of international consensus achieved to provide rules on specific areas of the dumping determination made by national authorities. Article 2 addresses certain parts of the calculation of exporter-specific dumping margins but does not begin to guide WTO Members through all the intricacies of various margin calculations. Article 2 does not include a standard computer program to be used by all national authorities to calculate dumping margins. Instead, Article 2 permits WTO Members to adopt their own antidumping duty laws as long as they are consistent with the rules provided in the Antidumping Agreement. Perhaps because of some of the limitations of Article 2 in terms of scope as well as the level of detail achieved in the final text, WTO Members have challenged a significant number of antidumping measures by requesting Panel and/or Appellate Body review.[18]

The Determination of Injury

Article VI:1 of the GATT 1994 condemns dumping if it causes or threatens to cause material injury to a domestic industry or materially retards the establishment of a domestic industry. Likewise, Antidumping Agreement Footnote 9

[18] For a discussion of Article 2 of the Antidumping Agreement, see generally *Guatemala – Cement I*, WT/DS60/R; *US – DRAMS*, WT/DS99/R; *Canada – Dairy*, WT/DS103/RW/2, WT/DS113/RW/2; *US – 1916 Act (EC)*, WT/DS136/R; *US – 1916 Act*, WT/DS136/AB/R, WT/DS162/AB/R; *US – 1916 Act (Japan)*, WT/DS162/R; *Thailand – H-Beams*, WT/DS122/R, WT/DS122/AB/R; *Guatemala – Cement II*, WT/DS156/R; *EC – Bed Linen*, WT/DS141/R, WT/DS141/AB/R, WT/DS141/RW, WT/DS141/AB/RW; *US – Stainless Steel (Korea)*, WT/DS179/R; *US – Hot-Rolled Steel (Japan)*, WT/DS184/R, WT/DS184/AB/R; *Argentina – Ceramic Tiles*, WT/DS189/R; *US – Steel Plate (India)*, WT/DS206/R; *Egypt – Steel Rebar*, WT/DS211/R; *US – Offset Act*, WT/DS217/AB/R, WT/DS234/AB/R; *EC – Tube or Pipe Fittings*, WT/DS219/R, WT/DS219/AB/R; *Argentina – Poultry*, WT/DS241/R; *US – Corrosion-Resistant Steel Sunset*, WT/DS244/R, WT/DS244/AB/R; *US – Final Softwood Lumber V*, WT/DS264/R, WT/DS264/AB/R; *US – Oil Country Tubular Goods Sunset Reviews*, WT/DS268/R; *US – Antidumping Measures on Oil Country Tubular Goods*, WT/DS282/R, WT/DS282/AB/R; *Korea – Paper*, WT/DS312/R; *US – Zeroing (EC)*, WT/DS294/R, WT/DS294/AB/R. Full citations to cases discussing the Antidumping Agreement are provided in Appendix 2 to this chapter. A bibliography of books and articles discussing the Antidumping Agreement is provided at the end of this chapter.

clarifies that the term "injury" means material injury, threat of material injury, or material retardation of the establishment of a domestic industry. In other words, dumping is permissible unless the national authorities of the WTO Member find that the action is "injurious" according to the requirements in Article VI:1 of the GATT 1994 and Article 3 of the Antidumping Agreement. According to the international trade rules governing WTO Members, it is only at the point at which dumping becomes injurious that the practice is deemed "unfair" and can be remedied.

As with the determination of dumping, the Antidumping Agreement envisions that "authorities" in the WTO Members will make injury determinations. Footnote 3 defines the term "authorities" to mean "authorities at an appropriate senior level." In the United States, the U.S. International Trade Commission is charged with determining whether an industry is materially injured or threatened with material injury or the establishment of an industry is materially retarded by reason of dumped imports.[19]

Unlike the determination of dumping, however, the determination of injury is not based on the application of a simple, objective mathematical equation. The Antidumping Agreement does not even attempt to define "material" injury. Instead, Article 3.1 requires an injury determination to be based on "positive evidence" and an objective examination of (1) the volume of the dumped imports, (2) the price effect in the domestic market for like products, and (3) the consequent impact of imports on domestic producers of such products. Articles 3.2 and 3.4 identify the various considerations or economic factors that must be considered with respect to volume, price, and impact in making any injury determination. Both Articles 3.2 and 3.4 recognize, however, that the factors listed in the agreement cannot "necessarily give decisive guidance." Article 3.5 requires authorities to demonstrate that the dumped imports are, through the effects of dumping as set forth in Articles 3.2 and 3.4, causing that injury to the domestic industry.[20]

[19] 19 U.S.C. §§ 1673b(a), 1673d(b), and 1677(2).

[20] For a discussion of Article 3 of the Antidumping Agreement, see generally *Guatemala – Cement I*, WT/DS60/R; *US – DRAMS*, WT/DS99/R; *Mexico – Corn Syrup*, WT/DS132/R, WT/DS132/RW, WT/DS132/AB/RW; *US – 1916 Act (EC)*, WT/DS136/R; *US – 1916 Act (Japan)*, WT/DS162/R; *Thailand – H-Beams*, WT/DS122/R, WT/DS122/AB/R; *Guatemala – Cement II*, WT/DS156/R; *EC – Bed Linen*, WT/DS141/R, WT/DS141/RW, WT/DS141/AB/RW; *US – Stainless Steel (Korea)*, WT/DS179/R; *US – Hot-Rolled Steel (Japan)*, WT/DS184/R, WT/DS184/AB/R; *US – Cotton Yarn*, WT/DS192/R; *Argentina – Ceramic Tiles*, WT/DS189/R; *US – Line Pipe*, WT/DS202/AB/R; *Egypt – Steel Rebar*, WT/DS211/R; *US – Offset Act*, WT/DS217/ARB/EEC; *EC – Tube or Pipe Fittings*, WT/DS219/R, WT/DS219/AB/R; *Argentina – Poultry*, WT/DS241/R; *US – Steel Safeguards*, WT/DS248/AB/R, WT/DS249/AB/R, WT/DS251/AB/R, WT/DS252/AB/R, WT/DS253/AB/R, WT/DS254/AB/R, WT/DS258/AB/R, WT/DS259/AB/R; *US – Corrosion-Resistant Steel Sunset*, WT/DS244/R; *US – Softwood Lumber VI*, WT/DS277/R, WT/DS277/RW; *US – Final Softwood Lumber V*, WT/DS264/R; *US – Oil Country Tubular Goods Sunset Reviews*, WT/DS268/R, WT/DS268/AB/R; *Mexico – Antidumping Measures on Rice*, WT/DS295/R; *US – Antidumping Measures on Oil Country Tubular Goods*, WT/DS282/R, WT/DS282/AB/R.

Volume Factors

According to Article 3.2, investigating authorities must consider whether there has been a significant increase in dumped imports, either in absolute terms or relative to production or consumption, in the importing Member. Article 3.3 further permits investigating authorities to cumulatively assess the effects of imports from more than one country if those imports are simultaneously subject to antidumping investigations and if the authorities determine that (1) the margin of dumping established for imports from each country is more than *de minimis* and the volume of imports from each country is not negligible, and (2) a cumulative assessment is appropriate in light of the conditions of competition between the imported products and between the imported products and the domestic like product.

Price Factors

In contrast to the dumping determination, which compares import prices with their normal values, the price analysis in injury determinations involves a comparison of import prices with the domestic prices of the importing Member. According to Article 3.2, investigating authorities shall consider (1) whether there has been significant price undercutting by the dumped imports, or (2) whether the effect of such imports is otherwise to depress prices to a significant degree or prevent price increases that would have occurred, to a significant degree.

Impact Factors

Article 3.4 requires the examination by investigating authorities of the impact of the dumped imports on the domestic industry, including "all relevant economic factors and indices having a bearing on the state of the industry...." Article 3.4 further identifies the following nonexhaustive list of factors to be considered:

- actual and potential decline in sales, profits, output, market share, productivity, return on investments, or utilization of capacity;
- factors affecting domestic prices;
- the magnitude of the margin of dumping; and
- actual and potential negative effects on cash flow, inventories, employment, wages, growth, and ability to raise capital or investments.

The Causal Relationship

Article 3.5 requires authorities to demonstrate a causal relationship between the dumped imports and the injury to the domestic industry. The authorities must examine "all relevant evidence" before them as well as known factors, other than the dumped imports, that are injuring the domestic industry at the same time. Article 3.5 contains a nonattribution requirement that prohibits authorities from attributing the injuries caused by "other factors" to the dumped imports. Article 3.5 further identifies a number of "other factors" that might be relevant, including:

- the volume and prices of imports not sold at dumping prices;
- contraction in demand or changes in the patterns of consumption;
- trade-restrictive practices of and competition between the foreign and domestic producers; and
- developments in technology and the export performance and productivity of the domestic industry.

Threat of Material Injury

Although the Antidumping Agreement may not define "material" injury in so many words, it does explain that a threat of material injury must be based on facts that lead to the conclusion that "further dumped exports are imminent and that, unless protective action is taken, material injury would occur." The threat must be "clearly foreseen and imminent." For example, as Footnote 10 points out, such a threat could occur if there was reason to believe that there would be, in the near future, substantially increased imports of the product at dumped prices.

Article 3.7 explains that a threat of material injury cannot be based merely on "allegation, conjecture or remote possibility." Rather, Article 3.7 requires authorities to consider the following nonexhaustive list of factors:

- a significant rate of increase of dumped imports into the domestic market indicating the likelihood of substantially increased importation;
- sufficient freely disposable, or an imminent, substantial increase in, capacity of the exporter indicating the likelihood of substantially increased dumped exports to the importing Member's market, taking into account the availability of other export markets to absorb any additional exports;
- whether imports are entering at prices that will have a significant depressing or suppressing effect on domestic prices, and would likely increase demand for further imports; and
- inventories of the product being investigated.

As with the material injury factors, Article 3.7 recognizes that these factors cannot "necessarily give decisive guidance." Instead, Article 3.7 explains that the "totality of the factors considered must lead to the conclusion that further dumped exports are imminent and that, unless protective action is taken, material injury would occur."

The Domestic Industry

According to Article 4.1(i), the relevant domestic industry is defined as those domestic producers as a whole of the like products or those whose collective output of products constitutes a major proportion of the total domestic production of those products. Under certain circumstances, however, domestic producers that import the allegedly dumped product or who are related to exporters or importers can be excluded from the domestic industry.[21]

Article 3.6 specifies that the effect of dumped imports should be assessed with respect to domestic production of the like product. If domestic production data are not available for the like product, then the effects of dumped imports should be assessed by examining the production of the narrowest group or range of products that includes the like product.

The relevant "domestic industry" for purposes of the injury determination is the domestic industry of the particular importing WTO Member. If two or more countries have achieved a level of integration characterizing a single, unified market within the meaning of customs unions under Article XXIV:8(a) of the GATT 1994, Article 4.3 specifies that the domestic industry will include the entire area of integration.

Article 4.1(ii) also recognizes that sometimes dumped imports injure only the domestic industry located in a particular region or territory of the Member. If the territory of a Member can be divided into multiple competitive markets, domestic producers within each market may be regarded as a separate domestic industry if (1) the producers within that market sell all or almost all of their production of the product in that market, and (2) the demand in that market is not to any substantial degree supplied by producers located elsewhere in the territory. In addition, there must be a concentration of dumped imports into the isolated market. In such a case, injury may be found to exist if dumped imports cause injury to producers of all or almost all of the production within the isolated market. Then Article 4.2 permits the collection of antidumping duties only on the products in question consigned for final consumption to that area. Separate rules regarding duty collection apply if the importing Member cannot collect antidumping duties on a selective basis.

The Application of Antidumping Measures

Article VI of the GATT 1994 and the Antidumping Agreement not only condemn injurious dumping, they authorize WTO Members to take remedial action

[21] For a discussion of Article 4 of the Antidumping Agreement, see generally *US – 1916 Act (EC)*, WT/DS136/R; *US – 1916 Act*, WT/DS136/AB/R, WT/DS162/AB/R; *US – 1916 Act (Japan)*, WT/DS162/R; *EC – Bed Linen*, WT/DS141/RW; *US – Hot-Rolled Steel (Japan)*, WT/DS184/R, WT/DS184/AB/R; *Argentina – Poultry*, WT/DS241/R; *US – Final Softwood Lumber V*, WT/DS264/R.

against dumped imports. Articles 1[22] and 18.1 of the Antidumping Agreement clarify that any such action must be consistent with the rules expressed in Article VI and the Antidumping Agreement. The Antidumping Agreement further authorizes different types of antidumping measures, such as provisional and final antidumping duties and price undertakings (or agreements).

Antidumping Duties

General

Article VI:2 of the GATT 1994 provides that antidumping duties may be "levied" or collected on any dumped product to offset or prevent dumping. According to Article VI:2 and Article 9.3 of the Antidumping Agreement, the amount of antidumping duty collected on dumped imports cannot exceed the margin of dumping found for that product. As explained earlier in this chapter, Article VI:2 defines the "margin of dumping" as equal to the price difference between normal value and the export price. Article 9.1 of the Antidumping Agreement further states that the decisions of whether to impose an antidumping duty and whether the amount should be the full margin of dumping or less are for the WTO Member's national authorities to make. Moreover, Article 9.1 expresses the desire that imposition of antidumping duties be permissive, rather than mandatory, in all WTO Members and that the duty be less than the margin of dumping if that would be adequate to remove the injury to the domestic industry.[23]

Article 9.2 requires duties to be collected on a nondiscriminatory basis on all imports of the dumped product from a particular country. Frequently, it

[22] For a discussion of Article 1 of the Antidumping Agreement, see generally *Guatemala – Cement I*, WT/DS60/R; *US – 1916 Act (EC)*, WT/DS136/R; *US – 1916 Act*, WT/DS136/AB/R, WT/DS162/AB/R; *US – 1916 Act (Japan)*, WT/DS162/R; *Guatemala – Cement II*, WT/DS156/R; *EC – Bed Linen*, WT/DS141/R; *US – Stainless Steel (Korea)*, WT/DS179/R; *US – Section 129(c)(1) URAA*, WT/DS221/R; *US – Offset Act*, WT/DS217/R, WT/DS234/R; *EC – Tube or Pipe Fittings*, WT/DS219/R, WT/DS219/AB/R; *Argentina – Poultry*, WT/DS241/R; *US – Softwood Lumber VI*, WT/DS277/R; *US – Final Softwood Lumber V*, WT/DS264/R; *US – Oil Country Tubular Goods Sunset Reviews*, WT/DS268/R; *Mexico – Antidumping Measures on Rice*, WT/DS295/R; *US – Antidumping Measures on Oil Country Tubular Goods*, WT/DS282/R; *Korea – Paper*, WT/DS312/R; *US – Zeroing (EC)*, WT/DS294/R.

[23] For a discussion of Article 9 of the Antidumping Agreement, see generally *US – 1916 Act*, WT/DS136/AB/R, WT/DS162/AB/R; *US – 1916 Act (Japan)*, WT/DS162/R; *Guatemala – Cement II*, WT/DS156/R; *EC – Bed Linen*, WT/DS141/RW, WT/DS141/AB/RW; *US – Hot-Rolled Steel (Japan)*, WT/DS184/R, WT/DS184/AB/R; *Argentina – Ceramic Tiles*, WT/DS189/R; *US – Steel Plate (India)*, WT/DS206/R; *US – Section 129(c)(1) URAA*, WT/DS221/R; *US – Offset Act*, WT/DS217/ARB/EEC; *EC – Tube or Pipe Fittings*, WT/DS219/R, WT/DS219/AB/R; *Argentina – Poultry*, WT/DS241/R; *US – Corrosion-Resistant Steel Sunset*, WT/DS244/AB/R; *US – Softwood Lumber VI*, WT/DS277/R; *US – Final Softwood Lumber V*, WT/DS264/R, WT/DS264/AB/R; *US – Oil Country Tubular Goods Sunset Reviews*, WT/DS268/AB/R; *Mexico – Antidumping Measures on Rice*, WT/DS295/R; *Korea – Paper*, WT/DS312/R; *US – Zeroing (EC)*, WT/DS294/R, WT/DS294/AB/R.

is impracticable for national authorities to investigate every foreign producer or exporter of the allegedly dumped product. Although Article 6.10 requires national authorities to determine an individual margin of dumping for each known exporter or producer of the product under investigation, authorities may limit their examination to a reasonable number of interested parties or products by using statistically valid samples. According to Article 9.4, the antidumping duty applied to those foreign exporters or producers that are not investigated as part of the sample must not exceed (1) the weighted-average margin established with respect to investigated exporters/producers, or (2) the difference between the weighted-average normal value established with respect to investigated exporters/producers and the export prices of uninvestigated exporters/producers (in a prospective normal value system). For example, in the United States, the U.S. Department of Commerce issues an antidumping duty order instructing Customs to collect antidumping duties on imports of a certain product from certain foreign producers and "all others" from a particular country.[24]

Provisional Measures and Retroactive Collection of Duties

In the context of an antidumping investigation, national authorities may decide to take "provisional measures" based on a preliminary finding of dumping and injury. According to Article 7.2, provisional measures can take the form of a duty or, preferably, a security (cash deposit or bond) equal to the amount of the estimated antidumping duties.[25] If the investigation ultimately results in a negative determination, Article 10.5 requires the national authorities to refund any cash deposit made and release any bonds expeditiously.

After the national authorities have made affirmative determinations of dumping and injury, Article 10.1 states that duties are generally collected on future imports entered after the decision. Article 10.2 identifies two scenarios permitting the retroactive collection of duties for the period in which provisional measures, if any, have been applied: (1) if a final material injury determination is made, or (2) if a final threat of injury determination is made where the effect of the dumped imports would, in the absence of provisional measures, have led to a determination of injury.[26]

Article 10.6 permits the retroactive collection of duties for the 90-day period preceding the application of provisional measures if the authorities find (1) that there is a history of injurious dumping or that the importer was, or should have

[24] *See* 19 U.S.C. §§ 1673d(c)(5), 1673e(a).

[25] For a discussion of Article 7 of the Antidumping Agreement, see generally *Mexico – Corn Syrup*, WT/DS132/R; *Guatemala – Cement II*, WT/DS156/R; *US – Offset Act*, WT/DS217/ARB/EEC.

[26] For a discussion of Article 10 of the Antidumping Agreement, see generally *Mexico – Corn Syrup*, WT/DS132/R; *EC – Bed Linen*, WT/DS141/RW; *US – Hot-Rolled Steel (Japan)*, WT/DS184/R; *US – Offset Act*, WT/DS217/ARB/EEC.

been, aware that the exporter practices dumping that would cause injury, and (2) the injury is caused by massive dumped imports in a relatively short time that is likely to seriously undermine the remedial effects of the antidumping duties. At no point, however, can antidumping duties be collected retroactively on products entered for consumption prior to the date the investigation was initiated.

Price Undertakings

If a foreign producer or exporter would rather commit to revising its prices or ceasing exports to the area in question at dumped prices, an antidumping investigation may be suspended or terminated without the imposition of provisional measures or antidumping duties. According to Articles 8.1 and 8.2 of the Antidumping Agreement, price undertakings are voluntary and may not be sought or accepted until after the national authorities have made an affirmative preliminary determination of both dumping and injury. National authorities are not required to accept an undertaking offered by a foreign producer/exporter if it would be impractical. If the undertaking is accepted during the investigation, however, Article 8.4 provides that the exporter or national authorities may decide to complete the investigation.[27]

To ensure compliance with the undertaking, Article 8.6 allows national authorities to require the exporter to provide supporting information periodically and to permit verification. If the exporter violates the undertaking, Article 8.6 further permits the authorities to apply provisional measures immediately. Any retroactive duty assessment may not apply to imports entered before the violation occurred.

Other Considerations

Even if a national authority has made an affirmative determination of both dumping and injury, there are two additional factors that must be considered before a Member can apply antidumping measures to imports. First, Article 3.8 cautions national authorities to consider and decide "with special care" whether to apply antidumping measures if the injury determination is based on a finding of threat, rather than material, injury. Second, Article 15 of the Antidumping Agreement requires national authorities to give "special regard" to the "special situation" of developing country Members when considering the application of antidumping measures. Accordingly, Article 15 states that the possibility of constructive remedies provided by the Agreement "shall be explored" before

[27] For a discussion of Article 8 of the Antidumping Agreement, see generally *US – Offset Act*, WT/DS217/R, WT/DS234/R, WT/DS217/ARB/EEC; *EC – Tube or Pipe Fittings*, WT/DS219/R.

applying antidumping duties "where they would affect the essential interests of developing country Members."[28]

Procedures

Initiation and Subsequent Investigation

Initiation

Antidumping measures are imposed following an investigation to determine the existence of margins of dumping, the existence or threat of material injury to the domestic industry, and a causal link. Per Article 5.1, antidumping investigations are typically initiated following the receipt by investigating authorities of an application (or "petition," in U.S. terminology) by or on behalf of the domestic industry. However, Article 5.6 permits authorities, in special circumstances, to self-initiate an investigation, but only where they have sufficient evidence of dumping, injury, and a causal link to justify initiation. In the United States, authorities rarely self-initiate an antidumping investigation.

Article 5.2 describes the information that must be included in a petition for an antidumping investigation. The petition must include evidence of dumping, injury or threat of injury, and a causal link between the alleged dumping and injury. Specifically, the petition must provide information on the identity of the petitioner; production data for the petitioner and the domestic industry; a description of the allegedly dumped product; the countries involved; any known exporters, foreign producers, and importers; price data for the dumped product in the home market and export markets; and information on the volume of allegedly dumped goods and the effect on prices and impact on the domestic industry. The evidence presented must be documented to the extent that information is reasonably available to the petitioners. Unsubstantiated assertions are not sufficient, so in practice a great deal of documentation is required. Typically, petitions filed with the U.S. Department of Commerce and U.S. International Trade Commission are lengthy documents with numerous attachments.

Article 5.3 requires that the authorities examine a submitted petition prior to initiating an investigation to determine whether it contains sufficient evidence to justify the initiation of an investigation. It is important to note that the evidence sufficient to justify initiation is different and less than the evidence necessary to warrant an affirmative final determination of dumping or injury after a complete investigation. Article 5.5 prohibits the authorities from publicizing the filing of a petition (or its preparation) prior to the initiation of an investigation. Thus, there is an opportunity for petitioners to consult with the authorities prior to

[28] For a discussion of Article 15 of the Antidumping Agreement, see generally *EC – Bed Linen*, WT/DS141/R, WT/DS141/RW; *US – Steel Plate (India)*, WT/DS206/R; *US – Offset Act*, WT/DS217/R, WT/DS234/R; *EC – Tube or Pipe Fittings*, WT/DS219/R.

filing a petition to determine whether the petition presents sufficient evidence to justify initiation. However, Article 5.5 also requires authorities to notify the government of the exporting Member concerned before proceeding to initiate an investigation. Per Article 5.7, the evidence of both dumping and injury is considered simultaneously in the decision whether to initiate an investigation.

Standing

Prior to initiating an investigation, the authorities must also determine whether the petitioner has standing to file the petition, in other words, whether the petition has been filed "by or on behalf of the domestic industry." Article 5.4 provides that a petition shall be considered filed by or on behalf of the domestic industry (1) if it is supported by producers representing 50% of the total production of the like product of producers indicating either support or opposition to the petition, and (2) if it is supported by producers representing at least 25% of overall production of the like product by the domestic industry. Both of these numerical thresholds must be met. In most cases, standing is not in doubt because many petitions include all members of a domestic industry as petitioners. However, in the case of fragmented industries involving an exceptionally large number of producers, Footnote 13 allows authorities to determine the level of support for the petition based on statistically valid sampling techniques.

Administrative Process

As with the decision whether to initiate, the investigation of dumping and injury proceeds simultaneously per Article 5.7. In the United States, the Department of Commerce investigates dumping while the International Trade Commission (a separate, independent agency) investigates injury. Other WTO Members maintain a unified authority, which considers evidence of both dumping and injury.

According to Article 5.10, antidumping investigations should normally take no longer than a year, and in no case should they last longer than 18 months. Article 5.9 states that, while the investigation is ongoing, customs clearance of imports of the product under investigation cannot be hindered. Quantitative restrictions or import prohibitions are not contemplated under the Antidumping Agreement as a remedy for dumping.

De minimis *Margins/Negligible Volume*

Article 5.8 requires the immediate termination of an investigation, as well as the rejection of a petition, if authorities determine that the dumping margin is *de minimis* or the volume of dumped imports is negligible. A dumping margin is considered *de minimis* if it is less than 2 percent when expressed as a percentage of the export price. The volume of dumped imports is considered negligible if the volume from a particular country is less than 3 percent of total imports of the like product, unless countries that individually account for less than 3 percent of imports collectively account for more than 7 percent of imports.[29]

Evidence

Antidumping investigations and review proceedings require authorities to collect and consider large amounts of evidence, including price data, production data, information on production processes, cost data, and financial data. Article 6 sets forth rules for the collection, treatment, and consideration of such evidence by authorities.

Right of Interested Parties to Defend their Interests

Much of Article 6 establishes the due process rights of interested parties that investigating authorities must recognize. Article 6.2, for instance, expressly states that "[t]hroughout the anti-dumping investigation all interested parties shall have a full opportunity for the defence of their interests."

"Interested parties" is defined in Article 6.11 as at least exporters, foreign producers, and importers of a product subject to investigation; trade or business associations a majority of the members of which are producers, exporters, or importers of such product; the government of the exporting Member; and producers of the like product in the importing Member or a trade or business association a majority of the members of which produce the like product in the territory of the importing Member. Members are not prevented by Article 6.11 from permitting other interested parties to participate in investigations. Article 6.12 requires authorities to permit industrial users and representative organizations of consumers of the product under investigation to provide information relevant to the investigation, but does not confer on these groups "interested party" status.

Article 6.1 requires authorities to provide interested parties notice of all information required to be submitted and "ample opportunity" to submit in writing all evidence they consider relevant. Much of the data for the dumping determination come from exporters or foreign producers who submit responses to questionnaires issued by investigating authorities. Article 6.1.1 requires that

[29] For a discussion of Article 5 of the Antidumping Agreement, see generally *Guatemala – Cement I*, WT/DS60/R, WT/DS60/AB/R; *US – DRAMS*, WT/DS99/R; *Mexico – Corn Syrup*, WT/DS132/R; *US – 1916 Act (EC)*, WT/DS136/R; *US – 1916 Act*, WT/DS136/AB/R, WT/DS162/AB/R; *US – 1916 Act (Japan)*, WT/DS162/R; *Thailand – H-Beams*, WT/DS122/R, WT/DS122/AB/R; *Guatemala – Cement II*, WT/DS156/R; *EC – Bed Linen*, WT/DS141/R, WT/DS141/RW; *US – Hot-Rolled Steel (Japan)*, WT/DS184/R, WT/DS184/AB/R; *US – Offset Act*, WT/DS217/R, WT/DS234/R, WT/DS217/AB/R, WT/DS234/AB/R, WT/DS217/ARB/EEC; *Argentina – Poultry*, WT/DS241/R; *US – Corrosion-Resistant Steel Sunset*, WT/DS244/R; *US – Final Softwood Lumber V*, WT/DS264/R; *Mexico – Antidumping Measures on Rice*, WT/DS295/R; *Korea – Paper*, WT/DS312/R; *US – Zeroing (EC)*, WT/DS294/R, WT/DS294/AB/R.

exporters and foreign producers be given at least 30 days to reply to questionnaires, and authorities must give due consideration to any request for an extension of time to file a response. Article 6.1.1 provides that such extensions should be granted whenever practicable. With the relatively tight one-year to eighteen-month deadline for completing an antidumping investigation, however, there is a limit on the flexibility authorities have to permit significant extensions. Article 6.13 requires authorities to take due account of any difficulties of interested parties, in particular small companies, in providing requested information, and to provide any assistance practicable.

Articles 6.1.2 and 6.1.3 require investigating authorities to disclose information received in writing from interested parties to the other interested parties participating in the investigation, subject to rules governing the treatment of confidential information (discussed later in this chapter). In particular, Article 6.1.3 requires that authorities provide the full text of the petition to known exporters and the authorities of the exporting Member as soon as an investigation has been initiated. However, when the number of exporters is particularly high, it is possible to provide the petition to the authorities of the exporting Member or a relevant trade association. Additionally, Article 6.4 requires authorities to permit interested parties to see all information that is relevant to the presentation of their cases and to prepare presentations based on such information. Article 6.9 requires that, before making a final determination, the authorities inform all interested parties of the essential facts under consideration on which the determination will be based, and provide sufficient time for the parties to defend their interests.

Articles 6.2 and 6.3 provide the possibility, upon request, for meetings of all interested parties, so that opposing views may be presented and rebuttal arguments offered, including the oral presentation of information. However, no interested party may be compelled to attend such a meeting, and the failure to attend a meeting cannot be prejudicial to a party's case. In addition, per Article 6.3, any information received orally must be reproduced in writing and made available to all interested parties if it is to be taken into account by the authorities.

Confidential Information

Much of the information provided to authorities by interested parties in an antidumping investigation is highly confidential, proprietary data. Pricing data, cost of production data, and financial data, as well as information about production processes, are not reported in public financial statements or reports, and the public release of such information would be harmful to the competitive interests of the submitter. However, this information is vital for authorities to make determinations based on accurate information.

Article 6.5 sets forth rules for the treatment of such confidential information. In general, authorities must not disclose confidential information submitted by an interested party without specific permission of the party submitting it. Footnote 17 recognizes, however, that some Members maintain "protective order" systems, wherein confidential information is released to the representatives of interested parties, for example, attorneys and trade consultants, so that they may adequately defend the interested party's position. However, these representatives are bound by the protective order to prevent disclosure of the confidential information released to them, even (and especially) to their clients, with severe sanctions for noncompliance.

Article 6.5.1 requires that interested parties furnish nonconfidential summaries of confidential information submitted, which must provide sufficient detail to permit a reasonable understanding of the substance of the information provided. If, in exceptional circumstances, the information is not susceptible of summarization, the interested party must explain why. Under Article 6.5.2, the authorities may disregard information submitted in confidence if they determine that the confidential treatment is not warranted and the submitting party refuses to permit disclosure. Footnote 18 recognizes that requests for confidential treatment should not, however, be arbitrarily rejected.

Verification

Authorities cannot simply accept information submitted by interested parties at face value. Article 6.6 requires that authorities satisfy themselves as to the accuracy of the information supplied. Article 6.7, and Annex I, set forth rules for a particular form of verification known as on-the-spot investigations. Article 6.7 establishes that authorities are permitted to carry out investigations in the territory of other Members, with the consent of the firms concerned and with notice to and no objection from the particular Member. Annex I provides procedures for such on-the-spot investigations, including timely notification of interested parties and exporting Member authorities, and advanced notice of the information to be verified. Verification should generally be carried out after the questionnaire response has been submitted, as the purpose is to verify the information provided.

Facts Available

As indicated above, much of the information required in an antidumping investigation is proprietary information in the possession of interested parties. It is, thus, essential that interested parties cooperate with investigating authorities and provide necessary information so that accurate determinations may be made. Where interested parties refuse to provide information, or where they significantly impede the investigation, Article 6.8 provides that authorities may rely on facts available to them.

Annex II elaborates and places limitations on authorities' use of the "best information available." Annex II reiterates the requirement of Article 6 that authorities notify interested parties early of the information that is required. Authorities must also notify parties that the consequence of failing to provide information is that authorities may make determinations based on the facts available, including those contained in the petition, which may be disadvantageous for the noncompliant party.

Annex II requires a degree of flexibility on the part of the authorities in accepting information (particularly information submitted on computer media) that does not precisely conform to a Member's regulations or guidelines. Paragraph 5, in particular, states that "[e]ven though the information provided may not be ideal in all respects, this should not justify the authorities from disregarding it, provided the interested party has acted to the best of its ability."

If the authorities determine to reject information supplied, they must explain why and provide an opportunity for the interested party to further explain or correct the problems identified. Additionally, when authorities rely on facts available, Annex II requires that they check the information used against other independent sources available.

Individual Margins of Dumping

Finally, Article 6.10 requires that authorities, as a rule, determine an individual margin of dumping for each known exporter or producer of the product under investigation. However, where there are a large number of exporters or producers, authorities may limit their examination to a reasonable number of interested parties or products using statistically valid sampling methods or the largest percentage of export volume from the country in question that can reasonably be investigated. It is preferable, according to Article 6.10.1, that the selection of sample producers, exporters, importers, and products be made in consultation with the interested parties.

If an interested party is not selected for the sample but nevertheless voluntarily submits information, Article 6.10.2 requires that authorities calculate a dumping margin for that party unless doing so would be unduly burdensome because of the number of exporters and producers. In any event, authorities may not discourage voluntary responses.[30]

Public Notice and Explanation of Determinations

Article 12 details requirements related to public notice and explanation of determinations. Per Article 12.3, these requirements apply *mutatis mutandis* to

[30] For a discussion of Article 6 of the Antidumping Agreement, see generally *US – DRAMS*, WT/DS99/R; *Thailand – H-Beams*, WT/DS122/R, WT/DS122/AB/R; *Guatemala – Cement II*, WT/DS156/R; *EC – Bed Linen*, WT/DS141/R, WT/DS141/RW, WT/DS141/AB/RW; *US – Stainless Steel (Korea)*, WT/DS179/R; *US – Hot-Rolled Steel (Japan)*, WT/DS184/R, WT/DS184/AB/R, WT/DS184/13; *Argentina – Ceramic Tiles*, WT/DS189/R; *US – Steel Plate (India)*, WT/DS206/R; *Egypt – Steel Rebar*, WT/DS211/R; *EC – Tube or Pipe Fittings*, WT/DS219/R, WT/DS219/AB/R; *Argentina – Poultry*, WT/DS241/R; *US – Corrosion-Resistant Steel Sunset*, WT/DS244/R, WT/DS244/AB/R; *US – Final Softwood Lumber V*, WT/DS264/R, WT/DS264/AB/R; *US – Oil Country Tubular Goods Sunset Reviews*, WT/DS268/R, WT/DS268/AB/R; *Mexico – Antidumping Measures on Rice*, WT/DS295/R; *US – Zeroing (EC)*, WT/DS294/AB/R.

the initiation and completion of reviews as well as to investigations. So, in any antidumping proceeding, Members must abide by the notice and transparency provisions of Article 12.

When investigating authorities initiate an antidumping investigation, Article 12.1 requires that they notify the Member or Members from which the product under investigation is exported as well as any known interested parties, and the authorities must publish public notice. That notice must identify the exporting country or countries, the product, the date of initiation of the investigation, the basis on which dumping is alleged, the factors on which injury is alleged, the address to which representations by interested parties should be directed, and the time limits for interested parties to make their views known.

Article 12.2 requires public notice of any preliminary and final determination, any determination to apply provisional measures, and any suspension of an investigation following the acceptance of an undertaking. Beyond mere notification of the decision, though, the authorities must set forth in sufficient detail the findings and conclusions reached on all issues of fact and law considered material by the investigating authorities. When authorities determine to apply provisional measures, or when they make an affirmative final determination or suspend an investigation following an undertaking, Article 12.2.1 requires that they specifically report the names of the suppliers or the supplying countries involved, a description of the product sufficient for customs purposes, the margins of dumping established and a full explanation of the methodology used, considerations relevant to the injury determination, and the main reasons leading to the determination.[31]

Antidumping Action on Behalf of a Third Country

Article 14 provides for antidumping action on behalf of a third country. Per Article 14.1, application for such action must be made by the authorities of the third country concerned, rather than by the domestic industry in the third country. As with applications under Article 5, Article 14.2 requires that an application for antidumping action on behalf of a third country be supported by detailed information showing dumping and injury. The government of the third country is required to provide necessary assistance to the authorities of the importing country to obtain further necessary information.

[31] For a discussion of Article 12 of the Antidumping Agreement, see generally *Mexico – Corn Syrup*, WT/DS132/R, WT/DS132/RW; *Thailand – H-Beams*, WT/DS122/R, WT/DS122/AB/R; *Guatemala – Cement II*, WT/DS156/R; *EC – Bed Linen*, WT/DS141/R; *US – Stainless Steel (Korea)*, WT/DS179/R; *US – Hot-Rolled Steel (Japan)*, WT/DS184/13; *Argentina – Ceramic Tiles*, WT/DS189/R; *US – Offset Act*, WT/DS217/ARB/EEC; *EC – Tube or Pipe Fittings*, WT/DS219/R, WT/DS219/AB/R; *Argentina – Poultry*, WT/DS241/R; *US – Corrosion-Resistant Steel Sunset*, WT/DS244/R; *US – Softwood Lumber VI*, WT/DS277/R; *US – Oil Country Tubular Goods Sunset Reviews*, WT/DS268/R; *Mexico – Antidumping Measures on Rice*, WT/DS295/R; *Korea – Paper*, WT/DS312/R.

Article 14.3 states that the injury determination must consider injury to the domestic industry of the third country as a whole, not merely injury to exports to the importing country or total exports. The decision to take antidumping action on behalf of a third country is discretionary with the importing Member. Article 14 does not require any Member to take such action under any circumstances.

The Review of Antidumping Measures

After national authorities decide to collect antidumping duties on imports or agree to a price undertaking, the Antidumping Agreement requires those decisions to be reviewed and, if necessary, revised over time. According to Article 18.3, the provisions of the Antidumping Agreement apply to every antidumping investigation, or review of existing measures, initiated pursuant to applications made on or after the date the agreement enters into force for a WTO Member.[32] By that time, each WTO Member must have taken all necessary steps to ensure the conformity of its laws, regulations, and administrative procedures with the provisions of the Antidumping Agreement. The Antidumping Agreement then includes several different requirements to ensure the WTO consistency of Members' antidumping laws or measures. As explained below, the Antidumping Agreement requires Members to provide some form of judicial, arbitral, or administrative tribunals or procedures for the review of administrative actions relating to antidumping measures. A Member's application of antidumping measures is also subject to WTO review by the Dispute Settlement Body (DSB) or the Committee on Antidumping Practices.

WTO Member Review

According to Article 13, the importing Member can be requested to conduct a national review of administrative actions relating to its final antidumping determinations and reviews. For example, Members like the United States that operate a retrospective duty assessment system will, upon request, make an Article 9.3.1 determination concerning the final amount of duties to be collected on earlier imports by conducting an administrative review. In the United States, administrative reviews of particular foreign producers'/exporters'

[32] For a discussion of Article 18 of the Antidumping Agreement, see generally *US – DRAMS*, WT/DS99/R; *US – 1916 Act (EC)*, WT/DS136/R; *US – 1916 Act*, WT/DS136/AB/R, WT/DS162/AB/R; *US – 1916 Act (Japan)*, WT/DS162/R; *Guatemala – Cement II*, WT/DS156/R; *US – Hot-Rolled Steel (Japan)*, WT/DS184/R, WT/DS184/AB/R; *US – Steel Plate (India)*, WT/DS206/R; *US – Section 129(c)(1) URAA*, WT/DS221/R; *US – Offset Act*, WT/DS217/R, WT/DS234/R, WT/DS217/AB/R, WT/DS234/AB/R; *US – Corrosion-Resistant Steel Sunset*, WT/DS244/R, WT/DS244/AB/R; *US – Softwood Lumber VI*, WT/DS277/R; *US – Final Softwood Lumber V*, WT/DS264/R; *US – Oil Country Tubular Goods Sunset Reviews*, WT/DS268/R; *Mexico – Antidumping Measures on Rice*, WT/DS295/R; *US – Zeroing (EC)*, WT/DS294/R.

imports subject to a particular antidumping duty order or price undertaking are conducted by the Department of Commerce, if requested.[33] According to Article 9.5, all Members are required to offer accelerated "new shipper" reviews for the purpose of determining individual margins of dumping for any foreign exporters/producers that did not export the product during the period of investigation and are not related to any exporters/producers that are already subject to antidumping duties. In the United States, administrative determinations are then subject to judicial review at the U.S. Court of International Trade and are appealed to the U.S. Court of Appeals for the Federal Circuit and (infrequently) to the U.S. Supreme Court.

According to Article 11.1, antidumping duties and price undertakings should remain in force only as long as and to the extent necessary to counteract injurious dumping. Therefore, Article 11 provides two forms of review.[34] First, Article 11.2 states that, on their own initiative or based on a substantiated request, national authorities are required by Articles 11.2 and 11.5 to review whether the continued imposition of the duty or price undertaking is necessary to offset dumping, whether the injury would be likely to continue or recur if the duty were removed or varied, or both. If the authorities determine that the antidumping duty or price undertaking is no longer warranted, they will terminate it immediately. Second, Articles 11.3 and 11.5 require national authorities to terminate antidumping duties or a price undertaking not later than five years from its imposition (or the most recent Article 11.2/11.3 review) unless the national authorities determine, on their own initiative or upon a duly substantiated request, that expiry of the duty or price undertaking would be likely to lead to continuation or recurrence of dumping and injury. In the United States, reviews implementing the requirements of Article 11.3 are called "sunset reviews" and are conducted by the Department of Commerce (with respect to dumping) and the International Trade Commission (with respect to injury).[35]

WTO DSB Review

WTO Members can also opt to challenge antidumping measures applied to their exports through a WTO dispute settlement. Annex 2 to the WTO Agreement contains the Dispute Settlement Understanding (DSU). The Antidumping

[33] 19 U.S.C. § 1675(a).

[34] For a discussion of Article 11 of the Antidumping Agreement, see generally *US – DRAMS*, WT/DS99/R; *US – 1916 Act (Japan)*, WT/DS162/R; *EC – Bed Linen*, WT/DS141/RW; *EC – Sardines*, WT/DS251/R; *US – Section 129(c)(1) URAA*, WT/DS221/R; *US – Offset Act*, WT/DS217/ARB/EEC; *EC – Tube or Pipe Fittings*, WT/DS219/R, WT/DS219/AB/R; *US – Corrosion-Resistant Steel Sunset*, WT/DS244/R, WT/DS244/AB/R; *US – Oil Country Tubular Goods Sunset Reviews*, WT/DS268/R, WT/DS268/AB/R; *Mexico – Antidumping Measures on Rice*, WT/DS295/R; *US – Antidumping Measures on Oil Country Tubular Goods*, WT/DS282/R, WT/DS282/AB/R; *US – Zeroing (EC)*, WT/DS294/R, WT/DS294/AB/R.

[35] 19 U.S.C. § 1675(c).

Agreement is one of the "covered agreements" subject to WTO dispute settlement. The DSU establishes a Dispute Settlement Body (DSB) charged with the authority to establish Panels, adopt Panel and Appellate Body Reports, and monitor the implementation of rulings and recommendations. Article 17 of the Antidumping Agreement establishes a number of rules regarding consultations and the settlement of disputes pertaining to the Antidumping Agreement.[36] Notably, the Antidumping Agreement is the only covered agreement that establishes special standards of review in Article 17.6 for Panel or Appellate Body review of factual and legal issues.

WTO Antidumping Committee Review

Article 16 continues the role of the Committee on Antidumping Practices originally established in the Kennedy Round Antidumping Code by allowing Members to consult on any matters relating to the operation of the agreement or the furtherance of its objectives in the context of the Committee. According to Article 18.6, the Committee is also charged with conducting an annual review of the implementation and operation of the agreement and informing the Council for Trade in Goods of any developments during the period of review.

The Committee is the recipient and repository of Member notifications regarding the Antidumping Agreement. For example, Article 16.4 also requires Members to report to the Committee (1) "without delay" all preliminary and final antidumping actions taken, and (2) on a semiannual basis any antidumping actions taken within the preceding six months. According to Article 16.5, each Member must notify the Committee concerning which of its authorities are competent to initiate and conduct Article 5 antidumping investigations and the domestic procedures governing the initiation and conduct of investigations. Finally, Article 18.5 requires each Member to inform the Committee of any changes in its laws and regulations relevant to the agreement and in the administration of such laws and regulations.

[36] For a discussion of Article 17 of the Antidumping Agreement, see generally *Guatemala – Cement I*, WT/DS60/R, WT/DS60/AB/R; *US – Lead and Bismuth II*, WT/DS138/R, WT/DS138/AB/R; *Mexico – Corn Syrup*, WT/DS132/R, WT/DS132/RW, WT/DS132/AB/RW; *US – 1916 Act (EC)*, WT/DS136/R; *US – 1916 Act*, WT/DS136/AB/R, WT/DS162/AB/R; *US – 1916 Act (Japan)*, WT/DS162/R; *Thailand – H-Beams*, WT/DS122/R, WT/DS122/AB/R; *Guatemala – Cement II*, WT/DS156/R; *EC – Bed Linen*, WT/DS141/R, WT/DS141/AB/R, WT/DS141/AB/RW; *US – Stainless Steel (Korea)*, WT/DS179/R; *US – Hot-Rolled Steel (Japan)*, WT/DS184/R, WT/DS184/AB/R; *Argentina – Ceramic Tiles*, WT/DS189/R; *US – Steel Plate (India)*, WT/DS206/R; *Egypt – Steel Rebar*, WT/DS211/R; *EC – Tube or Pipe Fittings*, WT/DS219/R, WT/DS219/AB/R; *US – Corrosion-Resistant Steel Sunset*, WT/DS244/R, WT/DS244/AB/R; *US – Softwood Lumber VI*, WT/DS277/R; *US – Final Softwood Lumber V*, WT/DS264/R, WT/DS264/AB/R; *US – Oil Country Tubular Goods Sunset Reviews*, WT/DS268/R; *Mexico – Antidumping Measures on Rice*, WT/DS295/R; *US – Zeroing (EC)*, WT/DS294/AB/R.

The Use of Antidumping Laws

The Competing Interests of Exporting and Importing WTO Members

Antidumping rules are an important part of the international framework of WTO rules established to encourage countries to reduce tariffs on imported goods and eliminate their nontariff barriers to trade. Those WTO Members that view themselves as exporters are free to minimize the importance of those tools in their national legislation, whereas those Members that are primarily importers may have a greater interest in ensuring that their domestic industries have access to effective remedial measures.

A number of provisions in the Antidumping Agreement reflect the tension between the interests of exporters and importers. For example, the standing provisions in Article 5.4 were included to protect a perceived need to ensure that antidumping investigations were actually supported by the domestic industry and not by a handful of producers. However, Footnote 13 to Article 5.4 provides a limited exception to those standing requirements to protect the interests of fragmented industries involving exceptionally large numbers of producers that are unable to coordinate themselves and respond *en masse* to injurious dumping.

The provisions of the Antidumping Agreement authorizing remedial action in response to injurious dumping also reflect the tension between exporting and importing interests. As explained earlier in this chapter, the purpose of antidumping measures is not to bolster an uncompetitive domestic industry but to eliminate the false market signals sent by dumped prices. For that reason, Article VI of the GATT 1994 and the Antidumping Agreement require affirmative determinations of dumping and injury, in addition to a causal relationship between the dumped imports and the injury to the domestic industry, before antidumping duties can be imposed on imports. Article VI:2 of the GATT 1994 and Article 9.3 of the Antidumping Agreement further limit the amount of duties collected to the margin of dumping found. Whereas antidumping remedies in the form of duties or price undertakings were included in the Antidumping Agreement for the benefit of domestic industries of importing Members, the Article 11.3 "sunset" requirements, which terminate those duties or price undertakings every five years in the absence of an affirmative determination to continue them, were included for the benefit of foreign exporters/producers.

Major Users of the Antidumping Laws

Although patterns of usage may shift over time, many countries have relied on their antidumping laws, at one time or another, to address injurious, unfair trade practices. An inverse correlation between resort to antidumping laws and the level of tariff bindings has been observed: the lower the tariffs on imports, the greater the use of antidumping laws to address instances of injurious dumping. For example, the large developed markets of the European Union, Canada, Australia, New Zealand, and the United States have historically relied on their antidumping laws to address unfairly dumped imports.[37] Since the WTO Agreement entered into force, developing countries have also become major users of trade remedy laws, including antidumping laws.[38]

For example, South Africa was historically a major user of antidumping laws.[39] During the 1980s and into the 1990s, however, South Africa's reliance on antidumping duty measures waned because of the international trade sanctions imposed against apartheid.[40] After apartheid was abolished, South Africa began to focus its efforts on lowering its tariffs in the 1990s,[41] and its resort to antidumping measures increased.[42] Mexico enacted its first antidumping law shortly after acceding to the GATT in 1986. As part of its accession, Mexico significantly liberalized its economy and became an active user of the antidumping remedy.[43] India's experience is similar. Prior to the Uruguay Round, despite being a Contracting Party to the GATT, India had bound only about 6% of its tariff lines, imposed quantitative restrictions on more than 2,000 tariff lines, and maintained other significant import-restricting measures.[44] It is not surprising, therefore, that India was not a user of the antidumping remedy. In the Uruguay Round, India agreed to bind 67% of its industrial tariffs and 100% of its agricultural tariffs. India then modified its antidumping laws to conform to the WTO Antidumping Agreement. As a result of a dispute settlement case brought by the United States, India eliminated the quantitative restrictions it had maintained for balance-of-payment purposes. With its market substantially liberalized, there has been a dramatic increase in its usage of antidumping remedies. Likewise, since joining the WTO, China has begun to use antidumping remedies.[45]

Based on the total number of initiations of antidumping investigations reported from 1995 through 2005, the major users of antidumping laws include not only the United States, the European Community (EC), Australia, and Canada, but also developing countries such as India, Argentina, South Africa, Brazil, China, Turkey, and Mexico (Table 1). While the United States may be among the eleven major users of the antidumping laws (based on initiations) and

[37] See T.P. Stewart, A.S. Dwyer, P.J. McDonough, M.M. Prado, and A.A. Karpel, *Rules in a Rules-Based WTO: Key to Growth; The Challenges Ahead* (Ardsley, NY: Transnational Publishers, Inc., 2002), 15.

[38] Ibid., 15–31.

[39] See Kommerskollegium/National Board of Trade, Sweden, *The Use of Antidumping in Brazil, China, India and South Africa – Rules, Trends and Causes* (February 2005), 53.

[40] Ibid., 49.

[41] Ibid., 51.

[42] See G. Brink, "The 10 Major Problems With the Anti-dumping Instrument in South Africa," 39 *Journal of World Trade* 2005, 147, 148.

[43] T.P. Stewart, A.S. Dwyer, P.J. McDonough, M.M. Prado, and A.A. Karpel, *Rules in a Rules-Based WTO: Key to Growth; The Challenges Ahead* (Ardsley, NY: Transnational Publishers, Inc., 2002), 17–21.

[44] Ibid., 21.

[45] Ibid., 22–23, 28.

Table 1. *Number of antidumping initiations*[46] *(1995–2005)*

WTO member	Number of initiations	Percent of total
India	425	15
United States	366	13
European Community	327	12
Argentina	204	7
South Africa	197	7
Australia	179	6
Canada	134	5
China, P.R.	123	4
Brazil	122	4
Turkey	101	4
Mexico	85	3
Subtotal	2,344	80
Total	2,840	100

a major importer, its initiations during the period from 1995 through 2005 individually accounted for only 13% of all initiations. Thus, a broad range of WTO Members have perceived a need for antidumping laws at one time or another since the Antidumping Agreement went into effect. During that same period, 38 WTO Members maintained at least one antidumping measure on imports.[47]

WTO Disputes Over Antidumping Laws and Measures

As this overview has explained, WTO panels and the Appellate Body have interpreted the Antidumping Agreement in a significant number of trade disputes[48] (Table 2). Of the 343 requests for consultations filed as of May 31, 2006, almost 50% involved the WTO Agreements on Antidumping, Subsidies and Countervailing Measures, or Safeguards.[49] Since January 1, 1995, WTO Panel or Appellate Body decisions have been adopted in more than 100 disputes, of which more than 25% involved the Antidumping Agreement.[50]

[46] AD Initiations: By Reporting Member from January 1, 1995 to December 31, 2005, available at http://www.wto.org/english/tratop_e/adp_e/adp_e.htm.

[47] AD Measures: By Reporting Member from January 1, 1995 to December 31, 2005, available at http://www.wto.org/english/tratop_e/adp_e/adp_e.htm.

[48] See, for example, Appendix 2. For lists of WTO dispute settlement reports and case summaries, see P. Pescatore and Stewart and Stewart in *Handbook of WTO/GATT Dispute Settlement.* Eds. T.P. Stewart, A.S. Dwyer, and E.A. Argenti (Ardsley, NY: Transnational Publishers, Inc., 2001–) (looseleaf); WTO Update of Dispute Settlement Cases, WT/DS/OV/*; WTO Dispute Settlement: One-Page Case Summaries (1995–Sept. 2006).

[49] Requests for consultations were identified by searching the WTO Web site for "G/ADP/D*," "G/SCM/D*," or "G/SG/D*." The number of requests for consultations citing a violation of the Agreement on Subsidies and Countervailing Measures (SCM Agreement) includes not only disputes involving countervailing duties but subsidies in general.

[50] See T.P. Stewart, A.S. Dwyer, and E.M. Hein, "Trends in the Last Decade of Trade Remedy Decisions: Problems and Opportunities for the WTO Dispute Settlement System," Paper presented at the ABA International Law Section's Fall Meeting (September 29, 2005) (as updated for publication).

Table 2. *List of WTO antidumping agreement disputes and major topics addressed (ranked by date of Panel Report)*

No.	Case name	WT/DS	Investigation	Review	Initiation	Margin calculation	Injury	Evidence	Zeroing	Other topics
1	*Guatemala – Cement I*	60	✓		✓		✓			notification
2	*US – DRAMS*	99		✓						revocation; *de minimis* margins
3	*Mexico – Corn Syrup*	132	✓		✓		✓			provisional measures
4	*US – 1916 Act (EC)*	136								antidumping measures (damages/criminal)
5	*US – 1916 Act (Japan)*	162								antidumping measures (damages/criminal)
6	*Thailand – H-Beams*	122	✓		✓	✓	✓			
7	*Guatemala – Cement II*	156	✓		✓		✓	✓		
8	*EC – Bed Linen*	141	✓			✓	✓		✓	
9	*US – Stainless Steel (Korea)*	179	✓			✓				
10	*US – Hot-Rolled Steel (Japan)*	184	✓			✓	✓	✓		
11	*Argentina – Ceramic Tiles*	189	✓			✓		✓		
12	*US – Steel Plate (India)*	206	✓					✓		
13	*US – Section 129(c)(1) URAA*	221								WTO decision implementation
14	*Egypt – Steel Rebar*	211	✓				✓	✓		

(*continued*)

Table 2 *(continued)*

No.	Case name	WT/DS	Investigation	Review	Initiation	Margin calculation	Injury	Evidence	Zeroing	Other topics
15	*US – Offset Act*	217/234								antidumping measures (distribution of duties)
16	*EC – Tube or Pipe Fittings*	219	✓			✓	✓	✓		
17	*Argentina – Poultry*	241	✓		✓	✓	✓	✓		
18	*US – Corrosion-Resistant Steel Sunset Review*	244		✓	✓				✓	*de minimis* margins; revocation
19	*US – Softwood Lumber VI note: ITC*	277	✓				✓			
20	*US – Softwood Lumber V note: AD*	264	✓		✓	✓			✓	
21	*US – Oil Country Tubular Goods Sunset Reviews note: Argentina*	268		✓						waiver of participation; revocation
22	*Mexico – Antidumping Measures on Rice*	295	✓				✓	✓		notification; termination
23	*US – Antidumping Measures on Oil Country Tubular Goods note: Mexico*	282		✓						causation; revocation
24	*Korea – Certain Paper*	312	✓			✓		✓		disclosure
25	*US – Zeroing (EC)*	294	✓	✓					✓	
26	*US – Zeroing (Japan)*	322	✓	✓					✓	
27	*US – Shrimp (Ecuador)*	335	✓						✓	
28	*Mexico – Steel Pipes and Tubes*	331	✓		✓		✓	✓		

The hyperfocus of WTO Members on challenging trade remedies in general and antidumping measures in particular is inconsistent with the negligible amount of trade actually affected by those measures. For example, the United States is a major importer and user of antidumping laws. The percentage of U.S. imports affected by antidumping and countervailing duty measures, however, has historically been small (i.e., typically between 0.5% and 2% of total U.S. imports).[51] Nevertheless, the availability of three tiers of review – whether administrative, judicial, or WTO – offered by the Antidumping Agreement not only protects the interests of exporting Members but also confirms the legitimacy of antidumping measures taken to address unfairly traded imports.

BIBLIOGRAPHY[52]

Adamantopoulos, K. and D. De Notaris, "The Future of the WTO and the Reform of the Anti-Dumping Agreement: A Legal Perspective," 24 *Fordham International Law Journal* 30 (2000).

Akakwam, P.A., "The Standard of Review in the 1994 Antidumping Code: Circumscribing the Role of GATT Panels in Reviewing National Antidumping Determinations," 5 *Minn. J. Global Trade* 277 (1996).

[51] Economic Effects of Antidumping and Countervailing Duty Orders and Suspension Agreements, Inv. No. 332–344, USITC Pub. 2900 at 4–1 (June 1995) (In 1991, hundreds of active antidumping [AD]/countervailing duty [CVD] orders affected $9.0 billion in imports from more than 1,300 10-digit HTS product categories from nearly fifty countries. This represents 1.8% of total U.S. merchandise imports, which was nearly $491 billion in 1991); WTO Trade Policy Review – United States, WT/TPR/S/16 at 65 (1996); Prepared Testimony of the Honorable William M. Daley, Secretary of Commerce, Before the Senate Finance Committee (September 29, 1999), available at http://www.ogc.doc.gov/ogc/legreg/testimon/106f/daley0929.htm (In 1998, AD and CVD orders covered only 0.50% of total U.S. imports); WTO Trade Policy Review – United States, WT/TPR/S/126 at 50 (2004) ("in FY2001 . . . imports subject to AD/CVD measures . . . accounted for less than 0.5% of total U.S. imports."). See also T.P. Stewart, A.S. Dwyer, P.J. McDonough, M.M. Prado, and A.A. Karpel, *Rules in a Rules-Based WTO: Key to Growth; The Challenges Ahead* (Ardsley, NY: Transnational Publishers, Inc., 2002), 32; T.P. Stewart, P.J. McDonough, and M.M. Prado, "Opportunities in the WTO for Increased Liberalization of Goods: Making Sure the Rules Work for All and that Special Needs are Addressed," 24 *Fordham International Law Journal* 2000, 652, 677.

[52] Reference list based, in part, on the WTO Antidumping Agreement bibliography database, available at: http://forms.wto.org/eradbibliographie/bibliography_displaycategory_e.asp; the USITC Bibliography of International-Trade-Related Law Journal Articles, available at: http://www.usitc.gov/law_journal_bibliog/; the Peace Palace Library, Bibliography on the World Trade Organization, available at: http://www.ppl.nl/bibliographies/all/showresults.php?bibliography=wto&code=WTG01 &topic=Goods%20>%20Antidumping; the Georgetown University Law Library, International Trade Law Research Guide, available at: http://www.ll.georgetown.edu/intl/guides/trade/print.html; the Georgetown University Law Library, "From the GATT to the WTO," available at: http://www.ll.georgetown.edu/intl/guides/FromtheGATTtotheWTO.cfm; and the Georgetown University Law Library, "International Trade Law," available at http://www.ll.georgetown.edu/intl/guides/International TradeLaw.cfm.

Almstedt, K.W., and P.M. Norton, "China's Antidumping Laws & the WTO Antidumping Agreement (Including Comments on China's Early Enforcement of its Antidumping Laws)," 34 *Journal of World Trade* 75 (December 2000).

Beckington, J.S., "The World Trade Organization's Dispute Settlement Resolution in United States–Antidumping Act of 1916," 34 *Vanderbilt Journal of Transnational Law* 199 (January 2001).

Berg, Gerald C., "An Economic Interpretation of 'Like-Product,'" 30 *Journal of World Trade* 195 (April 1996).

Bhala, R., "Rethinking Antidumping Law," 29 *George Washington Journal of International Law & Economics* 1 (1995).

Blonigen, B.A., and T.J. Prusa, "Antidumping," in Choi, E.K. and Harrigan, J., eds., *Handbook of International Trade*, Blackwell (2003).

Boscheck, R., "The Governance of Global Market Relations: The Case of Substituting Antitrust for Antidumping," 24 *World Competition* 41 (March 2001).

Bown, C.P., "Antidumping Against the Backdrop of Disputes in the GATT/WTO System," Working Paper, Department of Economics, Brandeis University (2000).

Bown, C.P., "Trade Remedies and World Trade Organization Dispute Settlement: Why Are So Few Challenged?" 34 *Journal of Legal Studies* 515 (June 2005).

Bown, C.P., B. Hoekman, and C. Ozden, "The Pattern of US Antidumping: The Path from Initial Filing to WTO Dispute Settlement," 2 *World Trade Review* 349 (November 2003).

Brink, G., "The 10 Major Problems With the Anti-dumping Instrument in South Africa," 39 *Journal of World Trade* 147 (February 2005).

Bronckers, M. and N. McNelis, "Rethinking the 'Like Product' Definition in WTO Antidumping Law," 33 *Journal of World Trade* 73 (June 1999).

Bronckers, M.C.E.J., "Rehabilitating Antidumping & Other Trade Remedies Through Cost-Benefit Analyses," 30 *Journal of World Trade* 5 (April 1996).

Bronckers, M.C.E.J., "WTO Implementation in the European Community – Antidumping, Safeguards and Intellectual Property," 29 *Journal of World Trade* 73 (1995).

Broude, T., "An Anti-dumping 'To Be or Not To Be' in Five Acts: A New Agenda for Research & Reform," 37 *Journal of World Trade* 305 (April 2003).

Buchs, T.D., "Selected WTO Rules and Some Implications for Fund Policy Advice," IMF Working Paper: WP/96/23 (1996).

Bundjamin, E., "The 10 Major Problems With the Anti-dumping Instrument in Indonesia," 39 *Journal of World Trade* 125 (February 2005).

Caetano, A., "The 10 Major Problems With the Anti-dumping Instrument in Brazil," 39 *Journal of World Trade* 87 (February 2005).

Cann, W.A. Jr., "Internationalizing Our Views Toward Recoupment & Market Power: Attacking the Antidumping/Antitrust Dichotomy Through WTO-Consistent Global Welfare Theory," 17 *University of Pennsylvania Journal of International Economic Law* 69 (Spring 1996).

Cartland, M., "Antidumping & Competition Policy," 28 *Law & Policy in International Business* 289 (Fall 1996).

Chung, M.Y., "U.S. Antidumping Laws: A Look at the New Legislation," 20 *North Carolina Journal of International Law & Commercial Regulation* 495 (Summer 1995).

Clough, M., "Anti-dumping and Jurisprudence of the WTO Panel and Appellate Body Reports (1995–2001)," 7 *International Trade Law and Regulation* 76 (2001).

Conrad, C.A., "Balancing the GATT Antidumping Code," 22 *World Competition* 123 (June 1999).

Conrad, C.A., "Dumping & Antidumping Measures from a Competition & Allocation Perspective," 36 *Journal of World Trade* 563 (June 2002).

Corr, C.F., "Trade Protection in the New Millennium: The Ascendancy of Antidumping Measures," 18 *Northwestern Journal of International Law & Business* 49 (Fall 1997).

Cunningham, R.O., "Commentary on the First Five Years of the WTO Antidumping Agreement and Agreement on Subsidies and Countervailing Measures," 31 *Law and Policy in International Business* 897 (2000).

Czako, J., J., Human, and J. Miranda, *A Handbook on Anti-dumping Investigations*, Cambridge (2003).

De Araujo, J.T. Jr., C. Macario, and K. Steinfatt, "Antidumping in the Americas," 35 *Journal of World Trade* 555 (August 2001).

de Lima-Campos, A., "Nineteen Proposals to Curb Abuse in Anti-dumping & Countervailing Duty Proceedings." 39 *Journal of World Trade* 239 (April 2005).

de Lima-Campos, A., and A. Vito, "Abuse & Discretion: The Impact of Anti-dumping & Countervailing Duty Proceedings on Brazilian Exports to the United States," 38 *Journal of World Trade* 37 (February 2004).

Didier, P., "The WTO Anti-dumping Code & EC Practice: Issues for Review in Trade Negotiations," 35 *Journal of World Trade* 33 (February 2001).

DiSalvo, N., "Let's Dump the 1916 Antidumping Act: Why the 1994 GATT Provides Better Price Protection for U.S. Industries," 37 *Vanderbilt Journal of Transnational Law* 791 (May 2004).

Dohlman, P.A., "Determinations of Adequacy in Sunset Reviews of Antidumping Orders in the United States," 14 *American University International Law Review* 1281 (1999).

Dong, Y., H. Xu, and F. Liu, "Antidumping & the WTO: Implications for China," 32 *Journal of World Trade* 19 (February 1998).

Dunn, A.M., contributing author, *Dumping, A Comparative Approach*, Institute of International Business Law and Practice (1995).

Dunn, A.M., "Antidumping," in *World Trade Organization: Multilateral Trade Framework for the 21st Century and U.S. Implementing Legislation*, American Bar Association (1996).

Durling, J.P., "Deference, But Only When Due: WTO Review of Anti-dumping Measures," 6 *Journal of International Economic Law* 125 (2003).

Durling, J.P., and M.R. Nicely, *Understanding the WTO Anti-dumping Agreement: Negotiating History and Subsequent Interpretation*, Cameron May (May 2002).

Ehrenhaft, P.D., "Is Interface of Antidumping & Antitrust Laws Possible?" 34 *George Washington International Law Review* 363 (2002).

Esch, M.D., and D.E. Walsh, "The Impact of the Uruguay Round Agreements on U.S. *Antidumping Laws*," 5 *Federal Circuit Bar Journal* 393 (1995).

Feaver, D., "Threat of Material Injury: One Ingredient in the Witches' Brew," 20 *World Competition* 91 (September 1996).

Fukunaga, Y., "An 'Effect-Based' Approach to Anti-dumping: Why Should We Introduce a "Mandatory Lesser Duty Rule?" 38 *Journal of World Trade* 491 (June 2004).

Gingerich, T., "Why the WTO Should Require the Application of the Evidentiary Threshold Requirement in Antidumping Investigations," 48 *American University Law Review* 135 (October 1998).

Gong, H., "Legal Strategies for Challenging the Current EU Antidumping Campaign Against Import from China: A Chinese Perspective," 27 *Brooklyn Journal of International Law* 575 (2002).

Harpaz, G., "'Dumping' the Anti-dumping Instruments in the Trade Relations Between the European Union & the State of Israel?–The European Union's Perspective," 39 *Journal of World Trade* 445 (June 2005) (Note).

Hawkins, Adam C., "Antidumping Beyond the GATT 1994: Supporting International Enactment of Legislation Providing Supplemental Remedies," 10 *Indiana International & Comparative Law Review* 149 (1999).

Henry, K., "Is the United States the World's Dumping Ground for Steel? Recent Influxes in Steel Imports in the United States, the Effects, and the Possible Remedies," 25 *Houston Journal of International Law* 381 (Winter 2003).

Hervey, C., "The Byrd Amendment Battle: American Trade Politics at the WTO," 27 *Hastings International & Comparative Law Review* 131 (Fall 2003).

Hoekman, B.M., and P.C. Mavroidis, "Dumping, Antidumping & Antitrust," 30 *Journal of World Trade* 27 (February 1996).

Holmer, Alan F., Gary N. Horlick, and Terence P. Stewart, "*Enacted and Rejected Amendments to the Antidumping Law: In Implementation or Contravention of the Antidumping Agreement?" The International Lawyer*, Vol. 29, No. 2 (Summer, 1995).

Horlick, G., "Antidumping at the Seattle Ministerial: With Tear Gas in My Eyes," 3 *Journal of International Economic Law* 179 (2000).

Horlick, G., and E. Vermulst, "The 10 Major Problems With the Anti-dumping Instrument: An Attempt at Synthesis," 39 *Journal of World Trade* 67 (February 2005).

Horlick, G.N., "The 10 Major Problems With the Anti-dumping Instrument in the United States," 39 *Journal of World Trade* 169 (February 2005).

Horlick, G.N., and E.C. Shea, "The World Trade Organization Antidumping Agreement," 29 *Journal of World Trade* 5 (February 1995).

Horlick, G.N., and S.A. Sugarman, "Antidumping Policy as a System of Law," in G. Horlick, ed., *WTO and NAFTA Rules and Dispute Resolution*, London (May 2003).

Huang, T.W., "The Gathering Storm of Antidumping Enforcement in China," 36 *Journal of World Trade* 255 (April 2002).

Hurabiell, M.L., "Protectionism Versus Free Trade: Implementing the GATT Antidumping Agreement in the United States," 16 *University of Pennsylvania Journal of International Business* 567 (Fall 1995) (Note).

Jung, Y., and S.H. Lee, "The Legacy of the Byrd Amendment Controversies: Rethinking the Principle of Good Faith," 37 *Journal of World Trade* 921 (October 2003).

Keppler, D.M., "The Geneva Steel Co. Decision Raises Concerns in Geneva: Why the 1916 Antidumping Act Violates the WTO Antidumping Agreement," 32 *George Washington Journal of International Law & Economics* 293 (1999).

Kerr, W.A., and L.J. Loppacher, "Anti-dumping in the Doha Negotiations: Fairy Tales at the World Trade Organization," 38 *Journal of World Trade* 211 (July 2004).

Killion, M.U., "Quest for Legal Safeguards for Foreign Exporters Under China's Anti Dumping Regime," 29 *North Carolina Journal of International Law & Commercial Regulation* 417 (Spring 2004).

Kim, J.B., "Currency Conversion in the Anti-dumping Agreement," 34 *Journal of World Trade* 125 (August 2000).

Kim, J.B., "Fair Price Comparison in the WTO Anti-dumping Agreement: Recent WTO Panel Decisions Against the 'Zeroing' Method, 36 *Journal of World Trade* 39 (February 2002).

Klitgaard, T., and K. Schiele, "Free Versus Fair Trade: The Dumping Issue," 4 *Current Issues in Economics & Finance* (Federal Reserve Bank of New York) 1 (August 1998).

Kommerskollegium/National Board of Trade, Sweden, "The Use of Antidumping in Brazil, China, India and South Africa – Rules, Trends and Causes" (February 2005).

Kufuor, K.O., "The Developing Countries and the Shaping of GATT/WTO Antidumping Law," 32 *Journal of World Trade* 167 (December 1998).

Kumaran, V.L., "The 10 Major Problems With the Anti-dumping Instrument in India," 39 *Journal of World Trade* 115 (February 2005).

Lasagni, A., "Does Country-Targeted Anti-dumping Policy by the EU Create Trade Diversion?" 34 *Journal of World Trade* 137 (August 2000).

Lee, S.Y., and S.H. Jun, "On the Investigation Effects of United States Anti-dumping Petitions," 38 *Journal of World Trade* 425 (June 2004).

Leycegui, E., and L.E.R. de la Torre, "The 10 Major Problems With the Anti-dumping Instrument in Mexico," 39 *Journal of World Trade* 137 (February 2005).

Lindsey, B., "The US Antidumping Law: Rhetoric versus Reality," 34 *Journal of World Trade* 1 (February 2000).

Lindsey, B., and D. Ikenson, *Reforming the Antidumping Agreement: A Road Map for WTO Negotiations,* Cato Institute (2002).

Liu, X., and H. Vandenbussche, "European Union Anti-dumping Cases Against China: An Overview & Future Prospects With Respect to China's World Trade Organization Membership," 36 *Journal of World Trade* 1125 (December 2002).

Lopez, D.M., "The Continued Dumping & Subsidy Offset Act of 2000: 'Relief' for the U.S. Steel Industry; Trouble for the United States in the WTO," 23 *University of Pennsylvania Journal of International Economic Law* 415 (Summer 2002).

Mabile, M.M., and J.M. Telep, "Emerging Customs Issues for Petitioners in Antidumping Countervailing Duty Cases," 38 *International Lawyer* 89 (Spring 2004).

Macrory, P.F.J., "The Antidumping Agreement," in Patrick F.J. Macrory, Arthur E. *Appleton, and Michael G. Plummer, eds., The World Trade Organization: Legal, Economic and Political Analysis,* Vol. I, at 485, Springer (2005).

Maur, J.-C., "Echoing Antidumping Cases: Regulatory Competitors, Imitation & Cascading Protection," 21 *World Competition* 51 (December 1998).

McClafferty, E.R., "Identifying 'Level of Trade' in U.S. Antidumping Law," 36 *Virginia Journal of International Law* 1021 (1995–96) (Note).

McGee, R.W., "Antidumping Laws, the World Trade Organization and the People's Republic of China," in C. Jayachandran and G. Lin, eds., *The Managerial Process and Impact of Foreign Investment in Greater China. Advances in Chinese Industrial Studies,* Vol. 6., at 141, JAI Press (1999).

Messerlin, P.A., "Should Antidumping Rules be Replaced by National or International Competition Rules?" 18 *World Competition* 37 (March 1995).

Messerlin, P.A., "Competition Policy and Antidumping Reform: An Exercise in Transition," in Jeffrey J. Schott, ed., *The World Trading System : Challenges Ahead,* Institute for International Economics (1996).

Miranda, J., "Should Antidumping Laws Be Dumped," 28 *Law & Policy in International Business* 255 (Fall 1996).

Miranda, J., R.A. Torres, and M. Ruiz, "The International Use of Antidumping: 1987–1997," 32 *Journal of World Trade* 5 (October 1998).

Monti, G., "When Does Dumping Cause Injury?" 18 *World Competition* 97 (March 1995).

Moore, M.O., "Antidumping Reform in the United State: A Faded Sunset," 33 *Journal of World Trade* 1 (August 1999).

Moore, M.O., "Department of Commerce Administration of Antidumping Sunset Reviews: A First Assessment," 36 *Journal of World Trade* 675 (August 2002).

Morgan, C., "Competition Policy & Anti-dumping: Is it Time for A Reality Check?" 30 *Journal of World Trade* 62 (October 1996).

Moulis, D., and P. Gay, "The 10 Major Problems With the Anti-dumping Instrument in Australia," 39 *Journal of World Trade* 75 (February 2005).

"New Battle Lines in the Antidumping War: Recent Movements on the European Fronts," 31 *Journal of World Trade* 135 (June 1997).

Niels, G., and A.T. Kate, "Trusting Antitrust to Dump Antidumping: Abolishing Antidumping in Free Trade Agreements Without Replacing it with Competition Law," 31 *Journal of World Trade* 30 (December 1997).

Ohnesorge, J.K.M., "States, Industrial Policies & Antidumping Enforcement in Japan, South Korea and Taiwan," 3 *Buffalo Journal of International Law* 289 (1996–1997).

Palmeter, D., "United States Implementation of the Uruguay Round Antidumping Code," 29 *Journal of World Trade* 39 (June 1995).

Palmeter, D., "A Commentary on the WTO Anti-dumping Code," 30 *Journal of World Trade* 43 (August 1996).

Parker, M.E., "The Impact of a Hyperinflationary Economy on the Determination of Dumping," 29 *Journal of World Trade* 193 (August 1995).

Pescatore P., and Stewart and Stewart (T.P. Stewart, A.S. Dwyer, and E.A. Argenti, eds.), *Handbook of WTO/GATT Dispute Settlement*, Transnational Publishers, Inc., 2001– (looseleaf).

Petersmann, E.U., "International Competition Rules for Governments & for Private Business: The Case for Linking Future WTO Negotiations on Investment, Competition & Environmental Rules to Reforms of Anti-dumping Laws," 30 *Journal of World Trade* 5 (June 1996).

Polouektov, A., "Non-Market Economy Issues in the WTO Anti-dumping Law & Accession Negotiations: Revival of a Two-Tier Membership?" 36 *Journal of World Trade* 1 (February 2002).

Qureshi, A.H., "Drafting Anti-dumping Legislation: Issues & Tips," 34 *Journal of World Trade* 19 (December 2000).

Regan, D., "Regulatory Purpose and 'Like Products' in Article III.4 of the GATT," 36 *Journal of World Trade* 443 (2002).

Reich, A., "Institutional & Substantive Reform of the Anti-dumping & Subsidy Agreements–Lessons from as Israeli Experience," 37 *Journal of World Trade* 1037 (December 2003).

"Rethinking the 1916 Antidumping Act," 110 *Harvard Law Review* 1555 (May 1997) (Note).

Rosenthal, P.C., and R.T.C. Vermylen, "The WTO Antidumping and Subsidies Agreements: Did the United States Achieve Its Objectives During the Uruguay Round?" 31 *Law and Policy in International Business* 871 (2000).

Seastrum, E.C., and M.S. Getlan, "The Globalization of International Trade Litigation: AD/CVD Litigation –Which Forum & Which Law?" 26 *Brooklyn Journal of International Law* 893 (2001).

Silberston, A., "Anti-dumping Rules–Time for Change?" 37 *Journal of World Trade* 1063 (December 2003).

Singh, H.V., "Consistency of Estimated Dumping Margins with other Relevant Data," 19 *World Competition* 121 (June 1996).

Sohn, C., "Treatment of Non-market Economy Countries under the World Trade Organization Anti-dumping Regime," 39 *Journal of World Trade* 763 (August 2005).

Spamann, H., "Standard of Review for World Trade Organization Panels in Trade Remedy Cases: A Critical Analysis," 38 *Journal World Trade* 509 (2004).

Steele, K., ed., *Anti-dumping under the WTO: A Comparative Review*, Kluwer Law International (1996).

Stewart, T.P., "Why Anti-dumping Laws Need Not Be Cloned After Competition Laws Nor Replaced by Such Laws," Centre for Applied Studies in International Negotiations Anti-dumping and Competition Policy, Geneva, Switzerland, (July 11–12, 1996).

Stewart, T.P., "The Uruguay Round Agreements Act: An Overview of Major Issues and Potential Trouble Spots," in *The World Trade Organization – The Multilateral Trade Framework for the 21st Century and US Implementing Legislation*, ABA Sec. of Int'l Law and Practice (1996).

Stewart, T.P., "Dealing with the Fallout of Foreign Economic Dislocations Under The Antidumping and Countervailing Duty Laws," Georgetown University Law Center's 13th Annual International Trade Update (December 10, 1998).

Stewart, T.P., "U.S.-Japan Economic Disputes: The Role of Antidumping and Countervailing Duty Laws," 16 *Arizona Journal of International and Comparative Law* 689 (1999).

Stewart, T.P., with the Trade Lawyers Advisory Group, "The Importance of Trade Remedies to the U.S. Trade Relationship with China – Challenges Facing the Use of Antidumping Law: A Critical Period for the Administration and Congressional Action," A Report to the U.S.-China Economic and Security Review Commission (May 16, 2005) (an Updated Report prepared July 20, 2005).

Stewart, T.P., and T.C. Brightbill, Some 'Heretical' Observations on the Interaction of U.S. Trade and Competition Laws: A Defense of U.S. Antidumping and Countervailing Duties," 4 *United States–Mexico Law Journal* 35 (1996).

Stewart, T.P., and A.S. Dwyer, "WTO Antidumping and Subsidy Agreements: A Practitioner's Guide to Sunset Reviews in Australia, Canada, the European Union, and United States," Kluwer Law International (July 1998).

Stewart, T.P., and A.S. Dwyer, "Sunset Reviews of Antidumping and Countervailing Duty Measures – U.S. Implementation of Uruguay Round Commitments," 32 *Journal of World Trade* 101 (October 1998).

Stewart, T.P., and A.S. Dwyer, *Handbook on WTO Trade Remedy Disputes: The First Six Years (1995–2000)*, Transnational Publishers, Inc. (Spring 2001).

Stewart T.P., A.S. Dwyer, and E.M. Hein, "Trends in the Last Decade of Trade Remedy Decisions: Problems and Opportunities for the WTO Dispute Settlement System," Paper Presented at the ABA International Law Section's Fall Meeting (September 29, 2005).

Stewart, T.P., A.S. Dwyer, P.J. McDonough, M.M. Prado, and A.A. Karpel, *Rules in a Rules-Based WTO: Key to Growth; The Challenges Ahead*, Transnational Publishers, Inc. (2002).

Stewart, T.P., A.S. Dwyer, and M.M. Prado, "Antidumping, Countervailing Duties & Trade Remedies: 'Let's Make a Deal'??–Views From A Domestic Practitioner," 37 *International Lawyer* 761 (Fall 2003).

Stewart, T.P., S.G. Markel, and M.T. Kerwin, "Antidumping," in *The GATT Uruguay Round: A Negotiating History (1986–1992)*, Vol. II, Kluwer Law & Taxation Publishers (1993).

Stewart, T.P., P.J. McDonough, and M.M. Prado, "Opportunities in the WTO for Increased Liberalization of Goods: Making Sure the Rules Work for All and That Special Needs Are Addressed," 24 *Fordham International Law Journal*, No. 1 (April 2001).

Stirk, J.D., "United States – Anti-dumping Measures On Certain Hot-Rolled Steel Products From Japan: Possibilities And Predictions For Compliance With The Appellate Body Report," 33 *Law & Policy in International Business* 683 (2002).

Sutham, A.J., P. Attavipach, and P. Eiamchinda, "The 10 Major Problems With the Antidumping Instrument in Thailand," 39 *Journal of World Trade* 159 (February 2005).

Tarullo, D.K., "The Hidden Costs of International Dispute Settlement: WTO Review of Domestic Anti-dumping Decisions," 34 *Law & Policy in International Business* 109 (Fall 2002).

Tarullo, D.K., "Paved With Good Intentions: The Dynamic Effects of WTO Review of Anti-dumping Action," 2 *World Trade Review* 373 (November 2003).

Van Bael, I., and J. Bellis, *Anti-dumping and other Trade Protection Laws of the EC* (2004).

Vermulst, E., "Adopting & Implementing Anti-dumping Laws: Some Suggestions for Developing Countries," 31 *Journal of World Trade* 5 (April 1997).

Vermulst, E., "The 10 Major Problems With the Anti-dumping Instrument in the European Community," 39 *Journal of World Trade* 105 (February 2005).

Vermulst, E., *The WTO Anti-dumping Agreement: A Commentary*, Oxford University Press (2005).

Vermulst, E., and F. Graafsma, "WTO Dispute Settlement with Respect to Trade Contingency Measures: Selected Issues," 35 *Journal of World Trade* 209 (April 2001).

Vermulst, E., and F. Graafsma, *WTO Disputes: Anti-dumping, Subsidies and Safeguards*, Cameron May (2002).

Vermulst, E., and N. Komuro, "Anti-dumping Disputes in the GATT/WTO: Navigating Dire Straits," 31 *Journal of World Trade* 5 (February 1997).

Walders, L.R., and N.C. Pratt, "Trade Remedy Litigation–Choice of Forum & Choice of Law," 18 *St. John's Journal of Legal Commentary* 51 (Fall 2003).

Wang, J., "A Critique of the Application to China of the Non-Market Economy Rules of Antidumping Legislation & Practice of the European Union," 33 *Journal of World Trade* 117 (June 1999).

Wang, L., "China's Anti-dumping Law & Its Implementation: A Practitioner's Perspective," 3 *Journal of World Intellectual Property* 561 (July 2000).

Wang, L., and S. Yu, "China's New Anti-dumping Regulations: Improvements To Comply with the World Trade Organization Rules," 36 *Journal of World Trade* 903 (October 2002).

Wellhausen, M., "The Community Interest Test in Antidumping Proceedings of the European Union," 16 *American University International Law Review* 1027 (2001).

Wenig, H., "The European Community's Anti-dumping System: Salient Features," 39 *Journal of World Trade* 787 (2005).

World Trade Organization (WTO), *WTO Analytical Index, Guide to WTO Law and Practice*, Vol. I (1st ed., 2003).

Yano, K., "Thirty Years of Being A Respondent in Antidumping Proceedings: Abuse of Economic Relief Can Have a Negative Impact on Competition Policy," 33 *Journal of World Trade* 31 (October 1999).

Yi, D., H.J. Xu, and F. Liu, "Antidumping and the WTO – Implications for China," 32 *Journal of World Trade* 19 (1998).

Yu, T., "The 10 Major Problems With the Anti-dumping Instrument in the People's Republic of China," 39 *Journal of World Trade* 97 (February 2005).

Appendix 1.

Kennedy Round AD Code (10 pages)	Tokyo Round AD Code (13 pages)	Uruguay Round AD Agreement (24 pages)
Art. 1: Limits imposition to circumstances of GATT Art. VI; notes that provisions of the Code govern application of Art. VI	Art 1: Principles – limits imposition of AD measures to circumstances provided for in Art. VI and pursuant to investigations initiated and conducted in accordance with Code	Art 1: Principles – limits imposition of AD measures to circumstances provided for in Art. VI and pursuant to investigations initiated and conducted in accordance with Agreement
Art. 2: Determination of Dumping (7 paragraphs)	Art. 2: Determination of Dumping (7 paragraphs)	Art. 2: Determination of Dumping (7 paragraphs, 8 subparagraphs, including sub-subparagraphs) (elaborates on comparison methodologies, Art. 2.4.2)
Art. 3: Determination of Injury (6 paragraphs)	Art. 3: Determination of Injury (7 paragraphs)	Art. 3: Determination of Injury (8 paragraphs, 4 subparagraphs)
Art. 4: Definition of Domestic Industry (3 paragraphs)	Art. 4: Definition of Industry (4 paragraphs, 2 subparagraphs)	Art. 4: Definition of Industry (4 paragraphs, 2 subparagraphs)
Art. 5: Initiation and Subsequent Investigation (4 paragraphs)	Art. 5: Initiation and Subsequent Investigation (5 paragraphs)	Art. 5: Initiation and Subsequent Investigation (10 paragraphs, 4 subparagraphs)
Art. 6: Evidence (9 paragraphs)	Art. 6: Evidence (9 paragraphs)	Art. 6: Evidence (14 paragraphs, 10 subparagraphs)
Art. 7: Price Undertakings (2 paragraphs)	Art. 7: Price Undertakings (7 paragraphs)	Art. 7: Provisional Measures (5 paragraphs, 3 subparagraphs)
Art. 8: Imposition and Collection of AD Duties (5 paragraphs)	Art. 8: Imposition and Collection of AD Duties (5 paragraphs)	Art. 8: Price Undertakings (6 paragraphs)
Art. 9: Duration of AD Duties (2 paragraphs)	Art. 9: Duration of AD Duties (2 paragraphs)	Art. 9: Imposition and Collection of AD Duties (5 paragraphs, 5 subparagraphs)
Art. 10: Provisional Measures (5 paragraphs)	Art. 10: Provisional Measures (4 paragraphs)	Art. 10: Retroactivity (8 paragraphs, 2 subparagraphs)
Art. 11: Retroactivity (2 paragraphs with 5 subparagraphs)	Art. 11: Retroactivity (3 paragraphs, 4 subparagraphs)	Art. 11: Duration of AD Duties (5 paragraphs) (includes "sunset" reviews, Art. 11.3)
Art. 12: AD Action on Behalf of a Third Country (4 paragraphs)	Art. 12: AD Action on Behalf of a Third Country (4 paragraphs)	Art. 12: Public Notice and Explanation of Determinations (3 paragraphs, 4 subparagraphs)
	Art. 13 Developing Countries (1 paragraph)	Art. 13: Judicial Review
	Art. 14: AD Committee (4 paragraphs)	Art. 14: AD Action on Behalf of a Third Country (4 paragraphs)
	Art. 15: Consultation, Conciliation, and Dispute Settlement (7 paragraphs, 2 subparagraphs)	Art. 15 Developing Countries (1 paragraph)
		Art. 16: AD Committee (4 paragraphs)
		Art. 17: Consultation, Conciliation, and Dispute Settlement (7 paragraphs, 4 subparagraphs) (includes special standard of review, Art. 17.6)

Notes: AD = antidumping; Art. = Article; GATT = General Agreement on Tariffs and Trade.

Appendix 2. *WTO reports citing the Antidumping Agreement (as referenced in chapter): An alphabetical list of citations**

Short title	Full case title and citation
Argentina – Ceramic Tiles	Panel Report, *Argentina – Definitive Antidumping Measures on Imports of Ceramic Tiles from Italy,* WT/DS189/R, adopted November 5, 2001
Argentina – Poultry Antidumping Duties	Panel Report, *Argentina – Definitive Antidumping Duties on Poultry from Brazil,* WT/DS241/R, adopted May 19, 2003
Canada – Dairy	Panel Report, *Canada – Measures Affecting the Importation of Milk and the Exportation of Dairy Products – Second Recourse to Article 21.5 of the DSU by New Zealand and the United States,* WT/DS103/RW2, adopted January 17, 2003, as modified by the Appellate Body Report, WT/DS103/AB/RW2, WT/DS113/AB/RW2
EC – Bed Linen	Appellate Body Report, *European Communities – Antidumping Duties on Imports of Cotton-Type Bed Linen from India,* WT/DS141/AB/R, adopted March 12, 2001
EC – Bed Linen	Panel Report, *European Communities – Antidumping Duties on Imports of Cotton-Type Bed Linen from India,* WT/DS141/R, adopted March 12, 2001, as modified by the Appellate Body Report, WT/DS141/AB/R
EC – Bed Linen	Appellate Body Report, *European Communities – Antidumping Duties on Imports of Cotton-Type Bed Linen from India – Recourse to Article 21.5 of the DSU by India,* WT/DS141/AB/RW, adopted April 24, 2003
EC – Bed Linen	Panel Report, *European Communities – Antidumping Duties on Imports of Cotton-Type Bed Linen from India – Recourse to Article 21.5 of the DSU by India,* WT/DS141/RW, adopted April 24, 2003, as modified by the Appellate Body Report, WT/DS141/AB/RW
EC – Tube or Pipe Fittings	Appellate Body Report, *European Communities – Antidumping Duties on Malleable Cast Iron Tube or Pipe Fittings from Brazil,* WT/DS219/AB/R, adopted August 18, 2003
EC – Tube or Pipe Fittings	Panel Report, *European Communities – Antidumping Duties on Malleable Cast Iron Tube or Pipe Fittings from Brazil,* WT/DS219/R, adopted August 18, 2003, as modified by the Appellate Body Report, WT/DS219/AB/R
Egypt – Steel Rebar	Panel Report, *Egypt – Definitive Antidumping Measures on Steel Rebar from Turkey,* WT/DS211/R. adopted October 1, 2002
Guatemala – Cement I	Appellate Body Report, *Guatemala – Antidumping Investigation Regarding Portland Cement from Mexico,* WT/DS60/AB/R, adopted November 25, 1998
Guatemala – Cement I	Panel Report, *Guatemala – Antidumping Investigation Regarding Portland Cement from Mexico,* WT/DS60/R, adopted November 25, 1998, as modified by the Appellate Body Report, WT/DS60/AB/R

(continued)

Appendix 2 *(continued)*

Short title	Full case title and citation
Guatemala – Cement II	Panel Report, *Guatemala – Definitive Antidumping Measures on Grey Portland Cement from Mexico,* WT/DS156/R, adopted November 17, 2000
Korea – Paper	Panel Report, Korea – Antidumping Duties on Imports of Certain Paper from Indonesia, WT/DS312/R, adopted November 28, 2005
Mexico – Antidumping Measures on Rice	Appellate Body Report, *Mexico – Definitive Antidumping Measures on Beef and Rice, Complaint with Respect to Rice,* WT/DS295/AB/R, adopted December 20, 2005
Mexico – Antidumping Measures on Rice	Panel Report, *Mexico – Definitive Antidumping Measures on Beef and Rice, Complaint with Respect to Rice,* WT/DS295/R, adopted December 20, 2005, as modified by the Appellate Body Report, WT/DS295/AB/R
Mexico – Corn Syrup	Panel Report, *Mexico – Antidumping Investigation of High Fructose Corn Syrup (HFCS) from the United States,* WT/DS132/R and Corr.1, adopted February 24, 2000
Mexico – Corn Syrup	Appellate Body Report, *Mexico – Antidumping Investigation of High Fructose Corn Syrup (HFCS) from the United States – Recourse to Article 21.5 of the DSU by the United States,* WT/DS132/AB/RW, adopted November 21, 2001
Mexico – Corn Syrup	Panel Report, *Mexico – Antidumping Investigation of High Fructose Corn Syrup (HFCS) from the United States – Recourse to Article 21.5 of the DSU by the United States,* WT/DS132/RW, adopted November 21, 2001, as upheld by the Appellate Body Report, WT/DS132/AB/RW
Mexico – Steel Pipes and Tubes	Panel Report, *Mexico – Antidumping Duties on Steel Pipes and Tubes from Guatemala,* WT/DS331/R, adopted July 24, 2007
Thailand – H-Beams	Appellate Body Report, *Thailand – Antidumping Duties on Angles, Shapes and Sections of Iron or Non-Alloy Steel and H-Beams from Poland,* WT/DS122/AB/R, adopted April 5, 2001
Thailand – H-Beams	Panel Report, *Thailand – Antidumping Duties on Angles, Shapes and Sections of Iron or Non-Alloy Steel and H-Beams from Poland,* WT/DS122/R, adopted April 5, 2001, as modified by the Appellate Body Report, WT/DS122/AB/R
US – 1916 Act	Appellate Body Report, *United States – Anti-Dumping Act of 1916,* WT/DS136/AB/R, WT/DS162/AB/R, adopted September 26, 2000
US – 1916 Act (EC)	Panel Report, *United States – Antidumping Act of 1916,* WT/DS136/R and Corr. 1, adopted September 26, 2000, as upheld by the Appellate Body Report, WT/DS136/AB/R, WT/DS162/AB/R
US – 1916 Act (Japan)	Panel Report, *United States – Antidumping Act of 1916,* WT/DS162/R and Add.1, adopted September 26, 2000, as upheld by the Appellate Body Report, WT/DS136/AB/R, WT/DS162/AB/R

Short title	Full case title and citation
US – Antidumping Measures on Oil Country Tubular Goods	Appellate Body Report, *United States – Antidumping Measures on Oil Country Tubular Goods (OCTG) from Mexico,* WT/DS282/AB/R, adopted November 28, 2005
US – Antidumping Measures on Oil Country Tubular Goods	Panel Report, *United States – Antidumping Measures on Oil Country Tubular Goods (OCTG) from Mexico,* WT/DS282/R, adopted November 28, 2005, as modified by the Appellate Body Report, WT/DS282/AB/R
US – Corrosion-Resistant Steel Sunset Review	Appellate Body Report, *United States – Sunset Review of Antidumping Duties on Corrosion-Resistant Carbon Steel Flat Products from Japan,* WT/DS244/AB/R, adopted January 9, 2004
US – Corrosion-Resistant Steel Sunset Review	Panel Report, *United States – Sunset Review of Antidumping Duties on Corrosion-Resistant Carbon Steel Flat Products from Japan,* WT/DS244/R, adopted January 9, 2004, as modified by the Appellate Body Report, WT/DS244/AB/R
US – Cotton Yarn	Panel Report, *United States – Transitional Safeguard Measures on Combed Cotton Yarn from Pakistan,* WT/DS192/R, as adopted November 5, 2001, as modified by the Appellate Body Report, WT/DS192/AB/R
US – DRAMS	Panel Report, *United States – Antidumping Duty on Dynamic Random Access Memory Semiconductors (DRAMS) of One Megabit or Above from Korea,* WT/DS99/R, adopted March 19, 1999
US – Hot-Rolled Steel	Appellate Body Report, *United States – Antidumping Measures on Certain Hot-Rolled Steel Products from Japan,* WT/DS184/AB/R, adopted August 23, 2001
US – Hot-Rolled Steel	Panel Report, *United States – Antidumping Measures on Certain Hot-Rolled Steel Products from Japan,* WT/DS184/R, adopted August 23, 2001, as modified by Appellate Body Report, WT/DS184/AB/R
US – Hot-Rolled Steel	Award of the Arbitrator, *United States – Antidumping Measures on Certain Hot-Rolled Steel Products from Japan – Arbitration under Article 21.3(c) of the DSU,* WT/DS184/13, February 19, 2002
US – Line Pipe	Appellate Body Report, *United States – Definitive Safeguard Measures on Imports of Circular Welded Carbon Quality Line Pipe from Korea,* WT/DS202/AB/R, adopted March 8, 2002
US – Offset Act	Appellate Body Report, *United States – Continued Dumping and Subsidy Offset Act of 2000,* WT/DS217/AB/R, WT/DS234/AB/R, adopted January 27, 2003
US – Offset Act	Panel Report, *United States – Continued Dumping and Subsidy Offset Act of 2000,* WT/DS217/R, WT/DS234/R, adopted January 27, 2003, as modified by Appellate Body Report, WT/DS217/AB/R, WT/DS234/AB/R

(continued)

Appendix 2 *(continued)*

Short title	Full case title and citation
US – Offset Act	Decision by Arbitrator, *United States – Continued Dumping and Subsidy Offset Act of 2000, Original Complaint by the European Communities – Recourse to Arbitration by the United States under Article 22.6 of the DSU,* WT/DS217/ARB/EEC, August 31, 2004
US – Oil Country Tubular Goods Sunset Reviews	Appellate Body Report, *United States – Sunset Reviews of Antidumping Measures on Oil Country Tubular Goods from Argentina,* WT/DS268/AB/R, adopted December 17, 2004
US – Oil Country Tubular Goods Sunset Reviews	Panel Report, *United States – Sunset Reviews of Antidumping Measures on Oil Country Tubular Goods from Argentina,* WT/DS268/R and Corr.1, adopted December 17, 2004, as modified by the Appellate Body Report, WT/DS268/AB/R
US – Oil Country Tubular Goods Sunset Reviews	Appellate Body Report, *United States – Sunset Reviews of Antidumping Measures on Oil Country Tubular Goods from Argentina,* WT/DS268/AB/RW adopted May 11, 2007
US – Oil Country Tubular Goods Sunset Reviews	Panel Report, *United States – Sunset Reviews of Antidumping Measures on Oil Country Tubular Goods from Argentina,* WT/DS268/RW, adopted May 11, 2007, as modified by the Appellate Body Report, WT/DS268/AB/RW
US – Section 129(c)(1) URAA	Panel Report, *United States – Section 129(c)(1) of the Uruguay Round Agreements Act,* WT/DS221/R, adopted August 30, 2002
US – Shrimp (Ecuador)	Panel Report, *United States – Antidumping Measure on Shrimp from Ecuador,* WT/DS335/R, adopted February 20, 2007
US – Softwood Lumber VI	Panel Report, *United States – Investigation of the International Trade Commission in Softwood Lumber from Canada,* WT/DS277/R, adopted April 26, 2004, DSR 2004:VI, 2485
US – Softwood Lumber VI	Appellate Body Report, *United States – Investigation of the International Trade Commission in Softwood Lumber from Canada – Recourse to Article 21.5 of the DSU by Canada,* WT/DS277/AB/RW, adopted May 9, 2006
US – Softwood Lumber VI	Panel Report, *United States – Investigation of the International Trade Commission in Softwood Lumber from Canada – Recourse to Article 21.5 of the DSU by Canada,* WT/DS277/RW, adopted May 9, 2006, modified by Appellate Body Report, WT/DS277/AB/RW
US – Softwood Lumber V	Appellate Body Report, *United States – Final Dumping Determination on Softwood Lumber from Canada,* WT/DS264/AB/R, adopted August 31, 2004
US – Softwood Lumber V	Panel Report, *United States – Final Dumping Determination on Softwood Lumber from Canada,* WT/DS264/AB/R, adopted August 31, 2004, as modified by the Appellate Body Report, WT/DS264/AB/R
US – Softwood Lumber V	Appellate Body Report, *United States – Final Dumping Determination on Softwood Lumber from Canada – Recourse to Article 21.5 of the DSU by Canada,* WT/DS264/AB/RW, adopted September 1, 2006

Short title	Full case title and citation
US – Softwood Lumber V	Panel Report, *United States – Final Dumping Determination on Softwood Lumber from Canada – Recourse to Article 21.5 of the DSU by Canada,* WT/DS264/RW, adopted September 1, 2006, reversed by Appellate Body Report, WT/DS264/AB/RW
US – Steel Plate	Panel Report, *United States – Antidumping and Countervailing Measures on Steel Plate from India,* WT/DS206/R and Corr.1, adopted July 29, 2002
US – Steel Safeguards	Appellate Body Report, *United States – Definitive Safeguard Measures on Imports of Certain Steel Products,* WT/DS248/AB/R, WT/DS249/AB/R, WT/DS251/AB/R, WT/DS252/AB/R, WT/DS253/AB/R, WT/DS254/AB/R, WT/DS258/AB/R, WT/DS259/AB/R, adopted December 10, 2003
US – Zeroing (EC)	Appellate Body Report, *United States – Laws, Regulations and Methodology for Calculating Dumping Margins ("Zeroing"),* WT/DS294/AB/R, adopted May 9, 2006
US – Zeroing (EC)	Panel Report, *United States – Laws, Regulations and Methodology for Calculating Dumping Margins ("Zeroing"),* WT/DS294/R, adopted May 9, 2006, as modified by the Appellate Body Report, WT/DS294/AB/R
US – Zeroing (Japan)	Appellate Body Report, *United States – Measures Relating to Zeroing and Sunset Reviews,* WT/DS322/AB/R, adopted January 23, 2007
US – Zeroing (Japan)	Panel Report, *United States – Measures Relating to Zeroing and Sunset Reviews,* WT/DS322/R, adopted January 23, 2007, as modified by the Appellate Body Report, WT/DS322/AB/R

* WTO reports can be downloaded from the WTO's website at http://docsonline.wto.org/gen_search.asp? searchmode=simple.

DAVID A. GANTZ

6.1 *A Commentary on the Stewart and Dwyer "Overview"*

I appreciate the opportunity to comment on the excellent and comprehensive overview of the World Trade Organization's (WTO's) Antidumping Agreement (ADA)[1] (hereinafter "Overview") written by Terence P. Stewart and Amy S. Dwyer. In this chapter, I offer a few observations on the operation of antidumping laws under national and international law, and provide an alternative view in several instances.

There are obvious differences in perception of the appropriateness and fairness of the antidumping laws, likely based in part on our differing experience. Mr. Stewart is the senior partner of one of the oldest and most successful international trade firms specializing in representing U.S. domestic industries in unfair trade cases, including (but not limited to) antidumping proceedings. I have been a full-time law professor for fourteen years, but prior to that time I spent sixteen years as an international trade lawyer in Washington, D.C., primarily representing foreign producers and U.S. importers, occasionally in the same proceedings as Mr. Stewart (but on the opposite side). As I tell my international trade law students on the first day of class, there is no one speaking and writing on this topic, including your instructor (and Mr. Stewart), who is entirely objective about unfair trade laws and practice. The same caveat applies to my comments here.

Certain of the contentions made in the Overview in my opinion justify further discussion and examination; that is the purpose of this chapter. I encourage the student who studies objectively the global and U.S. antidumping laws (and who is reading the Overview and the various responses) to look carefully as well at their implementation by the national administering authorities, including the U.S. Commerce Department and the U.S. International Trade Commission (ITC).

[1] Article VI of the GATT; *Agreement on Implementation of Article VI of the General Agreement on Tariffs and Trade*, Annex 1A of the Marrakech Agreement Establishing the World Trade Organization (hereinafter the "*WTO Agreement*"), April 15, 1994, available at http://www.wto.org/english/docs_e/legal_e/legal_e.htm (last visited September 24, 2007).

 I thank Professor Petros Mavroidis and Columbia Law School for the opportunity to participate in the seminar for which these comments were prepared.

Here, as in so many other areas of the law, the "devil is in the details" and process often trumps substance. It is an unfortunate fact that the international rules providing for and attempting to regulate the use of the antidumping remedy function far better in theory than in actual practice.

Justification for the Antidumping Laws

Despite extensive discussion among economists, academics, lawyers, and policy makers,[2] an economic justification for the current international rules is difficult to make.[3] The Overview quotes with approval a statement of Assistant Attorney General Samuel Graham in 1916, providing the policy reasons for not permitting sales of imported goods at *less than cost of production.* This is a reasonable assertion, although it of course neglects any likely benefit to U.S. users and to the U.S. economy of lower-cost imported industrial goods (e.g., steel) or consumer products (e.g., footwear).[4] However, the Overview then jumps to the conclusion that condemnation of *international price discrimination* is equally justified. These are two different concepts; it is possible (and entirely rational) economic behavior to sell goods at different prices in segregated markets, above fully allocated cost of production, so as to maximize total profits. Indeed, the best justification for antidumping laws would likely occur if such laws punished only predatory pricing, that is, sales below marginal cost (or average variable cost), but that is not, of course, the law.

In my view, the only colorable economic argument in favor of punishing international price discrimination is that, in the absence of tariff or nontariff barriers in the exporting market, such price discrimination would not be any more feasible than it would be in a single national market, because entrepreneurs would purchase the lower priced goods and re-sell them in the higher-priced market. However, other factors may make it practical for a seller to price a product differently in two different markets; these factors can be freight costs, restrictions on "gray market" goods, distribution issues, and the like.

In my view, national antidumping laws can are justified primarily on political and practical, rather than economic, grounds. Economic analysis seems

[2] See, for example, M.J. Trebilcock and R. Howse, *The Regulation of International Trade* (London, Routledge, 3rd ed., 2005) 250–256, reviewing the various rationales for antidumping laws, including international price discrimination, predatory pricing, and intermittent dumping).

[3] See the remarks of economist Professor Thomas J. Prusa elsewhere in this volume.

[4] Under current U.S. law and under the Antidumping Agreement, there is no requirement that consumer (as distinct from producer) interests be taken into account, although it has been proposed that such interests be taken into account in a recent Doha Round draft on modifying the Antidumping Agreement. See D. Pruzin, "Brazil Criticizes WTO Draft Rules Text as 'Major Step Backward' for Global Trade," 24 *International Trade Reporter (BNA)* 2007, 1718 (noting the proposal to have consumer group interests taken into account in antidumping investigations).

largely absent from the drafting of antidumping rules at both the global and national level. However, this does not mean that there is no justification for the current system, imperfect as it may be. The evidence in the Overview of an inverse relationship between a country's aggressiveness in imposing antidumping duties and tariff reduction under WTO or other auspices is telling. Most trade agreements that reduce tariffs, remove nontariff barriers, and otherwise liberalize world or regional trade simply could not be enacted in many countries, including the United States, without the existence of the antidumping remedy.

For example, the U.S. Congress has consistently opposed any weakening of U.S. antidumping (and countervailing duty) laws in international trade negotiations such as the current Doha Round, and the U.S. Executive Branch has been warned against accepting further restrictions on their use.[5] No one believes that this is an idle, albeit implied, threat of Congressional nonapproval of future multilateral trade agreements; a recent December 2007 draft of proposed Doha Round modifications of the ADA by the Uruguayan chair of the "rules" negotiations somewhat surprisingly would permit the Members (read "United States") the right to continue "zeroing" in antidumping investigations,[6] despite a series of WTO Appellate Body decisions holding zeroing to be inconsistent with the ADA in most respects.[7] The only logical explanation for the explicit endorsement of zeroing is to placate the United States Congress, even though most other WTO Members consider the practice abhorrent and will not likely accept it in any ultimate revision of the ADA.

When high tariffs are no longer available to protect domestic industries, and most nontariff barriers, such as quotas, are outlawed as they have been in the WTO system,[8] the only remaining effective means of protecting domestic industry is through the trade remedy laws. Politically, it is easier for a government to punish "unfair" trade practices and to give protection to domestic producers through imposition of penalty antidumping or countervailing duties (the latter against actionable, trade-distorting government subsidies in the exporting country) than to impose higher tariffs or quotas on domestic producers who are unable to compete (fairly) with imports. Nor is it particularly popular in the United States, Canada, or the European Union (EU) to provide direct subsidies to U.S. producers (except for a variety of reasons with regard to agriculture), because such subsidies may cause unhappiness among groups that do not benefit directly from them. Most WTO Members other than the United States,

[5] See B. Lindsey and D. Ikenson, *Reforming the Antidumping Agreement: A Road Map for WTO Negotiations*, December 11, 2002, at p. 2, available at http://www.freetrade.org/pubs/pas/tpa-021.pdf (last visited September 24, 2007) (discussing the Congressional restrictions on preserving U.S. antidumping laws in Trade Promotion Authority, and the limited mandate given to Doha Round negotiators on this issue).

[6] See D. Pruzin, *supra* note 4 (noting Brazilian criticism of the draft text for, *inter alia*, permitting zeroing).

[7] See Zeroing, *infra*.

[8] GATT, Article XI.

Canada, and the EU, either for policy reasons or because of lack of the necessary government analytical and administrative skills, do not commonly use the countervailing duty laws, so it is appropriate to focus here on the antidumping laws.

The use of safeguard measures, additional tariffs, or quotas imposed when increasing imports are causing serious injury (without any evidence of "unfair" trading practices), is enshrined in the General Agreement on Tariffs and Trade (GATT) and in the Safeguards Agreement.[9] However, the safeguards remedy is today more apparent than real. First, as noted earlier, protecting domestic industries against fairly (rather than "unfairly") traded imports may be unpopular for domestic political reasons, and with other industry sectors that may be harmed. Second, under the Safeguards Agreement, the imposition of safeguards measures normally requires compensation to the exporting Member, which can also adversely affect unrelated industries.[10] Finally, the WTO's Appellate Body has made it almost impossible for a WTO Member to impose safeguard measures legally.[11]

Also, although the use of safeguards measures in many circumstances that are now subject to the antidumping laws would be much more appropriate as well as more honest intellectually (avoiding the sham of national administrative authorities finding dumping where none actually has occurred), that approach would require amendment of the Safeguards Agreement so as to eliminate the conflicts with Article XIX of the GATT that have led the WTO's Appellate Body to treat many national administrative actions imposing safeguards measures as inconsistent with Article XIX.[12] However, to the best of the author's knowledge, amendment of the Safeguards Agreement is not on the Doha Development Round agenda, which means use of safeguards instead of the antidumping laws in the foreseeable future is unlikely. Thus, the antidumping remedy is left as the default mechanism for protecting domestic industry against imports.

[9] Agreement on Safeguards, Annex 1A of the WTO Agreement, *supra* note 1.

[10] Ibid. Article 8 (with some limitations).

[11] See, for example, Appellate Body Report, *United States – Definitive Safeguard Measures on Imports of Certain Steel Products*, WT/DS248, 249, 251, 252, 253, 254, 258, 259/AB/R, adopted on December 10, 2003; Appellate Body Report, *Argentina – Safeguard Measures on Imports of Footwear*, WT/DS121/AB/R, adopted on January 12, 2000.

[12] Article XIX of the GATT permits the application of safeguards measures "as a result of unforeseen developments and of the effect of the obligations incurred by a contracting party under this Agreement...." In other words, safeguards are permitted only for "unforeseen circumstances" arising from tariff concessions. Because tariff concessions are presumably intended to permit increased imports, proof that the increased imports are "unforeseen" is problematic. The laws of the United States, the EU, and other safeguards users in force for decades incorporated no such conditions on the use of safeguards, and they are absent from the Safeguards Agreement. However, the Appellate Body, following reasonable rules of treaty interpretation but ignoring state practice and the Uruguay Round negotiators' intent, effectively reinstated the Article XIX preconditions. See, for example, *Argentina – Footwear, supra* note 11.

It is also worth emphasizing that the antidumping remedy is frequently the trade remedy of choice for domestic industry petitioners as well. In the United States, after the Commerce Department has determined the existence of dumping, and the ITC has found material injury or threat thereof, antidumping duties *will* be imposed (in the absence of a suspension agreement resulting in an increase in prices of dumped imports); there is little or no administrative or presidential discretion not to provide relief, or to delay relief. Moreover, administrative antidumping and countervailing duty final (and some preliminary) determinations have since 1980 been subject to judicial review by the U.S. Court of International Trade and Court of Appeals for the Federal Circuit.[13] The ADA requires Members that apply national antidumping laws to provide judicial, arbitral, or administrative tribunals to review national authority determinations.[14]

This contrasts again with other trade remedies, such as safeguards, where under U.S. law the president may decline to impose safeguards measures despite a serious injury finding and recommendation for relief by the ITC.[15] Similarly, relief provided under Section 301 for violations of obligations to the United States under trade agreements remains subject to considerable executive branch discretion.[16] Neither safeguards nor Section 301 determinations are effectively subject to effective judicial review in the United States. Under such circumstances, it is no wonder that for domestic industries (and their counsel), the antidumping remedy is most often the national remedy of choice.

Challenges in International Regulation of National Antidumping Proceedings

The Overview clearly demonstrates that, with the expansion of the antidumping rules beyond Article VI of the GATT of the Kennedy Round and Tokyo Round Codes, and now with the WTO ADA, the discretion that can be exercised by national administering authorities has been substantially reduced in favor of agreed international parameters. The ADA, in particular, requires a level of transparency, and procedural protections for exporters and importers, that has dictated a fairer process, particularly when coupled with the availability of review of national antidumping determinations under the WTO's Dispute Settlement Understanding (DSU),[17] as discussed further *infra*. In particular, the detail provided in Article 2 (margin determination), Article 3 (injury determination), and

[13] 28 U.S.C. § 1581(c) (jurisdiction); 19 U.S.C. § 1516A (standard of review).

[14] Anti-Dumping Agreement, *supra* note 1, Article 13.

[15] Under Section 202(a)(1)(A) of the Trade Act of 1974, as amended, 19 U.S.C. § 2253(a)(2)(F), "... the President may deny relief from increasing imports as recommended by the International Trade Commission based on the "national economic interest."

[16] Sections 301 *et seq.* of the Trade Act of 1974, as amended, 19 U.S.C. §§ 2411–2416.

[17] *Understanding on Rules and Procedures Governing the Settlement of Disputes*, Annex 2 of the WTO Agreement, available at http://www.wto.org/english/docs_e/legal_e/28-dsu.doc (last visited September 26, 2007).

Article 6 (due process rights of interested parties) is extremely significant, as is the requirement of Article 13 that any WTO Member using antidumping laws provide judicial, arbitral, or administrative review of agency determinations.

Also, as noted earlier, determinations by the administering authorities in the United States and elsewhere have been subject to court review. In the United States at least, such judicial review has encouraged a relatively high degree of transparency and consistency in the administrative process.

However, despite these protections, considerable discretion on the part of national administering authorities remains, and such authorities are still able to favor strongly their domestic constituencies, particularly in politically sensitive cases (such as those involving steel, tomatoes, and softwood lumber in the United States). This result is not surprising. The determination of the margin of dumping is made by an office in the U.S. Department of Commerce, a government agency the constituents of which are overwhelmingly domestic producers of goods.[18] Nor is there much Congressional support for making it easier for foreign firms to export low-cost goods to the United States. Also, under the U.S. antidumping laws, consumer interests (e.g., firms that use steel in making washing machines or automobiles, TV buyers) are for all practical purposes ignored; although the U.S. ITC routinely hears from consumers in the course of their injury proceedings, the ITC has no statutory authority other than to determine whether a domestic industry producing the like product is being injured or threatened with material injury.[19]

Although national antidumping laws among the more than one hundred WTO Member countries that have enacted them vary, many observers who have participated in the process elsewhere (including the EU, Argentina, Canada, and Korea) would likely agree that, in terms of transparency, procedural due process, and the effectiveness of judicial review, the U.S. administering authorities have few equals, although Canada comes close.[20] (That being said, many of them

[18] This is not unusual. In Mexico, both dumping and injury determinations are made by the Secretariat of Economy, earlier called the Secretariat of Commerce and Industrial Development.

[19] But see *supra* note 4, indicating that consumer interests may have to be taken into account in a future, revised WTO Anti-Dumping Agreement.

[20] The author has been involved directly or indirectly in proceedings in those four countries as well as in the United States. In the author's experience, Canada's federal courts on the whole do a competent job of judicial review, although the expertise of specialized review courts is lacking and the degree of deference to administrative agency determinations is probably greater than in the United States. Canada's International Trade Tribunal, which functions in a manner generally similar to the U.S. International Trade Commission, demonstrates a generally respectable level of fairness, independence, and competence in making material injury determinations. In the author's view, the bifurcated system in which the material injury determination is made by an independent agency rather than the Ministry of Economy (e.g., Mexico) or the Directorate General of Trade (EU) is more likely to provide objectivity in such determinations.

would be far less satisfied with the substantive analysis performed by the U.S. authorities or the fairness of the results.)

When determining dumping margins (usually the difference between the "Normal Value" of sales in the home market and the "Export Price" of sales in the export market), the Commerce Department retains extensive discretion in making such calculations as allocations of circumstance-of-sale adjustments or indirect selling expenses in exporters' sales price calculations over different models or product lines. The ADA, especially its Article 2, does provide considerable detail regarding the conduct of national antidumping proceedings, but as the Overview correctly indicates, the ADA is silent on some issues because the Uruguay Round negotiators could not agree.

It is admittedly difficult to determine to what extent the silence of the ADA on a particular issue leaves national administrative authorities free to do as they please. The Overview contends essentially that where the Agreement is silent, such discretion exists. However, it must be remembered that the ADA states: "A *fair comparison* shall be made between the export price and the normal value."[21] It also requires that authorities make "due allowance" for, *inter alia*, "other differences affecting price comparability."[22] To what extent do these general principles restrict national authority discretion? Clearly, the Overview is correct in that the Agreement "was not drafted to cover each and every possible question or concern that might arise regarding the dumping margin calculation." Under those circumstances, however, if the Appellate Body is to decide the controversies brought before it, it will be forced to interpret these general principles as well as very specific language in the ADA. The balance of this section discusses some examples of the dilemma.

De minimis Margins

Although Article 5.8 of the ADA specifies that antidumping investigations must be discontinued if the dumping margins are less than 2% for the initial investigation, the Agreement is silent as to any particular *de minimis* level that may be applied to administrative reviews, making it legal for the United States to continue to apply the former U.S. 0.5% *de minimis* level in such reviews.[23] In contrast, there is some justification for use of a smaller *de minimis* level in reviews; after the initial investigation is completed, foreign producers should be able to estimate actual dumping margins with a reasonable degree of precision, and thus avoid future dumping when the margins are reviewed annually by the administering authority. However, from a policy point of view, it is difficult to

21 ADA, *supra* note 1, Article 2.4; emphasis supplied.

22 Ibid., Article 2.4.

23 Appellate Body Report, *United States – Sunset Review of Antidumping Duties on Corrosion-Resistant Carbon Steel Flat Products from Japan*, WT/DS244/AB/R, adopted on January 9, 2004.

justify the costs both to interested parties and to administering governments, and the potential disruption of trade flows, where dumping margins have dropped to less or much less than 2%, and are thus in most cases economically insignificant.

Non–Market Economy Analysis

The ADA itself silent on the legality of using non–market economy (NME) procedures for calculating Normal Value in antidumping actions brought against NMEs such as China and Vietnam. When NME analysis is utilized, publicly available surrogate values for the factors of production (e.g., labor, materials, electricity) from market economies (such as India or Bangladesh) are substituted for the values for factors of production in the NME (such as China or Vietnam). This approach is said to be justified by the assumption that such local factor values are suspect because those values are determined by central planners rather than by market forces. A GATT "Ad Article" does give some very limited support to the NME approach, recognizing that "in the case of imports from a country which has a *complete or substantially complete monopoly* of its trade and where *all domestic prices are fixed by the State*, special difficulties may exist in determining price comparability..." thus permitting the authorities to deviate from a "strict comparison with domestic prices...."[24] The Ad Article, however, provides no effective guidance as to how an NME analysis is to be conducted. In my view, it is a considerable stretch to argue today that either China or Vietnam falls into the "substantially complete monopoly" and "all domestic prices" categories, even though there are some inputs in some sectors for which prices may still be affected by government fiat.

In any event, the United States effectively obtained the consent of China, as part of the WTO accession process ending in 2001, to continue use of NME surrogate procedures for 15 years.[25] Vietnam agreed to similar language prior to its WTO accession process culminating in 2007.[26]

Although there is an underlying economic justification to the NME principle, it is often applied in an illogical or inconsistent manner that fails to recognize differences among producers and sectors and fails to use market-based inputs even when such specific inputs are available. As far as I am aware, in current Commerce Department practice, no effort is normally made to use surrogate

24 GATT, Ad Article VI(1); emphasis supplied.

25 Protocol of Accession for the People's Republic of China, November 23, 2001, available at http://www.wto.org/english/docs_e/legal_e/28-dsu.doc (last visited September 26, 2007); see also the Working Party Report (discussing further the obligations assumed by China in the Protocol of Accession).

26 Accession of the Socialist Republic of Vietnam, November 15, 2006, available at http://docsonline.wto.org/DDFDocuments/t/WT/L/662.doc (last visited September 26, 2007); see also the Working Party Report (incorporating most of the obligations undertaken by Vietnam).

country values only for factors of production that are not determined by market forces within the NME exporting country, with NME exporting country production values used when the values for those factors of production are clearly determined by market forces.[27] There is also considerable discretion within the administering authority as to which surrogate country to use in a particular case. Further potential distortion may occur simply because Commerce is willing to use only publicly available data from the surrogate country, and some relevant data in particular cases may be proprietary.

A particularly egregious example of the distortions possible with NME procedures is evidenced by parallel U.S. antidumping cases against color television receivers from China and from Malaysia in 2003 through 2004. The imported televisions manufactured in China and Malaysia, respectively, were essentially identical and used the same internationally available parts and components. Yet, although the Commerce Department found no dumping in the action against Malaysia, weighted-average dumping margins of up to 78% were found in the proceeding against Chinese producers![28]

Material Injury Determinations

Even though Article 3 of the ADA attempts to provide guidance to national authorities on determining material injury, or threat thereof, as discussed much more fully in the Overview, the concept of material injury itself is sufficiently nebulous, with determinations of injury to a domestic industry, increasing imports (actually or relative to domestic consumption), and a causal relationship between the two, as to make the process both difficult and imprecise, despite considerable guidance provided by the ADA and in various rulings by the WTO's Appellate Body.

Under the ADA, the material injury investigation must be based on "positive evidence" and comprise an "objective examination" of the volume of dumped imports, the effect on prices, and the impact on domestic producers.[29]

The examination of the impact of the dumped imports on the domestic industry concerned shall include an evaluation of all relevant economic factors and indices having a bearing on the state of the industry, including actual and potential decline in sales, profits, output, market share, productivity, return on investments, or utilization of capacity; factors affecting domestic prices; the magnitude of the margin of dumping; and actual and potential negative effects on cash flow, inventories, employment, wages, growth, and ability to raise capital or investments. This list is not exhaustive, nor can one or several of these factors necessarily give decisive guidance.[30]

[27] See 19 C.F.R. § 351.408 (1997) (setting out statutory authority for NME calculations).

[28] R. Brevetti, "Commerce's ITA Sets Hefty Duties on Color Television Receivers from China," 21 *International Trade Reporter (BNA)* 2004, 700.

[29] ADA, *supra* note 1, Article 3.1.

[30] Ibid., Article 3.4.

Moreover, although the ADA cautions that "[a] determination of a threat of material injury shall be based on facts and not merely on allegation, conjecture or remote possibility" and that the "change in circumstances which would create a situation in which the dumping would cause injury [if no antidumping duties are applied] must be clearly foreseen and imminent,"[31] determinations of threat are inherently speculative, as the administering authority is effectively required to try to predict the future.

Zeroing

Another contemporary example is the concept of zeroing, a Commerce Department practice that has now been held illegal by the WTO's Dispute Settlement Body (DSB) in a growing series of cases.[32] As discussed in the Overview, calculation of dumping margins requires a comparison of Normal Value (prices based on home market sales or a surrogate for them) and Export Price (generally the price of the like product exported to the country seeking to apply antidumping duties, as indicated in the Overview). Prior practice in a number of countries, including the United States, has typically been to compare a weighted average of home market prices either to a weighted average of export prices or (more frequently) to export prices individually.[33] However, when making such comparisons, U.S. practice (and until recently, that of the EU) had been to treat all export sales above Normal Value (i.e., the sales that were not dumped) as having a margin of zero, rather than at the actual algebraic value (less than zero). For example, consider the following universe of sales:

Sale	Normal value	Export price	Margin
1	100	90	10
2	100	100	0
3	100	110	0 or −10

The first sale has a dumping margin of 10. The second sale has no margin; it is fairly traded. The third sale has a negative margin, as the price is higher in the export market. If the third sale is treated as zero, the weighted-average margin (three sales) is 10/300 or 3.3%. (This percentage is computed as "NV – EP/NV".)

[31] Ibid., Article 3.7.

[32] See, for example, Panel Report, *United States – Antidumping Measure on Shrimp from Ecuador*, WT/DS335/R, adopted on February 20, 2007; Appellate Body Report, *United States – Measures Relating to Zeroing and Sunset Reviews*, WT/DS322/AB/R, adopted on January 23, 2007; Appellate Body Report, *United States – Laws, Regulations and Methodology for Calculating Dumping Margins ("Zeroing")*, WT/DS294/AB/R, adopted on May 9, 2006; Appellate Body Report, *United States – Final Dumping Determination on Softwood Lumber from Canada*, WT/DS264/AB/R, adopted on August 31, 2004.

[33] Both are permitted under the ADA, Article 2.4.2, although the latter requires special justification on the part of the authority.

However, if the third sale is treated as –10, the weighted-average margin is 0/300 or zero.[34]

Inherent Prejudice Against Foreign Producers

Despite the efforts of the ADA to achieve transparency and procedural fairness, and entirely apart from the substantive methodology used by the Commerce Department, the ITC, and other national administering authorities, the process is inherently weighted against foreign producers. First, the domestic industry controls the timing of the filing of petitions seeking antidumping duties. The petitioner industry group or trade association likely will file its petition only after it has been carefully drafted and discussed with the domestic administering authorities in draft form and after the industry or trade association has raised sufficient funds for the proceedings. The foreign producers must then react immediately to retain counsel, raise funds for the defense if the producers are small companies, organize a response team, and prepare data because of the short statutory deadlines in the United States and in many other countries.

For example, the first administration determination, as to whether there is a "reasonable indication of material injury or threat thereof," is made by the U.S. ITC only 45 days after the petition is filed.[35] The foreign producers remain at a disadvantage because of the remaining statutory deadlines as well, and can be punished for failing to provide complete information in a timely manner by the use of "facts available" by the Commerce Department.[36] Moreover, even where the administering authority ultimately determines that there is no dumping and/or no material injury or threat thereof, the nearly year-long administrative process is likely to result in disruption of imports from the accused foreign producers for the entire period, because the importers are understandably wary of purchasing goods that may be retroactively subject to antidumping duties.[37]

Impact of the DSB on National Antidumping Practices

Perhaps the most significant change in worldwide antidumping practice after the Uruguay Round, beyond the promulgation of the ADA, which was

[34] See the detailed discussion of zeroing by Professor Prusa elsewhere in this volume.

[35] 19 U.S.C. § 1673b(a)(2)A)(i). At least one Washington law firm (not Mr. Stewart's) had a practice of filing antidumping petitions right before major long-weekend holidays; for example, at 5:00 p.m. on the Wednesday before Thanksgiving, presumably to put additional time pressure on foreign respondents, their counsel, and the U.S. administering agencies.

[36] 19 U.S.C. § 1677e(a)(B); this is specifically authorized under the Antidumping Agreement, Article 6.8.

[37] The ADA, *supra* note 1, provides in Article 7 that antidumping duties may be imposed under certain circumstances for months before any preliminary determination of dumping is made, up to only 60 days after the date of initiation of the investigation.

obligatory for all WTO Members (rather than optional as with the Tokyo Round "Code"), is the fact that national antidumping determinations are effectively reviewable by the DSB,[38] just as are virtually all other Member actions or measures that are allegedly inconsistent with any of the WTO Agreements.

However, the ADA is unique among the WTO Agreements in one respect: It is the only one with a distinct standard of review that is designed (in Article 17.6) to provide the responding Member (or its administering authorities) with a higher level of deference than is afforded generally under the system. When it is charged by a Member that the Member's benefits under the ADA have been nullified or impaired by the responding Members or the objectives of the ADA are being impeded:

(i) [I]n its assessment of the facts of the matter, the Panel shall determine whether the authorities' establishment of the facts was proper and whether their evaluation of those facts was unbiased and objective. *If the establishment of the facts was proper and the evaluation was unbiased and objective, even though the Panel might have reached a different conclusion, the evaluation shall not be overturned;*

(ii) [T]he Panel shall interpret the relevant provisions of the Agreement in accordance with customary rules of interpretation of public international law. *Where the Panel finds that a relevant provision of the Agreement admits more than one permissible interpretation, the Panel shall find the authorities' measure to be in conformity with the Agreement if it rests upon one of those permissible interpretations.*[39]

This language, which is conceptually derived from *Chevron*,[40] was clearly incorporated at the insistence of the United States. However, on the whole there seems to be little evidence that the Panels or the Appellate Body have given investigating authorities much more leeway as to the review of facts than they would have in the absence of a requirement that multiple interpretations be countenanced, or if the standard of review were simply Article 11 of the DSU, as with most other covered agreements.[41] Also, the Appellate Body has pointed out that Article 17.6(ii) applies only when there is more than one permissible interpretation

[38] Created under the Dispute Settlement Understanding (DSU), *supra* note 17.

[39] ADA, *supra* note 1, Article 17.6.

[40] *Chevron v. Natural Resources Defense Council*, 467 U.S. 837, 843–45 (1984) (standing generally for the proposition that a reviewing court in the United States must afford a high degree of deference to the decisions of administrative agencies under review, respect the agency's construction of the statutory scheme the agency is entrusted with administering, and avoid reversal even where the reviewing court might on first impression have decided the issue differently).

[41] See Appellate Body Report, *United States – Antidumping Measures on Certain Hot-Rolled Steel Products from Japan*, WT/DS184/AB/R, adopted on August 23, 2001, para. 55 (comparing the Panel's obligations under Article 17.6(i) of the ADA to Article 11 of the DSU).

of a provision of the ADA,[42] which is not often the conclusion of the Appellate Body.

As the data provided in the Overview demonstrate, the existence of effective dispute settlement has changed the trade remedy world. More than 25% of all DSB cases are in the area of trade remedies. Although many of these cases have delved into the details of calculating dumping margins or determining the existence or threat of material injury, several have made it clear that the only antidumping laws that are permitted post–Uruguay Round are those that are fully consistent with the ADA. Even if the dollar volume of total U.S. imports subject to antidumping duties is small compared with total U.S. imports, as discussed in the Overview, the significance of the volume of affected exports for the foreign producers (and their governments) may be very substantial, particularly if the result of the antidumping duties is to bar those producers from the highly lucrative U.S. market. This factor may largely explain why, as the Overview shows, more than half of the DSB rulings under the ADA (16 of 28) have been brought against the United States.

Perhaps most significantly, two major U.S. statutes (with no counterparts in any other WTO Member nation), the 1916 Antidumping Act[43] (in reality an antitrust law masquerading as a dumping law) and the "Byrd Amendment"[44] (a much more recent mechanism to transfer collected antidumping duties from the U.S. Treasury to successful domestic industry petitioners), have been determined by the Appellate Body to be inconsistent with U.S. obligations under the ADA.[45]

The Future of Antidumping Actions

As the Overview explains, the use of the antidumping remedy through national laws on dumping has spread. From 1980 through 1988, the four principal users (the United States, Australia, Canada, and the EU) accounted for 97.5% of worldwide antidumping actions,[46] compared to the participation of dozens of countries today, particularly Mexico, Brazil, India, and South Africa. However, according to WTO data supplied by Members, ten nations accounted for 80% of the antidumping initiations reported to the WTO since 1995. Just three of those, India, the United States, and the EU, accounted for 40%. During that period, the United States was the second largest user, after India, of the antidumping remedy.

[42] Ibid., paras. 57, 59–60.

[43] Revenue Act of 1916 ("1916 Act"), 19 U.S.C. § 72 (repealed 2004).

[44] Continued Dumping and Subsidy Offset Act of 2000 (Byrd Amendment), 19 U.S.C. § 1675(c) (2000) (repealed 2006, although certain provisions remained in force until October 1, 2007).

[45] Appellate Body Report, *United States – Continued Dumping and Subsidy Offset Act of 2000*, WT/DS217, 234/AB/R, adopted on January 27, 2003; Appellate Body Report, *United States – Anti-Dumping Act of 1916*, WT/DS136, 162/AB/R, adopted on September 26, 2000.

[46] Trebilcock and Howse, *supra* note 2, at 232–233.

Nevertheless, examination of data on new antidumping investigations reported to the WTO annually from 1995 through 2006 shows a significant decline. Worldwide annual antidumping actions increased from 157 in 1995 to a peak of 364 in 2001, and then declined to 193 in 2006.[47] U.S. antidumping case initiations followed a similar pattern, increasing from fourteen in 1995 to seventy-five in 2001, and then declining to only seven in 2006.[48] During the same twelve-year period, the United States imposed antidumping "measures" (usually duties but occasionally suspension agreements or other mechanisms for limiting dumped imports) in 239 instances, of which 52, or nearly 25%, were against Chinese imports.[49] In the EU, which as of June 30, 2007, had 133 antidumping orders in force (46 against China), *no* new investigations were launched during the first 6 months of 2007.[50]

This decline suggests, to the author at least, that the balance between the traditional domestic industries (e.g., steel, automobiles, textiles, and footwear in the United States), which generally favor strong antidumping laws, and the export-oriented industries in the same country (e.g., computers and telecommunications equipment), which do not, may be shifting, at least in developed nations such as the United States and the EU, to the point where in another decade or less the political pressures supporting these laws may change to favor U.S. and EU exporters (which often face antidumping actions or other import restrictions in the destination country).

One can speculate on other causes of the decline. They likely include the broader sourcing by major multinational enterprises of some of their production abroad, so that a U.S.-based enterprise that is supporting an antidumping or countervailing duty action brought in the United States against foreign imports risks endorsing an action that would adversely affect some of its own imports. The NME may also worry that if it supports an unfair trade action against a major foreign competitor, the competitor will retaliate by bringing a similar action to protect its own domestic market.

Also, as a general rule, when the decision on injury is made in an objective and independent manner, it is more difficult to prove material injury when the local economy is strong, as it has been in the United States and much of the rest of the world in recent years. Even though national authorities have some leeway in the manner in which the factors discussed in the Overview are to

[47] WTO, *AD Initiations: By Reporting Member from 01/01/95 to 31/12/06*, available at http://www.wto.org/english/tratop_e/adp_e/adp_stattab2_e.xls (last visited September 25, 2007).

[48] Ibid.

[49] WTO, *AD Measures: Reporting Member vs. Exporting Country from 01/01/95 to 31/12/06*, available at http://www.wto.org/english/tratop_e/adp_e/adp_stattab8_e.xls (last visited September 25, 2007).

[50] *EU Reports New Antidumping Cases Dropped to Zero in First Half of 2007*, 24 *International Trade Reporter (BNA)* 2007, 1239.

be analyzed,[51] according to the Appellate Body, all must be evaluated. Such an analysis will normally result in findings of no material injury where a decline in "sales, profits, output, market share, productivity, return on investments, or utilization of capacity" cannot be documented. In fact, such declines are much less likely in good economic times than in times when the economy is weak.

It also seems self-evident that it is far easier to show that a domestic industry is being injured if there is a general downturn in company financial results and in other factors such as employment. For example, if increasing imports cause most of the members of the domestic industry to experience traditional annual returns of, say, 6% on investment decrease to negative numbers, with accompanying layoffs, the evidence of injury is relatively clear. However, it is likely more difficult for the members of a domestic industry to demonstrate that an industry currently realizing a 6% return would be experiencing a 10% return, and hiring more workers, if it were not for increasing volumes of dumped imports, and thus is also suffering from material injury. (In countries where the material injury finding is more *pro forma*, these factors are of course much less significant.)

As in most other litigation, whether national or international, the sheer costs of bringing an antidumping action can also be an impediment to initiation and to defending the action once brought. An antidumping proceeding before the Department of Commerce and the U.S. ITC can easily result in legal and economic consulting fees in excess of $1 million, and sometimes much more, particularly when the administrative determinations are challenged in court. For example, the U.S. shrimping industry considered the initiation of an antidumping action for nearly a year before it had put together sufficient financial and political support to pursue the action through the administrative process.[52] It is also questionable whether the shrimping industry would have moved forward without the promise of recovery of much of the funds expended through the Byrd Amendment, which provided for the payment of antidumping duties collected on the dumped product by U.S. authorities to the affected domestic industry,[53] repealed after the WTO DSB held the mechanism to be inconsistent with the ADA.[54]

Under these circumstances, one may reasonably expect the global decline in new antidumping actions to continue over the longer term, although not in a linear manner. For developing countries, the decline may be over a long term

[51] Appellate Body Report, *European Communities – Anti-Dumping Duties on Malleable Cast Iron Tube or Pipe Fittings from Brazil*, WT/DS219/AB/R, adopted on August 18, 2003, para. 131.

[52] See E.H. Buck, *Shrimp Trade Dispute: Chronology*, August 2, 2004, available at http://www.cnie.org/nle/crsreports/04Aug/RS21776.pdf (last visited September 25, 2007) (setting out the various steps taken by the industry toward presenting antidumping petitions to Commerce, including securing a pledge of financial assistance from the Louisiana state government).

[53] Byrd Amendment, *supra* note 44.

[54] Appellate Body Report, *United States-Byrd Amendment, supra* note 45.

indeed, and increases can be expected for some WTO Members other than the United States, the EU, and Canada. As the Overview suggests, there is often an inverse relationship between the number of antidumping actions brought in a country and its level of tariffs. If and when the Doha Round is concluded, and at least some developing countries agree to reduce their bound tariffs on manufactured goods by a significant percentage, one can expect an increase in the number of antidumping actions brought by adversely affected domestic industries in those countries. Thus, for example, if Brazil, India, South Africa, and others ultimately agree to reduce nonagricultural tariffs, an increase in the number of antidumping actions in those nations (already major users) is likely.[55]

Also, if there were to be a major recession, either worldwide or in specific WTO Members such as the EU and the United States, one could reasonably expect an increase in new antidumping filings there, even if the increase would also only be temporary, until the local economies recover and major industries return to profitability.

[55] The popularity of antidumping actions in developing countries may also be affected by weaknesses in the administrative and judicial systems, which makes it less likely that a successful imposition of antidumping duties can be successfully challenged for foreign producers in the local courts or tribunals.

THOMAS J. PRUSA

6.2 *Comments on "Antidumping: Overview of the Agreement"*

Antidumping looms large among the laws governing international trade. Between 1995 and 2005, World Trade Organization (WTO) Members initiated more than 2,800 antidumping investigations.[1] By contrast, over the same time period, there were only 182 countervailing duty investigations and 142 safeguard actions.[2] By 2005, almost two-thirds of WTO Members had imposed antidumping measures. Moreover, about half of all requests for WTO Appellate Body consultations have involved antidumping.

Given the prominence of antidumping law, it seems sensible for anyone interested in practicing international trade law to have at least a familiarity with its basic workings. For such students, Chapter 6 by Stewart and Dwyer is an excellent starting place. They give a broad overview of the legal underpinnings of antidumping and summarize virtually all key aspects of antidumping law. As befitting a legal practitioner of Stewart's stature, the chapter includes dozens of relevant citations to guide the more interested reader to longer treatises on specific topics. The chapter is a first-rate summary of the antidumping agreement from a purely legal perspective.

From an economic perspective, however, the chapter is severely lacking. In fairness, this is not entirely the fault of Stewart and Dwyer. As antidumping has evolved over time, the economic foundation for its practice and administration has been systematically eradicated. Under current WTO rules, pricing and sales decisions that are entirely consistent with basic economic theory are sanctionable. At least as disconcerting, the antidumping agreement means that foreign and domestic transactions are treated differently. Said differently, pricing and sales decisions that are perfectly legal domestically are illegal under antidumping law.

Although such duties may be consistent with the WTO Agreement, firms, legal practitioners, and policy makers must ask whether such rules are consistent

[1] Statistics from WTO Web site, http://www.wto.org.
[2] Statistics from WTO Web site, http://www.wto.org.

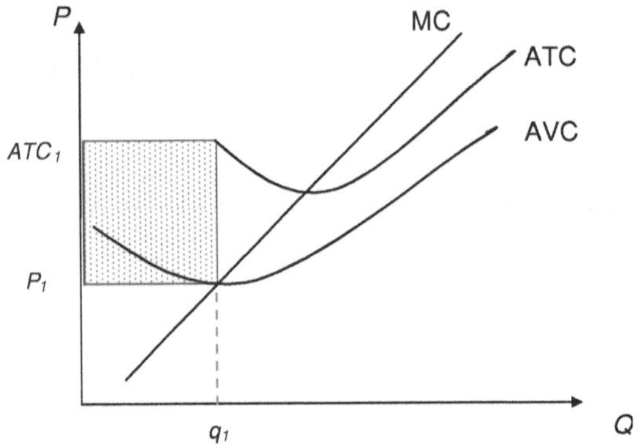

Figure 1. Profit-maximizing behavior and short-run losses.

with the primary objectives of the WTO – to promote free and fair trade. To be clear, the issue is not that economists view antidumping as bad and lawyers view it as good. I think few would disagree with the statement Stewart and Dwyer give as rationale for antidumping:

> [G]enerally accepted principles of political economy hold that it is not sound policy for any Government to permit the sale in its country by foreign citizens of material at a price below the cost of production at the place produced, for the reason that such a system, in its final analysis and on a sufficient scale, spells bankruptcy. (U.S. Assistant Attorney General Samuel Graham)

A serious problem with this quote is that Graham does not define what he means by the term "cost of production." Sales below marginal costs? Sales below average variable costs? Sales below average total costs? Sales below average total costs plus additional markups? Depending on the concept to which Graham was referring, economists may or may not agree with his conclusion regarding the need to impose duties, and this vagueness about meaning and intent is a serious flaw in the rhetoric surrounding antidumping.

Stewart and Dwyer fail to acknowledge that current antidumping law defines "price below the cost of production" in such a way that the foreign firm can be making an economic profit on each and every transaction and still be found to have dumped! That is correct. A firm charging higher export prices than at home and making a positive profit will likely find itself to have dumped. The failure to acknowledge antidumping's protectionist intent is the main shortcoming of the chapter. The current antidumping law is seriously disconnected from basic economic principles.

Let's consider an extended example of the disconnect. In Figure 1, I depict a standard cost chart. Similar figures can be found in virtually any introductory microeconomics textbook.[3] In the figure, the typical relationship between the quantity of product sold (the variable measured on the x-axis) and the price and cost per unit (the variables measured on the y-axis) are plotted. To make the discussion concrete, imagine that the variables measured on the y-axis are measured in dollars. Furthermore, for the rest of the discussion I will be referring to the quantity of the good produced (and sold) as imports to the country considering imposing an antidumping order. With only slightly more complicated economic analysis, we can extend the discussion to allow the firm to sell in its own home market and/or sell to other countries. However, for the sake of simplicity, the discussion will presume that the foreign firm only sells to one foreign-destination market. Because antidumping allows duties to be imposed on "sales below cost," this stylized situation is certainly subject to antidumping scrutiny.

The curve labeled MC depicts the firm's marginal cost. Marginal cost is defined as the extra cost required to produce one more unit of the good. As graphed, I have assumed that marginal costs are increasing with production. This is not a crucial assumption, and everything I have to say can just as easily be argued if I instead assume constant marginal costs.[4]

I have also graphed the firm's average variable cost (labeled AVC) and average total cost (labeled ATC) curves. The difference between the two curves is fixed costs. When marginal cost is below (above) average variable cost, average variable cost declines (increases) toward it. The relationship between average total cost and marginal cost is exactly the same. Hence, we have familiar U-shaped cost curves.

One of the important lessons taught in a basic microeconomics course is that firms will maximize profits by selling output as long as the price they receive is more than the average *variable* cost of production. If the price is less than the average variable cost of production, the firm will find it optimal to shut down and simply incur losses on the fixed costs. In the longer run, if prices persist below P_1, the firm will exit the industry (or, as U.S. Assistant Attorney General Samuel Graham indicated, face bankruptcy). Conversely, as shown in Figure 1, this means that the firm maximizing profits will sell its product as long as the price is at P_1 or above.

There are two important lessons we can gather from this diagram. First, just because a firm maximizes profit does not mean that it will be making a positive profit. For example, suppose the price is exactly P_1. In this case, the firm just meets its average variable costs and hence will find it profitable to produce q_1 units. At this level of production, the firm's average total cost is ATC_1; the firm is earning negative profit given by the shaded area in Figure 1.

[3] See Cass and Fair (Chapters 7 and 8), Hubbard and O'Brien (Chapters 10 and 11), Hall and Lieberman (Chapters 6 and 8).

[4] The discussion is a bit more long-winded if marginal costs are declining. However, in this case the argument against modern antidumping rules is even stronger. See, for example, Clarida (1993).

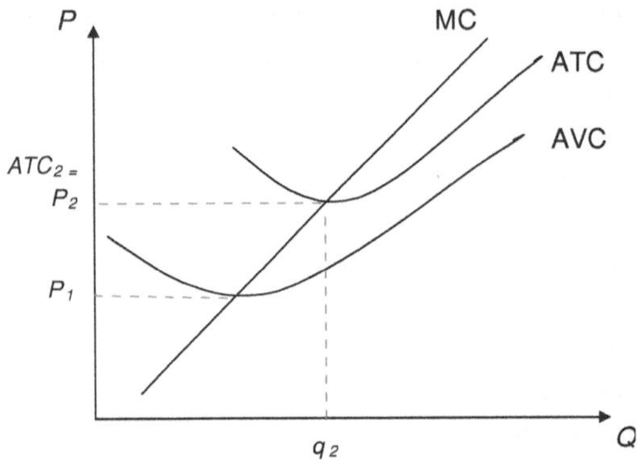

Figure 2. Profit-maximizing behavior and zero profits.

Are such losses a sign of unfair behavior or some nefarious attempt by the foreign firm to destroy the domestic industry? No. The firm is simply maximizing profits. Any firm that has ever announced negative profits has priced below its average total cost curve. If negative profits were a sign of unfair pricing, then it is safe to say that virtually every company has engaged in unfair pricing. This discussion implies that antidumping imposes a burden on foreign firms' pricing behavior to which domestic firms are not subject.

Second, from an economic perspective, the key criterion as to whether a firm is behaving unfairly by "selling below cost" is if the firm is selling below average *variable* costs! That is, if the firm continued to sell even though it was receiving a price below P_1, then one might want to investigate its pricing behavior.[5] However, to my knowledge there is no country in the world that interprets antidumping's "pricing below cost" in such a way. Countries consider unfair pricing as pricing less than average *total* costs. Yet, as long as a firm is receiving a price more than its average variable costs, it is not engaged in any type of economically unfair or questionable behavior. Again, this means that antidumping defines "unfair" pricing differently than even the most basic economics theory suggests is truly unfair.

Let us now consider the case in which the market price rises to the level as depicted in Figure 2. In this case, the firm is receiving a price (P_2) that exactly equals its average total cost of production (ATC_2). As an economist, I would say that the firm is "breaking even" or making zero profits. Is this unfair? Well, given that it is impossible to say that the firm is selling less than cost – either variable or total – I would say that there is no question that this is "fair" pricing.

[5] Even in this case, when a firm is selling less than short-run average variable costs, it is quite possible that the firm's actions are economically sensible (e.g., if the firm's technology is characterized by dynamic economies of scale or learning-by-doing).

Yet, under modern antidumping law, this firm would be subject to duties, as the firm is not making a sufficiently large positive profit. Historically, the United States required that the foreign firm make at least an 8% profit margin on its sales. At this statutorily mandated rate, a foreign firm would be found to have priced unfairly unless it earned a higher profit rate than the vast majority of U.S. manufacturing firms. According to the data reported by the U.S. Census Bureau, more than 80% U.S. manufacturing industries earn *less* than an 8% profit rate.[6] In the Uruguay Round, the minimum profit margin was changed from 8% to a "reasonable amount." In practice, "reasonable" has been interpreted as the average profit rate for the industry. Although this change is an improvement, it still means that any firm making a positive profit but less than the average profit for the industry will be found to have priced unfairly! This is hardly what Attorney General Samuel Graham meant in the quote cited by Stewart and Dwyer.

Unfortunately, the economic problems with antidumping are even more perverse than profitable transactions being deemed to be unfair. In most cases, the agency assessing the foreign firm's costs will levy duties on the foreign firm if its overhead costs (or, in the language of the statute, the firm's "administrative, selling, and general costs") are too low. Historically, the United States would add-in a 10% overhead rate on the foreign firm's operating costs. With the Uruguay Round agreement, the overhead rate was changed to be a "reasonable" rate. Whether the 10% standard or the "reasonable" standard is used, a foreign firm that has invested to become more efficient (say, lowering its overhead costs so that they are less than the average of its industry) will face dumping margins based on the actions of its inefficient (and perhaps nonexporting) competitors. The imposition of *ad hoc* profit rates and overhead margins reveal the statute's true protectionist purpose.

Finally, the above issues are exacerbated by the challenges of accurately measuring the foreign firm's costs. As discussed by Blonigen (2006), agencies assessing duties have considerable discretion in determining costs. Blonigen argues (and statistically documents) that the extent of the discretion has increased over the past two decades. He shows that, as a result of the growing use of administrative discretion when imposing duties, the average U.S. antidumping margin has risen from about 15% in the early 1980s to more than 60% in recent years.

Blonigen argues that the U.S. Department of Commerce imputes the foreign firm's costs to be well above the firm's actual costs. As shown in Figure 3, rules such as minimum profit margins and overhead rate and discretion by authorities means that antidumping authorities act as if the foreign firm's costs are ATC_{cc} (denoting constructed costs) rather the economically meaningful ATC_3. Imagine you observe a foreign firm pricing at price P_3. Most observers would

[6] See various issues of *Quarterly Financial Report for Manufacturing, Mining, and Trade Corporations*, U.S. Census Bureau.

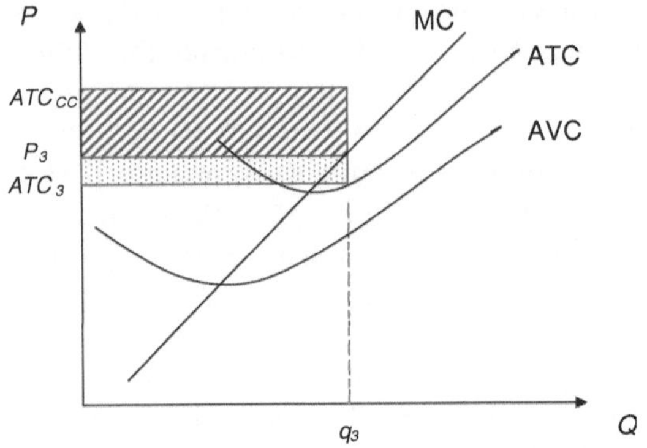

Figure 3. Economic profits and dumping still found.

conclude that the firm is making a profit (denoted by the hatched region). Under current antidumping rules, however, the firm's costs will likely be marked up to ATC_2, leading an affirmative dumping determination. I again ask whether this is what Attorney General Samuel Graham meant in the quote cited by Stewart and Dwyer.

There are numerous other issues with antidumping law that simply are inconsistent with basic economic principles. Injury analysis is exceedingly simple under antidumping rules compared with any other type of litigation. Think of the decades of litigation involving the question of whether smoking cigarettes "causes" cancer. If the antidumping approach were relevant, all that would be required is a short note that pointed out that people smoke and people get cancer. Whether the people who smoke also work in an asbestos factory would not be needed. In fact, it is likely that one would not even have to show that the same people who smoked were the people who got cancer!

I should emphasize that the lack of economically (and econometrically) grounded margin calculations and injury analysis is found across all antidumping using countries. Because of the lax standard, new antidumping users like India find injury in well over 90% of their cases and determine that the foreign firm has priced unfairly in almost 100% of the investigations.

My own view is that antidumping is perhaps the most powerful reason why all law students should be required to take a basic microeconomics course either prior to law school or as part of their required studies while in law school. Even with only a basic understanding of economics, aspiring lawyers would recognize the flaws in the current antidumping statutes. Although I enjoyed reading Stewart and Dwyer's review of the antidumping agreement, I found the lack of attention paid to the "economic sensibleness" of the statute frustrating. The time is right for a legal scholar to make the effort.

REFERENCES

Blonigen, B. A. 2002. "Evolving Discretionary Practices of U.S. Antidumping Activity." *Canadian Journal of Economics* 39:874–900.

Cass, K. E., and R. C. Fair. 2004. *Principles of microeconomics*, 7th ed. Upper Saddle River, NJ: Prentice-Hall.

Clarida, R. 1993. "Entry, Dumping, and Shakeout." *The American Economic Review* 83:180–203.

Hall, R. E., and M. Lieberman. 2008. *Microeconomics: Principles and applications*, 4th ed. Mason, OH: Thomsom Southwestern.

Hubbard, R. G., and A. P. O'Brien. 2008. *Microeconomics*, 2nd ed. Upper Saddle River, NJ: Prentice-Hall.

U.S. Census Bureau. Quarterly Financial Report for Manufacturing, Mining, and Trade Corporations. Series QFR-98-3. Washington, DC: GPO, various years. Available at www.census.gov.

WILLIAM E. KOVACIC

7 Price Differentiation in Antitrust and Trade Instruments

Introduction

Competition policy overlaps with many forms of government intervention that seek to regulate conduct that falls within the ambit of antitrust statutes.[1] From their origins in the late nineteenth and early twentieth centuries, antitrust and antidumping legal systems have shared an interest in price differentiation – the practice by which a single supplier charges different prices for the same product to distinct classes of customers.[2] Antidumping mechanisms generally forbid a firm from "selling a product in an export market at a price below that which is charged for the same or comparable merchandise in the home market."[3] Various antitrust commands – for example, prohibitions on predatory pricing – can be interpreted to limit the ability of a firm to use localized price cuts to deter entry or chasten existing rivals.

At times in the twentieth century, both the antitrust and antidumping regimes in the United States treated price differentiation with acute skepticism. In the past three decades, however, U.S. antitrust law has taken a more tolerant view of price differences. Courts and enforcement agencies have embraced analytical approaches for monopolization and attempted monopolization that have

[1] See W.E. Kovacic, and A.P. Reindl, "An Interdisciplinary Approach to Improving Competition Policy and Intellectual Property Policy," 28 *Fordham International Law Journal* 2005, 1062 (discussing relationship between competition law and intellectual property law).

[2] This chapter uses the term "price differentiation" rather than the economic term "price discrimination," as the former term seems to capture more closely what various antitrust and antidumping provisions seek to regulate – namely, price differences, rather than what economists would define technically as price discrimination.

[3] T.P. Stewart, et al. Antidumping: Overview of the Agreement 1 (2006) (prepared for the Columbia University Law School WTO Seminar in Law & Public Policy 2006–2007).

I am grateful to Gary Horlick for many useful suggestions. The views expressed here are the author's alone and not necessarily the views of the Federal Trade Commission or any of its individual commissioners. Parts of this chapter are adapted from 'W. Kovacic, "The Intellectual DNA of Modern U.S. Competition Law for Dominant Firm Conduct: The Chicago/Harvard Double Helix," 2007 *Columbia Business Law Review* 1.

given firms progressively greater freedom to choose pricing strategies with the effect of making it more difficult for plaintiffs to sustain claims based on unlawful price differentiation. Since the 1980s, judicial interpretations of the Robinson–Patman (RP) Act have eroded the force of anti–price differentiation provisions that Congress enacted in 1936 with the express purpose of protecting smaller enterprises from the efforts of larger rivals to prevail by extracting special discounts and other concessions from their suppliers. As a consequence, U.S. law and policy today feature a genuine divergence in the way antitrust policy and antidumping policy treat price differentiation.

The relaxation of antitrust controls on price differences has accorded with the views of the many commentators who have scorned the controls of the RP Act and criticized the tendency of earlier antitrust decisions involving monopolization and attempted monopolization to discourage larger incumbent firms to use price cuts as a competitive tactic.[4] The commentary of economists and lawyers has influenced antitrust rules most deeply by discouraging a tendency to equate the distress of individual firms – or the distress of domestic producers – with damage to the competitive process or with harm to consumer interests. This is most evident in the analysis of predatory pricing, in which courts and enforcement agencies have pressed claimants to demonstrate not only that the defendant has set its prices below some accepted measure of its own costs, but also that market conditions (including the state of barriers to entry or expansion by rivals) will enable the predator to recover its investment in below-cost sales once the plaintiff has been suppressed.

The variation in the treatment of price differences by, respectively, U.S. antitrust doctrine and antidumping policy has attracted extensive attention from commentators. A central focus of discussion has been whether antidumping policies that focus on injury to domestic suppliers might be modified to account for the effect of challenged behavior on competition in the relevant market. This would involve a reinterpretation or redrafting of antidumping laws to use the type of competitive effects analysis commonly used to resolve antitrust disputes. Other observers have proposed mechanisms for engaging the antitrust and trade communities in discussions aimed at achieving a deeper mutual understanding of the aims and operations of the antitrust and antidumping systems and perhaps reaching a consensus on methods for reducing conflict between the two.

This chapter considers the treatment of price differentiation under antitrust and antidumping laws from three perspectives. It begins by mapping out the elements of the antitrust and antidumping systems that give agency officials and courts discretion to determine the impact of statutory commands. The second part of the chapter then describes the manner in which antitrust courts have adjusted the application of controls on price differentiation. The third part

4 See J.C. Cooper, et al. "Does Price Discrimination Intensify Competition? Implications for Antitrust," 72 *Antitrust Law Journal* 2005, 327.

considers how the treatment of price differentiation under antitrust law and antidumping law accords with the views of economists and business school instructors about how firms should make pricing decisions.[5]

The Antitrust and Antidumping Systems

Antitrust and antidumping laws in the United States today differ significantly in their treatment of price differentiation. As embodied in standards established in the framework of the World Trade Organization (WTO) and in the decisions of U.S. antidumping authorities, the antidumping regime defines dumping as the sale of goods in the importing jurisdiction at a price below their normal value. The economic literature equates the implementation of this command as triggering scrutiny of suppliers that sell their goods in the importing jurisdiction at or above long-run average cost.[6] A finding of liability typically requires a showing of actual material injury or threatened material harm to the industry of the importing nation where the injury is caused by the challenged export behavior.

The U.S. antitrust regime under the Sherman Act's controls for attempted monopolization and monopolization is more forgiving. With some variation, U.S. courts generally have established a rebuttable presumption of legality for prices set at or above average variable costs. A plaintiff who proves pricing below average variable cost can prove liability only by taking the additional step of showing that market conditions will enable the predator to recoup its investment in below-cost sales once the target of its predatory campaign has been subdued.

The RP Act's price differentiation provisions establish nominally more powerful restrictions on price differentiation, and their origins and application traditionally have evoked the spirit, and sometimes the form, of antidumping policy. Judicial decisions since the early 1980s gradually have endorsed interpretations that pull the operation of the RP Act closer to the meaning of modern applications of the Sherman Act. One line of decisions has ruled that the RP statute's predatory pricing provision – the ban on primary line price differentiation contained in Section 2(a) of the Act – are to be interpreted in a manner consistent with predatory pricing standards established under the Sherman Act.[7] A second group of modern decisions involving the secondary line price differentiation provisions[8] of the RP Act has imposed progressively greater demands on

[5] The author is grateful to Luke Froeb, Michael Sallinger, and David Scheffman for extensive discussions about the manner in which economics departments and business schools teach business strategy courses related to various competitive techniques that involve price differentiation, including predatory pricing, bundling, and loyalty discounts.

[6] See A.O. Sykes, "The Economics of 'Injury' in Antidumping and Countervailing Duty Cases," in S. Jagdeep, Bhandari, and A.O. Sykes (Eds.), *Economic Dimensions in International Law: Comparative and Empirical Perspectives* (2001), 83.

[7] *Brooke Group Ltd. v. Brown & Williamson Tobacco Corp.*, 509 U.S. 209 (1993).

[8] The secondary line provisions of the RP Act police injury to downstream purchasers that arises when a single supplier sells the same product at different prices to two rival enterprises.

plaintiffs seeking to establish liability. The Supreme Court's most recent decision, *Volvo Trucks N. Am. v. Reeder-Simco GMC, Inc.*,[9] suggests that the Court may be inclined to insist that the injury required in secondary line cases be injury to competition and not simply injury to the complaining downstream firm. Were the Court to take this step in a future case, it would go a long distance toward demanding the type of competitive effects analysis that takes place in cases decided under the Sherman, Clayton, and Federal Trade Commission (FTC) Acts.

One way to assess the possibilities for the exercise of discretion in the application of the antidumping laws and the antitrust laws is to highlight the operational elements of the two regimes that require interpretation, and invite, at least to some degree, judgments about the economic rationality of each system. The degrees of interpretational flexibility in the antitrust and antidumping systems are not identical. For the most part, the adoption of the U.S. antitrust statutes entailed a deliberate congressional delegation of authority to federal judges to adjust the interpretation of the statutes over time to conform to current ideas about economics and law.[10] This gives judges a large measure of freedom to depart from existing interpretations of the statutes when changes in economic and legal thinking call for adjustments.[11] By contrast, the antidumping laws and the RP Act are more expressly concerned with the welfare of individual firms, or classes of firms, that are adversely affected by price differentiation in import commerce. The texts and legislative histories of the laws arguably do not permit decision-making tribunals to ignore this purpose and to adopt interpretations that conform the laws to the evolving jurisprudence of antitrust courts. Nonetheless, in the case of the RP Act, modern judicial decisions have tended to bend the application of the statute toward a consideration of consumer welfare effects and away from a single-minded focus on the effect on the supplier's rivals or downstream firms.

Consider the key decision-making variables in an antidumping case and a predatory pricing case under the antitrust laws. In an antidumping case, the key operational elements that permit some exercise of discretion include:

- Determination that sales involved identical or comparable products
- Calculation of costs

[9] 546 U.S. 164 (2006).

[10] W.E. Kovacic and C. Shapiro, "Antitrust Policy: A Century of Economic and Legal Thinking," 14 *Journal of Economic Perspectives* 2000, 43.

[11] See *State Oil Co. v. Khan*, 522 U.S. 3, 20 (1997) (describing Supreme Court's distinctive role under antitrust statutes "in recognizing and adapting to changed circumstances and the lessons of accumulated experience"); *PolyGram Holding, Inc.*, (F.T.C. July 24, 2003) (courts and FTC have refined operational content of antitrust laws over time "to account for insights gained from adjudication experience and from developments in economic and legal learning"), order enforced, 416 F.3d 29 (D. C. Cir. 2005). See also P. Areeda, "Monopolization, Mergers, and Markets: A Century Past and the Future," 75 *California Law Review* 1987, 959, 981. ("The weakness of the common law approach to antitrust is its uncertainty; its strength is its adaptability and thus survivability.")

- Determination and calculation of injury
- Determination of causation.

In an antitrust case involving a claim of monopolization by means of predatory pricing, the key operational elements are:

- Definition of the relevant market
- Finding that the defendant possesses substantial market power
- Definition of the requisite price–cost relationship
- Requirement of recoupment
- Finding that plaintiff's injury corresponded to harm to competition.

An examination of the elements suggests that a court would have some freedom to adapt operational principles to account for changes in economic and legal thinking about the social benefits and costs of price differentiation. The next part of this chapter indicates how that discretion has been used in the interpretation of the RP Act and the Sherman Act.

Evolution of Antitrust Law and Policy

The enforcement of the U.S. antitrust laws in recent decades demonstrates the acceptance of a competitive effects test that focuses on consumer welfare rather than on the fortunes of individual enterprises. The discussion that follows examines experience with the RP Act and Sherman Act separately and indicates how courts have used the interpretational power described earlier in this chapter to adopt more tolerant views of price differentiation.

RP Act

As noted above, the RP Act forbids various forms of price differentiation. Since enactment of the measure in 1936, the statute and its enforcement have attracted greater hostile commentary than has any other substantive command in the U.S. competition policy system.[12] Despite intense criticism, Congress has not repealed the statute or seriously considered doing so.

Although the statute has remained essentially the same since its adoption in 1936 and throughout its subsequent implementation, federal enforcement activity has decreased dramatically during the past 40 years. Table 1 presents the number of RP Act cases filed by the FTC from 1961 through 2008.[13] The table

[12] See T. Calvani and G. Breidenbach, "An Introduction to the Robinson-Patman Act and Its Enforcement by the Government," 59 *Antitrust Law Journal* 1991, 765, 770–772 (describing scholarly views of aims and effects of government RP Act enforcement).

[13] The Justice Department has brought no RP cases since initiating a small number of RP matters in the early 1960s. See T.E. Kauper, "The Justice Department and the Antitrust Laws: Law Enforcer or Regulator?" 35 *Antitrust Bulletin* 1990, 83, 99. (During Kauper's tenure as Antitrust Division head in the 1970s, "the Division used its understanding with the FTC that the latter would be responsible for government enforcement of the Robinson-Patman Act to

Table 1. *Federal Trade Commission Robinson–Patman Act Enforcement Actions – 1961 through 2008*

President	Number of complaints issued	Matters per year
Bush II (2001–2008)	0	0
Clinton (1993–2000)	1	0.125
Bush (1989–1992)	0	0
Reagan (1981–1988)	5	0.625
Carter (1977–1980)	8	2.0
Nixon/Ford (1969–1976)	41	5.125
Kennedy/Johnson (1961–1968)	518 (134)	64.75 (16.75)

records the number of complaints issued in the period indicated. Some matters took the form of consent decrees; others were litigated on the merits.

Counting RP cases requires several judgment calls. Perhaps the most important is whether to treat selected, industry-wide enforcement projects as one case, or to treat all consent decrees or other enforcement actions taken pursuant to the industry-wide project as separate enforcement events. During the Kennedy and Johnson administrations, the FTC undertook major industry-wide initiatives involving the citrus and apparel industries. The citrus initiative yielded 45 consent decrees, and the Commission conducted apparel industry sweeps that yielded batches consisting of 163 matters, 27 matters, 33 matters, and 56 matters. If one treats each large grouping of consents as one matter, one generates the total of 134 RP cases for the period. If one treats each consent as a separate event, the number of matters is 518.

The matters presented in Table 1[14] are organized by presidential administration. The grouping of matters does not track the tenure of Reagan appointees at the FTC. Ronald Reagan's first appointee to the Commission, James C. Miller III, did not begin his term as FTC chairman until September 30, 1981. Between Reagan's inauguration in January 1981 and Miller's arrival at the FTC, the Commission accepted consent orders in two RP matters[15] and initiated a matter that was resolved by a settlement in 1983.[16] Table 1 includes all of these matters in the Reagan totals, even though Miller was involved neither in accepting the consent orders in 1981 nor in commencing the third matter that ultimately was settled during his tenure.

However one resolves issues of classification, the enforcement data from 1961 through 2008 reveal a striking change in the FTC's norm for enforcing the RP Act. After a robust period of activity in the 1960s, FTC enforcement

avoid any involvement under a statute it thought economically unwise.") Table 1 presents data involving only the FTC, which has provided the federal enforcement presence since the early 1960s.

[14] The data in Table 1 are derived mainly from the CCH Trade Regulation report looseleaf service and transfer binders on *FTC Complaints, Orders, Stipulations* for 1961 through 2000.

[15] Miles Laboratories, Inc., 98 F.T.C. 29 (1981); YKK (U.S.A.) Inc., 98 F.T.C. 25 (1981).

[16] Gillette Co., 102 F.T.C. 1351 (1983).

declines progressively during the past three decades. The Nixon and Ford FTC shifted resources away from RP enforcement and increased scrutiny of dominant firm behavior, vertical restraints, and some horizontal behavior. During Jimmy Carter's presidency, the agency initiated an average of two RP matters per year. The Commission announced five matters during the Reagan administration, including a much-publicized action involving the book-publishing sector[17] issued during the chairmanship of Daniel Oliver. The FTC issued no RP cases during the chairmanship of Janet Steiger, who was appointed by George Bush in 1989 and continued as chair until Bill Clinton's first appointee to that post, Robert Pitofsky, took office on April 12, 1995. Under Pitofsky's chairmanship, the FTC initiated one new RP matter (*McCormick*[18]), a consent decree accepted in 2000, and dismissed the RP case begun during the Oliver chairmanship. Thus, from the initiation of the book-publishing case in 1989 until the consent decree in *McCormick* in 2000, the Commission issued no RP matters.

This history illustrates how an antitrust enforcement norm changes over time. The acceptance of a norm of limited activity can be inferred not only from enforcement patterns, but also from the statements of FTC leaders indicating that the antitrust community should not regard the amount of contemporary federal RP enforcement outputs as remarkable.[19]

Why did the RP enforcement norm change within the FTC? Congress did not alter the relevant statute, and there is no observable evidence that Congress or its committees told the FTC that the Commission could dispense with RP enforcement. Several phenomena explain the change of the FTC's enforcement norm.

Consensus of Commentators

Extensive, repeated criticism of the RP statute and enforcement patterns through the 1960s suggested that the consensus within the larger community of antitrust academics and practitioners favored retrenchment.

Consensus of Agency Leadership

Beginning with the selection of Miles Kirkpatrick as FTC chair in 1970, presidents from Richard Nixon through George W. Bush appointed leaders who either

[17] Harper & Row Publishers, Inc., 122 F.T.C. 113 (1996) (dismissing complaint charging six of the largest U.S. book publishers with unlawful price discrimination).

[18] McCormick & Co. (FTC Complaints & Orders 1997–2001 Transfer Binder), Trade Reg. Rep. (CCH) para. 24,711 (FTC 2000).

[19] Soon after the Commission announced its McCormick settlement in 2000, the agency's first RP complaint since 1989, FTC Chairman Robert Pitofsky gave a tongue-in-cheek explanation for the decision to prosecute: "I only voted for that case," Pitofsky explained during a panel discussion at the Annual Spring Meeting of the American Bar Association's Section of Antitrust Law, "because I couldn't bear to come back here for a fifth year and say that Robinson-Patman enforcement was imminent. Some of you might have said I was losing credibility." "Roundtable Conference with Enforcement Officials," 68 *Antitrust Law Journal* 2000, 581, 611.

doubted the value of robust RP enforcement or believed that other applications of the agency's enforcement resources promised greater returns. At the Commission level and in the agency's operating bureaus, the injection of new members into the agency's policy-making group caused the group to reconsider the RP enforcement norm that had prevailed in the 1960s.

Judicial Interpretation

The formal rulings and the perspective of contemporary court decisions forced FTC leadership to reassess the RP enforcement norm. The federal courts in the 1970s and 1980s imposed greater burdens on plaintiffs seeking to establish liability under the RP statute. Courts toughened standards that plaintiffs must satisfy to prevail,[20] and the Commission's own experience in defending RP administrative decisions in the 1980s showed the agency that future orders would have to survive review by an increasingly skeptical judiciary.[21]

Private Enforcement Alternative

Private enforcement of the RP statute continued at substantial levels, providing some assurance that the Act's commands would be implemented, albeit by private rather than public prosecutors.[22]

These and other factors suggest how the RP federal enforcement norm accepted a progressive reduction in the number of cases initiated. The change in the RP enforcement norm over time is evident, and the reasons for the transformation are probably not in dispute. This leaves open the question of whether the transformation is appropriate. Recall that the adjustment occurred without alternations in the underlying statute or some other form of dispensation from Congress. If a drop in federal enforcement matters from 518 (or 134) from 1961 through 1968 to a total of one case from 1990 through 2008 without a statutory amendment is acceptable, on what basis can one object to a reduction in activity in other enforcement areas, such as scrutiny of other distribution practices? Is it appropriate to rely on adjustments in a public agency's enforcement norm to calibrate public enforcement activity to match an apparent consensus within the competition policy community about suitable levels of activity?

One response is that the evolution of a more permissive federal enforcement norm is less important if other prosecutorial agents (consumers, injured firms, or state governments) are able to increase their activity. Suppose, however, that the intuition supporting the federal enforcement norm is substantively correct

[20] See T.E. Kauper, "The Report of the Attorney General's National Committee to Study the Antitrust Laws: A Retrospective," 100 *Michigan Law Review* 2002, 1867, 1874. (RP Act "has been significantly curtailed through judicial interpretations contracting expansionary decisions of the sixties.")

[21] See Boise Cascade Corp., 107 F.T.C. 76 (1986), rev'd, 837 F.2d 1127 (D.C. Cir. 1988), on remand, 113 F.T.C. 956 (1990).

[22] In explaining why it dismissed the *Harper & Row* complaint, the FTC said that one factor was the existence of a private RP suit challenging the conduct at issue in the FTC's case.

in its doubts about the social benefits of RP enforcement. In such circumstances, the performance of the competition policy system suffers if other prosecutorial agents can pursue matters that contradict the sensible federal enforcement norm. If the federal prosecutorial norm is wise, one might prefer that federal prosecutors take measures to promote broader acceptance of the norm.

This may suggest the value of fuller efforts by federal prosecutors to engage the competition policy community in a discussion that permits public officials to explain transparently why the federal agencies have embraced a different norm for a specific area of enforcement over time. If the federal agencies have discovered that there are instances in which enforcement of the formal legal command undermines consumer interests, perhaps it is best to identify areas in which enforcement is beneficial. At any one time, the aim should be to make the actual enforcement norm transparent to outsiders and to promote consideration about how the formal legal command and relevant doctrine might be conformed to the enforcement norm.

Predatory Pricing

It is useful to begin by considering how an antitrust specialist would have counseled a dominant firm about price-cutting when the 1960s drew to a close. The most recent Supreme Court guidance on the question appeared in *Utah Pie Co. v. Continental Baking Co.*[23] in 1967. The decision, which analyzed predatory pricing claims under the RP Act, strongly suggested that the pricing above average total costs could be unlawful predation.[24] The Court also relied on what might be characterized as general expressions of the defendant's intent to exclude a competitor.[25] Effects on the well-being of rival firms, rather than effects on consumers, also seemed paramount. One passage in *Utah Pie* noted, as a factor weighing for a finding of liability, that the market in question had featured a "declining price structure" as a consequence of the defendant's pricing tactics.[26]

A counselor giving advice in the 1960s and 1970s also would have to warn his or her clients that the federal enforcement agencies were willing to police dominant firm price cuts aggressively. In 1963, the Department of Justice had brought criminal charges under the Sherman Act and the RP Act against a dairy in New England for selling milk below its costs.[27] In 1963, the Justice Department had obtained an indictment under Section 2 of the Sherman Act against a firm and several of its executives for oversupplying the market in Los Angeles with bananas.[28] The possibility that the Justice Department would use its criminal enforcement powers to attack predatory pricing persisted well into the 1970s. In

23 386 U.S. 685 (1967).

24 386 U.S. at 698.

25 Ibid., at 696–97.

26 Ibid., at 703.

27 *United States v. H.P. Hood & Sons, Inc.*, (1961–1970 Transfer Binder), Trade Reg. Rep. (CCH) para. 45,063, at 52,519 (D. Mass., filed March 15, 1963).

28 *United States v. United Fruit Co.* (1961–1970 Transfer Binder), Trade Reg. Rep. (CCH) para. 45,063, at 52,528 (C.D. Ca., filed on July 16, 1963).

a speech in 1977, Griffin Bell, the Attorney General of the United States, provided the following warning:

> Predatory pricing is another subject toward which I expect to direct more criminal enforcement. Persistent below cost pricing well within the boundaries of traditional criminal antitrust enforcement. Where predatory conduct is uncovered, I support the use of all our criminal enforcement resources against it.[29]

The Department of Justice never brought a criminal case of the type Bell described in his 1977 speech. At that time, however, one could not idly disregard the promise of the chief law enforcement officer of the United States to prosecute price-cutting as a crime. Antitrust counselors also had to advise clients that the possibilities for government civil cases were genuine. The Justice Department's monopolization lawsuit against IBM including a claim of predatory pricing,[30] and the FTC in the 1970s initiated predatory pricing lawsuits against ITT-Continental (bread),[31] Borden (lemon juice),[32] and General Foods (instant coffee).[33]

The doctrinal environment changed dramatically in the 1970s, and the inspiration for the adjustment was an intellectual revolution inspired significantly by the Harvard School. The principal stimulus was an article by Phillip Areeda and Donald Turner that has a strong claim to be the most influential law review article ever written on an antitrust topic. In 1975, Areeda and Turner published a proposal that courts use the relationship of the dominant firm's prices to its variable costs to determine the legality of a challenged pricing strategy.[34] Within months, two courts of appeals relied heavily on the article to dismiss predatory pricing allegations.[35] In the years to follow, the article became the starting point for judicial analysis of below-cost pricing claims.[36] Although many decisions declined to embrace the Areeda–Turner test in all of its features, the article transformed the way that federal judges analyzed predatory pricing allegations.[37] The 1975 article, the proposal of which Areeda and

[29] Griffin Bell, Harvard Law School Address (1977).

[30] *United States v. International Business Machines Corp.*

[31] *In re* ITT Continental.

[32] *In re* Borden.

[33] *In re* General Foods.

[34] P. Areeda and D. Turner, "Predatory Pricing and Practices Under Section 2 of the Sherman Act," 88 *Harvard Law Review* 1975, 697.

[35] Hanson v. Shell Oil Co., 541 F.2d 1352 (9th Cir. 1976); Int'l Air Indus., Inc. v. Am. Excelsior Co., 517 F.2d 714 (5th Cir. 1975)."

[36] W. Kovacic, "The Intellectual DNA of Modern U.S. Competition Law: for Dominant Firm Conduct: The Chicago/Harvard Double Helix," 2007 *Columbia Business Law Review* 1, 46–47.

[37] See R.O. Zerbe Jr. and M.T. Mumford, "Does Predatory Pricing Exist? Economic Theory and the Courts After Brooke Group," 41 *Antitrust Bulletin* 1996, 949, 950–951 (noting influence of the Areeda–Turner predatory pricing proposal in the courts; observing that "the legacy of the Areeda-Turner rule continues to inform the debate about predatory pricing, making standards of evidence more objective and rigorous").

Turner incorporated and refined in 1978 in the third volume of their treatise,[38] also set off an academic debate about predatory pricing that continues to this day.[39]

One major conduit for bringing the Areeda–Turner proposal into the mainstream of antitrust jurisprudence was the opinion writing of Stephen Breyer, who taught with Areeda and Turner on the Harvard Law School faculty in the 1970s before joining the First Circuit in 1980. In 1983, Breyer's opinion for the court in the *Barry Wright Corp. v. ITT Grinnell Corp.*[40] case drew heavily from the technical details and philosophy of the Areeda–Turner article. "Antitrust laws," Breyer wrote, "very rarely reject beneficial birds in the hand for the sake of more speculative future low price; birds in the bush."[41] This passage endorsed the policy trade-off between short-term and long-term effects that animated the Areeda–Turner test – let consumers take the short-term benefits of price-cutting now, and worry about the longer-term harms (which Areeda and Turner in 1975 regarded to be speculative) later,[42] if and when they come about.

Barry Wright proved to be influential. The Supreme Court's decision in 1986 in *Matsushita Electric Industrial Co. v. Zenith Radio Corp.*[43] prominently cited Breyer's *Barry Wright* opinion and echoed its philosophy.[44] The Court endorsed the scrutiny of the relationship between the defendant's prices and its costs and approved the further requirement that the plaintiff show how the defendant, after excluding the plaintiff, could recoup the sacrifice of short-term profits that the below-cost pricing strategy entailed.[45] Although the recoupment test had gained prominence in the work of other scholars who were responding to the Areeda–Turner proposal, the 1975 article of the two Harvard scholars also had anticipated such a test.[46]

[38] P. Areeda & D. Turner, III Antitrust Law Paras 710–22 (1978).

[39] The catalytic effect of the Areeda–Turner predatory pricing proposal within academia was immediate and powerful. In 1981, in the introduction to a book that collected papers At an FTC conference on business strategy and predatory conduct, Steven Salop commented:

> Any modern discussion of predatory conduct must begin with Areeda and Turner's seminal article. Few scholarly works have had so much influence on such a diverse group of researchers and practitioners in so short a time. More than any other article, it has led courts to begin taking an economic view of predation, either by actually adopting the rule or by using it as a starting point. Indeed, the progress the courts have made in the past 6 years in increasing their own economic sophistication has been dramatic. The Areeda and Turner article has also been a strong source of stimulation for economists, spawning a variety of commentary and further research. . . . Although all the economists contributing to the debate take some exception either to Areeda and Turner's static, nonstrategic mode of analysis, all have benefited from the path they have provided.

S.C. Salop, "Strategy, Predation, and Antitrust Analysis: An Introduction," in S.C. Salop (Ed.), *Strategy, Predation, and Antitrust Analysis* (Volume 1, FTC, September 1981), 10–11.

[40] 724 F.2d 227 (1st Cir. 1983).

[41] 724 F.2d at 234.

[42] Areeda & Turner, *Antitrust Law, supra* note 38, at 166–68.

[43] 475 U.S. 574 (1986).

[44] 475 U.S. at 594.

[45] Ibid., at 590–91.

[46] Areeda & Turner, *Predatory Pricing, supra* note 34, at 698.

Antitrust and Antidumping: Consistency with Commentary

Even though courts in recent decades have adopted antitrust rules that are more tolerant of price differentiation, existing antitrust rules and antidumping principles continue to attract criticism in the economic and legal literature, including from academics who teach business strategy in economics departments and business schools. Recent criticism falls into roughly three categories.

The first is that reliance upon price–cost relationships is difficult to apply in practice. Even though many commentators and business managers applaud the greater permissiveness embodied in modern predatory pricing jurisprudence, they emphasize that firms rarely have the ability to make accurate computations of their likely average variable costs within the times needed to make decisions about how to respond to the efforts of their rivals. Many observers argue that the most important screens established in modern antitrust cases are the requirements that the alleged predator have substantial market power and that the plaintiff demonstrate the feasibility of recoupment. Antitrust and antidumping tests that are tied to price–cost relationships promise to remain troublesome grounds for counseling in the foreseeable future.

The second critique is that the acceptance of greater permissiveness in either antidumping or in antitrust policies ignores strategic considerations that make price differentiation a successful strategy for excluding rivals on grounds other than superior performance. This theme is most pronounced in the literature on predatory pricing that emphasizes the utility of price-cutting in establishing a reputation for toughness or in sending confusing signals to entrants about their prospects for success. This literature would entertain consideration of a wider range of quantitative and qualitative factors in assessing the validity of a chosen strategy.

The third critique is that, to the extent that antitrust and antidumping systems continue to discourage firms from engaging in price differentiation, such policies retard the use of tactics that improve consumer welfare. To overcome the limits of existing policies, firms are advised to resort to techniques other than simply price-cutting to achieve the benefits of differentiation. This accounts in part for the popularity of bundling and loyalty programs in the sale of various products. These strategies often defy simple application of traditional antitrust rules that control price differentiation (e.g., bans on predatory pricing, tying, or exclusivity).

STEFANO INAMA[1] AND EDWIN VERMULST[2]

8 Nonpreferential Origin Rules in Antidumping Law and Practice

Introduction

This article first examines the efforts made at a multilateral level to establish disciplines on rules of origin and the various techniques that may be used in drafting rules of origin. The second part discusses the role of origin rules in antidumping law and practice, with a focus on the European Union (EU) system. It analyzes the use of such rules as an operative tool during the investigative process and as an enforcement mechanism when antidumping measures are imposed. It concludes with an overview on the status of the Harmonization Work Programme (HWP) under the World Trade Organization (WTO) Agreement on Rules of Origin (ARO) and the recent proposals on anticircumvention made in the negotiating group on rules.

Although the use of harmonized nonpreferential origin rules in the context of antidumping proceedings remains a desirable goal, it should realistically go hand in hand with the establishment of third-country anticircumvention legislation.

Nonpreferential Rule of Origin and Methodologies for Drafting Rules of Origin

Efforts to Establish Multilateral Rules and Methodologies Used

The issue of rules of origin (as opposed to origin markings, to which Article IX of the General Agreement on Tariffs and Trade [GATT] is devoted, because of U.S. influence) did not attract much attention in the negotiation of the

[1] The opinions expressed in this article are those of the author and do not represent the official views of the United Nations Conference on Trade and Development (UNCTAD) or any other UN agency.

[2] Edwin Vermulst thanks Wim Keizer and Marcel Van Marion for their helpful comments.

original GATT. On the contrary, during the second session of the Preparatory Committee in 1947, a subcommittee considered that "it is to be clear that it is within the province of each importing member to determine, in accordance with the provisions of its law, for the purpose of applying the most-favoured-nation (MFN) provision whether goods do in fact originate in a particular country."[3] Only later – in 1951 and 1952[4] – were the first attempts made (without success) to address the question of harmonization of rules of origin.

The scant attention devoted to the issue of rules of origin in the original GATT was probably because of the preoccupation of the drafters with establishing the unconditional MFN principle contained in Article I. In an MFN world, there is no need to examine the origin of goods. This association implied that, as a general concept, origin entered into world trade with a discriminatory bias: Origin needs to be ascertained whenever a discriminatory measure is in place.[5]

Efforts to codify and strengthen a general concept of origin in the absence of multilateral disciplines were made at the multilateral level during the Kyoto Convention negotiations in 1973.[6] However, Annex D I of the Convention, containing guidelines, was not sufficiently detailed and left Member States freedom to choose different and alternative methods of determining origin. The low level of harmonization achieved, combined with the fact that few countries ratified this annex, meant that the annex became little more than general guidance used in determining origin at the national level.

These meager results achieved at the multilateral level with regard to harmonizing rules of origin or even determining a valid method of origin assessment contrast with the efforts to negotiate the Customs Valuation Code, negotiated during the Tokyo Round in 1979, and the entry into force of the International Convention on the Harmonized Commodity Description and Coding System, negotiated under the auspices of the Customs Cooperation Council (now World Customs Organization) in 1988. Thus, until the Uruguay Round Agreement, rules of origin remained the only one of the three basic customs laws operating at the national level not subject to multilateral discipline.

[3] See EPCT/174, pp. 3–4.

[4] See, for instance, the 1951 Report on "Customs Treatment of Samples and Advertising Material, Documentary Requirements for the Importation of Goods, and Consular Formalities: Resolutions of the International Chamber of Commerce" (GATT/CP.6/36, adopted on October 24, 1951, II/210) and the 1952 Report on "Documentary Requirements for Imports, Consular Formalities, Valuation for Customs Purposes, Nationality of Imported Goods and Formalities connected with Quantitative Restrictions" (G/28, adopted on November 7, 1952, 1S/100).

[5] This consideration, however, does not fully explain why an origin determination was not considered necessary in the framework of Article VI of the GATT on antidumping, although an explicit reference is made to the cost of production in the country of origin in Paragraph I B ii.

[6] International Convention on the Simplification and Harmonization of Custom Procedures, adopted in 1974 by the Customs Cooperation Council at its 41st and 42nd sessions, held in Kyoto. See H. Asakura, "The Harmonized System and Rules of Origin," 27(4) *Journal of World Trade* August 1993.

Annex D I of the Kyoto Convention was one of the multilateral attempts to clarify some of the conceptual issues arising from the definition of "substantial transformation." As of today, the observations and comments contained therein are still useful and valid.

In substance, Annex D I of the original Kyoto Convention did not provide for ready-to-use rules of origin. Nevertheless, the Convention provided a series of key concepts and practices that are still valid today. These key concepts and practices were extremely useful in guiding the reader toward a better understanding of the different practices and methods of defining rules of origin.

Although the criterion for products "wholly produced in one country" was sufficiently precise, the "substantial transformation criterion when two or more countries have taken part in the production" was not specified other than by listing the three different ways in which the substantial transformation may be interpreted:

- by a rule requiring a change of tariff heading in a specified nomenclature, with lists of exceptions, and/or
- by a list of manufacturing or processing operations that confer, or do not confer, upon the goods the origin of the country in which those operations were carried out, and/or
- by the *ad valorem* percentage rule, where either the percentage value of the materials used or the percentage of the value added reaches a specified level.

The revised Kyoto Convention contains in Annex K guidelines concerning rules of origin in Chapter 1, documentary evidence of origin in Chapter 2, and control of documentary evidence of origin in Chapter 3. As in the old convention, the revised text covers a number of areas (such as certification and verification) that are still the only multilateral rules in this area. It also contains in its annexes a format for certificate of origin.

The revised text is rather different in substance on the options to define the substantial transformation criterion. Inspired by the WTO ARO, it does not dwell on discussing the pros and cons of the different methodologies in drafting rules of origin, and it recommends the use of the harmonized system (HS) to determine substantial transformation.

Translated into plain language, the Kyoto Convention recommends a change of tariff classification (and not a change of tariff heading as in the original Kyoto Convention) as the best criterion to determine substantial transformation. The *ad valorem* percentage used in the revised Kyoto Convention is based on the use of a percentage criterion calculation based on import content as the numerator and the ex works price as the denominator.

The option to define substantial transformation on the basis of manufacturing or processing operations is no longer present, although it is still being used in a number of preferential rules of origin and in the HWP for certain HS chapters like chemicals. To a certain extent, these changes represent the evolution of the methodologies used in drafting rules of origin by the main users – basically the EU and the United States.

In portraying what could be defined as the current menu in drafting rules of origin, the following options may be identified:

- Across-the-board criteria, across the board with product specific, or product specific only;
- Change of tariff heading simple or with exceptions;
- Tariff shift at change of tariff subheading (CTSH) with exclusions of specific headings and subheadings and regional value content;
- Percentage criterion based on (a) value added, (b) import content, or (c) value of materials;
- Specific working or processing; or
- A mix of criteria.

None of these methodologies are perfect in drafting rules of origin, and generally speaking, the pros and cons of each methodology as contained in the original Kyoto Convention are still applicable. However, additional remarks may be made from the experience gained since the first Kyoto Convention.

- An across-the-board percentage may be an attractive option given its simple nature and apparently transparent application. However, experience has shown that rules of origin starting as an across-the-board percentage have later evolved into a product-specific approach to regulate sensitive sectors. Even the latest attempt made by the EU Commission to adopt an across-the-board percentage in the context of its own reform of the Generalised System of Preferences (GSP) rules of origin has resulted in product-specific exceptions.[7]
- The change of tariff heading or change of tariff classification methodology is progressively gaining international recognition as the most predictable criterion to determine origin. The preference given to this methodology by the Uruguay Round Agreement has contributed to its popularity. However, because the HS was not conceived to draft origin rules, the adoption of a change of tariff heading or change of tariff classification methodology implies the development of product-specific rules of origin to take into account those cases in which the architecture of the HS does not reflect substantial transformation. This limitation may open a Pandora's box scenario where lobbies, industrialists, and trade negotiators intervene in drafting product-specific rules of origin that reflect their narrow interests and turning the issue of rules of origin into a restrictive and time-consuming exercise. The North American Free Trade Agreement (NAFTA) rules of origin were the first example in this area, followed recently by the negotiations in

[7] See TAXUD document 2046/2007 of December 2007.

The Southern Africa Development Community (SADC) and The Association of Southeast Asian Nations (ASEAN).
- Percentage criteria are increasingly considered with suspicion, especially by U.S. and Japanese administrators; surprisingly, they are still viewed favorably by the EU.

The difficulties encountered in administering the net cost method in the NAFTA context have progressively persuaded the United States to reduce to a minimum the use of percentage rules in their latest free trade agreements.

In adopting a percentage calculation, there is a tendency (if not a consensus) among exporters and/or manufacturers to prefer the adoption of a maximum imported inputs allowance rather than a minimum value-added requirement. There are two reasons for this preference:

The percentage calculation of the value of the imported input or materials is easier to compute, and the value of the imported input may be supported by suppliers' invoices. It has been used by the EU for a long time. The term "value of imported material," rather than being left vague and subject to the discretion of Customs authorities, may be anchored to the customs value as determined in accordance with the Agreement on Implementation of Article VII of the GATT 1994. Most recently, in the Central American Free Trade Agreement (CAFTA), the materials-based calculation has been defined in two ways: the build down and built up methods. Although methodologies for the calculation may vary according to the EU or U.S. approach, the essence of the calculation is the same because both approaches refer to "materials" and not to complex calculations referring to value added.

In fact, the calculation of the value added is complex, as it entails:

- a distinction of costs, which could be computed as local value added;
- itemization of such costs to the single unit of production. As a consequence, it often requires accounting, and discretion may be used in assessing unit costs. Additionally, currency fluctuations in beneficiary countries may affect the value of the calculation; and
- low labor costs, which in developing countries may result in low value added and instead of being a factor of competitiveness may turn out to be a factor penalizing producers based in developing countries.

These elements may be familiar only to accountants. As prices, costs, and quantities change, recalculation will be necessary to ensure compliance. Although some of these tasks may form part of the normal accounting procedures required for commercial purposes, some may not. In such cases, therefore, additional professional expertise may be required.

Obviously, there are still important differences among the United States and the EU in the formulas and the definition of the numerator and denominator.

The use of the percentage criterion in the HWP for machinery and electronics is still one of the most divisive issues.

Origin and Anticircumvention

The first cases in which the absence of multilateral disciplines on nonpreferential rules of origin started to attract the attention of policy makers and analysts occurred in the 1980s in connection with the enforcement of antidumping duties and other trade contingency or protectionist measures.

The emergence of antidumping law as one of the most important trade policy instruments during the 1980s and 1990s has been largely responsible for the growing attention to the use of rules of origin as commercial policy instruments that could influence the interaction between the internationalization of production and its location. Imposition of antidumping duties coinciding with increasing globalization of production created the first tangible relocation cases of certain companies in strategic markets such as the European Community (EC) and the United States. Claims by EC and U.S. domestic industries regarding the establishment of screwdriver factories on their territories led the two jurisdictions to adopt anticircumvention legislation in the 1980s.[8]

As examined later in this chapter, the absence of multilateral disciplines on rules of origin left a free hand to Administrations, especially those of the EU, to use *ad hoc* origin rules to counteract circumvention.

From a legal point of view, the basic problem of anticircumvention measures is the absence of multilaterally agreed-on rules and the resulting unilateral discretionary practices of the investigating authorities. Until recently, neither the United States nor the EC – the main users of such measures – had codified detailed nonpreferential rules of origin. Moreover, they sometimes applied different tests of origin depending on the trade instruments within which the origin determination had been carried out.

For example, in U.S. practice, the origin of semiconductors determined by the U.S. Department of Commerce in the context of antidumping proceedings was different from that determined by the U.S. Customs Service.[9] Codification of nonpreferential rules was rare or totally absent in EC legislation until the entry

[8] See, for the U.S. legislation, Pub. L. No. 100–418, § 1321, 102 Stat. 1192, adding § 781 to the Tariff Act of 1930, as amended, 19, USCA § 1677j. For an analysis of the U.S. anticircumvention measures, see N. Komuro, "US Anti-circumvention Measures and GATT Rules," 28(3) *Journal of World Trade* June 1994. For the EC legislation on anticircumvention, see, as originally adopted, Council Regulation 1761/81 of June 22, 1987, O.J. 2167 (1987). For a detailed discussion of EC antidumping and the new anticircumvention measures, see E. Vermulst and P. Waer, *EC Anti-Dumping Law and Practice* (London, Sweet and Maxwell, 1996).

[9] See Palmeter, "Rules of Origin in the United States" in Vermulst, Waer, and Bourgeois, op. cit., p. 74, and the following decision where Customs concluded that assembling and testing conferred origin on a semiconductor: C.S.D. 80–227, 14 Cust. b and Dec. 1133 (1980). In the following case, the Commerce Department decided that, for antidumping purposes,

into force of the common customs code in 1992. Even at that time, such codification was incomplete. Only after the progress made in the HWP did the EU start to apply a consistent policy on nonpreferential rules origin adopting, on a *de facto* basis, the preliminary results of the HWP. Before these developments, the EC Commission investigations relied on a rule of thumb of a 45 percent value-added test.[10] This value added text, however, did not prevent the EC authorities from developing *ad hoc* rules on assembly products where the circumstances of the case so required, as further discussed later in this chapter.

The draft Antidumping Agreement (ADA) of the December 1991 Draft Final Act (referred to as the "Dunkel Draft") contained detailed provisions on circumvention. However, the U.S. negotiators were of the opinion that the provisions were "weak," and succeeded in deleting these provisions from the final ADA.

The Draft was replaced by a Ministerial Decision that recognizes the "problem" of circumvention and the desirability of having uniform rules on anticircumvention as soon as possible. The Decision referred the matter to the Committee on Anti-Dumping Practices for resolution. The United States and other WTO members hold that the Ministerial Decision constitutes recognition of the legitimacy of anticircumvention measures and does not preclude members from maintaining, modifying, or enacting anticircumvention measures.

In the aftermath of the Uruguay Round ARO, it was considered and hoped that the results of the HWP could be used to satisfactorily address the issue of anticircumvention. As the ARO expressly provided that the results of the HWP would be used in the context of antidumping proceedings, the HWP could be consistently used to determine if a product exported via a third country is truly originating in that country or if it has been exported via that third country only to circumvent the antidumping duty. However, the actual status of the negotiations in the HWP seems to have dashed such hope, as briefly examined later in this chapter.

Nonpreferential Rules of Origin and Antidumping

Conceptually, nonpreferential[11] origin rules may be relevant both in the course of an antidumping investigation and in its aftermath, when antidumping measures are imposed.

assembling and testing did not confer origin: Erasable Programmable Read Only Memories (EPROMs) from Japan; Final determination of sales at less than fair value, 51, Fed. Reg. 39680, 39692 (1986). See also D. Palmeter, "Rules of Origin or Rules of Restrictions: A Commentary on a New Form of Protectionism," 11(1) *Fordham International Law Journal* 1987.

10 See E. Vermulst and P. Waer, "European Community Rules of Origin as Commercial Policy Instruments?" *Journal of World Trade*, 1990.

11 Preferential origin rules are not used in this context and therefore fall outside the scope of this chapter.

To determine whether dumping is taking place, the investigating authorities must select a country that will form the basis for the calculation of the normal value. For this selection process, the authorities may use origin rules (see section later in this chapter).

To determine whether the dumping is causing material injury to the *domestic industry* of the like product, the authorities may use origin rules to decide whether the *domestic* producers allegedly comprising the domestic industry qualify as such (see "Origin in the Injury Determination" in this chapter).

Following the imposition of antidumping measures, exporters may initiate or increase shipments from other countries. The authorities could then use origin rules to determine whether the antidumping measures imposed on the original exporting country should also apply to the shipments from the third countries (see "Origin after the imposition of antidumping measures").[12]

Origin During the Investigative Process

Origin in the Dumping Determination

The WTO and GATT do not provide a conclusive answer to the question of whether normal value should be based on prices and/or costs in the country of export, the country of origin, or the country of production, all three of which might potentially differ.

The language used in Article VI of the GATT is imprecise. In Article VI:1, for example, the Contracting Parties recognize that:

> ... dumping, by which *products of one country* are introduced into the commerce of another country at less than the normal value of the products, is to be condemned.... A product is to be considered as being introduced into the commerce of an importing country at less than its normal value, if the price of the *product exported from one country* to another
>
> (a) is less than the comparable price ... for the like product when destined for consumption in the *exporting country*, or
>
> (b) in the absence of such domestic price, is less than either
>
> ...

[12] They might also use anticircumvention rules. For the time being, there is no multilateral agreement on the use of anticircumvention rules in antidumping proceedings. In the absence of international agreement, the EU, the United States, and some Latin American countries have unilaterally adopted anticircumvention rules in the framework of their antidumping legislation. A recently tabled draft Anti-Dumping Agreement provides for the possibility of anticircumvention rules (Valles draft November 30, 2007). Anticircumvention rules are not further discussed in this chapter.

(ii) the cost of production of the like product in the *country of origin.* (emphasis added)

Similar language is used in Articles VI:4,[13] VI:5,[14] and VI:6[15] of the GATT, as well as in the two supplementary provisions to Article VI:1.[16]

The explanation for this lack of clarity (apart from bad drafting) might be that the typical case that the GATT drafters presumably had in mind in 1947 would have been the case in which products are (wholly) produced in one country and then exported (dumped) from that country to the importing country. Indeed, in such a case, the countries of export, origin, and production are identical.

A report by a GATT Group of Experts[17] established in 1958 to examine the operation of antidumping laws in various countries for the first time reflected recognition that the country of export might not be the same as the country of production, a situation they referred to as *indirect dumping*:

> . . . the Group then considered the question of dumping of goods where the *exporting country* is not the *producing country* of the goods concerned. Most members of the Group reported that their countries had little or no experience of indirect dumping and that, where legislation existed to deal with this problem, the legislation had not been used. The Group noted that since the wording of Article VI, paragraph 1(a), referred only to the comparable price

13 No product of the territory of any Contracting Party imported into the territory of any other Contracting Party shall be subject to antidumping or countervailing duty by reason of the exemption of such product from duties or taxes borne by the like product when destined for consumption in the country of origin or exportation, or by reason of the refund of such duties or taxes.

14 No product of the territory of any Contracting Party imported into the territory of any other Contracting Party shall be subject to both antidumping and countervailing duties to compensate for the same situation of dumping or export subsidization.

15 No Contracting Party shall levy any antidumping or countervailing duty on the importation of any product of the territory of another Contracting Party unless it determines that the effect of the dumping or subsidization, as the case may be, is such as to cause or threaten material injury to an established domestic industry, or is such as to retard materially the establishment of a domestic industry.

16 1. Hidden dumping by associated houses (i.e., the sale by an importer at a price below that corresponding to the price invoiced by an exporter with whom the importer is associated, and also below the price in the exporting country) constitutes a form of price dumping with respect to which the margin of dumping may be calculated on the basis of the price at which the goods are resold by the importer. 2. It is recognized that, in the case of imports from a country which has a complete or substantially complete monopoly of its trade and where all domestic prices are fixed by the State, special difficulties may exist in determining price comparability for the purposes of Paragraph 1, and in such cases importing Contracting Parties may find it necessary to take into account the possibility that a strict comparison with domestic prices in such a country may not always be appropriate.

17 Anti-Dumping and Countervailing Duties, Report adopted on May 13, 1959 (L/978), GATT, B.I.S.D., 8th Supp., 145–153 (1960).

> in the exporting country, there was some doubt whether action against indirect dumping was strictly in accordance with the letter of the Agreement. However, despite this doubt, the Group was generally of the opinion that it was reasonable for countries to have the right to protect themselves against indirect dumping (whether of processed or unprocessed goods).... [18]

Presumably as a result of the Group's discussion, a special provision was devoted to this problem in the Kennedy[19] and the Tokyo Round Anti-Dumping Codes and in the Uruguay Round ADA. Article 2:5 of the ADA provides that:

> ... [i]n the case where products are not imported directly from the country of origin but are exported to the importing Member from an intermediate country, the price at which the products are sold from the country of export to the importing Member shall normally be compared with the comparable price in the country of export. However, comparison may be made with the price in the country of origin, if, for example, the products are merely transhipped through the country of export, or such products are not produced in the country of export, or there is no comparable price for them in the country of export.

Thus, under the ADA, the starting point for the normal value calculation is the country of *export*. However, the normal value may be based on the prices and/or costs in the country of *origin* where

- the exported products are only transshipped through the country of export,
- the exported products are not produced in the country of export, or
- a comparable price for the exported products in the country of export does not exist.

By essentially focusing on transshipments, the provision therefore does not address the cases in which the country of origin and the country of production and/or assembly differ.

Until now, classical transshipment issues have mainly[20] come up in the case of products manufactured in China, but exported from Hong Kong. When the cases targeted both customs territories, the authorities considered China the relevant starting point for the normal value selection and terminated the investigations against Hong Kong on the grounds that products with Hong Kong origin did not exist.[21]

[18] Ibid., at 148–149.

[19] See Article 2(c) of the Kennedy Round Anti-Dumping Code, Agreement on Implementation of Article VI of the GATT (1967), GATT, B.I.S.D., 15th Supp., 24–36 (1968).

[20] But see, for example, *Potassium permanganate from USSR*, [1991] OJ L14/56 (termination).

[21] See, for example, *Silicon metal from China, Hong Kong*, [1990] OJ L80/9 (definitive); *Tungsten ores and concentrates from China, Hong Kong*, [1990] OJ L83/23 (provisional, termination). Compare *Gas-fuelled non-refillable pocket lighters from China*, [1991] OJ L326/1 (definitive); *Gas-fuelled, non-refillable pocket flint lighters from China*, [1995] OJ L101/38

The assessment becomes more complicated if the activities in an intermediate country can no longer be characterized as mere transshipment. In *Aspartame*,[22] for example, the question arose as to what should be done with aspartame originating in Japan but exported to the EU from the United States. The Commission decided to use U.S. prices; in other words, prices in the exporting country, as the basis for normal value:

> [t]he investigation revealed that the product was not merely transhipped through the USA but was actually sold to and imported by the US producer/exporter in the USA before exportation to the EC. The investigation also showed that there was substantial production within the USA and that there was a comparable price for aspartame in the USA. In these circumstances the conditions under which . . . the country of origin might be considered appropriate as a basis for establishing normal value are not fulfilled. In addition, the investigation showed that the Japanese product was fully interchangeable with the US material, and that almost the entire production of the Japanese manufacturer was purchased and warehoused by the US exporter which subsequently sold the product both in the USA and for export to the EC. The Commission therefore based normal value on US domestic prices.

An even more complex situation arose in *Small Screen Colour Televisions*,[23] where a number of Hong Kong producers assembled the product concerned in Hong Kong without the televisions obtaining nonpreferential Hong Kong origin in the process. Although the country of production and the country of export were the same, the country of origin differed. In this case, the Commission based normal value on Hong Kong sales or on Hong Kong constructed value.

In a subsequent proceeding targeting exports of color televisions of all sizes from China, Korea, Malaysia, Singapore, and Thailand,[24] in contrast, the Commission used constructed normal values in the country of origin in cases where the country of origin and the country of production differed.

The cases just discussed all concerned initial investigations. However, it may also happen that when antidumping duties are imposed, the producers concerned start or increase exports from other countries. The authorities may then decide to start a new antidumping investigation against such third countries, normally following an application by the relevant domestic industry, and decide in the course of that investigation that the products manufactured in third

(amendment definitive), where the EC rejected claims by Chinese producers that normal value be based on Hong Kong prices on the grounds that there was no Hong Kong production of lighters.

22 *Aspartame from USA, Japan*, [1991] OJ L134/1 (definitive).

23 *Small screen colour televisions from China, Hong Kong*, [1991] OJ L14/31 (provisional).

24 *Colour televisions from China, Korea, Malaysia, Singapore, Thailand*, [1994] OJ L255/50 (provisional).

countries actually did not obtain local origin but rather still have the origin of the country against which the original antidumping measures were imposed.[25]

This happened, for example, in *Ball Bearings from Thailand*[26] and *Electronic Typewriters from Taiwan*.[27] In these cases,[28] the European Commission terminated antidumping proceedings that it had initiated on the grounds that the production processes carried out in these countries were not sufficient to confer, respectively, Thai and Taiwanese origin on the products manufactured in those countries. The practical consequence of these findings was that the products assembled in Thailand and Taiwan were effectively considered to have Japanese origin, as a result of which they were subject to the antidumping duties imposed with respect to such products originating in Japan.

Following a subsequent investigation of the Taiwanese producer concerned – the Japanese company Brother – the German customs authorities decided to levy the Japanese antidumping duty applicable to Brother *retroactively*. The consequence was that Germans customs ordered Brother to pay more than 3 million DM in antidumping duties. Brother appealed against this decision on the grounds that the typewriters produced in Taiwan should be considered as originating in Taiwan on the basis of application of the EU's nonpreferential origin rules: Although most of the parts came from Japan, they were mounted and assembled in Taiwan in a fully equipped factory into ready-for-use typewriters.[29]

With reference to the third standard of Annex DI of the Kyoto Convention,[30] the European Court of Justice (ECJ, where the case eventually ended up) distinguished between *simple* assembly operations and other types of assembly operations. It defined simple assembly operations as operations that do not require staff with special qualifications for the work in question or sophisticated tools or specially equipped factories for the purposes of assembly. Such simple operations could never confer origin because they do not "*contribute to the essential characteristics or properties of the products in question*."

Other types of assembly *could* confer origin depending on fulfilment of one of two tests, in order of precedence:

- an assembly process representing (from a technical point of view and with regard to the definition of the goods in question) the decisive production stage during which the use to which the component parts are to be put becomes definite and the goods in question are given their specific qualities; or

[25] They may also decide to investigate the origin of the products, see Section 3.2 below.

[26] *Certain ball bearings from Thailand*, [1985] OJ L59/30 (notice of termination).

[27] *Electronic typewriters from Taiwan*, [1986] OJ L140/52 (notice of termination).

[28] See, for more detail, Vermulst and Waer, "European Community Rules of Origin as Commercial Policy Instruments?" 24(3) *Journal of World Trade* 1990, 55–100.

[29] Case 26/88, *Brother International GmbH v. Hauptzollamt Giessen*, [1989] ECR 4253.

[30] International Convention on the simplification and harmonization of customs procedures, accepted on behalf of the Community by Council Decision 77/415/EEC, [1977] OJ L166/1.

- where the above technical test does not lead to a decisive answer, the technical test plus a value-added test as an "*ancillary criterion.*"

Specifically with respect to the value-added test, the Court held that the assembly operations as a whole must involve an appreciable increase in the commercial value of the finished product at the ex-factory level. The ECJ did not lay down a concrete percentage of value added sufficient to confer origin, but noted that, in a production process in which only two countries are involved, a value added of less than 10% in the assembly process is insufficient.[31]

The German Finanzgericht of Hessen subsequently ruled that the operations performed by Brother in Taiwan fell into the category of "simple assembly" because the assembly operations of Brother in Taiwan did not employ staff with special qualifications for the work in question, did not involve use of sophisticated tools, and did not involve specially equipped factories for the purposes of the assembly of the typewriters.[32]

Origin in the Injury Determination

Antidumping measures may be imposed only if the dumped imports cause material injury to the domestic industry of the like product. The domestic industry is defined as all domestic producers or a major proportion thereof.

Most user countries do not employ origin rules for purposes of the definition of the domestic industry.[33] In fact, Footnote 1 to Article 2(1) of the WTO ARO explicitly states that Article 2(1) is without prejudice to determinations made for purposes of the "domestic industry" definition, thereby authorizing investigating authorities to ignore rules of origin in this context.

Where the origin of the products manufactured by the domestic producers and/or applicants is questioned, the authorities tend to analyze the situation on a case-by-case basis.[34] The following examples taken from EU practice may serve as an example.

In *Outboard Motors*,[35] several of the Japanese producers questioned whether the major EC complainant, Outboard Marine Belgium, qualified as a European producer. The Commission concluded that, on the basis of application of the

[31] In Case 93/83, *Zentralgenossenschaft des Fleischergewerbes e.g. (Zentrag), v. Hauptzollamt Bochum*, [1984] ECR 1095, the Court issued a similar judgment in a situation in which only two countries were involved and the value added in the last country was 22%.

[32] Hess, FG, Urteil vom 25.5.1992 – 7 K 552/91; rechtskräftig, reproduced in 6 Recht der Internationalen Wirtschaft, 522–524 (1993).

[33] By way of exception, Australian antidumping law provides by analogy to Australian origin rules that an Australian producer must add at least 25% value in Australia to qualify as a domestic producer. See Steele, "The Australian Anti-Dumping System," in Jackson and Vermulst (Eds.), *Anti-Dumping Law and Practice: A Comparative Study* (1989) 223–286, at 265.

[34] For an overview of the Canadian Import Tribunal's practice, see Magnus, "The Canadian Anti-Dumping System," *id.*, 167–222, at 209–210.

[35] *Outboard motors from Japan*, [1983] OJ L152/18 (provisional).

EU's nonpreferential origin rules, the outboard motors produced by Outboard Marine Belgium originated in the Community.

In *Photocopiers*,[36] the EU had to determine whether the factories of the main EU complainant Xerox in the Netherlands and in the United Kingdom could be included in the definition of the domestic industry. As regarded the Dutch plant (mid-volume machines), the European Commission found that integrated manufacturing operations were carried out by or on behalf of Xerox in the EU, that the value added within the EU in these manufacturing operations exceeded 70%, and that the Dutch-produced photocopiers had Community origin. However, in the United Kingdom plant (low-volume machines), the photocopiers were found to have been manufactured predominantly from Japanese parts. The production processes carried out in the United Kingdom consisted of the construction of certain subassemblies[37] for the production line, completion of the frame assembly, and the final mainline assembly of subassemblies and components by testing and packing of the photocopiers. During the investigation period, the EU value added in the United Kingdom plant was found to be between 20% and 35% (this would not have been sufficient under the EU's nonpreferential origin rules to confer EU origin on the products). However, the weighted-average value added in the Community for all Parts of Photocopiers (PPCs) manufactured by Xerox was in excess of 50%. On this basis and taking into account Xerox's policy of obtaining an increasing proportion of its components from within the Community, the EU decided that Xerox qualified as a domestic producer.[38]

In dynamic random-access memory (DRAMs)[39] and erasable programmable read-only memory (EPROMs),[40] the European Commission distinguished between front-end (wafer diffusion and sorting) and back-end (assembly and testing) operations in the production of semiconductors and found that wafer diffusion was from a technological and capital investment point of view more significant than the assembly and testing operations, even though, as a ratio of total production costs, assembly costs were generally significant, and in some cases exceeded wafer diffusion costs. This finding was significant because the EU producers were generally performing the diffusion process in the EU and the assembly and testing in third countries, whereas a number of Japanese manufacturers did the diffusion in Japan and the assembly and testing in the EU.

While the investigation into these antidumping cases was in progress, the EU also adopted a product-specific origin Regulation on Integrated Circuits providing that diffusion[41] (rather than assembly and testing) constituted the last

[36] *Photocopiers from Japan*, [1987] OJ L54/12 (definitive).

[37] The fusers, modules, develop boxes, cassettes, semiautomatic document handlers, optics, and other minor assemblies.

[38] *Photocopiers from Japan*, [1987] OJ L54/12 (definitive).

[39] *DRAMs from Japan*, [1990] OJ L20/5 (provisional); [1990] OJ L193/1 (definitive).

[40] *Erasable programmable read-only memories from Japan*, [1991] OJ L65/1 (definitive).

[41] Diffusion is the process whereby integrated circuits are formed on a semiconductor substrate by the selective introduction of an appropriate dopant, see Annex 11 to the ICCC, consolidated version, July 1, 2006.

substantial process or operation. The Integrated Circuits Regulation came at a convenient time for these proceedings because some Member States' customs authorities had held until then that the process of assembly and testing was origin-conferring. If applied to the definition of the domestic industry in the antidumping cases, this would have entailed that the EU complainants would not have had standing to bring the case.

In *Certain Ring Binder Mechanisms*,[42] the Commission relied on the origin rules to include EU-originating ring binder mechanisms assembled in Hungary by one of the two EU complainants and to exclude Hungary-originating ring binder mechanisms.

Thus, the tendency of the authorities in the cases just mentioned has been to apply nonpreferential rules of origin to define the domestic industry where the complaining producers meet such rules and to rely on softer criteria to include them where this is not the case.

In the recent *Footwear*[43] investigation, it was relatively clear from an origin perspective that the complaining producers made footwear with EU origin whereas major successful European and international brands and other entities imported footwear with Chinese and/or Vietnamese origin.[44] Yet the importers added high value in the EU through pre- and postproduction activities.[45]

Although the EU authorities used their traditional methodology to define the domestic industry and to eventually impose antidumping measures, the underlying policy issue was subsequently raised in the context of the reflection process on the use of the EU's trade defense instrument in a globalized economy,

[42] *Certain ring binder mechanisms from Malaysia, China*, [1997] OJ L22/1 (definitive):

> *...it was found that a limited portion of the sales of one of the complainant Community producers related to products which had undergone their last substantial processing in Hungary and had therefore to be excluded from its Community production. On the other hand, it was established that some products, which were reported in import statistics as being of Hungarian origin, were merely assembled in Hungary from Austrian parts and were therefore considered to be part of the Community production of the producer concerned, since the assembly operation which the products in question had undergone in Hungary did not, on the basis of non-preferential rules of origin, confer Hungarian origin on the finished products. The fact that such products had been reported in import statistics as being of Hungarian origin was considered irrelevant, since their origin had been declared on the basis of the preferential rules of origin, which are not applicable to this investigation.*

[43] *Certain footwear with uppers of leather from China, Vietnam*, [2006] OJ L 275/1 (definitive).

[44] The EC has a product-specific, nonpreferential origin rule for Chapter 64 footwear providing that origin is conferred from manufacture from materials of any tariff heading except for assemblies of uppers affixed to inner soles or to other sole components of heading 6406 (see Annex 11 to the ICCC, consolidated version, July 1, 2006). In other words, the assembly process should at a minimum include the affixing of the uppers to the (inner) soles.

[45] Design, research and development, marketing, advertising, and distribution. See also Isakson, "When Anti-dumping Meets Globalisation: How Anti-dumping Can Damage the Supply Chains of Globalised European Companies, Five Case Studies from the Shoe Industry," 3(3) *Global Trade and Customs Journal* 2007.

Box 2: Case study – Antidumping measures on leather shoes, August 2006

In October 2006, the EU imposed duties of 16.5% and 10% on certain leather shoes imported to the EU. These duties were the result of an investigation that found both dumping of these exports from certain third countries and consequent injury to EU producers. The application of EU and WTO rules in this highly complex case provoked divisions among EU economic operators and EU Member States. The case illustrated two important issues.

initiated by Directorate-General (DG) Trade Commissioner Mandelson in the aftermath of the case in December 2006.[46]

Outsourcing by EU Producers

Although many EU companies still produce leather footwear in the EU, a significant number of EU companies have outsourced the production of footwear to third countries while keeping other parts of their operations in the EU. Those EU companies that produce leather shoes in the third countries concerned are subject to the antidumping duty. Moreover, under the existing rules for antidumping investigations, only producers that keep their production within the EU are considered in determining whether the required proportion of Community industry for the case to be initiated is met. Yet the number of EU companies that are moving elements of their production is growing, and these companies account for thousands of jobs in the EU.

Consumer Interest

The footwear case also illustrates another problem in the context of determining what is in the wider economic interest of the EU. In the majority of cases, especially those that do not concern consumer products, the impact of antidumping measures on the prices paid by the consumer has typically not been significant. Nonetheless, it is important to reflect on the question of whether and how consumer interests can be better reflected in antidumping investigations, and any measures taken.

Similar issues arose again in the *Energy Saving Lamps* review case, this time, however, pitting multinationals such as Osram/Siemens (complainant) and Philips and GE (respondents) against each other.[47]

[46] Global Europe, Europe's Trade Defence Instruments in a Changing Global Economy, A Green Paper for Public Consultation (December 6, 2006).

[47] *Integrated electronic compact fluorescent lamps (CFL-i) from China and extending to imports of the same product consigned from the Socialist Republic of Vietnam, the Islamic Republic of Pakistan and the Republic of the Philippines,* [2007] OJ L272/1.

Origin After the Imposition of Antidumping Measures

As we have just seen, when antidumping measures are imposed, it is possible that exporters or third parties start or increase exports from third countries.

Rather than opening a new antidumping proceeding against these third countries,[48] the EU (or EU Member States' customs authorities) may dispute the origin of the products now coming from such countries and conduct an origin investigation. When the investigation reveals the existence of fraudulent[49] or incorrect origin declarations, the correct amount of duties due, including antidumping duties,[50] may be collected retroactively and fines imposed. In cases of clear-cut fraud, the importers may also be criminally prosecuted.

The best-known examples of origin investigations are those that involved the photocopier plants of Ricoh in California and Mita in Hong Kong. Following an on-the-spot investigation in California by officials of DG Trade and DG Taxation and Customs Union (TAXUD), the Commission took the view that the photocopiers produced by Ricoh in the United States should be denied U.S. origin. In the absence of a qualified majority within the Origin Committee and the Council, the Commission adopted a product-specific origin rule in the form of Regulation (European Economic Community [EEC]) No. 207/89 on the origin of photocopiers.[51] Although couched in general terms, the regulation was essentially tailor-made for the Ricoh situation. It provided that the manufacture of photocopiers accompanied by the manufacture of the harness, drums, rollers, side plates, roller bearings, screws, and nuts (i.e., the production processes carried out by Ricoh in California) shall *not* confer origin. On the basis of an origin investigation conducted at Mita's Hong Kong premises, the Commission arrived at the conclusion that the photocopiers made by Mita in Hong Kong *did* possess Hong Kong origin and advised the members of the Origin Committee accordingly. As the members of the Origin Committee agreed unanimously with the conclusions of the Commission, the case was dealt with informally. The *negative* Ricoh origin rule was much criticized and became the inspiration for the restrictions on the use of such negative standards in the WTO ARO.[52]

[48] See Section 3.1.1, above.

[49] Fraud normally requires guilty knowledge.

[50] False declarations of origin can be used not only to avoid payment of antidumping duties, but also to claim preferential treatment.

[51] Commission Regulation (EEC) No. 2971/89 of July 11, 1989, on determining the origin of photocopying apparatus, [1989] OJ L196/24, see also Annex 11 to the ICCC, consolidated version July 1, 2006.

[52] Article 2(f) of the WTO ARO requires members to base their rules of origin on a positive standard during the transition period. During that same period, rules of origin that state what does not confer origin (negative standard) are permissible only as part of a clarification of a positive standard or in individual cases in which a positive determination of origin is not necessary.

Less visible origin investigations include those conducted with respect to *Car Radios*, assembled in Indonesia (in the aftermath of antidumping duties imposed on Korean car radios), *Compact Disc Players* assembled in Singapore and Malaysia by Japanese producers (in tandem with antidumping investigations of the same producers), *Steel Wire Ropes* assembled in the United Arab Emirates (following imposition of antidumping duties on India and later on China), *Persulphates* from various countries (following imposition of antidumping duties on China), *Ring Binder Mechanisms* from Thailand (following imposition of antidumping duties on China), *Energy Saving Lamps*, initially from Macao and later from Indonesia, Malaysia, Pakistan, the Philippines, Sri Lanka, Thailand, Tunisia, the United Arab Emirates, and Vietnam (following imposition of antidumping duties on China), *Non-Refillable Lighters* from Indonesia and Malaysia (following imposition of antidumping duties on China), and *Certain Footwear with Leather Uppers* from Macao (following the imposition of antidumping duties on China and Vietnam). Some of these cases were relatively clear because they involved pure transshipments and falsified origin certificates, but others involved at least a certain degree of assembly.

EU customs legislation contains an anticircumvention provision in Article 25 of the European Common Customs Code (ECCC) stipulating that "[a]ny processing or working in respect of which it is established, or in respect of which the facts as ascertained justify the presumption, that its sole object was to circumvent the provisions applicable in the Community to goods from specific countries shall under no circumstances be deemed to confer on the goods thus produced the origin of the country where it is carried out within the meaning of Article 24."

Thus far, this provision has been invoked only once in the context of enforcement of antidumping duties. That case concerned a producer of video cassettes that switched production of video cassettes from China to Macao following imposition of antidumping duties on China (the case concerned not only retroactive collection of antidumping duties but also of regular customs duties, as the producer had benefited from GSP treatment for an estimated total of ECU 20 million).[53] Presumably the reason why Article 25 is used only rarely is that it is difficult to apply in practice. Although the avoidance of payment of antidumping duties may be one reason for the shift in production, it will seldom be the *sole* reason.

Table 1 provides a schematic overview of these and other cases, the customs violations found, and the amount of duties involved, to the extent publicly available.

[53] Annual Report from the Commission on the Fight against Fraud – 1992 Report and Action Programme for 1993–COM (93) 141 Final, at 15–16 (April 20, 1993).

Table 1. *Overview of cases*

Antidumping measures	Third countries	Customs violations	Duties involved
Car radios from Korea[54]	Indonesia	Incorrect origin declarations; assembly	€14.4 M
Bicycles from China[55]	Vietnam	Incorrect origin declarations; assembly	€16.5 M
Video cassettes from China[56]	Macao	False origin declarations	ECU 20 M
Silicon from China[57]	Australia	Falsified origin declarations; pure transshipment	€0.5 M
Silicon carbide from China[58]	Czech Republic	False origin declarations	
Footwear from China[59]	Cambodia	False origin declarations	€1.4 M
Persulphates from China (83.3%)[60]	Taiwan	False origin declarations; wrong classification; pure transshipment	>€4 M
Color televisions from China, Korea, Malaysia[61]	Turkey, Thailand	Incorrect origin declarations; assembly	€18 M
Ring binder mechanisms from China (78.8%)[62]	Thailand	False/incorrect origin declarations; assembly; transshipment	>€3–6 M
Steel wire ropes from India (up to 55.6%)[63]	United Arab Emirates	False origin declarations; assembly	>€6 M

54 Report from the Commission, Report on the follow-up of traditional own resources in cases of fraud and irregularities, at 31–32, COM(2004) 850 final/2 (Brussels, February 4, 2005).

55 Report from the Commission, Report on the follow-up of traditional own resources in cases of fraud and irregularities, at 31–32, COM(2004) 850 final/2 (Brussels, February 4, 2005).

56 Annual Report from the Commission on the Fight against Fraud–1992 Report and Action Programme for 1993–COM(93) 141 Final, at 15–16 (April 20, 1993).

57 Report of the European Anti-Fraud Office, [Second] Activity Report for the period from June 1, 2000, to May 31, 2001, at 19 (2001). See also Report from the Commission, Report on the follow-up of traditional own resources in cases of fraud and irregularities, at 21–22, COM(2004) 850 final/2 (Brussels, February 4, 2005).

58 Report of the European Anti-Fraud Office, [Second] Activity Report for the period from June 1, 2000, to May 31, 2001, at 19 (2001).

59 Report from the Commission, Report on the follow-up of traditional own resources in cases of fraud and irregularities, at 20–21, COM(2004) 850 final/2 (Brussels, February 4, 2005).

60 Report of the European Anti-Fraud Office, Fourth Activity Report for the year ending June 2003, at 29 (2003). See also Report from the Commission, Report on the follow-up of traditional own resources in cases of fraud and irregularities, at 19–20, COM(2004) 850 final/2 (Brussels, February 4, 2005).

61 Report of the European Anti-Fraud Office, Sixth Activity Report for the period from July 1, 2004, to December 31, 2005, at 50 (2006).

62 Report of the European Anti-Fraud Office, Sixth Activity Report for the period from July 1, 2004, to December 31, 2005, at 50 (2006). Compare: Evasion of anti-dumping duties under scrutiny, http://ec.europa.eu/anti_fraud/press_room/pr/2006/07_en.html, accessed August 12, 2007 (May 22, 2006); Report of the European Anti-Fraud Office, Fourth Activity Report for the year ending June 2003, at 28–29 (2003).

63 Report of the European Anti-Fraud Office, Fifth Activity Report for the year ending June 2004, at 49 (2004).

Antidumping measures	Third countries	Customs violations	Duties involved
Steel wire ropes from China[64]	United Arab Emirates	Fraudulent origin declarations; pure transshipment	€2 M
Bicycles from China (up to 30.6%)[65]	Philippines	False origin declarations; pure transshipment (through Hong Kong)	€1.5 M
Energy saving lamps	Macao	False origin declaration	€7.2 M
Energy saving lamps (up to 66.1%)[66]	Indonesia, Malaysia, Pakistan, the Philippines, Sri Lanka, Thailand, Tunisia, United Arab Emirates, Vietnam	Falsified origin declarations; incorrect origin declarations; assembly or pure transshipment	€37 M
Nonrefillable lighters from China (€0.065 p/u)[67]	Malaysia, Indonesia	Malaysia: Fraudulent origin declaration; pure transshipment Indonesia: transshipment through Hong Kong/Singapore	Malaysia: €19.5 M Indonesia: Pending
Leather uppers from China (15%), Vietnam (10%)	Macao	Investigation pending	Pending

Sanctions for Violations of Origin Rules

Fraudulent or incorrect customs declarations can result in severe financial penalties for companies and criminal proceedings against individuals, in accordance with the laws of the individual EU Member States. In general, where there is sufficient *prima facie* evidence that an importer knew that his action was in contravention of customs law, the matter is initially nearly always dealt with as a criminal matter. Mere incorrect reports to the customs authorities can also be dealt with criminally, although this is rare (i.e., normally there has to be some suspicion of guilty knowledge by the party concerned with the import declaration). When incorrect customs declarations are found to exist, the customs authorities

[64] Evasion of anti-dumping duties under scrutiny, http://ec.europa.eu/anti_fraud/press_room/pr/2006/07_en.html, accessed August 12, 2007 (May 22, 2006).

[65] Report of the European Anti-Fraud Office, Seventh Activity Report for the period from January 1, 2006 to December 31, 2006, at 36 (2007).

[66] Illegal trade with energy saving lamps, http://ec.europa.eu/anti_fraud/press_room/pr/2006/21_en.html, accessed August 12, 2007 (December 4, 2006).

[67] OLAF stubs out illegal trade in cigarette lighters, http://ec.europa.eu/anti_fraud/press_room/pr/2007/1_en.html, accessed August 12, 2007 (January 30, 2007).

can go back three years and levy the correct duties by means of the postclearance recovery procedure. When fraud is involved, the time limit of three years can be lengthened if fraud can lead to criminal court proceedings in a Member State. The time limit will then be determined according to the rules in force in that Member State.[68]

Antidumping and the ARO

As discussed earlier, in the case of anticircumvention, the absence of a clear and binding multilateral discipline in the field of rules of origin has been one of the reasons for opening the way to the utilization of rules of origin as a trade policy instrument. The growing concern over trade policy implications of rules of origin ultimately generated efforts that matured into the long-awaited multilateral discipline.[69] In comparison with past multilateral negotiations on this subject, the Uruguay Round ARO (hereinafter the Agreement) broke new ground in several aspects and clearly defines the difference between, and the field of application of, nonpreferential and preferential rules of origin systems.

The Issue of Equally All Purposes

Article 1 Paragraph 1 of the Agreement defines nonpreferential rules of origin as follows:

> "For the purposes of Parts I to IV of this Agreement, rules of origin shall be defined as those laws, regulations and administrative determinations of general application applied by any Member to determine the country of origin of goods provided such rules of origin are not related to contractual or autonomous trade regimes leading to the granting of tariff preferences going beyond the application of paragraph 1 of Article I of GATT 1994."

Paragraph 2 of Article 1 provides that:

> "Rules of origin referred to in paragraph 1 shall include all rules of origin used in non-preferential commercial policy instruments, such as in the application of: most-favoured-nation treatment under Articles I, II, III, XI and XIII of GATT 1994; anti-dumping and countervailing duties under Article VI of GATT 1994; safeguard measures under Article XIX of GATT 1994; origin marking requirements under Article IX of GATT 1994; and any discriminatory quantitative restrictions or tariff quotas. They shall also

[68] See Article 221 (3) and (4) ECCC. The ECJ has ruled that longer time periods for postclearance recovery can only apply to acts that are classified as offenses under national criminal law. See Case C 273/90, *Meico-Fell v. Hauptzollamt Darmstadt v. Germany,* [1991] ECR 5569.

[69] On the United States approach leading to the Agreement on Rules of Origin, see D. Palmeter, "The US Rules of Origin Proposal to GATT: Monotheism or Polytheism," 2 *Journal of World Trade* 1990.

include rules of origin used for government procurement and trade statistics."[70]

Thus according to Paragraph 2, rules of origin are to be utilized to determine the origin of goods for the following purposes:

- MFN tariffs and national treatment,
- Quantitative restrictions,
- Antidumping and countervailing duties,
- Safeguards measures,
- Origin marking requirement,
- Any discriminatory quantitative restriction and tariff quotas,
- Government procurement,
- Trade statistics.

The commitment of using the harmonized rules of origin for the trade policy instruments mentioned above including antidumping was one key objective of the Agreements.

Article 3 Paragraph (a), regulating disciplines after the transition period, is clear that when the HWP is over, the harmonized rules should be equally utilized for all purposes:

> Taking into account the aim of all Members to achieve, as a result of the harmonization work programme set out in Part IV, the establishment of harmonized rules of origin, Members shall ensure, upon the implementation of the results of the harmonization work programme, that:
>
> a) they apply rules of origin equally for all purposes as set out in Article 1...

The relationship between the results of the HWP and the other WTO agreement listed in Paragraph 2 of Article 1 of the ARO is commonly referred as the "implications issue."

Such implications of the rules of origin for other WTO agreements were first openly raised in a submission from India in 1998, other developing countries, and the United States.[71] In this latter submission, the possible implications of the application of the ARO for a series of agreements (such as the Agreement on Textile and Clothing, marks of origin, Trade-Related Aspects of Intellectual Property Rights [TRIPS], Sanitary and Phytosanitary Measures [SPS], etc.) were openly unveiled, with a series of illustrative examples. It was noted that such implications affect the flexibility of Members in attaining consensus on a number of

[70] It is understood that this provision is without prejudice to those determinations made for purposes of defining "domestic industry" or "like products of domestic industry" or similar terms wherever they apply.

[71] For more information, see WTO documents: G/RO/W/42, G/RO/W/48, G/RO/W/50, and G/RO/W/65.

issues, because there were concerns on how to maintain integrity of certain trade policy measures or regimes affecting particular products or product areas.

The United States suggested that one possible solution to this impasse was to agree on a common interpretation of the future obligation of applying rules of origin for "*equally for all such purposes*" does not necessarily entail that Members have "*to use rules of origin for all such purposes.*" Undoubtedly, for some Members this kind of "à la carte menu" may facilitate the creation of a consensus; however, for other Members this flexibility may greatly diminish the value of the whole HWP exercise because it will impair the legal certainty and predictability that the whole agreement was designed to fill in the absence of multilaterally agreed-upon rules.

As pointed out by the United States,[72] according to the Secretariat, thirty-six Members have indicated that they do not have nonpreferential rules of origin.[73] Although many of these same Members are known to utilize antidumping measures, it would appear that rules of origin are not being used for such measures – given that these Members have indicated that they do not have nonpreferential rules of origin. These Members, many of which are active in the HWP, are likely to support the U.S. position on the scope of application to maintain their discretional practices in antidumping proceedings.

Moreover, the Republic of Korea[74] argues that antidumping measures are based on the concept of "exporting country" rather than "origin country." To calculate the dumping margin, derived from the difference between export price and normal price, the domestic price of the like product in the exporting country is used as the normal price. Only in exceptional cases referred to in Articles 2.2 and 2.5 does the country of origin play a role in the Agreement on Antidumping. The first case (Article 2.2) refers to a situation in which there are no sales of the like product in the ordinary course of trade in the domestic market of the exporting country, or a low level of sales in the domestic market of the exporting country is not appropriate to be used for normal price. In such case, the origin country of that product is meaningful. The second case (Article 2.5) refers to a situation in which products are imported through an intermediate country (exporting country). If the products are merely transshipped, or such products are not produced in the exporting country, or there is no comparable price for them in the exporting country, the comparison for dumping margin may be made with the price in the origin country.

The view set forth in this description by the Republic of Korea may be difficult to apply in the situation cited earlier in text involving the thirty-six

[72] See WTO document G/RO/W/65, Implications of the Implementation of the Harmonised Rules of Origin on Other WTO Agreements.

[73] See WTO document G/RO/W/73, Committee on Rules of Origin – Draft – Seventh Annual Review of the Implementation and Operation of the Agreement on Rules of Origin – Note by the Secretariat.

[74] See WTO document G/RO/W/38, Implications of the Implementation of the Harmonized Rules of Origin on Other WTO Agreements.

Members that have notified the WTO that they do not have nonpreferential rules of origin, even though many of these Members are known to utilize antidumping measures. There is, in fact, an apparent wide variety of practices as to "exporting country" versus "origin country" in antidumping regimes, and there is also an apparent absence of a common understanding of the implications of the prospective obligation to apply equally the harmonized rules of origin for all purposes.

A footnote at the end of Article 1, Paragraph 2 of the ARO states that: "it is understood that this provision is without prejudice to those determinations made for purposes of defining 'domestic industry' or 'like products of domestic industry' or similar terms wherever they apply." In India's opinion,[75] could it mean that the Member applying a restriction might define domestic industry by a criterion that is different from the rule of origin applicable to the products in question? This interpretation could lead to a situation of domestic industry appearing to suffer greater damage than may be the case if domestic production were defined according to the harmonized rules of origin. If, for the purpose of antidumping, the term "like product" may be defined differently than for the harmonized rule, then it would be contrary to the principle of the ARO to apply rules of origin equally for all purposes.

Nonpreferential Rules of Origin and Circumvention: Recent Developments in Negotiation Group on Rules

Pending absence of an agreement on the issue of third country circumvention, a substantial number of countries, including not only the United States and the EC, but also Latin American developing countries, have unilaterally adopted anticircumvention provisions. Thus, nonharmonized, nonpreferential rules of origin continue to be used to enforce antidumping duties and, consequently, to combat third country circumvention.

It was suggested and hoped that when the harmonization program has been completed, the rules of origin may help to resolve the issue of third country anticircumvention actions. Some countries also argued that the utilization of harmonized residual rules of origin in the case of third country circumvention, coupled with Rule 2(A) of the HS,[76] should allow this issue to be addressed. This line of reasoning is fiercely opposed by those who are of the view that origin and circumvention should de-linked.

[75] See WTO document G/RO/W/42, Implications of Certain Major Proposal for Harmonized Rules of Origin for Access Under the Agreement on Textile and Clothing: An Analysis of Possible Effects.

[76] The first part of Rule 2(a) extends the scope of any heading that refers to a particular article to cover not only the complete article but also that article incomplete or unfinished, provided that, as presented, it has the essential character of the complete or finished article. The second part of Rule 2(a) provides that complete or finished articles presented unassembled or disassembled are to be classified in the same heading as the assembled article. When goods are so presented, it is usually for reasons such as requirements or convenience of packing, handling, or transport.

In a submission[77] to the negotiating group on rules, Brazil strongly argued that origin determination made by antidumping investing authorities are different from those made, for instance, by customs valuation authorities. According to Brazil, "there seems to be no conceptual or theoretical reason to tie the concept of origin in the ADA to the one in the ARO. Although using the same concepts of 'substantial transformation' and 'value added,' anti-dumping investigating authorities and custom valuation authorities will look at the same t-shirt and ask themselves different questions regarding the origin of that t-shirt. The answers, of course, may differ."

It follows that, according to Brazil: "Any future multilateral disciplines on circumvention shall explicitly recognize that rules of origin, in the sense of the ARO, do not apply in anti-circumvention."

A proposal by the United States[78] further de-link any consideration of origin in possible discipline over anticircumvention. The United States proposes the insertion in the ADA and in the Agreement on Subsidies and Countervailing Measures of language aimed at: (1) providing explicit recognition of the two forms of circumvention traditionally recognized by Members using trade remedies; and (2) adopting uniform and transparent procedures for conducting anti-circumvention enquiries.

The first paragraph of the proposal codifies the practice of enlarging the scope of an antidumping order without engaging on a new antidumping investigation:

> Notwithstanding any other provision of this Agreement or of Article VI of the GATT 1994, the authorities may impose [an anti-dumping duty] [a countervailing duty] with respect to a product that was not within the product under consideration in an investigation which resulted in imposition of a duty, if the authorities determine, pursuant to a review carried out in accordance with this paragraph, that exports of the product are in circumvention of the [anti-dumping duty] [countervailing duty] originally imposed.

In a nutshell, the U.S. proposal aims at inserting in the ADA and in the Agreement on Subsidies and Countervailing Measures provisions ensuring that both Agreements should make explicit the right of authorities to examine the facts and make a determination based on those facts. One may then legitimately wonder what would change from the current *status quo* of the absence of multilateral rules.

Subsequently, the U.S. proposal provides examples of circumvention based on the key concept that the alteration of the original product may be relatively minor, such that the altered product has essentially the same characteristics and uses as the original product covered by the measure. For example, if an exporter adds an additional low-value ingredient to a chemical product (thus changing

[77] See WTO document TN/RL/W/200 of March 3, 2006.
[78] See WTO document TN/RL/GEN/71 of October 14, 2005.

the chemical product's classification), but does not change its essential nature from the point of view of customers, authorities may conclude that the altered product has circumvented the measure on the original product. After the product has been de-linked from origin, authorities will have a free hand in determining if the alteration has changed the commercial use of the good.

The wide discretion left to the authorities may be drawn from the following language:

> Exports of a product that is not within the product under consideration are in circumvention of the [anti-dumping duty] [countervailing duty] originally imposed if:
>
> (i) subsequent to the filing of the application, exports of the product under consideration have been supplanted, in whole or in part, by exports from the same country of another product that has the same general characteristics and uses as the product under consideration; or ...

A second form of circumvention involves replacement of trade in a product with trade in its subcomponents, which are then assembled or finished either in a third country or in the country of import. According to the U.S. proposal, as long as the assembly or finishing operation is relatively minor, there is no reason to consider that moving the location of this operation should have any effect on the antidumping or countervailing duty measure.

This statement seems to forget that issues of what constitute simple assembly and assembly involving substantial transformation have been largely debated during the HWP and a number of technical solutions have been agreed upon.

The real point is that, although the United States recognizes that some assembly or finishing steps may be complex and their location is of great commercial significance, it does not wish to tie its hands and prefers to delegate to the authorities the right to examine the facts and make a determination based on those facts as contained below:

> Exports of a product that is not within the product under consideration are in circumvention of the [anti-dumping duty] [countervailing duty] originally imposed if: (i) [see above]; or
>
> (ii) subsequent to the filing of the application, exports of the product under consideration have been supplanted, in whole or in part, by exports of parts or unfinished forms of the product under consideration, where only a minor or insignificant process of finishing or assembly is necessary to convert the parts or unfinished forms into the product under consideration.

Recently, a proposal on circumvention was contained in the Chairman's Draft[79] of the Negotiating Group on Rules:

[79] See WTO document TN/RL/W/213 of November 30, 2007.

Circumvention

9bis.1 "The authorities may extend the scope of application of an existing definitive anti-dumping duty to imports of a product that is not within the product under consideration from the country subject to that duty if the authorities determine that such imports take place in circumstances that constitute circumvention of the existing anti-dumping duty."[80]

9bis.2 "Authorities may only find circumvention within the meaning of paragraph 1 if they demonstrate that:

(i) Subsequent to the initiation of the investigation that resulted in the imposition of the existing definitive anti-dumping duty, imports of the product under consideration from the country subject to that duty have been supplanted, in whole or in part[81]:
  - by imports from the country subject to the anti-dumping duty of parts or unfinished forms of a product for assembly or completion into a product that is the same as the product under consideration;
  - by imports of a product that is the same as the product under consideration and that has been assembled or completed in a third country from parts or unfinished forms of a product imported from the country subject to the existing anti-dumping duty; or
  - by imports of a slightly modified product[82] from the country subject to the existing anti-dumping duty;

(ii) The principal cause of the change described in subparagraph 2(i) is the existence of the anti-dumping duty on the product under consideration from the country subject to the duty rather than economic or commercial factors unrelated to that duty[83]; and

[80] Throughout this Article, antidumping duty will be understood as duty or undertaking.

[81] Factors pertinent to a consideration of whether imports of the product under consideration have been supplanted include whether there has been a change in the pattern of trade of the exporters subject to the antidumping duty, the timing of such change, and any association or compensatory arrangement between the exporter and the importer or a third party. No one or several of these factors can necessarily give decisive guidance.

[82] A slightly modified product is a product that is not within the product under consideration but that has the same general characteristics as the product under consideration. Factors pertinent to a consideration of whether a product is a slightly modified product include general physical characteristics; purchaser expectations; end uses; channels of trade; the interchangeability of the products; the processes, facilities, and employees used in production of the products; differences in the costs of production; the manner in which the products are advertised and displayed; and the costs to transform the slightly modified product into the product under consideration. No one or several of these factors can necessarily give decisive guidance.

[83] Factors pertinent to a consideration of the possible role of economic or commercial factors unrelated to the duty include technological developments, changes in customers' preferences, and changes in relative costs. No one or several of these factors can necessarily give decisive guidance.

(iii) The imports that have supplanted the imports of the product under consideration from the country subject to the existing anti-dumping duty undermine the remedial effect of that duty."[84]

9bis.3 "With respect to imports referred to in 9bis.2 of parts or unfinished forms of a product and imports referred to in 9bis.2 of a product assembled or completed in a third country, the authorities shall only find circumvention if they establish that (i) the process of assembly or completion is minor or insignificant[85] and (ii) the cost of the parts or unfinished forms makes up a significant proportion of the total cost of the assembled or completed product. The authorities shall in no case find that circumvention exists unless they determine that the value of the parts or unfinished forms is 60 per cent of the total value of the parts or unfinished forms of the assembled or completed product or more, and that the value added to the parts or unfinished forms during the assembly or completion process is 25 per cent of the total cost of manufacture or less."

9bis.4 "The authorities may extend the scope of application of an existing definitive anti-dumping duty to imports of parts or unfinished forms of the product under consideration assembled or completed in a third country only if they find that such imports are dumped pursuant to Article 2."

9bis.5 "A determination of the existence of circumvention within the meaning of this Article shall be based on a formal review initiated pursuant to a duly substantiated request. Except in special circumstances, such a review shall not be initiated unless the authorities have determined, on the basis of an examination of the degree of support for, or opposition to, the request expressed by domestic producers of the like product that the request has been made by or on behalf of the domestic industry within the meaning of Article 5.4."

9bis.6 "The provisions regarding evidence and procedure in Article 6 shall apply to any review carried out under this Article. Any such review shall be carried out expeditiously and shall normally be concluded within 12 months of the date of initiation of the review."

[84] Factors pertinent to a consideration of whether the remedial effect of an existing antidumping duty is undermined include the evolution of the prices and quantities of the product assembled or completed in the importing country or in a third country or of the slightly modified product and whether those products are sold to the same customers and for the same uses as the product subject to the existing definitive antidumping duty. No one or several of these factors can necessarily give decisive guidance.

[85] Factors pertinent to a consideration of whether a process of completion or assembly is minor or insignificant include the level of investment, research and development related to the completion or assembly, the nature and cost of the production process, and the extent of the facilities used for completion or assembly. No one or several of these factors can necessarily give decisive guidance.

9bis.7 "If the authorities have determined in accordance with this Article that circumvention exists, they may apply the anti-dumping duty to the imported products found to be circumventing the existing definitive anti-dumping duty,[86] including retroactively to imports entered after the date of the initiation of the review."

This draft calls for the following preliminary comments:

- The three indents of Paragraph 9bis.2 identify the three classic forms of circumvention: (i) import of disassembled products into parts, (ii) circumvention by third country operations, and (iii) minimal alteration of the original product, and do not significantly differ from previous practice or the U.S. proposal above given the latitude of discretion that the authorities may exert in interpreting these forms of circumvention.
- There are a number of conditions to be filled for imposing antidumping duties, most notably the one contained in the second paragraph of Article 9.3: *The authorities shall in no case find that circumvention exists unless they determine that the value of the parts or unfinished forms is 60 per cent of the total value of the parts or unfinished forms of the assembled or completed product or more, and that the value added to the parts or unfinished forms during the assembly or completion process is 25 per cent of the total cost of manufacture or less.*

However, although the formula for the calculation of the first criterion is straightforward because it is a value of parts test (even if it does not say how the value of materials could be assessed; one may argue according to the WTO agreement on customs valuation), the methodology for calculating the second criterion does not sufficiently clarify the numerator and denominator.

It is not clear at all how the total cost of manufacturing is calculated – which costs can be counted as costs of manufacturing and which cannot. As noted earlier, this is one of the inherent difficulties of a value-added calculation of this nature.

Finally, these requirements appear restrictive if we generally compare them to the rather liberal approach adopted in the HWP. Perhaps this once again explains the resistance of some administrations, namely that of the United States, to adopt the results of the HWP for antidumping purposes.

- Paragraph 9bis.4 provides for a fundamental condition because finding of dumping is now required before extending the scope of the antidumping duties.

[86] If a review under this Article has been initiated on a country-wide basis, the authorities shall exempt imports from particular exporters from the scope of any extended antidumping duty if they find that those imports take place in circumstances that do not constitute circumvention of an existing antidumping duty.

Summing up the proposal could be read as a compromise that may allow some progress on the issue of circumvention and may indirectly facilitate a final agreement of the HWP under the ARO.

Conclusions

Nonpreferential origin rules may play a role in the dumping determination (selection of normal value), the injury determination (determination of domestic producers), and in the enforcement of antidumping measures (to combat third country circumvention). In the absence of harmonized nonpreferential origin rules, each importing country is free to use its own origin rules for these purposes.

Even though this lack of harmonization already grants administering authorities substantial discretion, our analysis of EU practice has shown that origin rules are not used in a consistent manner in the context of the dumping and the injury determination.

In the enforcement phase, rules of origin can be applied (as an alternative to or in tandem with third country anticircumvention legislation) to extend the application of antidumping measures to third countries, sometimes retroactively. The use of origin rules in this context works well where multinational companies are involved. However, in the case of smaller "fly-by-night" operators, the actual collection of antidumping duties due has proven difficult, because of both country-hopping by exporters and rapid changes of the importers on record.

The eventual harmonization of nonpreferential origin rules will be helpful to limit administrative discretion and arbitrary application. However, in light of the relatively liberal character of the harmonized origin rules, it seems likely that countries will insist on the use of third country anticircumvention rules in the context of antidumping legislation as an alternative mean to fight third country circumvention.

PIET EECKHOUT

8.1 *Nonpreferential Origin Rules in Antidumping Law and Practice: A Comment on Inama and Vermulst*

Stefano Inama and Edwin Vermulst provide an excellent analysis of the connections between rules of origin and antidumping law and practice. The authors' combined expertise produces a chapter that leaves no stone unturned. Highly technical issues are made accessible and comprehensible in an exemplary fashion.

My short comment does not aim to engage with the technicalities of applying nonpreferential rules of origin in antidumping proceedings. It focuses on a couple of broader considerations that should also be looked at and borne in mind.

The difficulties associated with devising and applying appropriate rules of origin for antidumping purposes need to be linked to the broader debate about antidumping. Indirectly, their chapter shows that antidumping policy is becoming ever more artificial and ineffective, even distortive. In a globalized world where the production of so many goods is an intricate business stretching across many different countries, the idea that a product is exported from just one country to another at dumped prices is losing all basis in economic reality. The authors point out that the language of Article VI of the GATT, which refers to products of a country (country of exportation or country of origin), is very imprecise. The world was, of course, a very different place in 1947 – one where the standard case was indeed one where country of production, country of origin, and country of exportation were one and the same. There was no need for the drafters to be more precise. Today's world is totally different. The Leather Footwear case to which the authors refer exemplifies this. Even a commodity as basic as footwear is no longer produced in a single country. Design, raw materials, production, and marketing involve many different businesses and countries.

These globalization trends affect protectionist policies such as antidumping. Newer forms of protectionism are focused, not so much on the origin of goods or services, but on the "nationality" of firms and businesses. As a single place of production is ever more difficult to determine, attention shifts to the location and identity of economic actors. At a European level we see this very clearly. In the European Union's (EU's) internal market, protectionism is oriented toward shielding domestic companies from competition, through, for example, "golden shares" and state aid, rather than through erecting barriers to trade as such. Global developments are comparable. Where public authorities are intent on protecting domestic interests (e.g., through antidumping measures), they are increasingly confronted with the issue of sorting out domestic and nondomestic companies. The former deserve protection (ultimately because they are seen to provide domestic jobs), and the latter have to be penalized (because they are seen to remove jobs). However, the realities of globalization do not permit such neat classifications. Domestic companies may be outsourcing large parts of their production processes, and nondomestic companies often contribute to the economy and labor market of the importing country.

The European Commission Green Paper, to which Inama and Vermulst refer, is an indicator of this trend. In the Paper, the Commission referred to the fact that:[1]

> Increasingly, European companies are using production bases outside the European Union whilst maintaining significant operations and employment in Europe. From the perspective of trade defence instruments, the challenge is to consider whether EU rules take sufficient account of the reality of outsourced production by European businesses, which are then in competition with EU-based production and might be negatively affected by trade defence measures.

The Green Paper also referred to the Leather Footwear case as an illustration of the increased complexity of the protectionist question (more neutrally referred to by the Commission as the "Community interest question"). The Commission noted that many European footwear companies had been outsourcing production, making them subject to antidumping duties. They nevertheless accounted for thousands of jobs in the EU.

The debate about rules of origin (as well as their application) risks being captured by these changes in the nature of protectionism. Rules of origin can be used as a tool for newer forms of protectionism. Those newer forms include the use of antidumping as an anticompetitive instrument, as again Leather Footwear illustrates: European companies that have not outsourced production bring an antidumping case against those that have. Rules of origin can also be used as a regulatory instrument for slowing down outsourcing, or even for forcing foreign companies to change to local sourcing.

At the seminar where the Green Paper was presented, many argued that the World Trade Organization (WTO) should develop much more detailed and specific disciplines regarding rules of origin, in particular in the context of

[1] COMMUNICATION FROM THE COMMISSION – GLOBAL EUROPE, Europe's trade defense instruments in a changing global economy – A Green Paper for public consultation, COM (2006) 763 final, p. 6.

antidumping. This commentator is highly skeptical about taking that route, for essentially two reasons.

First, the complexity of this project is enormous. There is not only the reality of globalized production, to which reference is made earlier in this comment. In addition, determining the "origin" of a product is inherently intricate, as it draws you into ontological questions of determining what makes up a product's essence. The example was given of the Apple iPod, which is designed in the United States; its manufacture and sourcing take place elsewhere (in many different countries). Where, then, is the iPod produced? In which country does it come into being? Any attempt to produce rules of origin that seek to serve as a tool for determining, objectively, the country of origin will struggle with those near-philosophical questions.

Second, if one abandons such attempts, and if one decides simply to draw up rules of origin that are "practical," one is still left with many questions. In the context of antidumping, rules of origin could be seen as purely functionalist. The problem here is that the very rationale for antidumping is contested, and increasingly contestable in a globalized economy. Is antidumping an instrument against anticompetitive behavior? Is it an instrument for safeguarding employment? Is it an instrument for protecting domestic companies? As long as there is no greater clarity and consensus about the basic rationale for antidumping, it will be difficult to formulate appropriate rules of origin that are specific to this policy. Perhaps that explains why, in practice, it is proving so difficult to make progress with the Harmonized Work Programme, as so eloquently set out in the chapter by Inama and Vermulst.

CLAUDIO DORDI

9 The Appellate Body Interpretation of "Sunset Reviews" Provisions of Anti-Dumping and Countervailing Measures Agreements: A Critical Analysis

Introduction

The World Trade Organization (WTO) Anti-Dumping (AD) Agreement and the Agreement on Subsidies and Countervailing Measures (SCM Agreement) require that AD duties and countervailing measures (CVMs) be terminated no later than five years from their imposition unless domestic authorities determine, with a specific review initiated before the mentioned deadline, that the expiry of the duty would likely lead to continuation or recurrence of dumping (or subsidization) and injury. If domestic trade authorities terminate the review with a negative determination of likelihood, either with respect to dumping (or subsidization) or injury, the duty expires (sunset).

However, the WTO sunset reviews rules provided in Article 21.3 of the SCM Agreement and in Article 11.3 of the AD Agreement are vague and do not accurately regulate all of the complex aspects of the sunset reviews procedure.[1] Indeed, in both agreements, the text of the articles regulating the sunset reviews was the result of complex negotiations, and the provision of an expiry deadline was an absolute novelty, as before the Uruguay Round there were no rules providing for the termination of AD and countervailing duties within a predetermined deadline.[2] The relevant articles in the AD and SCM Agreements provide only a

[1] See C. Brown and J. Wauters, *United-States Anti-Dumping Measures on Oil Country Tubular Goods (OCTG) from Mexico*, P. Mavroidis (Ed.) (Geneva, Staiger, 2006).

[2] In the report of the Negotiating Group on Multilateral Trade Negotiation (MTN). Agreements and Arrangements (doc. MTN.GNG/NG8/W/83/Add.5, adopted on July 23, 1990), where we can find the first proposal of an article regarding the expiry of AD duties, Article 11.3 was drafted as follows: "Notwithstanding the provisions of paragraphs 1 and 2, any definitive anti-dumping duty shall be terminated within 5 years of its imposition, unless the authorities determine on the basis of a review carried out before the date of termination that there is good cause for the continuation of the anti-dumping duty, after all parties referred to in Articles 6:10 and 11 have had a full opportunity to present information." Afterward, the text of Article 11.3 has been modified, in particular, following the proposals of the United States and of the EC. According to the U.S. proposal, "the investigating authorities shall review the need for the continued imposition of the duty, where warranted, *on their*

generic discipline, which is only partially complemented by the rules applicable to basic proceedings. Indeed, Article 11 of the AD Agreement and Article 21 of the SCM Agreement make a reference, respectively, to Article 6 of the AD Agreement and to Article 12 of the SCM Agreement regulating the procedural part of the sunset reviews. However, it is generally agreed that the same rules and definitions provided for basic AD and countervailing duty (CVD) proceedings are not applicable to sunset reviews, with some exceptions. In reality, Article 11 of the AD Agreement and Article 21 of the SCM Agreement do not make any reference to the substantial rules provided in the AD Agreement for the basic procedure; this silence has been interpreted by the Appellate Body as the desire of the drafters to exclude sunset reviews from the application of the basic rules for AD and SCM proceedings. This is mainly caused by the differences existing between the objectives and the aims of the two procedures. Whereas in basic AD and CVD proceedings it is required to ascertain the existence of dumping (subsidy), injury for national producers, and causal link, in the sunset reviews it suffices that the national authorities prove that "the expiry of the duty would be likely to lead to continuation or recurrence of dumping (subsidy) and injury."

The very general formulations of Article 21.3 of the SCM Agreement and Article 11.3 of the AD Agreement have had the effect of creating a "legislative vacuum" and allocating wide discretionary powers to national investigating authorities.

The Appellate Body and the Panels' final reports tried to fill in the legislative vacuum in a number of cases; however, although some decisions imparted some indications that can be helpful in defining the national authorities' powers in this field, most of the actual discipline in the field is still dominated by uncertainty. This chapter will analyze some of the issues covered by the decisions of the Appellate Body dealing with sunset reviews. In these cases, the Appellate Body interpreted WTO rules in a way that promoted the application of the same discipline for sunset reviews that is provided for AD and CVMs. It will also be clarified whether the decisions of the Dispute Settlement Body (DSB) filled, at least partially, the regulatory gap left by the AD and SCM Agreements' discipline on sunset reviews.

Furthermore, the substantial differences between original and sunset procedures highlighted by the Appellate Body will be emphasized, and attention

own initiative or if any interested party so requests and submits positive information substantiating the need for review. In assessing the need for the continued imposition of the duty, the authorities may take into account the existence *of recurrent injurious dumping*, as defined in paragraph 4 of Article 5, or *repeat corporate dumping*, as defined in paragraph 1 (iv) of Article 11. Whenever the authorities initiate or complete a review, the authorities shall publish notice thereof, and publish the findings of the review consistent with the requirements of Article 8:5. The provisions of Article 6 shall apply to a review." According to the EC, the measures shall terminate except "where an interested party shows that the expiry of the measure would lead again to injury or threat of injury."

will be focused on the method adopted by the Panels and the Appellate Body for interpreting sunset reviews rules contained in the AD and SCM Agreements.

Last, this chapter provides some answers to the following questions: Are the results obtained with these methods of interpretation satisfactory? Is the discipline of sunset reviews as regulated by the AD and SCM Agreements and as interpreted by the Appellate Body in line with the rationale of AD and CVM? Does the discipline of sunset reviews distort trade?

Five decisions of the Appellate Body will be analyzed: Three addressed the AD sunset review provision (*US – Corrosion-Resistant Steel Sunset Review, US – Oil Country Tubular Goods Sunset Reviews from Argentina,* and *US – Oil Country Tubular Goods from Mexico*), and two addressed the analogous provision of the SCM Agreement (*US – Carbon Steel* and *US – Countervailing Measures on Certain EC Products*).

First, it is worthwhile to point out that:

(i) All five decisions involved complaints regarding sunset reviews in the United States. Before the application of WTO agreements, the U.S. AD orders had no set date when they were terminated and they were revoked only if the Department of Commerce (DOC) – the U.S. agency responsible for assessing dumping margins – established in administrative reviews that three consecutive years of nondumping prices at commercial levels of import had occurred[3]; and

(ii) the European Community (EC) has introduced some new practices concerning the duration of AD duties. For example, in the *Leather Footwear* AD investigation (Council Regulation n. 1472/2006), in *Plain Photocopiers from Japan,*[4] the duration of AD duties was limited to two years, whereas it was four years in *Electronic Weighing Scales from Japan and Magnetic Disks from China, Japan and Taiwan*[5] (the five-year time limit provided in Article 11.3 is not mandatory: According to Article 11.1 of the AD Agreement, an AD duty shall remain in force only as long as and to the extent necessary to counteract dumping that is causing injury). Similarly, in the sunset (expiry, according to the EC regulation) review of AD duty against *Ethanolamine from the United States* and in the later sunset reviews of *Ammonium Nitrate*

[3] See M. Moore, "Commerce Department Anti-Dumping Sunset Reviews: A First Assessment," in 36(2) *Journal of World Trade* 2002, 675 ff.

[4] Council Regulation (EC) No. 2380/95 of October 2, 1995, imposing a definitive antidumping duty on imports of plain paper photocopiers originating in Japan, O.J. L244/1 of October 12, 1995.

[5] Council Regulation (EC) No. 468/2001 of March 6, 2001, imposing a definitive antidumping duty on imports of certain electronic weighing scales originating in Japan, O.J. L67/24 of March 9, 2001; Council Regulation (EC) No. 312/2002 of February 18, 2002, imposing a definitive antidumping duty on imports of certain magnetic disks (3.5 microdisks) originating in Japan and the People's Republic of China and terminating the proceeding in respect of imports of 3.5 microdisks originating in Taiwan, O.J. L50/24 of February 21, 2002.

from Ukraine,[6] after the positive determination of likelihood of dumping and injury, the EC decided to maintain AD duty for only two years, whereas in the *Electronic Compact Fluorescent Lamps* proceedings, the final AD duty will be maintained for one year only.[7] This increasing attitude of the EC, if followed by other WTO Member States, will make the sunset reviews provisions useless.

The Overarching Principles of Sunset Review According to the Appellate Body Case Law and Their Application in Recent EC Cases

In paragraph 88 of *US – Carbon Steel*, the Appellate Body pointed out that "a termination of a countervailing duty is the rule, while the continuation is the exception." Therefore, the degree of diligence required by the domestic trade authorities in sunset reviews proceedings is particularly qualified. In fact, "the continuation of a countervailing duty must therefore be based on a properly conducted review... and a fresh determination, based on credible evidence." The Appellate Body drew similar conclusions for the sunset reviews under Article 11.3 of the AD Agreement. In *US – Corrosion-Resistant Steel Sunset Review*, it is stated that the reviews combine "investigatory and adjudicatory aspects." For that reason, "Article 11.3 assigns an active rather than a passive decision-making role to the authorities," which "must act with an appropriate degree of diligence and arrive at a reasoned conclusion on the basis of information gathered as part of a process of reconsideration and examination." Moreover, the adoption of the term "likely" in Article 11.3 of the AD Agreement implies that an affirmative likelihood determination "may be made only if the evidence demonstrates that dumping would be *probable* if the duty were terminated – and not simply if the evidence suggests that such a result might be possible or plausible" (paragraphs 110–111).

Therefore, an affirmative likelihood determination of dumping depends on "a firm foundation" (paragraph 178). The same consideration is valid also for the likelihood of injury: In *US – Country Tubular Goods Sunset Reviews* (paragraph 284) the Appellate Body stated that the determination of likelihood must "rest on a 'sufficient factual basis' that allows the agency to draw 'reasoned and adequate conclusions.'"

Other peculiarities of the sunset reviews can be drawn from the comparison that the Appellate Body made between original and sunset review investigation. In the *US – Corrosion-Resistant Steel Sunset Review*, the Appellate Body pointed out that, in the original investigation, "investigating authorities must determine whether dumping exists during the period of investigation," whereas in a sunset

[6] See EC Regulation n. 442/2007, in OJ L106/2007, p. 1 ff.

[7] See EC Regulation n. 1205/2007.

review, "investigating authorities must determine whether the expiry of the duty that was imposed at the conclusion of an original investigation would be likely to lead to continuation or recurrence of dumping" (paragraph 107). Regarding CVMs, the differences existing between original and sunset review have been clearly pointed out in *US – German Steel CVDs* by the Appellate Body. In this case, according to the Appellate Body, "original investigations and sunset reviews are distinct processes with different purposes. The nature of the determination to be made in a sunset review differs in certain essential respects from the nature of the determination to be made in an original investigation. For example, in a sunset review, the authorities are called upon to focus their inquiry on what would happen if an existing countervailing duty were to be removed. In contrast, in an original investigation, the authorities must investigate the existence, degree and effect of any alleged subsidy in order to determine whether a subsidy exists and whether such subsidy is causing injury to domestic industry so as to warrant the imposition of a countervailing duty" (paragraph 87).

In this case, the Appellate Body had to review the conclusion of the Panel that the 1 percent *de minimis* standard expressly provided as grounds for ending a basic CVM proceeding in Article 11.9 of the SCM Agreement should be "implied" in Article 21.3 of the SCM Agreement. However, Article 21.3 neither mentions the existence of any *de minimis* standard nor makes any express reference to the above-mentioned provision in Article 11.9. According to the Panel interpretation, U.S. CVD law and its accompanying regulations, which contain a 0.5 percent *de minimis* standard for sunset review, violate Article 21.3. The Appellate Body reversed the Panel's conclusion because, as previously mentioned, Article 21.3 does not refer to any *de minimis* standard to be applied in sunset review proceedings, nor does it make any express reference to the *de minimis* standard contained in Article 11.9. As the Appellate Body noted that "the technique of cross-referencing is frequently used in the SCMA" and that "when the negotiators of the SCMA intended that the disciplines set forth in one provision be applied in another context, they did so expressly," it stated that the silence "must have some meaning" and concluded that the lack of any mention of a *de minimis* standard in Article 21.3 indicates that the 1 percent *de minimis* standard requirement does not exist for the sunset review procedure.[8] However, embracing the reasoning of the Panel, the Appellate Body also pointed out that "the task of ascertaining the meaning of a treaty provision with respect to a specific requirement does not end once it has been determined that the text is silent on that requirement. Such silence does not exclude the possibility that the requirement was intended to be included by implication" (paragraph 64). With this in mind, the Appellate Body, noting that Article 11.9 of the SCM Agreement refers neither to Article 21.3 nor (more generally) to CVD reviews, affirmed that none of

[8] See, in general, N.P. Meagher, "The Sound of Silence. Giving Meaning to Omissions in Provisions of the WTO Agreements," 37(2) *Journal of World Trade* 2003, 417.

the words in Article 11.9 "suggests that the *de minimis* standard... is applicable beyond the investigation phase" (paragraphs 66–68).

The circumspection adopted by the Appellate Body in this circumstance has been justified by the fact that the adoption of a *de minimis* standard for investigations and the introduction of a sunset provision were regarded as "important additions" to CVD rules in the SCM Agreement (paragraph 69). However, this view is not consistent with the well-known obligations provided in Article 3.2 of the Dispute Settlement Understanding (DSU) (... "recommendations and rulings of the DSB cannot add or diminish the rights and obligations provided in the covered agreements").

In another decision, the Appellate Body addressed the differences between original investigation and sunset review; in the case of *US – Oil Country Tubular Goods Sunset Reviews*, the Appellate Body emphasized that "original investigations require an investigating authority, to impose an AD duty, to make a determination of the existence of dumping in accordance with Article 2, and subsequently to determine, in accordance with Article 3, whether the domestic industry is facing injury or a threat thereof at the time of the original investigation. In contrast, Article 11.3 requires investigating authorities, to maintain an AD duty, to review an AD order that has already been established – following the prerequisite determinations of dumping and injury – so as to determine whether that order should be continued or revoked" (paragraph 279).

The Appellate Body was aware that the above-mentioned interpretation would have left the "likelihood" investigation completely at the mercy of the importing authorities. Therefore, it specified in the next paragraph that some of the factors listed in the paragraphs of Article 3, even if they are not mandatorily applicable in a sunset review investigation, "may prove to be probative, or possibly even required, in order for an investigating authority in a sunset review to arrive at a 'reasoned conclusion.'" The Appellate Body, in more detail, further refined its view by stressing that "factors such as volume, price effects, and the impact of domestic industry of dumped imports, taking into account the conditions of competition, may be relevant to varying degrees in a given likelihood of injury determination." However, it refrained from providing a general, mandatory rule. Indeed, for the Appellate Body, the above-mentioned factors "may prove to be probative, or possibly even required," leaving the determination of whether those factors are "required" to be decided on a case-by-case review basis. Again, in general terms, "the fundamental requirement of Article 3.1 that an injury determination be based on 'positive evidence' and an 'objective examination' would be equally relevant to likelihood determinations under Article 11.3." However, "the necessity of conducting such an analysis in a given case results from the requirement imposed by *Article 11.3* – not Article 3 – that a likelihood-of-injury determination rest on a "sufficient factual basis" that allows the agency to draw "reasoned and adequate conclusions." The above-mentioned analysis does not clarify whether a likelihood-of-injury determination based on the rules of Article 3 of the AD Agreement would be considered to be conducted on a "sufficient factual basis," allowing "reasoned and adequate conclusions" to be drawn. It would be more helpful if the Appellate Body were to conclude that a likelihood determination based on Article 3 criteria would be presumed to be conducted on a "sufficient factual basis." This rebuttable presumption would switch the burden of proof in the proceedings before the DSB and would provide investigation authorities with a useful guide in sunset reviews.

Some guiding principles regarding the content of the likelihood determination in a countervailing proceeding can be found in the *US – German Steel* case. In its report, the Appellate Body (paragraphs 136–137) makes a reference to the Panel's interpretation of Article 21.3 (not appealed) to ascertaining what kind of activity that provision requires of investigating authorities making a "determination" in a sunset review. The Panel, recognizing that "the facts necessary to assess the likelihood of subsidisation in the event of revocation may well be different from those which must be taken into account in an original investigation," further elaborated that, in "assessing the likelihood of subsidisation in the event of revocation of the CVD, an investigating authority in a sunset review may well consider, *inter alia*, the original level of subsidisation, any changes in the original subsidy programmes, any new subsidy programmes introduced after the imposition of the original CVD, any changes in government policy, and any changes in relevant socio-economic and political circumstances."

The Appellate Body, in Many Decisions, Decided Not to Apply the Same Provisions Regulating Original Investigations to the Sunset Review

An analysis of Appellate Body case law shows a tendency of the Appellate Body to interpret the sunset review provisions contained in the AD and SCM Agreements in a restrictive and strictly literal manner. Moving from the assumption that basic and sunset reviews proceedings are substantially different, the Appellate Body has refrained from applying to sunset reviews the procedural and substantial rules disciplining basic AD and CVM proceedings, except in situations in which articles regulating sunset reviews expressly make applicable the basic rules through a direct reference (i.e., Article 11.4 of the AD Agreement, which makes reference to the procedure regulating the basic procedure).

Regarding the initiation phase of sunset reviews of CVM, the evidentiary standard provided in Article 11.6 of the SCM Agreement requires domestic authorities in an original CVM investigation to initiate an investigation in the absence of a written application from the domestic industry "only if they have sufficient evidence... to justify the initiation of an investigation." However, according to the Appellate Body, this is not applicable in a sunset review, as

Article 21.3 does not contain an explicit cross-reference to Article 11.6 (*US – Carbon Steel*, paragraph 105). As a consequence, no evidentiary standards apply to sunset reviews launched on the domestic authority's own initiative (*US – Carbon Steel*, paragraphs 104 and 106–116).

A similar method of interpretation has been adopted by the Appellate Body regarding the existence of dumping in the *US – Corrosion-Resistant Steel Sunset Review*. In this case the Appellate Body highlighted the fact that "Article 11.3 neither explicitly requires authorities in a sunset review to calculate fresh dumping margins, nor explicitly prohibits them from relying on dumping margins calculated in the past." The "silence in the text of article 11.3 suggests that no obligation is imposed on investigating authorities to calculate or to rely on dumping margins in a sunset review" (paragraph 123). What is really relevant, in this case, is that the Appellate Body noted that "in a sunset review, dumping margins may well be relevant to, but they will not necessarily be conclusive of, whether the expiry of the duty would be likely to lead to continuation or recurrence of dumping" (paragraph 124). The Appellate Body then concluded that there is "no obligation under Article 11.3 for investigating authorities to calculate or rely on dumping margins in determining the likelihood of continuation or recurrence of dumping," however, "should investigating authorities choose to rely upon dumping margins in making their likelihood determination, the calculation of these margins must conform to the discipline of Article 2.4."

An interesting point regards the application in sunset reviews of the term "dumping," as defined in the section of the AD Agreement that regulates the applicable basic procedure. In its *US – Corrosion-Resistant Steel Sunset Review* final report, the Appellate Body had to ascertain whether the word "dumping," as used in Article 11.3 of the AD Agreement, had the same meaning as the one used in Article 2.1. Again, the Appellate Body highlighted that the absence of a cross-reference in Article 11 to Article 2 (and vice versa) "may be of some significance." However, in this case, "the opening words of Article 2.1 (for the purpose of this Agreement) go beyond a cross-reference and indicate that Article 2.1 applies to the entire ADA." As a consequence, "the word dumping in Article 11.3 has the meaning described in Article 2.1" (paragraphs 121–126).

In the same case, the Appellate Body decided that some provisions applicable in the basic procedure were not applicable to sunset reviews, even if cross-referenced in the relevant articles of the AD Agreement. Among others, Japan challenged the U.S. DOC practice (established by the Sunset Policy Bulletin) of making determinations on an "order-wide" basis (i.e., to determine whether the expiry of the AD duty order on all exporters and producers from the relevant country is likely to lead to a continuation or recurrence of dumping). Even if Article 11.3 does not provide any procedures to be followed by national authorities in conducting sunset review investigations, Article 11.4 makes applicable the procedures provided for the basic AD contained in Article 6 to all the reviews disciplined in Article 11.

As Article 6.10 requires investigating authorities to make separate determinations with respect to each exporter or producer as to whether the expiry of the duty would likely lead to continuation or recurrence of dumping, Japan (the recurrent) argued that the same rules, as Article 11.4 makes a specific reference to Article 6, have to be applied to sunset reviews. As the Appellate Body reiterated that "Article 11.3 does not prescribe any particular methodology to be used by investigating authorities in making a likelihood determination in a sunset review," one would expect that the provisions of Article 6 were applied without any other limitation to sunset reviews. That was not the case in the Appellate Body interpretation, which adopted a curious methodology.

First (paragraph 151), the Appellate Body recognized that "certain provisions in Article 6 are expressly applied to sunset reviews by virtue of the cross-reference contained in Article 11.4" ("the provisions of Article 6 regarding evidence and procedure shall apply to any review carried out in this article"). Afterward, the Appellate Body identified that only some provisions contained in Article 6 (Articles 6.1, 6.2, 6.4, and 6.9) that commit investigating authorities to take in particular consideration "interested parties" (distinguished from exporters taken as a general category) were applicable, thereby demonstrating that when the AD Agreement drafters "intended to impose obligations on authorities regarding individual exporters or producers, they did so explicitly." However, and this is the first conclusion that seems questionable, according to the Appellate Body, the provisions of Article 6 "are silent on whether the authorities must make a separate likelihood determination for each exporter or producer." First of all, it has to be highlighted that Article 6 is silent on all the "due process" requirements applicable to sunset reviews. Second, if the Contracting Parties were to provide a specific "due process" discipline to be applied to reviews, they would have inserted it directly into Article 11.4, instead of incorporating a simple cross-reference in the same article.

Finally, the conclusions reached by the Appellate Body regarding Article 6.10 appears debatable; in other words, the fact that Article 6.10, which obliges the authorities to calculate an individual margin of dumping for each known exporter or producer concerned, refers to *the product under investigation* implies for the Appellate Body that it is "primarily directed to original investigation." The Appellate Body had previously concluded that in sunset reviews, authorities "are not *required* to calculate or rely on *dumping margins* in making a likelihood determination in a sunset review under Article 11.3." Therefore, the provision of Article 6.10 requiring that dumping margin, as a rule, has to be calculated "for each known exporter or producer concerned" for the Appellate Body is not, in principle, "relevant to sunset reviews."

The methodology adopted by the Appellate Body for settling this issue is questionable. In fact, instead of giving effect to a treaty provision expressly made applicable to sunset reviews through the direct reference, presuming that it is consistent with the main discipline regulating the issue (Article 11.3), it adopted an interpretation of Article 11.3 that made it inconsistent with the referred Article 6.10. The interpretation adopted by the Appellate Body would render most of the provisions of Article 6 ineffective when they are to be applied to sunset reviews. As stated by the Appellate Body in *Standards for Reformulated Conventional Gasoline*, "an interpreter is not free to adopt a reading that would result in reducing whole clauses or paragraphs of a treaty to a redundancy or inutility."[9]

As highlighted by Bown and Wouters,[10] this interpretation brings the consequence that a company "can remain subject to an anti-dumping order even though it is no longer dumping; its sales will continue to be monitored and remain under threat of anti-dumping action for another 5 years." As the two authors rightly pointed out, it is difficult to see how this interpretation can fit with the perseverance of the Appellate Body on stressing that the duty can be maintained only on a sufficient factual basis, as AD duties will remain in force against all exporters when the facts support that even only one exporter is likely to continue or restart dumping.

The same methodology of interpretation has been adopted by the Appellate Body with regard to the determination of likelihood of injury in a sunset review. Without going into detail, we can summarize as follows some decisions of the Appellate Body demonstrating its reluctance to extend the rules and procedures provided for original investigation regarding injury to sunset reviews:

- Regarding the existence of injury in *US – Oil Country Tubular Goods Sunset Review* the Appellate Body did not agree with Argentina that any reference to injury in the AD Agreement means that a determination of injury must be made in accordance with Article 3 of the AD Agreement (paragraph 275). Argentina argued that the definition of injury contained in Footnote 9 of Article 3 of the AD Agreement means that a determination of likelihood of continuation or recurrence of injury in a sunset review under Article 11.3 must be made in accordance with Article 3 of the AD Agreement. Argentina sustained this point of view, arguing that likelihood-of-injury determinations are "determinations of injury" for purposes of the AD Agreement. Again, the Appellate Body emphasized the differences between original investigation and sunset review, pointing out that "the ADA distinguishes between 'determinations of injury', addressed in Article 3 (the investigating authorities must determine "whether the domestic industry is facing injury or a threat thereof at the time of the original investigation") and determinations of 'likelihood of continuation or recurrence of injury,' addressed in Article 11.3" (paragraph 280). Furthermore, Article 11.3 does not contain

[9] *Gasoline*, WT/DS2/AB/R, adopted on May 20, 1996, p. 23.

[10] *United States – Anti-Dumping Measures on Oil Country Tubular Goods (OCTG) from Mexico*, article reviewing the WTO Appellate Body Report United States – Anti-Dumping Measures on Oil Country Tubular Goods from Mexico.

any cross-reference to Article 3, and there is not any provision in Article 3 indicating that, wherever the term "injury" appears in the AD Agreement, a determination of injury must be made following the provisions of Article 3.

- Regarding the possibility of cumulating the effects of imports of a product from more than one country, where these imports are simultaneously subject to AD investigations in a determination of likelihood of injury, the Appellate Body (in the *US – Oil Country Tubular Goods* case above mentioned) rejected Argentina's argument (Argentina maintained – paragraph 287 – that cumulation is not permitted under a sunset review or that, if it is permitted, it must satisfy the conditions of Article 3.3) by noting that Article 11.3 does not refer to Article 3.3 and that Article 3.3 is directed toward AD investigations, rather than sunset reviews (paragraphs 292 and 294). Moreover, it held that the "rationale for cumulation . . . applies to original investigations as well as to sunset reviews," such that investigating authorities may conduct a cumulative assessment in sunset reviews (paragraph 297). Finally, the Appellate Body, although it disagreed with Argentina that the provisions of Article 3.3 are applicable to sunset reviews, pointed out that a sunset review's determination must nonetheless be "based on a rigorous examination leading to a reasoned conclusion" (paragraph 302).
- Finally, regarding the time frame in which injury is likely to continue or recur, the Appellate Body rejected, in the same *US – Oil Country Tubular Goods* case, Argentina's argument that the temporal limitation provided in Article 3.7 of the AD Agreement (". . . the change in circumstances which would create a situation in which the dumping would cause injury must be clearly foreseen and imminent") must also be applied for sunset reviews. This conclusion was based on the fact that, as discussed above, Article 3 is not applicable to sunset reviews. (However, the Appellate Body pointed out that a time frame focusing "too far in the future" is difficult to justify, whereas the United States contested time frame, as it was based on a "reasonably foreseeable time," was acceptable).[11]
- In the *US – Oil Country Tubular Goods* from Mexico, the Appellate Body held the view that, contrary to the original investigation, in the sunset reviews the national authority is not obliged to prove the existence of a causal link between likely dumping and likely injury. The Appellate Body justified its conclusion confirming that a sunset review is a distinct process with a different purpose from an original investigation, and that, as Article 11.3 does not

[11] In the recent sunset review case of *Ethanolamines originating in the United States* (Reg. 1583/2006), the EC, after having concluded that the "expiry of the duty would be likely to lead to continuation of dumping," approved the maintenance of an AD duty for only two years after having ascertained (the examination was based on the submissions of the interested parties) that the most important factor which would likely lead to continuation of dumping terminates in two years.

require the importing authority to demonstrate the existence of the above-mentioned causal link, "adding such a requirement would have the effect of converting the sunset review into an original investigation, which cannot be justified."[12] However, the further legal reasoning added by the Appellate Body to justify its decision raises some doubts as to its accuracy. The Appellate Body decision regarding this specific issue is mainly based on the assumption that, as original investigation and sunset reviews are "different," "[t]he disciplines applicable to original investigations *cannot, therefore, be automatically imported* into review processes" (paragraph 119). The Appellate Body, then, stressed the differences between the two procedures in general by referring to a previous decision,[13] and later it tried to emphasize the differences between an AD duty that came into existence after an original investigation and the AD duty subject to a revision in a sunset review procedure. Whereas the former "comes into existence following an original investigation that has established a causal link between dumping and injury to the domestic industry in accordance with the requirements of Article 3 of the *Anti-Dumping Agreement*, including, in particular, the requirement that the injury caused by any other known factor not be attributed to dumping," the latter is the result of an investigation aimed at ascertaining whether the "expiry of the duty" would "likely . . . lead to continuation or recurrence of dumping and injury." For this reason, it seems, the Appellate Body believes that it is "reasonable to assume that, where dumping and injury continues or recurs, the causal link between dumping and injury, established in the original investigation, would exist and need not be established anew." It is apparent that what is "reasonable" for the Appellate Body might not be in the reality. Even without analyzing the relationship between injury and causation, which has been already carried out by Bown and Wouters,[14] it would

12 Appellate Body Report, *US – Anti Dumping on Oil Country Tubular Goods from Mexico*, para. 123.

13 The Appellate Body Report (para. 279) of *US – Oil Country Tubular Goods Sunset Reviews* decision, where it clarified the main differences existing between original investigation and sunset reviews: "Original investigations require an investigating authority, in order to *impose* an anti-dumping duty, to make a determination of the existence of dumping in accordance with Article 2, and subsequently to determine, in accordance with Article 3, whether the domestic industry is facing injury or a threat thereof at the time of the original investigation. In contrast, Article 11.3 requires an investigating authority, in order to *maintain* an anti-dumping duty, to review an anti-dumping duty order that has already been established – following the prerequisite determinations of dumping and injury – so as to determine whether that order should be continued or revoked."

14 See C. Bown and J. Wouters, cit., p. 21. The two authors criticized the artificial separation between injury and causation introduced by the Appellate Body, "since the only relevant injury under the AD agreement is the injury caused by the dumped imports." According to the authors, in the text of the AD agreement, causation is always dealt with injury (there is no separate provision dealing with causation). As a consequence, the "examination of likelihood or recurrence or continuation of injury must refer to likelihood of injury in so far as it is caused by dumping, and not just any injury."

suffice to point out that sunset reviews start at least five years after the original investigation has ended, and it is easy to guess that many conditions, in these years, could have changed. However, it is puzzling to realize that the conclusion of the Appellate Body regarding the "causation" issue in sunset reviews is in clear contrast with the text of Article 11.1: "an anti-dumping duty shall remain in force only as long as and to the extent necessary to counteract dumping which is *causing* injury." This contrast should not come as a surprise, as the Appellate Body never referred to the provision of paragraph 1 for filling in the deficiencies of paragraph 3, even if, according to the Panel Report in the case *EC – Tube or Pipe Fittings*, "Article 11.1 contains a general, unambiguous and mandatory requirement that anti-dumping duties 'shall remain in force only as long as and to the extent necessary' to counteract injurious dumping. It furnishes the basis for the review procedures contained in Article 11.2 (and 11.3) by stating a general and overarching principle, the modalities of which are set forth in paragraph 2 (and 3) of that Article." Article 11.1 plainly states that one of the overarching principles of reviews is that they are served to ascertain whether to maintain in force "dumping causing injury." As it is unquestionable that likely injury might be caused by different factors from likely dumping, it is obvious that the analysis of the causation link between the two is necessary.

Only in Few Decisions Did the Appellate Body Decide in Favor of a Strict Standard for Sunset Reviews

The following cases represent the few instances in which the Appellate Body opted for a strict standard to be respected by national authorities when carrying out sunset reviews:

(i) Regarding the participation of interested parties in sunset reviews, Article 11.4 of the AD Agreement makes applicable the rules provided for original investigation contained in Article 6. In particular, Articles 6.1 and 6.2, as pointed out by the Appellate Body, "set out the fundamental due process rights to which interested parties are entitled in anti-dumping investigations and reviews" (*US – Oil Country Tubular Goods*, paragraph 241). In this context, the Appellate Body considered inconsistent with the abovementioned articles a national regulation requiring the national authority in charge of sunset reviews to disregard evidence submitted by respondents in an incomplete manner (i.e., not answering properly to the national authority's questionnaires), preventing as well their participation in a hearing during a sunset review procedure (*US – Oil Country Tubular Goods*, paragraph 246).

(ii) A proper determination of likelihood of dumping under Article 11.3 of the AD Agreement "cannot be based solely on the mechanistic application of presumptions." As a consequence, in the case *US – Corrosion-Resistant Steel Sunset Review*, the Appellate Body considered inconsistent with Article 11.3 a national practice/regulation instructing the national authority to treat dumping margins and/or import volumes as determinative or conclusive of the likelihood of future dumping (paragraph 178).

(iii) The obligations in Articles 19.4 and 21 of the SCM Agreement, aimed at limiting CVDs to the amount and duration of the subsidy found to exist, are applicable both to original investigations and to administrative and sunset reviews covered under Article 21 of the SCM Agreement (*US – Countervailing Measures on Certain EC Products*; paragraph 139). The Appellate Body, confirming the conclusions of the Panel, stated that investigating authorities must determine in a sunset review whether a benefit (which is one component of the subsidy definition according to Article 1 of the SCM Agreement) continues to exist after the privatization of the subsidy beneficiary resulting in a change of ownership (paragraphs 149–150).

Final Considerations Regarding the Appellate Body Case Law

It is possible to summarize our analysis of case law of the Appellate Body as follows:

- The Appellate Body considers sunset reviews as being different from original investigations, from both substantial and procedural points of view. As a consequence, the rules applicable to original investigations cannot be applied *tout court* to sunset reviews.
- The rules provided for original investigations are applicable to sunset reviews only when there is a specific cross-reference in the text; moreover, even in those cases, the Appellate Body excluded the application of part of these rules when they are in conflict with the general characteristics of sunset reviews as, according to the Appellate Body, it is not reasonable to apply the same rules for proceedings that are substantially different.
- The WTO discipline on sunset reviews allows Member States to behave in a very protectionist manner (after being applied, in a few cases AD duties have been terminated after a sunset review) allowing Member States to give priority to the interest of domestic industries at the expense of the interests of consumers and of the other stakeholders (importers, distributors, workers in the distributors' companies, etc.).
- Recent EC practice shows that AD duties have been applied for a limited period of time (one or two years). In another case, a sunset review provided a deadline (two years) for AD duties. Through these decisions, EC authorities (the EC in particular) have indicated that AD duties might not be beneficial for the all the importing States' stakeholders.

The Interpretation of Sunset Review Provision in the EC: An Example of a Different Methodology

The purpose of this paragraph is not to provide a comparative analysis of the EC discipline on sunset (expiry) reviews, but to verify whether the European Court of Justice (ECJ) adopted, at least for some specific issues, different methods than those applied by the Appellate Body for interpreting the EC provisions dealing with sunset reviews. In particular, we will focus our attention on one of the provisions contained in the EC discipline on AD that is not mandated by the WTO AD Agreement: the "community interest" clause. According to the EC basic AD regulation, the imposition of definitive AD and CVMs may be applied if it can be demonstrated, after the existence of dumping and injury is established, that they are not against the "Community interest." This evaluation is based "on an appreciation of all the various interests taken as a whole, including the interests of the domestic industry and users and consumers" (Article 21 of the EC basic AD regulation).

In the Euroalliages case,[15] the Court of First Instance, after having ascertained that "Article 11(2) of the basic regulation (dealing with sunset reviews) does not refer expressly to the Community interest as one of the conditions for retaining a measure that is due to expire,"[16] recognized that "Article 11(5) ... provides that the expiry review should be conducted in accordance with the relevant provisions of that regulation concerning the procedures and conduct of investigations." Moreover, according to Article 11(9) of the basic regulation, "in all review or refund investigations ... the Commission shall, provided that circumstances have not changed, apply the same methodology as in the investigation which led to the duty, with due account being taken of Article 2 (determination of dumping), and in particular paragraphs 11 and 12 (dealing with dumping margin) thereof, and of Article 17 (sampling)." Of course, in contrast to the AD Agreement, there is a direct reference to some articles of the regulation dealing with substantial issues such as dumping margin and sampling of companies during investigation. For this reason, the Tribunal inferred from those provisions "that the conditions for retaining a measure that is due to expire are *mutatis mutandis* the same as those for the imposition of new measures." As the substance of sunset (expiry) reviews does not differ from original investigations in EC basic AD regulation, there is no need to reject the application to the former of all the procedures provided for the latter. This solution differs substantially from the Appellate Body's position (i.e., applying the same requirement provided

[15] *Euroalliages v. Commission of the European Communities*, Case T-188/99, Judgment of the Court of First Instance of June 20, 2001, [2001], ECR-II 1757.

[16] See Council Regulation (EC) No. 384/96 of December 22, 1995, on protection against dumped imports from countries not members of the European Community, OJ L 56, 6.3.1996, p. 1.

for original investigation to sunset reviews "would have the effect of converting the sunset review into an original investigation, which cannot be justified"[17]), as the Tribunal maintains that the substantive discipline of the original investigation is applicable to sunset reviews, including the "community interest" test, even in the absence of a clear cross-reference.

This conclusion did not impede the Court, in a later judgement, from clarifying that "a review procedure is, as a rule, objectively different from that of an initial investigation, which is governed by other provisions of the same regulation."[18] The Court explained that "the objective difference between the two proceedings lies in the fact that imports subject to a review proceeding are those on which definitive anti-dumping duties have already been imposed and in respect of which sufficient evidence has generally been adduced to establish that the expiry of those measures would be likely to result in a continuation or recurrence of dumping and injury. On the other hand, where imports are subject to an initial investigation, the purpose of that investigation is precisely to determine the existence, degree and effect of any alleged dumping even if the initiation of such an investigation presupposes the existence of sufficient evidence to justify the initiation of that procedure/proceeding."

Without going into the details of the dispute, it is relevant to highlight that the Court did not see any obstacles in applying the same rules for original and sunset investigation (Euroalliages), even while recognizing that initial investigations and sunset reviews are different, from both a substantial and a formal point of view (*Europe Chemi-Com* case).

Puzzling Situation in Sunset Reviews in the EC Practice

Despite the situation detailed above, in the EC, much like in the United States, a restrictive interpretation of the relevant rules regulating sunset reviews often prevails, especially among investigating authorities. A good example of the substantial effects following from the application of a restrictive interpretation of the current discipline regarding sunset reviews can be derived from some excerpts of a recent EC regulation imposing AD duties on *Electronic Compact Fluorescent Lamps* originating in the People's Republic of China following an expiry review investigation.[19] Paragraph 21 of the above-mentioned regulation reads as follows:

> In accordance with Article 11(9) of the basic Regulation, the same methodology was used as in the original investigation. As an expiry review does not

[17] Appellate Body Report, *US – Anti Dumping on Oil Country Tubular Goods from Mexico*, para. 123.

[18] *Europe Chemi-Com v. Council and Commission*, Case C-422/02 P, Judgement of the Court of Justice, Instance of January 22, 2005, para. 49.

[19] See Council Regulation (EC) No. 1205/2007 of October 15, 2007, in OJ, L 272, p. 1.

provide for any examination of changed circumstances, it was not reconsidered whether producers merited or not to be granted market economy treatment (MET).

In AD proceedings dealing with goods exported from a "non–market economy" country, the normal value is established on the basis of the information submitted by a producer in a market economy third country (the so-called "analogue country"). As a general rule, that normal value is compared with the average export price of all the product under investigation imported from the non–market economy country; this comparison then leads to a calculation of a country-wide AD duty. This duty normally results in a higher dumping margin and in a higher AD duty. However, according to both the EC and U.S. legislation, enterprises located in a non–market economy country may claim a "market economy" treatment if they can demonstrate that they compete in a market economy arena. Whereas the "market economy" status granted to a State, even if it is formally based on specific criteria elaborated by the EC Commission, is mainly a decision depending on political evaluations, the market economy treatment granted to enterprises is based on some criteria defined by Article 2.7 of Regulation 384/96.[20] The Chinese companies were denied the "market economy" treatment based on an investigation that ended more than five years before the conclusion of the sunset review proceedings. Any comments on this puzzling and illogical treatment would be superfluous.

Another similarly strange example is provided by the description in paragraph 41 of the same regulation:

> During the RIP (review investigation period), export prices to third countries were generally higher than those achieved by the three cooperating Chinese exporting producers for comparable models on their domestic market. However, they were lower than the normal value determined in the analogue country. There is no reason to assume that this latter pattern would be different for exports to the Community if measures were lifted. Therefore, these facts support the conclusion that there is continuation and at least a risk of recurrence of dumping regarding most Chinese exports.

[20] According to Article 2.7, the following criteria are applicable for granting the market economy status:

- Decisions of firms regarding prices, costs, and inputs, including raw materials, cost of technology and labor, output, sales, and investment, are made in response to market signals reflecting supply and demand, and without significant State interference in this regard, and costs of major inputs substantially reflect market values.
- Firms have one clear set of basic accounting records that are independently audited in line with international accounting standards and are applied for all purposes.
- The production costs and financial situation of firms are not subject to significant distortions carried over from the former non–market economy system, in particular, in relation to depreciation of assets, other write-offs, barter trade, and payment via compensation of debts.
- The firms under investigation have to be subject to bankruptcy and property laws that guarantee legal certainty and stability for the operation of firms.
- Exchange rate conversions are carried out at market rate.

The position described in the above-mentioned quotation is equally absurd so as not to deserve any further comment.

Another interesting example can be found in the *Ammonium nitrate originating in Ukraine*,[21] where the Ukraine was denied market economy status during the investigation, although the EC granted that status a few days before the end of the review investigation period.

Paragraph 24 of the regulation 442/2007 provides that:

> Since Ukraine was not yet considered a market economy country at the time of the lodging of the request for the expiry review, the normal value had to be determined on the basis of data obtained from a producer in a market economy third country, in accordance with Article 2(7) of the basic Regulation. In the notice of initiation, the USA and Romania were envisaged as appropriate analogue countries. It should be recalled that in the original investigation, Poland was selected as an analogue country. Since Poland entered the European Union in May 2004, it is no longer a possible choice. All interested parties were given the opportunity to comment on the choice of the USA and Romania as analogue countries.

Of course, the expiry review ended with the application of an AD duty. However, the decision of the investigating authorities seems questionable according to the ECJ of the case law evaluating the factors that can be taken into consideration in a sunset (expiry) review proceeding.

In the Euroalliages case,[22] the Court of First Instance dealt with the provision of Article 6(1) of the basic regulation, which provides that "information relating to a period subsequent to the investigation period shall, normally, not be taken into account." According to the Tribunal (paragraph 74):

> Fixing an investigation period and precluding consideration of factors arising subsequently are intended to ensure that the results of the investigation are representative and reliable. This applies as regards both investigations conducted in the context of a review and those initiated in accordance with Article 5 of the basic regulation. Consequently, the rule that information relating to a period subsequent to the investigation period is not, normally, to be taken into account applies also to investigations relating to expiry reviews.

The Tribunal subsequently (paragraph 75) highlighted the fact that:

> By using the term normally, Article 6(1) of the basic regulation does, however, allow exceptions to that rule. In that regard, it has been held that the Community institutions cannot be required to incorporate in their calculations data relating to a period after the investigation period unless such data

[21] See Council regulation (EC) No. 442/2007 of April 19, 2007, imposing a definitive antidumping duty on imports of ammonium nitrate originating in Ukraine, OJ, L 106/2007.

[22] *Court of First Instance, Euroalliages et al. v. Commission, 20 June 2001, case T-188/99.*

> disclose new developments which make the proposed anti-dumping duty manifestly inappropriate." (Case T-161/94 *Sinochem Heilongjiang v. Council* [1996] ECR II-695, paragraph 88)

Indeed, the decision of the investigating authority in the *Ammonium nitrate originating in Ukraine* should not be considered consistent with the above-mentioned principle established by the Tribunal. Moreover, the new situation came into existence even before the end of the investigation period.

It is quite interesting to note that, in the Euroalliages case, the Tribunal analyzed whether the above-mentioned exception to Article 6.1 provisions "concerns only the situation referred to by the Court of First Instance in *Sinochem*... that is to say where developments arising after the investigation period preclude the imposition of measures, or whether such factors may also be taken into consideration as regards, in particular, measures in the case of an expiry review, in order to justify retention of those measures."

In interpreting the provision of the basic regulation, the Court then highlighted the "strict conditions" laid down by Article 11.2 of the WTO AD Agreement (paragraphs 76–77) in respect of both the imposition and the retention of measures.

In particular, Article 11(2) of the basic regulation makes the retention of protective measures after the expiry of a five-year period conditional upon the conduct of an investigation in accordance with the basic regulation to establish the factual data from which the likelihood of recurrence of injury may be inferred. However, when the results of such an investigation are insufficient to justify retaining AD duties, the basic regulation provides that they should expire. That means that factors that arise after the investigation period cannot be taken into account for duties to be retained. Consequently, the judgment in *Sinochem*, cited in paragraph 75 above, concerns only the case in which factors arising after the investigation period that have not been established by means of an investigation conducted in accordance with the procedural safeguards required by the basic regulation and the WTO AD Agreement are taken into account in the decision not to impose, or to retain, AD duties.

In light of such a clear interpretation of the AD Agreement and its implication in case law, it is interesting to pose this question: Would the Appellate Body have adopted the same methodology?

THOMAS J. PRUSA

9.1 *Comments on "The Appellate Body Interpretation of 'Sunset Reviews' Provisions of Anti-Dumping and Countervailing Measures Agreements: A Critical Analysis"*

Claudio Dordi offers a fine discussion on the sunset provisions in the World Trade Organization (WTO) agreement. One aspect of Dordi's approach that I particularly like is that he does not limit himself to discussing only the sunset provisions as incorporated in the Uruguay Round. Rather, Dordi takes the reader considerably further by discussing the Appellate Body and Panel decisions regarding sunset reviews. Dordi also discusses specific examples of the sunset review issues for the European Union and the United States. It is through this extended discussion that Dordi is able to effectively convey some of the key legal issues surrounding the sunset provisions.

Beyond the specifics of sunset rules, Dordi's chapter highlights a key lesson for trade negotiators. Namely, the same agreement might mean something very different to different parties. Your partners might think that you have agreed to one thing and you might justifiably think the agreement says something very different, and you both may be correct – the difference of opinion may be valid.

Just because an issue has been agreed to and enacted as part of the WTO is not a guarantee that countries know what it means for their own or others' practice. The reason is not necessarily because one side is violating the agreement. Rather, the issue is caused by the deliberate generality of the agreement text. I should emphasize that although Dordi discusses the issue in the context of sunset provisions, the issue is certainly not limited to that issue. Member States are learning that a poorly drafted or vaguely worded provision may well be worse than no provision at all.

In the case of sunset reviews, the general formulation in the agreement created what Dordi calls a "legislative vacuum." This vacuum has had the effect of endowing national authorities with a great deal of discretion over how to implement sunset rules. Whether this result was intentional is subject to debate. Discretion is efficient because it allows countries to respond to new developments and changes in the trading environment. In addition, a broadly worded agreement facilitates members reaching a consensus on a WTO agreement. Narrowly crafted rules and precise language expose the drafts to intensive criticism, likely resulting in an agreement that no party can agree.

In contrast, discretion is not wholly virtuous. Excessive discretion can lead to a situation where the negotiation's implicit and required *quid pro quo* may not be satisfied. Excessive discretion will make it impossible for negotiators to commit to a proposal that requires meaningful changes in behavior and policy. Said differently, negotiations that involve broadly worded text may well result in agreements that achieve little practical benefit – on any matter.

Consider the following example. Suppose Thailand gives concessions on a key issue, say, intellectual property, to obtain concessions in other areas. Suppose one of these other areas of interest to Thailand is the termination of AD duties after a definite period of time – for example, five years. Suppose another country (e.g., the United States) is opposed to sunset provisions but agrees to them to secure the strengthened intellectual property provisions. With both sides giving and taking, the agreement is signed and each goes home, perhaps not entirely happy, but understanding that bargaining was necessary. After the celebration and parades conclude, countries will ask what changes must be made per the agreement.

Suppose the country that begrudgingly accepted sunset reviews (in my hypothetical example, the United States) exploits the vagueness of the sunset provision and enacts domestic legislation that allows for the termination of orders, but in such a way that the termination of duties will only rarely happen. Rather than being the norm, the termination of duties may happen rarely after five years and often not after even ten years.

After a few years of experience and observation, the other country (Thailand) will realize that it received little substantive for its intellectual property concessions. Even if it initially began to offer more stringent intellectual property protection, seeing so little change in sunset provisions might lead Thailand to start to interpret the intellectual property provisions in a markedly different way. It is easy to imagine the Thai intellectual property regime being different from what U.S. negotiators imagined when the agreement was enacted.

Assuming that Thai exports are disproportionally exposed to antidumping (AD) duties, whereas U.S. exports are weighted more heavily toward intellectual property–related trade, both sides might be understandably upset with the other party's interpretation of the agreement. In this case, discretion can lead to the unraveling of the promise of the agreement.

With that backdrop, let's take a closer look at the specifics of the sunset provisions. Before the Uruguay Round, the General Agreement on Tariffs and Trade (GATT) AD code did not require any firm date when AD and countervailing duty orders were terminated. Prior to 1995 in the United States, for example, AD orders normally were revoked only if the Department of Commerce (DOC) determined via administrative reviews that imports at commercial levels had occurred for three consecutive years at nondumped prices. Thus, even if the economic condition of U.S. industry had improved significantly so that there was no ongoing injury as a result of foreign dumped imports, duties could remain in place as long as any non–*de minimis* dumping margin had been found. Many observers found these procedures deeply disturbing, especially given what many believed was the DOC's biased methods for calculating dumping margins. To many, AD duties seemed to be essentially permanent. In fact, at the conclusion of the Uruguay Round, more than thirty U.S. AD orders originally introduced *before* 1980 were still in place, some dating back to the 1960s.

As part of the greater endgame of the Uruguay Round, member countries finally agreed to institute a "sunset review" process under which orders would be terminated after five years unless an investigation determined that dumping and material injury were likely to recur if the order were revoked. Although the U.S. Congress incorporated the sunset changes into law in the Uruguay Round Agreements Act, there was substantial uncertainty over implementation. Given the U.S.'s public commitment to a rules-based system of law, one would think that it would live up to the letter of the agreement. In contrast, given the strong political support that AD enjoys in Congress, there was also concern that politics would demand that sunset reviews be weakly implemented and rarely result in the termination of orders.

It turns out that the latter view was correct. To get a sense of why I say this, consider the data and analysis in two fine articles by Mike Moore (2002, 2006). In both articles, Moore analyzes so-called transition orders. The term "transition orders" refers to U.S. AD orders in place on January 1, 1995, when the Uruguay Round commitments took force.

Moore analyzed 222 transition AD orders that were subject to the new sunset review process. Figure 1 (taken from Moore, 2006) gives the broad details. The first decision is made by the domestic industry and involves whether to even request a sunset review. If the industry decides not to request a review, the AD duties will be revoked. As shown, Moore finds that, in about 20 percent of cases, the domestic industry did not even ask for a review – effectively ending the AD order. Said differently, this means that in 20 percent of the cases, the domestic firms had so little interest in the continuation that they did not even bother to ask for the sunset review investigation to be initiated – even though the old rules meant the duties would have remained in place.

The second decision is made by the DOC, which has to determine whether it is likely that dumping will reoccur if the order is revoked. As shown in Figure 1, the DOC *did not revoke a single case* in the sunset review process. As discussed in Moore (2002), this is not surprising given the rules the DOC follows. According to Moore, the DOC announced that it will normally determine that dumping is likely to continue or recur if: (a) dumping has continued at any level above *de minimis* (i.e., 0.5%) during the order; (b) imports under an order have ceased; or (c) dumping margins are zero after the issuance of the order and import market share has declined "significantly."

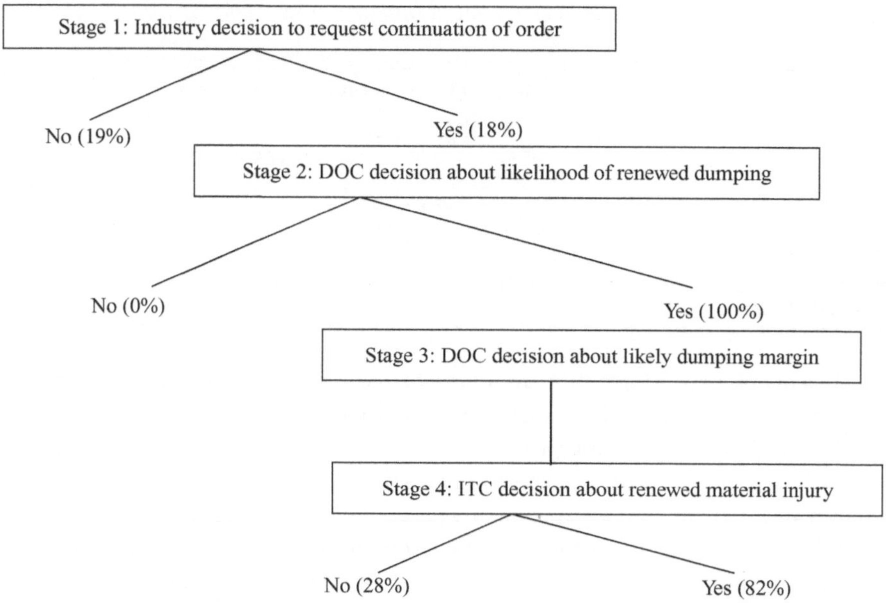

Figure 1. Decisions in U.S. Sunset Reviews (transition orders). DOC = Department of Commerce; ITC = International Trade Commission.[1]

To get a clearer idea of how perverse the DOC rules are, let's look at what the DOC said the margin of dumping would be if the order were revoked. To be precise, recall that the DOC calculates margins in original investigation, administrative reviews, and sunset reviews at the individual firm level. So, in Table 1 I will report firm-specific margins. In Table 1 I present information on the average the margin reported to the International Trade Commission (ITC) in contested cases and the margin in the original investigation.[2] As shown, the DOC almost always reported a margin equal to the margin in the *original* investigation, which means that the DOC relies almost exclusively on analysis often done more than a decade earlier.

In Moore's data, we see that of the 313 individual sunset margins reported to the ITC, 297 (94%) were exactly the same as in the original investigation. The DOC reported a sunset review margin that exceeded the original investigation margin in fourteen cases. For these cases, the average margin of the original investigation was 29%, whereas the average sunset review margin was 89%. The DOC reported a margin to the ITC below that of the original investigation for only two firms in the sample. In both of these cases, a lower margin was reported, not

[1] Figure from Moore (2006).

[2] In this part of Moore's analysis, he limits himself to only antidumping cases initiated after January 1, 1980; cases before that time were administered by the Department of the Treasury. Hence it would be difficult to know what the DOC would have done during the original investigation.

Table 1. *Post-1980 U.S. Sunset Review (individual firm cases)*[3] *comparison of margins*

	Number of firms/cases	Original investigation (average margin)	Sunset Review (average margin)
Sunset Review = Original Margin	297	47%	47%
Sunset Review > Original Margin	14	29%	89%
Sunset Review < Original Margin	2	58%	22%

because of any new information about the firms, but instead because each of the firms had been purchased by another firm so that the DOC simply reported the purchasing firm's original margin.

Although the WTO agreement delegates how sunset margins were to be calculated, one can hardly imagine that any party (with the possible exception of the United States) thought that the sunset agreement would involve all determinations saying that dumping would reoccur and that nearly all of these reoccurring margins would be the same as the margins from decades earlier.

The third decision is made by the ITC. At the time of the original investigation, the ITC is the agency empowered to determine if dumped imports have caused, or threaten to cause, material injury. For the sunset review, the ITC determines if revocation of the order will result in renewed injury. According to Moore (and as shown in Figure 1), among the 181 contested orders (i.e., for which there was domestic interest in continuation), the ITC revoked only about 28% of the contested orders. What is noteworthy is that Moore's data involve the oldest, longest-lived AD cases in the U.S. system. Moore's database is composed of many orders that had already been in place for many years. One would expect these cases to have fairly high termination rates, certainly higher than for the orders that were only five years old. Taking the DOC and ITC decisions together, it is fair to conclude that the U.S. sunset review process did not routinely terminate cases.

Moore's results are consistent and reinforce many of the points made by Dordi. Moore's data suggest that, under the U.S. approach, sunset provisions do not result in a marked decrease in the duration of AD orders – less than 30% of all contested sunset cases were terminated and none by the DOC. As Dordi points out, it is hard to believe such a low percentage is consistent with the presumption (stated in the agreement) that the orders would be terminated.

These trends certainly make one doubt the importance of the sunset provision (as implemented). Even more damning is what they mean for future rounds. After seeing what the United States does with an area that it offered as a concession for other issues, one wonders what trading partners will assume that any

[3] Table from Moore (2006).

new agreement will mean. Clearly, the sunset provisions have shown that one must be very careful with what is negotiated with the United States. This doubt is surely part of why the Doha Round seems impossible to conclude. Given the broad language in many aspects of the agreement, can countries trust their trading partners to follow the intent of the new agreement? Will their partners exercise protectionist discretion? As the saying goes, "Fool me once, shame on you! Fool me twice, shame on me!"

REFERENCES

Moore, M.M., Commerce Department Antidumping Sunset Reviews: A First Assessment. *Journal of World Trade* 36 (2002).

Moore, M.M., An Econometric Analysis of US Antidumping Sunset Review Decisions. *Review of World Economics/Weltwirtschaftliches Archiv* 142 (2006).

JASPER M. WAUTERS

10 The Safeguards Agreement – An Overview

Introduction

The Agreement on Safeguards (the Safeguards Agreement or SA) establishes rules for the application of safeguard measures, a term understood to mean those measures provided for in Article XIX of the General Agreement on Tariffs and Trade (GATT), entitled "Emergency Action on Imports of Particular Products."[1] Although the World Trade Organization (WTO) SA was an agreement that did not exist in the form of a plurilateral code prior to the conclusion of the Uruguay Round, it is thus nevertheless clearly rooted in the GATT system and in Article XIX of the GATT in particular. More than with any other of the WTO's Agreements, it is the relationship between the new WTO Agreement on Safeguards and the original "safeguard" provision in the GATT that proved to be problematic.

In this chapter, first, safeguard measures are discussed in the larger context of the WTO system in general and WTO trade remedies in particular. Second, the conditions for the imposition of safeguard measures will be examined. Third, the chapter addresses the application of safeguard measures in place and time, and distinguishes between the various types of measures that may be imposed as a safeguard. Some conclusions are formulated at the end.

Safeguards in the WTO Context

Safeguards as a Trade Remedy

A safeguard measure is a unilateral way of providing additional protection to the domestic industry. In that respect, safeguards are akin to other forms of contingent trade protection, such as antidumping (AD) and countervailing measures (CVMs). Actually, these three types of measures are often grouped together as different types of *trade remedies*. All three types of measures allow a WTO Member

[1] Article 1 of the SA.

country to backtrack from some of the concessions made, and this unilaterally, provided that an investigation is conducted by the competent authorities of the Member in question and that reasoned conclusions are provided supporting the need for such measures. In all three cases, the protection offered is of a temporary nature only, and is conditional. Although the conditions for imposing such protection are slightly different for each of the three types of measures, injury to the domestic industry is central in all three cases.

At the same time, however, safeguards are different. The history of safeguards, their rationale, and their function within the system distinguish safeguard measures from other types of contingent trade protection such as AD measures or CVMs. Whereas AD measures and CVMs have historically been justified by the perceived need to protect an industry faced with alleged unfair competition in the form of imports that have benefited from a subsidy or that are sold at dumped prices, the safeguards provision in Article XIX of the GATT functions as a pure escape clause.

The Appellate Body, in its Report on *United States – Definitive Safeguard Measures on Imports of Circular Welded Carbon Quality Line Pipe from Korea (US – Line Pipe)*, had the opportunity to underscore its understanding that safeguards should be distinguished from other contingent protection in that they do not address what the Appellate Body termed "unfair trade":

> Before turning to the first issue raised in this appeal, it is useful to recall that safeguard measures are extraordinary remedies to be taken only in emergency situations. Furthermore, they are remedies that are imposed in the form of import restrictions in the absence of any allegation of an unfair trade practice. In this, safeguard measures differ from, for example, anti-dumping duties and countervailing duties to counter subsidies, which are both measures taken in response to unfair trade practices. If the conditions for their imposition are fulfilled, safeguard measures may thus be imposed on the "fair trade" of other WTO Members and, by restricting their imports, will prevent those WTO Members from enjoying the full benefit of trade concessions under the *WTO Agreement*.[2] (italics in the original)

This observation serves as a discouragement to have "light-hearted" recourse to safeguard measures. This chapter will return to a discussion of this point *infra*, when discussing the standard of review applied by WTO adjudicating bodies.

The Role of Safeguards in the GATT/WTO

Although this chapter does not want to dwell on the rationale for safeguards (an issue discussed in a different chapter on the same topic of safeguards), it is

[2] Appellate Body Report, *United States – Definitive Safeguard Measures on Imports of Circular Welded Carbon Quality Line Pipe from Korea* WT/DS202/AB/R, adopted on March 8, 2002 *("US – Line Pipe")*, para. 80.

important to briefly explain the role and position of safeguards in a multilateral trade agreement such as the GATT.

Article XIX of the GATT, entitled "emergency action on imports of particular products," was incorporated into this multilateral trade agreement as an escape clause. In essence, what Article XIX of the GATT provides for is a fall-back option in case the effects of trade liberalization are more damaging than expected for a particular industry. In other words, although the granting of trade concessions could be expected to lead to more imports entering the country, and thus more competition for the domestic industry, Contracting Parties are given an opportunity to scale back some of the concessions granted if, because of some unforeseen developments, imports had increased to such an extent that the domestic industry is suffering serious injury as a consequence, a result obviously not intended by the negotiators of the importing country when they granted the concession. The price to pay for using this escape clause is to allow the affected Contracting Party to suspend substantially equivalent concessions.

Various rationales have been offered for the inclusion of a safeguards clause in a trade agreement. The political rationale for explaining safeguards as a mechanism that allows the negotiators/politicians to go further in trade liberalization than they otherwise would have been able to because of domestic pressure has been convincingly argued by Sykes.[3] In other words, safeguards function as a type of insurance mechanism that allows a country to take certain risks it would otherwise not dare to take. Another rationale offered is that safeguards assist countries in temporarily reducing the rate of adjustment to trade liberalization, and hence reduce the total cost of adjustment.[4]

The inclusion of such an escape clause in the GATT back in 1947 made a lot of sense in light of the groundbreaking endeavour that was undertaken by the original Contracting Parties of liberalizing trade, shortly after the end of the Second World War. Moreover, as we all know, the GATT was supposed to be a temporary arrangement, awaiting the final formation of an International Trade Organization (ITO). In this temporary setting, an escape clause such as that of Article XIX of the GATT 1947 is all the more understandable. The ITO never became a reality in the years following,[5] and the escape clause of Article XIX of the GATT 1947 remained in place, to be supplemented by a more detailed SA only at the conclusion of the Uruguay Round in 1994.

[3] A.O. Sykes, "The Safeguards Mess: A Critique of WTO Jurisprudence," 3 *World Trade Review* 2003, 261–295. (Sykes 2003)

[4] This is at least one of the rationales offered for justifying safeguards in a multilateral trade agreement. See, *inter alia*, A.O. Sykes, "Safeguards Reform: The Injury Test," in M. Trebilcock and R. York, *Fair Exchange: Reforming Trade Remedy Laws* (Toronto: C.D. Howe Institute, 1990); H. Horn and P. Mavroidis (Eds.), "US – Lamb: What Should Be Required of Safeguards Investigations?" in *The WTO Case Law of 2001* (ALI Reporters series, Cambridge Press, 2003).

[5] J.H. Jackson, W.J. Davey, and A.O. Sykes, *International Economic Relations* (Minneapolis West Group, 2002), 211–216.

It is not surprising that the escape clause just described was placed right before Article XX, entitled "General Exceptions" and Article XXI, "Security Exceptions." Actually, Article XIX of the GATT also provides for an important exception, as it allows a Contracting Party to suspend in whole or in part *any* obligation incurred by a Contracting Party under the GATT, including tariff concessions, or to withdraw or modify the concession. This exception is broadly defined and does not limit the types of emergency measures to tariff increases only. Rather, it links the emergency safeguard measure to the type of obligation, the effect of which has led to imports increasing in such a way as to cause serious injury to the domestic industry. This obligation can be anything. The difference with the exceptions set forth in Articles XX and XXI of the GATT is that the imposition of an emergency safeguard comes at a cost: allowing the suspension of an equivalent level of concessions by the affected parties. No costs are involved in the case that a country is justified to rely on the exceptions of Articles XX and XXI.

The Uruguay Round Agreement on Safeguards was the result of an effort to give more practical meaning to the escape clause of Article XIX of the GATT, which, for various reasons, had hardly been used in the decades following the conclusion of the GATT. Whereas little use had been made of Article XIX of the GATT safeguards, an important number of measures with an effect equivalent to that of a safeguard (so-called "grey area measures"[6]), were used in a number of industries such as steel, automobiles, and electronic equipment.[7] Such grey area measures were considered problematic for a number of reasons, such as the lack of information and transparency with regard to such grey area measures, the fact that such measures were often taken by importing countries (or imposed on exporting countries accepting to restrict exports on a "voluntary" basis) where it would otherwise not have been possible for the importing country to justify an Article XIX action, and their obvious effect of restricting trade.[8] These reasons explain why an agreement was negotiated in the Uruguay Round to bring all forms of safeguard action back into the framework of the GATT, and Article XIX in particular. The preamble of the Agreement on Safeguards reflects this historical evolution, as it recognizes "the need to clarify and reinforce the disciplines of the GATT 1994, and especially those of Article XIX (Emergency Action on Imports

[6] The term "grey area measures" refers to various types of export restraint agreements, such as voluntary export restraints, orderly marketing arrangements, export forecasts, basic price systems, and so forth, which are taken by contracting parties in situations similar to the one addressed in Article XIX of the GATT, but without following the disciplines of Article XIX of the GATT. Such measures were selective, in the sense that only products from particular countries were targeted, whereas Article XIX required Most-Favored-Nation (MFN) application of the safeguard, and was entered into "voluntarily" by the affected countries.

[7] For an interesting overview of such grey area measures and their importance in relative terms compared to Article XIX of the GATT safeguards, see "Inventory of Article XIX Actions and Other Measures Which Appear to Serve the Same Purpose," Background Note by the Secretariat, MTN.GNG/NG9/W2/Rev.1.

[8] See Background Note by the Secretariat on Grey Area Measures, dated September 16, 1987, MTN.GNG/NG9/W/6, p. 5.

of Particular Products), to re-establish multilateral control over safeguards and eliminate measures that escape such control."[9]

The Agreement on Safeguards builds on Article XIX of the GATT by adding further disciplines, introducing increased transparency, clarifying a number of terms, and prohibiting the use of alternative "safeguards" others than those allowed by the Agreement. In essence, the Agreement on Safeguards deals with (a) the conditions for the lawful imposition of a safeguard measure, (b) the lawful application of such a measure, (c) procedural requirements, (d) the requirement to maintain an equivalent level of concessions, and (e) the elimination of grey area measures. Each of these aspects of the Agreement will be addressed in the order mentioned above.

Conditions for Imposing Safeguards Action

In WTO case law, the *right to impose* safeguard measures has been distinguished from the lawful *application* of such measures. For a *right* to exist, a WTO Member must ensure that it has met all of the requirements set forth in Article 2.1 of the SA *and* Article XIX of the GATT; namely, it must show that its domestic industry has suffered serious injury as a result of unforeseen developments that have led to increased imports; for an *application* to be lawful, the safeguard measure may be applied only to the extent necessary to counteract the resulting damage.[10] This distinction, first made by the Appellate Body in its Report on *US – Line Pipe*, has been faithfully (indeed, sometimes *verbatim*) reproduced in subsequent case law.[11]

As the Panel in *United States – Definitive Safeguard Measures on Imports of Certain Steel Products* (*US – Steel Safeguards)* pointed out, Articles 2, 3, and 4 of the Safeguards Agreement and Article XIX of the GATT are relevant to examine whether a *right* to impose measure exists, whereas Article 5 of the Safeguard Agreement concerns the *application* of such measures.[12]

Three conditions are provided for in Article 2 of the SA (entitled *Conditions*): (a) increased imports, (b) serious injury to the domestic industry, and (c) the causal link between the imports and such injury. Case law added a fourth condition: The increased imports have to be the result of *unforeseen developments*. Each of these conditions will be discussed in turn, starting with the condition that was unforeseen by the Safeguards Agreement: unforeseen developments.

[9] Article 11.1(b) of the SA further clearly provides that a Member shall not seek, take, or maintain any voluntary export restraints, orderly marketing arrangements, or any other similar measures on the export or the import side.

[10] Appellate Body Report, *US – Line Pipe*, paras. 83–84.

[11] See, for example, Panel Report on *United States – Definitive Safeguard Measures on Imports of Certain Steel Products* WT/DS248, 249, 251, 252, 253, 254, 258, 259/R, adopted on December 10, 2003, as modified by the Appellate Body Report, WT/DS248, 249, 251, 252, 253, 254, 258, 259/AB/R (*US – Steel Safeguards*), para. 10.14.

[12] Panel Report, *US – Steel Safeguards*, para. 10.16.

Condition 1: Unforeseen Developments

(i) A Requirement, According to the Appellate Body

The Appellate Body, in its Report on *Argentina – Footwear (European Community [EC])*, held the view that meeting the three conditions mentioned above (increased imports, causing, serious injury) does not suffice for safeguards to be lawfully imposed; a WTO Member must further demonstrate that imports increased *as a result of unforeseen developments*. To reach this conclusion, the Appellate Body borrowed from Article 1 of the SA, which states that safeguard measures will be understood to be the measures provided for in Article XIX of the GATT. According to the Appellate Body, any safeguard action must *conform with* the provisions of Article XIX of the GATT 1994 *as well as* with the provisions of the *Agreement on Safeguards*.[13] The "emergency actions" provided for in Article XIX of the GATT are to be invoked only in situations when, as a result of obligations incurred under the GATT 1994, a Member finds itself confronted with developments it had not "foreseen" or "expected" when it incurred that obligation.[14]

The soundness of this construction is doubtful. Article 1 of the SA is entitled "General Provision" and, if at all, refers to the types of safeguard measures that can be lawfully imposed. It does not purport to regulate the conditions under which a safeguard can be lawfully imposed. By contrast, Article 2 of the SA ("Conditions") does *not* mention *unforeseen developments* among the conditions that must be observed. The fact that the Appellate Body itself considered the "unforeseen developments" not to be a "condition" for imposing safeguard measures, but rather "a circumstance which must be demonstrated as a matter of fact," only adds to the confusion.[15] In any case, for all practical purposes, it seems that the Appellate Body added a condition and thus, as will be discussed later in this chapter, opened the door to additional problems.[16]

[13] Appellate Body Report, *Argentina – Safeguard Measures on Imports of Footwear*, WT/DS121/AB/R, adopted on January 12, 2000. [*Argentina – Footwear (EC)*], para. 83.

[14] Appellate Body Report, *Argentina – Footwear (EC)*, paras. 93–94.

[15] Appellate Body Report, *Argentina – Footwear (EC)*, para. 92; Appellate Body Report, *Korea – Definitive Safeguard Measure on Imports of Certain Dairy Products*, WT/DS98/AB/R, adopted January 12, 2000 (*Korea – Dairy*), para. 85. In effect, this distinction is meaningless, as the Appellate Body required, as for any other condition, the same reasoned and adequate demonstration of the existence of this "circumstance" (i.e., of unforeseen developments resulting in increased imports). The Appellate Body thus rejected a U.S. argument that a different standard of review should be applied to "unforeseen developments" because it was not a "condition" but merely a "circumstance." Appellate Body Report, *US – Steel Safeguards*, paras. 274–276.

[16] Remarkably, the Appellate Body did not spend any time discussing the historical context and the preparatory work in general when deciding on this issue. As a result, the Appellate Body Report reflects no official account of the will of the founding fathers on this issue. The two Panels on *Korea – Dairy* and *Argentina – Footwear (EC)* that examined the same issue reached the conclusion that "unforeseen developments" is not a condition for imposing safeguards. Although they did so without expressly referring to the negotiating history, they did attempt to explain the absence of this criterion from the SA by pointing to the rationale for this criterion in the original Article XIX of the GATT 1947 and to past practice, which

A necessary by-product of this *extension* of the conditions under which safeguards can be lawfully imposed is the incorporation in the Safeguards Agreement of the language in Article XIX of the GATT that imports must have increased "as a result of *obligations assumed* under the GATT." Arguably, this language does not add much to Article 2 of the SA: In the absence of committing to tariff bindings, a WTO Member flooded with imports will simply increase its applied rate of duties, instead of conducting a full-fledged safeguards investigation and be requested to comply with various requirements.[17]

(ii) Developments that are "Unforeseen"

By introducing this requirement, the Appellate Body requests from WTO Members that increased imports were caused by unforeseen developments, and not by the normal course of trade.

In its report on *Korea – Definitive Safeguard Measure on Imports of Certain Dairy Products ("Korea – Dairy")*, the AB had, *inter alia*, the opportunity to explain its understanding of the term *unforeseen*. In its view, *unforeseen* should be read as synonymous to *unexpected*, as opposed to *unpredictable*, which would be synonymous to *unforeseeable*.[18]

The next question is, of course, "When should developments be unforeseen?" The Panel Report on *Argentina – Definitive Safeguard Measure on Imports of Preserved Peaches (Argentina – Preserved Peaches)*, reflecting prior case law by the Appellate Body, records the view that developments should be unforeseen *at the time when concessions were made*.[19] This test has been criticized as being highly unworkable. Sykes (2003) explains that, in light of the variables that might influence a potential trade outcome, it is simply impossible to reasonably request a WTO Member to foresee events that will occur in the not-immediate future. To make matters worse, it could, *theoretically* at least, be the case that the time span is quite long: What if a WTO Member did not make any bindings[20] after the Kennedy or the Tokyo Round?[21] Should it still be held liable for not having foreseen events occurring thirty years later? Grossman and Mavroidis (2004) advanced a proposal to the effect that the last round of trade negotiations should be the point in time that counts for the purposes of this exercise. Still, the authors accept that even such delimitation cannot by itself take care of all problems to

ignored this criterion. See Panel Report, *Korea – Dairy*, paras. 7.42–7.49 and Panel Report, *Argentina – Footwear (EC)*, paras. 8.64–8.66.

17 See, however, Horn and Mavroidis (2003) for a comprehensive discussion of this issue.

18 Appellate Body Report, *Korea – Dairy*, para. 84.

19 Panel Report, *Argentina – Definitive Safeguard Measure on Imports of Preserved Peaches*, WT/DS238/R, adopted April 15, 2003 ("*Argentina – Preserved Peaches*"), paras. 7.26–7.28.

20 As we will see *infra*, usually recourse to safeguards will take place against imports of products that a WTO Member has included in its list of concessions (bindings).

21 The first Round took place in the 1960s, whereas the second took place in the 1970s.

which the satisfaction of the *unforeseen developments* requirement might give rise.[22]

(iii) What Could Constitute "Unforeseen Developments"? Lessons from Case Law

It is interesting to note that, so far, none of the safeguard measures challenged before the WTO passed the "unforeseen developments" hurdle. Actually, domestic investigating authorities started to look into the question of unforeseen developments only after the rulings of the Appellate Body in *Korea – Dairy* and *Argentina – Footwear (EC)* established the need to demonstrate such unforeseen developments in early 2000.[23] Not surprisingly, in all cases, Panels and the Appellate Body found an inconsistency based on an absence of a reasoned and adequate explanation in the report of the investigating authorities of the existence of unforeseen developments and their logical link to increased imports. The *US – Steel Safeguards* case was the first case that dealt with a decision by an investigating authority that explicitly decided to address the question of unforeseen developments in an attempt to comply with this "new" condition. Actually, the U.S. authorities had done so by preparing a Second Supplementary Report addressing, in particular, unforeseen developments.[24] Still, the measure failed to pass muster, as the authorities were still found to have failed to provide a sufficient, adequate, and reasoned explanation linking the possible unforeseen developments to the specific increase in imports of the products covered by the measure. In the words of the Panel:

> the weakness of the USITC Report is that, although it describes a plausible set of unforeseen developments that may have resulted in increased imports to the United States from various sources, it falls short of demonstrating that such developments actually resulted in increased imports into the United States causing serious injury to the relevant domestic producers.[25]

[22] Grossman, G., Mavroidis P.C. "Not for attribution," U.S. – Line Pipe, in Hern and Mavroidis (eds), The WTO Case Law of 2002: The Amercan Law Institute Reporters' Studies, (Cambridge, Cambridge University Press, 2004).

[23] This became painfully clear in the Appellate Body Report on *US – Lamb*, where the Appellate Body confronted the United States with its earlier expressed view that there was no need for a demonstration of unforeseen developments. The absence of any explanation of unforeseen developments in the U.S. authorities' report of the Lamb safeguard measure thus did not come as a surprise to the Appellate Body. See Appellate Body Report, *US – Lamb*, paras. 73–74.

[24] As the Panel noted, "at no point in the initial USITC Report is the issue of 'unforeseen developments' *per se* mentioned, except, as the complainants have pointed out, in a footnote in the separate view of one commissioner explaining that although such a demonstration is required in WTO law, it is not required by U.S. law." Panel Report, *US – Steel Safeguards*, para. 10.116.

[25] Panel Report, *US – Steel Safeguards*, para. 10.122. The Panel's ruling in this regard was upheld by the Appellate Body, which also emphasized the importance of an adequate and

So, really, we do not know what could be considered as "unforeseen developments." What the Panel referred to as a "plausible set of circumstances" that the U.S. authorities had identified concerned the Asian and Russian financial crisis at the end of the 1990s and the strong U.S. dollar and economy.[26] In the words of one of the U.S. Commissioners,

> It is apparent that these increased imports were the result of the unforeseen global financial crises in Asia and Russia, as well as unanticipated levels of global steel overcapacity, the collapse of foreign steel markets, emerging countries beginning massive steel production, and foreign producers focusing their sales into the lucrative US market.[27]

With respect to the type of facts that may be considered as "unforeseen developments," the Panel, in its report on *United States – Safeguard Measures on Imports of Fresh, Chilled or Frozen Lamb Meat from New Zealand and Australia (US – Lamb)*, referred with approval to the 1951 GATT report of the Working Party in *US – Fur Felt Hats*, a case relating to the withdrawal of a concession by the United States on women's fur hats and hat bodies. The members of the Working Party agreed that

> "the *fact that hat styles had changed did not constitute an 'unforeseen development'* within the meaning of Article XIX," but that the effects of the special circumstances of this case, and "particularly the *degree to which the change in fashion affected the competitive situation*, could not reasonably be expected to have been foreseen by the United States authorities in 1947, and that the condition of Article XIX that the increase in imports must be due to unforeseen developments and to the effect of the tariff concessions can therefore be considered to have been fulfilled."[28] (emphasis added)

What is clear is that the unforeseen developments cannot be equated with increased imports; rather, the increased imports are *the result of* the unforeseen developments. Unforeseen developments and increased imports are two distinct matters.[29]

reasoned explanation of the link between the unforeseen developments and the resulting increased imports. Appellate Body Report, *US – Steel Safeguards*, para. 330.

[26] Panel Report, *US – Steel Safeguards*, para. 10.121. For the complete description of the U.S. authorities' discussion of the unforeseen developments, see Panel Report, *US – Steel Safeguards*, para. 10.110.

[27] Panel Report, *US – Steel Safeguards*, para. 10.111.

[28] *Report of the Intersessional Working Party on the Complaint of Czechoslovakia Concerning the Withdrawal by the United States of a Tariff Concession under Article XIX of the GATT* (*US – Fur Felt Hats*), GATT/CP/106, adopted on October 22, 1951, at para. 12, as quoted in Panel Report, *United States – Safeguard Measures on Imports of Fresh, Chilled or Frozen Lamb Meat from New Zealand and Australia*, WT/DS177/R, WT/DS178/R, adopted on May 16, 2001, as modified by the Appellate Body Report, WT/DS177/AB/R, WT/DS178/AB/R (*US – Lamb*), para. 7.23.

[29] Panel Report, *Argentina – Preserved Peaches*, paras. 7.17–7.18.

Condition 2: Increased Quantities of Imports

(i) Role of "Increased Imports" Compared with Other Contingent Trade Remedy Instruments

Article 2.1 of the SA provides that, for safeguards to be imposed, a product must be imported in such *increased quantities, absolute or relative to domestic production,* so as to cause serious injury.[30] In the safeguards context, increased imports is an independent condition for imposition of a measure. Its importance is similar to a finding of dumping or subsidization in the AD/countervailing duty (CVD) context. Without an increase in imports, no safeguard measure.

The term *increased quantities of imports* was interpreted by the Appellate Body in its Report on *Argentina – Footwear (EC)*, in which it ruled that Panels should be looking at *trends* instead of isolated transactions or absolute numbers based on an end-point to end-point comparison.[31] Moreover, in its report on *Argentina – Footwear (EC)*, the Appellate Body emphasized that not just any increase over a period of time will do – rather, it is necessary for the competent authorities to examine recent imports.[32] The Appellate Body summarized its position by concluding that the increase in imports must have been *recent, sudden, sharp,* and *significant enough, both quantitatively and qualitatively,* so as to cause serious injury.[33] (emphasis and italics in the original)

Although, on the basis of the Appellate Body's reasoning, one could have come to the conclusion that, in the absence of a sudden and sharp increase during the most recent period examined, no safeguard measures may be imposed, later case law showed that this is not necessarily so. A recent decrease does not necessarily prevent an investigating authority from finding that, nevertheless, products continue to be imported "in such increased quantities." According to the Appellate Body, what is important in such a case is the reasoned and adequate explanation to be provided by the authorities as to why, in the presence of a recent decrease in imports, the "increase imports" condition is nevertheless met.[34]

[30] Economic theory suggests that imports *per se* can never be a cause of injury, for they represent the difference between consumption and domestic production at a given price level: Imports are a *proximate* and not the *ultimate* cause. Sykes (2003) has correctly criticized the SA for being economically naïve in this respect. See A.O. Sykes, "The Safeguards Mess: A Critique of Appellate Body Jurisprudence," 2 *World Trade Review* 2003. One possible way to avoid this issue is to interpret the term "increased imports" as a pure procedural requirement and also request that investigating authorities have the duty to investigate the reasons that explain *why* imports have increased. Such an approach has been advanced as a possible second best that helps avoid a costly renegotiation of the SA by Grossman and Mavroidis, "US – Line Pipe," in H. Horn, and P. Mavroidis (Eds.), *The WTO Case Law of 2002* (ALI Reporters Series, Cambridge Press, 2004).

[31] Appellate Body Report, *Argentina – Footwear (EC)*, para. 129.

[32] Appellate Body Report, *Argentina – Footwear (EC)*, para. 130.

[33] Appellate Body Report, *Argentina – Footwear (EC)*, para. 131.

[34] Appellate Body Report, *US – Steel Safeguards*, paras. 368 and 370. The Panel in this case had stated that, in an evaluation of a recent decrease, "factors that must be taken into account

Actually, the Panel in *US – Steel Safeguards* correctly, albeit somewhat cynically, reworded the Appellate Body's famous "sudden, recent and sharp" mantra to find that an increase that "evidences a *certain degree of* recentness, suddenness, sharpness and significance"[35] (emphasis added) is an increase in the sense of Article 2.1 Safeguards.

Condition 3: Serious Injury or Threat of Serious Injury to the Domestic Industry

(i) Serious Injury

The Safeguards Agreement allows the imposition of safeguard measures if the WTO Member concerned has shown either *serious injury* or *threat of serious injury.* Serious injury is defined in Article 4.1 of the Safeguards Agreement as "a significant overall impairment in the position of the domestic industry."[36]

The Appellate Body, in its Report on *US – Lamb,* supplied its understanding of these terms.[37] It considered that the adjective "serious" implies that "serious injury" is a higher standard than "material" injury. Although it may be so that *serious injury* is a higher standard than material injury, it needs to be said that we do not really know what the *material injury* standard is in the first place. What is "significant" or "serious" is of course very subjective. It remains to be seen whether in practice there is any meaningful difference between "material" injury and "serious" injury, or whether it would not be more correct to state that, in both cases, a finding of injury that is *not insignificant* will be upheld by WTO Panels.

The Agreement requires an authority to evaluate all relevant factors and mentions eight factors that must be examined in particular: the rate and amount of the increase in imports of the product concerned in absolute and relative terms; the share of the domestic market taken by increased imports; and changes in the level of sales, production, productivity, capacity utilization, profits and losses, and employment.[38] The Appellate Body in *Argentina – Footwear (EC)* emphasized that, in addition to a technical examination of all the listed factors and any other relevant factors, an authority is to examine the overall position of the domestic industry.[39] Authorities are not required to show that each listed

are the duration and the degree of the decrease at the end of the relevant period of investigation, as well as the nature, for instance the sharpness and the extent, of the increase that intervened beforehand." Panel Report, *US – Steel Safeguards,* para. 10.163.

[35] Panel Report, *US – Steel Safeguards,* para. 10.167. A statement the Appellate Body actually agreed with as being a correct interpretation of what it had said in *Argentina – Footwear (EC).* Appellate Body Report, *US – Steel Safeguards,* para. 361.

[36] No similar definition of the term "material injury" exists in the Anti-Dumping Agreement (AD Agreement) or the Subsidies and Countervailing Measures Agreement (SCM Agreement).

[37] Appellate Body Report, *US – Lamb,* paras. 124–125.

[38] Article 4.2(a) of the SA.

[39] Appellate Body Report, *Argentina – Footwear (EC),* para. 139.

injury factor is declining; rather, they must reach a determination in light of the evidence as a whole.[40]

It is interesting to note that no price analysis is required by the Safeguards Agreement,[41] although the negotiating history clearly shows that safeguards were intended to address situations of low-priced imports that were not dumped or subsidized.[42] Nevertheless, although no price analysis is required for a safeguard to be imposed lawfully,[43] it may be a very "relevant factor" that needs to be examined and that may be important in a causation analysis as part of the conditions of competition, as underlined by the Panel in its report on *United States – Definitive Safeguard Measures on Imports of Wheat Gluten from the European Communities (US – Wheat Gluten).*[44]

(ii) Threat of Serious Injury

Article 4.1 of the SA states that "threat of serious injury" shall be understood to mean serious injury that is clearly imminent, adding that a determination of the existence of a threat shall be based on facts and not merely on allegation, conjecture, or remote possibility.[45] Therefore, according to the Appellate Body in *US – Lamb*, for a threat determination, it must be manifest that the domestic industry is on the brink of suffering serious injury.[46]

The Safeguards Agreement thus contains a definition of a threat of serious injury, but does not list any specific factors that need to be taken into account, as was the case in Article 3.7 of the AD Agreement/15.7 Agreement on Subsidies and Countervailing Measures (SCM Agreement) for AD/CVD proceedings. This omission is surprising, not in the least because the factors to be examined in the AD/CVD context relate to the possibility of further future increased imports. In light of the important role given to increased imports in the safeguards context, it would have made even more sense in the safeguards context to require an

[40] Appellate Body Report, *US – Lamb*, para. 144; Panel Report, *US – Lamb*, para. 7.203. According to the Panel in *US – Lamb*, for example, this implies that authorities "may arrive at a threat determination *even if the majority of firms within the relevant industry is not facing declining profitability*, provided that an evaluation of the injury factors *as a whole* indicates threat of serious injury." (emphasis added) Panel Report, *US – Lamb*, para. 7.188.

[41] Contrary to what is the case in the AD and Countervailing Duty CVD context (Article 3.2 of the AD Agreement and Article 15.2 of the SCM Agreement, respectively).

[42] MTN.GNG/NG9/W/1, para. 7; BISD9S/26.

[43] Panel Report, *Korea – Dairy*, para. 7.51. The Panel on *Argentina – Footwear (EC)* similarly held that the phrase "under such conditions" does not constitute a specific legal requirement for a price analysis. Panel Report, *Argentina – Footwear (EC)*, para. 8.249.

[44] Panel Report, *United States – Definitive Safeguard Measures on Imports of Wheat Gluten from the European Communities*, WT/DS166/R, adopted on January 19, 2001, as modified by the Appellate Body Report, WT/DS166/AB/R (*US – Wheat Gluten*), para. 8.109.

[45] Article 4.1(b) of the SA. These general requirements are similar to those set forth in Articles 3.7 of the AD and 15.7 of the SCM Agreements.

[46] Appellate Body Report, *US – Lamb*, para. 125.

authority in a threat determination to be examining the same projected future increase in imports.

Of course, and as noted by the Appellate Body in its Report on *US – Lamb*, there is an unavoidable tension between requesting a future-oriented study (such as the one required for threat of injury to be determined) and, at the same time, obliging the investigating authority to come up with hard data. Future incorporates uncertainty. An investigating authority must provide adequate justification for its final findings. To do that, it should certainly examine recent data, as "data relating to the most recent past will provide competent authorities with an essential, and, usually, the most reliable, basis for a determination of a threat of serious injury."[47]

(iii) The Domestic Industry Producing the Like or Directly Competitive Product

Article 4.1(c) provides that, in determining injury, a "domestic industry" shall be understood to mean the producers as a whole of the like or directly competitive products operating within the territory of a member, or those whose collective output of the like or directly competitive products constitutes a major proportion of the total domestic production of those products. This definition raises the issue of the scope of *like* or *directly competitive* products.

While the AD and SCM Agreements contain a definition of the term "like product," the Safeguards Agreement does not. It seems justified to assume, however, that the same definition of a like product applies in this context: a product that is identical to the imported product; in other words, alike in all respects, or, in the absence of such a product, a product that has characteristics closely resembling those of the imported product.[48] In the AD/SCM Agreement context, this definition has led to a focus on the physical characteristics of the product.

The term "directly competitive products" seems to refer to a wider group of products; in other words, those products that are not necessarily physically alike but nevertheless compete in the same market. The term has not been interpreted in the context of a dispute concerning the Safeguards Agreement. However, the Appellate Body did express its views on this term as it also appears in the now defunct Agreement on Textiles and Clothing (ATC) as part of the special safeguard provision in that Agreement. According to the Appellate Body, two products are "competitive" if they are *commercially interchangeable* or if they offer *alternative ways of satisfying the same consumer demand.* They do not actually have to be presently competing with one another for these two products to be competitive products. It is the capacity of products to compete in the same market, which is important.[49] Because of the qualifier "directly," the Appellate Body

[47] Appellate Body Report, *US – Lamb*, para. 137. Panel Report, *US – Wheat Gluten*, para. 8.81.

[48] Article 2.6 of the AD Agreement; Footnote 46 of the SCM Agreement.

[49] Appellate Body Report, *United States – Transitional Safeguard Measure on Combed Cotton Yarn from Pakistan*, WT/DS192/AB/R, adopted on November 5, 2001 (*US – Cotton Yarn*), para. 96.

was of the view that "a safeguard action will not extend to protecting a domestic industry that produces unlike products which have only a remote or tenuous competitive relationship with the imported product."[50]

A similar emphasis on consumer preference, both actual and future potential, as well as on substitutability as determinative in the consideration of two products as directly competitive, can be deduced from jurisprudence of Article III of the GATT, which seems to be obviously relevant in this respect.[51] In terms of substitutability, the difference between like products and directly competitive products is that "like" products are perfectly substitutable and that "directly competitive" products are characterized by a high, but imperfect, degree of substitutability.[52] So, although wooden matches are not "like" plastic disposable lighters, it could probably be argued that these two products are directly competitive products.[53] A safeguard measure on imports of matches could thus be based on a finding of serious injury to the domestic industry producing disposable lighters.

It is therefore clear that the definition of what constitutes the domestic industry for purposes of the injury analysis in the Safeguards context (producers of the like or directly competitive product) is wider than the scope of the domestic industry in the AD/CVD case, which was limited to the like product producers only.[54] Still, the coverage is not so wide as to include, for example, producers of the input product in the definition of the domestic industry producing the final product. The fact that there is a high degree of vertical integration between an input producer and a producer of the final like product is not relevant in defining the domestic industry producing the like product.[55] The Appellate

[50] Appellate Body Report, *US – Cotton Yarn*, para. 98.

[51] In *US – Cotton Yarn*, the Appellate Body referred to its analysis concerning the term "directly competitive products" in its reports on *Korea – Taxes on Alcoholic Beverages*, WT/DS75/AB/R, WT/DS84/AB/R, adopted on February 17, 1999 (*Korea – Alcoholic Beverages*) and *Japan – Taxes on Alcoholic Beverages*, WT/DS8/AB/R, WT/DS10/AB/R, WT/DS11/AB/R, adopted on November 1, 1996 (*Japan – Alcoholic Beverages II*). It even provided a summary of its relevant findings in this respect as the basis for its analysis of the term in the safeguards context of the ATC. Appellate Body Report, *US – Cotton Yarn*, para. 91.

[52] Appellate Body Report, *US – Cotton Yarn*, 68; Also see, for example, *Korea – Alcoholic Beverages*, para. 118.

[53] Although a counterargument could be made that the difference in physical characteristics is such that, even in the presence of consumer preference, matches and lighters are not directly competitive products. Any like or directly competitive product determination is of course to be made on a case-by-case basis and will depend on the available evidence.

[54] Panel Report, *US – Lamb*, para. 7.117:

> This being said, it is clear on the face of the Safeguards Agreement that the product coverage of a safeguard investigation can potentially be broader than in an anti-dumping or countervail case, to the extent that "directly competitive" products are involved. In our view, this apparent additional latitude that exists under the Safeguards Agreement may be related to the basic purpose of the Safeguards Agreement and Article XIX of the GATT, namely to provide an effective safety valve for industries that are suffering or are threatened with serious injury caused by increased imports in the wake of trade liberalization.

[55] Appellate Body Report, *US – Lamb*, para. 94.

Body in its Report on *US – Lamb* thus considered that the United States was wrong to include in its safeguards investigation of imports of lamb meat not only the domestic producers of lamb meat (the breakers and packers) but also the growers and feeders of live lamb (the input for lamb meat) in the United States.[56]

Condition 4: Existence of a Causal Link Between Increased Imports and Serious Injury

A determination that increased imports caused or are threatening to cause serious injury may be made only in a case in which the investigation demonstrates "the existence of the causal link" between the increased imports and serious injury. When factors other than increased imports are causing injury to the domestic industry at the same time, "such injury shall not be attributed to increased imports." Hence, the (very realistic) working hypothesis of this second sentence is that it could be the case that more than one factor affects a particular outcome. This is what Article 4.2(b) of the Safeguards Agreement stipulates: a causation requirement and a nonattribution requirement.

(i) Nonattribution

There is an important body of WTO case law on this issue by now, under the Safeguards Agreement as well as under the AD and SCM Agreements, which contain similar provisions.[57] In a nutshell, case law stands for the proposition that, under the nonattribution requirement, an investigating authority will be requested to *separate and distinguish the effects* of increased imports from the effects that other factors might have had on the state of its domestic industry producing the like or directly competitive product. What is required under the nonattribution requirement of Article 4.2(b) of the SA is that the authority identify the nature and extent of the injurious effects of the known factors other than increased imports.[58] It is only after having complied with this so-called nonattribution requirement that the causal link between increased imports and injury may be established.

The Agreement does not specify the method to be used for separating and distinguishing these various effects as confirmed by the Appellate Body in its Report on *US – Lamb*:

> We emphasize that the method and approach WTO Members choose to carry out in the process of separating the effects of the other causal

[56] Appellate Body Report, *US – Lamb*, para. 90. The Appellate Body thus concluded that by expanding the "domestic industry" to include producers of other products, namely, *live lambs*, the USITC defined the "domestic industry" inconsistently with Article 4.1(c) of the SA, as this should have been limited only to *packers and breakers of lamb meat*. Appellate Body Report, *US – Lamb*, paras. 95–96.

[57] The relevance of the AD case law for the causation requirement under the SA (and vice versa) was explicitly recognized by the Appellate Body Report on *US – Line Pipe*. Appellate Body Report, *US – Line Pipe*, para. 214.

[58] Appellate Body Report, *US – Line Pipe*, para. 215.

> factors is not specified by the *Agreement on Safeguards*. What the Agreement requires is simply that the obligation in Article 4.2 must be respected when a safeguard measure is applied.[59]

The obvious question, however, is whether one can actually properly separate and distinguish the effects of increased imports from the effects of other factors without in some way or another quantifying these various factors' effects. Although there does not seem to exist an explicit legal obligation in the Safeguards Agreement to do so, the Panel in *US – Steel Safeguards* did consider that "quantification may be particularly desirable in cases involving complicated factual situations where qualitative analyses may not suffice to more fully understand the dynamics of the relevant market."[60] The Panel went on to consider that, in certain circumstances, quantification may even be *necessary* to establish nonattribution explicitly on the basis of a reasoned and adequate explanation:

> [...] we believe that a competent authority may find itself in situations where quantification and some form of economic analysis are necessary to rebut allegedly plausible alternative explanations that have been put forward. While the wording of the provisions of the Agreement on Safeguards does not require quantification in the causal link analysis *per se*, the circumstances of a specific dispute may call for quantification.
>
> Having said that quantification may be desirable, useful and sometimes necessary depending on the circumstances of a case, the Panel recognizes that quantification may be difficult and is less than perfect. Therefore, the Panel is of the view that the results of such quantification may not necessarily be determinative. We consider that an overall qualitative assessment that takes into account all relevant information, must always be performed.[61] (footnotes omitted)

To separate and distinguish the effects of other factors is one thing, but what is the authority supposed to do with the results? Two Panels on *US – Wheat Gluten* and *US – Lamb* had been of the view that, after the effects of the other factors were separated and distinguished from the effects of the imports, an authority was required to determine that the imports *in and of themselves* were responsible for the serious injury. The Appellate Body rejected this approach. It emphasized the fact that the text of Article 4.2(b) only requires that a causal *link* be established, which it viewed as a requirement to establish that imports *contributed to* the injury, rather than being the necessary and sufficient cause of such injury. The Appellate Body thus advocated a two-step approach, requiring the authority to (1) distinguish the effects of increased imports from that of other

[59] Appellate Body Report, *US – Lamb*, para. 181. Although the methodology is not prejudged, it is difficult to imagine how an investigating authority can honor this test without recourse to econometrics.

[60] Panel Report, *US – Steel Safeguards*, para. 10.336.

[61] Panel Report, *US – Steel Safeguards*, paras. 10.340–10.341.

factors, and (2) attribute to increased imports, on the one hand, and by implication, to other relevant factors, on the other hand, "injury" caused by all of these different factors (attribution).[62] It rejected the idea that, following the attribution of the effects to these other factors, and thus by implication to imports, there was a need to exclude the effects of other factors (what the Appellate Body considered to be the Panel's step 3) or to determine that imports alone were capable of causing serious injury (considered to be the Panel's step 4).[63]

The question of causation (and nonattribution in particular) has led to many conceptual discussions and linguistic analyses. At the end of the day, however, what is required is that an authority provide an adequate and reasoned explanation as to the impact of other factors on the state of the domestic industry.[64]

(ii) A Relationship of Cause and Effect: Theory and Practice

Postseparation, the *causal link* between imports and serious injury must be established.[65] This implies that it must be established that increased imports contributed to "bringing about," "producing," or "inducing" the serious injury.[66]

In *US – Wheat Gluten*, the Appellate Body explains that a *genuine* and *substantial* relationship between cause and effect must exist for the causality requirement to have been met.[67] This genuine and substantial relationship language should not be confused with substantial cause-standard, which is the standard applicable in the context of safeguards by U.S. investigating authorities.[68] Althoughthe Appellate Body has yet to issue a definitive ruling on

[62] Appellate Body Report, *US – Wheat Gluten*, para. 69.

[63] Appellate Body Report, *US – Wheat Gluten*, paras..66 and 79.

[64] See Appellate Body Report, *US – Lamb*, para. 175.

[65] The important problem is of course that imports are an endogenous variable and as such can never *cause* injury. Sykes (2003) explains as much when stating that imports are simply the difference between consumption and domestic supply (at a given price, of course). The same set of factors (exogenous variables, like technology and cost structure) that influence imports also influence domestic supply. Hence, it can never be the case that imports cause injury. Rather, investigating authorities should look elsewhere (to exogenous variables) for what causes injury to their domestic production. Hence, in Sykes's view, the WTO judge has in his/her hands an intellectually unworkable tool in the form of the causality requirement. Also see A.O. Sykes, "The Persistent Puzzle of Safeguards, Lessons from the Steel Dispute," (2003) 7(3) *Journal of International Economic Law*. Grossman and Mavroidis (2004) agree with Sykes's analysis. They argue, however, that unless the WTO judge is imaginative, he/she risks penalizing WTO Members for failing to meet an unworkable (and hence impossible-to-meet) standard. In their view, one way out would be for the judge to interpret the causality requirement as tantamount to permitting the imposition of safeguards every time there are changes in the import supply curve (which in turn are caused by exogenous variables). G. Grossman, and P. Mavroidis, *US – Line Pipe*, in H. Horn and P. Mavroidis (Eds.), *The WTO Case Law of 2002* (ALI Reporters Series, Cambridge Press, 2004).

[66] Appellate Body Report, *US – Wheat Gluten*, para. 68.

[67] Appellate Body Report, *US – Wheat Gluten*, para. 69.

[68] The U.S. Court of Appeals for The Federal Circuit (CAFC), in its *Gerald Metals Inc.*, decision of December 23, 1997 (97–1077), describes as follows the *substantial cause-standard* which is reflected in U.S. statutes:

this U.S. standard as such, the U.S. causation analysis in all cases challenged so far was found to have been inconsistent, and this finding tends to suggest that the substantial cause standard may not be adequate to comply with the causation requirement of Article 4.2(b) of the Safeguards Agreement.

In practice, what does the expressed need to establish a genuine and substantial relationship require an authority to do? How does one go about establishing that the serious injury is caused by the increased imports? In *Argentina – Footwear (EC)*, the Appellate Body agreed with the following analysis by the Panel of what is required to comply with the causation requirement of Article 4.2(b)[69]:

> ...we will consider whether Argentina's causation analysis meets these requirements on the basis of (i) whether an upward trend in imports coincides with downward trends in the injury factors, and if not, whether a reasoned explanation is provided as to why nevertheless the data show causation; (ii) whether the conditions of competition in the Argentine footwear market between imported and domestic footwear as analysed demonstrate, on the basis of objective evidence, a causal link of the imports to any injury; and (iii) whether other relevant factors have been analysed and whether it is established that injury caused by factors other than imports has not been attributed to imports.[70]

In other words, in an analysis of causation, it is the *relationship* between the movements in imports (volume and market share) and the movements in injury factors that must be central to a causation analysis and determination.[71] In its report on *Argentina – Footwear (EC)*, the Appellate Body referred with approval to a statement by the Panel establishing a negative presumption in the case of an absence of correlation.[72]

In addition to a trends/correlation analysis, a causation analysis requires an examination of the conditions of competition between the imported products

> ...the statute requires the injury to occur "by reason of" the LTFV imports. This language does not suggest that an importer of LTFV imports goods can escape countervailing duties by finding some tangential or minor cause unrelated to the LTFV goods that contributed to the harmful effects on domestic market prices. By the same token, this language does not suggest that the Government satisfies its burden of proof by showing that the LTFV goods themselves contributed only minimally or tangentially to the material harm. ...Hence, the statute requires adequate evidence to show that the harm occurred 'by reason of' the LTFV imports, not by reason of a minimal or tangential contribution to material harm caused by LTFV goods. (pp. 9–10 of the decision. **NB.** LTFV stands for "Less Than Fair Value.")

[69] Appellate Body Report, *Argentina – Footwear (EC)*, para. 145.

[70] Panel Report, *Argentina – Footwear (EC)*, para. 8.229. For the use of a similar test, see Panel Report, *US – Wheat Gluten*, para. 8.91; Panel Report, *US – Lamb*, para. 7.232. Also see Panel Report, *US – Steel Safeguards*, paras. 10.297 *et seq.*

[71] Appellate Body Report, *Argentina – Footwear (EC)*, para. 144.

[72] Panel Report, *Argentina – Footwear (EC)*, para. 8.238, as quoted in Appellate Body Report, *Argentina – Footwear (EC)*, para. 144. In other words, the authorities will need to provide more of an explanation when there is no time coincidence between increased imports and injury.

and the like or directly competitive products. In other words, "for an analysis to demonstrate causation, it must address specifically the nature of the interaction between the imported and domestic products in the domestic market of the importing country."[73] Although this analysis may imply a price analysis, it is not necessarily so, as much will depend on the product in question.Other bases on which products may compete include physical characteristics (e.g., technical standards or other performance-related aspects, appearance, style, or fashion), quality, service, delivery, technological developments, consumer tastes, and other supply and demand factors in the market.[74]

The Lawful Application of Safeguard Measures

A Typology of Safeguard Measures

A list of all possible *forms* of safeguard measures is not explicitly reflected in the WTO Safeguards Agreement or Article XIX of the GATT 1994.[75] The latter simply provides that, under certain circumstances, a Member may be free "to suspend the obligation in whole or in part or to withdraw or modify the concession." Thus, tariff increases above the bound rate may clearly be used as a safeguard measure. Actually, Article 7 of the SA provides that provisional safeguard measures should take the form of such tariff increases, but definitive safeguard measures could take the form of quantitative restrictions or any type of quota system as well, as becomes evident from Article 5 of the SA. Article 5.1 of the SA, for example, states, "... *if* a quantitative restriction is used." (emphasis added) Article 5.2 deals with "cases in which a quota is allocated among supplying countries." Article 5.1 *in fine* states that Members should choose measures most suitable for the achievement of the objectives (i.e., to prevent or remedy serious injury and to facilitate adjustment).

Actually, based on the notifications by WTO members to the Safeguards Committee, it appears that *ad valorem* tariff increases are the most widely used safeguards instrument. Almost as popular are tariff rate quotas (TRQs) whereby Members reserve a favorable tax rate for a small initial quantity imported. Specific tariff increases are third in the ranking. Quantitative restrictions with some quota system are a distant fourth.[76] In other words, although one often associates

[73] Panel Report, *Argentina – Footwear (EC)*, para. 8.250.

[74] Panel Report, *Argentina – Footwear (EC)*, para. 8.251. Also see Panel Report, *US – Wheat Gluten*, paras. 8.109–8.110; Panel Report, *US – Steel Safeguards*, para. 10.318.

[75] This is one the many differences between the SA and the AD, SCM/CVD Agreement where the three types of measures are exhaustively listed: provisional measures, antidumping/countervailing duties in the form of tariff increases, and undertakings. No other "specific action against dumping/subsidization" may be taken. Article 18.1 of the AD Agreement; Article 32.1 of the SCM Agreement.

[76] Based on the notifications until November 7, 2005, we counted 24 *ad valorem* tariffs, 21 tariff rate quotas, 18 specific tariff increases, and 7 quantitative restrictions/quota measures. Two variable tariff increases complete the picture.

safeguard measures with quantitative restrictions, a quantitative restriction clearly does not exhaust the realm of possible safeguard measures that can be lawfully imposed under the Safeguards Agreement – quite to the contrary.

The Level of Safeguards

General Rule: Only to the Extent Necessary

Article 5.1 of the SA requires WTO Members to "... apply safeguard measures only to the extent necessary to prevent or remedy serious injury and to facilitate adjustment."

Based on this provision, the Appellate Body in *US – Line Pipe* expressed the view that, by virtue of this provision, an investigating authority that has separated the effects caused by imports and other factors can apply the safeguard only up to the level of that part of the injury attributable to imports in isolation.[77] Assuming, for example, that it can be shown that increased imports account for twenty percent of the total injury suffered, a WTO Member, by virtue of Article 5.1 of the SA, can impose safeguards to counteract the twenty percent only, and not the total amount of injury suffered.

It is noteworthy that the AD and SCM Agreements contain nonattribution language in their respective provisions dealing with injury and causation (Article 3.5 of the AD/15.5 of the SCM) similar to the nonattribution language of Article 4.2(b) of the Safeguards Agreement. However, in terms of the legitimate level of the measure to be imposed upon a finding of dumping/subsidization, injury, and the causal link, the texts of the various Agreements differ and the situation is more complicated.

On the one hand, in the AD and CVD context, the Agreements clearly link the maximum amount of the duty/measure to the margin of dumping or subsidization rather than to the injury.[78] Therefore, the argument used by the Appellate Body in *US – Line Pipe* to support its reasoning is factually inaccurate: The Appellate Body argues that, because in case of "unfair" trade remedies (AD/CVD), the measure is limited by the amount of the injury inflicted, then, *a fortiori*, such limitations should also apply to "fair" trade actions such as safeguard measures.[79] However, in the AD/CVD context, the amount of the duty is limited by the margin of dumping or subsidization and *not* necessarily by the amount of the injury caused by dumping or subsidization. In other words, and unless the Appellate Body is suggesting that the lesser duty rule is in fact mandated by the

[77] Appellate Body Report, *US – Line Pipe*, para. 260. The Appellate Body considered that textual reasons (the wording of Article 5.1 of the SA), contextual reasons (the wording of other SA provisions closely relating to the subject matter of Article 5.1 of the SA), as well as the object and purpose of the SA supported this view. Appellate Body Report, *US – Line Pipe*, paras. 249–250, 252, 257, and 258.

[78] Article 9.3 of the AD Agreement; Article 19.4 of the SCM Agreement.

[79] Appellate Body Report, *US – Line Pipe*, para. 257.

nonattribution language in the AD/SCM Agreement,[80] it is not so that the WTO Agreement limits a countermeasure to the extent of the injury caused by unfair practices.

Safeguard Measures: The Special Case of Quantitative Restrictions

(a) Minimum Quantity of Imports in Case of Quantitative Restrictions

As stated earlier, Article 5 does not specify which kind of measures can be used as a safeguard measure,[81] but quantitative restrictions are certainly permitted, as Article 5 expressly provides for a number of specific disciplines concerning such restrictions in terms of quota allocation and quota modulation. The basic rule in the case of safeguards in the form of quantitative restrictions is that

> ...such a measure shall not reduce the quantity of imports below the level of a recent period which shall be the average of imports in the last three representative years for which statistics are available, unless clear justification is given that a different level is necessary to prevent or remedy serious injury.[82]

The overall quantity of imports that, at a minimum, should be allowed to enter the country is the average of the last three representative years for which statistics are available. If imports increased during the last three years from 100 tons over 150 tons to 200 tons in year three, at least 150 tons should be allowed to enter the country after imposition of a safeguard quota. There is of course a question about the meaning of the term "representative." It could be argued that, in the case of a sudden and sharp increase in imports in the last year of the period of investigation (the ideal safeguards situation, according to the Appellate Body), this last year was not "representative" of normal import volumes, but rather the result of some unforeseen developments. Excluding this last year from the representative period would, of course, have serious implications on the minimum amount of imports to be allowed into the country.

Restricting imports to a higher degree; in other words, imposing a quantitative restriction that lowers the amount of imports to below the average of the last three representative years for which statistics are available (in our example, anything below 150 tons, whether 120 tons, 50 tons, or 0 for that matter) is possible if a *clear justification* is given that such a different level is necessary to prevent or remedy serious injury.

[80] Or even by customary international law and the rules on state responsibility, as the Appellate Body seems to consider that nonattribution is really an expression of the principle of proportionality of countermeasures in public international law. See Appellate Body Report, *US – Line Pipe*, paras. 256–259.

[81] The Appellate Body in *Korea – Dairy* referred to three types, it seems, by way of example: quantitative restrictions, tariffs, and tariff rate quotas. Appellate Body Report, *Korea – Dairy*, para. 98. We discussed the various types of safeguard measures notified to the Committee on Safeguards at the beginning of this section.

[82] Article 5.1 of the SA.

(b) Quota Allocation and Quota Modulation

When safeguard measures are imposed in the form of quantitative restrictions, quotas, by virtue of Article 5.2(a) of the SA, shall be allocated to supplying members by reference to their *share* in the import market *during a previous representative period.*[83] Article 5.2(a) does not specify (contrary to what is the case in Article 5.1) that this representative period consist of the last three years. Any representative period will do, so it seems.[84] Essentially, although the idea is often expressed that safeguards must be imposed in a nondiscriminatory manner, what happens through the imposition of a safeguard in the form of a quota is that *historic* market shares are being *maintained* throughout the period when the safeguard is in place.[85]

In contrast, WTO Members can depart from the obligation to respect historic market shares in their import market and target the relatively more efficient sources of supply by allocating them quotas that are less than their market share as observed during the investigation period. This will be the case if certain WTO Members have increased their market share in the market of the Member imposing a safeguard in *disproportionate* quantities. This is what *quota modulation* under Article 5.2(b) of the SA amounts to.

Article 5.2(b) of the SA allows such quota modulation, in case a *clear demonstration* has been given to the Committee on Safeguards that:

(i) imports from certain Members have increased in disproportionate percentage in relation to the total increase of imports of the product concerned in the representative period;
(ii) the reasons for the departure from the historic patterns are justified; and
(iii) the conditions of such departure are equitable to all suppliers of the product concerned.[86]

It is noteworthy that the Agreement does not provide that the Committee has to *authorize* such a departure from historical patterns, but who can decide

[83] Actually, Article 5.2(a) first provides that the Member imposing the safeguard measure may seek agreement with respect to quota allocation with all other Members having a substantial interest in supplying the product concerned. It is, when this method is not reasonably practicable, that the Member imposing the Safeguards measure "shall allot... shares based upon the proportions supplied by such members during a previous representative period... due account being taken of any special factors which may have affected... the trade in the product." Article 5.2(a) of the SA.

[84] Article 5.2(a) of the SA does specify that an authority is to take "due account... of any special factors which may have affected... the trade in the product." This could be interpreted to use a "representative" period that does not include the most recent period of increased imports.

[85] For an interesting article on safeguards and nondiscrimination, see C. Bown and R. McCulloch, "Non-discrimination and the WTO Agreement on Safeguards," 2(3) *World Trade Review* 2003, 327–348.

[86] The duration of any such measure shall not be extended beyond the initial period of four years. Such targeted safeguard measures may only be used in case of a finding of current serious injury and not in the case of a threat of serious injury. Article 5.2(b) of the SA.

whether a clear demonstration has been given to the Committee: a Panel or the Committee itself? The answer is unclear.

(c) Measures Other than Quantitative Restrictions

It seems that the obligations discussed (of allowing a certain minimum amount of imports to enter the country and of respecting historical patterns) apply only in cases in which the safeguard measure takes the form of a quantitative restriction. They do not apply in cases of safeguard measures in the form of tariff increases or tariff quotas, which, according to the Panel on *US – Line Pipe*, are not a form of quotas/quantitative restrictions.[87] The only obligation in such cases is the one discussed earlier, of ensuring that the level of the tariff increase is not higher that the amount of injury caused by increased imports alone.

The MFN Application of Safeguards

Article 2.2 sets forth the important obligation that safeguard measures be imposed on the imported product "irrespective of its source." In other words, and different from the country-specific application of AD duties and CVD measures, safeguard measures are in principle imposed on an Most-Favored-Nation (MFN) basis. It is an all-or-nothing type of measure, taken in reaction to an increase in imports, from whatever source (and not imports from a particular country).[88]

In a number of cases involving the application of a safeguard measure by a member of a customs union or a free trade area, *in casu*, Argentina, as a member of MERCOSUR (Common Market of the South), and the United States, as a member of the North American Free Trade Agreement (NAFTA), the question of application of safeguard measures on an MFN basis was addressed. Both Argentina and the United States had excluded from the scope of their challenged safeguards measures imports from the other customs union/free trade area members.[89]

The special situation of a customs union or a free trade area as an area in which duties and other restrictive regulations of commerce are eliminated on substantially all the trade between the union or area members (as required by Article XXIV.8 of the GATT 1994) raises two questions: The first is whether members of such an area or union are *required to* impose safeguard measures on other area or union members because of the MFN requirement in Article 2.2 of the

[87] Panel Report, *US – Line Pipe*, para. 7.69.

[88] The accession of China to the WTO introduced a special country-specific safeguards regimen for imports of Chinese products, in the form of (i) a China-specific transitional safeguard and (ii) a textile-specific safeguard concerning Chinese textile products. These country-specific safeguards are based on China's Accession Protocol (WT/L/432) and the Report of the Working Party on the Accession of China (WT/MIN (01)/3).

[89] Although these cases thus involved free trade area members rather than members of a customs union, it appears that the relevant findings of the Panels and Appellate Body in these free trade area cases can be applied in a customs union context as well.

SA. A second question that arises is whether free trade area or customs union members are actually *allowed* under Article XXIV.8 of the GATT 1994 to impose such trade-restrictive measures as safeguard measures on each other. Of crucial importance in the discussion is the fact that the last sentence of Footnote 1 to the SA provides that "Nothing in this Agreement prejudges the interpretation of the relationship between Article XIX and paragraph 8 of Article XXIV of GATT 1994."

In the cases dealt with so far, the Appellate Body avoided answering these two questions by pointing to the particular facts of the cases and by applying the "parallelism principle." Both Argentina and the United States had included in their examination of *increased imports* and consequent *serious injury* imports from their customs union/free trade area partners. In so doing, Argentina and the United States were not allowed to subsequently exclude from the measure their customs union or free trade area partner imports. In *Argentina – Footwear (EC)*, the Appellate Body emphasized that it was not facing a situation in which a customs union applied a measure on behalf of a member of the customs union. Rather, an individual WTO Member, Argentina, which happened to be in a customs union, examined imports from all sources and was thus under Article 2.2 of the SA obliged to impose its safeguard measure on imports from all sources, including those from other MERCOSUR countries.[90]

What is of importance in these situations is that there exists a necessary parallelism between the imports examined and the imports covered by the measure. An authority that examines imports from *all* sources is precluded from applying the measure only to a *subset of such imports* examined (i.e., those of non-free trade area partners only).[91] In other words, such an authority is in any case behaving in an inconsistent manner.[92] Whether complying with the parallelism principle necessarily implies a WTO consistent measure, *ceteris paribus*,[93] is not

[90] Appellate Body Report, *Argentina – Footwear (EC)*, paras. 112–113. The Appellate Body did not consider whether Article XXIV of the GATT could be used as a defense to a violation of Article 2.2 of the SA, as Argentina did not argue before the Panel that Article XXIV of the GATT 1994 provided it with a defense to a finding of violation of a provision of the GATT 1994. Appellate Body Report, *Argentina – Footwear (EC)*, para. 110.

[91] The Appellate Body summarized its case law in the *US – Steel Safeguards* case. Appellate Body Report, *US – Steel Safeguards*, paras. 441–442.

[92] Appellate Body Report, *US – Wheat Gluten*, para. 96:

> In the usual course, therefore, the imports included in the determinations made under Articles 2.1 and 4.2 should correspond to the imports included in the application of the measure, under Article 2.2.

[93] The point is this: In all cases before the WTO so far, the authorities themselves started by including in the examination imports from their partners. They were then precluded from excluding such imports later without a new determination that the remaining imports alone satisfied the requirements of the Safeguards Agreement. However, no case addressed the question of whether, in case an authority decides not to apply the measure to its partners, and excludes their imports from the examination, such a measure would – assuming that the conditions for imposition of a measure are met by the remaining imports – necessarily be WTO consistent. In other words, we know what is not consistent, but we do not know yet for sure what is consistent.

clear from the Appellate Body's Reports, as the facts of the case examined in, for example, *Argentina – Footwear (EC)* did not require it to make such statements.[94]

However, it seems reasonable to extend the application of the parallelism principle to state that, in situations in which customs union or free trade area partner imports were excluded from the coverage of the examination, such imports may also be excluded from the coverage of the measure. This may be concluded on the basis of the fact that in *US – Wheat Gluten, US – Line Pipe,* and *US – Steel Safeguards,* the Appellate Body examined whether a reasoned and adequate explanation had been provided by the United States that imports other than those from NAFTA partners were causing serious injury to the domestic industry.[95]

It is important to recall that the parallelism principle, as discussed in the various cases mentioned, was clearly linked to the special case of free trade area partners or custom union members and the text of Footnote 1. It would not be correct to say that the Appellate Body was suggesting that any country could impose safeguard measures on a selective basis as long as there was a parallelism between the imports examined and the imports targeted in the measure. A safeguard measure is not an AD measure or a CVM. The question only arises because an argument could be made on the basis of Footnote 1 and the relationship between the Safeguards Agreement and Article XXIV of the GATT 1994 that it would be legitimate to exclude such free trade area/customs union partner imports. Similarly, the parallelism principle has been applied in one other situation in which the SA itself explicitly provides for an exception to the MFN principle of Article 2.2, the case of negligible imports from developing countries under Article 9. We refer to our discussion of this matter later in this chapter. In the absence of such an authorization from the SA itself or the GATT in general, there is no basis for not applying the measure on an MFN basis and the parallelism question thus does not even arise.

The response to the second and more fundamental question (i.e., "Are customs union members or free trade area partners even allowed to impose such trade-restrictive measures as safeguard measures on one another?") depends on the interpretation of the so-called *internal* requirement set forth in Article XXIV.8 of the GATT (e.g., the obligation for members of a customs union to liberalize substantially all trade among them, certain exceptions notwithstanding). Article XIX of the GATT does not feature in Article XXIV.8 of the GATT 1994 among the measures that can be exempted from this rule. The Panel in *Argentina – Footwear*

[94] Appellate Body Report, *Argentina – Footwear (EC)*, para. 114. Similarly, while summing up prior case law, the Appellate Body, in its report on *US – Line Pipe*, shied away from clarifying in more general terms the relationship between Article XXIV of the GATT and Article 2.2 of the SA and avoided directly addressing the issue. Appellate Body Report, *US – Line Pipe*, para. 198.

[95] Appellate Body Report, *US – Wheat Gluten*, para. 98; Appellate Body Report, *US – Line Pipe*, para. 188.

(EC) addressed the question and came to the conclusion that Article XXIV does not prohibit customs union members from imposing safeguard measures on each other.[96] On appeal, the Appellate Body reversed the Panel's ruling in this respect, as it was of the view that, in the absence of any Article XXIV defense by Argentina, the Panel was not justified in considering the relevance and scope of Article XXIV.[97] Nevertheless, the case law that requires a parallelism and thus also the application of safeguard measures on customs union or free trade area partners in case their imports were covered by the examination clearly indicates that to do so is not prohibited; quite the contrary, it seems.

In accordance with Article 9 of the SA, a safeguard measure is not to be applied against imports from developing country members in case their share of imports does not exceed 3 percent. In case there are several of such developing country members, safeguard measures may still be applied against such imports if the imports from these developing country members collectively account for more than 9 percent of total imports of the product concerned.

Similar to the views expressed regarding the possible exclusion of free trade area or customs union partners, in cases in which developing country imports are excluded from the measure, it must also be demonstrated that the imports that *are* covered by the measure, alone, in and of themselves, were sufficient to cause serious injury. In other words, if imports from developing countries are excluded on the basis of Article 9 of the SA, an authority must establish in a clear manner that imports from sources other than the excluded developing countries fulfilled all of the conditions for the imposition of a measure.[98]

The Duration of Safeguards

A safeguard measure can be imposed for an initial period of up to *four years* (Article 7.1 of the SA). It can be *extended for a maximum of four years more*, in case it has been determined that (a) the safeguard measure continues to be necessary to prevent or remedy serious injury, and (b) there is evidence that the industry is adjusting. Such an extended measure may not be more restrictive than it was at the end of the initial period.[99] In general, eight years is the maximum period for a safeguard measure (Article 7.3 of the SA), an exception being made for developing countries. A safeguard measure imposed by a developing country is allowed to stay in place for a maximum period of *ten* years.[100]

One might find it counterintuitive that safeguard measures will be imposed for a period longer than three years: In practice, as discussed later in text,

[96] Panel Report, *Argentina – Footwear (EC)*, para. 8.97.
[97] Appellate Body Report, *Argentina – Footwear (EC)*, para. 101.
[98] Appellate Body Report, *US – Steel Safeguard*, para. 472.
[99] Article 7.4 *in fine*.
[100] Article 9.2 of the SA.

no compensation is due when safeguards do not extend for three years, and there is no need for a review of the measure. This rule contrasts with the situation in the case of a safeguard measure of more than three years. In other words, the Member imposing a maximum three-year safeguard does not impose costs on other producers' interests,[101] because no compensation will be paid. This rule is all the more relevant given the fact that the WTO Member imposing a safeguard cannot choose the area where it will be paying compensation: *Affected* WTO Members might suspend concessions in fields of *their* interest; all they have to ensure is substantial equivalence between damage and concessions withdrawn.[102] Still, based on the notifications of safeguard measures to the Committee on Safeguards, we notice that, in fact, quite a number of safeguard measures are imposed for a period exceeding three years.[103]

Procedural Obligations

The Need to Conduct an Investigation

A WTO Member may apply a safeguard measure only following an investigation by the competent authorities of that Member pursuant to procedures previously established and made public.[104] As in the case of AD measures and CVMs, an investigation is required before a safeguard measure may be imposed.

As is the case with other instruments of contingent protection, *due process* considerations guide the investigation process. However, as will be shown in what immediately follows, *due process* types of clauses are far less ambitious in the context of the SA than are their counterparts in the context of the AD and SCM Agreements.

(a) Initiation

There is nothing in the SA relating to the pre-initiation phase. There is nothing subjecting the decision to initiate an investigation to certain procedural or substantive conditions. Unlike other contingent protection instruments, there is nothing like a distinction between *self-initiated* (*ex officio*) and *upon request* investigations. This does not mean that an investigation cannot be requested by a private party. The SA does not prejudge this issue.

[101] Consumer welfare will of course be negatively affected, because consumers will now have to pay a higher price for the good on which a safeguard has been in place. The relative importance of consumers' interests, however, has been weighed before the decision to take safeguards was taken (and obviously, set aside).

[102] Article 22 of the Dispute Settlement Understanding is legally irrelevant here, because there is no dispute between the parties. The *affected* Members are free to choose the sectors where they will impose countermeasures.

[103] See, for example, WTO Docs. G/SG/N/8/EEC/2, G/SG/N/10/EEC/2, and G/SG/N/11/EEC/2/Suppl. 1 of March 16, 2004.

[104] Article 3.1 of the SA.

In fact, the legislative requirements are the same irrespective of how an investigation has been initiated by a private party or *ex officio*. What is clear is that, contrary to the AD and SCM Agreements, there are no standing requirements reflected in the SA and no other threshold conditions that must be met for an investigation to be lawfully launched. It could be, for example, the case that one economic operator representing a minor proportion of the domestic industry requests initiation of investigation: An investigation *could* be launched, assuming the investigating authority agrees. That is, there is no need for *either* the private party *or* the investigating authority to show some preliminary evidence of increased imports resulting from unforeseen developments and causing injury to the domestic industry. It suffices that the investigating authority has decided to initiate the process.

The mere fact of initiating an investigation may have a trade-distorting effect, however. That is why, in the AD/CVD context, the requirements imposed on both applicants and the investigating authority to provide sufficient evidence to justify initiation and of sufficient support for an investigation are important in avoiding frivolous investigations. These rules play an essential role in maintaining the balance between the authorities' right to investigate and impose measures and the exporters' right to be able to trade without undue interference or harassment. Surprisingly hence, an instrument that is supposed to, in the words of the Appellate Body, combat *fair* trade and should be used in extraordinary circumstances only, is not associated with a legal framework that will impose stringent conditions on WTO Members wishing to avail themselves of this possibility.

(b) Article 3.1 and the General Due Process Requirement

The main, if not the only, due process provision of the SA is Article 3, which, unlike its counterparts in the AD Agreement or SCM Agreement, is of a general nature and lacks specification as to how the various due process obligations listed therein are to be complied with. Article 3.1 of the SA requires from an investigating authority of a WTO Member (a) to provide reasonable public notice to all interested parties; (b) to provide all such parties with the opportunity to present evidence and their views and to respond to the presentations of other parties; and (c) to publish a report setting forth their findings and reasoned conclusions reached on all pertinent issues of fact and law (Article 3.1 of the SA).[105] Article 3.2 of the SA incorporates the requirement to protect confidential information, a requirement which is similarly present in Article 6.5 of the AD Agreement and Article 12.4 of the SCM Agreement. Such confidential information may not be disclosed without the permission of the party submitting it.

Perhaps the most important procedural obligation is the requirement to provide reasoned conclusions reached on all pertinent issues of fact and law.

[105] The only other obligation is that Members conduct such safeguards investigations in accordance with procedures previously established and made public.

The absence of an explicit (in the sense of "clear and unambiguous") explanation of a pertinent issue of fact and law as, for example, the existence of unforeseen developments in the published report was considered WTO inconsistent by the Appellate Body.[106] For compliance with Article 3.1 of the SA to be achieved, a WTO Member must set forth findings and reasoned conclusions on *all* pertinent issues of facts and law because this is the only basis (along with requirements under Article 4 of the SA[107]) upon which Panels can base their findings.[108]

Publication and Notification

The SA does not impose any detailed *publication* requirements, so, whereas Articles 12 of the AD Agreement and 22 of the SCM Agreement contain specific obligations concerning public notice of the initiation of the investigation and the measures taken, both provisional and final, there is nothing of that kind in the SA. All that Article 3.1 of the SA requires is that the investigation shall include "reasonable public notice to all interested parties," and that the authorities "shall publish a report setting forth their findings and reasoned conclusions reached on all pertinent issues of fact and law." It does not in any way specify this obligation further.[109]

In contrast, a separate and important *notification* requirement is included in Article 12 of the SA, which requires that the WTO Committee on Safeguards be duly notified, in a timely manner. Assuming that a WTO Member wishes to initiate an investigation, it will have to notify the *Committee on Safeguards* of its decision (Article 12.1[a] of the SA). The same duty exists with respect to the decision to impose provisional measures, to impose or extend definitive measures, as well as to report all findings of injury or threat thereof caused by increased imports (Article 12.1[b] and [c]). The Appellate Body in *Korea – Dairy* agreed with the view of the Panel that the notification serves essentially a transparency and information purpose.[110]

The Price to Be Paid for a Safeguard – Balancing the Level of Concessions

Article 8 of the SA ensures that the overall *level of concessions* will not be altered as a result of a safeguard measure. It relevantly provides that, *before* imposing safeguard measures, the WTO Member will enter into negotiations

106 Appellate Body Report, *US – Steel Safeguards*, para. 297.

107 Article 4.2(c) of the SA has a much narrower scope compared to Article 3 of the SA, as it requires WTO Members to publish their findings on injury (or threat thereof).

108 Appellate Body Report, *US – Steel Safeguard*, para. 299.

109 There is, of course, a clear difference between notice *to interested parties* and *public* notice (i.e., to the public in general).

110 Appellate Body Report, *Korea – Dairy*, para. 111, referring to Panel Report, *Korea – Dairy*, para. 7.126.

with the affected Members, the object of which is to compensate through concessions in another product market for loss of market shares in the product market where a safeguard is being taken (Article 8.1 of the SA).[111] In other words, a Member imposing safeguard measures has to "pay" for offering this protection to its domestic industry. Such an obligation to compensate does not exist in other contingent protection instruments (neither in AD measures nor in CVMs).

Assuming that there is no agreement within 30 days between the *affected* WTO Member(s) and the Member proposing to impose the safeguard, the *affected* Member(s) can withdraw *substantially equivalent concessions or other obligations* under the GATT 1994, unless the Council for Trade in Goods (CTG) disapproves of such action.[112] It is highly unlikely, however, that the CTG will disapprove of such action because the *affected* Members will, in all likelihood, be blocking a consensus to this effect.[113]

In fact, the obligation to compensate can be avoided, however, if the WTO Member concerned proposes a safeguard action the maximum duration of which will not exceed three years. Article 8.3 provides that the right of suspension of an equivalent level of concessions by the affected members shall not be exercised for the first three years that a safeguard measure is in effect. The condition is that the measure (a) was taken as a result of an absolute increase in imports and (b) was taken in conformity with the provisions of the Agreement (Article 8.3 of the SA).

The obvious next question is, of course, "Who will determine whether the measure conforms with the provisions of the SA?" In other words, can an affected Member suspend an equivalent level of concessions effective from the moment of imposition of the measure, unilaterally determining that the measure does not conform with the provisions of the SA? This approach would in effect force the Member taking the safeguards action to establish before a WTO Panel that its measure conforms with the SA and thus that the suspension of concessions during the first three years was illegitimate. The other possibility, and the one followed in practice, is that an affected Member first suspends an equivalent level of concessions to then suspend its suspension, while bringing a case before the

[111] Hence the importance of the notification requirement under Article 12.3 of the SA, which will form the basis for any meaningful consultations under Article 8.1. See Panel Report, *US – Wheat Gluten*, para. 8.206.

[112] Article 8.2 of the SA. This provision further states that a Member should do this, at the latest, ninety days following imposition of the measure. It must give the Committee thirty days to disapprove the proposed suspension. So it seems that a Member has to announce its suspension, at the latest, sixty days following application of the safeguard measure.

[113] This might give the *affected* Members the incentive to overshoot their injury. The tables will now be turned, and this time it is the Member imposing the safeguard that will feel affected by the amount of countermeasures imposed against it. In such a case, it can only initiate dispute settlement proceedings against the Member(s) imposing countermeasures. Assuming that overshooting takes place, it might provide the Member imposing the safeguard with a disincentive to do so. Article 8.1 of the SA seems to have been drafted in a sloppy manner because it can be abused in both directions.

WTO to establish the lack of conformity of the safeguard measure with the SA. This is what happened, for example, in the *US – Steel Safeguards* case.[114] When a finding of inconsistency would be obtained from the WTO, the affected Member would reactivate the suspension of an equivalent level of concessions. In this case, however, the United States repealed the steel safeguard shortly after the Appellate Body issued its ruling, and even before the DSB had had a chance to adopt the report.[115] The announced countermeasures were abandoned shortly thereafter.

The Elimination of Measures Having Equivalent Effect – No Grey Area Measures

Article XIX of the GATT and Article 2.2 of the SA (as of the advent of the WTO) request WTO Members to apply safeguard measures irrespective of their origin. Hence, the WTO regime does not allow interested states to *target* particular exporters (sources of supply). This regime was perceived as quite inflexible by countries interested in targeting specific sources of supply. Hence, as was explained earlier, a practice parallel to that of safeguards developed in the 1970s and 1980s was that some GATT Contracting Parties, upon request, would agree to limit their export toward particular destinations. This is how the notorious *voluntary export restraints* (VERs) saw the light of day. A VER is not a formal treaty; it is, in practice, a unilateral reduction of exports.[116]

The legality of VERs was not formally tested by a GATT Panel.[117] There were admittedly few, if any, incentives to mount a legal challenge: The requesting state would not normally be attacking a practice it requested, and the country limiting its exports was adjusting itself in a comfortable second-best position, whereby it could capture monopoly rents while rethinking its output strategies. The absence of a formal condemnation notwithstanding, a series of good arguments could be advanced in support of the opinion that they violate both Article XI of the GATT (because they effectively amount to a quantitative restriction) and Article XIX of the GATT (in light of their discriminatory character).

Article 11.2 of the SA put an end to this discussion, as far as its legal dimension is concerned, by outlawing recourse to VERs: A Member shall not seek, take,

[114] Actually, the EC first published a list of products on which additional duties were going to be levied as of the third birthday of the U.S. Safeguard Measure, or the fifth day following the date of a decision by the WTO Dispute Settlement Body that the measure is incompatible with the WTO Agreement, if that is earlier. Council regulation (EC) No. 131/2002 of June 13, 2002.

[115] The measures were repealed on December 4, 2003, whereas the reports were adopted by the DSB on December 10, 2003 only. The EC repealed its planned countermeasures on December 12, 2003. See Council Regulation (EC) 2168/2003 of December 12, 2003.

[116] The reduction, of course, would not take place absent a request to this effect.

[117] Although the Panel Report *Japan – Trade in Semiconductors* faced facts that closely resemble a VER.

or maintain any VERs, orderly marketing arrangements, or any other similar measures on the export or the import side.[118]

Conclusions

The goal of this chapter was to give an overview of the provisions of this Agreement and its interpretation by WTO Panels and the Appellate Body. As noted on a couple of occasions, this Agreement has certain shortcomings. The Appellate Body's jurisprudence has not contributed much to rectifying these shortcomings. To the contrary, on certain occasions it has confused matters even further.

First, the Agreement sets forth the conditions for a lawful imposition of a safeguard measure but does not address two elements that were clearly present in Article XIX of the GATT (i.e., unforeseen developments and tariff concessions) as preconditions for the imposition of safeguard measures. This is not to say that the Appellate Body was right in re-introducing these conditions. The Appellate Body actually only contributed to the problem by adding "unforeseen developments" to the list of conditions of Article 2, but then failing to explain what those developments could be, or by whom and at what time they had to be unforeseen. Nevertheless, it is an important oversight of the Agreement because these "forgotten conditions" may have an important role to play in solving what has been exposed as another problem of this Agreement: the need to demonstrate that increased imports are causing serious injury. As argued convincingly in the economic literature, imports can never be the ultimate cause of injury, as they are a mere reaction to the forces of supply and demand. They can perhaps constitute the proximate cause, the ultimate cause being the granting of a tariff concession or some other, unforeseen, exogenous variable.

Second, the Agreement does not contain many of the important due process provisions of other trade remedies instruments such as the AD Agreement or the SCM Agreement. These procedural obligations play an important role in the AD and CVD context in ensuring an investigation that is as transparent, objective, and fair as possible. The Appellate Body intervened to give more body to the SA in this respect. It showed a great willingness to conclude a lot from very little, incorporating almost all of the procedural safeguards of the AD/SCM Agreements into the one paragraph of the SA dealing with the investigation. Its contribution in this respect was welcome.

Third, the Agreement fails to explain in a satisfactory manner what a situation of serious injury is and in which way it differs from the material injury standard in the AD/CVD context. Although the Appellate Body emphasized the exceptional emergency nature of these measures, it unfortunately failed to give specific meaning to these terms.

[118] Article 11.1(b) of the SA.

Fourth, the Appellate Body has turned one of the more innocent provisions of this Agreement into an important limitation on the level of any safeguard measure by limiting the level of the safeguard to that part of the injury caused by increased imports in isolation from other factors. It is noteworthy that the Appellate Body, in the context of a causation and nonattribution analysis, had been lenient in requiring the authority merely to separate and distinguish the injury caused by other factors to examine whether imports contributed to the situation of serious injury. However, when dealing with the question of the application of the measures, the Appellate Body unexpectedly became very demanding. In other words, the Appellate Body seemed willing to take a more deferential approach when it came to the question of whether a right to impose a measure existed, while being more demanding with respect to the lawful application of such a measure. One may wonder whether this is the correct approach. The explanation offered by the Appellate Body and its erroneous reading of the AD/CVD parallel provisions are hardly convincing.

In sum, given these shortcomings, and in light of the controversial Appellate Body jurisprudence in the safeguards area, it is unfortunate that the Safeguards Agreement does not form part of the Doha mandate, and that we will have to live with this Agreement for many years to come. It remains to be seen whether the result of all this may not be a return of the "grey area measures" of the 1970s and 1980s. To be continued...

MARCO BRONCKERS

10.1 *Nondiscrimination in the World Trade Organization Safeguards Agreement: A European Perspective*

This chapter submits that the arguments that have traditionally been advanced in favor of a nondiscriminatory application of safeguard measures are not convincing within the regime of the World Trade Organization (WTO) Safeguards Agreement (SA). Furthermore, if selective safeguards were plainly accepted in this Agreement, it would no longer be necessary to design country-specific mechanisms, such as the China-specific safeguard clause. In the 1970s and 1980s, the European Community (EC) was a major proponent of selective safeguards. However, with the advent of the WTO SA, the EC seems to have lost interest in taking safeguards. This situation may change, when the European Union (EU) Reform Treaty (the Lisbon Treaty) enters into force, and the European Parliament for the first time will obtain important powers in EU trade policy.

This chapter accompanies Jasper Wauters's splendid overview of the WTO SA. He has packed a lot of punch in a few pages. His chapter not only contains an excellent description of the WTO safeguards law as it stands, but it also highlights some important developments in the case law that offer food for thought.

Nondiscrimination

During the 1970s and 1980s, at the time of the General Agreement on Tariffs and Trade (GATT), there had been much debate as to whether safeguards could be applied "selectively" – that is, to only those countries that were held responsible for disrupting the domestic market of an importing country. When the negotiations on safeguards were concluded at the end of the Uruguay Round, there seemed to be agreement that safeguard measures had to be applied on a Most-Favored-Nation (MFN) basis. A selective safeguard was only envisaged in the transitional WTO Agreement on Textiles and Clothing (which applied from 1995 through 2004).[1] Yet, according to the general WTO SA, safeguard measures

[1] See Article 6.4 of the WTO ATC.

The author appreciates the comments he received from Lothar Ehring on an earlier draft.

must be imposed on an imported product "irrespective if its source."[2] Wauters does not investigate whether that provision makes sense,[3] and it is this question I want to look at a bit more closely.

In addressing this question, I confess to a personal interest. When I joined the European Commission's Legal Service as a young intern in 1981, I learned that one of the EC's negotiating aims in reforming the GATT was to obtain the possibility of applying safeguard measures selectively, and I was assigned the task of investigating how this could be legally defended. The topic fascinated me, and ultimately became the subject of my PhD dissertation.[4] Revisiting this old battleground now, I am struck by a couple of things.

Given that the WTO SA stipulates that safeguard measures must be imposed on an imported product "irrespective of its source," the EC seems to have lost the battle on selectivity. Or did it? The first observation to be made is that the WTO SA continues to allow Members to impose safeguards by way of quantitative restrictions. It is difficult to reconcile the precepts of nondiscrimination with quantitative restrictions. Unless one allocates quota shares through auctions, the distribution of quotas usually ends up discriminating against the most efficient suppliers. This is a point I made when looking at the practice under Article XIX of the GATT.[5] It has been confirmed through empirical research of safeguard measures taken since the entry into force of the WTO SA.[6] Moreover, the WTO Agreement goes one more step down the path of discrimination in cases in which the importing Member shows that "imports from certain Members have increased in disproportionate percentage in relation to the total increase of imports of the product concerned." In those cases, quotas can be "modulated" to target imports from the country deemed to be the most distorting.[7]

Accordingly, the position that the WTO Agreement maintains the MFN application of safeguard measures appears to be a sleight of hand. As long as safeguards formally cover imports "from every source," the importing country can select its targets and effectively discriminate. Thus, the most efficient importers are not protected by this MFN rule. In addition, within the context of the present WTO Agreement, the MFN rule also fails to deliver on the other, more important objective originally ascribed to it by its defenders in the 1970s and 1980s. That objective was to deter countries from taking safeguard measures to begin with.[8]

[2] See Article 2.2 of the WTO SA.

[3] See Wauters, at §§ 68–77.

[4] Bronckers, "Selective Safeguard Measures in Multilateral Trade Relations: Issues of Protectionism" in *GATT, European Community and United States Law* (Kluwer, 1985).

[5] Ibid., 20–24, 58–63, 83–84.

[6] See Brown and McCulloch, "Nondiscrimination and the WTO Agreement on Safeguards," 2(3) *World Trade Review* 2003, 327.

[7] See Article 5.2(b) of the WTO SA. Wauters mentions this possibility in a different section of his article, at §§ 63–66.

[8] Bronckers, *supra* note, at 69–70.

Under the GATT's original safeguard clause, Article XIX, countries resorting to safeguard measures had to pay compensation to all affected suppliers.[9] Accordingly, the thought was that countries would think twice before imposing a safeguard as they would realize that this was going to be expensive because of the compensation claims (or retaliation rights) of all these countries. What happened, in fact, was that countries increasingly ignored the escape clause and resorted to bilateral "grey area measures" (such as voluntary export restraints) so as to escape all these compensation claims.

The negotiators of the WTO SA tried to put some order into this messy situation and bring Members back into the fold of the multilateral system. On the one hand, they strengthened the WTO safeguards regime. They prohibited grey area measures.[10] They introduced floor levels below which imports ought not be cut whenever a quantitative restriction was used.[11] They stipulated that provisional safeguard measures could only take the form of tariffs,[12] and they limited the duration of safeguard measures.[13] On the other hand, they relaxed certain requirements of Article XIX of the GATT. For example, some people, including myself, thought that part of this grand bargain was that the "unforeseen developments" requirement of Article XIX had been dropped.[14] However, as Jasper Wauters recalls, the Appellate Body opined differently and revived this requirement, yet without specifying what it is supposed to mean.[15]

Another requirement that was indisputably relaxed was the obligation for the importing country to pay compensation to affected suppliers. At least if the safeguard meets certain conditions (i.e., is otherwise WTO-compatible, does not last longer than three years, and follows an absolute increase in imports), compensation is no longer due.[16] Now consider again the second objective ascribed to the MFN obligation as it applies to safeguards: deterring countries from imposing safeguard measures as they realize that they will have to pay a lot of compensation. This logic no longer applies to the extent that the compensation obligation has disappeared from the WTO SA.

Expressed differently, within the context of the present SA, the MFN rule does not live up to its expectations. It does not protect the most efficient suppliers, given that quantitative restrictions, and even modulated quotas, are allowed.

[9] See Article XIX.1(b) of the GATT.

[10] See Article 11.1 of the WTO SA.

[11] See Article 5.1 of the WTO SA.

[12] See Article 6 of the WTO SA.

[13] See Article 7 of the WTO SA.

[14] Bronckers, "Voluntary Export Restraints and the New GATT Safeguards Agreement," in Bourgeois, Berrod, and Gippini-Fournier (Eds.), *The Uruguay Round Results: A European Lawyer's Perspective* (Brussels, European Interuniversity Press, 1995), 273,275.

[15] Wauters, §§ 17–19. I do not agree with Wauters that the drafters of the WTO Agreement committed an "oversight" by not explaining what the "unforeseen developments" requirement is supposed to mean. More likely, the drafters saw no need to provide such explanation as they felt they had deleted the "unforeseen developments" requirement from WTO safeguards law. See Wauters, § 97.

[16] See Article 8.3 of the WTO SA.

It does not operate as much of a deterrent to the imposition of safeguards as the obligation to compensate exporting countries has largely disappeared.

One counter might be that even a formal MFN rule ensures that many countries will, if only mildly, be affected by a safeguard, so that all of them may have sufficient interest to challenge a safeguard in WTO dispute-settlement proceedings. This combined interest to litigate, in turn, could operate as some deterrent to the imposition of safeguard measures. In support of this conjecture, one might cite the example of the safeguards imposed by the United States on imports of steel in 2002, which provoked a spate of legal challenges in the WTO.[17] I do not find this comeback convincing. Even if the MFN rule might have some such effect, it could only deter the imposition of safeguards that are WTO-illegal, and there is no immediate reason why the regular dispute settlement system would not suffice to combat WTO-illegal safeguard measures. Accordingly, safeguards need not be singled out and endowed with additional protection (e.g., an incentive for collective dispute settlement action through the MFN rule).[18]

In sum, the MFN rule in the WTO SA is in need of justification – or an overhaul. This demand is not just theoretical. The absence of a justification puts into a different light, for instance, the difficult negotiations on a selective safeguard with new Members joining the WTO, such as China in the recent past.[19] Creating different norms for only some Members understandably provokes their resistance and lingering resentment. A lot of political acrimony might have been (and might still be) avoided if no separate safeguard mechanism would need to be maintained in respect of certain new Members because selective safeguard measures would be admitted under the SA.

Wauters does engage with another controversy on discrimination, which currently attracts more attention, as to whether imports from free trade agreement partners can be excluded from a global safeguard measure. This debate was also played out in the 1980s. In those days the EC, both in policy documents as well as through actual measures, took the position that it could exclude preferential trading partners from global safeguard measures taken under Article XIX of the GATT. Other countries, like Norway, took a position similar to that of the

[17] Eight WTO members challenged the U.S. safeguards on steel: Brazil, China, EC, Japan, Korea, New Zealand, Norway, and Switzerland. See WTO Appellate Body Report, *US – Definitive Safeguard Measures on Steel* (November 10, 2003).

[18] Of course, the fact that WTO dispute settlement takes several years and that rulings have no retroactive effect creates a particular problem for safeguard measures that last no more than three years. See Ahn, "Restructuring the WTO Safeguard System," in Matsushita, Ahn, and Chen (Eds.), *The WTO Trade Remedy System: East Asian Perspectives* (Cameron May, London, 2006), 11–31. Those measures cannot be properly disciplined through WTO dispute settlement. However, adding multiple complainants by requiring safeguards to be applied on an MFN basis does not improve this situation.

[19] See Bronckers, "The Special Safeguard Clause in respect of China: (How) Will It Work?" in Matsushita, and Ahn (Eds.), *WTO and East Asia: New Perspectives* (Cameron May, London, 2004), 39–50.

EC, and exempted their partners in preferential trade agreements from safeguard measures with an appeal to Article XXIV of the GATT. Furthermore, the EC and others believed that any safeguards it imposed on its preferential partners did not need to be extended to other GATT Contracting Parties through a more global measure notified under Article XIX of the GATT. These views were never challenged in GATT dispute-settlement proceedings.[20] Having concluded no free trade agreements at the time, the United States did not seem particularly interested in these questions.[21]

Let us turn to the present and inquire where WTO law stands. Jasper concludes rather summarily that, if customs and free trade area partners were not included in the importing country's safeguard investigation, they can also be excluded from the coverage of a safeguard measure that applies to other WTO members.[22] This view, which has been expressed by others as well,[23] does not go unchallenged.[24] Although not yet authoritatively decided by the Appellate Body, Jasper also submits that it is not inconsistent with Article XXIV for countries to impose – discriminatory – safeguard measures on their free trade agreement partners. Again, this view has been disputed,[25] but I do note that if Jasper's views are ultimately upheld, the EC will have obtained virtually all of its negotiating demands, which it formulated in the late 1970s and early 1980s, on the issue of selective safeguards. Patience pays, also in international trade relations. Or does it?

The EC's Current Position on Safeguards

Intriguingly, although it seems to be on a winning streak, the EC appears to have lost interest in taking safeguard measures.[26] If anything, rather than

20 See, for example, GATT Panel Report, *Norway – Restrictions on Imports of Certain Textile Products,* 27th Supp. BISD 119, at § 14(a) (1981).

21 Bronckers, *supra* note, at 86–87. The United States concluded its first free trade agreement, with Israel, in 1985. A free trade agreement with Canada followed in 1989, which was combined with NAFTA in 1994. The United States only accelerated its free trade agreement negotiations from 2000 onward.

22 Wauters, § 73.

23 See Pauwelyn, "The Puzzle of WTO Safeguards and Regional Trade Agreements," 7(1) *Journal of International Economic Law* 2004, 109, 137 note 60.

24 See Ahn, "Foe or Friend of GATT Article XXIV: Diversity in Trade Remedy Rules," 11(1) *Journal of International Economic Law* 2008, 107.

25 See, generally, Estrella, and Horlick, "Mandatory Abolition of Anti-dumping, Countervailing Duties and Safeguards in Customs Union and Free Trade Areas Constituted between WTO Members: Revisiting a Long-Standing Discussion in Light of the Appellate Body's Turkey–Textiles Ruling, in Bartels, and Ortino (Eds.), *Regional Trade Agreements and the WTO Legal System* (Oxford University Press, 2006), 109–148 (arguing that all trade remedy measures must be abolished in free trade agreements).

26 See the recent statistics on safeguard measures published by the WTO Secretariat on November 7, 2007, http://www.wto.org/english/tratop_e/safeg_e/safeg_e.htm.

imposing safeguards itself, the EC's policy seems to be to attack safeguard measures and to constrain their use by other Members. What happened? Does the EC not realize that it (almost) got what it wanted?

The EC trade policy makers may or may not realize that they are close to obtaining the goals they originally set for themselves,[27] but they have become mired in other complications. Internal decision-making procedures make it difficult for the EC to actually impose safeguard measures. Under EC law, safeguards are treated differently than antidumping (AD) and countervailing duty (CVD) measures. To begin with, private parties have no right to petition the European Commission for safeguards. They have to pass through an EC Member State, which has to put a request to the European Commission.[28] This is a considerable deterrent. The subsequent procedural steps do not make things easier.

If the European Commission were to impose a provisional or definitive safeguard, any Member State can refer this measure to the Council of Ministers. If the Council does not confirm the Commission's measure by qualified majority within three months, the Commission's measure expires.[29] Given the diverging economic and geopolitical interests of the Member States, which invariably come into play when the EC is to take a controversial trade policy measure, this decision-making process puts an effective brake on EC safeguard measures. In contrast, in AD and countervailing investigations, the Commission can take provisional measures as well, and its proposal for definitive measures to the Council becomes law *unless* a majority of the Council opposes the Commission's proposal.[30] This arrangement is conducive to the EC taking trade remedy measures, as it puts the Commission in the driver's seat – although this arrangement does not stop the Council from trying to unseat the Commission in politically sensitive cases.[31] Accordingly, whenever possible, the EC Commission seeks to transform safeguard action into AD or, to a far lesser extent, CVD measures.[32]

27 In its third-party submission in one case, the EC seemed to be backtracking from its original position, when criticizing the exclusion of NAFTA imports from a U.S. safeguard measure. See WTO Appellate Body Report, *US – Safeguards on Line Pipe from Korea*, at § 66 (February 15, 2002). However, this seems to be an isolated incident that does not reflect current policy.

28 See Article 16.1 of the Council Regulation 3285/94, OJ 1994 L349/1 (as subsequently amended).

29 Ibid.

30 See Article 9.4 of the Council Regulation 384/96, OJ 1996 L 56/1 (as subsequently amended).

31 For example, see Council Regulation 1472/2006, imposing a definitive antidumping duty on imports of certain footwear originating in the People's Republic of China and Vietnam, OJ 2006 L 275/1 (where, to avoid a reversal by the Council, the Commission reduced the initial duration of the antidumping measure to two years).

32 See, for example, the definitive safeguard measure on imports of farmed salmon imposed by the Commission on February 4, 2005, OJ 2005 L 33/8, which the Commission revoked already a few months later, on April 22, 2005, when it imposed provisional antidumping measures on imports of farmed salmon from Norway. See Commission Regulation 627/2005, OJ 2005 L104/4; definitive antidumping measures on salmon from Norway were imposed by Council Regulation 85/2006, OJ 2006 L 15/1.

The EC's previous interest in selective safeguards, in the 1970s and 1980, dates from a time when the European Commission (and some of the Member States) bypassed these internal decision-making constraints in EC safeguards law by negotiating VERs and other grey area measures directly with exporting countries. The frequent target in those days was Japan[33]; China had not yet become the trading force it is today. However, when the WTO SA outlawed these grey area measures in 1994,[34] the EC was confined to its formal decision-making processes regarding the imposition of safeguard measures. The essential features of this machinery (i.e., no private petition right, automatic expiry of Commission measures when referred to the Council, and not adopted by qualified majority) were never changed, perhaps because of a desire among the more liberal Member States to maintain these obstacles so as to forestall an all-too-easy slide of the EC toward protectionism.

Interestingly, these liberal Member States seem to have had insufficient faith that the multilateral constraints imposed by the WTO SA could have achieved the same objective. Rather than relying on third countries to push back on unwarranted safeguards from the EC, the liberal EC Member States seem to have preferred maintaining internal constraints. Having thereby rendered EC safeguards law by and large ineffective, these Member States also contributed to an informal policy choice of the EC in recent years to attack the safeguard measures of other countries.

The outlook for EC safeguards law may change though. As a result of the new European Reform Treaty (the Lisbon Treaty), the European Parliament for the first time is to acquire co-decision-making powers in the area of international trade.[35] What this implies for the direction of EC trade policy remains to be seen, but it seems a fair guess that the formulation of EC trade policy will become less technocratic and more politicized. Industries and other constituents will have more outlets to exercise their political clout. They may well ask, more insistently than they were able to do in the past, why it is that the EC offers them fewer effective trade remedies than competing industries in other major trading partners, like the United States. If one follows this scenario, it is not inconceivable that the EC may soon renew its interest in safeguard measures, selectively applied.

33 See Bronckers, "A Legal Analysis of Protectionist Measures Affecting Japanese Imports into the European Community – Revisited," in Völker (Ed.), *Protectionism and the European Community* (2nd ed., Kluwer, 1987), 57, 69–82.

34 See, *supra*, note.

35 See Article 188C EC (Lisbon version), replacing Article 133 EC (Nice version).

KAMAL SAGGI

10.2 *The Agreement on Safeguards: Does It Raise More Questions Than It Answers?*

ABSTRACT. This chapter argues that, although the economic rationale underlying the Safeguards Agreement (SA) is sound, the same cannot be said about the structure of the agreement and its subsequent interpretation by the Appellate Body. In fact, the SA appears to be fraught with ambiguity, and its insistence that safeguards be used when imports are an unforeseen cause of injury to domestic industry appears to be misguided in two key respects. First, at a conceptual level, it seems difficult to see how one could ever convincingly establish that a given surge in imports was unforeseen in the past. Second, the notion of a causal link between imports and injury is devoid of economic logic: Domestic production and imports of like goods are jointly determined in the marketplace, and it makes little sense to attribute a reduction in domestic output to an increase in imports.

In his insightful chapter, Jasper Wauters (2010) provides a comprehensive overview of the SA. The chapter is well written and clear, and I have learned much from reading it. The following comments draw extensively upon Wauters's analysis, and my contribution, if any, lies in providing further critical discussion of the economics underlying some of the issues raised in his chapter. Furthermore, my comments focus mainly on the key conditions under which safeguards are permitted, and the reader is referred to Wauters (2009) for a detailed discussion of other aspects of the agreement. In a nutshell, I shall argue that, whereas the economic rationale underlying the SA is sound, the same cannot be said about the structure of the agreement and its subsequent interpretation by the Appellate Body. I begin by reviewing the basic economic rationale underlying the use of safeguards and then critically discuss some key aspects of the SA.

Given that multilateral trade liberalization is the *raison d'etre* of the World Trade Organization (WTO), the existence of the General Agreement on Tariffs and Trade (GATT) Article XXIX and the SA raises a fundamental question: Why should a system the major stated goal of which is to liberalize world trade permit temporary protectionist measures? From an economic perspective, the basic justification for the SA (and GATT Article XXIX) is captured clearly in the following passage from Dam (1970):

> "...a system that made withdrawals of concessions impossible would tend to discourage the making of concessions in the first place. It is better, for example, that 100 commitments should be made and that 10 should be withdrawn than that only 50 commitments should be made and that all of them should be kept."

Thus, safeguards act as a safety valve: They allow a country to temporarily undo a previously granted concession to protect domestic industry from "fair" foreign competition (in contrast to antidumping [AD] duties and countervailing duties [CVDs] that are to be used in case of "unfair" foreign competition). From this perspective, one should expect a government to use safeguards in those states of the world in which maintaining previously granted trade concessions becomes too costly in political economy terms. Knowing that such problematic states can arise in the future, countries may be unwilling to grant certain types of concessions if they lack access to a safety valve.

The basic economic principle underlying this *ex ante* rationale for safeguards is relevant under a variety of circumstances. For example, when faced with strict labor regulations that make it extremely difficult to lay off workers during adverse times, employers will typically decide to hire fewer workers to avoid being stuck with a large wage bill and/or idle workers. Similarly, when faced with irreversible costs of entry, potential entering and existing firms in an industry may exercise an optimal degree of inertia – those inside may be hesitant to exit and those outside may be reluctant to enter. However, as Mavroidis (2007) astutely notes, the need for some sort of a safety valve or an escape clause does *not* imply that Article XXIX of the GATT or the SA deal with this need in an efficient manner.

According to the text of the SA and its subsequent interpretation by the Appellate Body, for a country to be able to use safeguards, four key conditions have to be met: (i) there should have been a recent, sudden, and sharp increase in imports; (ii) domestic industry should have either suffered serious injury or been faced with the threat of serious injury; (iii) the injury itself should have been caused by the increase in imports; and (iv) the increase in imports must have been a result of unforeseen developments. Before further consideration of each of these four conditions, it is worth noting that, although the notion of unforeseen developments was an integral part of Article XXIX of the GATT, it does not appear in the text of SA and has found its way back into the process because of the manner in which the Appellate Body has interpreted the SA.

Consider condition (i) first. Little reflection reveals that even this seemingly straightforward condition is fraught with ambiguity: How much of an increase in imports should be considered sharp? Who determines whether the increase was sudden? And how can anyone determine that something is "sudden" without knowledge of past expectations? Although it may be too much to expect the SA or the Appellate Body to provide concrete answers to such questions, they do help highlight a general problem: By its very design, the SA tries to deal with a quantitative issue in purely qualitative terms. This tendency to shy away from quantification has created confusion and doubt regarding circumstances under which countries can legally use safeguards, and this may be one reason why they are not used frequently.

On first glance, the injury criterion specified in condition (ii) seems simple enough. After all, whether a certain domestic industry is going through a troubled phase ought to be relatively easy to determine – a variety of economic indicators such as sales, profits, investment, and employment can help make such a determination. However, deciding that a domestic industry has suffered *serious* injury is a much more complicated and ambiguous matter. For starters, how much reduction in local profits and/or sales constitutes serious injury? The problem is compounded by the fact that the SA allows the threat of injury to substitute for actual injury. Perhaps the justification for this is that if safeguard action is taken early or as a preventive measure, the trade policy measures required may be less restrictive and the duration for which they have to be implemented might be shorter. Such justification has to be balanced against the potential for misuse as well as nonuse that ambiguity necessarily creates.

Perhaps the causation condition is the one that irks economists the most. The problem is quite simply stated: Domestic production and imports of like or directly competitive products are jointly determined in the marketplace, and it makes no economic sense to say that an increase in imports can "cause" domestic injury. Imports can increase because of a variety of changes in domestic or world market conditions. For example, there could be a decrease in price abroad or an improvement in quality of foreign products. Alternatively, domestic industry might be faced with adverse macroeconomic conditions that lower aggregate consumer demand. Of course, such domestic and foreign forces can be at work simultaneously. The key point is that, quite often, changes that lead to an increase in imports of a given product will occur in conjunction with a decline in sales of competing or substitutable domestic products. Such correlation surely should not be confused with causation. Although the Appellate Body has acknowledged the distinction between correlation and causation, it has implied that the two generally go hand in hand. It has further noted that imports need not be the sole cause of serious injury; they only need to have contributed to such injury. Pushing this logic further leads one back to an issue raised earlier: How does one isolate the relative contributions of domestic and foreign factors to injury without conducting a quantitative analysis? Such quantification appears essential for the matter at hand but is somehow not required. Note also that determining the role of domestic and foreign *factors* is quite distinct from the view that imports can somehow cause injury – this view implicitly acknowledges that something *other than* imports is the ultimate cause of domestic injury.

The causation criticism, although important for its own sake, also has a useful policy implication. For domestic policies to appropriately target the problem at hand, a proper determination of why a domestic industry is suffering is essential. Without an accurate diagnosis of the problem, what hope is there of implementing the correct policy response? For example, the real cause of injury might be inadequate investment in research and development by domestic industry (which may also result from the moral hazard that safeguards create), it might be the case that the domestic exchange rate has become overvalued, making imports cheaper, or it simply might be that the long run pattern of comparative advantage has shifted permanently against domestic industry and the only reason to protect it is to ease the transition path (i.e., slow down its inevitable decline). One does not have to be a professional economist to see that the optimal policy response varies across these scenarios. Simply saying that imports "caused" the injury not only makes little sense, it does nothing to help identify the true underlying problem and the appropriate policy response.

Consider now the notion of "unforeseen developments." As Mavroidis (2007) notes, Dam's often-cited rationale for safeguards does not make any reference to unforeseen developments. This is just as well because it appears to be an impossible criterion to satisfy and its inclusion in the SA is perhaps a key reason that the present situation with respect to safeguards at the WTO has become a "mess" (Sykes, 2003). The rather slippery notion of unforeseen developments raises some fundamental questions [most of which Wauters (2009) discusses in detail]: Unforeseen by whom? At what time? How does one verify today that something was unforeseen in the past? Although partial answers to such questions can be provided, it seems fair to say that the inclusion of this condition creates more problems than it solves. One can only wonder why the Appellate Body found it necessary to reintroduce this condition given that it was explicitly dropped during the negotiations that led to the SA.

To conclude, although a sound economic rationale for the use of safeguards certainly exists, the structure of the SA (and its subsequent interpretation) is rather puzzling. Overall, the system does not appear to be working too well, and it is unclear if it can be fixed easily because some fundamental, and perhaps unanswerable, challenges confront the SA. For example, the Appellate Body's insistence on the condition that imports should have increased as a result of unforeseen developments certainly does not appear to have helped matters. It is difficult to understand how one could ever prove that something was unforeseen in the past. Similarly, the notion of a causal link between imports and injury really does not have a leg to stand on: Imports and domestic production of like goods are simultaneously determined in the global market place. It also seems difficult to justify a blanket policy of allowing safeguards for a three-year period without compensating exporters. For example, why should the duration for which safeguards are permitted for manufacturing be the same as that for agriculture? A bad weather shock can be reversed the next season whereas the long-term decline of an industry might require a longer response period. Given that the duration of protection required is likely to be context specific, it might be useful to allow the duration of safeguards to be a part of the initial negotiations between concerned parties. Such inclusion has the potential to deliver a more efficient package of safeguards: By being able to optimize both the level and the duration of protection, an injured party might be able to provide the desired level of relief to domestic industry while inflicting less harm on exporters (who in turn ought to be less inclined to raise a challenge at the WTO).

REFERENCES

Dam, K. 1970. *The GATT: Law and International Economic Organization.* Chicago: University of Chicago Press.

Mavroidis, P. 2007. *Trade in Goods.* New York: Oxford University Press.

Sykes, A. 2003. The Safeguards Mess: A Critique of WTO Jurisprudence. *World Trade Review* 3:216–296.

Wauters, J. 2010. "The Safeguards Agreement – An Overview," this volume.

MEREDITH A. CROWLEY

11 Why Are Safeguards Needed in a Trade Agreement?

This chapter reviews the theoretical and empirical literature on the use of safeguards in a trade agreement. It then analyzes the available data on the use of safeguards by World Trade Organization (WTO) members to examine two hypotheses in the economics literature: (i) that safeguards improve welfare by facilitating tariff reductions and (ii) that safeguards improve welfare by providing insurance against adverse economic shocks. I find that countries that undertook larger tariff reductions during the Uruguay Round conducted more safeguards investigations after the WTO was established. This finding suggests that the presence of a safeguard clause in the WTO agreement may have facilitated greater tariff reductions during the Uruguay Round. I find no evidence that safeguards are used more intensively by countries exposed to more aggregate economic uncertainty. It thus seems unlikely that safeguards provide insurance against aggregate economic shocks.

Introduction

Economists have a love–hate relationship with the idea of contingent policies in general and the use of safeguards in a trade agreement in particular. On the one hand, because the economic environment is constantly bombarded with sudden and unexpected changes in everything from technology, to individual preferences, to the weather, it makes sense to give the parties to a trade agreement some flexibility to change the terms of the agreement when something unexpected occurs. On the other hand, depending on the rules of the agreement, it is not clear that the benefits of flexibility outweigh their costs. If too much flexibility is allowed, the credibility of the agreement could be undermined, and the agreement might provide few or no benefits.

I thank Gadi Barlevy, Patrick Bolton, and, especially, Jeff Dunoff for thoughtful comments and suggestions.

In this chapter, I review the economics literature, both theoretical and empirical, on the use of safeguards in a trade agreement. Are they necessary? Do they improve welfare? After outlining the theoretical arguments in favor of and against the use of safeguards as a welfare-improving component of a trade agreement, I turn to the empirical literature on the use of safeguards and, because there is little empirical research on safeguards, other forms of contingent protection.

The chapter's main contribution is to analyze the available data on the use of safeguards by WTO members to examine two hypotheses in the economics literature: first, that the presence of a safeguard option in a trade agreement facilitates greater tariff reductions during the negotiation of a trade agreement, and, second, that safeguards improve welfare by acting as a form of insurance against an unexpected change in the economic environment. More specifically, imposing a safeguard during a period when the volume of imports is unexpectedly high can be thought of as an insurance payout in which the safeguard mitigates the adverse consequences of an unexpected import surge.

An ideal test of the hypothesis that safeguards facilitate tariff reductions would be to conduct a counterfactual experiment in which we compare the tariff reductions undertaken by one group of countries under the auspices of a trade agreement with no safeguard provision against the reductions undertaken by a second group that participates in a trade agreement with a safeguard option. Unfortunately, conducting this type of experiment in the real world is not possible. Instead, I conduct an empirical exercise in which I develop an econometric model that exploits variation across countries that participated in the Uruguay Round to try to infer if the presence of a safeguard option in a trade agreement can facilitate greater tariff reductions. The empirical model relates the number of safeguards investigations initiated by WTO members to the magnitude of tariff reductions undertaken during the Uruguay Round and two measures of economic uncertainty: the volatility of the aggregate economy and the variability of the exchange rate.

The analysis provides some evidence in support of the hypothesis that safeguards facilitate greater tariff liberalizations. I find that countries that undertook larger tariff reductions during the Uruguay Round conducted more safeguards investigations after the WTO was established. The evidence is strongest when the analysis is restricted to developing countries. When we include both developed and developing countries in the analysis, the findings vary across different specifications of the model. Interestingly, within this mixed pool of developed and developing countries, omitting the steel industry from the analysis results in a strong relationship between the frequency of safeguards and the magnitude of the tariff reductions.

In summary, it appears that developing countries that undertook large tariff reductions during the Uruguay Round tended to use safeguards more frequently under the WTO regime. Although this type of exercise cannot provide definitive proof of the safeguards-as-facilitator-of-tariff-reductions hypothesis, the empirical findings are supportive of the hypothesis.

I find no evidence that the frequency of safeguards increases with increasing aggregate economic uncertainty. There is no statistically significant relationship between the number of safeguards investigations conducted by WTO members and the variance of gross domestic product (GDP), consumption or aggregate import growth, or the variance of the nominal exchange rate. The empirical analysis finds no evidence to support the hypothesis that safeguards provide insurance aggregate uncertainty. However, this analysis should not be construed as a definitive rejection of the safeguards-as-insurance hypothesis. It is often difficult to find clear relationships between microeconomic policies like safeguards and macroeconomic variables like GDP. Future research that uses measures of economic uncertainty at the detailed sector or product level could yield different results.

The chapter is organized as follows. The second section provides general information on safeguards. The third section reviews the economics literature on safeguards. The empirical model relating safeguards use to tariff reductions is presented in the fourth section. The fifth section describes the data used in the empirical exercise. Results from the empirical analysis are presented in the sixth section, and the last section concludes.

Background: What Is a Safeguard?

A safeguard is a temporary import restraint that is used to protect a domestic import-competing industry from foreign competition.[1] Under the General Agreement on Tariffs and Trade (GATT)/WTO system, when countries negotiate reciprocal tariff concessions, they commit themselves to maximum "binding" tariffs. These commitments restrict, to a considerable extent, a domestic policy maker's authority to unilaterally raise its tariffs at some later date. The GATT of 1947 included two provisions under which countries could reintroduce protective trade policies. Countries remained free to temporarily raise a tariff above the maximum tariff binding or introduce a temporary quantitative restriction under the Article XIX "safeguard" provision. Countries wishing to permanently raise their bindings could do so under Article XXVIII. The GATT of 1994 provides for the use of safeguards under the Agreement on Safeguards (AS).

The text of the AS states that safeguards may be used when there is an increase in imports, either absolute or relative to domestic production, which is causing or threatens to cause injury to the domestic import-competing industry. Sykes (2007) notes that various WTO Appellate Bodies have resurrected two other requirements for safeguards that were present in Article XIX, but which were essentially ignored between 1947 and 1999. These are that safeguards may

[1] Bown and Crowley (2005) provide a good overview of the economics of safeguards.

be used in response to "unforeseen developments" and if the imposing country previously committed to a "tariff concession" on the product in question. Whereas the vagueness of these conditions might make their usefulness doubtful from a policy perspective, these requirements make sense from an economic viewpoint. Prominent arguments in favor of safeguards are that they can facilitate greater tariff concessions and that they provide insurance against unforeseen developments.

Safeguards are temporary measures that face a basic time limit of four years. Under exceptional circumstances, protection can be extended to eight years. Importantly, after a safeguard has been in place for three years, affected exporting partners can retaliate against the safeguard by withdrawing substantially equivalent tariff concessions. Thus, safeguards-imposing countries have an incentive to abide by the time limits.

The AS states that safeguard measures should be nondiscriminatory, or Most-Favored-Nation (MFN), but many countries use discriminatory safeguards, especially in the context of exemptions for regional trade agreement members. This practice is contentious and frequently challenged before the WTO's Dispute Settlement Body (DSB). Pauwelyn (2004) discusses this unresolved issue.

Lastly, safeguards are included among the trade policies known as "trade remedies," "administered protection," or "contingent protection." Safeguards are distinct from other trade remedies – antidumping duties and countervailing duties – in that they are intended to be used to prevent or reduce injury to an import-competing sector that is not competitive with foreign goods. Although each trade remedy has a different set of criteria that should be satisfied before the policy can be imposed, there is some overlap in these criteria, which means that, in practice, these policies are to some degree substitutable. Consequently, when analyzing safeguards, it is important to be cognizant of these alternative policies and how they may be interacting with or substituting for safeguards.

Previous Economic Research

Economic arguments explaining the inclusion of safeguards in trade agreements are founded in an analysis of the effects of safeguards on welfare. This literature can be divided into arguments based solely on efficiency – that is, arguments that safeguards improve the sum total welfare of all members of a trade agreement. More precisely, efficiency arguments assume that the welfare of each individual is weighted equally and then demonstrate that, even though some individuals may experience gains and others may experience losses as a result of a policy change, the sum total change in welfare is positive. Political economic or distributional arguments, in contrast, accept that safeguards do not necessarily improve total welfare. Rather, they assign some actors; for example, governments, firms, and/or workers, more weight than others in welfare calculations. They then show that this specially weighted measure of welfare is improved by a policy change. Often these weights are thought to reflect political power. Even though safeguards may reduce measures of worldwide welfare in which each individual merits equal weight, safeguards are understood to be included in the trade agreement because those who benefit wield enough political power to see that the policy is included in the trade agreement.

Do Safeguards in a Trade Agreement Improve Worldwide Welfare?

Safeguards add flexibility to trade agreements. Theoretically, this flexibility can improve welfare by making the trade agreement more responsive to a constantly changing economic environment. Alternatively, it can reduce welfare by undermining the credibility of the agreement. Both arguments have been made in the economics literature. As an empirical question, the issue is unresolved.

Safeguards Facilitate Greater Trade Liberalizations

Perhaps the most widely cited argument in favor of safeguards is that they can facilitate greater tariff liberalizations by governments during trade negotiations. Because a government has an escape valve if a tariff reduction causes pain to its producers, it has more freedom to make larger and potentially more risky tariff reductions. Because there are large gains from permanent tariff reductions and relatively small costs from imposing temporary safeguards in a few sectors, the world gains by having safeguards in a trade agreement, even if they are not used. Jackson (1997) provides an intuitive discussion of how safeguards facilitate tariff reductions.

Ethier (2002) asks: How does the interaction between unilateralism and multilateralism affect the pace of trade liberalization? His central concern is to analyze a trading system like the GATT/WTO, which is characterized by the general practice of negotiating tariff reductions to benefit all members and the occasional use of temporary unilateral tariff increases through safeguards or antidumping duties. He develops a multicountry model in which countries grow at different rates. He shows, first, that the pace of trade liberalization is constrained by the slowest-growing countries in the world. He then illustrates how allowing these countries to temporarily raise their tariffs can accelerate the pace of worldwide trade liberalization. The key insight is that, when countries negotiate tariff reductions, they do not know if their growth will be fast or slow. In a trade agreement that does not allow temporary tariff increases, countries fear their growth will be slow and will negotiate only small tariff reductions. When safeguards are added to the trade agreement, countries negotiate large tariff reductions because they know that if they turn out to have slow growth, they can temporarily increase their tariffs.

Klimenko, Ramey, and Watson (forthcoming) arrive at a similar result by examining the question of why the WTO's DSB exists. In their article, they show that, when countries regularly renegotiate their tariffs, as in the WTO's trade rounds, a DSB is necessary for the trade agreement to survive. A DSB makes it possible for countries to punish each other for violations. Because countries want to avoid punishment, they will not violate the trade agreement when it includes a DSB. As an extension to their article, they also show that, if the DSB allows countries to temporarily raise their tariffs (as is the case with safeguard measures) in response to some unexpected change in the economic environment, they will negotiate larger tariff reductions initially.

How can the theories of the role that safeguards play in facilitating tariff reductions be verified empirically? In some ways this is an impossible task – how can we prove that countries negotiate lower tariffs when a safeguard is part of a trade agreement when all the trade agreements in existence include safeguards? In the fourth section of this chapter, I present an empirical model of the relationship between safeguards and tariff reductions by WTO members that attempts to quantify this relationship by using cross-country variation in safeguards use and tariff reductions. My results are generally supportive of the hypothesis that safeguards facilitate tariff reductions. An interesting study of India's trade policies by Bown and Tovar (2007), which exploits cross-product variation in the magnitude of tariff reductions, finds that safeguards and antidumping duties are applied more frequently to products that experienced large tariff cuts in the 1990s. Thus, their findings appear generally consistent with the idea that an "escape clause" in a trade agreement can facilitate greater tariff reductions *ex ante*.

Safeguards Provide Insurance

Another economic argument in favor of the inclusion of safeguards in a trade agreement is that they act as a form of insurance against adverse economic shocks. When an unexpected change in the economy occurs (e.g., a price falls, the volume of imports rises), imposing a safeguard can partially mitigate the effect of the change (by stemming the price fall, restricting imports, etc.) and, thus, acts as something similar to an insurance payout.

Bagwell and Staiger (1990) explore how price fluctuations affect large players in a trade agreement – countries like the United States, European Union (EU), and Japan who have markets that are so large that their safeguard measures can significantly alter world prices. They argue that, because of the self-enforcing nature of the trade agreement, in periods of large import volumes, a safeguard measure acts as a pressure valve to enable countries to sustain cooperation by temporarily raising tariffs. In the absence of a safeguard clause, countries would not be able to sustain cooperation, and the result would be a costly trade war of high levels of tariff retaliation.

Fischer and Prusa (2003) show that small countries, which cannot affect world prices, can use safeguards to insure themselves against international price shocks. In their multisector model, imposing a safeguard in the face of a negative world price shock improves national welfare by improving the welfare of the import-competing sector.

While I am aware of no empirical research on the use of safeguards as insurance, two empirical articles (Knetter and Prusa, 2005; Staiger and Wolak, 1994) from the literature on antidumping can offer insights into the relationship between economic shocks and contingent trade protection. Knetter and Prusa (2003) estimate a negative binomial model of the relationship between the number of antidumping investigations initiated in four countries – Australia, Canada, the EU, and the United States – and macroeconomic factors. They find that a one-standard-deviation real appreciation of the importing country's currency increases filings by thirty-three percent and a one-standard-deviation decrease in the importing country's real GDP growth increases filings by twenty-three percent. One interpretation of these results is that domestic import-competing firms use antidumping duties to maintain their market shares and profits in the face of adverse economic shocks.

Staiger and Wolak (1994) estimate a negative binomial model of antidumping investigations using a panel of U.S. industries. They find that industries are more likely to file petitions for antidumping protection when the market share of imports is high and the industry's capacity utilization is low. This behavior is consistent with two ideas. First, industries in the United States respond to the incentive structure of U.S. antidumping law. Second, industries use antidumping policy to insure themselves against positive import shocks and negative shocks to the demand for their products.

Safeguards Undermine the Credibility of a Trade Agreement

Staiger and Tabellini (1987) provide an argument against safeguards by showing that safeguards could reduce the credibility of a trade agreement. If governments are not fully committed to liberal trade, the productive factors in their economies may not efficiently reallocate because firms expect their governments to use safeguards in the future. Because productive factors are not efficiently allocated in a trade agreement with a safeguard, but would be in a trade agreement that did not include a safeguard, there is a relative welfare loss associated with the inclusion of the safeguard in a trade agreement.

Staiger and Tabellini (1999) compare tariff policies made under two different policy environments – the U.S. escape clause and the Tokyo Round GATT negotiations over sectoral exclusions – to empirically investigate the question of whether GATT rules help governments make trade-policy commitments to their private sectors. Although they do not find direct evidence that U.S. safeguards undermine the U.S. government's ability to commit to a particular trade policy, they find evidence using the Tokyo Round exclusions data that support the claim that GATT rules do give governments commitment power. This finding indirectly provides support for the hypothesis that the inclusion of safeguards in a trade agreement can erode a government's ability to commit to liberalization.

Do Safeguards in a Trade Agreement Improve National Welfare?

An alternative set of arguments for why safeguards are needed in a trade agreement is that they improve national welfare for politically powerful countries or that they improve the welfare of politically powerful agents in politically powerful countries. Without the participation of these powerful countries, the agreement might not be formed. These articles, which were founded on strong assumptions about redistribution,[2] do not try to explain why safeguards are needed in a trade agreement. Instead, they offer explanations for why safeguards are included in trade agreements.

Infant Industry Arguments

Several theoretical articles (Crowley, 2006; Matsuyama, 1990; Miyagiwa and Ohno, 1995, 1999) explore how safeguards benefit import-competing firms that are technologically behind their foreign competitors. These articles examine the consequences of using a temporary safeguard to induce domestic firms to adopt newer, more efficient production technologies.[3]

Matsuyama (1990) and Miyagiwa and Ohno (1995) provide theoretical support for the WTO's practice of setting a strict termination date for safeguard protection and allowing exporting countries to retaliate against safeguard measures that extend beyond this limit. Miyagiwa and Ohno (1995) find that safeguards provide an incentive for protected firms to innovate quickly only if the cost of the new technology is decreasing over time and the termination date for safeguard protection is credibly enforced by foreign retaliation. One implication of their article is that the exact length of time that a safeguard must be in place to induce a domestic firm to acquire a new technology will depend critically on how quickly the cost of the new technology is decreasing. Thus, the WTO's three-year time limit will provide too much protection in some cases and not enough in others. The cases in which it provides too little protection are particularly troubling. The safeguard will force consumers to pay very high prices but will not yield any benefit to the economy.

Crowley (2006) finds that a nondiscriminatory safeguard tariff can accelerate technology adoption by a domestic import-competing firm, but will slow down technology adoption by foreign exporting firms. Because an MFN safeguard tariff can delay a foreign firm's adoption of new technology, its worldwide welfare costs may exceed its benefits.

There is little empirical evidence on the effect of safeguards on technology adoption, and it is not very encouraging. A 1982 study by the U.S. government's administrative body that reviews safeguard petitions, the U.S. International Trade Commission (USITC), found that most safeguards failed to promote

2 Note that redistribution in political economy models can be redistribution from a weak or impoverished group to a strong or wealthy group.

3 Economists have long understood that a government subsidy is better than a tariff for helping a firm adopt a new technology. A direct subsidy can achieve the same result as a safeguard, but because it doesn't increase the price consumers will face, it's less costly to society as a whole. Dixit and Norman (1980); Caves, Frankel, and Jones (2002); and Krugman and Obstfeld (2000) are a few standard textbooks that make this point.

positive adjustment to import competition. Rather than assisting companies in upgrading their facilities, in most cases safeguards merely slowed an industry's inevitable decline. There are some exceptions: Harley-Davidson, a motorcycle producer, received safeguard protection in 1983 and successfully retooled its plants. However, successful cases are the exception to the rule. A review of U.S. safeguard cases since 1974 shows that some industries seek and receive protection repeatedly – for example, stainless alloy tool steel was granted safeguard protection in 1976 and again in 1983.

Recent empirical work by Konings and Vandenbussche (2007) on antidumping protection in the EU finds evidence that antidumping measures are associated with improvements in the total factor productivity of firms that are technologically lagging behind. However, these authors also find that the total factor productivity growth of the most efficient firms falls under antidumping protection. This finding suggests that the use of safeguards to promote technological improvement would be a costly policy at best.

Adjustment Cost Arguments

Another group of theoretical articles shows how firms in declining industries can use political support to maintain protection. Hillman (1982), Brainard and Verdier (1994, 1997), and Magee (2002) all examine the use of tariff protection to allow a dying industry to collapse slowly, rather than quickly. Because these articles all assume that there are high costs to quickly scaling back production, they find that a temporary tariff that can slow an industry's decline can improve an importing country's welfare. However, this type of policy also slows the reallocation of capital and labor into other industrial sectors in which they would be more productive. This loss of productivity is an indirect welfare cost to the country imposing the safeguard measure.

In summary, a number of explanations have been put forward in the economics literature to explain the use of safeguards in a trade agreement. In my opinion, the two most compelling are that the presence of a safeguards provision facilitates greater tariff reductions and that safeguards can provide insurance against economic shocks. There is no empirical research that proves or disproves the first hypothesis. The idea that safeguards could provide insurance against economic shocks finds some support in the empirical work on antidumping of Knetter and Prusa (2003) and Staiger and Wolak (1994). In the next section, I present an empirical model to examine both hypotheses.

Empirical Model

This section presents an empirical model of the number of safeguards investigations by countries that participate in a trade agreement. The model relates the number of safeguards investigations conducted by trade agreement members to tariff reductions negotiated under the trade agreement, the variance of the macroeconomic environment, the variance of the exchange rate, and country size.

This model will allow us to answer the following questions: Did WTO members that undertook greater tariff liberalizations during the Uruguay Round use more safeguards than other countries? Does aggregate uncertainty, measured as the variance of GDP, consumption, or import growth, affect the frequency with which safeguards are used? Is a more volatile nominal exchange rate associated with more safeguards investigations?

The number of safeguards investigations conducted in a particular time period is a non-negative count variable that exhibits over dispersion. That is, the variance of the number of investigations exceeds the mean (see Table 2). This type of count data can be generated by a negative binomial distribution. In this model, the number of safeguards investigations, y_i, follows a Poisson process after conditioning on the explanatory variable, x_i, and an unobserved variable, u_i. Specifically,

$$y_i \sim Poisson(\mu_i^*) \quad \text{where}$$

$$\mu_i^* = \exp(x_i\beta + u_i) \quad \text{and} \quad e^{ui} \sim gamma\,(1/\alpha, 1/\alpha).$$

I estimate the relationship between the number of safeguards investigations, tariff reductions, and aggregate uncertainty using maximum likelihood.

In the Poisson model, it is assumed that the incidence rate r_j (the rate per unit time at which events occur) is a function of the explanatory variables:

$$r_j = \exp(\beta_0 + \beta_1 x_{1j} + \cdots + \beta_k x_{kj}).$$

In interpreting the coefficient estimates from this model, it is useful to calculate incidence rate ratios (IRRs), the ratio of counts predicted by the model when the variable of interest is some magnitude above its mean value and all other variables are at their means to the counts predicted when all variables are at their means. The IRR for a one-standard-deviation change in x_i is given by:

$$IRR_i = \exp(\beta_i) = \frac{\exp(\beta_0 + \beta_1 x_1 + \cdots + \beta_i(x_i + stddev(x_i)) + \cdots + \beta_k x_k)}{\exp(\beta_0 + \beta_1 x_1 + \cdots + \beta_i x_i + \cdots + \beta_k x_k)}.$$

Theoretical research in the economics literature suggests that safeguards may improve worldwide welfare by encouraging countries to undertake larger tariff liberalizations when negotiating a trade agreement. To test this hypothesis, we would need data from a counterfactual experiment in which a country negotiated tariff reductions as part of an identical trade agreement that included safeguards and as part of a trade agreement that did not include safeguards. Unfortunately, we are not able to observe data from this kind of counterfactual experiment.

Consequently, I try to infer something about the role of safeguards in trade agreements by looking at the cross-sectional variation across WTO members in the number of safeguards investigations conducted during the five-year period,

1995 through 2000, and the ten-year period, 1995 through 2005, and the magnitude of tariff reductions arising from the Uruguay Round negotiations. A finding that the number of safeguards investigations is increasing in the magnitude of the tariff reduction undertaken during the Uruguay Round would lend support to the hypothesis that the presence of safeguards in a trade agreement facilitates greater tariff liberalizations.

Other research suggests that safeguards may improve global welfare by providing insurance in the face of economic shocks. I look for evidence that supports this hypothesis by estimating the relationship between the number of safeguards investigations and the variance of the growth rate of real GDP, real consumption, and real aggregate imports and the variance of the exchange rate. A finding that countries that have more variability in their economic aggregates or exchange rate also have more safeguards investigations would provide support to the hypothesis that safeguards improve global welfare by providing insurance.

Last, because the number of safeguards investigations is likely to increase with the scope of economic activity, I include a control for country size, the level of real GDP.

Data

Data on the number of safeguard investigations initiated in each year, 1995 through 2005, by each WTO member were collected from the annual "Report (year) of the Committee on Safeguards to the Council for Trade in Goods" (WTO, 1995–2005). Two measures of safeguards investigations are used. The first measure counts an investigation into any group of products initiated on a given day as a unique investigation. The second measure defines a unique investigation as each six-digit harmonized system (HS) product investigated by a country. According to Finger, Ingco, and Reincke (1996), most Uruguay Round tariff concessions were implemented by 1999. The total number of safeguards investigations conducted during the period from 1995 through 2000 serve as a measure of use during the transition to the new, lower tariff levels, whereas the total number of safeguards investigations conducted during the period from 1995 through 2005 serve as a measure that combines use associated with the transition with use after full implementation of the new tariff rates. Although I have data on the number of investigations by all WTO members, the empirical analysis is restricted to those 62 countries that joined the WTO in 1995, participated in the Uruguay Round, and for which tariff reduction data are available. See Table 1 for a list of countries. For two reasons, the analysis uses data on the number of investigations rather than the number of preliminary or final safeguard measures imposed. First, previous empirical work on antidumping by Staiger and Wolak (1994) suggests that investigations alone reduce imports. Second, not all safeguard investigations reported to the WTO had their ultimate outcomes fully reported.

Table 1. *Safeguard investigations by World Trade Organization member*

Country	No. of investigations initiated between 1995 and 2000	No. of investigations initiated between 1995 and 2005	No. of six-digit product investigations initiated between 1995 and 2000	No. of six-digit product investigations initiated between 1995 and 2005	No. of six- digit product investigations excluding steel, initiated between 1995 and 2000	No. of six-digit product investigations excluding steel, initiated between 1995 and 2005	Percent tariff reduction (Source: Finger et al.)	Percent tariff reduction (Source: WDI)
Argentina	3	5	44	46	44	46	4.2%	–
Australia	1	1	1	1	1	1	8.0%	–
Bahrain	0	0	0	0	0	0	–	0.0%
Brazil	1	3	15	16	15	16	1.1%	–
Bulgaria	1	7	1	27	1	4	–	5.8%
Canada	0	2	0	3	0	3	4.7%	1.0%
Colombia	1	3	4	6	4	6	3.6%	–
Congo Dem	0	0	0	0	0	0	–	1.0%
Costa Rica	0	1	0	2	0	2	–	4.4%
Cote d'Ivoire	0	0	0	0	0	0	–	19.8%
Croatia	0	0	0	0	0	0	–	1.3%
Czech Republic	3	9	34	70	34	37	1.4%	–
Dominican Republic	0	0	0	0	0	0	–	9.9%
El Salvador	3	3	25	25	25	25	3.8%	–
Estonia	0	1	0	6	0	0	–	0.7%
European Communities	0	4	0	97	0	8	3.1%	–
Ghana	0	0	0	0	0	0	–	–1.2%
Guatemala	0	0	0	0	0	0	–	2.8%
Hungary	0	4	0	76	0	6	2.8%	–
Iceland	0	0	0	0	0	0	15.8%	–
India	11	16	14	46	14	46	16.5%	16.3%
Indonesia	0	2	0	9	0	9	11.1%	2.0%
Jamaica	0	1	0	2	0	2	12.5%	1.3%
Japan	3	3	3	3	3	3	2.7%	–
Jordan	2	11	4	18	4	16	–	5.7%
Kenya	0	0	0	0	0	0	–	–2.6%
Korea	4	4	16	16	16	16	8.5%	1.2%
Kuwait	0	0	0	0	0	0	–	–0.5%
Kyrgyz Republic	0	0	0	0	0	0	–	0.3%

To examine the relationship between the number of safeguards investigations and tariff concessions agreed to during the Uruguay Round, the ideal tariff information is the change in the MFN bound tariff negotiated during the Uruguay Round. Unfortunately, these data are not readily available or, in the case of a product that had an unbounded tariff prior to the Round, this change is not well-defined. In this chapter, I use two measures of tariff changes, both of which are derived from *applied* tariff rates. Data on the magnitude of Uruguay Round tariff reductions come from two sources. The primary source is the book *The Uruguay Round: Statistics on Tariff Concessions Given and Received* (World Bank, 1996) by J. Michael Finger, Merlinda Ingco, and Ulrich Reincke. From this source, I use the variable "tariff reduction" from the Group G1 Tables on Concessions granted. This variable is the import-weighted average at the tariff line level of the reduction in the applied MFN tariff rate, where the reduction is defined as $(\tau_{\text{pre UR}} - \tau_{\text{post UR}})/(1 + .5(\tau_{\text{pre UR}} - \tau_{\text{post UR}}))$. This variable was available for 34 countries (see Table 1). To augment this variable, I turn to a secondary source, the *World Development Indicators* (WDI) CD ROM (World Bank, 2006). From this source, I calculated the average applied *ad valorem* tariff rates in 1994 and 2000 (or closest year available) using data on the nominal value of imports and total trade taxes. I then constructed an average tariff reduction variable using the formula of Finger et al. to augment the data series on tariff reductions. Unfortunately, this average tariff reduction measure does not embody the detailed product weights used by Finger et al. and may confound unilateral tariff reductions or tariff reductions under regional trade agreements with reductions agreed to as part of the Uruguay Round. As an alternative measure of the tariff reduction, I also constructed the simple difference in pre- and post–Uruguay Round average applied tariff rates from the WDI.

An important caveat about using applied tariff rates is that, during the Uruguay Round, many developing countries bound their tariffs on some products at rates much higher than the (pre and/or post) applied level. Consequently, for these countries, there is no need to use a safeguards measure to temporarily protect against imports of these products so long as the tariff increase remains below the bound level. For these countries, we may not observe any relationship between the change in the applied tariff rate and the number of safeguards used. Moreover, many developing countries that had not previously bound their tariffs at any level offered tariff commitments during the Uruguay Round. In these cases, the reduction in the bound tariff is not well-defined. Furthermore, because I do not have data on the pre- and post–Uruguay Round bound tariff rates, I don't know if the changes in the applied tariff rates are larger or smaller than the changes in the bound rates.

Macroeconomic data on real GDP, consumption, and imports come from the Organisation for Economic Co-operation and Development (OECD) whenever available and the International Financial Statistics (IFS) otherwise. For each variable, I calculated the annual growth rate for the years 1995 through 2005.

Table 2. *Summary statistics*

Variable	62-country sample	41-country sample
No. of safeguard investigations initiated between 1995 and 2000	0.806 (1.974)	0.561 (1.871)
No. of safeguard investigations initiated between 1995 and 2005	1.952 (3.216)	1.512 (3.31)
No. of six-digit HS product investigations initiated between 1995 and 2000	2.344 (0.666)	1.732 (0.778)
No. of six-digit HS product investigations initiated between 1995 and 2005	10.448 (3.149)	13.268 (7.245)
No. of six-digit HS product investigations, excluding steel products, initiated between 1995 and 2000	2.12 (0.635)	1.171 (0.544)
No. of six-digit HS product investigations, excluding steel products, initiated between 1995 and 2005	6.336 (2.467)	12.049 (7.176)
$\tau_{pre} - \tau_{post}$	0.031 (0.043)	0.031 (0.043)
% change in $\tau_{pre} - \tau_{post}$	0.066 (0.047)	0.049 (0.055)
Var(GDP growth$_{1995-2000}$)	0.001 (0.001)	0.001 (0.002)
Var(GDP growth$_{1995-2005}$)	0.001 (0.001)	0.001 (0.001)
Var(log of nominal exchange rates$_{1995-2000}$)	0.161 (0.504)	0.181 (0.596)
Var(log of nominal exchange rates$_{1995-2005}$)	0.392 (1.482)	0.355 (1.540)
Logged level of PPP adjusted GDP in 2000	4.532 (1.938)	3.887 (1.706)
Number of observations	62	41

Notes: GDP: gross domestic product; PPP: purchasing power parity.

The variance of the growth rates over two periods, 1995 through 2000 and 1995 through 2005, serve as measures of aggregate uncertainty.

Quarterly nominal exchange rate data (end-of-period domestic currency/ U.S. dollar) come from the OECD when available and the IFS otherwise.[4] The variance of the logged level of the quarterly nominal exchange rate between 1995 and 2000 and between 1995 and 2005 are the two measures of exchange rate uncertainty used.

The measure of country size, the logged level of purchasing power parity (PPP) – adjusted real GDP (chain-weighted measure) in 2000, comes from the Heston, Summers, and Aten (2002).

Summary statistics for all variables are reported in Table 2.

[4] Real exchange rate data were available for too few countries to conduct a useful analysis.

Table 3. *Maximum likelihood estimates of the negative binomial model*

Explanatory variables	Dependent variable: Number of investigations initiated between 1995 and 2000					
Absolute tariff reduction (Source: WDI)	14.98 (10.23)			22.28** (11.30)		
Percent reduction in tariff (Source: Finger et al. and WDI)		5.72 (6.40)	18.28* (9.59)		5.69 (6.48)	18.92** (8.99)
Variance of real GDP growth between 1995 and 2000				542.53 (438.07)	−85.32 (231.47)	278.49 (360.74)
Constant	−1.34** (0.63)	−0.55 (0.46)	−1.97*** (0.76)	−2.39** (0.98)	−0.45 (0.53)	−2.40*** (0.91)
Observations	41	62	41	41	62	41

Notes: WDI: World Development Indicators; GDP: gross domestic product. The numbers in parentheses are standard errors. ***, **, and * denote variables statistically different from zero at the 1, 5, and 10 percent levels, respectively.

Empirical Results

The negative binomial model of safeguards investigations by WTO members indicates that developing countries that undertook large tariff reductions during the Uruguay Round conducted more safeguards investigations after the establishment of the WTO. This finding provides some support for the hypothesis that safeguards facilitate greater tariff concessions during trade agreement negotiations. However, when the sample is expanded to include developed and developing countries, the results are mixed, with some specifications confirming the relationship between tariff reductions and safeguards investigations and others finding no statistically significant relationship. The model finds no evidence of a statistically significant relationship between safeguards investigations and aggregate economic shocks, measured as the variance of GDP growth or the variance of the logged exchange rate. This result implies that it is unlikely that safeguards provide insurance against aggregate economic uncertainty.

Tables 3 and 4 present results from the negative binomial model of safeguards investigations between 1995 and 2000. Tables 5 and 6 present results for investigations between 1995 and 2005.

Results in columns 1 through 3 of Table 3 present evidence on the relationship between the magnitude of tariff reductions and the number of safeguards investigations conducted between 1995 and 2000. Tariff reductions enter the model as positive numbers, so a positive coefficient on a tariff reduction variable implies that a larger tariff reduction is associated with more safeguards investigations. Beginning with column 1, the coefficient on the absolute reduction in the tariff, 14.98, can be restated as an IRR of 4.46 in response to a ten-percentage-point increase in the tariff reduction variable, or as an IRR of 1.9 in response to a one-standard-deviation increase in this variable. That is, if the magnitude of tariff reductions were to increase by ten percentage points, the predicted number

Table 4. *Maximum likelihood estimates of the negative binomial model*

Explanatory variables	Dependent variable: Number of investigations initiated between 1995 and 2000					
Absolute tariff reduction (Source: WDI)	22.55**	3.53	−0.50			
	(11.11)	(11.08)	(12.76)			
Percent reduction in tariff (Source: Finger et al. and WDI)				5.52	−1.71	−1.72
				(6.41)	(5.65)	(5.66)
Variance of real GDP growth between 1995 and 2000	628.02	60.27	−153.15	−11.31	−74.50	−79.47
	(477.94)	(313.07)	(450.89)	(260.89)	(185.74)	(217.73)
Variance of the log of the nominal exchange rate between 1995 and 2000	−0.91		0.90	−0.59		0.04
	(1.63)		(1.45)	(0.89)		(0.98)
Logged level of PPP adjusted real GDP in 2000		0.59**	0.70**		0.50***	0.50***
		(0.28)	(0.33)		(0.15)	(0.15)
Constant	−2.40**	−3.62***	−3.78***	−0.46	−2.60***	−2.60***
	(0.96)	(1.21)	(1.25)	(0.53)	(0.81)	(0.81)
Observations	41	33	33	62	53	53

Notes: WDI: World Development Indicators; GDP: gross domestic product; PPP: purchasing power parity. The numbers in parentheses are standard errors. ***, **, and * denote variables statistically different from zero at the 1, 5, and 10 percent levels, respectively.

of safeguards investigations would increase by a factor of 4.5. If the magnitude of tariff reductions were to increase by one standard deviation (4.3 percentage points), the predicted number of safeguards investigations would increase by a factor of 1.9.

Turning to column 2 of Table 3, which uses a percentage change measure of the tariff reductions, the coefficient estimate of 5.72, although positive, has a

Table 5. *Maximum likelihood estimates of the negative binomial model*

Explanatory variables	Dependent variable: Number of investigations initiated between 1995 and 2005					
Absolute tariff reduction (Source: WDI)	16.44*			20.29**		
	(8.49)			(8.83)		
Percent reduction in tariff (Source: Finger et al. and WDI)		4.91	17.32**		4.99	18.20**
		(5.34)	(8.09)		(5.26)	(7.76)
Variance of real GDP growth between 1995 and 2005				364.78	70.51	248.49
				(283.99)	(168.69)	(243.16)
Constant	−0.34	0.40	−0.74	−0.93	0.31	−1.10*
	(0.45)	(0.36)	(0.55)	(0.61)	(0.41)	(0.63)
Observations	41	62	41	41	62	41

Notes: WDI: World Development Indicators; GDP: gross domestic product. The numbers in parentheses are standard errors. ***, **, and * denote variables statistically different from zero at the 1, 5, and 10 percent levels, respectively.

Table 6. *Maximum likelihood estimates of the negative binomial model*

Explanatory variables	Dependent variable: Number of investigations initiated between 1995 and 2005					
Absolute tariff reduction	20.15**	10.48	7.17			
(Source: WDI)	(8.75)	(8.75)	(9.42)			
Percent reduction in tariff				4.86	−0.70	−0.55
(Source: Finger et al. and WDI)				(5.22)	(4.50)	(4.50)
Variance of real GDP growth	421.21	194.04	−213.32	160.42	84.84	154.29
between 1995 and 2005	(302.75)	(222.07)	(500.59)	(192.64)	(137.43)	(169.72)
Variance of the log of the	−0.34		1.87	−0.40		−0.28
nominal exchange rate between 1995 and 2005	(0.66)		(2.08)	(0.39)		(0.40)
Logged level of PPP		0.31	0.37*		0.36***	0.35***
adjusted real GDP in 2000		(0.19)	(0.20)		(0.11)	(0.11)
Constant	−0.92	−1.54*	−1.50*	0.32	−1.10*	−1.09*
	(0.60)	(0.83)	(0.81)	(0.41)	(0.59)	(0.59)
Observations	41	33	33	62	53	53

Notes: WDI: World Development Indicators; GDP: gross domestic product; PPP: purchasing power parity. The numbers in parentheses are standard errors. ***, **, and * denote variables statistically different from zero at the 1, 5, and 10 percent levels, respectively.

low IRR of 1.3 for a one-standard-deviation increase and is not statistically different from zero. Column 3 attempts to discern if the difference between results using the absolute reduction in the tariff versus the percent reduction is caused by differences in the measurement of the variable or differences in the samples. In this column, the model is estimated on the relatively small sample of countries for which the WDI tariff reduction data are available, but uses the percent reduction measure, which combines data from Finger et al with those from the WDI. Here, the coefficient on the tariff reduction of 18.28 is large and statistically significant. Transforming this coefficient yields an IRR of 6.2 in response to a ten percent increase in the tariff reduction or an IRR of 2.7 in response to a one-standard-deviation (0.055) increase in the tariff reduction. This result suggests that, if countries had undertaken greater tariff liberalizations during the Uruguay Round, we would see six times as many or two and a half times as many safeguards, depending on the magnitude of the additional reduction.

Columns 4 through 6 of Table 3, which also control for the variance of real GDP growth between 1995 and 2000, present results on the magnitude of tariff reductions that are qualitatively and quantitatively similar to those in columns 1 through 3. In all specifications, the estimate on the variance of GDP growth is not statistically different from zero. Similar statistically insignificant results are obtained if one uses consumption or aggregate import growth. To quantify the results, in column 4, the IRR for a one-standard-deviation increase in the tariff reduction variable is 3.4, whereas the IRR for a one-standard-deviation increase in the variance of GDP growth is 2.9, although the IRR for the GDP growth variable is not statistically different from 1.

Table 4 builds on the results in Table 3 by including controls for the variance of the exchange rate and country size. Overall, the results confirm the basic findings presented in Table 3. In the small sample of 41 countries, tariff reductions are associated with more safeguards investigations, but there is no clear or statistically significant pattern between the variance of GDP growth or the nominal exchange rate and safeguards investigations. As expected, larger countries (measured by PPP-adjusted GDP) conduct more safeguards investigations. Tables 5 and 6 present results that are qualitatively and quantitatively similar to those in Tables 3 and 4 using data from a longer time period, 1995–2005.

Table 7 adds additional insight into the relationship between tariff reductions and safeguards. The dependent variable in Table 7 counts the number of six-digit HS products that were subject to a safeguard investigation between 1995 and 2005. Because most safeguard investigations cover groups of six-digit products, this variable is a more precise measure of how much protection is sought by a country through safeguards. It also tells us how robust our previous results are to a slight change in the definition of a key variable – the number of safeguard investigations.

The left side of Table 7 (columns 1 through 4) uses a dependent variable that counts every six-digit HS product investigated as a separate safeguard investigation. The results are qualitatively and quantitatively the same as those presented in Tables 3 through 6. From column 2, the IRR associated with the tariff reduction coefficient of 24.682 tells us that, if the magnitude of the tariff reduction during the Uruguay Round had been one standard deviation larger (i.e., if average tariffs had been reduced by an additional 5.5 percentage points), then we would have observed 3.9 times as many products investigated for safeguard protection over the period from 1995 through 2005.

Turning to the right side of Table 7 (columns 5 through 8), the dependent variable counts all products subject to a safeguard investigation between 1995 and 2005 with the *exclusion* of steel products. Notably, this excludes the products investigated in the U.S. Global Steel Safeguard of 2001. Interestingly, in column 7, the effect of average tariff reductions on safeguard use is large and statistically significant in the 62-country sample of industrialized and developing countries. The IRR associated with an additional one-standard-deviation reduction (4.7-percentage-point reduction) in the tariff is 2.1. That is, if an industrialized or developing country had reduced its average tariff by an additional 4.7 percentage points, we would expect that that country would have conducted twice as many safeguard investigations into nonsteel products.

The puzzle of why the coefficient on the tariff reduction variable is large and statistically significant in the small 41-country sample, but small and insignificant in the larger 62-country sample in Tables 3 through 6 and on the left side of Table 7 can be somewhat resolved by looking at the countries and products used in the estimation. Table 1 presents the countries, the number of safeguards investigations conducted by product group and by individual six-digit HS product,

Table 7. *Maximum likelihood estimates of the negative binomial model*

Explanatory variables	Dependent variable: Number of six-digit HS products investigated between 1995 and 2005				Dependent variable: Number of six-digit HS products investigated (excluding steel products) between 1995 and 2005			
Percent reduction in tariff (Source: Finger et al. and WDI)	6.973	24.682**	6.981	28.322***	14.991	26.605***	15.359**	28.324***
	(8.229)	(10.676)	(8.284)	(9.862)	(6.914)	(9.610)	(6.747)	(9.535)
Variance of real GDP growth between 1995 and 2005			−50.197	621.387			160.706	376.416
			(258.266)	(471.036)			(264.095)	(496.951)
Constant	2.533***	0.703	2.584***	−0.322	1.400***	0.342	1.190**	−0.187
	(0.539)	(0.695)	(0.607)	(0.878)	(0.468)	(0.646)	(0.554)	(0.878)
Observations	62	41	62	41	62	41	62	41

Notes: WDI: World Development Indicators; GDP: gross domestic product; HS: harmonized system. The numbers in parentheses are standard errors. ***, **, and * denote variables statistically different from zero at the 1, 5, and 10 percent levels, respectively.

and the tariff reduction data available from the two sources, Finger et al. and the WDI. Notably, many large industrialized countries – Australia, the European Communities, Japan, and the United States – do not have tariff data available in the WDI and, consequently, are omitted from the smaller forty-one-country sample. As these countries are relatively heavy users of safeguards, but engaged in only small average tariff reductions during the Uruguay Round, it is unsurprising that their inclusion in the sample leads to small and statistically insignificant estimates on the tariff reduction variable. Because the smaller forty-one-country sample consists almost entirely of developing countries, one interpretation of the empirical results is to say that the inclusion of safeguards in the GATT facilitated greater tariff reductions by developing countries. The results on the right side of Table 7 suggest that steel products are unique in their policy treatment in industrialized countries. For nonsteel products, the results in Table 7 are consistent with the hypothesis that the presence of a safeguard option in the GATT facilitated greater tariff reductions during the Uruguay Round.

Conclusion

Safeguards have been part of the GATT–WTO system for more than fifty years. Although the arguments in favor of them are theoretically appealing, empirically we do not know if safeguards are a welfare-improving policy tool. The fact that they are used only rarely suggests that the direct costs associated with distortions in the sectors in which they are used are probably small. However, there are potentially large costs associated with an inefficient allocation of resources that occurs because governments' commitments to trade liberalizations are not credible. In contrast, the potentially large benefits of safeguards, the additional trade, and more efficient allocation of resources arising from greater tariff reductions cannot easily be quantified.

This chapter has shown, using data on developing countries, that countries that undertook greater tariff liberalizations during the Uruguay Round undertook more safeguards investigations after the establishment of the WTO. This finding suggests that the inclusion of safeguards played a role in facilitating greater tariff reductions during the Uruguay Round. Moreover, this result is robust to a larger sample that includes industrialized and developing countries, but which excludes safeguards investigations into steel products. In finding that there is no relationship between the number of safeguards investigations conducted and the variance of macroeconomic aggregates, this chapter suggests that safeguards are not providing insurance against macroeconomic shocks. This finding is surprising in light of the empirical research on antidumping.

Although the theoretical and empirical research discussed in this chapter could lead one to conclude that the benefits of safeguards likely outweigh their costs, that conclusion might be premature. Although safeguards have been used relatively rarely to date, that could change. Perhaps the best argument against including safeguards in a trade agreement is the concern that they could evolve into a protectionist tool like the antidumping duty, a policy instrument that was conceived to serve an economically sound objective, but that today simply enriches import-competing producers at a high cost to consumers.

REFERENCES

Bagwell, K., and R. W. Staiger. 1990. A theory of managed trade. *American Economic Review* 80:779–795.

Bown, C. P., and M. A. Crowley. 2005. Safeguards in the WTO. In *The World Trade Organization: Legal, economic and political analysis*, eds. A. Appleton, P. Macrory. Dordrecht: Springer.

Bown, C. P., and P. Tovar. 2007. "Protecting India's Trade Liberalization? Tariff Reform, Antidumping and Safeguards." Brandeis University working paper.

Brainard, S. L., and T. Verdier. 1994. Lobbying and adjustment in declining industries. *European Economic Review* 38:586–595.

Brainard, S. L., and T. Verdier. 1997. The political economy of declining industries: Senescent industry collapse revisited. *Journal of International Economics* 42:221–237.

Caves, R. E., J. A. Frankel, and R. W. Jones. 2002. *World trade and payments: An introduction.* Ninth ed. Boston: Addison-Wesley.

Crowley, M. A. 2006. Do antidumping duties and safeguard tariffs open or close technology gaps? *Journal of International Economics* 68:469–484.

Dixit, A. K., and V. Norman. 1980. *Theory of international trade.* Cambridge, UK: Cambridge University Press.

Ethier, W. J. 2002. Unilateralism in a multilateral world. *Economic Journal* 112:266–292.

Finger, J. M., M. Ingco, and U. Reincke. 1996. *The Uruguay Round: Statistics on tariff concessions given and received.* Washington: World Bank.

Fischer, R. D., and T. J. Prusa. 2003. WTO exceptions as insurance. *Review of International Economics* 11:745–757.

Heston, A., R. Summers, and B. Aten. 2002. Penn World Table Version 6.1, Center for International Comparisons at the University of Pennsylvania (CICUP).

Hillman, A. 1982. Declining industries and political-support protectionist motives. *American Economic Review* 72:1180–1187.

Jackson, J. H. 1997. *The world trading system: Law and policy of international economic relations.* Second ed. Cambridge: The MIT Press.

Klimenko, M., G. Ramey, and J. Watson. 2008. Recurrent trade agreements and the value of external enforcement. *Journal of International Economics* 74: 475–499.

Knetter, M. M., and T. J. Prusa. 2003. Macroeconomic factors and antidumping filings: Evidence from four countries. *Journal of International Economics* 61:1–17.

Konings, J., and H. Vandenbussche. 2007. Antidumping protection and the productivity of domestic firms. CEPR Discussion Paper 4620.

Krugman, P. R., and M. Obstfeld. 2000. *International economics: Theory and policy.* Fifth ed. Reading, MA: Addison-Wesley.

Magee, C. 2002. Declining industries and persistent protection. *Review of International Economics,* 10.

Matsuyama, K. 1990. Perfect equilibria in a trade liberalization game. *American Economic Review* 80:480–492.

Miyagiwa, K., and Y. Ohno. 1995. Closing the technology gap under protection. *American Economic Review* 85:755–770.

Miyagiwa, K., and Y. Ohno. 1999. Credibility of protection and incentives to innovate. *International Economic Review* 40:143–163.

Pauwelyn, J. 2004. The puzzle of WTO safeguards and regional trade agreements. *Journal of International Economic Law* 7:109–142.

Staiger, R., and G. Tabellini. 1987. Discretionary trade policy and excessive protection. *American Economic Review* 77:823–837.

Staiger, R., and G. Tabellini. 1999. Do GATT rules help governments make domestic commitments? *Economics and Politics* 11:109–144.

Staiger, R. W., and F. A. Wolak. 1994. Measuring industry-specific protection: Antidumping in the United States. *Brookings Papers: Microeconomics* 51–118.

Sykes, A, O. 2007. "Trade remedy laws." In *Research handbook of international economic law*, ed. A. T. Guzman and A. O. Sykes. Cheltenham, UK: Edward Elgar Press.

United States International Trade Commission. 1982. The Effectiveness of Escape Clause Relief in Promoting Adjustment to Import Competition. USITC Publication 1229, Investigation 332–115, March.

World Trade Organization (WTO). 1995–2005. Report (year) of the Committee on Safeguards to the Council for Trade in Goods. Geneva: WTO.

JEFFREY L. DUNOFF

11.1 *How* Not *to Think about Safeguards*

In this short chapter, I explore the question posed by the title of Meredith Crowley's thoughtful chapter, *Why Are Safeguards Needed in a Trade Agreement?* In particular, I consider whether framing an inquiry into the purpose of the safeguards mechanism in this form is likely to generate fruitful insights, or whether asking this question may instead be more likely to lead us astray. This exploration raises larger methodological questions concerning whether, at this point in time, there are limits to what either legal or economic analysis can add to current understandings about the purpose and function of safeguards.

The Puzzle of Safeguards

Article XIX of the General Agreement on Tariffs and Trade (GATT) permits a state to restrict imports of a product temporarily (take "safeguard" actions) if its domestic industry is injured or threatened with serious injury caused by a surge in imports. Although this provision was part of the original GATT, over the years safeguards were used relatively infrequently.[1] Instead, over time, many governments increasingly chose to protect their domestic industries through so-called "grey area measures"; that is, these governments persuaded trading partners to restrain exports "voluntarily" or to agree to other means of sharing markets. Over time, the number of these agreements grew dramatically,[2] and grey area

[1] GATT members notified 150 actions under Article XIX over GATT's history. GATT Analytical Index, Vol. I, pp. 539–559.

[2] For example, according to GATT figures, in early 1991, 24 formal Article XIX measures were in effect; at the same time, some 284 grey area measures were in effect. See A. O. Sykes, *The WTO Agreement on Safeguards: A Commentary* (2006). Of course, these figures may substantially understate the number of grey area measures, as by definition they were outside of the GATT system and were not systematically reported or notified to the GATT. See also GATT

This essay is based on remarks delivered at the Seminar on WTO Law at Columbia Law School, and preserves much of the brevity and informality of those remarks. In preparing this paper, I benefited from conversations about safeguards with Kyle Bagwell, Jagdish Bhagwati, Patrick Bolton, Meredith Crowley, and Petros Mavroidis.

agreements covered a wide range of important products, including automobiles, steel, semiconductors, footwear, and machine tools.

In the Uruguay Round negotiations, trading nations negotiated a detailed and comprehensive Safeguards Agreement. This agreement clarifies and elaborates many issues addressed by Article XIX of the GATT. Specifically, the Safeguard Agreement prohibits grey area measures and sets time limits (a "sunset clause") on all safeguard actions. The agreement provides that safeguards should only be undertaken when World Trade Organization (WTO) Members with substantial interests have been consulted and agree to the restraint or receive appropriate compensation in the form of offsetting trade concessions.

Thus, the trade community now has more than sixty years of experience with the use of safeguard provisions in trade agreements. In light of this substantial experience, one might wonder why a leading scholar would need to write an article exploring why safeguards are needed in trade agreements. By way of contrast, this volume on trade remedies does not include chapters addressing why antidumping or subsidy provisions are needed in trade agreements, and earlier volumes in this series do not explore why other features of the WTO agreements are necessary.[3] What lies behind the felt need to articulate a justification for safeguards?

The answer, I believe, is that safeguards have long been thought of as something of an anomaly in the trade system. The conventional wisdom, of course, is that the trade regime's primary purpose is to constrain protectionism and liberalize trade. Thus, a new and authoritative history of the GATT's origins concludes that "the most central motivation for the GATT seems to be along the lines of unwinding the retaliatory trade policies and other protectionist measures that had built up during the 1930s."[4] Other leading accounts confirm that the GATT's drafters sought to substantially reduce barriers to international trade by constraining use of discriminatory and protectionist trade policies,[5] but juxtaposing these accounts of the trade regime's origins and purpose with its safeguard provisions raises an immediate puzzle: Why would a trade system designed to constrain governments' ability to enact protectionist policies explicitly authorize safeguard measures? This puzzle prompts Crowley's chapter, which should

Secretariat, Background Note: Inventory of Article XIX Actions and Other Measures Which Appear to serve the same purpose, MTN.GNG/NG9/W2/Rev.1. An interesting history of the use of grey area measures can be found in W.H. Maruyama, "The Wonderful World of VRAs: Free Trade and the Goblet of Fire," 24 *Arizona Journal of International and Comparative Law* 2007, 149.

[3] See, for example, G.A. Bermann and P.C. Mavroidis (Eds.), *WTO Law and Developing Countries* (2007); G.A. Bermann and P.C. Mavroidis (Eds.), *Trade and Human Health and Safety* (2006) Cambridge University Press: Cambridge.

[4] D.A. Irwin, P.C. Mavroidis, and A.O. Sykes, "The Genesis of the GATT," p. 268 (unpublished manuscript).

[5] See, for example, J.H. Jackson, *World Trade and the Law of GATT – A Legal Analysis of the General Agreement on Tariffs and Trade* (Indianapolis, The Bobbs-Merrill Company, 1969), 53–57.

be understood in the context of a much larger body of scholarship that seeks to rationalize safeguards within the larger trade system.

For current purposes, we can understand the safeguards literature as falling into one of two camps. The first camp uses legal, or doctrinal, analysis to explain and justify both treaty language and Appellate Body and Panel Reports in disputes addressing safeguard issues. As a general matter, the legal literature is highly critical of the Appellate Body Reports in these disputes. Professors Mavroidis, Sykes, and others have persuasively demonstrated that the jurisprudence developed in these cases is incoherent, irrational, or both.[6]

As a result, the picture here is quite unsatisfactory, at least from the legal perspective. The relevant legal texts, including the terse and "extraordinarily oblique" Article XIX of the GATT[7] and the rather more wordy WTO Safeguard Agreement, do little to illuminate the nature or purpose of the safeguards regime. The case law developed in Appellate Body Reports is, in Syke's accurate and memorable characterization, a "mess." As a result, we cannot meaningfully understand the relevant treaty provisions and Appellate Body Reports without looking beyond the legal texts.

For this reason, most of the safeguards literature is, like Crowley's chapter, functionalist in orientation. That is, most of the scholarship on safeguards attempts to identify the purpose or function of the safeguards provisions within the larger WTO system. To oversimplify – although not misleadingly so – much of this functionalist scholarship advances one of three rationales to explain the safeguard puzzle. We can label these rationales as the equity, efficiency, and political efficacy arguments.[8]

The Equity Rationale

Some scholars argue that safeguards should be understood as a form of compensation for groups harmed by trade liberalization. The logic of this argument starts from the observation that a government decision to liberalize trade

[6] See, for example, G.M. Grossman, and P. Mavroidis, "United States – Definitive Safeguard Measures on Imports of Circular Welded Carbon Quality Line Pipe from Korea," in H. Horn, and P. Mavroidis (Eds.), *The WTO Case Law of 2002* (Cambridge, Cambridge University Press, 2004); AO. Sykes, "The Persistent Puzzles of Safeguards: Lessons from the Steel Dispute," 7 *Journal of International Economic Law* 2004, 523; H. Horn, and P. Mavroidis, "United States – Safeguard Measures on Imports of Fresh, Chilled or Frozen Lamb Meat from New Zealand and Australia: What Should be Required of a Safeguard Investigation," in H. Horn, and P. Mavroidis (Eds.), *The WTO Case Law of 2001* (Cambridge, Cambridge University Press, 2003); A.O. Sykes, "The Safeguards Mess: A Critique of Appellate Body Jurisprudence," 2 *World Trade Review* 2003, 261.

[7] Jackson, *supra* note 5, at 557.

[8] Others have used similar categories. See, for example, R.Z. Lawrence, and R.E. Litan, *Saving Free Trade: A Pragmatic Approach* (Washington, DC, The Brookings Institution, 1986); C.M. Aho, "U.S. Labor-Market Adjustment and Import Restrictions," in E.H. Preeg (Ed.), *Hard Bargaining Ahead: U.S. Trade Policy and Developing Countries* (New Brunswick, NJ, Transaction Books, 1985), 87.

creates winners and losers. Simple fairness suggests that, if a government policy is visiting foreseeable harms upon particular groups of citizens, then the government should pursue policies – including safeguards – that alleviate these adverse impacts.[9]

This stock justification for safeguards has, in turn, generated a series of stock objections. First, as a matter of equity, it is not clear why those who lose from liberalized trade have a greater claim to government assistance than those who work in sectors harmed by factors other than trade.[10] Moreover, even if trade-related economic injury is somehow particularly deserving of government attention, a large literature argues that trade protection is a rather clumsy and inefficient tool for effecting redistribution to vulnerable workers.[11] For one thing, trade restrictions may help displaced workers, but they also help wealthy managers and shareholders. Moreover, the costs that import restraints impose upon consumers are often greater than the gains they produce for affected workers.[12] Finally, there is little in the language of Article XIX or the Safeguards Agreement to suggest that this is the purpose of safeguards.

In addition to these theoretical issues, there is an empirical problem with claims that safeguards provide a form of social insurance for vulnerable workers. Crowley's sophisticated research suggests that there is little empirical support for the claim that states use safeguards to provide social insurance. For all of these reasons, the equity rationale for safeguards is deeply problematic; perhaps as a result, the scholarly literature has advanced alternative justifications for the presence of the safeguards provisions in trade agreements.

The Efficiency Rationale

All students of the trade system are familiar with arguments concerning the various ways that trade measures such as tariffs and quotas reduce aggregate welfare, but are there circumstances where interference with free markets is welfare enhancing?[13] More specifically, can the temporary use of safeguards

[9] For statements of this argument, see, for example, A.V. Deardorff, "Safeguards Policy and the Conservative Social Welfare Function, in Protection and Competition" in H. Kierzkowski (Ed.), *International Trade: Essay in Honor of W.M. Corden* (Oxford, Blackwell, 1987), 2.

[10] A.O. Sykes, "Protectionism as a 'Safeguard': A Positive Analysis of the GATT 'Escape Clause' with Normative Speculations," 58 *University of Chicago Law Review* 1991, 255, 272.

[11] P. Messerlin, *Measuring the Costs of Protection in Europe: European Commercial Policy in the 2000s* (Washington, DC, Institute for International Economics, 2001); Y. Sazanami, et al., *Measuring the Costs of Protection in Japan* (1995); G.C. Hufbauer, and K.A. Elliot, *Measuring the Costs of Protection in the United States* (1994).

[12] See M.J. Trebilcock, and R. Howse, *The Regulation of International Trade*, 314 (3rd ed., New York, Routledge, 2005) (providing statistics on cost to consumers per job saved and average compensation per work in affected industries). See also R.C. Feenstra, *How Costly is Protection?* 12 *Journal of Economic Perspectives* 1992, 159.

[13] Economists have identified a number of circumstances in which departures from the competitive model may be justified. See, for example, A.K. Dixit, and V. Norman, *Theory of International Trade* (Cambridge, Cambridge University Press, 1980) and J. Rander, and

promote the restructuring of firms in import-damaged industries? Some scholars argue that safeguards can provide time for ailing firms to invest in new technology and make other changes that will enable them to compete successfully in international markets. A U.S. Senate Finance Committee Report on the Trade Act of 1974 provides a justification for safeguard provisions found in U.S. law along these lines:

> The rationale for the "escape clause" has been, and remains, that as barriers to international trade are lowered, some industries and workers inevitably face serious injury, dislocation and perhaps economic extinction. The "escape clause" is aimed at providing temporary relief for an industry suffering from serious injury ... so that the industry will have sufficient time to adjust to freer international competition.[14]

Once again, a relatively stock response has generated a series of stock objections. For example, many scholars suggest that this efficiency argument presupposes a major failure in the capital market.[15] If a firm or an industry can be profitable once it has modernized and retooled, it should be able to enter the capital market and obtain funds to tide itself over until it can restructure and compete. In particular, in highly developed economies with sophisticated capital markets, we should expect potential suppliers of capital to recognize and finance firms that could become internationally competitive. Moreover, even if we believed that the capital markets would regularly fail to recognize these opportunities, there is little in theory or practice to suggest that government officials would be better able to predict which failing firms could become internationally competitive in the future.

Mavroidis and others have suggested a different efficiency rationale for safeguards. They suggest that, by slowing the rate of dislocation, safeguards may lessen the dislocation costs associated with the movement of workers out of declining firms,[16] but as advocates of these arguments usually recognize, safeguards can only increase efficiency in this sense under a quite limited (and unrealistic) set of facts.[17] Moreover, as noted earlier in this chapter, safeguards are an expensive way to address adjustment issues. Finally, there is nothing in the language of Article XIX or the Safeguards Agreement to suggest that this is the purpose safeguards are designed to serve.

B. Spencer, "Tariff Protection and Imperfect Competition," in H. Kierzkowaski (Ed.), *Monopolistic Competition and International Trade* (Oxford, Oxford University Press, 1984). However, the fact patterns and arguments underlying these claims are not relevant to the use of safeguard measures.

[14] S. Rep. No. 1298, 93d Cong., 2d Sess. 119 (1974). This argument bears a strong family resemblance to the "infant industry" argument that small, developing industries need a period of protection while they move up the "learning curve" and become competitive with larger, established rivals.

[15] See, for example, Lawrence and Litan, *supra* note 8; Sykes, *supra* note 10, at 264.

[16] Horn and Mavroidis, *supra* note 6, at 76–77. Sykes discusses, and rejects, this rationale as well. Sykes, *supra* note 10, at 265.

[17] Horn and Mavroidis, *supra* note 6.

The Political Economy Rationale

Given the difficulties with the standard equity and efficiency rationales, the more recent analytic move has been to advance political economy justifications for safeguards provisions. Like many political economy claims, the basic insight driving the analysis is that collective action problems can often lead to suboptimal results. More specifically, liberalized trade produces highly asymmetrical costs and benefits. On the one hand, the benefits of lower prices are widely diffused across the general public. On the other hand, the dislocations and other costs associated with trade liberalization fall upon narrow and well-organized groups. These groups may generate significant pressures upon elected officials, and the resulting political pressures may generate trade-restrictive policies that benefit the few at the expense of the many. Hence, one version of the political efficacy argument is that safeguards permit policy makers to deflect protectionist pressures into limited and temporary provisions, while permitting policy makers to maintain an overall commitment to freer trade.[18]

Of course, even if this argument justifies safeguards provisions in domestic law, it does not necessarily follow that safeguard provisions should be included in international trade agreements. Presumably, domestic safeguards clauses should be narrowly drawn, so that the safeguards exception cannot swallow the trade-liberalization rule. The presence of an escape clause in an international agreement can be seen as legitimating domestic protection. As Sykes argues, the ability of domestic governments "to resist special interest pressures for protection, therefore, would likely be greater in the absence of Article XIX, given that Article XIX facilitates the very measures that special interests groups seek."[19]

A variation on the political efficacy theme is the argument that the use of safeguards in trade agreements can prompt states to undertake greater trade liberalization in the first place.[20] States negotiate trade agreements under conditions of substantial uncertainty. They cannot know with a high degree of certainty, *ex ante*, the future results of any particular tariff reduction, let alone the domestic impacts of the hundreds or thousands of changes required by complex trade agreements. As a result, risk-adverse states may be highly reluctant to enter into trade agreements. However, rational states can attempt to factor uncertainty into treaty design.[21] Hence we might understand the escape clause as a mechanism to mitigate the risks associated with liberalizing trade. Safeguards clauses

[18] A similar argument is developed in K. Bagwell, and R. Staiger, *The Economics of the World Trading System* (Cambridge, MA, MIT Press, 2002), 104–106 and K. Bagwell, and R.W. Staiger, *A Theory of Managed Trade*, 80 *American Economic Review* 1990, 779.

[19] Sykes, *supra* note 10, at 273–274.

[20] This argument was first suggested by Kenneth Dam, and has been more fully developed in the legal literature by Alan Sykes. See, for example, K. Dam, *The GATT: Law and International Economic Organization* (1970), 99; Sykes, *supra* note 10.

[21] For a more generalized version of this argument, see J. Fearon, "Bargaining, Enforcement, and International Cooperation," 55 *International Organization* 1998, 269.

do so by providing *ex ante* authorization for states to escape from their liberalization commitments if, *ex post*, these commitments become politically too onerous. From this perspective, safeguards clauses are just one type of flexibility mechanism that states might use in the "rational design" of international agreements and institutions.[22] This sort of argument has recently proven to be quite influential as a matter of theory.[23] In seeking to investigate the empirical support for this argument in the specific context of safeguards, Crowley's chapter addresses an important and underexplored aspect of the safeguards puzzle. However, as Crowley notes, it is virtually impossible to measure directly whether the presence of a safeguards clause induces states to negotiate larger tariff reductions. Crowley creates an indirect measure that examines cross-country variations in tariff reductions and numbers of safeguards actions. Unfortunately, the data she examines are inconclusive; different results obtain depending on the data sample used and the way the model is specified. In short, the data Crowley examines do not provide robust empirical support for the political economy rationale.

New Approaches to Safeguards

The highly truncated overview of the safeguards literature presented highlights the difficulty that the functionalist strand of this literature has encountered in attempting to generate persuasive answers to the question posed by Crowley's chapter. As summarized, efforts to generate a functionalist rationale for safeguard provisions have come up short on both theoretical and empirical grounds. For current purposes, however, tracing the historiography of safeguards scholarship may be of less utility than seeking to shape its future. Of course, this history is not irrelevant to the design of a future research agenda. Indeed, any sensible scholarly agenda would account for both the successes and failures of past efforts. The history outlined earlier raises the following question: If, despite many years of effort and a great deal of ingenuity, functionalist accounts have proven unpersuasive, should we continue to engage in this effort? Or might it be sensible to consider using heretofore unexplored methodologies or

22 B.P. Rosendorff and H.V. Milner, "The Optimal Design of International Trade Institutions: Uncertainty and Escape," 55 *International Organization* 2001, 829; Sykes, *The Safeguards Mess*, *supra* note 6; Sykes, *supra* note 10.

23 Important contributions to the "rational design" literature include B. Koremenos, "Contracting Around International Uncertainty," 99 *American Political Science Review* 2005, 549; B. Koremenos, C. Lipson, and D. Snidal, "The Rational Design of International Institutions," 55 *International Organization* 2001, 761; Rosendorff and Milner, *supra* note 22. In the legal literature, rational design approaches to treaty architecture are explored in K. Raustiala, "Form and Substance in International Agreements," 99 *American Journal of International Law* 2005, 581; A.T. Guzman, "The Design of International Agreements," 16 *European Journal of International Law* 2005, 579; L.R. Helfer, "Exiting Treaties," 91 *Virginia Law Review* 2005, 1579.

interpretative strategies? In the remainder of this chapter, I will identify two distinct, albeit related, types of inquiry that might be more likely to advance our understanding of safeguards.

Divide and Conquer

For current purposes, let me suggest the possibility that functionalist accounts have failed, at least in part, because no "grand narrative" to explain safeguards exists. That is, different states use safeguard measures for different purposes at different times. Indeed, Crowley's chapter hints at the potential for a disaggregated approach to the use of safeguards when she suggests that one way to interpret her empirical results is that safeguards clauses may facilitate greater tariff reductions by developing states.[24] The question is whether we can push this sort of inquiry much further.

Thus, for example, instead of seeking a master narrative that explains the overall function of safeguards in the trade system, we might explore a number of country-specific questions: Why, for example, are safeguard petitions more common in Argentina than in Brazil?[25] Why is the ratio of antidumping to safeguard petitions in Colombia nearly one to one, when the global number of antidumping petitions dwarfs the number of safeguard petitions?[26]

Alternatively, we might explore patterns across states in the use of safeguards. For example, are there significant differences in the use of safeguard actions between states that are relatively new to the trade system – and hence may not be terribly experienced in predicting the likely consequences of liberalization – and those states that have long been GATT members? Do we see more or fewer safeguard actions in economic sectors in which the domestic economy is highly concentrated?[27] Are states with "left" leaning governments, which may be more sympathetic to the plight of those harmed by globalization, more likely to invoke safeguards than are states with "right" leaning governments, which may be less willing to attempt to address the distributional consequences of liberalized trade? Does regime type matter? For example, is there any difference in

[24] The idea that patterns and rationales of protection may be different in developing states is, of course, not new. See, for example, B. Balassa, *The Structure of Protection in Developing Countries* (Baltimore, Johns Hopkins Press, 1971).

[25] See, for example, J.M. Finger and J.J. Nogues (Eds.), *Safeguards & Antidumping in Latin American Trade Liberalization: Fighting Fire with Fire* (Washington, DC, World Bank Publications, 2005).

[26] According to statistics available on the WTO's Web site, between January 1, 1995, and until October 23, 2006, WTO Members initiated a total of 155 safeguard investigations, and imposed a total of 76 safeguard measures. During roughly the same period, WTO members initiated 2,938 antidumping investigations and imposed 1,875 antidumping measures.

[27] For example, in Brazil, more than 40% of antidumping restrictions apply to products for which there is only one domestic producer, and 80% of antidumping orders protected industries where there are five or fewer domestic producers. Finger and Nogues, *supra* note 25, at 8.

numbers of safeguard measures imposed by, say, parliamentary as opposed to presidential systems? Are there any differences between states that have proportional representation as opposed to single-member electoral systems?

We might undertake a series of longitudinal or historical inquiries: Do states tend to use safeguards for one purpose at one point in time, but for another purpose at another point in time? A quick example might help illustrate this point. There is broad consensus that the original GATT safeguards clause grew out of preexisting U.S. practice.[28] Drawing this connection simply raises the question of when and why the United States began to use safeguards clauses.

The conventional wisdom suggests that the first formal safeguard mechanism was found in a 1942 bilateral trade agreement between the United States and Mexico.[29] However, historical research calls this conventional wisdom into question. For example, the United States negotiated safeguards clauses in a number of bilateral agreements prior to the agreement with Mexico, including bilateral agreements with Brazil, Belgium, and other states during the 1930s. Interestingly, there is some historical evidence that these safeguards clauses were inserted to address the problem of unanticipated surges from third states, not party to the agreements.[30] Thus, as drafted in the Belgian agreement, the safeguards clause stated:

> "Each of the two Governments reserves the right to withdraw the concession granted on any article under this agreement... if at any time there should be evidence that, as a result of the extension of such concession to third countries, the latter will obtain the major benefit of such concession and that, in consequence thereof, any unduly large increase of the importations of such article will take place."[31]

Over time, the concern with states not party to the underlying trade agreement shifted to a concern with states party to the underlying agreement. This

[28] See, for example, GATT Secretariat, Drafting History of Article XIX and Its Place in GATT, MTN.GNG/NG9/W/7 (Kluwer Law International, 1987).

[29] See, for example, T.P. Stewart (Ed.), *II The GATT Uruguay Round: A Negotiating History* (1986–1992) (1993) at 1719 ("formal safeguard mechanism was first introduced by the United States in the U.S. Reciprocal Trade Agreement Act of 1942 with Mexico"); *Raj Bhala International Trade Law: Theory and Practice* (2nd ed., Lexus Publishing, 2000), 1117. Article XI of the U.S.–Mexico agreement provided:

> If, as a result of unforeseen developments and of the concessions granted on any article enumerated and described in the Schedules annexed to this Agreement, such article is being imported in such increased quantities and under such conditions as to cause or threaten serious injury to domestic producers of like or similar articles, the Government of either country shall be free to withdraw the concession, in whole or in part, or to modify it to the extent and for such time as may be necessary to prevent such injury.

Agreement on Reciprocal Trade, December 23, 1942, U.S. – Mexico, Article XI, 57 Stat. 833, 845–846 (Effective January 1, 1943).

[30] See, for example, A. Eckes, *Opening America's Market: U.S. Foreign Trade Policy Since 1776* (Chapel Hill, University of North Carolina Press, 1995).

[31] Ibid., 221.

example illustrates the point that historical investigation may reveal that safeguards are inserted in trade agreements for different purposes at different times.

The Flip

The approaches to safeguards mentioned above share a common methodological orientation in that they break the puzzle of safeguards into smaller and more discrete, and perhaps therefore more tractable, inquiries. Future inquiries into safeguards might also consider using an alternative approach, which I call "the flip." The flip reverses the direction of the questions we usually ask; it turns conventional analysis upside down. To explain how it does so, let me offer a constitutional law analogy.

Like trade scholars, constitutional law scholars have tried to justify and explain an anomaly that is central to their field: judicial review. Judicial review is anomalous because it seems difficult to justify the puzzle of judicial review by unelected and unaccountable federal judges within a democratic system like that found in the United States. By what rationale are unelected and unaccountable federal judges able to overturn the considered decisions of majoritarian, electorally accountable branches of government? It is no exaggeration to claim that the anomaly of "judicial review... ha[s] framed the central debates in American constitutional theory during the past fifty years."[32] For constitutional law scholars, the practice of judicial review is an enduring puzzle because it seems to contradict basic premises of a majoritarian, democratic system. In much the same way, safeguards are an enduring puzzle to trade scholars because they similarly seem to be inconsistent with the basic premises of the trade system.

The conventional inquiry seeks to justify an anomaly, like judicial review, within a larger democratic system. What happens if we reverse – or flip – the inquiry? Instead of using the larger system to understand judicial review, maybe we should use judicial review to understand the larger system. Is the antidemocratic nature of judicial review really so anomalous? Alternatively stated, is the U.S. legal and political system really so democratic? Adopting this perspective might enable us to see patterns across various features of U.S. law and politics

[32] M.J. Horowitz, "Foreword: The Constitution of Change: Legal Fundamentality Without Fundamentalism," 107 *Harvard Law Review* 1993, 30, 63. For similar characterizations of the importance of this problem, see, for example, B. Friedman, "The History of the Countermajoritarian Difficulty, Part One: The Road to Judicial Supremacy," 73 *New York University Law Review* 1998, 333, 334 ("The 'countermajoritarian difficulty' has been the central obsession of modern constitutional scholarship."); A.R. Amar, "The Consent of the Governed: Constitutional Amendment Outside Article V," 94 *Columbia Law Review* 1994, 457, 495 (noting that current generation of constitutional law scholarship is "[p]reoccupied with the 'countermarjoritarian difficulty'"); M.V. Tushnet, "Anti-Formalism in Recent Constitutional Theory," 83 *Michigan Law Review* 1985, 1502 ("Almost all recent work in the field [of constitutional theory] takes as its central problem what Alexander Bickel called the 'countermajoritarian difficulty' with judicial review.") (footnote omitted).

that appear problematic from the view of democratic theory, such as provisions that do not permit the direct election of the president[33] and laws that permit forms of gerrymandering that in effect let sitting officials choose their voters rather than the other way around.[34] In other words, engaging in the flip helps shift our attention from the antidemocratic nature of judicial review and encourages us to question the supposedly democratic nature of the larger system.[35]

The open question is whether a similar reversal of the usual line of inquiry would be useful for trade scholars. Should we continue our efforts to justify safeguards, which appear to be inconsistent with the basic purposes of the trade system, or, given the failure of efforts to explain safeguards, might we use the anomaly of safeguards to revisit our understandings of the trade system?

Conclusion

Where does this analysis leave us? Despite significant scholarly energies, we are unable to provide an adequate functional account of the role of safeguards. That is, we cannot answer the question posed in the title of Crowley's chapter: Why are safeguards needed in a trade agreement? I believe that this suggests a choice between two paths. One path would continue the search for a satisfactory functional justification. Given our experience with this endeavor, perhaps we should try a different tack. We might, for example, explore the different uses of safeguards by different states at different times, or otherwise attempt to disaggregate the problem of safeguards. We might use the puzzle of safeguards as an opportunity to revisit our understandings of the trade system. My limited suggestion in this short essay is that these strategies are more likely to be fruitful than continued efforts to try to determine why safeguards are needed in trade agreements.

33 The electoral college has selected presidents who did not get a majority of the popular vote as well as those who did not capture the greatest number of votes. Since World War II alone, Presidents Truman, Kennedy, Nixon (1968), Clinton, and George W. Bush were all elected without receiving 50% of the popular vote, and neither Kennedy nor George W. Bush captured first place in the popular vote.

34 See, generally, M. Kang, "The Bright Side of Partisan Gerrymandering," 14 *Cornell Journal of Law & Public Policy* 2005, 443; T.A. Aleinikoff and S. Issacharoff, "Race and Redistricting: Drawing Constitutional Limits After Shaw v. Reno," 92 *Michigan Law Review* 1993, 588.

35 For extended discussions of the antidemocratic elements embedded in the U.S. constitutional system, see, for example, S. Levinson, *Our Undemocratic Constitution: Where the Constitution Goes Wrong (And How We the People Can Correct It)* (Oxford, Oxford University Press, 2006); R.A. Dahl, *How Democratic Is the American Constitution?* (New Haven, CT, Yale University Press, 2002).

Index

accounting-based subsidies, 104–107
actionable subsidies, 34, 49–52. *See also* serious prejudice, in actionable subsidies
  injury to domestic industry in, 49
  nullification in, 49–50
  under SCM Agreement, 168–169
Aggregate Measure of Support (AMS), 77–79
Agreement on Agriculture (AoA)
  AMS and, 77–79
  Canada–Dairy Article 21.5 and, 80
  domestic support for, 75–79
  export subsidies under, 73–75, 128–129
  in GATS, 72–73
  in GATT, 71–72
  SCM Agreement and, 79–81
  subsidies in, 7, 71–81
  Uruguay Round, of SCM and, 117–118
  in *U.S.–FSC*, 73
Agreement on Rules of Origin (ARO). *See also* Nonpreferential Origin Rules
  antidumping measures and, 296–304
  for Brazil, 300
  circumvention of, 281–282, 299–304
  equality of application for, 296–299
  GSP and, 279
  Kyoto Convention and, 277–278
  Republic of Korea under, 298–299
  Uruguay Round and, 276, 279
  for U.S., 300–301
  in WTO, 276, 292
Agreement on Safeguards (AS), 381–382
Agreement on Subsidies and Countervailing Measures (SCM Agreement), 7–84, 103–114. *See also* sunset reviews
  actionable subsidies under, 168–169
  AoA and, 79–81
  arbitration process with, 164
  Article 1.1(1) of, 23–25
  Article 14 of, 114–115
  benefits of, 25–28
  Brazil–Aircraft under, 13
  competition charter perspective on, 92–94
  CVDs under, 7, 90, 103, 163–164
  Doha Round for, 86, 100–101
  domestic efficiency perspective on, 88–91
  DSB in, 56–60
  DSU in, 55–59
  equitable shares with, 72
  export subsidies under, 127–129
  fundamental research in, 52–53
  GATT and, 8–13
  global subsidiary perspective on, 97–100
  good governance perspective on, 95–97
  Illustrative List in, 136–139
  inputs in, 42
  like products under, 61
  nonactionable subsidies under, 53–54, 86
  peace clause in, 79–80
  prohibited subsidies under, 85, 127, 168–169
  purpose of, 13, 103
  remedies to subsidies under, 55–64
  serious prejudice in, 51–52
  subsidies in, 7, 28–29, 103, 105, 130–133, 168, 171
  sunset clause in, 97
  tariffs under, 89–90
  taxing of income under, 18
  territorial tax systems under, 32
  Uruguay Round of, 85–86
  U.S.–Lumber CVDs under, 13
amber box subsidies, 75, 77
American Tariff Act of 1890, 107
Ammonium Nitrate from Ukraine, 311–312, 326, 327
AMS. *See* Aggregate Measure of Support
anticircumvention discipline, 75
  circumvention of ARO and, 283
  for Nonpreferential Origin Rules, 283
Antidumping Act of 1916 (U.S.), 253
Antidumping Act of 1921 (U.S.), 198
Anti-Dumping Agreement, 13, 197–240, 266. *See also* duties, under Anti-Dumping Agreement; injury under Anti-Dumping Agreement; investigation procedures, under Anti-Dumping Agreement; Nonpreferential Origin Rules; price comparisons, in Anti-Dumping Agreement; sunset reviews; Tariff Act of 1930
  Article 2 in, limitations of, 204
  circumvention of, 281–282
  commentary on, 241–256
  consumer interests under, 242
  CVDs under, economic effects of, 227
  CVMs under, 309
  development background for, 197–200
  "Dunkel Draft" of, 282
  economic effects of, 227
  expiration clause of, 309–310
  injury determination under, 204–208, 249–250, 320
  during Kennedy Round of Multilateral Trade Negotiations, 199–200

Anti-Dumping Agreement (*cont.*)
legal cases, 225–240
market economy status under, establishment of, 325
modified products under, 302
Nonpreferential Origin Rules in, 276–283, 305
overview of, 257–262
price adjustment/selection in, 203–204
price undertakings for, 211
safeguard measures under, 244
sunset reviews provision in, 309–327
during Tokyo Round of Multilateral Trade Negotiations, 200
WTO Committee for, 221
antidumping measures, 197–200, 224
antitrust statutes and, 264–266, 268
ARO and, 296–304
in Australia, 198, 288
in Canada, 246
circumvention of, 299–304
Contracting Parties in, 284
costs of production for, 258
critique of, 274–275
under DOC, 246, 247, 330–332
DSB review of, 220–221, 251–253
DSU review of, 220–221, 245
foreign firm production costs as factor in, 261–262
future applications of, 253–256
under GATT, 198–199, 284–285
hidden dumping and, 284
in India, 223
international price discrimination and, 242
international regulatory challenges for, 245–251
interpretational flexibility within, 267
ITC and, 331, 332
justification of, 242–245
in LDCs, 256
as legislation, 198
in Mexico, 223, 246
modified products under, 302
in New Zealand, 198
Nonpreferential Origin Rules and, 292, 293
operational elements of, 267–268
prejudice against foreign producers under, 251
in South Africa, 198, 223
transition orders and, 330
unfair pricing and, 260
in U.S., 198, 246
U.S. DOC overview of, 220
use of, 222
users of, 222–224
WTO Member review of, 219–220, 257
antitrust statutes, 264–269
antidumping measures and, 264–266, 268
Clayton Act, 267
critique of, 274–275
under FTC, 267
interpretational flexibility within, 267
operational elements of, 268
price differentiation and, 264, 266
under Robinson-Patman Act, 265–272
under Sherman Act, 266–267
in U.S., evolution of, 264–265, 268–274
AoA. *See* Agreement on Agriculture
Appellate Body Reports, 104–106
benefits under, 104–105
for *Canada–Autos*, 35–36
CVDs in, 37–38
ETI Act in, 38
on sunset reviews, 328–333
for *U.S.–Oil Country Tubular Goods Sunset Review*, 320
Areeda, Philip, 273
Areeda-Turner proposal, on predatory pricing, 273–274
Argentina–Footwear, 339–340, 351, 357
Argentine-Definitive Safeguard Measures on Imports of Preserved Peaches, 340
ARO. *See* Agreement on Rules of Origin
articles, in state aid laws for EC, 173–174
AS. *See* Agreement on Safeguards
ASEAN. *See* Association of Southeast Asian Nations
Association of Southeast Asian Nations (ASEAN), 280
Australia
antidumping laws in, 198, 288
export subsidies in, 39
Australia–Automotive Leather, 134–135
obligations under domestic law in, 154
payment schedule in, 146, 147
withdrawal of remedies in, 145–150
Australia–Leather Article 21.5, 57

Ball Bearings from Thailand, 287
Barry Wright Corp. versus ITT Grinnell Corp., 274
Bell, Griffin, 273
below-market loans, 111
benefits, of subsidies, 25–28
under Appellate Body Reports, 104–105
calculation of, 114–115
in *Canada–Aircraft*, 26
competitive, 104, 107
definition of, 25–26, 131
in *Japan–DRAMS Countervailing Duties*, 26–27
in *Korea–Commercial Vessels*, 26, 27
private investor test for, 26
in *U.S.–CVDs on EC Products*, 28
in *U.S.–Lumber CVDs*, 26–28
in *U.S.–Lumber CVDs Final*, 28, 29
blue box subsidies, 75–77
Boeing Corporation, in EC, subsidiaries of, 173
Boeing–Airbus, 172–196
EIB loans in, 187, 190–191
French government involvement in, 188

German government involvement in, 188, 193–194
infrastructure-related grants in, 187–188, 191–192
"launch aid" in, 186–190
multinationals in, 195–196
R&D support as issue in, 188, 194–195
subsidy issues in, 186–188
Brander-Spencer model, for strategic trade policy, 123, 169
Brazil
ARO for, 300
CIRRs in, 137
export subsidies and, 116
PROEX in, 137, 150–152
Brazil–Aircraft, 47–48
export credits in, 43–44
export subsidies in, 39
OECD arrangements in, 46
under SCM Agreement, 13
withdrawal of subsidies in, 58
Brazil–Desiccated Coconut, 105
Brazil–Export Financing for Aircraft, 137, 140–141
obligations under domestic law and, 154
withdrawal of remedies in, 150–152, 156
Breyer, Stephen, 274
Bush, George H.W., 270
"but for" test, 17, 51
Byrd Amendment (U.S.), 253

CAFTA. *See* Central American Free Trade Agreement
Cairns group, 11
Canada
antidumping measures in, 246
export contingencies in, 37
export subsidies and, 116
International Trade Tribunal in, 246
MFN provision in, 20
subsidies in, with U.S., 30
Canada–Aircraft
benefits in, 26
contingent subsidies in, 36, 133–134
export subsidies in, 131
subsidy legislation and, 140
withdrawal of remedies in, 147–148
Canada–Autos, 20, 35
Appellate Body Reports for, 35–36
contingent subsidies in, 36–37, 133
Canada–Certain Measures Affecting the Automotive Industry (Complaint by Japan and the European Communities), 129–133
Canada–Dairy Article 21.5, 80
Canada–Export Credits for Aircraft, 138–139
EDC in, 140
obligations under domestic law in, 154–155
withdrawals of remedies in, 152, 156–159
Canada–Periodicals, 20–21
Canadian Value Added (CVA) requirements, 37
capital subsidies, 111–112
fungibility and, 111–112
Car Radios, 292–293
Carter, Jimmy, 270
CASA. *See* Construcionnes Aeronauticas, SA
Central American Free Trade Agreement (CAFTA), 280
Certain Footwear with Leather Uppers, 293
in Green Paper, 307
Certain Ring Binder Mechanisms, 290, 293
CFI. *See* Court of First Instance
Chevron versus National Resources Defense Council, 252
China, under SA, 356
circumvention, of ARO, 281–282, 299–304
anticircumvention discipline and, 283
definition of, 302–304
CIRR. *See* Commercial Interest Reference Rate
Clayton Act (U.S.), 267
Clinton, Bill, 11, 270
Commercial Interest Reference Rate (CIRR), 43–45, 58
in Brazil, 137
Common Market of the South (MERCOSUR), 356
Community Framework for State Aid for Research and Development and Innovation, 194
Compact Disc Players, 293
compensatory justification principle, 178
competitive benefits, of subsidies, 104, 107
CVDs and, 109–111
framework of, 107–109
Construcionnes Aeronauticas, SA (CASA), 189–190
contingent subsidies
in *Australia–Automotive Leather*, 134–135
in *Canada–Aircraft*, 36, 133–134
in *Canada–Autos*, 36–37, 133
de facto, 134, 166
export subsidies and, 133–139
in *Korea–Commercial Vessels*, 137
as prohibited, 35–38
in *U.S.–Cotton Subsidies*, 135–136
in *U.S.–FSC*, 37–38, 135
contract remedies, to subsidies, 144
Contracting Parties, in antidumping measures, 284
corporate mergers, opposition to, 185
countermeasures, for withdrawal of remedies, 155–156, 165
WTO members and, 159–160
countervailing duties (CVDs), 7
under American Tariff Act of 1890, 107
in Anti-Dumping Agreement, economic effects of, 227
in Appellate Body Reports, 37–38
below-market loans and, 111
competitive benefits and, 109–110
definitive *versus* provisional, 66–67
equity infusions and, 111

countervailing duties (CVDs) (*cont.*)
  under GATT, 126
  importing countries and, 122
  imposition of, in subsidies, 65–68, 84, 85, 104
  injury and, 113
  in *Japan–DRAMS Countervailing Duties*, 67–68
  loan guarantees and, 111
  NVCs and, 171
  purpose of, 104
  retroactivity of, 66
  under SCM Agreement, 7, 90, 103, 163, 164
  S&D treatment and, 71
  simultaneous, among numerous nations, 110–111
  under Subsidies Code, 10–11
  in sunset reviews, 310
  under Tariff Act of 1930, 107
  with unilateral remedies to subsidies, 60–64, 163
  in *U.S.–Lumber CVDs Final*, 66
  WTO members and, 65–66
countervailing measures (CVMs), 309
Court of First Instance (CFI), 173
Crowley, Meredith, 401
currency retention schemes, 39–40
Customs Act of 1904 (Canada), 198
Customs Cooperation Council, 277
CVA requirements. *See* Canadian Value Added requirements
CVDs. *See* countervailing duties
CVMs. *See* countervailing measures

de facto contingent subsidies, 134, 166
de minimis margins, under Anti-Dumping Agreement, 213–214, 247–248
decoupled payments, 76
definitive CVDs, 66–67
Department of Commerce (DOC), U.S., 220
  dumping margins determined by, 246, 247, 330–332
  ITC and, 331
  sunset provisions under, 329–330
  "zeroing" by, 243, 250–251
developing nations, export subsidies and, 124–125, 129
direct taxes, 21, 40
Dispute Settlement Body (DSB), 56–60, 103, 143, 172
  anti-dumping measure review under, 220–221, 251–253
  multilateral remedies to subsidies and
  repayment of subsidies in, 57–58
  safeguards under, 383, 384
  sunset reviews and, 310
  withdrawal of remedies and, 155–156
  on "zeroing," 250–251
dispute settlement system
  DSB, 56–60
  DSU, 55, 59
Dispute Settlement Understanding (DSU), 55, 59
  antidumping measure review under, 220–221, 245
  cases under, 118
  equivalence in, 58
  GATT and, 91
  multilateral remedies to subsidies and, 55–60
  withdrawal of remedies and, 156
DOC. *See* Department of Commerce, U.S.
Doha Round, for SCM, 86
  export subsidies during, 117
  failure of, 101–102
  nonactionable subsidies in, 100, 101
  trade distortion issues during, 101
domestic efficiency perspective, on SCM Agreement, 88–91
domestic subsidies, 113
  in AoA, 75–79
  decoupled payments in, 76
  international *versus*, 30–33, 75–79, 106
  in *U.S.–FSC*, 31–32
Dordi, Claudio, 328
DRAMs, 289–290
DSB. *See* Dispute Settlement Body
DSU. *See* Dispute Settlement Understanding
dumping. *See* Anti-Dumping Agreement; antidumping measures; hidden dumping
"Dunkel Draft," 282
duties, under Anti-Dumping Agreement, 209–211, 251
  provisional measures as, 210–211
  retroactive collection of, 210–211
Dwyer, Amy, 241–256

EC. *See* European Commission
EC Treaty, 92
  exclusions in, 94–95
EC–DRAMs Countervailing Measures, 62
ECJ. *See* European Court of Justice
EC-Tube or Pipe Fittings, 321
EDC. *See* Export Development Corporation of Canada
"efficient breach" approach, to remedies, 144
EIB. *See* European Investment Bank
Electronic Compact Fluorescent Lamps, 312, 324–325
Electronic Typewriters from Taiwan, 287
Electronic Weighing Scales from Japan and Magnetic Disks from China, Japan and Taiwan, 311
embedded liberalism, 87
Energy Saving Lamps, 293
environmental subsidies, 53
EPROMs, 289–290
equity infusions, 103, 115
  CVDs and, 111
equivalence, in DSU, 58
Ethanolamine from the United States, 311, 319

ETI Act. *See* Extraterritorial Income Exclusion Act
EU. *See* European Union, protectionism within
Euroalliages versus Commission of the European Communities, 323–324, 326–327
European Commission (EC). *See also* state aid laws, for EC
  EIB and, 187
  Framework Programmes of, 194
  Green Paper of, 307–308
  on infrastructure financing, 192
  "launch aid" by, 186, 187, 189–190
  multinationals within, 195–196
  Nonpreferential Origin Rules for, 290
  SA for, 371–373
  state aid laws for, 173–196
  sunset reviews, for Anti-Dumping Agreement/SCM, 323–327
  treaties within, 92
  in *U.S.–FSC,* arguments in, 16–17, 169
  withdrawal of remedies and, preexisting commitments for, 166–167
European Community (EC)–Commercials Vessels, 91
European Court of Justice (ECJ), 191
  Nonpreferential Origin Rules and, 287, 296
  sunset reviews under, 323–327
European Investment Bank (EIB), 187, 190–191
  loans as subsidies, 187, 191
European Union (EU), protectionism within
  export contingencies, 37
  in Canada, 37
  legislation for, 140–143
export credit guarantees, 42
  in *Brazil–Aircraft,* 43–44
  under OECD, 43
Export Development Corporation of Canada (EDC), 140
Export Development of Canada (EDC), 140
export restrictions, 106
export subsidies, 39–48, 106, 169–170
  under AoA, 73–75, 128–129
  in Australia, 39
  Brander–Spencer model for, 123
  Brazil and, 116
  Canada and, 116
  in *Canada–Aircraft,* 131
  contingent subsidies and, 133–139
  currency retention schemes as, 39–40
  definition of, 117, 119, 129–143
  developing nations and, 124–125, 129
  direct taxes as, 40
  discipline mechanisms for, 126, 127
  during Doha Round, for SCM, 117
  efficiency of, 125–126
  export credit guarantees and, 42
  exporting countries and, 122–123
  "fairness" issues with, 121–122
  fiscal incentives and, 40–42
  through freight charges, 39–40
  under GATT, 121–122, 126–127
  global benefits of, 117–118
  from governments, 39
  import charge drawbacks and, 42
  importing countries and, 122
  indirect taxes as, 41
  between multiple countries, 124
  nonlisted, 74–75
  product quality of, 120–121
  prohibition of, 119–126, 150
  public account charges as, 40
  remedies to, 143–165
  resource allocation distortion from, 119
  under SCM Agreement, 127–129
  S&D treatment and, 70
  in strategic trade theory, 120
  under strategic trade theory, 122–123
  Subsidies Code and, 13
  for subsidizing country, 119–120
  tax deferrals as, 40–41
  terms of trade with, 119
  transaction costs and, 161
  during Uruguay Round, for SCM, 117, 127
  in *U.S.–FSC,* 130–131
  as welfare reducing, 119, 123, 124
  under WTO, 116–129, 171
Extraterritorial Income Exclusion (ETI) Act, 38, 138–152

Federal Trade Commission (FTC), 267
  Robinson–Patman Act enforced by, 269–270
financial contributions by governments, as subsidies, 14, 15, 19, 82
  as benefits, 25–28
  direct, 22–23
  from incomes/price supports, 23–82
  from tariffs, 19–20
  types of, 14–15
  WTO case law and, 16
Footwear, 290–291
foreign sales corporations (FSCs), 17
  rules for, in U.S., 116–117
foreign source incomes, 41
Framework Programmes, 194
  grant value assessments under, 188
France, *Boeing-Airbus* and, 188
FSCs. *See* foreign sales corporations
FTC. *See* Federal Trade Commission
fungibility, 111–112

GATS. *See* General Agreement on Trade in Services
GATT. *See* General Agreement on Tariffs and Trade
GDP. *See* gross domestic product

General Agreement on Tariffs and Trade (GATT), 9. *See also* Anti-Dumping Agreement; Safeguard Agreement
amendments to, 9
antidumping measures under, 198–199, 284–285
AoA in, 71–72
Article 3.8(b) of, 20–21
Article 16 of, 23–48
Article 23 of, 8
Article 26.4 of, 8
Article 29 of, 8
AS under, 381–382
Contract Parties under, 8–9
CVDs under, 126
DSU and, 91
escape clause in, 8
export subsidies under, 121–122, 126–127
GATS and, 11–13
global subsidiary perspective and, 98
multilateral system in, 9
Nonpreferential Origin Rules and, 276–277, 279
nullification of subsidies under, 91
primary *versus* nonprimary goods, 9
prohibition of export subsidies under, 121–122
purpose of, 103
SA and, 335–338
SCM Agreement and, 8–13
Subsidies Code in, 9–11
subsidies under, 8–13, 85
sunset provisions under, 329–330
tariffs under, 89, 244
Tokyo Round of, 9–11
Uruguay Round of, 11, 23
General Agreement on Trade in Services (GATS), 11–13
AoA in, 72–73
MFN provision in, 12
subsidies under, 12–13
Generalised System of Preferences (GSP), 279
Germany, *Boeing–Airbus* and, 188, 193–194
global subsidiary perspective, on SCM Agreement, 97–100
GATT and, 98
NVNI in, 98
good governance perspective, on SCM Agreement, 95–97
governments
export subsidies from, 39
financial contributions by, as subsidies, 14, 15, 19, 82
provision of goods and services by, 115
Graham, Samuel, 197–198, 242, 261
grants, 103
green box subsidies, 75–77
green light subsidies. *See* nonactionable subsidies
Green Paper, 307–308
Certain Footwear with Leather Uppers in, 307
grey area measures, under SA, 337, 364–365
gross domestic product (GDP), 381
GSP. *See* Generalised System of Preferences

Harmonization Work Programme (HWP), 276
hidden dumping, 284
HWP. *See* Harmonization Work Programme

Illustrative List, in SCM Agreement, 136–139
import charges, drawbacks of, 42
import duties. *See* tariffs
Inama, Stefano, 306–308
incomes, 19
as financial contributions by governments, 23–82
from foreign sources, 41
price supports and, 23–67, 82
taxing of, in SCM Agreement, 18
India, antidumping laws in, 223
indirect taxes, 21, 41
prohibited studies and, 41
Indonesia–Autos, 20
serious prejudice in, 52
infant industries, safeguards for, 386–387, 405
injury provisions, in unilateral remedies, 63–64
in *U.S.–Lumber ITC Investigation Article 21.5*, 64
injury to domestic industry, 49
injury under Anti-Dumping Agreement, 204–208
causal relationships as factor for, 206–207
causation and, 320
to domestic industry, 208, 255
impact factors for, 206
material determinations for, 249–250
under Nonpreferential Rules of Origin, 288–291
price factors for, 206
threats of, 207
volume factors for, 206
WTO Member determination of, 205
insurance programs, 42
international subsidies
domestic *versus*, 30–33, 106
in *U.S.–FSC*, 31–32
International Trade Commission (ITC), 241
antidumping measures and, 331, 332
on safeguards, 386–387
International Trade Tribunal, 246
investigation procedures, under Anti-Dumping Agreement, 212–221
administrative process of, 213
confidential information in, 215–216
de minimis margin for, 213–214, 247–248
evidence in, 214–217
increasing costs of, 255
individual margins of dumping in, 217, 246, 247
initiation of, 212–213
NME analysis in, 248–249
Nonpreferential Origin Rules and, 283–296

petitioner standing and, 213
public notice of, 217–218
rights of defense for interested parties in, 214–215
in sunset reviews, 315–321
on third country behalf, 218–219
use of/verification of information in, 216–217
"zeroing" in, 243, 250–251
Italy, social security system in, 175
ITC. *See* International Trade Commission

Japan–DRAMS Countervailing Duties, 15
benefits in, 26–27
imposition of CVDs in, 67–68

Korea. *See* Republic of Korea, under ARO
Korea–Commercial Vessels, 22, 137, 142
benefits in, 26, 27
"but for" test in, 51
contingent subsidies in, 137
serious prejudice in, 51
Korea–Definitive Safeguard Measures on Imports of Certain Dairy Products, 340
Kyoto Convention, origin of rules from, 277–278

"launch aid," 186, 187, 189–190
LDCs. *See* least-developed countries
least-developed countries (LDCs)
antidumping measures in, 256
S&D treatment for, 68–71, 83
Leather Footwear, 311
legislation, on subsidies, 140–143
in *Brazil–Export Financing for Airport*, 140–141
in *Canada–Aircraft*, 140
discretionary, 140–141
mandatory, 140–141
strategic trade theory and, 142
in *U.S.–Corrosion-resistant Steel Sunset Review*, 141–142
in *U.S.–Section 301*, 141
in *U.S.–Zeroing of Dumping Margins*, 142
liability rules, in remedies to subsidies, 163
like products, 61
Lisbon Treaty, 373
loan guarantees, 111, 115
loans, 103
below-market, 111
from EIB, 187, 190–191
government, 14, 15, 82
as subsidies, 106, 115, 191
local content subsidies, 48, 49
in LDCs, 70
TRIMs and, 49

market economy investor principle, 176
Matsushita Electric Industrial Co. versus Zenith Radio Corp., 274
MERCOSUR. *See* Common Market of the South
mergers. *See* corporate mergers, opposition to
Mexico, antidumping laws in, 223, 246
MFN provision. *See* Most-Favored-Nation provision
Miller, James C, III, 269
Moore, Mike, 330
Most-Favored-Nation (MFN) provision
in Canada, 20
in GATS, 12
Nonpreferential Origin Rules and, 277
in SA, 356–359
safeguards and, 382
WTO on, 367–371
multilateral remedies, to subsidies, 55–60
Multilateral Trade Negotiations, Anti-Dumping Agreements during
Kennedy Round, 199–200
Tokyo Round, 200
multinationals, corporations as, 195–196

NAFTA. *See* North American Free Trade Agreement
The Netherlands and Leeuwarder Papierwarenfabriek BV-Commission, 175
New Zealand, antidumping laws in, 198
NGOs. *See* nongovernmental organizations
Nicolaidis, Kalypso, 87
Nixon, Richard, 270
NME analysis. *See* non–market economy analysis
nonactionable subsidies, 29, 34, 53–54
for disadvantaged regions, 53
in Doha Round for SCM, 100, 101
environmental, 53
R&D as, 53, 106
under SCM Agreement, 53–54, 86
Venezuela and, 100–101
nondiscrimination
MFN and, 367–371
in SA, 367–373
nongovernmental organizations (NGOs), 88
nonlisted export subsidies, 74–75
anticircumvention discipline in, 75
in *U.S.–Cotton*, 74–75
non–market economy (NME) analysis, 248–249
Nonpreferential Origin Rules
anticircumvention discipline for, 283
Anti-Dumping Agreement and, 276–283, 305
antidumping measures and, 292, 293
in *Ball Bearings from Thailand*, 287
in *Car Radios*, 292–293
in *Certain Footwear with Leather Uppers*, 293
in *Certain Ring Binder Mechanisms*, 290, 293
circumvention of, 281–282
codification of, 281–282

Nonpreferential Origin Rules (*cont.*)
in *Compact Disc Players*, 293
consumer interest and, 291
critique of, 306–308
drafting methodologies for, 276–282
in *DRAMs*, 289–290
for EC, 290
ECJ and, 287, 296
in *Electronic Typewriters from Taiwan*, 287
in *Energy Saving Lamps*, 293
in *EPROMs*, 289–290
in *Footwear*, 290–291
GATT and, 276–277, 279
harmonization of, 305
injury determination under, 288–291
during investigative process, 283–296
MFN provision and, 277
modified products under, 302
multilateral rules in, 276–281
in *Non-Refillable Lighters*, 293
in *Outboard Motors*, 288–289
outsourcing by EU producers and, 291
in *Persulphates*, 293
in *Photocopiers*, 289
in *Small Screen Colour Televisions*, 286
in *Steel Wire Ropes*, 293
trade pattern changes and, 302
violation of, sanctions for, 295–296
nonprimary goods
under GATT, 9
under Subsidies Code, 10
nonrecurring subsidies, 28
Non-Refillable Lighters, 293
Non-Violation and Nullification Impairment (NVNI), 89
in global subsidiary perspective on SCM, 98
in WTO rules, 89, 91
nonviolation complaints (NVCs), 171
CVDs and, 171
North American Free Trade Agreement (NAFTA), 279
under SA, 356
nullification, of subsidies, 49–50
under GATT, 91
under WTO, 91
NVCs. *See* nonviolation complaints
NVNI. *See* Non-Violation and Nullification Impairment

OECD. *See* Organisation for Economic Cooperation and Development
Office of Fair Trading (OFT), 175
OFT. *See* Office of Fair Trading
Oliver, Daniel, 270
Organisation for Economic Cooperation and Development (OECD), 43, 138
in *Brazil–Aircraft*, 46
CIRR under, 43–45, 58
exports credits under, 43
Outboard Motors, 288–289

Permanent Group of Experts (PGE), 56
Persulphates, 293
PGE. *See* Permanent Group of Experts
Photocopiers, 289
Pitofsky, Robert, 270
Plain Photocopiers from Japan, 311
predatory pricing, 272–274. *See also* antitrust statutes
Areeda-Turner proposal on, 273–274
in *Barry Wright Corp. versus ITT Grinnell Corp.*, 274
in *Matsushita Electric Industrial Co. versus Zenith Radio Corp.*, 274
under Sherman Act, 272
in *Utah Pie Co. versus Continental Baking Co.*, 272–273
price comparisons, in Anti-Dumping Agreement, 200–203
for constructed normal values, 201–202
export price options in, 202–203
for intermediate countries, 202
for non–market economy, 202
normal value options in, 201–202
for third country, 201–202
price differentiation, 264–269
antitrust statutes and, 264–266
definition of, 264
under Robinson-Patman Act, 265
price supports, as financial contributions by governments, 23–82
primary goods, 9
under GATT, 9
principle of proportionality, 159
private investor test, 26
production subsidies, 106
PROEX, 137, 150–152
prohibited subsidies, 34–49, 82. *See also* export subsidies
as contingent, 35–38
CVA requirements for, 37
indirect taxes and, 41
local content, 48–49
PGE and, 56
under SCM Agreement, 85, 127, 168, 169
in U.S., 34
property rules, in remedies to subsidies, 163
prospective withdrawal, of remedies, 146–148
provisional CVDs, 66–67

R&D. *See* research & development
Reagan, Ronald, 269
regulatory subsidies, 21–22
remedies, to subsidies, 54–64, 143–165. *See also* Dispute Settlement Body; Dispute Settlement Understanding; withdrawal of remedies
auctioning of retaliation as, 162
in *Australia–Leather Article*, 57
collective, 162
contract, 144

"efficient breach" approach to, 144
flexibility in, 144–145
monetary compensation as, 162
multilateral, 55–60
NVCs as, 171
property rule *versus* liability rule and, 163
reform for, 162
SA as, 334–335
tariff reduction as, 165
unilateral, 60–64, 163–165
withdrawal of repayments in, 57–58, 145–155
under WTO, 144
Republic of Korea, under ARO, 298–299
research & development (R&D)
in *Boeing-Airbus*, 188, 194–195
as nonactionable subsidies, 53, 106
retrospective withdrawal, of remedies, 148–149
in *Australia–Automotive Leather*, 148–149
in *U.S.–FSC*, 148
Revenue Act of 1916 (U.S.), 198
Robinson-Patman Act, 265–272
agency leadership under, 270–271
criticism of, 270
FTC enforcement of, 269–270
judicial interpretation of, 271
private enforcement of, 271–272
rules, of WTO, 88–100

SA. *See* Safeguard Agreement
SADC. *See* South African Development Community
Safeguard Agreement (SA), 244, 334–366
application of, 244, 352–360
Argentina-Footwear and, 339–340, 351, 357
Argentine-Definitive Safeguard Measures on Imports of Preserved Peaches and, 340
causation conditions under, 376–377
China under, 356
concessions for, 362–364
conditions for imposition of, 338–352
consumer welfare under, 360
context for, 353–354
critique of, 369, 374–378
for EC, 371–373
economic principles of, 375
GATT and, 335–338
GDP under, 381
grey area measures under, 337, 364–365
imports increase under, 343–348, 352
investigation requirements under, 360–362
Korea-Definitive Safeguard Measures on Imports of Certain Dairy Products and, 340
for MERCOSUR nations, 356
MFN provision of, 356–359, 367–371
for NAFTA nations, 356
nondiscrimination in, 367–373
notification requirements under, 362
procedural obligations under, 360–362
publication requirements under, 362
quantitative restrictions under, 354–356
serious injury to domestic industry under, 344–352
as trade remedy, 334–335
unforeseen developments under, 338–342, 377
United States–Definitive Safeguard Measures on Imports of Certain Steel Products and, 338, 343–344
United States–Definitive Safeguard Measures on Imports of Circular Welded Carbon Quality Line Pipe from Korea and, 335
United States–Definitive Safeguard Measures on Imports of Wheat Gluten from the European Communities and, 344–346, 350–351
United States–Safeguard Measures on Imports of Fresh, Chilled or Frozen Lamb Meat from New Zealand and Australia and, 341, 342
U.S.–Fur Felt Hats and, 342
VERs and, 364
WTO and, 335–338, 357
safeguards, 401–411. *See also* Agreement on Safeguards; Safeguard Agreement
adjustment costs under, 387
definition of, 381–382
under DSB, 383–384
as economic insurance, 384–385
economic welfare influenced by, 383–387
efficiency rationale for, 404–405
empirical model for, 387–389, 393–395, 397
equity rationale for, 403–404
historical development of, 409–410
for infant industries, 386–387, 405
investigation data for, 389, 390–392
ITC on, 386–387
MFN provision and, 382
political economy rationale for, 406–407
in trade agreements, 379–385, 399
trade liberalization from, 383–384
use patterns for, factors for, 408, 409
Salop, Steven, 274
Sanitary and Photosanitary Measures (SPS), 297
SCM agreement. *See* Agreement on Subsidies and Countervailing Measures
S&D treatment. *See* special & differential treatment
serious prejudice, in actionable subsidies, 50
in *Indonesia-Autos*, 52
in *Korea-Commercial Vessels*, 51
in SCM Agreement, 51–52
Sherman Act (U.S.), 266–267
predatory pricing under, 272
Slot, Piet Jan, 185–196
Small Screen Colour Televisions, 286

South Africa
antidumping laws in, 198, 223
SADC in, 280
South African Development Community (SADC), 280
special & differential (S&D) treatment, 68–71, 83
CVDs and, 71
export subsidies and, 70
for LDCs, 68–71
SPS. *See* Sanitary and Photosanitary Measures
standstill clause, 180, 185
state aid laws, for EC, 173–196
Articles in, 173–174, 178–184
block exemption regulations in, 180
CFI and, 173
compensatory justification principle in, 178
competition effects of, 175–176
de minimis rule for, 175
definition of, 174
exceptions to, 177–178
for existing aid, 179–180
formal investigation procedures for, 181
general *versus* specific measures in, 174–175
for infrastructural projects, 191–193
"launch aid" and, 186–187, 189–190
market economy investor principle and, 176
material principles of, 174–178
for new aid, 180–184
preliminary examination procedure for, 180
procedural rules for, 178–184
regulations for, 173, 178–184
selectivity in, 174–175
standstill clause in, 180, 185
trade between Member States and, 175–176
Steel Wire Ropes, 293
Steiger, Janet, 270
Stewart, Terence, 241–256
strategic trade theory, 120
Brander-Spencer model for, 123, 169
export subsidies under, 122–123
legislation on subsidies and, 142
principle of proportionality and, 159
withdrawal of remedies in, 159
subsidies, 13–33. *See also* actionable subsidies; benefits, of subsidies; contingent subsidies; export subsidies; international subsidies; legislation, on subsidies; local content subsidies; nonactionable subsidies; nullification, of subsidies; prohibited subsidies; remedies, to subsidies; withdrawal of remedies
accounting-based, 104–107
actionable, 49–52
amber box, 75, 77
in AoA, 7, 71–81
below market inputs as, 106
blue box, 75–77
in *Boeing-Airbus*, 186–188
capital, 111–112
categories of, 33–54
competitive benefits of, 104, 107
as concession-erosion instrument, 170
CVDS and, imposition of, 65–68, 84, 85, 104
definition of, 14, 24, 25, 33, 82, 103, 105, 130–133
differential treatment of, 68–81
discipline strategies for, 171
domestic *versus* international, 30–33, 75–79, 106
EIB loans as, 191
equitable shares with, 72
equity infusions as, 103, 115
export contingencies and, 37
under GATS, 12–13
under GATT, 8–13, 85
government financial contributions as, 14, 15, 82
grants and, 103
green box, 75–77
income/price support as, 23–67, 82
injury *versus*, 113
"launch aid" as, 186–187
legalization of, 85–102
loans as, 103, 106
local content, 70
nonactionable, 53–54
nonrecurring, 28
production, 106
regulatory, 21–22
repayment of, 57–58
in SCM Agreement, 7, 28–29, 103, 105, 130–133, 168–171
S&D for, for developing nations, 68–71, 83
specificity of, 28–29, 127, 132
tariff binding and, 89
by U.S., a financial contributions, 19
withdrawal of, in cases, 58–60
under WTO, 87–88, 168–171
WTO member opinions on, 32–33, 82–83
Subsidies Code, in GATT, 9–11, 22
CVDs under, 10–11
export subsidies and, 13
nonprimary goods as exports under, 10
from Tokyo Round, 127
sunset clause, in SCM Agreement, 97
sunset reviews
for *Ammonium Nitrate from Ukraine*, 326, 327
in Anti-Dumping Agreement, 309–327
Appellate Body case law and
critiques of, 328–333
CVDs in, 310
CVMs in, 309
de minimis standards in, 313–314
DSB and, 310
EC interpretation of, 323–327

under ECJ, 323–327
for *EC-Tube or Pipe Fittings*, 321
for *Electronic Compact Fluorescent Lamps*, 324–325
for *Ethanolamine from the United States*, 311, 319
for *Euroalliages versus Commission of the European Communities*, 323–324, 326–327
for investigation procedures under Anti-Dumping Agreement, 315–321
"legislative vacuum" with, 328–329
principles of, 312–315
in SCM Agreement
standards for, 321–322
for *U.S.-Carbon Steel*, 312
for *U.S.-Corrosion-Resistant Steel Sunset Review*, 141–142, 312–313, 316, 321–322
for *U.S.-German Steel*, 313, 315
for *U.S.-Oil Country Tubular Goods Sunset Review*, 312, 314, 318–321

Tariff Act of 1930 (U.S.), 107
tariffs, 19–20
complaints about, 162
under GATT, 89, 244
reductions of, 165
under SCM Agreement, 89–90
subsidies and, 89
trade distortion from, 169
tax deferrals, 40–41
tax incentives, 103
targeted, 106
Taxation and Customs Union (TAXUD), 292
taxes
direct, 21, 40
incomes and, in SCM Agreement, 18
indirect, 21, 41
territorial systems for, 32
TAXUD. *See* Taxation and Customs Union
Tokyo Round, of GATT, 9–11
Subsidies Code from, 127
trade agreements. *See also* Association of Southeast Asian Nations; Central American Free Trade Agreement; General Agreement on Tariffs and Trade; North American Free Trade Agreement
safeguards in, 379–385, 399
trade distortion, 101
from import tariffs, 169
Trade-Related Investment Measures (TRIMs), 49
Trade-Related Aspects of Intellectual Property Rights (TRIPS), 88, 297
transaction costs, export subsidies and, 161
transition orders, 330
TRIMs. *See* Trade-Related Investment Measures
TRIPs. *See* Trade-Related Aspects of Intellectual Property Rights
Turner, Donald, 273

unilateral remedies, to subsidies, 60–64, 163–165
consultation invitations in, 61–62
with CVDs, 60–64, 163
in *EC–DRAMS Countervailing Measures*, 62
injury provisions with, 63–64
procedural requirements of, 60–62
substantive requirements of, 63–64
in *U.S.–Lumber ITC Investigation Article 21.5*, 64
United States (U.S.). *See also* Department of Commerce, U.S.
Antidumping Act of 1916 in, 253
Antidumping Act of 1921 in, 198
antidumping laws in, 198, 246
antitrust statutes in, evolution of, 264–265, 268–274
ARO for, 300–301
Byrd Amendment in, 253
Clayton Act in, 267
financial contributions by, as subsidies, 19
FSCs in, rules for, 116–117
prohibited subsidies in, 34
Revenue Act of 1916 in, 198
Robinson–Patman Act in, 265–272
Sherman Act in, 266–267
subsidies in, Canada, 30
Tariff Act of 1930 in, 107
USTR for EC state aid, 186
United States–Definitive Safeguard Measures on Imports of Certain Steel Products, 338, 343–344
United States–Definitive Safeguard Measures on Imports of Circular Welded Carbon Quality Line Pipe from Korea, 335
United States–Definitive Safeguard Measures on Imports of Wheat Gluten from the European Communities, 344–346, 350–351
United States–Foreign Sales Corporation (U.S.-FSC), 16–17
AoA and, 73
"but for" test in, 17
contingent subsidies in, 37–38, 135
domestic *versus* international subsidies in, 31–32
EC arguments in, 16–17, 169
export subsidies in, 130–131
withdrawal of remedies in, 148, 152, 156, 157, 160
withdrawal of subsidies in, 59, 60
United States–Malt Beverages, 21
United States–Safeguard Measures on Imports of Fresh, Chilled or Frozen Lamb Meat from New Zealand and Australia, 341–342

Upland Cotton User Marketing Certificate Program, 135
Uruguay Round, of GATT
 AoA during, 117–118
 ARO from, 276, 279
 export subsidies during, 117, 127
 of GATT, 11, 23
 rules of origin from, 277
 of SCM, 85–86
U.S. *See* United States
U.S. Trade Representative (USTR), 186
U.S.–Carbon Steel, 312
U.S.–Corrosion-Resistant Steel Sunset Review, 141–142, 312–313, 316, 321–322
U.S.–Cotton Subsidies, 42, 74–75
 contingent subsidies in, 135–136
U.S.–DRAMS CVD Investigation, 22–23
U.S.–Export Restraints, 15, 19–20, 25
U.S.–FSC. See United States-Foreign Sales Corporation
U.S.–Fur Felt Hats, 342
U.S.–German Steel, 313, 315
U.S.–Lumber CVDs
 benefits in, 26–28
 under SCM Agreement, 13
U.S.–Lumber CVDs Final, 16
 benefits in, 28, 29
 imposition of CVDs in, 66
U.S.–Lumber ITC Investigation Article 21.5, 64
U.S.–Oil Country Tubular Goods Sunset Review, 312, 314, 318–321
U.S.–Section 301, 141
U.S.–Softwood Lumber, 93–94
USTR. *See* U.S. Trade Representative
U.S.–Zeroing of Dumping Margins, 142
Utah Pie Co. versus Continental Baking Co., 272–273

Venezuela, nonactionable subsidies and, 100–101
Vermulst, Edwin, 306–308
VERs. *See* voluntary export restraints
Vienna Convention on the Law of Treaties, 99, 154
voluntary export restraints (VERs), 364
Volvo Trucks N. Am. versus Reeder-Simco GMC, Inc., 267

Wauters, Jasper, 374
withdrawal of remedies, 57–58, 145–155
 in *Australia–Automotive Leather*, 145–150
 in *Brazil–Export Financing for Aircraft*, 150–152, 156
 in *Canada–Aircraft*, 147–148
 in *Canada–Export Credits for Aircraft*, 152, 156–159
 countermeasures to, 155–156, 165
 DSB and, 155–156
 DSU and, 156
 by EC, 166–167
 obligations under domestic law and, 153, 155
 preexisting commitments for, 149–153
 prohibition on export subsidies and, 150
 prospective, 146–148
 retrospective, 148, 149
 in strategic trade theory, 159
 in *U.S.–FSC*, 148, 152–157, 160
World Trade Organization (WTO). *See also* Agreement on Subsidies and Countervailing Measures; Anti-Dumping Agreement; Safeguard Agreement
 Anti-Dumping Agreement under, committee for, 221
 ARO in, 276, 292
 DSB of, 56–60, 103, 172
 exports subsidies under, 116–129, 171
 financial contributions by governments and, case law for, 16
 members, opinions of, 32–33
 on MFN, 367–371
 multilateral remedies to subsidies by, 55–60
 nullification of subsidies under, 91
 NVNI under, 89, 91
 remedies to subsidies under, 144
 rules of, 87–100
 SA and, 335–338, 357
 SCM Agreement, 7–84
 subsidies under, 87–88, 168–171
 TRIPS under, 88
WTO members
 antidumping measures and, review of, 219–220, 257
 countermeasures for withdrawal of remedies and, 159–160
 imposition of CVDs by, 65–66
 injury under Anti-Dumping Agreement by, 205
 on multilateral remedies, 55–60
 on subsidies, 32–33, 82–83

yellow light subsidies. *See* actionable subsidies

"zeroing," 243, 250–251